THE CONSUMER
IN AMERICAN SOCIETY
PERSONAL AND FAMILY FINANCE

McGRAW-HILL SERIES IN FINANCE
Professor Charles A. D'Ambrosio, Consulting Editor
University of Washington

FIFTH EDITION
THE CONSUMER
IN AMERICAN SOCIETY
PERSONAL AND FAMILY FINANCE

ARCH W. TROELSTRUP

Emeritus Professor
of Family Economics
Stephens College

McGRAW-HILL
BOOK COMPANY

New York
St. Louis
San Francisco
Düsseldorf
Johannesburg
Kuala Lumpur
London
Mexico
Montreal
New Delhi
Panama
Paris
São Paulo
Singapore
Sydney
Tokyo
Toronto

This book was set in Musica by University Graphics, Inc.
The editors were Jack R. Crutchfield, Hiag Akmakjian, and Annette Hall;
the designer was J. E. O'Connor;
and the production supervisor was Sam Ratkewitch.
New drawings were done by B. Handelman Associates, Inc.
The printer was The Murray Printing Company;
the binder, The Book Press, Inc.

**THE CONSUMER IN SOCIETY:
PERSONAL AND FAMILY FINANCE**

3 4 5 6 7 8 9 0 MUBP 7 9 8 7 6 5

LIBRARY OF CONGRESS CATALOGING IN PUBLICATION DATA

Troelstrup, Archie William, date
     The consumer in American society.

     (McGraw-Hill series in finance)
     First ed. published in 1952 under title: Consumer
problems; 2d–3d ed.: Consumer problems and personal
finance.
     1. Consumer education. 2. Home economics—
Accounting. 1. Title.
TX335.T76 1974   640'.73   73-17256
ISBN 0-07-065210-4

TO

Ann and our four children,
Bill, Glenn, John, Susan Lee —
whose patience has been tested
through five editions —and
to our several
grandchildren.

CONTENTS

FOREWORD

The college student of today is likely to have the challenge, the joy, and the opportunity of spending more than half a million dollars in his or her lifetime.

This half a million or more in earnings is an economic foundation. The goal is to build this income, received week by week or month by month, into a way of life. A paycheck is, after all, only a piece of paper with some numbers on it. The creative and demanding process of converting a series of paychecks into a way of life is what constitutes our role as consumers.

Consumers in the United States have the good fortune to live in a nation well endowed with natural resources. We have developed our technology to a high degree. We have maintained the same form of government for almost 200 years. In no other country does the great majority of citizens have such a wealth of consumer opportunities. But ours is an increasingly complex economy. More and more young people are recognizing that it is imprudent to undertake the spending of their earnings without training for that responsibility by developing purchasing skills.

This fifth edition of Arch Troelstrup's *The Consumer in American Society,* retains the basic fundamentals of consumerism; yet it is replete with up-to-date information about the fast-changing marketing scene. The year 1973 will go down in history as a year of upheaval in the United States farm and food affairs. Food prices skyrocketed, and in protest consumers first boycotted meat and then radically altered their food-buying patterns. This revolution in food-buying practices and the changes that consumer indignation and determination have been able to effect in food labeling and packaging are fully covered in the new edition.

The discussion of consumer problems in relation to family responsibilities has been expanded to include findings from recent studies by Bert Barlow and Wesley R. Burns, family relations and marriage researchers. Also, an innovative and more flexible approach to budgeting the family income is offered.

Professor Troelstrup does more than impart consumer knowledge. He enables the reader to realize what it means to be a consumer and to understand the consumer's role in relation to the economy. He recognizes that though we are all consumers, we are still individuals. The constant attention Professor Troelstrup gives to special consumer concerns of minority and disadvantaged peoples, combined with his understanding that we often wish to adhere to our own ethnic cultures, is particularly helpful. It is this respect for the rightness and the richness of individuality and free choice that makes his book an invaluable guide to that admonition which consumers disregard at their peril: "Know thyself."

In interpreting the economy to consumers, Professor Troelstrup pulls no punches. He documents the reluctance of business to compete for the consumer's dollar on the straightforward bases of price and quality; he relates business's efforts, too often successful, to secure government regulations that hamper the growth of competition; and he explains, in example after example, how business is constantly "taking" the consumer. His conclusion is that consumer advocacy is indispensable in our market economy.

In a simpler society, the consumer's vote at the cash register would more directly influence the decisions on what and how to produce than it does in our complex economy. Consumerists insist that to be truly effective, public influence in the marketplace must begin at an earlier stage. As demonstrated by Professor Troelstrup, through the five editions of this book, the proper place to begin is in teaching the consumers of tomorrow how to handle their money today. *The Consumer in American Society* serves as an excellent introduction to this emerging role, indeed, this emerging profession, of consumer advocate.

Helen Ewing Nelson

President, Board of Directors,
of Consumer Federation of America
Member, Board of Directors,
Consumers Union

PREFACE

For over thirty years I have been teaching consumer and personal finance to undergraduates and graduate students. This textbook is the product of continuous evaluation of present and foreseeable future needs of college students as consumers and as responsible citizens. Some four hundred college graduates have contributed to the textbook by volunteering after marriage to describe in detail the most important consumer problems and issues facing them in actual family situations.

In addition to the contributions of undergraduates and the approximately four hundred married couples who had been out of college from four to fifteen years, I have had the benefit of the advice of a committee of Stephens College instructors who represented a cross section of related disciplines—child study, clothing, foods and nutrition, health, economics, marriage and the family, household economics, psychology, and sociology. This committee met in two-hour sessions, twice monthly for two semesters, to analyze the contents, methods, and contributions of their special fields as they related to a course in the consumer in American society.

The cordial reception that college professors, businessmen, and particularly college students and homemakers gave the first four editions is evidence of the need for such a book. But in a dynamic society such as ours, a book and its author should grow. It is my hope that this fifth edition represents growth.

Much has happened in the areas of consumer problems and issues and personal finance since the fourth edition was published in 1970. Since 1970, the consumer has been "up in arms"—and rightly so. Consumers across the country have widely shared feelings of being ill-served by our present production and marketing arrangements, and they are aware of the need for corrective actions. Their present complaints concern inadequate information, poor quality, poor service, high food costs, dishonored promises, unsafe products, polluting products, deceptive advertising, and fraud. There is also a high volume of unsatisfactorily resolved consumer grievances. These consumer grievances include performance failures; misunderstandings between seller and buyer; misrepresentation; deception; fraud; the failure of manufacturers to take the environmental effects of certain products into account; and the failure of local, state, and federal governments to act wisely in matters pertaining to consumer protection and inadequate information concerning consumer products at the point of sale.

In the early 1970s, there was a trend toward dealing with consumer issues in most statehouses. All but two states presently have some type of office of consumer affairs. Unfortunately, most of these offices are woefully understaffed because they have impossibly low budgets. The future activities of state and local consumer organizations could be very exciting if adequate funding were provided for consumer complaint handling, for new authority to handle various frauds and deceptive practices, and for adequate public information and consumer education.

At the federal level, the activities of the federal regulatory agencies are seriously hindered by politics, inadequate powers, and lack of enthusiasm for the consumer interest. There are also many consumer issues that need attention, such as effective no-fault legislation, unfinished legislation in truth-in-lending, state usury laws, holder-in-due course and related problems, lack of basic information on selecting life insurance, mail-order insurance policies, health insurance, innercity property insurance, flood damage claims, and credit insurance. Perhaps the most important federal legislative need is for an independent consumer agency.

There is also the so-called energy crisis, as well as problems concerning use of the automobile and future development of public transportation. Meanwhile, it looks as if fuel shortages, blackouts, and rising prices may be with us for some time.

It appears that more consumer advocates will participate in local, state, and federal advisory councils, regulatory boards, and similar groups. In other words, consumers increasingly will discover the importance of installing the consumer interest in the mechanism of government.

These and many other dramatic changes are discussed and evaluated in this fifth edition of *The Consumer in American Society*. In fact, new knowledge, new legislation, and a widening of information density in the whole field since 1970 have made necessary a complete rewriting of most chapters. Chapter 1, for example, in addition to containing updated consumer income and expenditure data, expands on the four traditional consumer rights outlined by President Kennedy and also discusses new responsibilities of consumers. There is also new information about economic concentration, pollution and waste, producerism and efficiency, and the New Consumerism. Chapter 2, "Consumer Decision Making and Advertising," has been completely rewritten to reflect recent research, the payoff of intelligent search for information before buying, truth-in-advertising, "open disclosure" and self-regulation of advertising, federal government regulation, the danger of the power of mass advertising, "counteradvertising," "corrective advertising," and substantiation of ad claims. Chapters 3 through 5, centering on money and family management, have been thoroughly revised to include recent research developments. Chapter 6, "Consumer Credit and Borrowing Money," discusses important recent legislation, the recent Hunt Commission report (reintroducing competition in our banks, etc.), new evidence on the "excessively indebted," wise use of credit, credit abuses, recent legislation, tricky billing, recent court decisions, and debt counseling.

The new emphasis in Chapter 7, "Buying Food," is on the revolutions in food labeling regulations and on trends toward open dating, unit pricing, indications of net weight rather than drained weight on labels, ingredient labeling, and nutrient labeling. Also presented is new evidence on changing food habits, recent nutritional surveys, food costs in the ghettos, chemicals in food and recent legislation, children's vitamins, organic foods, and mechanized meals.

Chapter 9, "A Home for Your Family," contains much new material on the influence of the "long-hair" culture (communal living), buying choices, the sudden surge of condominiums and mobile living, recent interest rates, variable rates, closing costs, fine print in mortgages, and moving costs and complaints.

Chapter 10, "Family Transportation," besides containing updated statistics, presents new information on changing attitudes toward cars, Detroit's continued disregard of the real needs of consumers, the stress on smaller cars, the high costs of repairs, the quality of repairs and remedies, questionable car ads, the "Car-Puter" system, car warranties, car insurance (no-fault), auto recalls, and the social responsibility of car manufacturers.

Chapter 11, "Buying Good Health Care and Services," has been almost completely rewritten and centers on recent information on the soaring costs of health care, unnecessary operations, fixed drug prices, over-the-counter drugs, hospital practices, consumer organizations for health care, building a national health care system, limitations in health care insurance, health maintenance organizations, and consumer health care choices.

Chapter 12, which deals with Social Security, life insurance, and annuities, contains substantial additions with regard to the latest changes in Social Security and planning and selecting life insurance protection. Suggestions from such authorities as Dr. Joseph E. Belth and Dr. Herbert S. Denenberg are included, as well as recommendations by Consumers Union. New material in Chapter 13, on savings and investments, centers on where to put your savings, the need for a truth-in-savings law, inflation, new problems facing the small investor, and alternative forms of investment. Chapter 14 adds new information on the important question of whose tax burden is the heaviest. Issues discussed include tax structures that are not progressive, redistribution of income goals, tax reforms that are in the air, the regressive Social Security tax, new revenue sources such as a value-added tax, property tax relief, and federal revenue sharing.

Chapters 15 through 17, on private, federal, state, and local aids to, and protection of, consumers, have been completely rewritten because of multiple changes in organizations and legislation at these levels. The closing chapter, "The International Consumer Movement," examines the global character of consumerism. The stress is on the importance of more efficient allocation of the world's resources through the movement of goods and services across international boundaries.

Appendix A ("A Summary of Ways to Save Money from Marriage to Retirement") and Appendix B ("Federal Agencies Serving the Consumer") have been updated. Appendix C ("The Metric System: What You Need to Know") is new. This edition also contains marginal notes, which are intended to aid students in easily identifying subtopics and to point up significant concepts.

A Readings book, *The Consumer in American Society: Additional Dimensions,* also accompanies this edition. The Readings provide additional information on certain consumer topics for those who desire more details than are given in the textbook. The Readings book contains selected articles from various sources on important consumer issues and concerns. The textbook refers the student to specific readings for more details. The purpose, then, of the Readings book is twofold: to save the student the time and energy necessary to locate good consumer readings from among the many different sources in the library and to supply him with more details and facts than can be presented in a single textbook.

I am indebted to many college teachers and other well-informed persons for helpful comments with respect to this edition. I am particularly indebted to my editor, Hiag Akmakjian, whose interest and fruitful ideas led to a good working relationship, and to artist Tomi Ungerer, who supplied the illustrations. Jan Van Veen, Executive Director of the International Organization of Consumers Unions (IOCU), gave generously of his time and expertise in revising Chapter 18. Professor Jack L. Taylor, Jr., assistant professor of marketing at Portland State University, was most cooperative and assumed responsibility for preparing the Readings book.

I am deeply indebted to several specialists who made a number of suggestions for improvements. Among these were E. Thomas Garman, associate professor of business education, Northern Illinois University; E. Scott Maynes, professor of economics, Center for Economic Research, University of Minnesota; Elkin Minter, assistant professor of home economics, University of Alabama; Richard L. D. Morse, professor and head of the department of family economics, Kansas State University; and Faith Prior, family economics extension specialist, University of Vermont.

Although I am indebted to many instructors and other well-informed persons and specialists, the responsibility for the final content of this edition, as well as for any errors and omissions, is mine.

In preparing the manuscript for publication, my job was lightened immensely by the patience and help of Ann, my wife, who is expert and wise in publishing matters and who lent her talents as both proof-reader and critic.

Arch W. Troelstrup

THE CONSUMER
IN AMERICAN SOCIETY
PERSONAL AND FAMILY FINANCE

CHAPTER 1
THE CONSUMER IN OUR SOCIETY

Consumption is the sole end and purpose of all production; and the interest of the producer ought to be attended to only so far as it may be necessary for promoting that of the consumer.

Adam Smith

What are the major challenges that face Americans in their role as consumers? First, consumers need to know their part in the economy. They should know what makes our economy "tick." Consumers should understand that fraud, deceit, and other undesirable practices persist in the economy because of their own lack of organized resistance as well as ineffective protection on all government levels. They need to realize the importance of substituting rationality for emotion in the marketplace.

Second, consumers need to be aware of the increasing efforts of business to deceive and misinform the consumer. The business of making and selling is highly organized and calls to its aid at every step complex and expert skills. The business of buying is conducted by the smallest unit, the individual or the family. The capacity of sales personnel to aid the consumer has deteriorated. Furthermore, the trend toward automatic services, self-service, discount stores, catalog buying, and persuasive advertising has increased the chances of buying uninformedly. The manufacturer and distributor speak with a well-organized and powerful voice in national affairs. The interest of the consumer is often overlooked because he is voiceless.

Third, consumers need to understand their function in the economy. Is their job to spend in order to keep the economy going? Is it to do the bidding of profit-seeking persuaders? Or is their job that of guiding and controlling the production of goods and services with which to satisfy their wants? In other words, what is the function of the consumer?

THE PURPOSE OF AN ECONOMY

The purpose of an economy is to produce goods and services, large in quantity, high in quality, reasonable in price for maximum satisfaction in consumer use. Every economic system, be it capitalist, Communist, or Socialist, faces three questions: What shall we produce? How much shall we produce? For whom shall we produce?

Different economic systems solve these problems differently. Today, most economic systems are "mixed" in the way they set up their goals and manage their resources. They are neither purely private enterprise nor purely Socialist. And most economic systems are changing constantly.

Business enterprise in the United States is largely private, and its rationale is that consumer demands determine what is produced. Business tries to produce the goods and services that consumers want. And business tries to do so at the lowest possible cost. In most cases, business also seeks to influence consumer demands through advertising and other selling devices. Business will use labor, land, and machinery to produce the goods and services consumers demand. Businesses, in turn, pay out income to workers, landowners, and other suppliers of productive services. These incomes make it possible for consumers, in turn, to buy the goods and services in the marketplace.

Markets are the places where prices rise and fall in response to changing demands and supplies, and they provide the links that mesh together consumers and businesses. Individuals and businesses save part of their income and invest those savings in new productive facilities.

The rationale of our economy also assumes that individual freedom of choice is central to our economic way of life. But individual freedom of choice is limited by laws and by social and moral pressures, for the protection of the individual and society. Thus markets and prices are the chief regulator of the allocation of scarce resources. But the government sets the ground rules under which competition takes place and sometimes participates actively in the processes of production and distribution. Thus we have a "mixed economy."

WHO IS THE CONSUMER?

Anyone who spends money for goods and services, directly or indirectly, is a consumer. By this definition we are all consumers.

We are all consumers
On January 1, 1972, our population was 208.5 million consumers. We had gained about 2 million during the year 1971—the result of 3.6 million births and 1.9 million deaths, plus a net immigration of about 400,000. The rate of growth of nearly 1 percent was about the same as it had been in recent years. The number of babies born continues to be about double the number of deaths. It would require a drop in the number of births to about half the present level, or a doubling of the number of deaths, to reach zero growth in the next few years.

The outlook for the next years is continued increase in the nation's population, even though the birthrate may continue downward. This is the consequence of the "baby boom" of the late 1940s and the 1950s. The babies of the 1947 boom celebrated their twenty-fifth birthdays in 1972, and the rest will be reaching maturity in the 1970s. There were about 17 million persons between the ages of 20 and 24 in 1970, by 1975 the number will be about 19 million, and by 1980 it will have reached 21 million. The number in the next 5-year-age group, 25 to 29, will increase by nearly one-half during the same ten years, from 14 million in 1970 to nearly 20 million in 1980. Therefore, it appears that we can expect continued population growth. A total population of 270 million to 280 million by the year 2000 is possible if present rates of growth continue.

Consumer income and expenditures
A brief look at the income of consumers and how they spend their money can help in understanding the modern consumer. The American consumer is the richest in the world and spends money at the rate of about $2 billion a day. He also has a higher annual disposable income (after taxes) than the average consumer in the world.

In 1971, the United States produced goods and services worth $1 trillion. Consumer expenditures accounted for two-thirds of the gross national product (GNP), including $103 billion for food, $107 billion for housing and shelter, and $42 billion for recreation.

The median income for all families in 1970 was about $9,867. This median family income in 1970 continues the trend of rising family income that has been evident during the past twenty-two years.

Changing income differences
Population experts predict that there will be about 230 million people in the United States by 1980. The National Industrial Conference Board predicts that there will be a continuing rise in family income. In terms of constant (1969) dollars, median family income increased from about $5,000 in 1947 to $9,867 in 1970.

The general rise in family income was accompanied by an upward shift in the income distribution. This shift can be illustrated by the decline in the percent of families with incomes below $4,000 (1969 dollar constant) between 1947 and 1969. In 1969, 15 percent of all families had incomes below $4,000, compared with 37 percent of all families in 1947.

Projections of these trends by the Conference Board indicate that by 1980, over 60 percent of all American families will have incomes of $10,000 and over (in 1968 dollars), compared with about 45 percent at the present time (Figure 1-1).

The results of changes in income distribution from 1971 to 1980 to 1990 are shown in Figure 1-2. In 1970 the income bulge was in the $10,000 to $15,000 category (in 1971 dollars). In 1980 and 1990 the income bulge will appear in the $15,000 to $25,000 category. By 1980 over 60 percent of families are likely to be above the $10,000 level, compared with about 45 percent at the present time.

Multiple income sources
Families receiving both earnings and other income had a median income of $10,742 in 1969, which was $1,635 (18 percent) more than that of families with earnings income only. In 1969, families with income from multiple sources constituted 54 percent of all families, in contrast to only 33 percent in 1956. The number of families receiving earnings income only declined from 61 percent in 1956 to only 38 percent in 1969. The proportionate increase in the number of families with other income and no earnings (from 5 percent in 1956 to 8 percent in 1969) represents for the most part a proportionate increase in the number of families headed by persons 65 years old and over or by females—families for which the probability of having no earners is greater than it is for other families. The adverse impact of this latter factor on median income is underscored by the fact that families with other income and no earnings had a median income of only $3,109. This small income was about one-third of that of all families in 1969.

FIGURE 1-1   Changing income distribution, 1947 to 1980

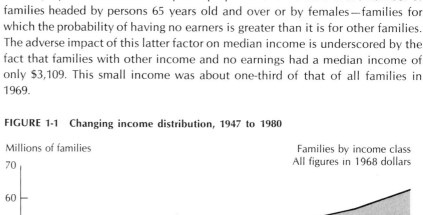

SOURCE: The Conference Board.

FIGURE 1-2   The changing pyramid of income distribution

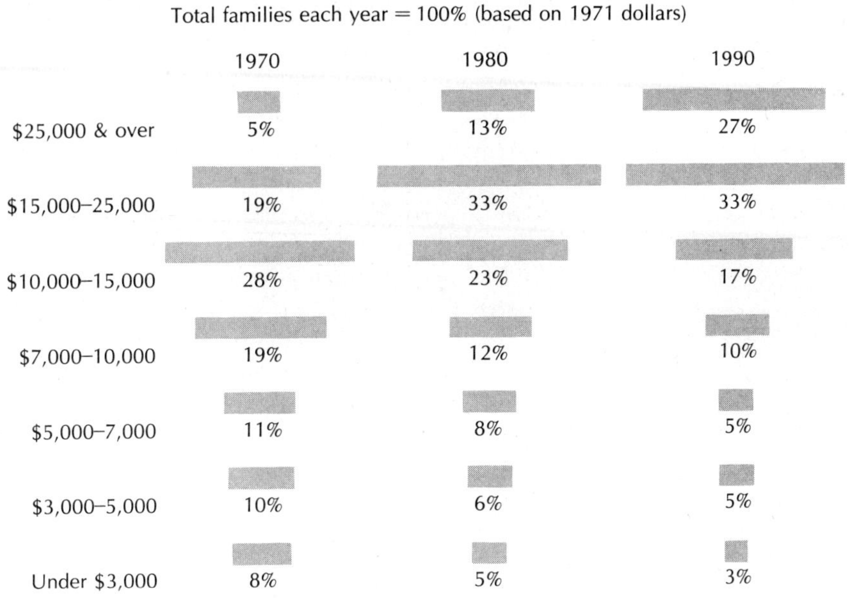

Total families each year = 100% (based on 1971 dollars)

	1970	1980	1990
$25,000 & over	5%	13%	27%
$15,000–25,000	19%	33%	33%
$10,000–15,000	28%	23%	17%
$7,000–10,000	19%	12%	10%
$5,000–7,000	11%	8%	5%
$3,000–5,000	10%	6%	5%
Under $3,000	8%	5%	3%

SOURCE: The Conference Board.

*Maldistribution
of income
and wealth*

A strong statistical underpinning for the idea of maldistribution of income and wealth in this country appears in a recent study by Letitia Upton and Nancy Lyons of the Cambridge Institute. In their opening sentence they state, "There is a startling and continuing inequality in the distribution of income in the United States, and the over-all pattern has remained virtually unchanged since World War II."

*The rich stay rich, and
the poor stay poor*

In other words, the rich are staying rich, and the poor are staying poor, despite rare and highly publicized exceptions. Moreover, the poor are paying relatively more in taxes, while the effective tax rate on the affluent has been declining since World War II.

The Upton-Lyons study makes these points:

1. In the postwar era, the income of the richest one-fifth of American families has been more than all the income received by the bottom three-fifths, since approximate income ranges have been as follows: the poorest one-fifth, under $5,000; the second one-fifth, $5,000 to $8,000; the middle one-fifth, $8,000 to $11,000; the fourth one-fifth, $11,000 to $14,000; and the richest one-fifth, $14,000 and over. The top 5 percent earn $24,000 and over.

2. The 10.4 million families in the poorest one-fifth receive less than 6 percent of total national money income, or an average of $3,054 annually, while the 10.4 million families in the richest one-fifth take over 40 percent, or an average of $23,100. If all money income had been divided equally among all families, the average would have been just over $11,000 in 1970.

3. Myth to the contrary, government "transfer payments" to the blind, the

unemployed, the aged, welfare mothers, etc., account for only 7 to 8 percent of all personal income, and over half of this amount goes to Social Security recipients, who not only were taxed to pay for their benefits but also are to be found throughout the income scale, not merely in the low-income groups; thus government subsidy has little if any impact on income distribution.

4. Capital gains, percentage depletion, depreciation, and interest exclusion provisions make federal income tax rates less progressive than they appear. Thus the effective rate of tax on the top 1 percent of income earners in 1967 was only 26 percent, and in 1962 the income share of the top one-fifth declined from only 45.5 percent before taxes to 43.7 percent after taxes, while the bottom three-fifths increased their income share from only 31.8 percent before taxes to 33.2 percent after taxes.

5. Percentages aside, the general rise in money income and living standards in the United States has only broadened the absolute dollar gap between rich and poor families. Calculated in 1970 dollars, the families in the bottom one-fifth gained income from $1,956 in 1958 to $3,085 in 1968, while the highest one-fifth gained from $15,685 in 1958 to $21,973 in 1968. Thus the gap between them increased from $13,729 to $18,888, as the rich got absolutely and relatively richer.

Distribution of wealth

Income is who gets what, wealth is who has what, and the wealth picture is even more inequitable than the income picture. The Upton-Lyons study shows, for example:

1. The top one-fifth of Americans, ranked by wealth, owned 77 percent of personal wealth in 1962—three times more than the entire wealth of the bottom 80 percent.

The top 1 percent of personal wealth-holders own 20 to 30 percent of personally held wealth

2. The top 1 percent of families and individuals receive only 9 percent of personal income, but the top 1 percent of personal wealth-holders own between 20 and 30 percent of all personally held wealth, and have done so for decades.

3. The number of individual stock investors increased from 9 million in 1956 to 31 million in 1970, but the proportion of corporate stock owned by the wealthiest 1 percent of the population increased from 69.5 percent in 1953 to 71.6 percent in 1962.

According to the Upton-Lyons study, then, the rich are staying rich and the poor are staying poor, and the wealth picture appears even more inequitable than the income picture.

Other changes in American society

There have been other major changes in American society that will affect people as consumers. We have become an urban society; our educational levels have increased substantially for both men and women; and we have become a more prosperous society. All these changes have served to reduce the size of families. Urban rates of childbearing are below those of the rural population. The higher a woman's educational level and, on the whole, the higher the family income, the fewer children she is apt to bear. We shall no doubt continue to become even more urban, and the proportion of women—and men—who complete high school and college will continue to increase. Finally, family incomes will increase in the foreseeable future.

Teen-agers   For many sellers, the teen-age market is important. Lester Rand, head of New York's Youth Research Institute, estimates that there are 25 million youths in the United States between 13 and 19 with more than $18 billion in earnings, gifts, allowances, and family "loans" to spend pretty much as they wish. According to a market study by Scholastic Magazines, Inc., 17 percent of the teen-agers owned their own TV sets, 18 percent owned tape recorders, 21 percent outboard motors, 42 percent electric razors, 68 percent cameras, and 87 percent watches. By 1970, Rand estimates that teen-agers will number over 30 million with disposable incomes totaling $30 billion.

In many cases, the teen-agers' spending far outweighs their numerical strength. Teen-age boys, for example, are only about 12 percent of the male population but buy more than 40 percent of all sportswear sold, while teen-age girls now purchase nearly a third of the nation's cosmetics output. Beyond their own purchases, they influence at least $35 billion of adults' spending, says Rand.

While most of the teen-agers are not in the market for homes and appliances, they soon will be. Over 40 percent of all brides are teen-agers; more wives have their first child in their nineteenth year than in any other, and one out of every six teen-age wives has two or more children. As consumers, many of these young marrieds believe in "go get tomorrow today." Advertisers are not unmindful of these teen-agers. For example, the senior editor of *Seventeen,* "America's Teenage Magazine," recently put it:

> Catch a teen-age girl and put her in your pocket now and you'll keep her forever. Now's the time to sew her up—before the rice is in her hair, before the stork is on the roof, before the wolf is at the door. Set her textured stockings on the path to your product now—and she'll come back blindfolded. . . .

Market consultant Bernice Fitz-Gibbon said to 1,500 leading merchants meeting in New York, "If you haven't struck the shimmering, glimmering teen-age lode, there must be something wrong with you."

What makes the economy tick?   Why are these consumer income figures important? Because the spending and saving of money, directly and indirectly, of our 210 million consumers today are what make our economy tick. In 1970, as in recent past years, consumer expenditures constituted about two-thirds of total expenditures in our economy. In 1971, for example, consumers collectively had over $741 billion in annual personal income and were spending over $616 billion annually. If family incomes increase, as they usually do for most consumers, their expenditures are likely to increase. If spending increases, the economy will grow. In fact, consumers are so important to a healthy economy that periodic reviews to ascertain the attitudes and buying intentions of consumers are made by the University of Michigan Survey Research Center and made public. Business, government, and consumers in general use these data for planning production, capital expenditures, and investing.

Consumers still have money (savings) left after all of their expenditures. The savings in recent years have been at a rate of 5 percent of total disposable income (amount left after deducting personal taxes). At the end of 1970, however, personal savings for the year amounted to $44.4 billion, or 7.3 percent of disposable personal income. This money is invested mostly in ways which help to lay the foundation for future business expansion. This is what we mean when we say that consumer spending and saving are what make our economy tick.

THE CONSUMER INTEREST—THE REAL ISSUE

The consumer is supposed to determine what is produced

Consumer sovereignty

The concept of consumer sovereignty still persists after nearly a century of experience. According to this theory, the role of the consumer is to guide the economy to the production of goods and services that he wants. In short, the consumer expresses his wishes by casting dollar votes. In this way, the consumer is supposed to determine what shall be produced.

Playing umpire is not a new role for the consumer. In theory, consumer sovereignty—consumer freedom of choice—is indeed the keystone of our economic system. It is from this assumption that the free competition, private enterprise system derives social justification for its division of rewards for effort. Withdraw consumer sovereignty from this concept, and free competition resembles a kind of economic jungle warfare. We are now fairly far along in the process of withdrawing true consumer sovereignty from the marketplace. The question is: Can we bring back into the marketplace a rational umpire—the consumer?

Consumer economic power

Dr. Robert D. Schooler, professor of marketing at the University of Missouri, states that the "reduction in consumer power is almost complete"; that the "maldistribution of power and the consequent abuse of the consumer are totally violative of the principles and rationale of a market economy"; that consumers and government are preoccupied with "consumer interest at the point of sale, with matters of packaging, advertising, and retail pricing methodology. While these are legitimate issues, they are secondary; if the consumer interest is to be served the issue of progress-sharing must take priority and the consumers' case against producers must be prosecuted vigorously."[1] In other words, consumers have lost their collective power in the marketplace. The road back is for consumers to act collectively in the marketplace.

Price and output are set in this market by supply and demand or by market power (monopoly), and the consumer can take it or leave it. The solution, according to some economists, is for consumers to organize effectively as a power group such as the founders of the Consumers' League relied upon in the 1890s and later. The only power the league had was the collective effort of every buyer to refuse to buy. The league founders were wealthy socialites in large urban centers who were primarily interested in poor working conditions in retail stores. The league made fairly successful use of consumer collective power in correcting some of the poor working conditions in retail stores. Perhaps this early illustration of the fairly effective use of consumer collective power offers some insight into the more complicated problems in our modern marketing system. The league defined its goals and pursued the means to accomplish these goals. For example, the league set up standards of fair practices for retailers, and later for manufacturers. It then publicized the firms which met these standards, and league members were asked to buy only at these stores. The league also adopted

[1]"The Consumer Interest: The Real Issue," *Journal of Consumer Affairs*, Summer 1967.

a label to identify goods made under approved conditions. Shoppers were alerted to look for this seal of approval.

Ultimately, the league urged legislation to require all firms to observe minimum standards for wages, hours, and working conditions. While the ultimate appeal was to law, the league tried to arouse public opinion. The league's policy expressed the value judgment that all consumers had a "moral duty" to carry out the goals of the national Consumers' League.

Today, however, consumer exploitation has replaced labor exploitation. Almost all consumer organizations agree that the consumer does not have the collective power to make effective changes in the marketplace. The newly created Consumer Federation of America with headquarters in Washington, D.C., could be the nucleus of a modern national consumer action group. Theoretically, collective consumer power is possible. But is it likely to come about under present and foreseeable conditions? In other words, is "consumer sovereignty," the collective power of all consumers, likely to come about even after great effort on the part of all consumer organizations working together for national consumer goals? (If you would like to know more about consumer action see the book that accompanies this text, Taylor-Troelstrup, *Consumer in American Society: Additional Dimensions* which will hereafter be referred to as Taylor-Troelstrup Readings.)

THE MODERN MARKET ECONOMY

The Consumers' League did not direct all of its economic power to getting remedial legislation. But the fact remains that it did effect legislation just as modern consumer organizations attempt to do. The league also used preferential buying and the boycott. These are weapons used today by black and other minority groups, by recent action of housewives boycotting retail food stores, and by affluent families reading *Consumers Union Reports* and following their recommendations for preferential buying and for government action. The real question is not whether the force of collective consumer demand is as great as it ever was. It is potentially as great today as in the decades of the league's activities. The realistic problem today is that the modern market economy, as described in economic texts, can rely upon what Adam Smith called the "invisible hand" to regulate it properly *only* if certain conditions exist. Dr. James Morgan, professor of economics at the University of Michigan, recently described these conditions:

> First, there must be enough competition among sellers, and among employers of labour, to assure no monopolistic restrictions of price or output, though sometimes countervailing power may help when two large units of labour and management clash.
>
> Second, there must be a *reasonably fair* distribution of income available for families to spend, so that individual market demands reflect real social needs and priorities.
>
> Third, there must be a proper and sufficient development of the public sector—the provision of goods and services by community or national action—where they cannot be provided by individual initiative. I refer, of course, to such things as parks, roads, clean water, and fresh air.

Fourth, there must be informed and intelligent consumers, with the understanding necessary to implement their desires effectively in the market place. This requires a proper mix of consumer education, consumer information, and consumer protection from fraud and harmful products.

Among all these requirements, the consumer interest threads, but in the first three of the four—preservation of competition, the equity in distribution of income, and the proper provision of public goods and services—the consumer can act only as a voter and our help is restricted to informing him as to his interests. Even in the fourth, where voluntary consumer organisations must focus, a major responsibility for general consumer education belongs in the school systems, and the major responsibility for protecting the consumer from fraud and dangerous products belongs to the Government.

Granting these limitations in our marketplace, how long do consumers have to wait for effective collective consumer power? Is effective collective

FIGURE 1-3   The power of the consumer illustrated by the recent nationwide boycotting of grapes grown in California. The boycott was in support of the organizing attempts of Mexican, Filipino, and other migratory workers in their fight to raise their wages to more than subsistence (or lower) levels. The boycott was so effective in 1968 alone (a 12 percent decline in profits for the large grape-growing combines) that supermarkets experienced a drop in sales of even those grapes coming from South America because for awhile consumers in some stores stopped buying *all* grapes unless they were sure of their origin—hence the sign displayed in a New York supermarket.

(Photograph by Mary Ann Schatz.)

consumer power possible today? It is hard to conceive of a time when consumers in a large, populous country like the United States can effectively balance the power of producers, corporations, labor, and government. Today we have in fact an industrial autocracy, an autocracy in which power rests with a managerial class believing basically in non-price competition. In regard to corporate power, there is also a real abuse most serious to the consumer welfare— the abuse of the power to price. Control of price is a different thing from effective competition among many producers.

Economic concentration and monopoly power

Not all segments of our economy can be characterized as either monopolistic (Xerox, Western Electric, and IBM, for example) or competitive (the wheat and fashion markets). Between the two are "shared monopolies"—a form of noncompetition or unreal competition in which a few large firms produce a particular product. Shared monopolists often act as a monopolist would, and the result is increased prices. For example, our steel industry, dominated by four firms controlling 54 percent of all shipments, periodically raises its prices despite idle capacity of some 33 percent and despite the availability of cheaper imported steel. Although big businessmen talk the language of competitive capitalism, each has sought refuge in price-fixing, parallel pricing, mergers, excessive advertising, quotas, subsidies, and tax favoritism.

Big business talks about free competition but really dislikes it

Industrial economists agree that when four or fewer firms control 50 percent or more of a market, a shared monopoly results. Collective or conspiratorial action, not competitive action, then pervades their productive activity. There are many such industrial giants: in automobiles (General Motors, Ford, Chrysler); in soap and detergents (Procter and Gamble, Colgate, Lever Brothers); in aluminum (Alcoa, Reynolds, Kaiser); in cereals (General Foods, General Mills, Kellogg, Quaker Oats); in light bulbs (General Electric, Westinghouse, Sylvania); in cigarettes (Reynolds, American, Philip Morris); and in other industries.

The extent of shared monopolies can be described as staggering. In 1971, economics professors William Shepherd and Richard Barber, authors of *Corporate America,* calculated that shared monopolies control about two-thirds of all industry. In terms of aggregate concentration, the ownership of all manufacturing assets by our biggest firms has been dramatic. While the top 200 industrial firms controlled 47 percent of total assets in 1950, by 1965 they controlled 55 percent. Dr. Willard Mueller, former chief economist of the Federal Trade Commission, testified in November 1969, that "today the top 200 manufacturing corporations already control about two-thirds of all the assets held by corporations engaged primarily in manufacturing."

A controlled market makes for overpricing

The disfiguring of free enterprise by monopoly and shared monopoly results in serious economic tolls. Foremost is overpricing by one firm or a very few firms who control the market. A Federal Trade Commission study estimates that "if highly concentrated industries were deconcentrated to the point where the four largest firms control 40 percent or less of an industry's sales, prices would fall by 25 percent or more." The examples are many:

1. Today the big three automobile firms in this country produce about 83 percent of all cars sold in our country and about 97 percent of all domestic models. Industrial economist Leonard Weiss, of the University of Wisconsin, estimated that the noncompetitive state of the auto industry costs consumers of cars $1.6 billion per year.

2.   Federal Trade Commission studies show that cereal prices are 15 to 25 percent higher than they would be under real competition because of the dominance of the industry by just four firms.

3.   The oil import quota, by keeping out much foreign competition, permits domestic firms to overcharge, according to a Presidential task force, by an estimated $5 billion to $7 billion per year.

Such overpricing leads to lost output. Monopoly misallocates scarce resources, creating excess capacity and a smaller gross national product (GNP) than is our national potential. In recent studies, William Shepherd and F. M. Scherer have tried to quantify this lost GNP. They concluded that the overall cost of monopoly and shared monopoly in terms of lost production is somewhere between $48 billion and $60 billion annually. The tax revenues from this wealth could go a long way toward ending poverty and pollution and reducing taxes for all consumers in this country.

Monopoly overcharging also results in an inequitable transfer cost. When consumers pay excessive prices for goods, monopoly profits then redistribute income from the consuming public to stock shareholders of large corporations. Professor Shepherd has estimated this redistribution at about $23 billion annually. However, a 1963 study showed that only 1.6 percent of the adult population in this country owned 82.4 percent of all publicly held stocks. Hence, very few extra dividends ended up in consumer pockets. Furthermore, this redistribution of wealth—accentuating the extremes in a society where the richest 1 percent receive more income than the bottom 20 percent and where the top 5 percent receive more than the bottom 40 percent—can have serious political and social consequences.

Private enterprise and free competition

Most mature Americans say they believe in private enterprise. However, for private enterprise to function at its best and fairest, we must also have free competition. And here is the rub. The expression "free enterprise" has become a meaningless political slogan used interchangeably with "free competition." Many, perhaps most, businessmen in this country believe in free enterprise, but in practice do not believe in free competition. Yet it is impossible to have one without the other. If business desired free enterprise without free competition, it would have socialism at the top—a few very large corporations, interlocking with other firms, reaping the extra profits of private enterprise without having to risk free competition. Such firms and conglomerate affiliations are thus in a position to enforce oligopoly or monopoly practices and replace the free market system with a closed market that assures larger profits but gives consumers no choice between real competitors. Those who pursue this policy really want two contradictory things: freedom to make profit without effective interference and protection from the nuisance of real competition. This is a paradox of free enterprise as we have known it. Such a system hurts consumers and most small manufacturing enterprises as well as millions of retailers because it makes free choice in the marketplace meaningless.

Private enterprise is meaningless without free competition

The not-so-free enterprise

Amtrak tells Congress it needs another large injection of federal funds to keep its passenger trains operating. United States airlines ask for more government help, too. Defense contractors lobby the Pentagon to boost profit margins and extend other aid to lift them from their current depressed state.

More and more, American industry—linchpin of the great free enterprise economy—seeks funds or tax advantages from the government. Lockheed gets special big federal loan guarantees and extra business to help it out of its troubles. The Navy sweetens the existing F-14 aircraft contract to bail out Grumman. The Pentagon earmarks more than $100 million to ease Litton Industries' pain. Why don't defense and aerospace corporations move more aggressively to take up their current slack with more work on mass transportation, pollution control, waste disposal, and other newly expanding areas? They lack the know-how; the technology is different, they claim; the market is uncertain. Yet these are precisely the problems that aggressive capitalism is supposed to specialize in overcoming. Obviously, many of these companies prefer to avoid the risks and to wait instead for a new cycle of defense orders or some special bailout, as in the case of Lockheed.

Clearly, there is a need for some sort of serious national discussion on how far we want to continue down the road to some modified form of state socialism. Whichever way the policy is to go, it certainly should be more carefully considered, more precisely planned.

And perhaps in the meantime, too, there could be less preaching about the wonderful principles of the free enterprise system by businessmen who frequently find these principles so difficult to practice.

Discrediting capitalism

We noted earlier that in the eighty years that antitrust laws have been in effect, guilty businessmen have been sent to jail for criminal price-fixing only three times. In 1969 the bathtub and bathroom plumbing fixtures industry became the second major segment of American private enterprise within that decade to be convicted of criminal conspiracy to overcharge its consumer customers. Evidently the plumbing manufacturers had not read or were unmoved by the words of Federal District Judge Ganey in handing down jail terms and fines in the earlier case of the electrical equipment industry, for they followed the same illegal path. Judge Ganey's statement deserves to be recalled:

> This is a shocking indictment of a vast section of our economy, for what is really at stake here is the survival of the kind of economy under which this country has grown great, the free enterprise system.
>
> The conduct of the corporate and individual offenders alike has flagrantly mocked the image of that economic system of free enterprise which we profess to the country, and it has destroyed the model, it seems to me, which we offer today, as a free world alternative to state control, to socialism, and eventual dictatorship.

Perhaps it is time to act on Ralph Nader's suggestion that antitrust crime be treated as a felony rather than as a misdemeanor. Nader said, "A successful price-fix can inflate consumer prices 25% or more over the competitive level."[2]

THE CONSUMER AND ENVIRONMENTAL AWARENESS

More recently, consumers have become concerned with the quality of the physical environment—air, water, soil, and noise pollution. The consumer movement has rearranged its priority list to take these critical issues into account. This rearrangement also follows naturally from consumers' long-standing

[2]*The Washington Post,* May 24, 1972, p. A2.

concern with built-in obsolescence and poor quality and repairability, for these problems contribute to pollution in a "disposable society."

As consumerists join with conservationists and interested legislators, there is an increasing likelihood of government action. Since most of the pollution comes from private corporate actions, business must play an important cooperative role in solving pollution contamination. Consumers, too, have a responsible role because household ecology today involves the need to dispose of human excrement, food wastes, packaging materials, used goods, etc. Households are a part of a larger ecological system, and no individual family can completely shelter itself from environmental pollution.

Corporate pollution   The corporation's structure, impact, and public accountability are the central issue in any program designed to curb or forestall air, water, soil, and noise pollution by industrial activity. While there are other sources of pollution, such as the dumping by municipalities of untreated or inadequately treated sewage, industrial processes and products are the chief contributors to the long-term destruction of natural resources that each year increases the risks to human health and safety.

The automobile manufacturers' cars, according to Department of Health, Education, and Welfare data, account for 55 to 65 percent of this nation's air pollution. There is enough smog in the air over Los Angeles so that schoolchildren are warned not to play too strenuously or breathe too deeply on the days of the amber cloud. We have put enough toxics in the air over New York City to make the result of a day's walking and breathing equal the intake of almost two packs of cigarettes. And between the two coasts, we have made eyes smart in mile-high Denver and not-so-high Phoenix and countless smaller cities.

We have put DDT in the shellfish in the waters off Martha's Vineyard in the Atlantic. We have mined enough coal and iron to sag and crack 2 million acres of land, and we have strip-mined enough to cause deadly floods in Kentucky, West Virginia, and elsewhere. Perhaps we need to find ways to quantify a good or bad polluter as well as the profit or loss a company achieves.

Government regulation of polluters

Pollution laws need teeth

The sanctions against polluters to date have been feeble, out of date, and rarely invoked. For example, the federal air-quality act to date has resulted in no criminal penalties, no matter how willful and enduring the violations. Most of the states have ineffective pollution laws. The existing requirements for disclosure of the extent of corporate pollution are weak and flagrantly flouted. Counties in California, for example, have been concealing from their citizens the identity of polluters and the amounts of pollution, using such weak arguments to support their cover-up as the companies' fear of revealing "trade secrets." State agencies in California have refused to disclose pesticide data to representatives of orchard workers being gradually poisoned by the chemicals. What must be made clear to both corporate and public officials is that no one has the right to a trade secret in lethality.

Government regulation and enforcement should come in various forms such as nonreimbursable fines (tax laws permit a considerable shifting of antipollution costs onto the general taxpayer), suspensions, dechartering of corporations, required disclosure of violations in company ads, and more severe criminal penalties.

**Household ecology:
consumer responsibility**

Householders no longer produce and process their own food and fibers. Just as ecology is a branch of science dealing with the interrelationships of living organisms and their environment, household ecology deals with the interrelationships of individuals, families, and other groups and their environment.

Today, consumers have sacrificed their independence for a higher standard of living. They need outside inputs of food, clothing, water, gas, electricity, and other goods and services to function as a household. And their homes cannot completely shelter them from environmental pollution.

Consumers can gain a greater appreciation of their householder relationship to the larger environmental problems if they ask a few questions: What happens to materials that constitute refuse—paper, plastics, metals, glass, aluminum, and other household wastes? Are paper, metal, and glass recycling facilities available in the community? Are they being used? Is the polluter trying to reduce pollutants to the air, water, and soil? In short, consumers have direct responsibilities to minimize environmental pollution and waste of limited resources.

In summary, industry, government, and consumers have joint responsibilities to solve our environmental pollution. We will not find a way out of our present ecological problems until we have the courage to look honestly at evil where evil exists, until we forswear hypocrisy, until we call injustice and dishonor by their right names, and until a large number of Americans from every sector of society and of all shades of opinion are willing to acknowledge their own special contributions to our troubles.

THE DIFFICULT ROLE OF CONSUMERS

Reflection and observation indicate that too many consumers are unprepared for the role of sovereignty in our present complex economy. They are easily manipulated and are ignorant concerning the ways of the ever-changing marketplace. For example, how many consumers ever consider these questions?

*The consumer is not
king*

1. Are present-day prices competitive?
2. Does present-day competition resemble competition fifty years ago?
3. To what extent are the prices of consumer goods a measure of the actual cost of producing and distributing them?
4. Do I know what goods and services are best in terms of my own needs?
5. Do I buy only the goods and services that are beneficial?
6. Am I able to judge quality?
7. To what extent can I check quantity measurements of my purchases?

Economists assume that consumers are rational. Psychologists and sociologists, however, insist that we are social men rather than economic men. Our motivations include a desire for status, for conformity, for prestige, and for power, to mention only a few.

Economists also assume that consumers buy only for individual or family consumption, whereas there is much institutional buying today. There is also considerable public buying by the military and by schools, parks, highways, and many other public bodies.

Another serious defect in the assumption that the consumer is king lies in the fact that income is unevenly distributed. Consumers with many dollars can cast many votes. Others have to be satisfied with casting fewer dollar votes. Obviously, such a system gives some consumers more influence than others.

The inarticulate consumer versus pressure groups

Another reason the consumer is not king in our mid-twentieth-century economy is that consumption is a function common to all and peculiar to none. We are all consumers, but we are first a worker, a manager, a producer, a government clerk, a teacher, a doctor, a farmer, a lawyer. In such roles, each person's interest is direct, and he is willing to promote his direct interest through group action, through organized effort, or through political appeals to governing bodies. In his role as a consumer, his interests are indirect and consequently are neglected. Nobody is willing to organize effort, to obtain political support, to rally his fellow consumers solely in behalf of consumer interests. It becomes apparent, then, that in our present-day democratic society, where government responds to pressure groups, inarticulate consumers are largely at the mercy of more effectively organized groups.

The inarticulate consumer is at the mercy of the organized group

Interest groups are organized primarily to improve the relative position of their members. They are never organized to improve the position of all the members in society. While groups attempt to present their own special interests as being identical with the interests of the general public, it frequently results that their behavior indicates a pathetic ignorance of the general welfare. Everybody is for the consumer until more direct interests conflict. Then nobody is for the consumer, and consumer interests are neglected.

As long as the marketplace was an adequate regulator and coordinator of economic activity, admittedly in the distant past, there was less need for government to act as protector of consumer interests against exploitation by producer interests. But as industrialization developed, with its urbanization, consumers' dependence on sources of supplies beyond their own control has continued to increase rapidly. This increasing consumer dependence, in turn, has been responsible for partial public realization that the material health of each individual is becoming inseparably bound to the economic health of the entire community.

Other significant economic changes that require revision of the consumer sovereignty assumption have taken place in the economy in the last twenty-five years. One important change has been the growth of giant corporations to a dominant position in our economy.

Another significant change has been the tremendous expenditures by the military for national security—expenditures of such magnitude that a sudden drastic curtailment would most likely cause a recession.

Corporate farming and labor unions have had increasing influence in our economy. Corporation farming is encroaching on family-type farming. Consumers pay an annual multibillion dollar subsidy for farming. When big business and giant unions reach an impasse, as in the 1959–1960 steel strike, the economy suffers and consumers usually pay higher prices.

Another change has been the tremendous power of radio and television in stimulating sales. Actually, the price competition of a simpler economy has been replaced by the non-price competition of giant corporations monopolizing the choice listening hours on radio and TV.

These changes can be in the consumer interest. In England, for example, the BBC television reports the results of independent testing of consumer goods, giving brand names and comparative prices.

What choice does the consumer have? Some economists would argue that the consumer choice remains the same regardless whether we have an ideal competitive-model market or a market powered by price controls. In both kinds of markets, these economists would say that the consumer is a price-taker. If the consumer does not like the price or the product, he can take it or leave it. This conclusion must assume that the real difficulties are not in price and other controls by power groups like business, labor, and government, but in ourselves as careless and uninformed buyers. Can enough buyers be taught to care? Can any consumer group organize the economic power of consumers to balance the present power groups? Perhaps the consumer weapons of boycotting and preferential buying can be applied here and there at different times. But the history of the use of these two weapons is not reassuring in the United States. Public involvement in consumer action in a large country like ours is possible but not likely except in very unusual situations like the recent housewives' strike against food prices. Such collective movements unfortunately are short-lived and therefore ineffective, on the whole. So, if the best method, collective consumer power, is not successful, consumers will have no alternative except to direct their energy toward real but secondary issues of adequate market information and supporting effective legislation so as to make free choice in the marketplace meaningful.

CONSUMER PRIORITIES IN THE NEXT DECADE

In the United States, consumption means more than merely acquiring the food, clothing, shelter, and other things we need to stay alive. It also means acquiring those things which will enrich life for the individual. We need, therefore, to be clear on the difference between a consumption-directed economy and a consumer-directed economy.

In a consumption-directed economy, almost anything would be permissible. Deceptive and false advertising would be permitted as long as it encouraged people to buy. Planned obsolescence as a means of increasing consumption would be the rule rather than the exception. Disregard for such public problems as poverty, the shrinkage of our natural resources, air and water pollution, and problems faced by the elderly and the low-income minority groups would be tolerated as long as the employment and gross national product statistics (economic growth) appeared favorable. All that is important is that there be many things to buy and they they be bought. Such a system contains the seeds of its own economic and moral destruction. Where people are encouraged to emphasize the materialistic way of life, without regard to skill, craftsmanship, and quality, satisfaction is more likely to give way to emptiness and joy to be replaced by excitement—a kind of excitement based on the sating of appetites dreamed up by copywriters. This excitement often turns into frustration when the promise of a mediocre product or service is not fulfilled.

In a consumer-directed economy, the individual is treated as something else than a "buying machine"—a robot created to consume the good, bad, and indifferent products and services of our economic system. Rather, he is treated as an individual where natural inclination is toward self-improvement and the improvement of his environment. For this to happen, we need to emphasize and educate for the pursuit of high standards in goods and services and of a better environment.

The quality of American life

The quality of life is at issue

Almost everywhere we turn, quality is becoming an issue: the quality of the air we breathe, the water we drink, the meat we buy, the repair services we need, and the TV and radio programs that stream endlessly into our homes. And beyond these are the quality of our urban centers and the quality of our relations with one another.

Why are we concerned about fraud, with lack of real choice, with the absence of meaningful competition, with poor housing, and with overpriced medical services? Why do we worry about consumer credit and collection practices, and why do we want truth-in-lending? Certainly to cure specific evils, but more fundamentally to help to make us as consumers meaningful participants in our economy and our government and to bring to our life a quality to match the quantity.

The world over, the "American way of life" stands for abundance and quantity. We can be proud of the abundance, though not in the way that we have excluded a sizable segment of our people from it. We face the difficult task of dealing with racism and poverty. We also face the challenge to develop in every facet of our lives, and especially in those who touch us as producers and consumers, as sellers and buyers, ever higher standards. In other words, we are called out not to build bigger junkyards and worse ghettos; not to turn out shoddier products; not to reduce the quality of repair services; not to set new records in obsolescence in consumer products or in the speed with which we waste our natural resources. We are called to seek higher standards, to do the best in what we produce, and to act as responsible consumers in the marketplace. This is not a remote ideal but an urgent necessity. Some of the recent consumer legislation, especially since 1962—the year when President John F. Kennedy proclaimed the consumers' four-pronged rights—the right to safety, the right to be informed, the right to choose, and the right to be heard—symbolized consumerism. They became the basis for important new consumer legislation.

Focus on consumers

The Kennedy consumer "rights" proclamation became the basis for enactment of several important new consumer laws and of amendments to other laws already on the books—Fair Packaging and Labeling Act, Consumer Credit Protection Act, Wholesome Meat Act, Fire Safety Act, Hazardous Products Commission Act, and Flammable Fabrics Act, to mention a few. More consumer protection legislation is in the works concerning areas such as fraud and deception in sales; automobile insurance; protection against hazardous radiation from television sets and other electronic equipment; closing the gaps in poultry inspection; the sale of unwholesome fish; the prevention of death and accidents on our waterways; warranties and guarantees; improving honesty and fairness in repair work and servicing; pipeline safety; electric power reliability; land sales frauds; mutual fund reform; the safety of natural gas lines; cigarette labeling and advertising; truth-in-trading stamps; full disclosure of costs when buying a home; advertising claims for dietary, vitamin, and mineral products; dishonest lumber grades; grade standards for more food products; and nutrient labeling. And there will be more consumer legislation in the years to come.

If it is good for the public, it is good for business

Business, in general, has discovered over the years that good consumer protection laws are in the interest of ethical, competitive business. E. B. Weiss, a veteran marketing and advertising executive, illustrates this point of view:

> Each industry affected by proposed legislation has tended, on balance, to oppose uncompromisingly each new legislative proposal on behalf of consumerism. The food industry fought truth-in-packaging bills for five years. Truth-in-credit legislation was opposed by the credit industry for seven years. . . . In short, after six years of tuning up, Washington is literally racing toward additional legislation, regulation, and organization. State governments are doing the same thing, and so are many city governments. But industry's attitude tends to remain a mixture of confrontation, lamentation, and pious posturing. The marketing fraternity, especially, is almost united in its opposition. Marketing conventions resound with wails of anguish, of frustration, of bewilderment.[3]

Mr. Weiss then predicted that continued opposition to consumer legislation will lead "to quasi-utility status for marketing. . . . Marketing will be regulated by law far more than it has ever been before. Most marketing leaders have only themselves to blame if they do not like this prospect."

This is a strong indictment of the general opposition of business and marketing men to consumer legislation, from a respected marketing and advertising executive. Mr. Weiss is receiving some support for his views from some leaders of business. Mr. Thomas J. Watson, Jr., International Business Machines board chairman, said, "If we businessmen insist that free enterprise permits us to be indifferent to those things on which people put high value, then the people will quite naturally assume that free enterprise has too much freedom."[4]

There are many evidences of new interest in consumer issues. In addition to the general support by the people for better consumer protection of goods and services, as indicated in all of the recent legislation, the Opinion Research Corporation in 1968 reported on home interviews at all income levels, and discovered that:

1. Seven out of 10 Americans feel that present federal legislation is inadequate to protect their health and safety;
2. Fifty-five percent feel that further laws are needed to help consumers get full value for their money;
3. Thirty-four percent would like to see packaging and labeling of grocery products further investigated; and
4. Sixty-two percent favor a proposed law requiring doctors to prescribe by generic rather than brand names.[5]

---

[3] In an article he wrote in the *Harvard Business Review,* July–August, 1968.

[4] Thomas J. Watson, Jr., *A Business and Its Beliefs,* McGraw-Hill Book Company, New York, 1963, pp. 88–90.

[5] Reported by the National Association of Manufacturers and reprinted in *Dollars and Decisions,* University of Vermont, Extension Service, Burlington, 1968.

Consumer issues and areas for attention

What are the issues and problems consumers are likely to be concerned with in the years ahead? Dr. Gordon E. Bivens, economist and professor in the college of Home Economics at the University of Missouri, prepared a paper in which he discusses some issues arising from urbanization, mobility, youthful spenders, rising consumer incomes, increasing complexity of consumer goods and services, depersonalization of the market, and increasing interdependence of nations. Dr. Bivens said that the consumer issues needing attention in the future are these:[6]

There are ten basic consumer needs

1. Need to rethink the ethics of consumption. An estimated three-fourths of the U.S. population will soon be living in urban areas. In such a highly urbanized society, consumption must take place in a setting of closeness to others. People both as individuals and as a society will need to give increasing consideration to ways of reducing noise, fumes, litter, and other by-products of their consumption activities that impinge on their neighbors.

2. Need to cope with increasingly complex market. The function of consumers as buying agents for households will become even more generalized than it is now, as the number and variety of goods and services on the market increase and the income consumers have to buy goods rises. Consumers will have to make decisions about so many items they cannot possibly have specialized information about all of them. At the same time, the selling side of the market situation undoubtedly will become more specialized—in advertising, selling, and promotional techniques.

3. Need to clarify values. As their buying functions become more complex, consumers will need to be honest with themselves and think through carefully the values and goals that guide their decisions. Otherwise, they may be too easily influenced in their buying by sales pressures.

4. Need to consider giving. Consumers are going to face important decisions about how much and what types of giving they want to support. The question will be how much of their private consumption they are willing to give up to contribute to peace at home and abroad. This will involve gifts for domestic relief and developing nations, both by public means (taxation) and private giving.

5. Need to consider public versus private consumption. Consumers will have to give more thought to which goods and services should be privately acquired and used and which provided by public means. Such decisions must be guided by considerations of how these can be provided at the lowest real cost, and what the long-time needs of society will be. An example is the need for setting aside public lands for play areas and parks, resulting from the increased urbanization. In any event, consumers will have to be concerned with public as well as private decisions. This means they will need to use their right to vote, so that the people most likely to act in accordance with their views are elected.

6. Need to relate present to future decisions. As goods become more complex and require more specialized service for repair and even maintenance, consumers must recognize more than ever before that their decisions today will affect those of the future. For example, deciding to buy an automatic washing machine this year commits one to future expense for repairs and maintenance if the washer is to be used and enjoyed. This precommitment of spending, then, restricts choices in other areas of future spending.

7. Relation to consumers in other countries. As countries become more interdependent, U.S. consumers will need to be concerned about such matters as (1) the effect of tariffs on potentials for growth in other countries as well as on prices at

[6]*Family Economics Review*, June 1968, pp. 9–12.

home, (2) standardization of sizes and terms used for consumer goods in international commerce, and (3) the effect of the quality of consumer goods we send abroad on international relations.

8. Need to appraise resource use and cost. The rates at which the various consumer resources—money, time, energy, skill, and interests—can be substituted for each other will have to be constantly reevaluated as incomes rise, goods on the market change, and opportunities to learn expand. For example, because of rapidly changing conditions, consumers will need constantly to reevaluate the relative importance of saving time in buying and saving money by searching the market.

As part of their appraisal of resource use, consumers may need to sharpen their figuring of costs of owning goods by counting as part of this cost what they could have earned in interest if they had saved or invested an amount equal to the purchase price. This type of calculation will be especially important in their decision to buy or to rent—houses and major durable equipment, for example. The option to lease, as an alternate to ownership, is likely to become important for more and more goods.

9. Need to know legal rights. In the years ahead consumers will be involved in more and increasingly complex contractual arrangements. They will need to be aware of their legal rights and responsibilities, and know when to consult legal experts.

10. Need to make likes and dislikes known. As markets become more impersonal and direct communication between consumer and decision-making personnel in the market becomes more limited, consumers may need to initiate—through group action or other means—ways to make their likes and dislikes constructively known. Although such communication is finally worked out through the market, it is only with a good bit of lag and then not perfectly.

This list of ten consumer issues, which will need attention in the coming years, aptly sums up the responsibilities of consumers in years to come.

The consumers' Magna Charta

On March 15, 1962, President John F. Kennedy proclaimed, as has been noted previously, a "declaration of rights" for consumers in a free society. This historic message to Congress was devoted entirely to a "Consumers' Protection and Interest Program." In this first consumer message to Congress the President listed the following consumer rights:

1. The right to safety—to be protected against the marketing of goods that are hazardous to health or life.

2. The right to be informed—to be protected against fraudulent, deceitful, or grossly misleading information, advertising, labeling, and other practices, and to be given the facts needed to make informed choices.

3. The right to choose—to be assured, wherever possible, access to a variety of products and services at competitive prices. And in those industries in which competition is not workable and government regulation is substituted, there should be assurance of satisfactory quality and service at fair prices.

4. The right to be heard—to be assured that consumer interests will receive full and sympathetic consideration in the formulation of government policy and fair and expeditious treatment in its administrative tribunals.

On February 5, 1964, President Johnson sent another historic message to Congress in which he reiterated the four consumer rights proclaimed by President Kennedy. On March 21, 1966, President Johnson transmitted a message to

Congress requesting effective laws on lending charges and packaging practices. Congress passed legislation on these matters in 1967 and 1968.

On February 6, 1968, President Johnson presented the fourth of these messages on the American consumer, enumerating the steps taken to achieve present progress and setting forth a new program for 1968. President Johnson said that this was not a partisan program or a business program or a labor program. It was, he said, a "program for all of us—all 200 million Americans."

President Nixon sent a message to Congress in October 1969 on the protection of interests of consumers in which he stated that "consumerism . . . is a healthy development that is here to stay." The consumers' rights he enumerated included:

1. The right to make intelligent choice among products and services.
2. The right to accurate information.
3. The right to expect that sellers have considered the health and safety of the buyer.
4. The right to register his dissatisfaction, and have his complaint heard and weighed.

Also, in the fall of 1969, the Congress of the International Co-operative Alliance in London adopted an international declaration of consumers' rights which affirms that consumers have a right to:

1. A reasonable standard of nutrition, clothing, and housing.
2. Adequate standards of safety and a healthy environment free from pollution.
3. Access to relevant information on goods and services and to education on consumer topics.
4. Influence in economic life and democratic participation in its control.

The consumers' rights were further extended by Mary Gardiner Jones, a member of the Federal Trade Commission, in an address to the Sixth Biennial Conference of the International Organization of Consumers Union, Baden-Vienna, Austria, on June 29, 1970. She said *consumerism* means that:

1. Advertisements must be free of lies and half truths.
2. Advertisements must cease being directed to irrational or irrelevant qualities.
3. Consumers want hard, affirmative facts about goods and services.
4. Consumers want what they paid for in appliance or product performance.
5. If there is a failure, consumers want satisfactory adjustment.

In 1971, the Committee for Economic Development, representing 200 top leaders in business and education in this country, issued a lengthy report entitled *Responsibilities of Business Corporations.* In it they listed the following goals:

1. Elimination of poverty and provision for good health care.
2. Equal opportunity for each person to realize his full potential regardless of race, sex, or creed.

3. Education and training for a fully productive and rewarding participation in modern society.

4. Ample jobs and career opportunities in all parts of society.

5. Livable communities with decent housing, safe streets, a clean and pleasant environment, efficient transportation, good cultural and educational opportunities. . . .

In short, these very broad goals concern a better quality of life for all our citizens, and they have expanded the meaning of consumerism today.

Finally, Ralph Nader, America's leading consumer advocate, made the following recommendations in a recent interview reported in the *New York Times,* February 17, 1971:

1. Federal chartering of corporations requiring that they issue annual reports on social cost accounting, that they establish complaint procedure, that they not be allowed to cover up antipollution abuses on the grounds that they must conceal trade-secrets, and that corporate officials be made personally responsible when a corporation is found guilty of fraud and deceit

2. New requirements for shareholders' rights

3. Social bankruptcy for a company found guilty of making people sick or of destroying and depreciating other people's property, without offering compensation, through contamination and pollution

Thus we see that consumerism has come to involve issues and responsibilities which were almost unheard of in the early sixties. Consequently, a new bill of rights for consumers is needed for the 1970s.

A new bill of rights for consumers

In light of the many concerns of consumers, including rearranging their list of priorities to include environmental and broadcasting demands, it is clear that basic consumers' rights have moved beyond those proclaimed by President Kennedy in 1962—the right to be heard, the right to be informed, the right to safety, and the right to choose. They have slowly expanded, brick by brick, from four to ten rights:

Basic consumer rights have expanded

1. The right to safety—to be protected against the marketing of goods that are hazardous to health or life.

2. The right to be informed—to be protected against fraudulent, deceitful, or grossly misleading information, advertising, labeling, and other practices, and to be given the facts needed to make informed choices.

3. The right to choose—to be assured, wherever possible, access to a variety of products and services at competitive prices. And in those industries in which competition is not workable and government regulation is substituted, there should be assurance of satisfactory quality and service at fair prices.

4. The right to be heard—to be assured that consumer interests will receive full and sympathetic consideration in the formulation of government policy and fair and expeditious treatment in its administrative tribunals.

5. The right to expect quality of design, workmanship, and ingredients in consumer products and services.

6. The right to be charged fair prices for consumer goods.

7.   The right to receive courteous and respectful treatment from the business firms which provide consumer products and services.

8.   The right to expect consumer products and services to be ecologically sound.

9.   The right to expect business firms to offer products and services whose uses by the consuming public are consistent with the values of a humane society.

10.   The right to redress of legitimate greivances relating to purchased products and services.

CONSUMER RESPONSIBILITY

How do you react to questionable methods and devices for selling the nation's abundant productivity? Are deceit, fraud, dishonesty, illusions, planned obsolescence, and plain cheating the only ways to utilize this abundant productivity? Is there no place for good standards, fairness, and honesty when exchanging dollars for goods and services? And, finally, do you agree with some marketing experts who say that the best way to utilize our abundant production is to "make consumption our way of life, that we should convert buying and use of goods into rituals, that we seek our spiritual satisfactions, or ego-satis-

To end glut, should we be gluttons?

factions, in consumption"? In short, these marketing experts say that "the way to end glut is to produce gluttons." What do you think?

Faced with these multiple issues, what can consumers do about it? In the first place, a consumer can become an alert, informed, and responsible person. Anyone can spend money. A responsible person, however, should know his role and function in the economy. In this way he can influence what is to be produced.

A second consumer responsibility is to exercise independence of judgment and action. Then he is not likely to yield to commercial selling pressures, to conspicuous consumption, to group pressures, and to the lure of excessive credit. This suggests that the mature consumer has a continuing need for consumer information and education.

A third consumer responsibility is to recognize the dangers inherent in needless waste of limited natural and human resources. Many of these resources are irreplaceable.

The consumer also has a responsibility to buy products and services that are produced most efficiently. Such efficiency, however, ought not to be at the expense of exploitation of people on the basis of sex, age, color, or national origin.

The responsible consumer should be honest in his dealings, just as he expects industry, merchants, and repairmen to be honest. He has the responsibility, for example, not to abuse the privilege of trying out merchandise.

He should also take the time to write protest letters to irresponsible industries, merchants, and repairmen. How else will irresponsible businessmen and servicemen know that you are aware of their deceitful and dishonest dealings? Lacking support of informed and responsible consumers, the fair-minded businessmen find it difficult to withstand dishonest and unethical competitors. Consumer awareness of deceit and fraud will help industry help itself. The consumer who knows how he is being ill-treated by dishonest merchants can exercise his sovereignty (his buying decision) by rewarding the honest and more efficient producer with his business.

Sometimes the collective effort of consumers brings about a change. The American consumers who protested against car design in the late 1950s showed their preference for smaller automobiles by purchasing such cars made in other countries. Likewise, consumer protest has led to the creation of new and different ways of distribution of goods and services—for example, discount stores, consumer cooperatives, and credit unions.

Producerism: another consumer responsibility

Consumerism is the other half of producerism. Because most of us tend to compartmentalize our roles in life, we generally view ourselves as consumers, overlooking our role as producers of goods and services consumed by others. Central to the long-range success of the consumer movement is the recognition that the dissatisfied consumer may himself be a less-than-satisfactory producer whose work elicits howls of protest from other consumers.

The focus of the consumer movement in its initial stages has been on the producer, on the giants of industry who determine whether the consumer will have effective safety devices in the car he drives, safe additives in the foods he eats, and honest packaging of the products he uses. There is strong news value in the lack of quality in the products we buy, and little in the story of the worker in the assembly line who turns out a defective product.

It is hard to determine when pride in accomplishment as a widespread concept came to an end—but it did. We must regenerate that sense of pleasure in accomplishment and motivate consumers to aim for high quality in their producer roles.

But quality of products or services is only one dimension of consumerism. Another, equally serious, is our current lack of increasing productivity, which is affecting the upward spiral of prices. From the industrial revolution until 1966, our economy each year benefited from increasing production per dollar of labor, a trend which kept costs of products and services in reasonable ratio to all the economic elements of our society. But those productivity increases can no longer be taken for granted. The tables of productivity gains by the world's industrial nations now show the United States far down the list. In the five years that ended in 1970, for example, manufacturing productivity rose 14.2 percent in Japan, 7.9 in Sweden, 6.6 in France, and 5.3 in West Germany. In the United States it rose only 2.1 percent.

America's productivity lags behind that of other countries

How do we solve the productivity problem in terms of both quality and quantity? The solution involves nothing less than the effort of every single working person.

Management, too, can be blamed for losing its edge in innovation, creativity, ingenuity, and planning. Perhaps Peter G. Peterson, President Nixon's Secretary of Commerce, identified one problem when he told a congressional group in 1972 that "management slipped into the habit of being more concerned with the short-term earnings statement than with the long-term earnings that would be seriously affected by lagging productivity."

Some manufacturers create built-in or planned obsolescence. According to Joseph Martin, general counsel to the Federal Trade Commission, obsolescence can be built into a product by failing to provide a source of spare parts for the reasonable life of the product, by making frequent style or nonfunctional changes so that the user feels he must turn in his old model, and by including certain components made of materials which have a shorter life expectancy than that of the product itself.

Government can be blamed. Why did the Federal Price Commission in 1972 seek, in its efforts to control inflation, solutions to symptoms instead of treating the basic underlying factors of inflation? Why did the Federal Price Commission try to keep prices down when production costs were rising?

Labor can also be blamed. Why is absenteeism in our manufacturing plants as high as 20 percent on certain days, and why did it average over 5 percent of the hourly work force between 1968 and 1972? This compared with only a 2 to 3 percent absentee rate in the early 1960s.

Perhaps we can solve the problems of lagging production and lack of pride in the quality of consumer goods by discovering how the individual worker can be motivated to do a better job through a cooperative management-labor program directed toward a renaissance of pride in the quality of goods produced — a program aimed at worker involvement not only in units per hour but also in well-made units.

If we don't produce efficiently, we won't consume efficiently

If we are to have an effective consumer revolution, we must effect a more efficient producer revolution. Almost every consuming unit in our society is also a producing unit, capable through greater care and efficiency of influencing the quality and price of a product or service. In the end, if we don't produce efficiently, we won't consume efficiently.

On July 10, 1972, a subcommittee of the Joint Economic Committee of Congress issued a special report, *American Productivity: Key to Economic Strength and National Survival,* calling for sharply expanding efforts to increase productivity in both the private and the public sectors. The report asserted that the National Commission on Productivity (NCP), established by President Nixon in 1970, has accomplished very little. The report also called on the commission to include in its report findings on causes for the lag in productivity in this country. (Productivity is defined usually as "output per man-hour" but also as "the relation of expansion in output to the increase in inputs of resources" in both industry and government.)

Increasing productivity is very important to all consumers. It is the key to the good life. With rising productivity we can pay higher wages, as workers share in the increased production. It is also a partial solution to inflation because unit prices of goods go down.

One major barrier to increased productivity is the persistent and continually high level of unemployment. Reducing unemployment is one way to increase productivity and bring about a better way of life.

The Joint Economic Subcommittee recommended that the NCP examine improvements in the service sector which can be brought about by government action. As an example, it mentioned the enforcement of increased standardization of packaging in certain industries, such as food retailing, as a way to implement increased productivity.

THE NEW CONSUMERISM

A middle western business executive, quoted by Albert Z. Carr in the *Harvard Business Review,* illustrates what the New Consumerism is not:

> So long as a businessman complies with laws of the land and avoids telling malicious lies, he's ethical. If the law as written gives a man a wide-open chance to make a killing, he'd be a fool not to take advantage of it. If he doesn't, somebody else will. There's no obligation on him to stop and consider who is going to get hurt. If the law says he can do it, that's all the justification he needs. There's nothing unethical about that. It's just plain business sense.[7]

In other words, if "legal" says "go ahead" regardless of other consequences to consumers and competition, only a fool would not take advantage of the situation. True, many business leaders today would not subscribe to this kind of business behavior.

Mrs. Virginia Knauer, Special Assistant to President Nixon for Consumer Affairs, has defined the New Consumerism as:

> . . . nothing more and nothing less than a challenge to business to live up to its full potential—to give consumers what is promised, to be honest, to give people a product that will work, and that is reasonably safe, to respond effectively to legitimate complaints, to provide information concerning the relevant quality characteristics of a product, to take into consideration the ecological and environmental ramifications of a company decision, and to return to the basic principle upon which so much of our nation's business was structured—"satisfaction guaranteed, or your money back."[8]

Mrs. Knauer spells out in more detail the classic "declaration of rights" for consumers proclaimed on March 15, 1962, by President John F. Kennedy. These four consumer rights—the right to safety, the right to be informed, the right to choose, and the right to be heard—remain basic rights for the New Consumerism in the United States today. Since 1962, however, the basic rights of consumers have expanded beyond these four. People who advocate the New Consumerism, including some political conservatives, realize that new effective state and federal laws will be needed to guarantee these rights whenever business leadership fails in its efforts to create effective change through self-regulation and cooperation with government and consumer groups.

The New Consumerism aims to revitalize our free enterprise and competitive system

The New Consumerism will seek to reassert both the dignity of the citizen and the primacy of the public interest. It will seek not to replace but to revitalize the free enterprise and competitive system—to make the corporate citizen as accountable for its actions as the human citizen is for his.

And, at the same time, the New Consumerism will demand that the consumer-citizen be more involved in the decisions affecting his well-being. More specifically, as consumers of products and services, we want the right to assess

[7] July 1971.
[8] Speech presented by Mrs. Knauer before the U.S. Jaycees Metro Chapter Conference, Indianapolis, Ind., Jan. 14, 1972.

the cost-benefit ratio in our terms, as we define cost to us and as we define benefit to us. Tell us all you know about the benefits and dangers of cyclamates, enzyme- and phosphate-laden detergents, plastic containers, SSTs, DDT, etc. Tell us all you know and don't know about the risks—the kind of risks and their probabilities or seriousness—to us as individuals and to society as a whole. Say it clearly and fully so that all involved can understand. Tell us about the alternatives in the same terms. And then let us decide whether we want to take the risks to get the benefits.

Makeup of the New Consumerism

Four groups are gradually beginning to see that they have more in common with the New Consumerism than they had thought. These four groups may well constitute the New Consumerism.

The first group is the one we now associate with consumerism, the middle-class consumers—restless, angry, and increasingly frustrated about shoddy goods, unsafe products, and inefficient services. But it should be recognized that the consumer movement involves much more than a mere concern for getting the best buy for our dollar—the activities of Ralph Nader alone show us that. The New Consumerism is concerned with "any pattern of behavior or course of events which reduces the income of any consumer or which exposes the consumer to hazards in terms of health and safety," says Mr. Nader.

The second group is made up of the black community and other minority groups. The emphasis of the black urban community, in particular, is shifting from social terms to economic terms. We are now beginning to get to the heart of the problem: It is not so much the irrational ill-will that some men of different races feel toward one another as it is the economic exploitation of the black man—to a far greater degree—by the same institutions that have aroused the middle-class white consumer, whose complaint has been largely about "shoddy goods and inefficient services." The black urban consumer is faced with the "worst" goods and the "worst" services and generally pays the highest prices for them. If the middle-class consumer is troubled by unsafe food additives, perhaps we can understand the feelings of the black parent who learns that his child has contracted lead poisoning from eating the chipping paint on the walls of their tenement rooms, despite city laws that are intended to protect children against such poisoning.

The reader may be surprised to learn that large numbers of political conservatives—the third group that is beginning to be allied with the New Consumerism—are beginning to realize, for example, that an oil company can, with impunity, befoul one of the nation's most beautiful shorelines. As a result of oil slicks, political conservatives in Santa Barbara, California, are starting to give some serious thought to the question of corporate irresponsibility. They are also thinking about a system that permits food processors to so pollute their food with pesticides that their children may be born with an amount of DDT residue in their blood that is five times greater than the amount the federal government allows in cow's milk shipped across state lines.

Political conservatives are concerned also with corporate irresponsibility. A 60-year-old man, apparently hard up for cash, broke into a phone booth in Maryland. He took $6 and was apprehended and sentenced to two years in jail. When General Motors' Allison Division was found to be culpable in the design of a particular engine in the Convair 580 that crashed and took thirty-eight lives, it was learned that GM knew about the defect beforehand but didn't warn the airlines that were using these planes to ground them immediately and disassemble the engines. The Federal Aviation Administration fined GM $8,000. No executive went to jail. We seem to have a double standard of sanction.

If political conservatives are still a little wary of consumerism, they may recall this public statement by a well-known conservative:

> I have reached the conclusion that, while large industry is important, fresh air and clean water are more important, and the day may well come when we have to lay that kind of a hand on the table and see who is bluffing.
> *Barry Goldwater.*

The government has failed to protect the consumer

Political conservatives are also beginning to take notice of the too frequent failure of government to protect the consumer as he deserves. It took the government six years to act against the Penn Central railway for a monumental pollution violation it was creating in the Hudson River. We know that if any of us were caught doing 80 miles per hour on a highway where the speed limit was 70, the government wouldn't wait six years to take action! But when a federal government official was asked why the government was not moving against the railroad more vigorously, he replied: "We're dealing with top officials in industry, and you just don't go around treating those people like that." The case did get to court finally, and Penn Central was fined $4,000—a cheap price for a convenient sewer pipe causing pollution for a forty-year period!

Retailers and consumers need a more efficient information system

Many retailers have an interest in consumerism. We are just beginning to work on a common marketing language that will enable all of us to talk to and understand one another. In the food area, for example, open dating, unit pricing, nutrient labeling, and percentage ingredient labeling will make it possible for retailers, producers, wholesalers, and consumers to communicate about what it is they are buying and selling. This is an important change because the retailer will begin to realize that he serves primarily as a buying agent for consumers rather than as a selling agent for producers.

The retailer, therefore, will have more in common with his consumer than he does with his supplier. He is learning that he is treated to the same kind of false and misleading advertising as the consumer. The retailer is involved in the same kinds of problems of product quality. In time—just maybe—he will begin to feel that his best interests lie in vigorously serving the best interests of his client, the consumer.

The fourth group that has recently become interested in the New Consumerism is college youth. Ralph Nader was perhaps the first consumer advocate to propose that students could help the cause of consumerism either through their own individual efforts or, more favorably, through organizing student action groups financed by student government organizations. In 1970, the Oregon Student Public Interest Research Group and the Minnesota Public Interest Research Group were established with offices in Portland, Oregon, and Minneapolis, Minnesota. Later, campus consumer organizations were established at St. Louis University and Washington University in St. Louis. These two student consumer organizations, situated on campuses in close proximity, plan to merge as one unit. At Kansas State University in Manhattan, the Student Governing

Association set up a Consumer Relations Board in 1971 financed by student fees. In its first year of operation, the Consumer Relations Board saved their students over $45,000. They were so pleased with the results that they published a seventy-one-page booklet, *University Consumer Protection,* describing this organization and its procedures.[9] Now, five of the six state colleges in Kansas have consumer protection agencies, and over two-hundred universities and colleges have purchased copies of *University Consumer Protection.* The keen interest in this extension of the consumer movement to the college campus resulted in the first National Conference on Student Consumer Action on May 3–6, 1972, at Kansas State University. This effort toward unity and a statement of guidance for student consumer protection agencies financed by student governing bodies is a good beginning of college-student-oriented interest and action in consumerism.

SUMMARY

The consumer movement in this country has been a "feeble animal." In recent years, however, vigorous debate about consumer issues has emerged as an important feature of the political scene. The initial impression was that the attention given to consumerism would be quite short-lived. This has proved to be in error. Interested legislators—urged by Consumers Union, reinforced by Ralph Nader and other young lawyers and writers, and more recently joined by college-campus consumer organizations financed by student government budgets and joined also by numerous local, state, and national organizations—have built up a base of support which assures continued interest and action for years to come.

Judging from recent concern over the economic role of advertising and promotion and over restrictive arrangements in the form of monopolies, "shared monopolies," and conglomerate mergers, it appears that antitrust action will be intensified.

Consumerism is identified with the quality of our physical environment

More recently, consumerism has become identified with the widespread concern over the quality of our physical environment. The consumer movement has rather rapidly rearranged its list of priorities to include its concern for problems contributing to pollution in a "disposable society" and to the problems of air, water, soil, and noise pollution.

Also, the present imperfections in the marketplace would not have generated the same depth of concern had it not been for the new visibility of our 25 million low-income consumers. These consumers suffer the most from fraud, excessive prices, and exorbitant credit charges, coupled generally with poor-quality merchandise and service.

"American society is characterized by injustice, insensitivity, lack of candor, and inhumanity"

There is, too, a basic dissatisfaction with the impersonalization of our society in general and of the marketplace in particular. The *Fortune* magazine (June 1969) student opinion poll found that 65 percent of the sample were in strong or partial agreement with the statement, "American society is characterized by injustice, insensitivity, lack of candor, and inhumanity."

[9] Available from Consumer Relations Board, Student Governing Association, K-State Union, Kansas State University, Manhattan, Kans. 66502.

The final and perhaps most enduring trend is reflected in the increasingly better-educated consumer. The Chamber of Commerce of the United States noted in 1969 that the present and future consumer "expects more information about the products and services he buys. He places greater emphasis on product performance, quality and safety. He is more aware of his 'rights' as a consumer and is more responsive than ever before to political initiatives to protect these rights." These better-educated consumers, many of them young people, are beginning to accept Ralph Nader's view that our institutions can be reshaped, can be remade so as to close the gap between the promise of America and its reality.

CHAPTER 2
CONSUMER DECISION MAKING AND ADVERTISING

The greatest gift is the power to estimate correctly the value of things.

de la Rochefoucauld

The real emphasis of this chapter is on decision making in the family and on advertising claims and corrective advertising.

GOALS AND CHOICE

Choice is a fundamental problem for all human beings, and it is also a complex problem—complex because we are living in an "embarrassment-of-riches" age. There are new products, new kinds of entertainment, new services coming along constantly. Shop windows, newspapers, magazines, radio, television, movies, and travel influence us to want more and more. Consumers are literally over-whelmed by a variety of goods and services. Choice making is therefore more difficult than in the make-what-you-need economy of pioneer times.

The choices we make, consciously and subconsciously, determine to a large extent the character of our lives. In other words, our choices determine what we get out of life. It goes without saying, however, that setting up goals of family spending is not enough. We need the ability to work them out. Nevertheless, if we can decide on major goals, we are doing something that many people seem unable to accomplish. The biggest determinant of what we *get* out of life is what we *want* out of life. It follows, then, that intelligent choice is the first important step in wise consumption.

One of the major aims of consumer education should be to teach consumers how to spend their money, time, and energy to bring expressed wants into harmony with considered needs. And all this should be done within the limits of the income of each family.

All people need food, shelter, clothing, and recreation. But many are not satisfied with supplying only these needs. They want a great many things they do not need, often more intensely than what is needed. A man may commit suicide if he is jilted by the lady he loves. Some parents risk all they have for the sake of sending a son or daughter to a university. So often, however, the things prized the most are the things needed the least. Why? Perhaps it is because people do not consciously and deeply consider what they want most out of life and how best to get it.

If consumers will probe through the surface reasons for wanting certain things, they may get down to the real reasons and thus make more intelligent choices and so get the fullest satisfaction out of supplying their important wants.

THE DECISION-MAKING PROCESS

The key to decision making is alternatives—to help us, as consumers, to learn how to evaluate alternative courses of action so that we may arrive at a better decision—a decision which will lead to results more satisfying than those made without the benefit of considering the alternatives. Most of us do not choose a product at random the first time it is purchased. We usually go through a process of careful selection called "decision making." Many products are purchased periodically and habitually. Products involving a relatively large outlay are more likely to be purchased after going through rather careful selection.

Usually we are not concerned with decision making until we are interested in buying a particular product. Having decided on the objective or use of the particular product desired, we may go through two or more of the following phases:

    1.   Searching for the best product for our purpose among the several commodities on the market

    2.   Determining relevant alternatives by making general evaluation of the products available

    3.   Appraising relevant alternatives seriously by securing important facts about the product

    4.   Making a final decision

The final decision may or may not lead to a purchase. We may decide not to buy if the net satisfaction derived is not large enough to offset the cost. In this case we may seek other alternatives or delay the purchase.

Decision making, however, is not a simple process. There are many external and internal forces acting upon the individual and the family.

The individual and decision making[1]

In making a decision, an individual is influenced by a number of basic forces. There are, also, subcategories too numerous to mention here.

Physical needs is a broad category which includes food, housing, clothing, and other items. Protein needs, for example, can be met with relatively low-cost foods such as variety meats and skim milk. On the other hand, they can be satisfied with more expensive exotic cheeses and steaks.

Social needs, another broad category, are important to many people for reasons other than attainment of physical pleasure. Some of the obvious social needs affecting decision making are achievement (highest satisfaction), affiliation (location of home in best neighborhood), prestige (keeping up with the Joneses), and exhibition (four-car garage).

There are many other social forces that play a role in consumer decision making, such as passively submitting to external forces, impulse, yielding to the influence of someone whom one admires, and purchasing to avoid humiliation.

Values and individual attitudes are other factors which account for differences in spending patterns. For example, some individuals place a higher value on savings than on spending. They value financial security higher than things.

A person's choice of alternatives is also influenced by day-to-day happenings. For example, there may be changes in income or prices, and there may be new information which may influence a decision.

Risk and uncertainty may also be influential in decision making. For example, the decision with regard to introducing a completely new food to the family presents an uncertainty situation.

These forces are interrelated and complex. Typically, one is influenced by a number of these forces simultaneously.

The family and decision making

Family-made decisions are far more complex than those made by the individual because they involve participation of family members. The same forces

---

[1] For details, see James N. Morgan, "Household Decision-Making," a paper presented at the University of Michigan; Calvin S. Hall and Gardner Lindzey, *Theories of Personality,* John Wiley & Sons, Inc., New York, 1957.

mentioned above may be involved, but the forces will have a varying impact on each participating family member. If tastes and preferences are relatively similar, no conflicts are apt to arise. But if there are differences in tastes and preferences, a decision can become involved and complex.

Family influences on consumer behavior

The influence of family members on decision making is complicated

How important are other family members in influencing what a consumer buys? What is the relative influence of the wife, husband, and children in the selection of a specific car model, a piece of furniture, or a breakfast cereal?

Family influences are important because they affect individual personality characteristics, values, and attitudes and because they affect the decision-making process involved in purchasing goods and services.

The influence of family members on decision making is likely to be more complicated than most people assume. For example, the husband may be responsible for recognizing the problem, and the wife may search for alternatives, or both may jointly evaluate alternatives, and the wife may purchase the product. This kind of family-member influence is thought to be not uncommon. When such influence does exist, it follows that meaningless answers are likely to be given to questions such as "Who makes the purchasing decision?" and "Who influences the purchasing decision?" What appear to be contradictory results may be due to the fact that respondents answer in terms of various stages in the decision process. Consequently, studies need to focus on the influence of family members at each of several stages in the decision-making process rather than simply on the purchase.

Children as consumers

There are few accurate studies attempting to measure the influence of children in purchasing decisions. In many husband-wife purchasing decisions, children are involved, although their influence is not obvious. It is well known, for example, that children influence soft drink and cereal purchases, but their influence on other purchases, such as dog food, is not so well known. Often, the influence of children is indirect in that the parent continues to purchase different brands until he or she finds one that the children like. Most studies grossly underestimate the influence of children in family purchasing decisions.

Cultural and group influences

All societies have somewhat different role specifications for men and women. These role specifications are learned early in life through social conditioning. Most families are generally characterized by an instrumental leader and an expressive leader. Usually the male is expected to be the instrumental leader, and the female is trained to be the expressive or morale leader in our society, according to Mirra Komarovsky.[2]

It is probably true to some extent that family role structures vary by ethnic groups, but the degree of variation can be exaggerated. For example, among certain foreign-born families, the husband-dominant roles are not necessarily more prevalent than they are among other families. There seems to be a tendency over a period of time for these foreign groups to divest themselves of the old family role characteristics of their native country.[3]

There is considerable evidence that many characteristics of the family affect

[2] *American Journal of Sociology*, November 1946.
[3] Robert O. Blood and Donald M. Wolfe, *Husbands and Wives: The Dynamics of Married Living*, The Free Press, New York, 1960.

role structures. Factors such as conflict with the mother and reaction to home discipline influence whether the general decision-making role structure is wife-dominant or husband-dominant.[4]

Friends, acquaintances, and members of other peer groups also influence the decision process in a family. In some cases peer-group influences may be even greater than those of the family.[5]

Characteristics of the family

In addition to cultural and group influences, certain family characteristics influence the role of family members in the purchasing process:

Family influences are important

1. *Stage of life cycle.* Studies indicate that the roles of family members in decision making change throughout the life of the family. The first few years of marriage are generally characterized by a large amount of joint husband-wife decision making and shopping. However, as the length of marriage increases, both spouses become more familiar with the attitudes and needs of the other family members. Consequently, the degree of joint decision making tends to decline over a family's life cycle.

2. *Social class.* Joint decision making is least common among upper and lower social classes (measured by income and occupation) and most common among middle social classes. Generally women tend to be more dominant in the lower-class family, and men have a greater tendency to dominate in upper-class families.[6]

3. *Employment status of wife.* Generally the wife has greater influence if she works for pay outside the home.[7] Her influence increases because she increases her intellectual and financial resources and becomes less dependent on her husband for the satisfaction of her needs.

4. *Location.* There is some evidence that joint decision making is more common among families living in rural areas.[8]

5. *Personality characteristics.* Wives who have a strong need for love and affection will generally have less influence in purchasing decisions.[9]

6. *Social networks.* There is some evidence that the degree of joint decision making varies inversely with the connectedness of a family's social network. When neither wife nor husband belongs to a closely knit group of friends, they tend to engage in joint decision making.[10]

7. *Relative contributions.* The greater a person's relative contributions,

[4] Yi-Chuang Lu, "Predicting Roles in Marriage," *American Journal of Sociology,* July 1952, pp. 51–55.

[5] Lional J. Neiman, "The Influence of Peer Groups upon Attitudes toward the Female Role," *Social Problems,* October 1954, pp. 104–111.

[6] Blood and Wolfe, op. cit., pp. 37–38.

[7] Ibid., pp. 40–41.

[8] Elizabeth Wolgast, "Do Husbands or Wives Make Purchasing Decisions?" *Journal of Marketing,* October 1958, p. 154.

[9] Donald M. Wolfe, "Power and Authority in the Family," in Darwin Cartewright (ed.), *Studies in Social Power,* Research Center for Group Dynamics, Ann Arbor, Mich., 1959, p. 109.

[10] Elizabeth Bott, *Family and Social Network,* Tavistock Publications, Ltd., London, 1957, pp. 59–60.

the greater his influence in decision making. For example, husbands who earn a high income and have high occupational prestige and high social status generally have more decision-making authority than husbands whose income is such that their wives must work.[11]

8.   *Least interested partner.*   This theory focuses not on the value to each spouse of the resources contributed by the other but on the value placed on these resources outside the marriage. In other words, the greater the difference between the value to the wife of the resources contributed by her husband and the value to the wife of the resources she might earn outside the existing marriage, the greater the influence of the husband in decision making.[12]

Type of product

The nature of joint decision making varies considerably from product to product. As the price of the product increases, the extent of joint decision making tends to increase. In the buying of lower-priced products, the purchase decisions are generally delegated to the husband or wife according to their respective knowledge and skills. For example, a man is supposed to know more about mechanical things and generally plays a more important role in selecting products with complex mechanical characteristics. On the other hand, a man is not supposed to know much about taking care of the family clothing, and thus he is likely to be less influential in selecting an iron.[13]

Variables that affect the extent of decision making

Consumers usually recognize that some risk is involved in buying and using certain goods and services. The risk may be financial, physical, social, or some combination of the three. Decision making, especially external search, occurs in order to reduce the risk.

There is some evidence which suggests that four kinds of variables affect the extent of decision making: (1) situational variables, (2) product characteristics, (3) consumer characteristics, and (4) environmental factors.

Situational variables[14]

Consumers have a higher probability of engaging in extended decision-process behavior when:

1.   They have had little or no experience with the product to be purchased.
2.   They have had no past experience with the product because it is new.
3.   They recognize their past experience as of no value because the product is bought infrequently.
4.   Their past experience with the product has been unsatisfactory.
5.   They consider the purchase to be discretionary rather than necessary.
6.   The product is important, perhaps intended as a gift.
7.   The purchase is socially "visible."

[11] Blood and Wolfe, op. cit., pp. 12–13, 30–33.

[12] David M. Heer, "The Measurement and Bases of Family Power: An Overview," *Marriage and Family Living,* 1963, p. 139.

[13] Wolgast, op. cit., pp. 151–158.

[14] George Katona, *The Mass Consumption Society,* McGraw-Hill Book Company, New York, 1964, pp. 289–290.

Product characteristics [15]

Extended decision-process behavior is more likely to occur when:

1. The consumer feels committed to the product for an extended period, in which case future needs and/or product performance is difficult to forecast.
2. The consumer perceives alternatives as having both desirable and undesirable qualities.
3. The product is expensive relative to the consumer's income.

Consumer characteristics [16]

Decision-process behavior is more likely to be extended rather than limited or habitual when:

1. The consumer has a college education.
2. The consumer is in the middle-income category, as opposed to the high- or low-income category.
3. The consumer is under 35 years old.
4. The consumer's occupation is in the white-collar class.
5. The consumer enjoys "shopping around."
6. The consumer sees no immediate need for the product.

Environmental factors. [17]

A consumer has a higher probability of engaging in extended decision-process behavior when:

1. He recognizes a difference between his customary behavior and that of the group to which he belongs.
2. There is a disagreement among family members about requirements and the desirability of alternatives.
3. There are strong new stimuli, such as news of a serious inflation, the threat of war, or news about a revolutionary product on the market.

In summary, many factors are likely to evoke extended decision-process behavior. The concept of the extended decision process is a sophisticated one, viewing consumer behavior as a process rather than as a separate or distinct act. It is as much concerned with how a consumer reaches a decision as it is with the decision itself.

[15] James F. Engel, "Psychology and the Business Sciences," *Quarterly Review of Economics and Business,* vol. 1, 1961, pp. 75–83.

[16] George Katona and Eva Mueller, "A Study of Purchase Decisions," in Lincoln H. Clark (ed.), *Consumer Behavior: The Dynamics of Consumer Reaction,* Consumer Behavior Series, New York University Press, New York, 1955, pp. 289–290.

[17] Katona, op. cit., pp. 289–290.

Family role involved in
problem recognition

Role refers to the behavior of family members at each stage in the decision-making process. We are concerned here with the first stage of decision making—problem recognition.

Table 2-1 presents part of the results of a *Life* magazine study that investigated the roles of husbands and wives in problem recognition. In general, the wife is involved more often in problem recognition than the husband. The data clearly indicate that the extent of husband-wife involvement varies considerably from product to product. The data in Table 2-1 support these generalizations:

1. The higher the price of the product, the greater the tendency for the husband to be involved in problem recognition—note automobiles.
2. The extent of husband-wife involvement in problem recognition tends to vary according to cultural norms of specialization. Husbands, for example, have a greater tendency to be involved in problem recognition when the product is technically or mechanically complex, as in the case of cars, refrigerators, and paint.

The statistic used in Table 2-1 to measure spouse involvement is the mean percentage. Means are likely to be deceiving in that there may be considerable interfamily variation in the degree of husband-wife involvement. Younger and higher-income husbands, for example, would be expected to play a greater role

TABLE 2-1   Life Magazine Study of the Roles of Husbands and Wives in Problem Recognition (percentages)

PRODUCT	SPOUSE INITIALLY RECOGNIZING PROBLEM*	
	HUSBAND	WIFE
Refrigerators	71.4	89.0
Vacuum cleaners	35.7	83.1
Automobiles	92.8	38.7
Pet foods	15.8	33.3
Frozen orange juice	31.4	82.0
Rugs and carpets	49.3	93.5
Paint	60.0	74.2
Coffee	40.0	43.8
Toothpaste	20.9	39.3

* The percentages are based on each spouse's self-appraisal and indicate whether the spouse in question was involved in problem recognition. Categories such as "both husband and wife" and "children" were not employed; thus the percentages sometimes total more or less than 100 percent.

SOURCE: *A Pilot Study of the Roles of Husbands and Wives in Purchasing Decisions,* study conducted for *Life* magazine by L. Jaffee Associates, Inc., 1965, parts I–X. The research design involved interviews with 301 middle- and upper-income households in Hartford, Cleveland, and Seattle.

in problem recognition than older and middle- and lower-income husbands.[18] Similarly, working wives would be expected to play a larger role in problem recognition than wives who are not employed outside the household.[19]

INTELLIGENT CONSUMER DECISION MAKING

Up to now we have been concerned largely with consumer behavior as a process rather than as a discrete or separate act, such as the purchasing of a new car. Dr. E. Scott Maynes, professor of economics at the University of Minnesota, writes about the "payoff" of intelligent search for information prior to purchasing a new car.[20] Generally, students of consumer economics offer the prescription that the use of more information will improve consumer decision making. Whether or not this is true depends upon the individual and the type of decision making he follows in a given situation. It must not be overlooked that costs are involved in information search which frequently lead to avoidance of information and establishment of buying routines. These costs include outlays of money, time, and energy. Unless the consumer perceives that the gains from the search outweigh the costs, he is not likely to seek out or use information.

Gains from search should outweigh costs

Why decide competently?

Dr. Maynes persuasively suggests that the search for information is apt to have rewarding consequences; for example, (1) you increase your purchasing power (you seldom get what you pay for—the less expensive product is often the best); (2) the savings from a competent search are untaxed; (3) it is open; (4) you can avoid being bilked, which no one relishes; and (5) there is a social payoff—namely, there is a chance not only that your own purchasing power will be increased but also that your intelligent search for information will have a disciplining effect on sellers, inducing them to offer better products on better terms to all buyers.

Costs of the search

If you consider the costs of the search to include anything that you undergo or forgo in order to obtain your information, it is possible that direct money costs such as expenditures for telephone calls, gasoline, and so on will be involved. There may also be indirect costs, such as giving up a day's pay or losing an afternoon of golf in order to visit car showrooms.

How many searches should you make? Keep working as long as the expected net payoff is positive. Generally, more searching is apt to be profitable:

1. When the cost of the product is relatively large in a particular household budget
2. When the cost of the search is low
3. When the expected variation in price and/or quality is large

[18] See, for example, Wolgast, op. cit., pp. 151–158; see also Nelson Foote (ed.), *Household Decision Making,* New York University Press, New York, 1961, pp. 259–264.

[19] David M. Heer, "Dominance and the Working Wife," *Social Forces,* vol. 36, 1958, pp. 341–347.

[20] E. Scott Maynes, "The Payoff for Intelligent Consumer Decision-Making," *Journal of Home Economics,* February 1969, pp. 97–103. Credit for considerable portions of the discussion of the "payoff" of search for more information goes to this excellent article.

Any source of product information available in your community—*Consumer Reports, Consumers' Research Magazine,* a classified telephone directory, and/or a Sears or Wards catalog—will do. The telephone can be used generally to get price information.

Determinants of price and quality variation

Usually, price and quality variations are greatest where:

1. Sellers practice price discriminations.
2. Product differentiation is substantial.
3. Consumer ignorance is great.
4. The number of sellers is large.
5. Price-fixing as practiced by manufacturers or regulated by law is at a minimum.

"Sales" occur when the retailer's usual products are sold at reduced prices. The retailer may have too high an inventory of certain products, he may wish to attract buyers to his place of business, or it may be a sale at a regular time.

Tentative operating rules for consumers

The climax of the searching process comes with the spelling out of tentative operating rules, says Dr. Maynes:

1. Before purchasing, ask yourself whether the product you are interested in purchasing is subject to price and quality variations.
   a. For fairly objective information on this point, consult *Consumer Reports, Consumers' Research Magazine,* and specialized publications such as *Popular Photography.*
   b. If objective information is unavailable, ask yourself:
      (1) Whether prices for the product are fixed by law, manufacturer, or retailers and how effective any price-fixing arrangements are.
      (2) Whether the product is subject to product differentiation as a result of a seller's reliability and friendliness or because of the store's location or the retailer's reputation for servicing his products.
      (3) Whether the product or service is subject to price discrimination.
      (4) Whether you can make valid comparisons of prices and qualities of different brands.
2. While purchasing:
   a. Deal in the market with the largest number of sellers.
   b. When there is a trade-in, always get the seller to make you a favorable price.
   c. When the price of goods or services is about $100 or more (set your own minimum), always visit at least three sellers.

There is nothing final about the above suggestions. Consumer decisions are too complex. However, these rules do provide you with an orderly framework within which to seek better consumer payoffs. For example, the above suggestions could be used to advantage when buying a new car. The problem is how to obtain the lowest price for a particular model with a particular set of accessories and how to get the highest trade-in for the old car. Let us say that in this particular deal, the well-informed consumer is able to secure a reasonably low offer from the dealer plus a good trade-in.

Close analysis has disclosed that this can be a very good price. But how is the buyer to know? Two bits of information are critical in evaluating the offer:

1. The wholesale price the dealer had to pay the manufacturer for the new car and accessories
2. The wholesale value of the used car

(See Taylor-Troelstrup Reading 17, for the details as well as the public sources of wholesale prices of all makes of new cars and accessories and a current used-car guide. A specific outline is provided telling you how to use the data.)

Understanding and predicting family expenditures

Income has been a favorite resource used by economists to explain consumer expenditures.[21] Not only do economists differ in interpretation of the impact of family resources on decision making, but their data do not help much in predicting or understanding individual or family purchasing behavior with respect to a particular product. Furthermore, these data reflect the end product or final choice of decision making. In a study at the University of Michigan, Katona found great variations existed in the way in which 1,000 different consumers went about buying the same type of commodity—durable goods such as TV sets, refrigerators, automatic washing machines, and kitchen stoves:[22]

1. Forty-six percent of them disregarded price.
2. Thirty-one percent were careful about brand.
3. Chief sources of information were friends and relatives.
4. Forty-seven percent shopped more than one store.
5. Thirty-five percent sought other facts than brand and price.
6. Those who preplanned their purchases tended to seek reliable information.
7. College-educated people sought reliable information in *Consumers Union Reports* and *Consumers' Research Magazine* and shopped around.
8. The older the head of the family and the higher the income, the less the care in arriving at a decision.
9. Repeat buying of the same brand was infrequent.

It would appear, then, that family resources are a factor influencing family decision making. Family resources, however, provide only a partial explanation

[21] Warren J. Bilkey, *Vector Analysis of Consumer Behavior,* University of Connecticut, Storrs, 1954; James S. Duesenberry, *Income, Saving and the Theory of Consumer Behavior,* Harvard University Press, Cambridge, Mass., 1949; Milton A. Friedman, *Theory of the Consumption Function,* Princeton University Press, Princeton, N.J., 1957; Ruby Turner Norris, *The Theory of Consumer's Demand,* Yale University Press, New Haven, Conn., 1941; and George Katona, *Psychological Analysis of Economic Behavior,* McGraw-Hill Book Company, New York, 1951.

[22] George Katona, "A Study of Purchase Decisions: Part I," in Lincoln H. Clark (ed.), *Consumer Behavior: The Dynamics of Consumer Reaction,* Consumer Behavior Series, New York University Press, New York, 1955, vol. 1, pp. 30–36.

of expenditure behavior. It is also necessary to consider family characteristics (noneconomic) such as family life cycle, occupation, level of education, residence, race, and religion. A considerable amount of data is available which illustrates the relationship between family characteristics and expenditures. One illustration may suffice. Food expenditures change as families move from the "newly married couple without children" stage to the period when they have children, to the time when the children are not on the family payroll, and finally to the retirement period. The change is likely to be attributable to changes in the family's income and their physical, social, and psychological needs.

While there are many internal and external factors influencing decision making (and much is still unknown), the American consumer apparently is no composite creature possessed of a single set of buying habits. He fits no single mold. He is not uniquely an apartment dweller, a suburbanite, a rural person, a ghetto dweller, or a trailer resident. He has no one level of buying competence. His purchasing habits reflect his position in the life cycle, his education, and his occupation and income as well as his nationality and cultural background. Indeed, he reacts with a highly variable degree of response to the numerous influences which surround him.

Considering the pitfalls American consumers may encounter, as well as their lack of adequate information, there is an alert contingent of buyers at one end of the buying spectrum—a group that purchases after considerable deliberation, particularly in the area of durable goods in which quality characteristics are important. At the other end of the spectrum is an equally substantial group being victimized by high-pressure selling and advertising and possessed of little discernment, a group which does not understand the new forces of hidden persuasion.

Between these extremes are the great mass of American consumers exercising varying degrees of intelligence in product purchasing. So it would seem that the Survey Research Center findings concerning durable goods afford some evidence that the American consumer is not a standardized creature in his buying deportment. As a matter of fact, we seem to be developing an ever-widening gulf between the discerning consumer and the backward consumer—the latter being a victim of his own ignorance and of manipulation by others.

Much of the problem of wisdom in consumer choice lies in little-explored territory. David Riesman, a sociologist, contends that the typical American middle-class family has, by social conditioning, set for itself a goal of acquiring a "standardized package of goods and services" containing such items as furniture, radio, TV, refrigerator, and standard brands of food and clothing. In his view this group is trained to spend up to and beyond their income and gradually accumulate the full basic package. How wise this basic spending pattern is remains open to question. There is undoubtedly much truth in William Whyte's somewhat cynical comment that the "consumer is trying to tune in on his fellow consumers to find out what is right, while they, equally baffled, are tuning in on him—and the producer is tuning in on them." This, in part at least, is the process of consumer choice, and we go round and round and come out in debt.

The task of becoming an intelligent consumer has become ever more difficult because of the nature of the American market, the spectacular development of new products, the persuasive influence of advertising, and the lack of quality information at the point of sale available to the consumer.

ADVERTISING: IS THE CONSUMER EXPLOITED OR SERVED?

Adequate information as a basis of purchase decisions is essential to the consumer; it is also important for effective functioning of our economic system. Real competition in the marketplace, however, is rapidly being reduced to competition in advertising.

Purpose of advertising   The purpose of advertising is to stimulate the sale of goods and services. It is a way of reaching many people via TV, radio, newspapers, direct mail, posters, placards, circulars, and other means. Perhaps the chief function of advertising today is that of a salesman. It can reach many millions of people more efficiently than can personal selling. The emphasis, therefore, is on preselling the consumer on a particular brand of service. And for this, and other advertising, consumers pay about $22 billion annually.

The justification for advertising, then, is to efficiently market products and services; to bring new and better products economically to the consumer; to contribute to a growing economy by expanding the consumption of goods and the circulation of capital; and to build a better way of life in an increasingly affluent and sophisticated society. There is no quarrel with these objectives. The basic quarrel with advertising is that this medium is misused and, under certain circumstances, the cost of advertising is excessive.

Advertising expenditures

Advertising expenditures in this country have been rising to a faster rate than most barometers of economic activity including gross national product and national income. The current estimate is about $22 billion annually. Advertisers claim that the typical consumer is exposed to 1,600 advertisements daily. The ads range from a local room to rent to the $270 million spent by Procter and Gamble. The top 125 advertisers spent over $4 billion in 1965. The biggest advertisers, in this order, were Procter and Gamble, General Motors, General Foods, Ford, and Bristol-Myers. Advertising expenditures, as a percentage of sales, were 27.6 for Bristol-Myers, 10.9 for Procter and Gamble, 8.7 for General Foods, 1.0 for Ford, and 0.8 for General Motors. Of the top 125 advertisers, 26 were food and soft drink producers, 16 drug and cosmetic firms, 9 brewers and distillers, and 8 tobacco manufacturers.

In a typical year advertisers spent about 30 percent of their advertising dollar for newspaper ads, 16 percent for television, 15 percent for direct mail, 8 percent for magazines, and 6 percent for radio. These media account for nearly 75 percent of all advertising expenditures in the United States.

When huge sums—$22 billion—are spent annually on one aspect of sales efforts, we need to ask: "Does advertising provide the answer to the consumer's need for important information about a product? Does advertising increase productivity? Does advertising aim to reduce costs or maximize profits? Does advertising increase competition and, thus, benefit the consumer?"

"Advertising's credibility gap"

In a recent report E. B. Weiss, formerly an advertising executive, editor of *Printer's Ink,* and in 1967 director of special merchandising for Doyle Dane Bernbach, Inc., concludes:

> There is ample cause to be concerned by the adverse image of advertising. . . . Who can dispute that the main causes for the criticisms lie not in Washington, not among rabble-rousers, but in the dull, boring commercials the public is forced to listen to; to bad taste of much advertising such as some of the proprietary drug commercials the public is forced to digest with dinner, and in the excessive buffoonery, unbelievability, bad taste, boorishness and boredom that characterizes so much of advertising today. There is also the over-commercialization of television with network commercials, station breaks, program promotion, etc., all tumbling over each other.
>
> A good part of the criticism directed against advertising is justified. An increasingly sophisticated public will become less tolerant of advertising's abuses. . . . It is entirely probable that in the decade of the 70's, advertising will come under more and more intelligent criticism than ever before in its history. This means that advertising must close its credibility gap . . . government will correct what advertising neglects to improve.[23]

How can advertising try on a halo for size when a slacks ad shows the boss's wife with her foot on a young man's ankle (under the slacks) while her husband dozes at the table; a swinger takes off his shirt for a final "permanent press test," while, superimposed on the ad, an apparently naked girl waits expectantly; a man is urged to "come on strong . . . go all the way" with a name-brand sports coat while a reclining girl with bared knee holds out her hand?

Since the problems of half-truths and pseudo-truths are also present in modern advertising, is it true that:

. . . a "woman in Distinction foundations is so beautiful that all other women want to kill her"?

. . . it "a woman gives in to her divine restlessness and paints up her eyelids with The Look, her eyes will become jungle green . . . glittery gold . . . flirty eyes, tiger eyes"?

. . . a "new ingredient in Max Factor Toiletries separates the men from the boys"?

Perhaps we have a new kind of truth emerging—pseudo-truth—which may be defined as a false statement made as if it were true but not intended to be believed. No proof is offered for pseudo-truth. Its proof is that it sells merchandise; if it does not, it is false. Is the function of language giving way to a misguiding function? If so, this is tragic to people who care about the quality and price of things. One wonders if *Esquire* magazine had a point in its January, 1961, issue when it stated in reference to advertising that the "only thing we have to fear is truth."

Abuse of advertising   The integrity of the whole marketing system depends in no small part upon adequate buyer information. Consequently, we cannot help but move to the

[23] E. B. Weiss, *A Critique of Consumerism,* Doyle Dane Bernbach, Inc., New York, 1967, chap. 4.

Open disclosure is the basis for truth-in-advertising

principle of "open disclosure" as exemplified recently in the call for open dating of food products and unit pricing. It is that simple and basic principle—open disclosure, as it pertains to advertising claims documentation—which forms the basis for truth-in-advertising. The consumer cannot possibly make decisions if relevant information needed to make intelligent choices is not available to him.

The Advertising Code of American Business recognizes the need for basic information. This code reads in part:

1. Advertising agencies and advertisers shall be willing to provide substantiation of claims made.
2. Advertising shall tell the truth, and shall reveal significant facts, the concealment of which would mislead the public.

Advertisers have been too often delinquent on both counts. In 1966 the National Association of Broadcasters conducted a nationwide survey, the results of which they attempted unsuccessfully to keep confidential. This survey revealed that:

1. A remarkable 60 percent of the respondents agreed with the statement that "many TV commercials claim too much for the product."
2. Forty-four percent had the same reaction to radio commercials.

In 1971, a nationwide poll conducted by Louis Harris and Associates for *Life* magazine found that:

1. Thirty-four percent of the public said that within the last year they had purchased a product which did not perform as the advertising said it would.
2. Forty-four percent mentioned misrepresentation and exaggeration more often than any other reason for disliking advertising.

When it comes down to the actual practice of providing claims documentation, many advertisers have a history of being guarded and extremely protective of their self-interests. In the 1950s, for example, advertisers didn't do much more than supply large media representatives, upon request, with a self-serving letter stating that they had evidence in their files to support their advertising. This practice proved futile and very frustrating from the purchaser's point of view.

As public pressures grew, it became the policy in the 1960s for television networks and a few publications to seek copies of the actual claims documentation. Yet, even under this procedure documentation is late in coming, sometimes is incomplete or inadequate, and often is accepted at face value with

Self-regulation of advertising may turn into a bargain counter for truth

superficial critical review from the consumer's point of view. If questions are raised by consumers, the advertising agency and legal counsel use subtle pressures and arguments which often turn self-regulation into a bargain counter for truth. And consumers are none the wiser since they do not have convenient access to the claims documentation.

The need for open disclosure

The need for open disclosure of claims information became apparent as far back as 1963. An internal memorandum circulated among members of the Code Authority questioned the content and believability of many commercial techniques such as:

1. Conflicting claims with regard to product superiority involving analgesics, razor blades, and gasolines
2. Demonstrations offered as proof of the effectiveness of cars, drugs, and other products
3. Dangling comparatives claiming, for instance, that "product X works better," leaving the consumer to ask, "Better than what?"
4. Surveys used as proof of product performance, as in claims that nine out of ten professionals recommend the ingredients contained in product X
5. References to clinical tests as proof of effectiveness
6. Claims that because a product contains more or added ingredients, performance is superior
7. Partial or biased disclosure of available facts relating to product performance

Businessmen's view of advertising

Advertising must close its credibility gap or "false promise is the soul of advertising"

The nation's businessmen aren't too happy with what they are getting for the $22 billion spent on advertising, Harvard Business School professors Stephen A. Greyser and Bonnie B. Reece found when they analyzed the results of an eight-page questionnaire on the subject returned by 2,700 readers of the *Harvard Business Review* (May–June 1971). For the nation's advertising agencies the findings produced more shock than satisfaction. The findings show that a majority of the responding businessmen agreed on these points:

1. Advertising increasingly irritates and insults "the public's intelligence--and their own."
2. Ads fail to give the true picture of the product they sell.
3. People shown in the ads are rarely representative of people in real life.
4. Generally, ads are an "unhealthy influence" on children.
5. Too much money is spent on advertising.
6. Advertising does not result in better or cheaper goods.

Most advertising does not necessarily result in better and cheaper goods

The opinion expressed by a majority of businessmen who believed that advertising does not result in better or cheaper goods is in harmony with a generally accepted theory that mass advertising reduces prices only when the industry is one whose costs of production per unit decline as production increases.

Advertising directed at children

Advertising directed at children comes under attack

One of the main criticisms of advertising is directed at advertising for children. In their race for the $50-billion youth market, advertisers in one year (1970) swamped youngsters with 1 billion square feet of advertising on the backsides of cereal boxes, according to Robert Choate, chairman of the Council on Children, Media and Merchandising. According to Dr. John Condry, a specialist in human ecology, the typical television-viewing youth is also exposed to 250,000 to 300,000 commercial messages by age 16! This senseless amount of exposure is questionable.

Only five countries allow any commercials on television programs aimed at children, according to the National Citizens Committee for Broadcasting. Two of these countries, Great Britain and Australia, set standards for such ads. Dr. Choate suggested an eleventh commandment: "Thou shalt not covet my child's purse," and this nutrition expert called for an end to "the advertisers' mad pursuit of your child and mine."

FTC gags on breakfast ad

Having trouble getting the children to eat a nutritious breakfast? Well, just give them two Toastems Pop Ups instead, General Foods told millions of parents in a television commercial, whereupon the Federal Trade Commission charged that General Foods and its advertising agency, Benton & Bowles, Inc., misrepresented Toastems as containing at least as many nutrients as a breakfast of two eggs, two slices of bacon, and two slices of toast.

Cited in the FTC complaint was a commercial showing a child mulling over a plate of eggs, bacon, and toast. A voice said, "Gerald! You're not eating your breakfast. . . . No breakfast will do a kid any good . . . if he leaves it on his plate. So give him something good for him you know he enjoys eating." The commercial then cut to a picture of two Toastems, and the voice continued, "Two hot Toastems provide 100 percent of the minimum daily requirement of vitamins and iron. . . . As long as you know that—let them think it's just a big cookie."

General Foods eventually signed an FTC consent order prohibiting it from making false nutritional claims for Toastems or any other consumer food product.

Self-regulation: National Advertising Review Board

Self-regulation is only as strong as the consumer protection laws that back it

An industrywide program to tackle advertising abuses was launched on September 28, 1971. The National Advertising Review Board (NARB) is a joint effort of the Council of Better Business Bureaus (CBBB), the American Advertising Agencies, and the Association of National Advertisers. The NARB set up a rather cumbersome system for handling advertising complaints. A complaint goes first to the National Advertising Division of the CBBB. If no resolution can be made, the complaint goes to a special panel. If the panel cannot resolve the complaint, an appropriate federal agency may be called in. It is too early to evaluate the plan. The guess is that such a cumbersome process was created to discourage consumer complaints. Mark Silbergeld, a former FTC lawyer, filed ten complaints, questioning ad practices that ranged from traditional puffery to the more recent testimonial huckstering. Among his exhibits were ads using allegedly misleading "medical" data and one ad that was said to give children the notion that indiscriminate consumption is fun. His complaints reflect some of the tricky, subjective questions of ethics and taste and of subtleties of psychology, morals, and politics that will need to be faced.

There are already skeptics within the advertising industry, such as Andrew Vladimer of Miami, Florida, who thinks "self-regulation will not work by itself in our industry." Dr. Robert Choate in his FTC testimony described a conversation he had with C. W. Cook, chairman of General Foods. "I suggested," said Choate, "that advertising men, afloat in a world of puffery, have lost the ability to judge when they are lying. Mr. Cook's response was: 'I fear you are correct.'"

It may be that self-regulation is only as strong as the consumer laws that back it up.

Magnitude of broadcast advertising

Two broad corrective approaches to the alleged abuses of advertising are open. The government, acting on behalf of the consumer, can turn advertising into a regulated industry by telling advertisers what they can or cannot do. Or industry can try again to purge itself of its bad habits through self-regulation (which it has not been able to do effectively up to now) and with cooperation from the federal government, attempt again to regain public confidence.

Broadcast advertising plays a predominant role in the marketing process. In 1970, advertising expenditures in this country totaled about $7 billion, or almost $115 per family; $3.6 billion of this, or about $60 per household, was devoted to broadcast advertising. The vast bulk of all broadcast advertising—$3.2 billion, or $52 per family—was television advertising.

Broadcast advertising: domination by major companies

Furthermore, broadcast advertising is dominated by relatively few major companies. In 1970, fewer than 100 firms accounted for 75 percent of all broadcast advertising expenditures. Only 10 firms were responsible for over 22 percent of all broadcast advertising expenditures, and the comparable figure for television advertising is even higher. The top 10 television advertisers spent almost one-quarter of the money spent for television; the top five alone accounted for over 15 percent. Moreover, more than half of all TV broadcast advertising expenditures were accounted for by five product categories—food, toiletries, automotive products, drugs, and soaps and detergents. Significantly, sales presentations for these products often raise issues that relate to the nation's most serious social problems—drug abuse, pollution, nutrition, and highway safety.

Much advertising is truthful, relevant, tasteful, and a valuable element in our free competitive economy. On the other hand, it is widely asserted that advertising is capable of being utilized to exploit and mislead consumers, to destroy honest competitors, to raise barriers to entry, and to establish market power, and it is also widely held that government regulation is needed to prevent such abuses. This is particularly true of television because it is largely a one-way street. Its usual technique is to provide only one carefully selected and presented aspect out of a multitude of relevant product characteristics. Advertising is about the only important form of public discussion where no public debate exists. This gives broadcast advertising enormous power to affect consumer and public welfare.

Role of the Federal Trade Commission in advertising regulation

The FTC, as a matter of first priority, is committed to a program to remedy the dissemination of false advertising. The FTC is empowered to proceed against such advertising primarily through administrative litigation.

The FTC has had limited success in regulating false and misleading advertising

It is important, however, to recognize two limitations upon litigation in the regulation of deceptive advertising. First, litigation is generally a lengthy and costly device; second, the litigation process may be an unsatisfactory tool for getting at the truth of certain kinds of advertising claims. The FTC has recently undertaken to recommend the use of "counteradvertising," "corrective advertising," and "advertising documentation" in advancing truth in advertising.

Counteradvertising

The FTC has announced, in a statement submitted to the Federal Communications Commission on January 6, 1972, that it supports the concept of counteradvertising, i.e., the right of access to the broadcast media for the purpose of expressing views and positions on controversial issues that are raised by commercial advertising. The FTC statement was submitted in response to the FCC's

New FTC regulatory tools are needed

Notice of Inquiry concerning the Fairness Doctrine. Counteradvertising, in the FTC's view, would be an appropriate means of overcoming some of the shortcomings of the FTC's regulatory tools and would be a suitable approach to some of the present failings of advertising which are now beyond the FTC's capacity. (See Taylor and Troelstrup Reading 16 for certain kinds of advertising which might appropriately call for counteradvertising.)

Corrective advertising

The Federal Trade Commission is trying out a new weapon in its fight against deceptive advertising—corrective ads. "The idea behind the approach is not to embarrass or disgrace corporations," commented Robert Pitofsky, director of the FTC's Bureau of Consumer Protection, "but to dissipate misleading impressions with a solid dose of accurate information." Corrective advertising is "an extremely logical concept," observes *Consumer Reports.* "It springs from the idea that it's not good enough for a manufacturer or advertiser simply to stop practicing deception whenever the FTC blows the whistle." Now the company must "repent" publicly and tell the consumer that he has been misinformed. This confession or disclosure has to constitute at least 25 percent of the total print advertising and 25 percent of the total broadcasting time. The ad must run for one year after the order becomes final. Future court tests will determine whether the FTC has the authority to elicit advertising confessions.

The idea of corrective advertising was originally introduced by eight law students working with John Banzhaf, associate law professor at George Washington University. The students had wanted the Campbell Soup Company to disclose in future ads that it had placed marbles in the soups used in advertisements in order to make the ingredients rise to the top. The case, however, was settled by a consent order when Campbell Soup agreed to drop this deceptive advertising technique. (A consent order is binding and cannot be appealed. Penalties can be enforced sixty days after the order is issued by the FTC. The maximum fine is $5,000 per violation. If a company does not agree to sign a consent order and claims that the FTC charges are false, the case is taken to court for a decision.)

Many of the Madison Avenue ad men believe that running corrective ads will result in product suicide. Pitofsky disagrees, maintaining that consumers will appreciate the candidness of the advertisers. At any rate, the latest battle between the FTC and the ad agencies should prove interesting and, according to one ad executive, tough.

The first corrective ads were run for Profile bread and acknowledged that in contrast to earlier descriptions, Profile is not good for weight reduction and is a bit lower in calories than other breads only because the slices are thinner.

In May 1972, the FTC obtained agreement from the makers of Ocean Spray cranberry juice cocktail to correct in future advertising allegedly false nutritional claims made in past ads. In the past the FTC had ordered only that such ads be stopped. Such a light tap on the wrist has seldom solved the problem. (See Taylor and Troelstrup Reading 15, for the FTC document on Ocean Spray cranberry juice cocktail.)

Substantiation of ad claims

On December 12, 1970, Ralph Nader proposed to the FTC that this agency require scientific proof for advertising claims that lack substantiation. Robert Pitofsky, director of the Federal Trade Commission's Bureau of Consumer Protection, said he was "very sympathetic to the idea." However, he said, "We don't have the staff to effectively monitor every piece of advertising. . . . By giving us the opportunity to fully see what's behind the claims, this would help us do our job and we could handle many more advertising cases."

Nader said at a press conference that his proposal would "shift the burden of proof from the consumer to the manufacturer." At present, the FTC must find proof of deception in advertising.

Under Nader's proposal, presented to the FTC, advertisers would have to give the agency scientific documentation for advertising claims. The data would be available to consumers, and the FTC could check the documentation against the ads and move against false or exaggerated claims.

Nader's petition included a report by two associates who monitored commercials and print ads for nearly a year and then asked fifty-eight companies for the scientific reports behind their claims.

Of the fifty-eight, three sent "clinical studies, the value of which was dubious," the petition said. The rest did not reply, refused to cooperate, or sent unsatisfactory answers, Nader said.

"But business almost systematically refuses to document its wide-ranging claims," Nader said. "Hundreds of millions of dollars are used not to inform the consumer, but to deceive.

"It undermines the cornerstone of the market, which is intelligent consumer buying so the consumer can reward quality and reject the shoddy."

Miles W. Kirkpatrick, FTC chairman, was sympathetic to Nader's suggestion. The Associated Press quoted the FTC chairman on February 7, 1972, as saying, "It would be my hope that they [advertisers] would think twice before they'd make a blunt factual claim without having some substantiation for it."

Since Kirkpatrick's statement was made in early February 1972, the FTC has requested many manufacturers of consumer products to file substantiation for the claims made in advertising certain products. Most firms document their claims and send the document to the FTC. The FTC does not have the budget to evaluate the substantiation document, but does make the firm's evidence available to the public in its various offices throughout the country; such documentation may be purchased from the National Technical Information Service. (See the FTC document entitled *FTC Makes Public Advertising Documentation Submitted by 11 Air Conditioner and 4 Electric Shaver Manufacturers*, Feb. 15, 1972, Taylor-Troelstrup Reading 14.)

The FCC: a push to place counterads on TV

"If you have one of these Chevrolets, it could cost you your life." So says actor Burt Lancaster in a proposed TV counteradvertisement warning the public to return 6.8 million Chevrolets recalled by General Motors for motor-mount defects.

The networks reject counteradvertising

Saying that all three networks have rejected the ad, the Stern Community Law Firm has announced that it will ask the Federal Communications Commission to force the networks to run the ad and another against a number of common headache remedies, including Excedrin, Empirin, Anacin, Cope, Vanquish, Bufferin, and Bayer aspirin.

The networks were asked to carry the countercommercials as free, public service spots.

At the same time, Stern said that it is sending five counterads—one on the Chevrolets, two on the headache remedies, one on pollution, and one on draft rights—to newspapers around the country. He hopes the papers will run the ads, but apparently has yet to devise any legal theory to force publishers to do so.

Requests for TV counteradvertising aren't new. "Public interest" groups and law firms have been deluging TV stations, the networks, and the FCC with requests for free television time to challenge the claims made in paid commercials.

Though some counteradvertisements have been run, the campaign is still largely a legal one, with the FCC and the courts attempting to decide whether broadcasters are obliged to run the counterads—and, if so, how many and what kind.

If the complaints are upheld, the practical effect would be to challenge the role of the Advertising Council—a nonprofit corporation composed of major companies, advertising agencies, and industrial associations—as the dominant supplier of public service spots for radio and TV.

Although GM is sending recall letters to car owners, the Stern firm says that past experience has shown that about 30 percent of recalled cars are not actually brought in for repairs.

The drug ads would highlight a recent report by the American Medical Association's Council on Drugs which concludes that straight aspirin is as effective in relieving headaches as combination analgesic drugs such as Excedrin, Vanquish, Empirin, Bufferin, and Anacin. The ad says that Bayer aspirin, more expensive than some other brands, is no more effective.

GM and Sterling Drug, maker of Bayer, Cope, and Vanquish, had no comment. Warren Jollymore, director of GM's news relations office in Detroit, said he knew nothing about the counterads. Edward Van Vlaanderen, a member of the New York public relations firm that handles the press for Sterling Drug, replied he had no comment at present. But he added, "Our advertising is accurate and truthful and based on scientific fact."

In the complaints, Stern argued that the networks have a public service obligation to broadcast the counteradvertisements; that is, the networks have a duty to tell viewers about the car recalls and the drug report as an aid to public health and safety.

Only once, in the case of cigarettes, has the FCC adopted this position. The Stern complaint would seek to expand the doctrine. Previously, requests for counteradvertisements have been based on the "fairness doctrine"—a legal obligation requiring broadcasters to give a "reasonable" opportunity for the airing of "conflicting views" on "controversial" questions.

Will candor in advertising pay off?

The integrity of our marketing system depends on buyer information

The integrity of our marketing system depends in no small way upon buyer information. Furthermore, it may well be that advertising is creating "psychological disbelief," which in turn results in a dangerous distrust in our society. Senator Philip Hart pointed out that one authority has stated that the public is automatically discounting 40 to 50 percent of what is said by advertisers.[24] Kenneth Mason, group vice president, Grocery Products, Quaker Oats, spoke of "the gathering evidence that advertising may be becoming less effective as a marketing tool." He said that 9 percent of the audience of six well-rated and regularly scheduled television shows didn't know what was being advertised when asked after viewing the program the night before.[25]

[24] *Advertising Age,* Sept. 11, 1967.
[25] *Of Consuming Interest,* May 25, 1972, p. 4.

Another sign of disbelief in the integrity of advertising, which just can't be missed, is the fact that the National Advertising Division (NAD) of the Council of Better Business Bureaus and the National Advertising Review Board, launched in September 1971, are just not handling many consumer complaints because they have preferred to keep their existence practically unknown to the public. Consequently, between September 1971 and about June 1, 1972, NAD reported receiving only 149 complaints; it said that 55 had been fully resolved, 49 were pending, and 42 had been dismissed as without merit. Of these 42 complaints, 6 had been appealed to the NARB. That's a very poor record, especially since the Consumer Federation of America alone had submitted about 25 of the 149 complaints. At this rate, advertising's self-regulatory mechanism is simply ineffective. One wonders why those who advertise and their advertising agencies continue to wait for action, either voluntary or governmental.

Will advertising candor pay off?

A good sign is that advertising candor seems to be paying off. During the annual 1972 American Advertising Federation meeting, FTC's consumer protection chief, Robert Pitofsky, told the gathering that Profile bread had agreed to use a corrective 25 percent of the time to let the public know that their bread is really not so great for reducing, although it is good for the whole family. Pitofsky said public response had been so good that corrective ads are being used in 60 percent of Profile ads. Esther Peterson, consumer advisor to the Giant Food Stores, made similar claims for the use of candor, saying that fish sales are booming because Giant Food Stores are now saying "previously frozen" rather than "fancy." If you're telling it like it is, just maybe, in today's climate, you've got the competitive advantage.

Consumer forces are presently seeking government aid in attempting to bring about advertising that is more useful to them. Consequently, the Truth in Advertising Act of 1971 was submitted to Congress in April 1971.

Truth in Advertising Act of 1971

Warren Braren, formerly manager of the New York office of the National Association of Broadcasters' Code Authority and now an associate director of Consumers Union, testified in favor of this act. He said:

Open disclosure is a basic part of the consumer's right to know

> Open disclosure is a fundamental part of the consumer's right to know and is essential if integrity in the marketplace is to be achieved. This is what the Truth in Advertising Act is all about. Its purpose is to help stimulate forthrightness and the flow of information. In so doing, it should help to hold shoddy practices up to public scrutiny. It most certainly will be no hindrance to those advertisers who observe the need to treat the consumer fairly, honestly and openly. If advertisers follow the law's spirit and intent, it could be the beginning of a newfound and much needed confidence between buyer and seller.[26]

Whatever happens legislatively to this act, it should be clear to both advertisers and their critics that public sensibilities have changed. What was once only "puffery" is now seen as effrontery. To a greater extent than before, advertising faces demands for information and accuracy. But the hard questions hover unanswered in the background. Has advertising passed its peak of effectiveness in pushing consumer goods and services? Is it simply a tool of the

[26] *Hearings before the Senate Committee on Commerce on Truth in Advertising Act of 1971,* Oct. 4, 1971, p. 53.

monopolists, lending a semblance of competition where little or none exists? Hard sell, soft sell, psychic sell—is truth serum the next step? Or did the Greeks, from whom we have adopted so much, speak a more constant truth when they said, "The market is a place set aside where men can deceive one another."

Actually, the outlook is likely to be for a better advertising world. Imagine a world where:

1.   Advertising battles are fought over the real merits of a product or service.

2.   Advertisers compete to give the consumer adequate and clear information about a product or service.

3.   Advertisers seek to demonstrate the quality of the product or service.

But we also have the world of the advertising huckster. Which world shall it be? The choice is yours. Choose the former, and quality and free informed choice will be the hallmark of tomorrow's consumer world. Choose the latter, and tomorrow may be George Orwell's *1984*.

QUESTIONS FOR DISCUSSION

1.   How do you explain the fact that on the whole, the higher the family income and the higher a woman's educational level, the fewer children she has?

2.   What responsibilities do citizens have as consumers?

3.   Monopoly overcharging results in an inequitable transfer cost. How do you explain this statement?

4.   Evaluate the statement, "If it's legal, go ahead regardless of other consequences to consumers or competition."

5.   Do you agree or disagree with the statement that consumerism is much more than a mere concern for getting the best buy for your dollar?

6.   Do we face a tomorrow where advertising is the master and not the servant of the public? Do we literally face George Orwell's *1984* or Aldous Huxley's *Brave New World*?

7.   What is the meaning of the statement, "You can't compare apples and oranges," as applied to advertising?

8.   "The consumer can be taught to prefer any product a marketing firm chooses to offer." Analyze this statement. Do you agree?

9.   How do you account for the recent interest of college youth in the consumer movement?

10.   Recently, consumerism has become identified with the widespread concern about the quality of our physical environment—air, water, soil, and noise pollution. How do you account for these new concerns?

11.   Who bears the responsibility for honest and informative advertising? The advertising agency? The manufacturer?

12.   What do you think about corrective advertising?

13.   Do you believe that private enterprise has a "social responsibility" to society? Explain your answer.

14.   Why is it difficult to judge how much influence family members have in purchasing consumer products and services? Explain.

15.   Why has self-regulation of advertising claims been almost a complete failure?

16.   From the viewpoint of the consumer, what advantages do you see coming from the FTC use of counteradvertising, corrective advertising, and substantiation of advertising claims?

17.   What evidence is there that advertising, especially mass advertising, may be becoming less effective as a marketing tool?

PROJECTS

1.   It has been said that "we face a tomorrow where never in the history of mankind have so many minds been manipulated by so few." Apply this pronouncement to mass advertising today. Be specific—check ads from the mass media against facts from *Consumer Reports* and *Consumers' Research Magazine*.

2.   After reading *The Nader Report on the Federal Trade Commission,* by Cox, Fellmeth, and Schulz, select specific evidence from Chapter 2 in the textbook and from Taylor-Troelstrup Readings 14–16, that appears to show that the FTC is seriously making an effort to be a better protector of consumer interest in the area of advertising abuses.

3.   Are advertising campaigns successful? Ad agencies would consider this question absurd, but perhaps they don't know whether their campaigns are successful. Do ad agencies know what their objectives are? Do they state their objectives in quantifiable or measurable terms? Maybe increased sales were due to such factors as price, competition, newness of product, and so on, rather than advertising. You might examine marketing journals such as the *Journal of Advertising Research,* the *Journal of Marketing,* and others for some answers to the question of success via advertising.

4.   Write to certain manufacturers of consumer products and ask them to substantiate their advertising claims. Names and addresses of firms can be found in *Standard and Poor's Register of Corporations, Directors, and Executives.* The nearest FTC office will also have copies of substantiation evidence of the ad claims of firms that have been under FTC investigation. What did you learn about the nature of evidence in substantiation of ad claims? Comprehending the evidence? Reliability of the evidence? Faking the evidence? Experts or authorities? Relating this investigation to the substantiation effort of the FTC, what conclusions do you come up with?

5.   The problem is how to purchase a new car at the lowest price consistent with allowing a fair profit for the sales agency. Read the latest evaluation of new cars in *Consumer Reports* (usually in the February through June issues). Settle on the make, model, and desired accessories. Get the facts on all wholesale costs to the dealer, using information sources provided in the Taylor-Troelstrup Reading 11. Follow the outline in the above Readings book. After getting all the data the final gross profit is your bargaining factor. What was the "payoff"?

6. It may be to your advantage to turn in your old car every year or every other year. Get all the facts and compare the cost data with the results from project 5 cost facts. Some dealers may give you a better deal if you turn your car in annually.

7. "Many mothers perceive that television advertising influences their children. They estimate the effect of commercials by the frequency with which their children attempt to influence purchases." How accurate is this statement? Are clear-cut measures of influence possible? Research-minded students should read recent consumer behavior textbooks.

SUGGESTED READINGS

Britt, Stewart H.: "Are So-Called Successful Advertising Campaigns Really Successful?" *Journal of Advertising Research,* June 1969.

Dunn, S. Watson: *Advertising: Its Role in Modern Marketing,* 2d ed., Holt, Rinehart and Winston, Inc., New York, 1969.

"Family Growth and Variation in Family Role Structure," *The Journal of Marriage and Family,* February 1970, p. 45.

Garoian, Leon (ed.): *Economics of Conglomerate Growth,* Oregon State University Press, Corvallis, 1972.

Hearings before the Committee on Commerce on S. 1461 and S. 1753, Oct. 4, 1971; *on Advertising,* 1971.

Katona, George: *The Powerful Consumer,* McGraw-Hill Book Company, New York, 1960, chap. 9.

Levitt, Theodore: "The Morality (?) of Advertising," *Harvard Business Review,* July–August 1970.

Nader, Ralph: *The Consumer and Corporate Accountability,* Harcourt Brace, Jovanovich, Inc., New York, 1973.

Packard, Vance: *The Hidden Persuaders,* David McKay Company, Inc., New York, 1957.

Sax, J. L.: *Defending the Environment,* Alfred A. Knopf, Inc., New York, 1971.

"Take Consumerism into Account or Government Will Act," *Advertising Age,* Mar. 9, 1970.

Troelstrup, Arch W.: "The Consumer Interest in Our Competitive System," in *Freedom of Information in the Market-Place,* University of Missouri, School of Journalism, Columbia, 1967, pp. 77–82.

"Values and Decision-Making," *Home Economics Research Abstract,* no. 6, 1968, Family Relations and Child Development, American Home Economics Association, Washington, D.C.

Ward, Scott: *Effects of Television Advertising on Children and Adolescents,* Marketing Science Institute, Cambridge, Mass., July 1971.

Weiss, E. B.: "Advertising's Crisis of Confidence," *Advertising Age,* June 26, 1969.

———: "Advertising's Triple Economic Threat," *Advertising Age,* July 3, 1967.

CHAPTER 3
MONEY AND MARITAL HAPPINESS

Spending money may be America's favorite sport, but marriage is our favorite institution. Ninety-two percent of our population marries. Why do so many marry? Ask the average married couple, and they will probably answer, "We love each other." Just as simple as that.

Most couples start out believing that they can have a happy and successful marriage. But love alone is not enough, apparently. More and more marriages end in divorce, annulment, or desertion.

THE FAMILY IS A THREATENED INSTITUTION

Of all our shaky institutions, none is more threatened than the family. Leaving aside divorce, annulment, and desertion, the increasing complexity of our interests, however legitimate they may be, serves as a centrifugal force, driving members of the family away from the center.

A Swiss pastor complained that it was almost impossible for him to find a half hour during the day when all members of his family could meet together, even for a meal. If a Swiss father, who has almost absolute authority, can't achieve family unity, what chance is there for an American father?

In many American families, the children take music lessons, riding lessons, voice lessons, and perhaps dancing lessons; they make trips to the orthodontist and are involved in Boy Scouts and Girl Scouts, school sports, band practice, play rehearsals, and all sorts of social life. There is a constant coming and going in the house at least until the college years.

Houses are now being built with separate wings just for the children, rather for the convenience of the parents than out of consideration for the children.

The English for centuries have relegated their children to nurseries—not, however, without adult supervision. On the island of Martinique, an American overheard an older woman reproaching a young mother for leaving her children alone with the maid.

"But I was left with the maid when I was a child."

"Never," said the old woman. "Your 'da' was always in the house." (The "da" is a black woman of great authority. Maids come and go, but the "da" of a family is a permanent resident. But what American can afford a "da"?)

Americans are about the only ones who argue that it is good to leave children without supervision. Children need mature companionship, too. Often, they crave it. They seek it elsewhere if the home fails to provide it.

Some writers describe the home as a "prison" or a "snake pit." Sometimes it is. Others describe it as a warm place—a refuge and a shelter. A family atmosphere of wholesome solidarity and unity gives a child a wonderful feeling of belonging.

The fact is that the American family as we have known it for decades is disintegrating. The family is worth preserving, but how can we safeguard it?

Marriage on the rocks

Marriage has been a solid rock in American culture for centuries, said Dr. Brent Barlow, family relations specialist, and he predicts that it still has a long way to go before it crumbles. Compared with 80 percent a century ago, Barlow said, 92 percent of today's adults have tried marriage at least once.

Although more people are marrying, more people are also marrying more than once. Dr. Barlow sees a trend toward serial mating or what he terms the "Hollywood style of marriage." In his words, "The age of pragmatism has caught up with marriage. Many people believe that if marriage doesn't work the first time, they should try another one. Marrying one person in a lifetime is still the norm, but a number of people who divorce marry again. About 90 percent of those under 30 who divorce do remarry."

Reasons for remarriage vary and may not always include love. People may desire another mate for economic reasons, in order to enjoy a more active social-life, for sexual fulfillment, or to serve as father or mother to their children.

After the honeymoon is over, the wife has to make greater adjustments than her husband. The woman undergoes changes, particularly if she's been working and later becomes pregnant and has to stay home. The husband goes on with his occupation, while the wife starts the household routine, which may prove a shock to her. She gives up her identity by changing her name and giving up some of her friends for his. In fact, she gives up many of her social claims to meet his.

Marriage counselors generally agree that many of the adjustments come during the first year of marriage, and therefore this period is often the most crucial one. Almost every marriage has to deal with certain problems. According to Dr. Barlow, the number one problem is finances. He said that the "amount of money couples have and the way they handle it is important, and at times triggers issues concerning differences in people's values and what they really want out of life."

Dr. Barlow ranks sexual adjustment as the second major problem in early marriage. This is followed by dilemmas in such areas as the in-laws, religion, child care, recreation, mutual friends, communication, drugs and what he calls "tremendous trifles" that are blown out of proportion.

Upturn in divorce and remarriage

Dr. Clifford R. Adams, professor emeritus of Penn State University, presented his latest findings to the Identity Research Institute in Washington, D.C., in 1969. After studying 6,000 couples, he said that federal government statistics showing that 28 percent of all marriages end in divorce are misleading. He said if you take annulments and desertions, which are not included in the government data, the figure would be nearer to 40 percent. Add to this the "morbidity marriage," where a man and a woman may continue living together just for appearances or convenience while hating each other, and you find that only about 25 percent of marriages are really happy.

Dr. Adams said that divorce is most likely to occur during the third year after the first marriage and that about one-half of all divorces are obtained within seven years of the first marriage.

A 1972 study, *Perspectives on the Recent Upturn in Divorce and Remarriage,*[1] covering a span of fifty years of marriage and divorce and remarriage, notes that the number of marriages has risen about one-third since 1960 but that the proportion of women remaining single in their early twenties also has risen by about the same percentage.

A key development behind this paradox, according to this study, is the upturn in divorce and subsequent remarriage during the 1960s and 1970s. During

[1] Financed by the National Institute of Child Health and Human Development, National Institutes of Health.

this period the annual number of divorces rose by 80 percent, and the annual number of remarriages rose by 40 percent.

The main reason for the continuing rise in remarriage has been the sharply advancing divorce rate, especially among women in their late 20s and early 30s.

The same study also makes these points:

1. About 25 to 29 percent of women in their late 20s or early 30s today may be expected to end their first marriage in divorce sometime during their lives. This is somewhat below the level of one divorce in every three marriages sometimes claimed.

2. About one-fifth of young women—aged 27 to 32 in 1971—whose first marriage ends in divorce may be expected to remarry and end that marriage in divorce.

3. Combining the 25 divorces for 100 women after the first marriage and the 5 divorces after remarriage yields a projected total of 30 divorces in a lifetime for 100 women born from 1940 to 1944.

4. Divorces that occur after remarriage seldom increase the proportion of women who have ever been divorced, inasmuch as about 95 percent of such divorces—according to data for women born from 1920 to 1924—are not the first divorce the person has experienced.

THE CONFUSED AMERICAN FAMILY

Why are American families the richest in the world and yet so often in debt and unhappy? First, we should be careful to avoid false and antisocial answers to the question of why American families are increasingly getting into debt. We need to consider the possibility that the real answer may be that many families are very confused about what standard of living they ought to have. Second, we should recognize that this confusion is not only the fault of the borrower. The confusion is probably the result of tremendous changes taking place in our society. The third idea is that American society is certainly going to keep on changing. And with change, we are likely to witness the rise of new standards and morals about borrowing and saving money. And some of us are going to disagree with the new standards.

It may be alarming to read about the $164.9 billion short-term consumer credit debt in 1971. Some people believe that most consumers are so deeply in debt that they cannot possibly get out. In fact, they have been saying that for decades. Yet somehow most debtors manage to liquidate their debts.

There must be a limit to debts, but the basic problem may not be whether or not the debts will be liquidated. They continue to be liquidated right along. The real problem is: Why has it become so common for families to have such worries and guilt feelings about their debts? The answers to this question are important because they are related to money and marital conflicts.

Many of us are familiar with the guilty suspicion that our neighbors are having less difficulty in paying their bills than we are having. Actually, this may not be true. In a study A. C. Spectorsky made of residents in the wealthier suburbs of New York City, where men were earning from $12,000 to $30,000 a year, he found that the average family was spending about 40 percent more than its annual income. He also found that every Tom or Harry in the community believed that he was the only man who had to borrow $500 to buy a hi-fi set, while his neighbor, Dick, could afford to go to Bermuda. Dick felt guilty about owing $500 for his "fly now, pay later" Bermuda vacation when his neighbor, Tom, could afford an expensive hi-fi set.

Tom and Dick illustrate a lot of boring statistics. Most families know that it has become quite common among American families, except the poorest and the richest, to owe enough money to feel anxious and guilty.

Individual worries are not the only problems resulting from the high consumer debt. Some economists mention it as a factor in the instability of our economy. And some sociologists have mentioned it as a factor in social disorganization. Psychiatrists mention it as a factor in the climbing rate of mental illness.

Willingness to incur debts: "I want tomorrow today"

So the fact that relatively well-off families are becoming more and more willing to incur debts is an important change in our society. One of the consequences of this change, especially for "young marrieds" and "growing families," is that this system is promoting debt as a way of life. In other words, more families want more immediate possessions than they can afford on a cash basis, and consumer credit is made to order for them.

Why has an increasingly large number of families changed from paying cash to assuming debts? There are many answers, but most of them appear to be unsatisfactory.

The first theory is found in most consumer-economics textbooks and in the Federal Reserve Board's excellent six-volume study of consumer credit. This answer says that people always have wanted more things than they could afford at a given time and that consumer credit was a natural evolution of merchandising methods to satisfy these wants. People used to buy laundry service from a man who owned a laundry, and transportation from a man who owned a livery stable, but nowadays they buy their own washer-dryer, their own automobile, and their own TV set. They can do this because they can get credit to buy these and many other expensive possessions immediately.

All this is true, but it is not the complete answer. People have always wanted more than they had, but Noah could not have paid for the Ark on the installment plan because such plans did not exist then. Credit is so much a natural evolution of distribution methods that you cannot help but wonder why it almost never existed until the twentieth century.

Part of the answer is simple. Throughout most of history, borrowing and lending at interest had been considered immoral and had been strictly taboo. The lender was usually considered a parasite and often a criminal. The borrower was usually considered improvident and even a sinner.

What happened to traditional morals?

Is borrowing immoral?

What changed such morals? Can it be that more people use more credit nowadays because they are economically more rational? The danger of this answer or theory is that it assumes the borrower is not confused by moral traditions and is acting by some kind of new, sensible standard. But the credit manager who assumes that every loan applicant knows what he is doing is asking for trouble.

The other two kinds of inadequate theory offer an answer to what happened to traditional morals, which is that people are becoming more immoral. There are the "naive moralists" who blame high debt levels on immoral individuals, and the "sophisticated moralists" who blame it on a bad system that forces people into debt. The naive moralists are people like John Keats, who said that immoral people are imitating the government's philosophy of deficit spending, and that we are becoming a nation of immature people who like to open Christmas presents the week before Thanksgiving. Or they are men like William Whyte, the sociologist, who says borrowers are immoral because of a contagious social-psychological neurosis called "budgetism"; or Eugene Barnes, a psychologist who believes that people have no "credit conscience."

But how can these explanations explain enough, especially when we consider that year after year the same percentage of different income classes have personal debts? About one-third of factory-worker families are in debt; about one-half of white-collar workers are in debt even though their average income is higher than that of the self-employed. It seems a strange thing when the same percentage of individuals decides to be "immoral" as concerns debt year after year in the different groups of our society. It is a little like criminals. Criminals have been considered immoral, and society has generally worked on them as individuals to mend their ways. But when society realized that slums turn out high percentages of criminals, a study of the effects of their environment began. We still don't know all that causes criminals, but at least society no longer believes that they are merely immoral individuals.

Involvement of the social system

In much the same way that slums help produce criminals, white-collar jobs help produce debtors. More white-collar workers have debts than self-employed people, whether the income of the self-employed is higher, lower, or the same. It would seem, therefore, that the social system is involved in some way.

The sophisticated moralists recognize this fact. The naive moralists still insist that borrowers are basically immoral, but they blame the system for making them that way. John McPartland, the novelist, blames the "easy credit system" for tempting him. A. C. Spectorsky, the sociologist who conducted the study in the wealthy New York City suburbs, blames the "status" system. John Kenneth Galbraith, the economist, blames the whole economic system for just plain overselling of consumer goods.

All these suggestions are part of an adequate explanation. Perhaps they explain too much. The systems they mention do exert constant pressure. But they do not explain why, year after year, one-third of blue-collar workers do not have debts, nor do two-thirds of the self-employed, nor one-half of the white-collar workers.

Besides, history shows that it is best to be suspicious of every generation that says that the younger generation is becoming more and more immoral. As often as not it has turned out that the morals were changing, and that often the new morals were better for their times.

We have to remember that before social morals were established, it was all right for a man to knock any other man over the head and drag away his property and his woman. Most husbands are grateful for the change in morals since that time.

Basic personal morals like the Ten Commandments remain generally unchanged. But specific little morals, in areas like economic and political behavior, change with the times. Economic behavior that produced the Robber Barons of two generations ago and was admired, or at least accepted, at the time would now be immoral and illegal.

Are credit users immoral?

It seems that when a set of morals becomes obsolete, and when there is no workable set of standards to replace the old ones, people become confused and begin experimenting until a suitable set of new morals is developed and accepted. Perhaps the rapid expansion of consumer credit represents that kind of experimenting, caused by that kind of confusion.

Has thrift become obsolete?

Let's consider the confusion that might make the former morals regarding thrift and debt become obsolete. In our early economy, capital had to be created largely by thrifty acts of individuals. Therefore, the virtue attributed to thrift, along with the moral taboo on using credit for consumer goods, was essential in causing a rapid rate of economic growth.

Thrift also had important motives for the individual. Before 1900, success came along usually with the "expansible possession"—that is, a little farm or a little shop or business that required only constant thrift to gain enough capital to become a big estate or a big factory or business.

But things have changed for the economic system and the individual. It appears at present that the economic system can form capital more easily than it can maintain purchasing power. And the individual does not as often find success with the expansible possession. Instead, he pins his hopes on the forward-looking job. To make the most of a job or position, thrift is not of much help. What is needed is a standard of living that will show that the family appreciate and want better things—even if they have to borrow to buy them.

So it seems that for both the economic system and the individual times have changed, and it makes more sense to attach moral virtue to spending than to thrift.

This is by no means a full explanation of the eagerness for credit. Perhaps social change could have removed the moral restrictions on credit without its resulting in a $465.8 billion *total* debt if American families were not so eager to borrow. Perhaps this eagerness may be the result, not of confusion about changing morals, but of confusion about standards of living.

Desire for change in standard of living

Your *level* of living is based on the amount of money you spend. Your *standard* of living is the way you want to live. One man's standard may require a shack by the seashore, one good suit, and regular meals. Another man's standard may require a trilevel home, two cars, and a yardman.

Where do these standards come from? Through most of human history, they simply became a part of a people during the process of their growing up in families. Chances are that most of us came from a middle-class family. Chances are that a majority had grandfathers or even fathers who were farmers, immigrants, or factory workers with less education than their children. The point

Standards change because each generation has a new environment

is that each generation could not live according to the standards of the preceding generation because each grew up in a different environment. And millions of American families have been experiencing this environmental change.

In a situation where every generation is living in a different kind of world from the preceding one, of what use are many of the living standards of grandfathers or even fathers? Each generation has to experiment with new standards. We are generally guided by our own ambitions and by the standards of friends—

the Joneses, who have debts we don't know about. Or maybe we are guided by the mass media—TV, motion pictures, magazines. If, under these circumstances, the average American family were not confused about an approximate standard of living, you would have something really difficult to explain.

The growth of consumer credit, then, may not be so much a matter of immorality as a consequence of confusion, and this confusion may be rooted in actual moral social change, not in bad psychology.

Near the beginning of this century, credit institutions and others helped make it respectable for people to admit that they needed to borrow in emergencies. At midcentury, it was standard practice for young married couples to place heavy mortgages on their future earnings in order to start out with a standard packet of durable goods when they needed them most. This packet might now include a stove, refrigerator, washing machine, dishwasher, a car, a television set, and a record player. By the end of the century, who knows? A family-size airplane, clothes that you toss into the ashcan after a 'few weeks' use—well, you guess!

The trend will likely be more use of "buy now, pay later," until we move out of the form of credit that has induced ownership and move into a system of less ownership but more continuous renting of needed goods and services. If this happens, credit will have a different meaning.

And perhaps we ought to do our part to eliminate the obsolete feelings of worry and guilt that keep people from talking about their use of credit. Too many people are like the man who went to the psychiatrist because he worried all the time. The doctor asked how he lived, and he listed numerous expensive habits. The doctor said, "This is wonderful, why worry?" The client said he was making only $5,000 a year. The psychiatrist answered, "My friend, you're not sick. You're simply overextended and overconfused."

Education neglects our needs

Most families perform their functions well when they have learned how. Grandmother's family, for example, taught children the kind of responsibilities they needed in their time. It was really an apprenticeship. And apparently they did a pretty good job as long as the family functions remained the same. But when the family functions changed, this system broke down. Something else was obviously needed.

The modern family has a real job in building personalities capable of adequately meeting the complexities of modern life. Understanding a child today is quite different and considerably more complicated or involved than it was years ago. Apprenticeship will no longer do the trick. Customs change too rapidly. We need families that can grow in their ability to live together happily and successfully. Divorce and separation statistics and other evidence of marital discord indicate that something is out of gear somewhere.

Money and quality of family life

The individuals entering into marriage bring attitudes, impressions, and expectations created throughout years of separate existence in a money society. They also use money in a variety of ways. Personal habits of spending are often used in instances of discordant marital relationships as a point of attack by the partner, or are viewed as an attack. For example, a husband may be dominating with regard to his wife, rigidly holding her to a tight budget. He may come from a home in which the father was the authoritative, thrifty provider, as responsible for the financial management of his home as for his business. On the other hand, this controlled disbursement of money may be a measure of the husband's recollections about a hungry youth in a period of economic depression and insecurity. To certain neurotic husbands, money may be an unconscious symbol of masculinity and power. This was illustrated in a 1971 Harris poll that revealed some storm signals in that 49 percent of all white women, 71 percent of all black women, and 55 percent of all women under 30 years of age said they believed that "most men find it necessary for their egos to keep women down." The wife's retaliation, irrespective of the factors underlying her husband's actions, may take several forms. She may spend money wastefully in order to express her hostility toward him or, perhaps at an unconscious level, in order to maintain a dominant role in her own right. She may handle the situation simply by making no effort to operate within the budget he has prescribed. To his practice of limiting her funds as a way of keeping his mate in a dependent relation to him, the wife may respond by setting limits of her own. She may deny his basic psychological needs—expressed, perhaps, through gambling, or excessive use of money for alcohol—in charges of inadequate support and by refusal to feed him properly.

Considerable tension may be aroused because of the wife's working for pay outside the home. Problems on this score are minimal if there are common goals understood and accepted by both partners. Many money problems grow out of environmental economic situations. There may be, for example, an unexpected loss of a job, or a reduction in income. Or the nature of the husband's work may involve considerable traveling. But if the partners have achieved a satisfactory joint ego ideal, and if they are reasonably well-integrated personalities, they are likely to make the necessary adjustments to situations.

In the remainder of the chapter we cannot hope to thoroughly explore marital adjustment with respect to a factor so important as the use of money. We shall only summarize a few studies on the use of money and point out the importance of seeking a practical, workable plan for meeting this inescapable aspect of marriage.

WHAT MONEY DOES TO MARRIAGE

Marriage experts, in general, agree that some conflict is inevitable. Some conflict is open quarreling. Then there may be what William Graham Sumner termed "antagonistic cooperation." This kind of conflict may be more subtle. Some couples learn to live with such problems. It would seem, then, that the attitude taken toward a disagreement is significant in working out a satisfactory solution.

Conflict in marriage

What causes marital conflict? Marriage counselors are not absolutely certain about the basic causes of conflict. As tensions develop in a family, any incident may spark the disagreement. The incident may not actually be the real cause for the conflict. Thus what seems to be the cause may not be so at all. An analysis of the major causes of conflict as reported by married couples may give us some tips for successful marriage.

The *Ladies' Home Journal* asked representative American women the question: "What things have you noticed husbands and wives quarrel about most frequently?" The reasons were given in this order: money, jealousy, rearing of children, little things, drinking, and in-laws.

Clifford Adams, Penn State psychologist, reported the testimony from 1,000

Money problems cause marital problems

married couples.[2] He selected the replies from 100 of the most unhappy marriages. The following reasons for marriage conflict are in the order of their frequency: lack of companionship, lack of money, sex, in-laws, housework, children, social life, personal traits, lack of affection, and religious differences.

Judson T. Landis, professor of sociology at the University of California, received information from 409 couples, married an average of twenty years, who were parents or friends of students taking the marriage course at Michigan State College.[3] This group was above average in income and education. Most of the husbands and wives agreed that it had taken longer to achieve sex adjustment than adjustment in any other area. The second most difficult adjustment was in reaching an agreement on how to spend the family income. For some of them, it took an average of seven years to end disagreement. About 10 percent were still quarreling over money problems. Other causes of conflict included quarreling over social and recreational activities, in-laws, religion and mutual friends.

Effectiveness of college education on marital conflict

C. Robert Pace reported on a study of 951 former University of Minnesota students between the ages of 25 and 34. Half were men, half were women; half had graduated, and half had left college after one to three years. The questionnaire aimed to probe the effectiveness of a modern college education. The results, shown in Table 3-1, throw light on the inadequacy of family relations education.

Disagreements occurred most frequently over the management of money. This is an interesting sidelight, because money management is the most frequent source of conflict among couples in the upper third or fourth of the na-

[2]*Ladies' Home Journal,* January 1949, p. 26. Reprinted with special permission. Copyright 1949. The Curtis Publishing Company.
[3]Associated Press report, May 29, 1948.

TABLE 3-1 Effectiveness of College Education

	PERCENTAGE OF HUSBAND'S WHO FREQUENTLY DISAGREED	PERCENTAGE OF WIVES WHO FREQUENTLY DISAGREED
Management of income	17	19
Religion	10	7
Politics	11	14
Relatives	16	20
Entertainment of relatives	7	9
Choice of friends	10	9
Ideals of conduct	9	10
Philosophy of life	12	12
Recreations	16	14
Entertainment of friends	7	9

SOURCE: C. Robert Pace, *They Went to College,* The University of Minnesota Press, Minneapolis, 1941, p. 82. Reprinted with permission.

tion's families according to economic status. Pace says that "bringing together evidence from all parts of the study relating to income management leads to the generalization that, although many of the young adults expressed a desire for more information about ways to economize, many were also engaging in uneconomical practices."

A brief analysis of the discrepancies and inconsistencies between attitudes and practices among this group is most revealing. In spite of relatively high incomes, most of them were dissatisfied with their incomes. While they said that they had good food, were well dressed, comfortable, and happy on their present incomes, nevertheless 35 percent of them found it difficult to keep out of debt. Over 40 percent expressed the need for money management information, yet less than half had a family spending plan. Furthermore, their marketing habits were needlessly expensive. About one-fourth had medical indebtedness, yet less than one-fifth of these took advantage of health insurance plans. With such discrepancies between feelings and practices, it is not difficult to understand why income mismanagement was a frequent source of conflict between these husbands and wives.

The case studies of about 100 college graduates from coast to coast (78 of whom were married) by the Merrill-Palmer School in Detroit throw further light on the nature of marital conflicts. Table 3.2, shows that one of the major issues for marital difficulties was the conflict over finances. More specifically, these conflicts were over (1) how the money was to be spent, and (2) who was to make the decision. Most of the women had taken a course in economics in college. Yet there seemed to be little or no carryover from such a course into the everyday problems of money management. When the counselors mentioned budgeting, nearly all the women resisted the idea as a device of Satan designed to restrict their spending habits. Nor did the size of income alter the general complaint that they could not make ends meet with the amount they had.

TABLE 3-2   Percentage of Problems of 78 Married Women

TYPE OF PROBLEM	PERCENT OF CASES
Personality	98
Financial	97
Health	96
Husband-wife	89
Relations with associates	88
Recreational	84
Housekeeping	82
Relations with relatives	80
Parent-child	78
Crisis	74
In-law	60
Sex	56
Religion	52
Vocation	34
Education	20

SOURCE: Reproduced from Robert G. Foster and Pauline Park Wilson, *Women after College.* Copyright 1942 by Columbia University Press, p. 27.

These women had almost entirely ignored the evident need to be prepared to meet certain inevitabilities in their lives—to be intelligent, effective, conscientious consumers. Most of them had prepared for a job, but neither college nor home had prepared them for the time when they would give up a job and manage a home.

It is strange that, although many college women expect to marry and have a home and children, few really prepare for this important function. Fewer yet do any mature thinking on combining homemaking and a career. Too many do not look on homemaking as a career for which they have to fit themselves. This fact goes a long way toward solving many of the problems that puzzle social economists and moralists. For it is at the bottom of much of the discontent that permeates many homes.

Problem of human relations   Money management may be the primary cause for marital discord. Behind the problems of money management, however, and all the other so-called big causes are the hard-to-analyze human behavior relationships. Whether the area of conflict concerns money or sex, characteristic and basic behavior patterns are revealed in subtle and, at times, unconscious ways. Along with each outward act go certain feelings and attitudes that are impossible or difficult to see.

In some cases, two persons will react differently to the same general problem. For example, a certain husband battled continuously with his wife over her "extravagant spending." Another husband's reaction to his wife's extravagant spending was: "I'll just prove to her that I can make more money than she can spend." The attitude toward the same general situation was quite different. Open conflict resulted in the one case, and an acceptance of the situation in the other.

It would seem logical to conclude that we need to discover the personality traits that lead married people to quarrel over money, sex, or any of the other "big" causes of family disagreements.

Psychologists tell us that the relationship between husband and wife is loaded with disguised impulses. And sometimes the least important part is what we see. Yet what we see and hear are extremely important, because they may be the advance signs—a symptom of what cannot be seen. A timely recognition of the symptom may give the clue that will lead to the solving of the difficulty.

An interesting study of 641 marriages in 1965 and 1966 identified patterns of marital problems encountered in marriage guidance clinics.[4] Thirty-two problems of counseling clients, nine of which are presented in the table on page 73, were identified in order of frequency of their occurrence.

In this study of 641 couples who were having marital difficulties to the point of receiving professional help, counselors noted that husband's management of money was fifth, inadequate income was eighth, and wife's management of money was twenty-ninth in order of frequency of incidence in a total list of thirty-two marital issues or problems. It would appear that the wife may be a better manager of the family income than her husband!

In another recent study, marriage researcher Wesley R. Burns investigated 147 middle-class couples, randomly selected from residential addresses and

[4] Jerzy Krupinski, Elizabeth Marshall, and Valerie Yule, "Patterns of Marital Problems in Marriage Guidance Clinics," *Journal of Marriage and Family*, February 1970, p. 138.

	PROBLEMS	PERCENTAGE OF INCIDENCE
1.	Lack of communication	41
2.	Quarreling	33
3.	Wife's neglect of, and indifference to, husband	30
4.	Wife's frigidity	30
5.	Husband's management of money	22
6.	Husband's intolerance	20
7.	Wife's desertion	20
8.	Shortage of money	19
9.	Wife's management of money	11

representing all age groups and all stages of the life cycle.[5] All the couples were interviewed in their homes by professionally trained persons and also filled in a long questionnaire. Satisfactions with various aspects of marriage and family living covering all the stages in the life cycle were identified. In the area of financial management such questions as these were discussed:

1. How often do I get mad or angry at something in regard to the way money is handled in our family?
2. How much improvement can there be in the way money is handled in our family?
3. How satisfied am I with the way our money is handled?

The Burns study concluded that most of the difficulties in management of money in the family come during the years the children are attending school. And this is true for both parents. Apparently, many young parents are more able to cope with income and spending issues that appear early in marriage. When children reach school age, more and more financial problems confront them as a whole set of new money demands comes into the picture.

Income versus success and happiness

In New York, a well-dressed woman called on a personal finance advisor at her bank. She said that, despite her husband's income of $18,000 a year, they had no money for fun. A Hollywood actor with an income of $100,000 a year went bankrupt. He had only $3,000 in assets to meet liabilities of $50,000.

Is more money the answer

The assumption of certain economists that most personal problems would be solved if the income of each couple could be raised sufficiently is not borne out by some studies of marital adjustment. In the case studies of seventy-eight married women, the Merrill-Palmer School clinicians found that regardless of their incomes—whether they had $3,000, $5,000, or $10,000—they felt that it was insufficient.[6] In fact, as income increased in arithmetical ratio, personal problems seemed to increase in geometric ratio.

Somewhat in contrast, Cottrell's study of 526 couples found that families

[5] "Satisfaction with Various Aspects of Marriage over the Life Cycle: A Random Middle-Class Sample," *Journal of Marriage and Family,* February 1970, p. 29.

[6] Robert G. Foster and Pauline Park Wilson, *Women after College,* Columbia University Press, New York, 1942, p. 51.

on moderate income seemed to have made better adjustments than when incomes were either high or low.[7] Terman found little relationship between happiness and income.[8]

Robert C. Williamson reported that economic variables are more important in marital adjustment than has been generally observed in previous investigations.[9] A total of 210 couples, representing a cross section of the Los Angeles white population, were interviewed in their homes by two interviewers. The husband and the wife were interviewed separately with a questionnaire that contained personal background and social and economic items, as well as a marital-adjustment test. On the scores secured in the adjustment test, the sample was divided into happily and unhappily married groups. The happy group totaled 86 men and 85 women; the unhappy group, 66 men and 62 women. There was an intermediate small group that could be considered neither happy nor unhappy. Some of the important economic variables in marital adjustment were these:

1. Lower incomes (below $436 a month) prevailed among the unhappy group. Conversely, higher incomes were found among happy husbands and wives.

2. Both the men and the women in the poor residential area were maritally less happy than those in the better areas.

3. It was found that for both partners there was a higher percentage of happy marriages among those having savings of at least $600.

4. The husbands who had no debts, or less than $300 in debts, were significantly happier than those who had $300 or more in debts.

5. The highest proportion of happy husbands and a still higher proportion of happy wives were among the highest security ratings (insurance, savings, debts, and type and regularity of employment).

6. There was no significant difference between the happy and unhappy groups in the matter of keeping budgeting records.

7. There was a significant difference favoring successful adjustment among those who did not overspend more than two months per year.

8. There was a significantly higher percentage of maladjustment among those who admitted having to borrow three or more times during the past five years than among those who borrowed less or not at all.

H. Ashley Weeks[10] and William J. Goode[11] in separate studies found an inverse relationship between economic level and divorce rate—the higher the economic level, the lower the rate, and vice versa. Even more important than

[7] Ernest W. Burgess and Leonard S. Cottrell, *Predicting Success or Failure in Marriage,* Prentice-Hall, Inc., Englewood Cliffs, N.J., 1939, pp. 152–153. A classic.

[8] Lewis M. Terman, *Psychological Factors in Marital Happiness,* McGraw-Hill Book Company, New York, 1938, pp. 169–171. A classic.

[9] Robert C. Williamson, "Economic Factors in Marital Adjustment," *Marriage and Family Living,* November 1952.

[10] "Differential Divorce Rates by Occupations," *Social Forces,* March 1943, pp. 334–337.

[11] "Economic Factors and Marital Adjustment," *American Sociological Review,* December 1951, pp. 802–812.

the quantity of the money are the couple's attitude toward it and the use to which it is put.

University of Pennsylvania researchers[12] interviewed 300 couples to determine why and how often they quarreled. Two hundred were chosen from families that had at one time sought family counseling help. The others were from a group of couples who considered their marriages sufficiently successful to compete in a nationwide contest for "representative families" from each state. The husbands and wives were given a list of possible points of disagreement and asked to indicate, independently of each other, what they fought about and how often. The 300 couples rated their problems in order, going from points of most conflict to those of least conflict. Fights over "finances" headed the list as the most common occasion for conflict.

When the answers of the two groups—the 200 and the 100—were tabulated separately, it was found that the couples who had had marital trouble ranked the problems in almost the same order as those who had considered themselves happily married. The difference was not in the nature of issues but in the extent of disagreement. Ironically, the one thing husbands and wives in both groups tended to agree on was which issues they disagreed about.

Economic factors in marital adjustment

Frances Lomas Feldman, who directed the research of the Money Management Project of the Welfare Planning Council of the Los Angeles Region, made these interesting observations of the feelings of people about money.

The world we live in is characterized by continual change. There are technological advances, increasing population with shifting urbanization and explosive suburbanization movements, economic depressions and recessions, wars, and changing fashions and standards of living. One pivotal factor, however, remains constantly important: money. But never before in the history of western civilization has the word "money" meant so much to so many. Money is the medium of exchange, a means for distributing the vast and increasing outpouring of the goods and services of our economic system. Money is a symbol of status and achievement, often the measure for human values and dignity. This is truly the age of the economic man.

Economists have tended to view money as having an objective reality, a life of its own, isolated from the emotional and intellectual life of the human beings whom it was designed to serve. They have applied complicated mechanistic concepts, frequently expressed in elaborate mathematical formulas, to describe objectively the flow and use of money. Recently, however, there has been a mounting awareness and emphasis on the importance of the so-called subjective aspects of money, on the unique significance of psychosocial influences. There is increasing cognizance that an essential ingredient in skillful working with people is the understanding of the objective and subjective influences which affect, and are the effect of, money —the understanding of the dynamics of the interactions in the socioeconomic and cultural climate in which the individual grows and develops.

The universality of money as a causative or symptomatic component in a strikingly high proportion of the problems and preoccupations of human beings in our culture is evidenced almost daily in the headlined stories in the public press. One reads about the distraught husband who kills his wife because of "arguments over finances," about the parent who solves his inability to provide for his children by ending their lives or by armed robbery. One reads about the divorce suit in which

[12] Reported in *Changing Times*, October 1966, pp. 21–22.

"stinginess" is offered as one justification for the action, or about the divorced wife petitioning for increased child support from the ex-spouse who has remarried and has another family to support.

The ironic humor of the many current cartoons with a money theme provides another barometer of the feelings of people in our society about money.[13]

Financial columnist Sylvia Porter quoted top jurists as saying: "Quarreling about money is a major reason for America's unprecedented divorce rate. It is difficult to overestimate the vicious part financial trouble is playing in destroying the American home."

There are other, unexpected areas where failure to manage money properly can produce dire results. More and more personnel officers are asking applicants direct questions about how they handle their family income.

Couples seeking to adopt children through reputable agencies also must account for the disposition of their income. One case worker said: "Young couples—both employed and with joint incomes of from $12,000 to $14,000— come in here and tell us they have assets of no more than $200 or $300. Before we will even consider their application, we ask them to demonstrate to us that they can change their values. We give them a year to do it."

From these studies and surveys it is evident that economic variables are more important in marital adjustment than has been generally recognized. The chain of cause and effect, however, is very complex in marital adjustment. The relationship that exists, for example, between savings and a happy marriage may be due in part to education or high intelligence. Or the negative relationship of loss of income to marital happiness may be a reflection of some other factor, such as illness. All this adds up to the fact that economic factors have never received sufficient attention in the studies of marital relations.

Attitudes toward spending money Happy working partnerships of husband and wife are not common according to many professional marriage counselors. They are difficult to achieve, largely because of the complicated attitudes of both husband and wife toward money and work. Contemporary society is regrettably money-conscious. Too often a husband is judged not by how fine a father he is but by how good a provider he is.

If money stands for success and perhaps authority, the manipulation of the family income and spending takes on emotional relationships. These relations may be handled satisfactorily or disastrously, depending on the attitudes of husband and wife. A husband might ask his wife to come to him for every little expenditure. He may be led to feel that he is not a good provider. This feeling can easily creep into ordinary discussions. Can we afford a new car? Can we go away for the summer? Each of these questions may be interpreted as an attack on the husband's ability to provide adequate income. On the other hand, such things need not be turned in the direction of conflict if the attitude itself is proper.

Money matters, however, cannot always be handled rationally. Psychological attitudes toward spending money are as real as the money itself. One family may agree, for example, to spend one-fourth of their income on clothes. "And why not?" they say. "We get more fun out of planning and wearing new

[13] *Journal of Home Economics*, December 1957, p. 267.

clothes than we do in seeing a dozen shows. We live within our income, and we like it this way." This attitude apparently is right for them. On the other hand, such disproportionate spending of money on clothes could be a focal point for a serious quarrel in another family.

"Living up to the Joneses"

Spending more money than your neighbors is not necessarily dangerous to family happiness. But "living up to the Joneses" is potential dynamite, because such a mental attitude leads to the strain of living beyond one's means. When John found that his promising insurance business could not provide for everything that Jane and he wanted, he gave it up to enter his father-in-law's business. Soon John became so resentful over his lack of vocational independence and his wife's extravagance that divorce was the result. John returned to his first love, insurance, and later married a girl whose charge accounts were in harmony with their income.

Helen, a society girl, married Dick, whose wholesale vinegar business went bankrupt two years after their marriage. Helen's friends were sure she was headed for divorce. Instead, Helen mastered typing and shorthand and pitched in as her husband's secretary. Several years later, their business was flourishing. A woman who marries with the expectation of mink is likely to prove an unhappy partner if she finds herself wrapped in rabbit—unless she does something about her attitude.

Foster and Wilson, in reporting on the case studies at the Merrill-Palmer School, concluded that the economic position of her associates may accentuate many of the individual's attitudes about her own position.[14] They report that among a few of the women of the study who belonged to the same sorority there were wide differences in income. One woman, who had the lowest family income and was unable to dress and entertain as elaborately as the others, accepted the situation, participated actively in the group, and took life in her stride. In this same set was a woman whose income was several times as great. But she constantly complained about her clothes, her home, and so on. She felt that her income was insufficient.

Attitudes toward housekeeping problems are important, too. Dislike for household tasks, lack of skill, and difficulties with household help are usually the foremost problems in this area.[15] These dislikes and difficulties are important because they are related to family happiness and success. Some women manage these tasks well and are able to use artistic and creative ability in many of the household duties. The new household aids might help to solve some of these problems. But modern appliances will not of themselves alter attitudes toward household duties.

Too high a financial goal

There is the danger, too, of setting the money goal too high. The young husband who is determined to make a million dollars before he reaches the ripe old age

---

[14] Foster and Wilson, loc. cit.
[15] *Ibid.*, pp. 48–50.

of 35 years is a menace to himself and his family. Edward was such a person.[16] Most of his friends and business associates thought he was a hard worker and never knew a day of worry in his life. He worked long and hard and seemed to thrive on it. Soon he had the highest salary in his office. Still he was not satisfied. A little success spurred him on to greater effort. He began to spend money lavishly, bought a large house, and put money in risky investments. He became so excited that he neither slept nor ate well.

Then Edward began to change. He lost his feeling of self-confidence. He was no longer so sure of his business judgment. He often stayed away from his office. He told his wife that he would soon lose his job and began to blame himself for ruining his family.

Most psychologists would call Edward's difficulty a "manic-depressive" illness. Manic-depressives become so when they are not attaining the goals they have set for themselves. Most of them are ambitious. They are overly anxious to achieve financial and social success. When they fall short, conflict results. Psychologists say that this kind of worry or moodiness is dangerous. Many of these people are potential suicides. Too high a financial goal is no solution to family happiness and success.

Money isn't everything

Money is not only dollars and cents. It is a symbol of personal attitudes toward marriage and life. The first essential is to acquire financial attitudes that will harmonize with what you and your family want out of life. It is not the amount of money but the way it is spent that counts.

It's not how much you have; it's how well you spend it

Some families, for example, have a savings complex. The desire to have excessive savings in proportion to income can lead to unhappiness. Generally, each spouse blames the other for spending too much money. These people usually do not realize that they are living so completely in the future that they cannot find happiness in their day-to-day lives. Perhaps this spending complex is related to what some psychologists refer to as "compulsive spending," which is merely an attempt to answer some other need.

THE WORKING WIFE AND MOTHER

A growing factor in the American economy is the influence and contribution of the working wife and mother. Besides making a contribution to the net income of her family, the working wife and mother is an increasingly important source of manpower in the American labor pool. However, the 1970 census data show that American women are changing fast in other ways besides holding down a job.

Profile of American women

According to the 1970 census data, there are 46.4 million married women in the United States, an increase of almost 3.9 million since the 1960 census and a gain of 8.9 million since 1950. Over one-third are under 35; one in twelve is 65 or over. One-fifth are in the 35 to 44 age range; 93 percent live with their husbands in their own households. Only 5.4 percent of married women live on farms. Almost 40 percent of married women over 18 work (a total of 16.8 million). Of those under 25, 43 percent work, and this proportion dips in the child-

[16] George Thorman, *Toward Mental Health,* Public Affairs Committee, New York, 1946, pp. 7–9.

rearing years (25 to 34) to 36.5 percent. Married women work because they want to supplement family income, help buy homes, pay for college tuition, or resume interrupted careers.

The American woman is now considerably more likely to attend college, to work, to live alone, to marry late, to be divorced or separated, and to outlive her husband than she was at the start of the 1960s.

Some of the changes continue trends dating back four or five decades. Others suggest new trends. Taken together, "these are social changes of the first magnitude," according to George Hay Brown, director of the Census Bureau. He also said that "women in the '70s are rapidly moving toward full equality."

Shifting makeup in the labor force

There is a bigger proportion of teen-agers and women, and a smaller proportion of men, in our labor force. In two decades, according to the U.S. Department of Labor, teen-agers and adult women have proportionally increased their makeup of the labor force, as indicated in the accompanying table.

TEEN-AGERS	ADULT WOMEN	ADULT MEN
Increase, 101%:	Increase, 69%:	Increase, 20%:
1952: 4,064,000	1952: 17,517,000	1952: 40,558,000
1972: 8,161,000	1972: 29,625,000	1972: 48,700,000

Teen-agers in 1972 made up 9.4 percent of the labor force, up from 6.5 percent in 1952. Adult women in 1972 made up more than one-third—34.3 percent—of the civilian labor force, up from 28.2 percent in 1952. Adult men in 1972 constituted 56.3 percent of the labor force, down from 65.3 percent in 1952.

Wives in the labor force

Married women have, in recent years, accounted for the largest portion of the labor-force gain, according to the Bureau of the Census. The number of working wives reached 18.4 million in March 1970, about 780,000 above March 1969. The number of working wives with children under 18 years old reached 10.2 million in March 1970, about 460,000 above March 1969.

Children of working mothers

The number of children whose mothers are in the labor force is increasing. In March 1970, 26 million children under 18 years of age had mothers who were working or looking for work, compared with 16 million in 1960. Children of working mothers accounted for 39 percent of all children in 1970, up from 26 percent ten years earlier. In both years, about 25 percent of these children were under the age of 6 and required some care in their mothers' absence.

There are now more children of working mothers, partly because there are now more children and partly because more mothers work. The labor-force participation of women with preschool children increased 60 percent in the last decade, compared with a 20 percent increase for mothers of older children. However, in 1970 as in 1960, mothers of schoolchildren were still more likely to be in the labor force than those with preschool children (see Figure 3-1).

Children of working mothers were found to come from families with higher incomes and fewer children than children whose mothers did not work outside

FIGURE 3-1   Wives in the labor force, by income of husband and age of children, 1970

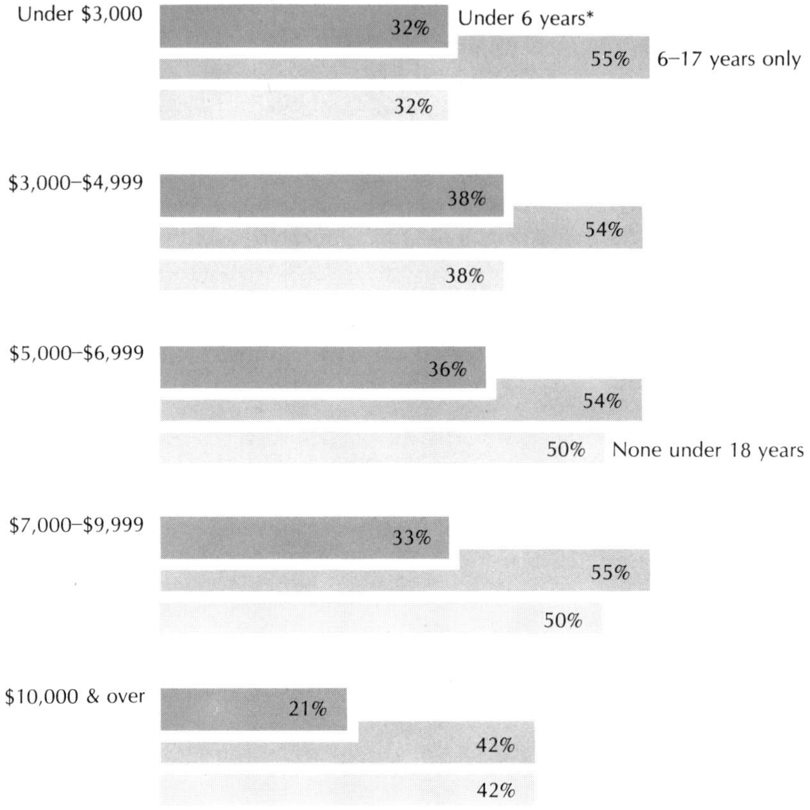

Under $3,000

32%   Under 6 years*

55%   6–17 years only

32%

$3,000–$4,999

38%

54%

38%

$5,000–$6,999

36%

54%

50%   None under 18 years

$7,000–$9,999

33%

55%

50%

$10,000 & over

21%

42%

42%

Wives with husbands present.
* May also have children 6–17 years.
SOURCE: U.S. Department of Agriculture.

the home. This was true for children in families headed by a woman as well as for children in husband-wife families. The accompanying table shows family size and family income data for children of working and nonworking mothers.

	AVERAGE NUMBER OF CHILDREN PER FAMILY	MEDIAN FAMILY INCOME IN 1969
Husband-wife families:		
Mother in labor force	2.19	$11,752
Mother not in labor force	2.42	9.884
Female family head:		
Mother in labor force	2.10	4,651
Mother not in labor force	2.73	2,988

Income in families with preschool children was lower than that in families with children 6 to 17 and was less affected by the mother's work status. Parents of younger children are likely to be younger themselves, probably earning less than the parents of older children. Also, because of the care required by the younger child, his mother is likely to work part time, adding less income than the mother of the older child, who is likely to be working full time. The median income of families with preschool children was only 8 percent higher when the mother worked ($10,000) than when she did not ($9,250), while that of families with children aged 6 to 17 was 14 percent higher when the mother worked ($12,423 versus $10,857). It is well to take note of the modest net income rise in families with working mothers.

A greater proportion of black than white children in two-parent families have both parents in the labor force. The median income in 1969 of black families with children and in which both parents worked was considerably lower ($8,944) than the median income of white families with children, regardless of whether the mother worked or not ($12,283 and $10,508, respectively).

We have seen, then, that the number of children whose mothers are in the labor market increased about 13 percent between 1960 and 1970. In the two decades ending in 1960 and 1970, mothers of schoolchildren were still more likely to be in the labor force than those with preschool children. Adult women in 1972 made up 34.3 percent of the total civilian labor force, up from 28.2 percent in 1952. The number of working wives reached 18.4 million in March 1970, an all-time high. In March 1970, 26 million children had working mothers, compared with only 16 million a decade earlier; 25 percent of the 26 million children were under the age of 6. Children of working mothers came from families with higher incomes and fewer children than children whose mothers did not work outside the home. The median income of families with preschool children was only 8 percent higher when the mother worked, while that of families with children aged 6 to 17 was 14 percent higher. Finally, the median income of black families with children and both parents working is considerably lower than that of white families.

Women in independent residence

The above conclusions concern the working wife and mother. There is also an increasing number of adult women, working and not working, who live alone or with unrelated roommates. We refer to them as *women in independent residence*.

The number of women in independent residence is increasing

The proportion of adult women living alone or with unrelated roommates jumped 50 percent to 7.6 million, about one-tenth of all adult women, according to the Census Bureau. Women over 65, some 4 million of whom now live independently, accounted for most of the increase. But the number of women aged 20 to 34 in this category increased at the fastest rate, jumping 109 percent to 800,000, according to the 1970 census.

Some of the increase in the number of women in independent residence is accounted for by a rise in the proportion of women who are divorced or separated. In 1960, both categories totaled about 7 percent of all women who were or ever had been married. In 1970, the figure approached 10 percent.

In the event young women are disturbed about these "living alone" statistics, let me remind them that almost 95 percent of all women eventually marry, but at a later age than they used to. After remaining stable for twenty years, the median age of marriage climbed half a year during the sixties to 20.8 years for women and 23.2 years for men.

Income, jobs, and employment

It was mentioned earlier that the number of working wives reached 18.4 million out of a total of 46.4 million married women in the United States in 1970. The total labor force averaged 85.9 million in 1970.

In 1971 total employment posted a modest gain of 490,000, compared with increases of 730,000 in 1970 and nearly 2 million in 1969. The 1971 gain was concentrated among 20- to 24-year-olds, mostly young men returning from the armed forces. Employment of men 25 years and over declined, while small gains were posted for women 25 and over and for teen-agers.

Since 1958, the proportion of the civilian labor force unemployed has ranged between annual averages of 3.5 percent in 1969 and 6.8 percent (1958). The average for 1971 was 5.9 percent, up from 4.9 percent in 1970. The greatest incidence of unemployment continues among teen-agers; 19.5 percent of the males and 16.2 percent of the females in the teen-age labor force were unemployed in January 1972 (see Figure 3-2).

The market for college graduates

The market for college graduates since the late 1960s has also been disappointing. In the late 1960s, for example, corporate recruiters flocked to the campuses. Graduates were in demand, even those with only average grades.

Those days are over for the time being. The 1971 hiring level was the lowest in many years, according to The College Placement Council, which surveys campus recruiting and job opportunities. Northwestern University, however, in the fall of 1971, anticipated an 11 percent increase in the employment of men by business and industry and a 15 percent increase in the employment of women. Michigan State University also sees slightly better prospects for women, particularly in accounting, engineering, and health services.

Salaries offered to women graduates lagged behind those offered to men in some jobs and were on a par with those offered to men in others. The accompanying table shows the results of a Northwestern University survey, taken in 1972, of beginning monthly salaries companies expected to offer to women.

Marketing, retailing	$672
Liberal arts	676
General business	690
Data processing	765
Science	818
Accounting	852
Engineering	880
Other fields	725

More schooling means higher income

Staying in school longer generally assures a young person a higher potential in career development as well as greater lifetime earnings. And for the economy, a better-educated labor force should generate higher levels of gross national product—in other words, it should be more productive.

The Census Bureau estimates indicate that completion of eight years of elementary school would point to a lifetime income of $277,000. Four years of high school should add about $94,000, making a total of $371,000. Four years of college should add another $213,000, bringing the lifetime income to about $584,000. One or more years of graduate study should add another $52,000, for a lifetime income of $636,000. These figures are only estimates and vary because education is only one of several factors that determine future earn-

FIGURE 3-2   Profile of the unemployed, by age and sex, January, 1972, in thousands (percentages shown are unemployment rate)

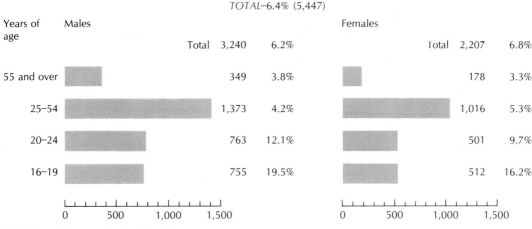

TOTAL—6.4% (5,447)

Years of age	Males		Total	3,240	6.2%	Females		Total	2,207	6.8%
55 and over				349	3.8%				178	3.3%
25–54				1,373	4.2%				1,016	5.3%
20–24				763	12.1%				501	9.7%
16–19				755	19.5%				512	16.2%

SOURCE: Bureau of Labor Statistics.

ings.[17] Future job prospects look promising, according to the Department of Labor, despite temporary setbacks from 1969 to 1972. Long a shortage occupation, teaching is undergoing a sharp change in prospects. Aggregate supply is expected to exceed demand if present patterns continue. Surpluses of elementary and secondary teachers, mathematicians, and life scientists may continue if students go on electing these fields in the same proportion as in the recent past. Areas for which potential shortages are in prospect include counseling, social work, urban planning, and a number of jobs related to the planning and administration of government, especially local government (see Figure 3-3).

Experts on future job prospects generally agree that the new entrant will face stiff competition. Young workers will have to prepare themselves for a rapidly changing and more complex world of work. They will need more and better education and more training with better guidance and counseling as they prepare to face keener competition for better jobs.

Other factors that determine future earnings

Differences in ability, type of training, kind of occupation, and number of years of formal education should be taken into account when deciding whether an individual should invest in additional education. Differences in ability are partly responsible for income differences. The more able are likely to have more education, and also to receive higher incomes, than the less able at the same level of education, according to several studies.[18] These studies also show that in the case of low achievers, investment in additional years of school does not yield a high rate of financial return.

The type of training an individual receives appears to make a difference in income, especially in the early earning years.[19]

[17] Frances M. Magrabi, "Education as an Investment," *Family Economics Review,* December 1971, pp. 3–6.

[18] Ibid., pp. 4–5.

[19] Ibid., p. 5.

FIGURE 3-3 Job outlook for future grads

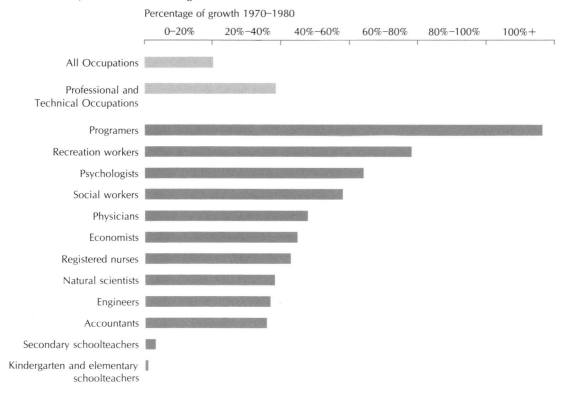

Percentage of growth 1970–1980

SOURCE: U.S. Department of Labor.

Studies also show that at least half of the income differential between persons at different levels of education is the result of employment in higher-paid occupations.[20]

In the next decade, with the supply of professional workers equal to or exceeding the demand, quality of preparation may have an even greater effect on income. For the person whose ability is limited, additional years of education may not result in higher income. Rather, his return on investment in education may depend on the amount and quality of vocational training he receives and on the occupational field he prepares to enter.

The decision, then, as to whether to invest in additional years of education should take into account:

1. *Ability.* If the individual's ability is below the average of those at the educational level he is considering, his income is likely to be lower.

2. *Expected demand.* If demand is low in the occupation he intends to enter he may be forced to accept a job in a lower-paying or less desirable field, even after completing additional education.

3. *Quality of training.* The earnings of those with vocational training are likely to be higher than the earnings of those with a more general education.

[20] Ibid., pp. 5–6.

**Why married women
work**

As mentioned earlier, wives work mainly for economic reasons, or so they say. A recent study of about 600 randomly chosen working wives in thirty-five states were given a list of nine reasons for working and asked to number them in order of importance.[21] Eighty-eight percent of the women listed a financial consideration first. The three reasons most frequently mentioned were: to provide better living for the family; to provide for the children's education; and to get out of debt. Table 3-3 is an interesting breakdown of this survey.

It is interesting to note that the nonfinancial reason for working—getting away from the boredom of housekeeping—was ranked first by only 8 percent of the wives. This is in contrast to a University of Michigan Survey Research Center study during which 1,925 girls (ages 11 to 19) were asked about their future plans. Although 94 percent said they hoped to marry, only 3 percent wanted to be housewives.

Although 88 percent listed a financial reason first, a Bureau of Labor study in 1964 reported only 49 percent of the wives in 1963 worked mainly for economic reasons.[22]

*Married women work
for different reasons*

A careful study of the *Changing Times* table will be rewarding in many ways. For example, the reasons for going to work varied by age, income group, and family situation; of the wives working between the ages of 18 and 24, 16 percent were working to help their husbands finish their education; working wives with preschool children or with no children are more likely to be saving for a home; and, as children get older, the emphasis shifts to education funds.

Like her pioneer forebears, today's housewife and mother is seeking the best the world has to offer for her family and herself. But there is still the question of how much net income a working wife can earn.

What is a wife worth?

How much income does it take for a family to maintain an adequate but modest standard of living? There are many answers to this question, so each family will need to come up with its own figure. The Bureau of Labor Statistics of the U.S. Department of Labor reported in a study completed in April, 1972, that the annual cost of a "moderate comfort" living standard for a family of four, son age 13 and daughter age 8, in an urban community ranged from $9,408 in Austin, Texas, to $14,867 in Anchorage, Alaska, in the autumn of 1971. The point of the above statistics is that it would be well for the family to study its own financial situation carefully before making a decision about a wife going to work. There are no simple answers to the question of a wife working. The answer that is right should be arrived at after the husband and wife have thought about it and discussed questions such as these:

What is the net income of the wife after deducting job-related and extra expenses and taxes?

Are the emotional as well as the material needs of the children being met?

Is there a woman in the household—a grandmother, an aunt, or an older sister—who can provide the children with the type of guidance which few servants can give?

Does the husband feel that the wife is competing with him?

[21] Conducted by *Changing Times* magazine and the Bureau of Laundry and Dry Cleaning Standards and reported in *Changing Times*, July 1965, pp. 7–10.

[22] *Monthly Labor Review*, September 1965, pp. 1077–1082.

TABLE 3-3 Some Things the Ladies Told Us

AMONG WORKING WIVES GROUPED BY...	Percent of Total	THIS MANY ARE WORKING FULL TIME	THIS MANY HIRE DOMESTIC HELP	AND THIS MANY GIVE AS THEIR REASON FOR WORKING....				
				Pay off Debt	Better Living	Saving for Home	Children's Education	Escape Boredom
Age								
18 to 24	9%	80%	2%	24%	34%	28%	6%	8%
25 to 34	20	66	11	35	30	15	10	8
35 to 44	29	69	26	18	28	11	26	18
45 to 54	25	73	18	17	40	7	31	10
55 to 64	12	76	30	7	35	11	20	14
Over 65	2	62	35	14	32	5	19	11
Children								
None	20%	83%	14%	14%	40%	20%	9%	14%
Preschool	16	56	12	40	30	17	15	12
Elementary	29	63	23	33	33	10	25	12
Junior High	19	63	26	23	29	8	37	12
Senior High	23	72	21	18	36	7	38	12
College	20	77	22	15	29	6	47	13
Family Income								
Under $5,000	9%	69%	13%	24%	42%	13%	13%	4%
$5,000 to $8,000	27	68	8	35	31	14	21	6
$8,000 to $10,000	23	69	15	14	38	11	20	13
$10,000 to $15,000	22	78	33	15	29	9	30	18
Over $15,000	10	78	43	7	21	9	17	28

Does the husband feel he is being deprived of his role as provider for the family?

The husband needs a wife, a companion in fun, and a social hostess. Can the working woman handle these responsibilities in addition to her job? If not, the marriage is in for trouble.

Is the husband willing and able to help the wife with household chores when they both come home from work?

Does the fact that both husband and wife work give them more in common?

Can the husband and wife arrange to take their vacations together?

Does the wife's employer know of her home responsibilities, and is he willing to make allowances for them?

Is there agreement between husband and wife about what is done with the money the wife earns?

Let's go back to the economic question: Can a wife afford to work? Expenses directly related to the working wife's job—taxes, getting to and from work, and extra clothing—were estimated at between $900 and $1,000 a year, according to a recent study in Ohio by the U.S. Department of Agriculture.[23] Gross earnings of 744 working wives averaged $2,900. The wife's net income, after taking out her job-related and extra expenses, amounted to about three-fifths of her gross earnings. This was so when the household consisted of adults and older children. In a household with preschool children, net income was about half of gross earnings. This was for 1964. Cost of living and taxes seem to go up every year, although wages go up, too. The big irritation is that every dollar she earns goes on top of her husband's pay for tax purposes. This means that it will probably be taxed in a higher bracket than his. The more the husband earns, the stiffer the tax bite on her income.

She will encounter other charges—transportation, lunches away from home, more and dressier clothes, laundry and more drycleaning, beauty treatments, and so on. These may come to $18 to $25 a week, or about $900 to $1,000 a year. Overall, the net increase in the family income is around $2,000. If her husband earns $15,000, taxes will take about one-third of her $3,900. The net increase for the family will be about $1,800. That's less than half her earnings, and it increases the family net by about 14 percent. If this information is discouraging, you might look at the hidden benefits.

Some hidden benefits of a working wife

There are some hidden benefits for the working wife that do not show up in the pay check. The Social Security benefits, after working a year and a half, have very substantial money value. And most workers get substantial fringe benefits in the form of insurance—medical and hospitalization—and pension funds. Women employed in stores usually get discount privileges and perhaps bargain-sale opportunities. Finally, by knowing how to handle a job, a wife is acquiring economic security that would be valuable in the event of premature death of her husband.

[23] "Job Related Expenditures of Gainfully Employed Wives in Ohio," *Home Economics Research Report*, no. 27.

But when all the dollars-and-cents benefits are taken into account, the fact remains that the vast majority of some 18.4 million working wives get anything but a glamorous financial deal. Even where the net addition to the family income made by wives is modest, many of them report that it makes the difference between "getting by" comfortably and having a nerve-jangling shortage of family income.

Two can live as cheaply as two

The persistent question that this chapter raises and attempts to settle is: "Will our pocketbook be ready when our hearts are ready for marriage?" The answer must depend largely on the young couple who are thinking of marriage. Some couples achieve a successful and happy marriage on a surprisingly low income during the first years. Such couples have an abundance of courage and faith and perhaps other sustaining forces.

This is no argument for a premature marriage. A couple very much in love is in the disquieting position of thinking via the heart. It is so easy to conclude that two can live as cheaply as one. It is wiser to figure that two can live as cheaply as *two*. We have pointed out that studies show that financial conflicts are the most-mentioned cause or symptom of marital unhappiness. While money in itself does not bring happiness, the absence of money can bring much unhappiness.

QUESTIONS FOR DISCUSSION

1. Why is the first year of marriage a crucial or critical period for many couples?

2. Is it possible to be successful in making money but a dismal failure in spending it? Explain.

3. It is said that American women shun success. They fear it will lead to loss of femininity and may be a threat to their husbands. Investigate this assumption.

4. Attitudes toward spending family money are more complicated than most people think. They take on emotional tones, social tones, economic tones, and psychological tones. Is it possible, for example, that some people's attitudes toward using family income are based on an attempt to answer some other need apparently quite unrelated to the immediate purpose of the expenditure? Try to pinpoint your real reasons for spending money for a particular dress, suit, pair of shoes, coat, car, etc.

5. "The more successful a man is in his work, the more attractive he becomes as a spouse and father. The more successful a wife becomes in a job outside the home, the more society believes that she has lost her femininity and therefore must be a failure as a wife and mother." What is your reaction to this observation?

6. The average share of income contributed by American husbands to

urban families was almost a constant 80 percent from 1900 to 1965. This statement is misleading even though accurate. Investigate.

7. Psychologists tell us that the relationship between husband and wife is loaded with "disguised impulses." Just what do they mean by "disguised impulses"?

8. How is our national income distributed among the population? Do the poor remain poor and the rich remain rich (in the last twenty years or so)?

PROJECTS

1. The 1970 Census Bureau report, covering the decade 1960–1970, tells us that big changes are taking place in the age pattern of our population. The report also says that the 1970s will be an "era of the young married" and that we are "heading into a society of an affluent majority." What does this really mean? Are our youth a "cop-out" generation? Are there more young leaders, more working women, rising incomes, etc.?

2. Every now and then we read or hear statements that a rise in the number of working wives results in a loss of jobs by husbands. Is this true? Go after the facts. A good source would be the 1970 census reports.

3. What are the characteristics of the income groups? In other words, who are the poor? Who are the rich? Able students who have the ability for graphic expression could devise a series of Lorenz curves and linear and bar graphs for families and unrelated individuals based on color, family type and size, occupation, region, etc. This should provide some understanding of the conditions of the human beings behind the statistics.

4. Many studies show that mismanagement of family income is often a major reason for disagreement and marital discord. Perhaps you know two or three families who feel that disagreements over family financing are largely responsible for some unpleasant family relations. Further investigations may reveal discrepancies and inconsistencies between attitudes and practices. For example, you might check on uneconomical practices such as (a) using credit cards, (b) eating meals at restaurants, (c) indulging in poor buying habits, (d) expensive recreation, and so on. If serious uneconomical practices seem to prevail among these families, what could be done to lessen such tensions?

5. Using the ideas in this chapter with regard to marital problems when both husband and wife work outside the home, prepare appropriate questions for interviewing married couples who have had or are now having this experience. A summary of these experiences could be the basis for a lively class discussion.

6. Should marriage be subsidized by parents? Invite married couples who have had such help to discuss this issue with the class.

7. What are lifetime income prospects for a boy or girl who does not finish high school? How many high school graduates go to college? How many complete college? What do current trends in employment and technology tell

us about employment opportunities in the future? What kinds of education and training will be needed in the future? Is a person's education ever finished?

SUGGESTED READINGS

College Educated Workers, 1968–80: A Study of Supply and Demand, Bureau of Labor Statistics Bulletin 1676, 1970.

Cotton, Dorothy W.: *The Case for the Working Mother,* Stein and Day Incorporated, New York, 1965.

Friedman, Betty: "Women: The Fourth Dimension," *Ladies' Home Journal,* June 1964, p. 48.

Horner, Matina: *Femininity and Successful Achievement: A Basic Inconsistency,* University of Michigan Research Study, Lansing, 1972.

Lobsenz, Norman N., and Clark W. Blackburn: "Hidden Meanings of Money," *Ladies' Home Journal,* July 1968.

Mayhew, H.: "Education, Occupation, and Earnings," *Industrial and Labor Relations Review,* January 1971, pp. 216–225.

Ross, Myron: *Income: Analysis and Policy,* 2d ed., McGraw-Hill Book Company, New York, 1968.

Sheldon, Eleanor B., and Wilbert E. Moore (eds.): *Indicators of Social Change: Concepts and Measurement,* Russell Sage Foundation, New York, 1968.

"So Mom Wants to Get a Paying Job," *Changing Times,* January 1969.

"The Working Wife and Mother," *Changing Times,* July 1965.

Waldman, Elizabeth, and Kathryn R. Gouer: "Children of Women in the Labor Force," *Monthly Labor Review,* July 1971.

CHAPTER 4

CHAPTER 4

MONEY AND DEMOCRACY IN HOME MANAGEMENT

All happy families are alike. All unhappy families are different, each in its own way.
Tolstoy, Anna Karenina

Money is not only dollars and cents. It is a symbol of personal attitudes toward marriage and life. It is in the early years of family life that the first tests of the quality of the partnership are made. The kind of relationship which the husband and wife establish, the nature of its strengths, and the depths of its weaknesses will largely determine the quality of the family relationships which will follow. Marital harmony has many qualities. Marital discord takes many shapes. If they are not understood and alleviated or resolved in the beginning, before the children arrive and complicate it, the family structure is placed in jeopardy.

THE QUALITY OF FAMILY RELATIONSHIPS

Marriage, parenthood, and all relationships within the family are affected by the inescapable psycho-socioeconomic demands of the money world. Individual attitudes are developed within the framework of each one's own immediate family as he grows from infancy through childhood and adolescence and is graduated into an adult world with adult responsibilities. The child's experiences during his growing-up years, the economic and social position of his family, the neighborhood environment (ghetto, urban, suburban, town, or farm), the attitudes and feelings of the family about money and social position, income and standard of living, and the way money is handled with the child inevitably will color the formulation of his own complex attitudes.

For example, children are particularly sensitive to parental anxieties about money and home surroundings. They sense the tension which is created when the father loses his job or brings home a smaller pay check. They quickly become aware of dissension centered around money matters. Their own feelings are aroused when parents quarrel over the management of money. In fact, an aura of awe and mystery surrounds money; it has importance for the parents and involves the children's own feelings of happiness and unhappiness, security and insecurity.

We are living in a money world today

Because the family is no longer a producing unit, the quality of family relationships in our current society is also related to the standard of living a family is able to secure in the labor market. Today, the family standard of living depends upon earning power and spending skills. Family earning power has been increasing each year, the result, to a considerable extent, of some 19 million wives in the labor force and a steady increase in real wages and salaries. And if there are teen-age children in the family, the son may be holding down a part-time job, and the daughter may be earning money by baby-sitting several nights a week. Thus each family member produces not goods primarily but income—an abstraction, a medium of exchange that must be translated into a standard of living. In short, the family is an *earning* and a *spending* unit. In a real sense, therefore, we are living in a money world today.

Over the years, the quality of our standard of living has changed greatly, just as our earning and spending capacity has changed. The traditional family made up of a wife and a husband, with children in the home until they leave for college or get married, is beginning to disappear. Many children leave home in their midteens; divorce and separation approach the 40 percent rate; and the generation gap grows wider.

**Experiments in marriage
and family living**

The gradual disintegration of the traditional American family has, again, led to experiments in marriage and family living. Experimental families are not new in our country. We hear much about "communes," serial mating, unstructured cohabitation prior to marriage, the single-parent family, and specialists in parenthood "for hire." Actually, experimental families have been with us since the last century and earlier. There existed in America such sects as the Shakers in Kentucky, who did away with marriage, children, and sex. There were also the members of the Oneida Community, who practiced a form of communal living; the men as a group married the women as a group, and every man had sexual access to every woman, and each woman had the same access to each man.

We also had specialists in parenthood who were well-trained people hired by parents to replace them during a certain period in the child's life. Not all parents who can conceive a child are able to bring him up properly.

Today, the long-haired culture is making itself heard, especially in relation to communal living.[1] Recently, even commune houses have been designed with large central meeting rooms leading to dormitory wings. Since the rearing of children is usually a group effort, "commune nurseries" will be built where each of the adults, male and female, will work with all the commune children one day a week.

Communal living

The kitchens will be large since many people will have to be fed. Bedrooms will be for individual couples because group sex is rare. Preferences will be for group showers and lavatories. These communal groups will practice ecological responsibility. Current youth values deemphasize material goods, and their homes will therefore be sparsely furnished or will have nonfurniture—multipurpose modular units. No draperies, no separate dining room, decreased dependence on the family car, and a more self-sufficient home should decrease the cost of living considerably.

Further changes in our traditional marriage and family living can be expected. There have been many family changes over the centuries, and there will be more experiments in family living in the hope of achieving the goals sought and a value system that makes more sense to the participants.

Regardless of the various experiments in living arrangements going on in our culture at the present time, most people seem to prefer monogamy, marrying one person in a lifetime or, at least, one person at a time.

MONEY

Money does more than buy the goods and services that we use every day. We live in a money world. Money influences us in our relationships with members of our family as well as with others around us. It affects our standard of living, our goals, and our emotions. It takes considerable experience to establish sound money values and to develop desirable relationships with all members of the family. In fact, close students of family relationships are beginning to see a correlation between distorted parental attitudes toward money and family

---

[1] James Croake, Mary Jo Weale, and W. Bruce Weale, "What Happened to the Parlor?" *The Journal of Home Economics,* April 1972, pp. 26–27.

unhappiness. Indulgent parents often deprive their children of the knowledge and experience that will help them to have the proper attitude toward money throughout their lives.

No one is born with ability to handle money intelligently. If children are to grow up as happy, independent, economically competent adults, they must learn to use money wisely, just as they learn to read, write, spell, and figure.

Normal and neurotic attitudes toward money

Psychologists and psychiatrists say that almost everyone has some form of money neurosis. A surprisingly large number of people act peculiarly in matters concerning money. Dr. Edmund Bergler, a psychiatrist, in his book *Money and Emotional Conflicts* identifies a few normal and abnormal attitudes toward money.

A case in point is that of a young husband with a wife and three small children who patronized the merchandisers of debt until he found himself in a psychologist's office. After considerable discussion of his attitudes toward money, he snorted: "Nonsense! There's nothing emotional about my money worries. I'm trying to pay off a mortgage, a washing machine, an automobile, and a fur coat. I'm not neurotic—I'm just broke!"

Attitudes toward money can be normal or neurotic

Under questioning, however, he revealed that he bought the expensive house to "knock the eyes out" of his patronizing in-laws, the mink coat so his wife could go to parties with his boss's wife, and the car, a European sports model, "just for fun." Clearly this highly emotional mixture of childish self-indulgence, antagonism, and snobbery (all common symptoms of a neurotic) was responsible for his agonizing money problems.

It is human to want to live a cut or two above one's means. It is probably all right to attempt it, especially during those years when family needs seem

Attitudes toward Money

Normally, money is a means to an end, that end the acquiring of things one desires.

Neurotically, money is an end per se.

Normally, one does not allow himself to be taken advantage of in money matters and will do his best to avoid it.

Neurotically, the fear of being taken advantage of in money matters is greatly out of proportion to the threat itself.

Normally, one tries to make money as best he can and as much as he can, but in the process will not sacrifice either health, love, hobbies, recreation, or contentment to this end.

Neurotically, money becomes the center of life; everything else—love, health, hobbies, recreation, and contentment—is subordinated to the urge to possess it.

Normally, money has no infantile strings attached to it.

Neurotically, money is a blind for existing and repressed infantile conflicts.

Normally, the spending of money is taken for granted; it needs no surgical operation to put a dollar into circulation.

Neurotically, the possession and hoarding of money becomes the predominant motif.

Normally, unjustified demands for money are warded off (out of necessity) in a matter-of-fact way.

Neurotically, demands or requests for money generate fury, excitement, and indignation.

Normally, the phrase "I cannot afford it" is a simple statement of an objective fact.

Neurotically, the phrase "I cannot afford it" represents a defensive triumph.

to grow faster than pay checks. We know the future can stand some mortgaging, but we may certainly question the emotional stability of the many thousands of irresponsible borrowers and spenders who have an adequate income but are outraged at the idea of being forced to live within it. Their homes are crammed with new furnishings and gadgets, yet they are not satisfied. Once the new acquisitions have been exhibited to admiring or envious neighbors, the proud owners lose much of their interest. It is the spending itself that gives these people a thrill.

At the other end of the scale are the people who find a miserable kind of happiness by living—and usually insisting that their families live—far below their real means. These people go in for endless shopping for bargains. They haggle over prices. They boast that they never buy anything on time. Every penny is accounted for. In such a family, the child who mislays a quarter is in for real trouble. In such a family, the money neurotic usually wears the pants.

It is obvious that both types, the penny pincher and his more wildly spending counterpart who cannot meet his bills, are tortured by inner anxiety. Both unfairly blight the lives of their mates and children.

The emotional power of money

Marriage counselors have taken a new look at money problems in marriage. They have found that it is no more possible to be objective about money than about love. If a husband and wife are constantly arguing about their spending, the source of the problem lies in their attitudes, not in their arithmetic. Dollars are important, but studies tend to show that marital happiness is less likely to be affected by the size of the weekly check than by the difference in opinions on how to spend it. Strangely enough, many married couples know little about each other's point of view when it comes to money and are often confused about their own attitudes. If you doubt this, ask a wife or a husband to guess how much the family spent on clothing in the last six months! Ask what each of them would do with a $500 legacy.

Almost invariably there is a breakdown in communications in a family because of the tremendous emotional power that money exercises over people's lives. To one person, money means love; to another, power; to another, a weapon to fight with; to yet another, protection from life's cruelties; and to others, comforts.

To a child, things = love

Emotional money disorders, like so many other disorders, grow out of the experiences of early childhood. When a little child is given a toy, which has cost money, he recognizes this as a gesture of love. Is it any wonder, then, that after several such experiences a child reasons that money (the receiving of things that cost money) means love? The child very early translates money and material things into symbols of love. Some parents try to get rid of their guilt feelings toward a child by material overindulgence. This is especially true in many white-collar and middle-income families where both parents work, particularly where the mother is working to buy nice things for the home. Feelings that the child is somehow being deprived often cause overgiving, even to a very young child.

Because of their personality structures, parents sometimes are unable to meet a child's emotional needs or to handle child-training problems constructively. Money then may become a substitute for love or an instrument for manipulation and control or a weapon for punishment. The use of money as a bargaining agent to secure a child's cooperation in doing his fair share of the family tasks is a poor substitute for helping him to achieve a sense of his importance, both as a contributing and as a receiving member of the family.

Bribing a child with money to put forth more effort in his schoolwork or to practice his music lesson sets up a false stimulus for achievement. It emphasizes the reward rather than the personal development and the increased satisfaction that come from accomplishment. Likewise, depriving a child of money to force him to atone for a misdeed or for an injury to another is also unwise, since the payment of money cannot in fact compensate for such actions and may actually lead him to believe that any kind of conduct is acceptable as long as he can pay his way out of consequences.

The real relation of money to life

The inappropriate use of money or its substitution for the basic elements in the parent-child relationship obscures the child's view of the value of money. The real relationship of money to life becomes clouded, and this creates a handicap for him when he grows up. And all of us know grownups whose money attitudes are still those of a child of 5. A woman who clings to the notion of equating love and money cannot tolerate a budget that threatens to deprive her of things—clothes and accessories—that to her mean love. Unfortunately, such a person has no idea that this belief—money or things equals love—and not her limited income may be the real cause of her budget trouble. If necessary, she will manufacture a dozen other reasons for her money difficulty.

Equating love with money causes problems

Dr. William Kaufman, a Boston psychiatrist, told the American Association for the Advancement of Science that "money sickness is the most common psychosomatic illness of our times." He said that the trouble does not necessarily come from how much money you have or don't have. It comes from the particular "meaning" you have come to place on money, and how you spend it. And he said it could come from the feeling that you need more money when actually you do not need it. He, too, believes that the attitude toward money you have as an adult begins in childhood. Most of us have experienced childhood disappointments when our parents were unable to provide all the things we desired. Dr. Kaufman said the manner in which a child resolves his early conflicts about money will determine some of his basic personality and behavior patterns. He goes on to say parental bribing, substitution of handouts for real love, or overcriticism of a child's use of money may establish habits that, if uncorrected, may set the stage for a money-sickness candidate in later life.

Analyzing attitudes toward money

Actually, how many ordinary people do you know who are well balanced in their attitude toward money? Do you know an embarrassingly stingy tipper? A couple always in debt? People who insist on telling how much they paid for everything? A family trying to keep up with other families in the neighborhood? Persons who find peace of mind through entrapment? People who are using installment credit without figuring total costs? You will probably discover that the percentage of level heads and the amount of good judgment based on known family goal values is frighteningly low!

Reports of many psychiatrists show that about 75 percent of their patients are suffering from some degree of abnormality in their attitudes toward money. This does not mean that you need to consult a psychiatrist about your attitude. Why not determine for yourself whether your attitude toward money is healthy and useful or damaging and potentially dangerous to a happy family life?

DEMOCRACY IN HOME MANAGEMENT

Fiction writers, sociologists, anthropologists, educational philosophers, psychologists, and others have recognized the importance of the home in promoting the democratic way of life. Jan Struther, for example, has written:

Home is the place to learn democracy

Democracy begins at home, and it begins very early in the morning—not at breakfast, but when the first reluctant eye is opened by the first devilish trill of the alarm clock and when everybody thinks that everybody else takes much too long in the bath. The home, and not a college of political science, is the place to learn democracy—but it's no good for us grownups to try to teach it to our children unless we teach it to ourselves as well—and oh my! we've certainly got a lot to learn. . . .[2]

Sait and Nimkoff, sociologists, expressed themselves as follows:

Consideration for others and willingness to cooperate are fundamental social attitudes. They are best secured through an orderly home routine, designed in such a way that, as early as possible, the child begins to help himself and to engage in communal tasks. . . .[3]

Science has established two facts meaningful for human welfare; first, the foundation of the structure of human personality is laid down in early childhood; and second, the chief engineer in charge of this construction is The Family.[4]

Margaret Mead, the well-known anthropologist, recognized the importance of the democratic family when she wrote: "Unless we democratize family life it is idle to talk of democracy."[5]

Democracy begins at home

What is democratic living? To answer this question is not easy. Definitions are tricky and inadequate, especially when they deal with an idea or a way of life. Fundamentally, democratic living means sharing—sharing of rights and responsibilities, duties and decisions based on beliefs. This definition is almost meaningless unless considered in relation to ordinary daily family experiences.

When turning the spotlight on daily family experiences, keep in mind that there is no one "right" way, no simple pattern. Democracy as a way of life may be expressed quite differently in different families. What is important is that the spirit of democracy—of cooperative sharing, of consideration for the rights of each in the family—is expressed through whatever is done. The following family rules, although incomplete and no doubt debatable, will help your family to lead a democratic life.

1. Assign well-defined chores to each person.
2. Talk over with the children decisions that affect the entire family.
3. Give the children a reasonable amount of privacy.

[2] "Democracy Begins at Home," *Adult Education Journal,* vol. 1, no. 3, July 1942, p. 118.

[3] Una B. Sait, *New Horizons for the Family,* The Macmillan Company, New York, 1938, p. 687.

[4] M. F. Nimkoff, *The Family,* Houghton Mifflin Company, Boston, 1934, p. ix.

[5] "The Comparative Study of Culture and the Purposive Cultivation of Democratic Values," *Science, Philosophy and Religion,* Conference on Science, Philosophy and Religion and Their Relation to the Democratic Way of Life, New York, 1942, p. 63.

4. Avoid favoritism.
5. Encourage the children to invite their friends into the home.
6. Encourage the children to help select their own clothing.
7. Have fun with your children.
8. Consider the family tastes when planning meals.
9. Allow the children freedom to be themselves.
10. Give fixed allowances to the children to cover ordinary expenses.

The child who learns democracy in his family circle will be better able to practice it as a member of his gang, as a student, and as a citizen. University of Chicago social scientists found that children from democratic homes were better equipped for the give-and-take of daily life. They seemed to get along better with their playmates and with teachers, church workers, and Scout leaders. They also rated higher in such traits as loyalty, honesty, moral courage, friendliness, and responsibility.

They were preferred by adults as after-school employees. They even tended to earn higher grades in school—perhaps because they were able to work to the full extent of their abilities.

There seems to be little doubt that the foundations of democracy are laid in the home. There, better than anywhere else, children can learn to do their share of the work and to make their share of the decisions, to respect each other's differences, to sacrifice together, and to have fun together. There they can learn to recognize the rights of others and to reject the idea of special privilege—even for themselves.

Evidence of sharing in homes

There are insufficient data on the evidence of the democratic way of life in the homes of this country. It seems probable, by the definitions given above, that only a modest percentage of American homes practice democracy as a way of life. Mary S. Lyle, in her study of 120 homes in a small town and surrounding area in Iowa, came to the following conclusions:

1. In 75 per cent of the homes the husband shared the financial management with his wife, but children had a voice in management in only about 17 per cent of the families.
2. Planning for the use of the total family income by all the family members mature enough to understand the situation was rather rare.
3. Slightly over 40 per cent of the 147 high school students reported that they "had no choice in the duties they did or how they were to be done." Only slightly over 18 per cent of the students "exercised some volition in what they did."
4. Over 53 per cent of the students claimed "home duties as a subject of some disagreement."
5. Recreational activities were shared by several family members in the majority of these homes but 30 per cent of these families did not share recreation.
6. Some families seemed to plan together for family projects and seemed to have a common understanding of the family goals, but the evidence was too meager to proclaim this as characteristic of the group.

7. The pattern of these families tended toward autocracy rather than democracy.[6]

This picture, if general among American families, is serious in terms of maximum development of all the members of the family. This is especially true if we agree that first among the values looked for in home life is the quality of family relationships that permits full development of the personalities that make up the family.

Achieving personality fulfillment

Studies show that families in which psychological relationships are sound can absorb severe strains in crises. These same studies reveal that the kind of personality each individual has is chiefly determined by the kind of family in which he grew up. When children are young, they need secure environment. They need to be loved generously and spontaneously. Children who experience rigid controls usually build up resentments that often are carried into adult life. Children need parents who can help them to build confidence in themselves and to feel that they have an important role to play in the family.

Children learn to be considerate of others and willing to cooperate for the family good when they are given increasing responsibility in family affairs. Even young children can help plan (1) how some of the family income is to be spent, (2) how leisure time is to be used, and (3) how, when, and by whom family chores are to be done. They, too, can contribute to discussions on how grievances and difficulties can best be handled.

This does not mean that parents should abdicate. Children cannot always have their way. But the chance to express themselves fully, to weigh ideas of others in the family, is important in development of personality. Procedures need to be planned for giving children more and more responsible independence, because eventually they must assume complete responsibility for their own actions. Many children have never had to think about the problems a family has to face. Someone else did all their thinking.

If family problems are shared according to age and ability, all members become aware of the realities of living. Thus they discover that family life consists of more than sweetness and love.

Division of work in the family

No one can prescribe exactly how work should be divided for every family. The family chores differ according to the financial status of the family and according to whether they live in the city or in the country, in a house or in an apartment. These differences must be recognized in family conferences about sharing activities and work.

Children's contributions to household tasks can be of considerable importance. In the pioneer family, the children were expected to assist with the

---

[6] Mary S. Lyle, *Adult Education for Democracy in Family Life,* The Iowa State University Press, Ames, 1944, pp. 65–69. Reprinted with permission.

homework as early as age and ability permitted. There never was a question about this matter in those days. Today there is much the same situation on the farms, according to Mary Lyle's study of democracy in family life. Her study of rural and small-town families in Iowa revealed that "in the majority of the farm families who had children, the children were cooperating in the daily tasks."[7]

The situation was different in the town families, for in "only 38.6 per cent of the homes with children were these children participating in the common tasks." This was not because the children of town families were too young to participate, for there were only three town families whose children were under the age of 6, as compared to 17 farm families with children younger than 6. On the farms, nearly "100 per cent of the children over six years of age shared the everyday tasks while in the town less than 50 per cent of the children over six years had this privilege."

Furthermore, many of them participated unwillingly in home tasks. Home duties expected of the children ranked fourth among sixteen subjects of possible disagreement with their parents. Mary Lyle concluded that "it may well be that the autocratic procedure followed by the parents was in a measure responsible for some of the conflict."[8]

Life in city apartments presents some problems when it comes to work in and around the home. There, almost all activities must relate of necessity to the household. Outside jobs are not available as a rule. The distinctions between the sexes in regard to household work become less marked than on farms or in small towns. Still, here as in rural homes, there are floors to be waxed, windows to be cleaned, some painting that can be done, and perhaps furniture to be repaired. These tasks are in addition to cleaning, preparing meals, bedmaking, dishwashing, and caring for babies and pets.

It is easier today, in contrast to pioneer days, for the family to neglect to plan work experience for their children. With fewer children per family, parents become more child-conscious and perhaps overprotective. It is so easy to decide: "I had to work too hard in my home when I was a child. I'm going to see that my child does not have to work so hard." While some parents, no doubt, had to work too hard at home, that fact does not justify taking the extreme opposite point of view. In a home dominated by that kind of philosophy, how are the children going to become mature and responsible persons? One cannot suddenly become mature through intellectualizing about the problem. Work experience is needed in the home, in an atmosphere where parents and children live, plan, and work cooperatively.

The chief reasons for having children work in and around the home are to give them a feeling of usefulness and importance in relation to their family and to society and to develop worthy attitudes and skills that will build family solidarity and happiness. Their help also reduces the time and energy spent by father and mother in home tasks.

However, there comes a time in many homes when the division-of-work concept breaks down because the kids "cop out" for any number of reasons.

---

[7] Ibid., p. 63.
[8] Ibid., p. 68.

Mom does most of the home chores, with Dad pitching in when convenient. A showdown comes sooner or later. And nothing compares with the strength of a mother who's decided she's had it. Perhaps she should post a bill for "Mom services!"

Posting a bill for Mom services

A bill for Mom services isn't something that mothers would expect to collect, but the accounting might have a calming effect on their offspring.

The accompanying table shows typical bills suggested by a couple of mothers based on standard charges in their communities.

Typical son's bill

Ironing shorts	
(5-day supply)	$ 1.75
Sewing new zipper on pants	3.00
Laundry	3.00
Cleaning his room	
(2 hours a week)	4.00
Chauffeuring (taxi rates)	8.00
Tutoring math and French	6.00
Cooking and serving	10.00
	$37.75

Typical daughter's bill

Setting hair	$ 2.00
Dressmaking, altering	10.00
Chauffeuring	5.00
Laundry	3.00
Slipcovering chair	15.00
Cooking, serving	10.00
	$45.00

Totaling these bills made one mother realize her versatility. Besides solving her family problem when the kids cop out, she thinks she may get a job working outside the home!

When the kids "cop out"

Maybe there are other ways to develop division-of-work responsibilities in the home when the kids cop out. The democratic concept of sharing may do the trick for some families.

DEMOCRATIC CONCEPTION OF THE FAMILY

There was a time when many families lived under the rule of a parent dictator or tyrant. In such homes, the parents were the source of all wisdom and control. In some of these homes, this control was stern and serious; in others, it took the form of benevolent despotism. In the latter type of family life, the parent may be a kindly person who believes that he is doing everything possible for the welfare of his family. He may, in fact, be completely self-sacrificing.

This kind of patriarchal or matriarchal family is gradually being replaced by the democratic family, which emphasizes the importance of the dignity and responsibility of the individual.

The democratic family (1) recognizes that human relations should be characterized by respect for each person in the family, (2) recognizes sharing according to age and ability in policy making as well as in the effort to achieve jointly determined goals, and (3) believes in intelligent discussion as to the means of successfully solving conflicts and settling family problems.

Both children and adults can assist in deciding (1) how to divide work, (2) who is to do it, (3) how to use family income for the maximum happiness of all, (4) how to participate in community activities; (5) how to use the vacation period, and (6) how to solve many problems of family life. Through sharing in the planning, all can feel the responsibility for carrying the plans through successfully.

The democratic process of sharing does not mean that there is no control and no direction. On the contrary, there are regulations; there is direction. The basic change is in the means to the end—the process. The rules and regulations are developed by those whom they directly affect.

Children, and everyone else, resent controls if they cannot see sense and purpose in them. Rules discussed and made by the group are more easily adhered to by the individuals who discussed and made them. If the regulations do not work out as planned or wished, each member of the group knows that they can be restudied and changed. Uncooperative action becomes the concern of all the members. As a result, disapproval by the group is often more effective than discipline by one member of the family.

There are always times in a family when adult control must swing into action. Safety of a child, for example, demands mature control when the child is too young to understand the consequences of dangerous actions. Gradually, as the child matures, he can take on more and more personal responsibility for his own and the family's safety.

The family as a problem-solving group

Using the family as a problem-solving group is one effective way in which to carry out the democratic idea in family life. Each family will have to decide on the kind of group best suited to its members.

Whether a family group session is formal or informal is of no great importance. There are times when informal sessions may be more appropriate—for such decisions as concerning holiday outings, preferred foods, clothes, play equipment, hours, and so on.

With added experience, an older child can have a part in the more difficult decisions. In time, the area of choice may be expanded until each child is able to make or help make major decisions.

When there is joint planning, suggestions made by the children should be accepted with an open mind. Even an impossible idea needs to be handled so that the child will continue to feel free to say what he thinks and know that his idea will be heard and treated fairly. He must be taught, however, to accept other points of view and in the end, possibly, negative group voting.

Discipline should not be handled in a family meeting. Cross-examinations of such matters as who daubed paint on the neighbor's garage or why the lawn wasn't mowed are best handled outside the group meeting. In fact, group meetings often help to prevent such problems.

What are some ways of making a family group session work successfully? Some family group experts are of the opinion that effective family problem solving requires:

How to make a family group session work

1. Open channels of communication for all family members competent to contribute to a problem solution
2. Sufficient flexibility in the group so that additional members can be admitted into critical communication networks at the stages in the family life cycle when they are able to make appropriate contributions

3. Some centralization of authority which serves to coordinate the problem-solving efforts of the family members

4. The ability of the family members to communicate and evaluate conflicting ideas

5. Consensus among family members as to family goals and the specific roles played by the various family members

When traditional homes collapse

Effective problem solving by the family group is not always possible for many modern families in our country. Many jobs keep the father or mother regularly away from home for a week or more at a time. A small family business, for example, may keep both parents away from the family for much of the daytime and evening. Then, too, we are experiencing a collapse of the household, as we have known it, all over this country as well as in many other countries. There is no opportunity or desire for the group process to function in many families. Not only does the generation gap seem to be wider than ever, but it also appears earlier in the family cycle. More children leave the family home before they complete high school. As pointed out earlier in this chapter, increasingly teen-agers join communes even before attending college, during college years, and frequently as young marrieds. For these youngsters, the traditional home collapsed. Think, also, of the thousands and thousands of families that left Appalachia for Detroit and other Northern urban centers seeking better jobs—and, they hoped, more civil rights—but left Grandma and Grandpa back home. This was tragic for the children because the grandparents traditionally took care of them when both parents worked. Now who cares for them? We are told that some of the preschool children are unable to talk when they first enter the public schools in their new Northern environment. Why? Both parents work, sometimes different shifts, and the grandparents were left in Appalachia! So, too often, the children are left unsupervised, and there is little opportunity to communicate with others in their new urban surroundings. In describing their situation, Dr. Kenneth Boulding referred to such a household as "Archilles' heel."[9] (See Taylor-Troelstrup Reading 22 for the story of a couple who shared a family-owned business, worked out the household chores, arranged a week-off switch from business duties and household duties, and encountered some problems mixed in with success.)

CHILDREN AND MONEY

The younger generation is "going to the dogs." A great philosopher said: "Our youth now love luxury. They have bad manners, contempt for authority. They show disrespect for elders and love chatter in place of exercise. Children are now tyrants, not the servants of their households. They no longer rise when elders enter the room. They contradict their parents, chatter before company, gobble up their food, and tyrannize their teachers."

If Socrates had not written this statement in the fifth century B.C., it would be considered a present-day comment. There are, of course, some differences

[9] Kenneth Boulding, "The Household as Achilles' Heel," Colston E. Warne Lecture at the American Council on Consumer Interests Annual Conference, Dallas, Apr. 12, 1972. From *The Journal of Consumer Affairs*, Winter 1972, pp. 110–119.

in the 1970s. Most children are urbanites. Nearly half of them live in suburbs surrounding a large city. There are fewer opportunities for parents to teach their children certain kinds of responsibilities. Homes are filled with laborsaving devices. As the children grow older, many mothers are reluctant to trouble them with the few chores that remain around the house. Instead, the drive is all for the children being "successful," and it is difficult for some parents to recognize how proficiency in bedmaking will contribute to their children's success in life. Many children won't mow the lawn or wash the car without pay.

The affluent child—and there is many a one—hears a good deal of talk at home about shortages of money, but usually these conversations make little sense to him. If parents are short of money, how come they have a second or third car? How come parents can go to Florida for two weeks to escape winter? Why talk about saving money when there is always more where the last supply came from? Can money really be short when a child can usually squeeze more cash or more presents out of his parents through tricks of the trade?

Teach your child the value of money: what not to do

Some parents seem determined to ruin their children's chances of ever being solvent—let alone financially astute—adults. After years of watching these spoilers at work, I feel I have a lot to offer new parents who would go the same route. Routinely follow three or more of the following practices and I'll practically guarantee you an offspring who doesn't know the value of a dollar or how to manage one.[10]

So wrote Martha Pattan, a family management columnist, for the *Chicago Daily News*. She listed thirty-three practices quite certain to produce a future immature manager of family expenditures. Here is a sample of "poor practices" from her extensive list:

Practices guaranteed to produce future poor managers of family income

1. Be sure your child is supplied with everything before either his age or stage would suggest it—a two-wheeler before he's old enough to ride it.
2. Get your little girl a fur coat.
3. Stand by helplessly while your teenager blows all his earnings and savings on a car. . . . "After all it's his money."
4. Be sure the gifts you give are geared to win your child's affection and approval.
5. Live vicariously—give your child all those things you never had.
6. Encourage your teenager never to work. "You have the rest of your life for that."
7. Pay for good grades. . . .
8. Make no plans with your child for a savings program.
9. Set a lousy example.

Mrs. Pattan mentions twenty-four more questionable practices that are likely to guarantee an offspring who doesn't know the value of money or how to manage it. (See Taylor-Troelstrup Reading 23 for the other twenty-four practices.)

Perhaps many of us will agree with Mrs. Pattan on some or all of the above

[10] *Chicago Daily News*, Sept. 26, 1970.

points. The question, then, is: How do we educate our children to eventually be reasonably good managers of their money?

Money training for children

Money affects everybody. In our homes, money determines our standard of living. More than that, money determines our outlook on life. Money also determines the relations of members of the family and, to a large extent, our relations to the community.

Said a regretful parent: "I wish somebody had given me the chance to have some sound and happy first impressions of money. I must have thought that money grew on trees by all the trouble I've had making it behave in my grownup years." The regret of this parent could have been prevented if his parents had realized that we learn how to handle money just as we master any other skill.

We are not born with "money sense." It takes time and experience on the part of parents to help children learn how to handle money for maximum use and happiness. The attitude of parents toward money, therefore, is of primary importance.

Children generally become conscious of money very early in life. Their attitudes toward money are shaped by much the same forces as their attitudes toward anything else—family, friends, school, hobbies, and many other forces. Advertising on radio and television and in newspapers, magazines, and movies leaves impressions of considerable weight. Then, too, children face some of the same problems that adults must face when managing money. Their wants are greater than their ability to purchase. They are tempted to buy things because friends have done so. Children, too, can become selfish or generous, conservative or impulsive, about spending money. They can easily mistake money as a "goal" in itself rather than as a means to good living.

In a certain sense, money training cannot be set apart from a child's general upbringing. Child-guidance and family-finance experts generally agree that money problems really stem from the more basic emotional and social problems of growing up. The two are easily confused. For example, a child needing social acceptance within his group may place the blame for his frustration on the lack of money. Therefore, parents need to be aware of the needs and drives, the pains and pangs, of their growing children. By identifying the underlying difficulties, they eliminate much needless bickering, and money training can be relatively free of emotional entanglements.

All this is consumer education at its best because consumer education should begin in the home.

Consumer education begins at home

The TV told him so!

Your child will be a consumer long before he reaches adulthood. In fact, a child's consumer consciousness begins to develop at a very young age. A good example is the tiny tot who pesters his mother to buy a box of cold cereal that contains a prize. How does he know about this prize? The TV told him so!

This is just the beginning of your child's involvement in the marketplace. He should learn at an early age some of the fundamentals of making wise purchases. One fundamental to teach your child is that although people have almost unlimited wants and desires, their resources are nearly always limited.

How and when do parents begin to instruct a young child in concepts of consumer efficiency? In the opinion of Doris Stalker, Director of Consumer Education in the U.S. Office of Consumer Affairs, [11] your child is ready for consumer instruction as soon as he begins to understand what he sees on television. Let him examine, for example, a toy he has seen advertised. A 3-year-old will recognize an unsafe toy if you point it out in the store. He knows the meaning of "hurt"—even if he protests your denial of his request.

When he begins to spend his own money, Mrs. Stalker believes that the child should make the final purchasing decision. The principle to learn early is that when the money is gone, it's gone, providing you can resist the temptation to bail him out.

Consumer education begins at home

Mrs. Stalker further suggests that you help your child understand income and outgo by exploring methods whereby he can earn money. Help him understand that parents have jobs that produce income for the family and that they then decide how the money is to be spent and saved.

Once a child can read, new opportunities for consumer education open up. He can read and mark the weekly grocery ads, indicating what looks like a good buy. In time, he can learn the principles of buying in quantity when good sales occur, buying different grades of meat for different dishes, and using substitutes for meat when meat prices are high.

Some food stores are beginning to use unit pricing, open dating, and nutrient and ingredient labeling, and the child can be introduced to these good, informative services. Perhaps he can decide on a best buy on the basis of some of the new labeling information. Older children should be able to learn the advantages of the nutrient and ingredient information that will be appearing on some food labels shortly.

THE TEEN-AGE CONSUMER

Teen-agers in America (26 million) are reputed to spend some $20 billion of their own each year. Additionally, they are said to influence the spending of some $35 billion of their families' money, according to Arthur Gross, Jr., marketing director for the F. W. Woolworth Company. [12] In all, purchases by teen-agers account for nearly 10 percent of the total consumer expenditures in this country annually.

Teen-age buying power

The following statistics, according to Gross, give some indication of teen-age purchasing power:

1.   About 13 million teen-agers play at least one musical instrument, 16 million own at least one camera, and 19 billion read one to five books (not textbooks) a month.

2.   Teen-agers own 1 million TV sets, 10 million record players, 20 million radios, and 1 out of every 10 cars.

3.   Each Christmas they spend some $1 billion on gifts.

[11] See *Everybody's Money,* Summer 1972, p. 26.
[12] *Parade,* July 6, 1969.

4.   Teen-age boys, 12 percent of the male population, buy over 40 percent of all sportswear sold to men and spend $120 million a year on cosmetics.

5.   Teen-age girls, about 11 percent of the female population, buy 20 percent of all women's apparel, 30 percent of all cosmetics, 50 percent of all record albums, and 25 percent of all greeting cards.

6.   One out of every five 17-year-old girls and two out of every five 17-year-old boys have their own charge accounts.

7.   The mythical average teen-ager is spending over $750 a year.

In 1967 the Associated Press ran a survey for a fashion magazine of high school and college girls' clothing expenditures. High school girls spent $1.44 billion on clothes and other needs in one year; college freshmen girls added another $320 million to the bonanza for women's shops. The average high school girl spent $240.32 a year; the average college freshmen spent $516.40.

But it's the roster of specifics that is awesome. In one year, the girls bought 19 million pairs of stockings, 30 million pairs of shoes, 3.5 million suits and pant suits, 13.8 million sweaters, and over 9 million coats.

Against this record, fathers will continue to wonder why the young ladies of the house complain that they don't have a "thing to wear."

With this kind of buying power exercised by some 26 million teen-agers, we can expect merchandisers to spend millions of dollars to exploit the youth market.

Commercial exploitation of teen-age consumers

One of the significant business trends of this midcentury is the effort to woo the teen-age market. A few years ago Charles and Bonnie Remsburg wrote: "Aided by a growing stable of researchers, promotion artists, public relations experts, merchandising consultants, ad agency psychologists and others who specialize in converting quirks of the teen-age psyche into cash receipts, our economy is mounting the biggest youth-kick ever."[13]

Apparently no area of retailing is omitted. Now there is a Teen-agers' Guide to the Stock Market which tells youth that they can now play the stock market and "enjoy a great experience" by learning how to sell short and reminds them that at stockholders' meetings they "frequently serve free luncheons."

Dr. Norma Werner, a psychologist who researched youth for the Leo Burnett advertising agency, points out that the main goal of a girl is marriage, and therefore she is interested in learning how to achieve the "body beautiful." This pressure makes girls "tremendously insecure about glamour." The Montgomery Ward Company, for about $10, offers a teen-age girl a six-week course in which she receives personal "charm counseling" from professional models.

The Ford Motor Company has been sending race drivers, mechanics, and car stylists to teen-age hot-rod and auto-customizing shows, where they offer "inside tips" on souping up cars, motor vehicles being the one item with which teen-age boys are likely to be intensely involved emotionally. When one consultant informed these boys that the family car could be given added power by installing a certain camshaft, Ford parts departments were sold out of the units within three months.

Many other appeals are made that are calculated to overcome teen-age em-

[13] The *New York Times Magazine*, June 5, 1966.

Commercial appeals to teen-agers

barrassment that inhibits 9- and 10-year-olds from spending money for bras; that employ youth panels to invent entirely new items for adolescents; that discover products and services which rebel against adult standards and yet remain within the framework of acceptability. For example, Dr. Irving White, founder of Creative Research Associates in Chicago, discovered most teen-agers would not go for goof-balls until a pill came out that had all the ingredients of milk, flavored like liquor, and called a "goof-ball." "Man, that would fly!"

Where does it all end? It doesn't. We already have shopping centers for teen-agers, complete with teen-age banks (California); a hospital has a special teen-age wing that offers unlimited snacks, jam sessions, and wheelchair races (Portland, Oregon); a doctor in Boston has launched a medical specialty, ephebriatrics—the treatment of teen-age ills. And more commercial exploitation of youth is on the drawing boards.

The big question is: Where and how can teen-agers learn how to use and control the use of money wisely and to their satisfaction? Some believe the place is in the home; some say the public schools; others believe it should be taught in both places. Even if we have not decided where it should be done, we can substantiate the need for it.

The teen-age consumer in the ghetto

Studies of teen-agers, as consumers , who live in the ghetto in urban centers, are rare indeed. The information and insights on the ghetto teen-ager as a consumer are taken from a series of conversations with teen-agers in various sections of Los Angeles—Watts (black), southeast (Mexican), and nearby Venice (Hippie Center). About forty of these youngsters were transported to a ranch some hundred miles from Los Angeles in order to get an away-from-home environment which might serve as a means of stimulating a free flow of ideas. The conversations were conducted by young men experienced in the ghetto sections. The study provides some hopeful insights into ghetto teen-age expenditures. The conversations also show how most of them are completely alienated from and hostile to the present system.

Insights into the ghetto teen-ager as a consumer

Some typical remarks[14]

One young Mexican said: "First of all, if this country continues to let poverty and racial injustice and prejudice exist, we won't have a country and we won't have to worry about what youths want."

And a black youth adds: "Everyone wants something nice. You work for a good car, then the cops come and ask where you got it. White people have good things. They don't stop them. Some say what the hell."

And a Mexican responds: "This is the attitude. You are Mexican. You are inferior. If you want to succeed, be like an Anglo. If you want to be a Mexican, forget about succeeding. Teachers say, 'If you can't dance to my music get out.'"

Another boy said: "As far as consumer goods go, I really don't feel it a part of my life because it doesn't relate to me ... . People just don't talk about it."

Many other insights are revealed in this study. They said that "prices are higher in our stores"; "there are no clothing stores in Watts"; buses are "too

[14] An unpublished report, *Los Angeles Teenager as a Consumer,* by Arthur Carstens, director of the study supported in part by a grant from Consumers Union.

expensive"; "very few own cars" because the "police will take it away"; the "personal touch is important, like a flower painted on the pants' leg"; a "car is just wheels, not a status symbol"; "the opinion of the peer group determines what a teen-ager buys."

It appears that their first problem is to exist—just exist. They want a good education, good jobs, and a nice home with all the consumer goods that the affluent class possesses. But, how? When? They also want to be respected and treated like white people. The feelings of many of the youth in Watts were stated by a black youth:

WHAT I WANT

I feel I want my people to be free. People think that Negro people are nothing but trouble makers, riot starters, and uneducated people. But they are not all of that. When people are being dogged around by police, and when they are aware that they do not have jobs, have run down homes, poor schools and not too many of them have a lot to eat, they feel like "so what, they hate us, we hate them." And this always leads to riots and race problems, but the way I see it the answer to this is:

1. Give my people more and better jobs
2. Give my people and their kids better schools
3. Let my people live where they want to
4. Give them better playgrounds to play in

These are only a few things that will help keep the riots down. These are not much to ask. The white people have these, and I do not know how come my people can't have them. Is it asking too much or is it because we are black? We must know this. We must try to live together, work together and try to solve the race problem together and stop these riots. Let us stop all of this. Let us make America and our city the greatest in the world. So this is why I want to see my people free.

It is clear, from this study, that teen-agers in the ghetto of Los Angeles, and probably in ghettos elsewhere, are more sensitive to the need for basic changes—better education, better jobs, open housing and decent housing, respect and fair treatment—than to the need for more and better consumer goods. A higher standard of living, they argue, will be a by-product of the basic needs mentioned above. This conclusion may not be as valid if applied to the parents of teen-agers. The Caplovitz study of the consumer behavior of low-income families in New York City, for example, indicates a keen interest and active participation in consumer durable goods. One wonders whether these two studies do not tell the deep, disturbing differences in attitudes of parents and their teen-agers.

"The consumer behavior of low-income families" [15]   This study by David Caplovitz, a sociologist at Columbia University, concentrated on consumer behavior of low-income, recent migrants to New York City—blacks from the South, Puerto Ricans, and whites—living in four low-income public housing projects. A summary of the findings is:

1. Most low-income families are consumers of high-cost durables.
2. Most families depend upon high-cost credit when making these pur-

[15] David Caplovitz, *The Consumer Behavior of Low-Income Families,* Bureau of Applied Social Research, Columbia University, New York, 1961.

chases. This restricts most purchases to their neighborhood stores and to door-to-door peddlers, who for the most part work for the small neighborhood stores. Their credit debts may not be larger than those of families of comparable income elsewhere, but they are much more likely to have less savings. About one-third of these families have such large debts in relation to assets that they border on insolvency.

3. These families are vulnerable to exploitation by unscrupulous merchants because of poor education and language difficulties, and because many are recent migrants and tend to be naive shoppers, vulnerable to the lure of "easy credit." About one-third of them suffer at the hands of unscrupulous merchants and door-to-door peddlers. Most of them who encounter severe consumer difficulties are not apt to know where to go for professional help, and consequently they respond with helpless resignation to their consumer problems. Furthermore, nonwhites are charged more for credit, so that blacks and Puerto Ricans are penalized in the marketplace.

Any solutions?

The buying patterns of low-income consumers need changing

These, in brief, are the major findings in the study. The question inevitably arises about what can be done to help these families with their consumer problems. More specifically, what can be done to change their consumer practices? What can be done to protect the consumers through control of the suppliers? To change buying patterns of low-income consumers is usually difficult. Underlying much of the problem confronting low-income consumers is the fact that their consumption goals tend to outstrip their means for realizing them. Can they save money for their major durable goods? Unless society can offer alternative sources for credit, these families are not apt to change their shopping habits, say some investigators.

This disparity of consumption goals and limited resources has its origins in the "revolution of expectations" in an affluent society. The very success of American people in raising their standard of living lies behind the runaway aspirations of low-income consumers. Goals that at one time did not seem possible—exposure to constant radio and TV advertising emphasizing better living—now appear to be obtainable. So we find that aspirations for material possessions are easily learned; earnings increase more slowly and consumer sophistication takes time to be acquired.

Besides education in better planning and buying habits, low-income consumers need legislation and law enforcement designed to protect the consumer from unscrupulous merchants and from himself—that is, from his own propensity to get into trouble as a consumer.

What has all of this to do with money and democracy in home management? We said earlier in this chapter that youngsters are particularly sensitive to parental anxieties about money and home surroundings. They sense the tensions between parents, and often they are the victims of such tensions. Admittedly, low-income families have more than a normal amount of tensions. It is a wonder that family dissension and discord have been kept down to an "almost tolerable" level. The ugly fact is that there is both an indirect and a direct relationship between family discord and disintegration and low income and low consumer sophistication.

To better understand some of the remarks made by the teen-age Mexican Americans, we should keep in mind the following current facts:

Mexican Americans as consumers—background

1.   Ten percent of all Mexican Americans were unemployed in March 1971—about 5 percent nationally.

2.   Twenty-eight percent of all Mexican Americans live below the "low-income level." compared with 12.6 percent of the population as a whole. [16]

3.   Discrimination against Mexican Americans exists—they are apt to be the last to be hired and the first to be fired.

4.   Unscrupulous employers illegally hire Mexicans who have no work permits, and then exploit them by threatening to report them to the immigration authorities if they complain about low wages and poor housing.

5.   Dropout rates among Mexican Americans are high. The education they receive is not relevant to their real-life problems, there is de facto school segregation, and schools tend to ignore Mexican culture.

6.   There has been a disintegration of the Mexican American family in recent years.

Many of us are more familiar with some of the disadvantages of the black teen-ager and his family. Among the blacks we find:

Blacks as consumers— background

1.   The poverty rate is higher than that for whites—24 percent in 1969, compared with 7 percent for white persons in urban areas; in rural areas, the poverty rate for blacks was about 50 percent, compared with about 14 percent for whites.

2.   In urban areas in 1969, about 64 percent of poor black families were headed by a woman, compared with about 38 percent of poor white families.

3.   In 1970, 15.9 percent of black male youths were high school dropouts; 13.3 percent of black females were dropouts, compared with 6.7 percent of white males and 8.1 percent of white females.

4.   Black Americans have suffered from a sense of racial, national, and cultural inferiority. The militancy and resentment of blacks today must be seen against the background of 300 years of subjugation in slavery and lower-caste status. Blacks were unable to participate in the American dream of equality of opportunity. The black unemployment rate, for example, is explosive today— more than twice that of whites. In some cities, as many as 35 percent of young black males and 50 percent of young black females are unemployed today. Consequently, it is the young adult or early-middle-aged who generally manifests black awareness, black consciousness, and black pride.

Money adulthood for the teen-ager

Many teen-agers are not prepared to shoulder, in later years, their own important personal or family financial responsibilities because their parents neglected this part of their education. This neglect is understandable, because nothing that concerns a teen-ager is easy, and money training is no exception.

There is, however, one important fact that parents can use to good advan-

[16] Census report, March 1971.

tage. The world of money and finance is an adult world. A teen-ager longs for adulthood. And learning how to handle money is one of the steps that carries him into that proud estate. But how can this objective be achieved?

Because family beliefs and goals as well as family situations vary greatly, it is difficult to give tips on how to teach money management to a teen-ager in ten easy lessons. Nevertheless, the following suggestions, coming from experienced child-guidance experts and from parents who have experimented with their adolescent children, should be of considerable help to other parents.

Parents have responsibilities in money training

1.   The example the parents set will be as influential as any specific training. If the family makes no attempt to plan its spending, the youngsters can hardly be expected to do so.

2.   Teen-agers should know the approximate family income and the major expenses.

3.   In the light of the family income and major expenditures, children's allowances should be discussed in relation to expected responsibilities. Family income is not pocket money, but each member shares in the family funds. A child's share should include as much of the money spent on him as is known. It certainly should include most or all of the money normally used for his clothing expenses.

4.   Let each child be responsible for his own money matters. Mistakes will be made. Let him learn from these mistakes. Almost overnight most youngsters will turn into thrifty shoppers. Advice, formerly unwanted and often viewed as nagging, will not only be accepted but sought.

5.   When the occasion arises, help each child to understand the legal rights of the retailer and the legal rights of the consumer. Sometimes guarantees of goods are confusing to the uninitiated. He will need and want help in these matters and in many other intricacies of the business world.

6.   Encourage children to use the services of a bank. Show them how to write a check, how to use charge accounts. Let them see how the family invests its money and how insurance is used to protect the family.

7.   Encourage teen-agers to earn money outside the home. They should not be paid for doing their share of routine work in and around the house.

8.   Do not discipline a child by withholding his regular share of the family income. Rather, investigate the real causes for the misbehavior or action.

9.   Encourage each child to become an "expert" on certain expenditures for the whole family. This helps to build confidence as well as to give a child the feeling of contributing to the well-being of the family.

10.   Do not treat matters that stem from more basic emotional and social problems of adolescence as money management problems. The two are easily confused.

Even if parents are knowledgeable in personal and family financial management, they may have difficulty in translating information into attitudes and finally into action.

Parental attitudes in money training

Unfortunately, many parents show extreme immaturity when it comes to helping their children learn how to manage money. Mary S. Lyle, in her study of families in a rural-town community in Iowa, came to the following conclusions:

1.   One hundred fifty-eight high school students, checking problems that troubled them most, mentioned "learning how to spend money wisely," "having to ask parents for money," and "having no regular allowance or regular income" more often than any other human relations problem. There were 330 problems listed in the check list.

2.   Nearly half of these boys and girls were "very sure they were not getting (intellectual) stimulation in money management."

3.   Less than one-third of their parents were providing stimulation for the children to learn to plan for and select most of their clothes within a given amount of money.

4.   "Planning for the use of the total family income by all the family members mature enough to understand the situation was rather rare."[17]

Children's allowances have a purpose

It was quite obvious that the parents of these 120 families were not helping their children to learn to handle money in the best way.

Why don't parents give their children a chance to handle the money that will be spent on them? Parents object to giving their children allowances for many reasons, such as:

"Money is a sordid business. I don't want my children to have to worry about it until they have to."

"I earned my own spending money when I was a boy."

"I'll give them money when they need it."

"My children spend enough money without giving them allowances, too."

All such arguments reveal poor insight with regard to the real purpose of children's allowances, and back of them are bits of family history, custom, folklore, inertia, and certainly lack of understanding.

Just how do most children get spending money? There are many schools of thought, each with its champions, on this question.

Whim of the parent

"He who pays the piper may call the tune" sums up one point of view. What the children are given depends on the whim of the giver. Some parents use this to show their "power." Others use it to purchase love. Such a parent tries to purchase the affection of his children, substituting material things for understanding. He has little to offer his family in the way of human understanding, capacity for play, imagination, humor, or simple sociability. He has one major virtue—a source for money. This virtue is made to work overtime. Consequently, his children's attitude toward money often tends to succumb to parental standards or to rebel against them, and to become warped in either case.

Money revealed to children only as a symbol of power and success may lead to feelings of inferiority, bitterness, and unhappiness in the parents. This same unhappiness and maladjustment tends to spread to the children. In such an atmosphere, money can easily seem to be the one good that has the power to dispel sorrow or, quite as falsely, become the root of some, if not all, evil.

[17] Lyle, op. cit., pp. 61, 66, 158. Reprinted with permission.

Wheedling and collusion

A second approach is the one of wheedling father or mother into buying things that previously have been refused by the other parent. Sometimes there may be collusion between parent and child. Mother, for example, may say to her child, "I'd try asking your father for money after he has had his second cup of coffee."

At times, wheedling takes on a "cute" manner. In this case, children master certain tricks that net the biggest returns. Parents of such children may be educating them unknowingly for future trickery in business.

Money as whip or reward

What not to do   A third approach is to use money as a whip or means of enforcing discipline. "If you are a good boy, I'll give you a nickel." Should a child grow up believing that virtue always is rewarded by cash? Sometimes business deals are made for music practice, for getting good or even passing marks in school, or for household chores. Or a child is fined for poor schoolwork or for lying.

When John comes home late from baseball practice two nights in a row, mother suddenly announces that she will deduct 15 cents from next week's allowance. In such a case, the mother reduces the responsibilities of her child to a cash basis. John will have to decide, when challenged again, between 15 cents less cash or more fun playing baseball.

The real issue, personal responsibility with regard to other members of the family, is completely disregarded. In the second place, John is entitled to a part of the family income because he is a member of the family. Money should not be used as a club to discipline a member of the family. Using money to discipline a child confuses his thinking with regard to his family responsibilities, the value of money, and its proper uses.

Adults frequently are confused over how to settle accidents caused by a child's carelessness. Bill broke a neighbor's window. His father decided that the cost of the new window must come out of Bill's allowance, so much each week. Is placing a mortgage on a child's allowance because of a careless act a wise policy? In a clear case of an act of carelessness resulting in a material loss, the parents might preferably decide to pay for replacement of the glass.

The important issue concerns the attitude of the child. Most children are sorry when they destroy someone's property. With a child, the problem is to ease his conscience and to help him make his peace with all parties concerned. Help him without reducing the issues to monetary discipline, which may only confuse the problem of wrongdoing. For Bill, the important thing is forgiveness, that no one will hold anything against him, and that he will want to be more careful in the future.

Reward a child after accomplishment

When parents "purchase" better grades and honors, they confuse buying and bribery. Most parents know that there is no relationship between scholastic attainment and cash. It seems to be the path of least resistance. But are there not better ways of showing parental appreciation and for giving praise and approval? To pay cash for success in school, for accomplishment that is for the good of the child, is to give the child a false scale of values and relationships. For example, is an A in history worth the same as an A in grammar or arithmetic?

Why not celebrate after something has been done unusually well? Everyone loves a celebration. A gift or money in appreciation *after* the accomplishment might be a nice gesture. The important thing is that the child understands the difference between a spontaneous gift and a calculated contract, such as "If you get a B in geography, I'll give you two dollars." It is preferable, after a child has accomplished a certain objective, for a parent to say, "Because you worked so hard to succeed, we are going to buy you that bicycle."

The problem is one of sharing, not making a deal. Those who have studied children have found that the way a child acts is not so important as *why* he acts a certain way. A child who usually carries out responsibilities within his ability range does so because he feels cooperative and because he gets parental approval. "We try to please those we love" is a more satisfactory approach to life than "We please those who pay us."

Should a child earn his allowance?

A fourth point of view of some parents is that children should not be given money unless they earn it. Such a parent says, "When a child needs money, make him earn it. He won't be handed money for nothing when he grows up." With as poor logic, you would refuse to button the dress of a 2-year-old because she will not be likely to have a maid when she grows up. After all, a small child is helped to do things until he can manage unaided. A healthy youngster wants to learn to do things alone. Children want to master buttons, to walk instead of being carried, because independence is an intriguing goal.

If a boy is taught that only earners can be spenders, is he likely to turn over most of his income to a wife for the family food, clothes, and rent? Grown up, he may feel that a full-time homemaker is not actually earning money and therefor is not entitled to a voice in how the family income is to be spent. A girl so taught may feel that as a housewife she is thwarted and be content only if she is actually receiving money earned outside the home.

If earning is to be the only source of a child's allowance, parents will find that they are paying for all home chores, since outside jobs available to children are strictly controlled by state labor laws. The family must decide which household jobs are to be done as a family team working together for the happiness of each member and which jobs can properly be paid for.

This is not a simple problem, because what is an outside hired job in one family may be just a family chore in another. Each family should discuss and come to an agreement on this matter. Usually it boils down to this proposition: "Here are some jobs we have to hire someone to do. If you want to do them, we'll pay you instead. How about it?"

Sharing family chores—pay or no pay

This leads to the fifth point of view, the most sound, with regard to children's allowances and work—making a child feel that all the family should share in the family work, pay or no pay. It should not be hard to impress upon all members of the family that they must share the family work just as they share the total family income.

It is easy to point out that there is really no way of paying mother for the thousands of dishes she is washing for the entire family. Likewise, there is no way of paying father for making a living for the family. And there is no way of paying for the love and care that both parents give to a child, especially in sickness. These things are taken for granted because parents want to do them.

When the family income and work are shared by every member of the family, it is not unreasonable to conclude that:

1. Every member of the family is entitled to a fair share of the family income, including an allowance, because he is a part of the family.
2. Every member of the family should do certain chores in and around the home to keep the family life happy and successful.
3. Jobs around the home that ordinarily involve hired help can be assumed by the children, according to their abilities and strength, for mutually agreed-on money payment.
4. Jobs for pay, outside the family, can be undertaken if such work is beneficial for all the family.

Reactions caused by parental attitudes

Inseparable from the children's allowance system is the way the parents manage the total family income. The spending pattern and the methods used by the parents are significant in terms of child development. First, family financial management determines the kind of living the child will experience for many years. Second, it influences his attitudes and feelings toward other people. Third, it sets before him a way of life in which relative values are revealed.

Most parents do not discover until a serious argument occurs that their attitude toward money is influencing all their relations with their children. In a study of 7,000 high school students, it was found that two-fifths of the quarrels between adolescents and their parents were over money matters.[18] In homes where money matters are permitted to become a focal point for argument, the children grow up with immature money concepts, which may continue for still another generation.

Immature money management concepts

Here are some of the techniques resorted to by children in families with immature money management concepts:

1. Having to beg for every cent of spending money is not foreign to some homes. The variations of method depend on the degree of resistance on the part of the parents and often on the child's skill of playing one parent against the other. Such a child knows that it is especially hard to resist appeals for money if a visitor is within hearing distance or if mother is very busy.
2. Some children take advantage of parents when on a shopping expedition. "Won't you buy me this?" pleads little Tommy. If mother refuses, Tommy says, "I'll lie down and scream unless you buy it." What should the mother do?

[18] Evelyn Millis Duvall, *Keeping up with Teen Agers,* Public Affairs Committee, New York, 1947, p. 77.

Call his bluff in a crowded store? Give him a sound spanking right there? Lack of money education on the part of Tommy's parents, or possibly always giving in to the child's way of handling a situation, invited such a public display. It is a human relations problem, not a mere matter of money management, though money is the focal point of the dispute.

3. In an effort to break through parental defenses, older children sometimes misuse the family charge account. This can be prevented by the parents, but too often the remedy comes after one or more bad experiences. For example, when a mother refused to give her daughter money for a birthday gift for a friend, the girl charged an expensive gift to the family account.

4. Children sometimes resort to pilfering in stores. It may be candy, gum, small toys at first, later perhaps a baseball, a doll, or even a clothing item. Usually, they are personal items that could be purchased by an adequate allowance. A variation of pilfering is shaking coins from the child's bank, "borrowing" cash from mother's purse, or shortchanging the parents when making a family purchase.

5. In some homes, the lack of an allowance system leads to seeking an outside job. This is not too bad if it is not forced on a child by parents who do not invite the child's confidence in money matters.

Today, youngsters spend more money than their parents spent in their day. Movies, soft drinks, milk shakes, and entertainment cost as much as the necessities of life may have cost a generation ago. But parents should remember that they helped to bring into existence these miracles of production and distribution. The problem cannot be solved simply by limiting a child's spending money or restricting it entirely. It must be met by helping a child to assume responsibility for spending his money intelligently—that is, teaching him to have money sense.

The allowance system

Children learn how to swim and to play baseball, hockey, and other games by experience in each of these sports. Likewise, they can learn how to use money by experiencing the spending of money. The best way to distribute family money to normal children is via the allowance system.

Learning how to spend money

An allowance gives a child a chance to handle some of the money that will be spent on him anyway. A child consumes food, clothes, and many other items from the time he is born. And he keeps this up on an ascending scale for many years.

Since youngsters must have certain essentials without actually earning them, why should money be an exception? Children should receive some money, then, just as they receive food and clothes. They can use such money to buy their own notebooks, paper, pencils, books, paints, and other personal items. This helps them to become acquainted with money, its limitations, potentialities, and value. They will learn money sense best by handling and spending money.

Even a preschool child can learn the use and value of money if he is permitted to hand the conductor the bus fare or to pay for things that mother buys in a store. In marketing, a child has the opportunity to see that mother has to make choices and decisions in buying.

Alice may say, "Mother! see the nice strawberries. May we have some for lunch?" Mother explains that those strawberries are expensive because they are out of season and she must plan to buy another fruit. Alice may be convinced after returning home if mother prepares another attractive dessert and compares its cost with the out-of-season strawberries. Add to these experiences, and soon even a preschool child begins to weigh the pros and cons of decisions in buying. Thus, when a child is put on an allowance and is confronted with the necessity for a decision, he will be more likely to weigh one desire against another.

What is an allowance?

An allowance is a specified sum of money given to a child at regular intervals, which is his to spend, save, give away, or even lose. It is cash received over and above any family income allotted for the child's normal care and necessities. As such, it should be set aside as a regular part of the family expenditures, like those for clothes, food, rent, and the car.

The allowance should not be treated as something earned or deserved; it should be distinct and separate from any form of discipline or parental desire. Also, it is desirable to avoid giving a child the feeling that his allowance is a gift from his parents. An allowance, no matter how small, should have no restrictions. Education, yes; but the child should have complete and exclusive control of the use of his allowance.

Restrictions, in place of information and education, reduce the experience to a point where the child is merely acting as a disbursing agent. This might rightly be called an allowance under false pretenses.

Guiding principles for allowances

Planning an allowance is not unlike any other educational venture. Certain fundamental principles are important. In addition to those given above, educational experts generally agree on the following:

1. Start a child on an allowance when he begins to make fairly regular requests for money for personal needs or desires. A child under 6 might need or desire such items as paints, crayons, ice cream cones, candy and chewing gum, Sunday-school money, gifts for others, children's books, and playthings. A child between the ages of 6 and 9 might begin to request money for magazines, movies, carfare, school lunches, box-top offers, and records, in addition to the items just listed.

2. The allowance should be matched with the child's ability to handle new responsibilities. Each child, even within the same family, is different. Usually you cannot handle two cases in the same way at the same age. A common mistake is to make the child assume too much responsibility or too little. Each year, additional responsibilities should be added, and corresponding increases in the allowance should be provided. By the time the child is of high school age, the allowance should cover most of his needs, including clothes.

3. The amount of the allowance should be determined after needs and costs have been listed by the child and discussed with the parents. Any cutting by the parents should be explained to the child and be fully understood and

accepted by him. The amount will have to be based on the financial circumstances of the family. If possible, the sum should include a fair amount above and beyond such necessities as carfare and school lunch money; otherwise, the child has no opportunity to decide how to spend his own money for his desires as well as needs. He must get sufficient experience in making decisions.

4.   The age and experience of a child will determine the length of time over which his money management has to stretch. If the family income is based on weekly payments, the allowance may have to fit into weekly spacing. Ordinarily, a young child, just beginning to have an allowance, might be paid twice a week; later, weekly or twice a month; and finally, monthly.

5.   It is important that full payment be made on the day agreed on. All the rules must be known and agreed on in advance. Then stick to this agreement until changes are mutually made. This is a good time to invite a child to participate in an informal family discussion of the total income and spending setup. As years go by, more and more of such information can be revealed, until by the time he is about ready for college, he will know the total financial situation. The sooner this is done, other things being equal, the easier it is to get cooperation without unpleasant bickering.

6.   After an allowance has been set up, the child should understand that part of it must be used for necessities and perhaps for savings, and the rest is his to spend as he chooses. Here is where parents need the patience of Job and the wisdom of Solomon. They must not expect too much. This might be illustrated by a remark that a student made in a money management conference: "When I was about twelve years old, my parents expected me to handle money as if I were thirty years old."

7.   An allowance should not be tied to jobs done at home. The allowance should be distributed because the child is a member of the family and is entitled to it as such. Work at home should be divided according to age and abilities. This is a separate responsibility, and each child should be expected to do his part.

8.   If a child requests more money, even though he understands the agreement, it is usually a good idea not to give him more money before his next allowance is due. While there are exceptions to all good rules in human relations, the exception can too easily become the rule. It might be wiser to say: "If your needs are more than your allowance, make a new list of them, and we'll talk it over again." Most children will consider that this is a fair attitude. At the same time, the parents are not placing themselves in the position of putting the child through a third degree. He, then, will have time to do a little adjusting for himself. This is sound psychology and good economics.

9.   If a child loses his allowance, it is important to take time to learn all the facts in a calm discussion of the matter. If money is needed for necessities, replace it to that extent. The extra amount should be deferred until the next allowance is due. This may seem to be a little rough, but it is conditioning the child for similar experiences that he will have later.

10.   If a child begins to hoard his money, observe whether it is a passing stage or whether it reflects maladjustment to living. Some children are influenced by their parents' attitude or by pressures and demands on them during their growing-up years. It may also be a symptom of personal insecurity.

11.   When a child is eager to contribute money to an organization or a school or community group, it is important that he understand its purpose. He should not give money to inflate his ego or just to hold his status among his friends. He should not derive satisfaction out of proportion to his allowance.

12.   Saving ought to be active and meaningful, not a routine stuffing of the child's bank. Saving can be encouraged if the objective is specific—for personal use or for a gift for someone the child loves—and the spending should not be delayed too long. A young child may save for a doll displayed in a window. A high school student may save for the annual dance. Saving for a rainy day—just putting away money—has no significance for a child.

A 4-year-old is not a saver. He must start with spending. In time, he may save to spend later. But the only way to learn this is by experience. When a child is 9 to 12 years old, he can begin to understand the principle of saving for future spending, but he must first discover the meaning of the future.

13.   If a loan is made to a child, repayment should be arranged within a reasonable time, but without too much sacrifice. Borrowing and lending are constantly going on in our society. A child needs sympathetic guidance if requesting a loan that is out of proportion to his ability to pay. Disappointment can be accepted gracefully if parents use tact and display friendly counsel in such matters. It is not easy for parents to judge the value of the things for which children want money. A seemingly small want can produce intense emotional stress. Many parents still carry such emotional scars from their own childhood.

14.   When a child is concerned because his friends have more money than he has to spend, two things are necessary. Discover what the allowances of the friends have to cover. Reexamine the child's needs and allowance. If the old agreement, or a new one, is consistent with the family income or with the needs of the child, he usually accepts it. Sometimes it is necessary to give him a clearer sense of values. Above all, a child must know why.

15.   If a child has experience in handling money, by the time he enters high school, he is ready to assume more responsibility. The urge for independence is strong when a child is of high school age. He begins to resent any attempt to keep him young and dependent. He insists on making his own decisions. His money needs are greater, too. The allowance should grow, but so should the responsibilities. The child now should learn how to handle a checking account, how to order merchandise and pay bills, how to decide on tips, how to buy his own clothing and care for it.

16.   Record keeping for a child is useless unless he can be made to feel a specific gain from the effort. A teen-ager may discover for himself that some records are necessary. This is especially true if he is granted increases in his allowance only on the basis of reasonably proved needs. Often this must take the form of evidence of where his money went.

Democratic ways to promote happy families   There is no substitute for happy, understanding family relationships. The best preparation for such relationships is for parents to teach their children to share the family chores, to cooperate in family discussions, and to handle money wisely. Children having such experience learn to face situations objectively, to analyze and solve difficulties and problems in later life.

This does not mean that children should be weighed down with family responsibilities before they are old enough to understand them. On the other hand, they should not be shielded or overprotected from the realities of family life. They should be allowed to join in family discussions and in final decisions as soon as they are old enough to understand what is involved.

QUESTIONS FOR DISCUSSION

1. Children are particularly sensitive to parental anxieties about income, making ends meet, a good home, vacations, credit, paying bills, and so forth. Should parents let their children know they feel anxious about such matters, these anxieties, which are the concern of most American families, including those in the upper-income brackets? Consider your answer from the point of view of philosophy, goals, values, and life-styles.

2. Can you identify persons you know who appear to have "normal" and "neurotic" attitudes toward money, as Dr. Bergler describes them? Do you agree with Dr. Bergler's identification of attitudes toward money? Explain.

3. Bribing a child with money to encourage him to get higher grades in school ($2 for A's, $1 for B's, 50 cents for C's) sets up a false stimulus for achievement because it emphasizes monetary reward rather than personal development and the increased satisfaction that comes with accomplishment. If you take issue with this point of view, what are your reasons?

4. If you can identify parents who use money as a symbol of power and success, try to discover the effect of this on the life-style of the family, especially on the children. Perhaps you can discuss it with the children.

5. Why are the attitudes of husband and wife toward family income and the spending of the income so important in maintaining reasonably happy family living?

6. After reading about the new house designs for communal living, with central meeting rooms leading to dormitory wings, nurseries, a large common kitchen, and so forth, do you think there may be some advantages in bringing up children in such an environment? What are the chances for having a more successful marriage as a whole? If you have communal homes in your locality, perhaps you can arrange to visit with the families and find out how they feel about their new way of life.

7. Do you think that posting a bill for Mom services is a proper way for a mother to confront her children when they neglect to do their chores? What would you do in such a case?

PROJECTS

1. Make a survey on how teen-agers spend their own money. Urge them to keep spending and income records for one month. What do they spend their money for? Do they spend beyond their income? Do they have any savings?

Make a summary of all spending, savings, income, overspending, etc. Prepare a report and discuss it with your class.

2. In what ways are parental attitudes toward money important in a family?

3. Ask a number of college students how they secured money for their own use from first grade through high school. How many had an allowance, begged, played one parent against the other, worked, etc.? Evaluate all the methods used in obtaining income. Which were best in their judgment? Why?

4. How would you teach a child to save money? Assume the child has never saved money for later use.

5. Make a list of the money management principles you think you will use in bringing up your child from preschool age through the twelfth grade. Can you support each of these principles if asked?

6. A University of Minnesota study concluded that "Negro and white shopping behavior is very similar at upper-income levels, but is different at lower-income levels." A black student may be interested in making his own investigation of the shopping behavior of low-income black consumers in the marketplace. Spending may be socially and psychologically unique.

7. If you are a black or Puerto Rican, you might enlighten your classmates with this report. Evaluate each of the sixteen guiding principles for allowances given in this chapter in terms of their usefulness in bringing up a Puerto Rican or black child in a low-income family.

SUGGESTED READINGS

Blum, Richard H.: *Horatio Alger's Children,* Jossey-Bass, San Francisco, 1972.

Facts and Figures on Older Americans: Income and Poverty in 1970, U.S. Department of Health, Education, and Welfare, Administration on Aging, Advance Report, June 1971.

Goulart, Ron: *The Assault on Childhood,* Sherbourne Press, Los Angeles, 1969.

Grebler, Moore: *The Mexican American People,* The Free Press, New York, 1970.

Hechinger, Fred, and Grace Hechinger: *Teen-Age Tyranny,* William Morrow & Company, Inc., New York, 1963.

Herrmann, Robert O.: "Young Adults as Consumers," *The Journal of Consumer Affairs,* Summer 1970, pp. 19–30.

Petgen, Albert: "The Spanish Market: $18 Billion Sleeping Giant," *Marketing Times,* June 1971.

Silberman, Charles: *Crisis in Black and White,* Random House, Inc., New York, 1964.

Stewart, Alice: *Consumer Close-Ups,* Cooperative Extension, Cornell University, Ithaca, N.Y., May 29, 1967.

Tallman, Irving: "The Family as a Small Problem Solving Group," *The Journal of Marriage and Family*, February 1970, p. 94.

Taylor, Jon: *My Allowance and How I Use It (ages 4–14)*, Impact Instructional Innovations, Salt Lake City.

U.S. Bureau of the Census, *Current Population Reports: Consumer Income*, ser. P-60, no. 77, May 7, 1971; May 20, 1971.

CHAPTER 5
MONEY MANAGEMENT

There is something funny
That isn't so funny
To have too much month
At the end of the money

Family money is the hardest in the world to manage. And why? Families have not discovered the secret of converting dollars into contentment.

And what is the secret? Good money management, largely. Considering what money can do to your marriage, for better or for worse, this is a good time to get your money thinking straight.

The marriage contract establishes an economic enterprise called a *family*. Like a business enterprise, a family sets out to operate at a profit. At the very best, it has to break even. If it doesn't, the enterprise goes under.

When a business fails, only the legal entity suffers. When a family goes under, human beings suffer. And, as we learned in earlier chapters, economic stress can put a marriage under great strain and may even destroy it.

College students, too, can wreck the opportunity to complete their college education because of financial mismanagement. In this day and age, almost any student of average ability with a desire to go to college is able to receive financing from several sources—his family, his own effort, loans, scholarships, work-study programs, National Defense Student Loans, educational opportunity grants, veterans of wars grants, and many others. But adequate financial aid does not, in itself, assure success in college. Many college students flunk out during the first year. Others mismanage their finances and join the labor force. Regardless of the reasons many college students leave school, they may not realize that the longer they stay in school, the greater their potential in career development and the larger their lifetime earnings. As noted in Chapter 3, the Census Bureau estimates that the average lifetime earnings of a four-year college graduate are about $584,000, in contrast to about $272,000 for an elementary school graduate and about $371,000 for a high school graduate. Of course, some of the highly specialized professional people—medical doctors, business administrators, government officials, and many others—will net lifetime incomes in the million-dollar bracket. Thus education is one of the most important determinants of income (see Table 5-1).

Education is an important determinant of income

Education increases the income of women, too. After the excitement of the wedding day, parents may ask themselves whether college was really necessary for their daughter. Rapidly rising college costs raise serious doubts for many parents. Research into this subject by the Institute of Life Insurance has found that a college degree for a woman is "likely to be valuable to her all her life." Most women find a college degree helpful in meeting the challenges of marriage and child rearing. The practical value of a college degree becomes evident later in life, when the children are less dependent. At this time a woman may decide to enter the working world. The U.S. Department of Labor has found that among college-educated women 45 to 54 years old, seven out of ten now hold jobs, and the chances improve with a year or more of graduate work.

Dropping out of college is not the end

About half of the entering college freshmen each year will probably drop out of college before receiving a degree. This 50 percent casualty rate has been constant since at least 1960.

This is not an entirely bleak picture, however. Even if a student does drop out of college, he is likely to return at a later date to finish his degree. The U.S. Office of Education reports that the one-out-of-two dropout rate is also balanced further by the fact that many of these students did not plan to go to college for the full four years.

A University of Illinois study reporting on the dropout problem says that

TABLE 5-1   Household Income by Education of Head of Household, 1970 (percentage of households in each group)

| Household Income | SCHOOLING COMPLETED | | | | | | |
| | ELEMENTARY | | HIGH SCHOOL | | COLLEGE | | |
	Less Than Eight Years	Eight Years	One to Three Years	Four Years	One to Three Years	Four Years or More	ALL HOUSE-HOLDS
Under $3,000	36.8	25.7	17.1	8.9	9.3	4.7	15.8
$3,000 to $4,999	19.5	17.1	13.6	9.1	7.9	4.7	11.6
$5,000 to $6,999	13.8	13.6	13.6	12.4	10.0	6.4	11.8
$7,000 to $9,999	13.7	18.1	20.6	21.4	19.6	13.2	18.5
$10,000 to $14,999	11.0	16.4	21.8	29.2	27.0	26.6	23.2
$15,000 and over	5.1	9.0	13.6	18.7	26.1	44.4	19.1
Total	100.0	100.0	100.0	100.0	100.0	100.0	100.0
Thousands of households	9,027	8,255	10,583	20,142	7,602	8,765	64,374
Mean income	$5,747	$7,253	$8,757	$10,422	$11,761	$15,980	$10,001
Median income	$4,290	$5,987	$7,833	$9,708	$10,506	$13,947	$8,734
Ratio of mean to median	1.34	1.21	1.12	1.07	1.12	1.15	1.15

SOURCE: Bureau of the Census.

NOTE: Parts may not add to totals because of rounding.

more than seven out of ten men and women who enter state-supported colleges and universities eventually acquire their degrees, although it may take ten years.

Many educators who have studied the dropout pattern are beginning to feel that four consecutive years of college may be economically or psychologically beyond the reach of a substantial number of students. For many youngsters an interruption provides needed cash or motivation to return to college to complete a degree.

Who pays for college education?   In a recent study reported in *Financing a College Education,* by the College Entrance Examination Board, one university indicated that its students paid approximately 25 percent of their college expenses from their own savings and earnings; parents paid 40 to 50 percent of the expenses from current income and another 10 to 15 percent, from savings and loans. The remaining 10 to 20 percent of the expenses came from various kinds of scholarships and gifts.

Most financial aid offices in colleges and universities are very familiar with the problems of parents whose income should be adequate to finance their children's higher education, who have every intention of providing for college, but who simply cannot meet college bills when they fall due. Typically, parents' lamentations are: "We thought we had planned well, but we just didn't save enough." "We never saved because we were sure our son would get a scholarship." Or, "We never imagined it would cost so much." Or, "We thought that by the time the children entered college the government would pay for it." Research by the Ford Foundation has shown that only half of parents set aside money for their children's education.

TABLE 5-2 Amount Saved Compared with Family Income

FAMILY INCOME	AVERAGE AMOUNT SAVED
$7,000 - $9,999	$185
10,000 - 11,999	211
12,000 - 14,999	335
15,000 - 19,999	353
20,000 - 24,999	438

The fact is that, according to a recent study,[1] only two out of every five families with upper-middle income (mean gross income of $14,000) have any savings plan for college, and most of these plans are dangerously inadequate. The average amount saved was only $310. As Table 5-2 shows, this amount varied directly with the family's net income.

The average amount saved and invested annually over ten to fifteen years might produce $2,000. But parents said that their savings would meet 40 percent of the college costs for one child. If college costs are around $3,000 per year or $12,000 over four years, savings should be $4,800 to meet the savings goal of 40 percent of costs. Clearly, actual savings are more than likely to fall short of the goal. Many parents seem unwilling or unable to save adequately to meet these costs. Unless affluent parents do a better job of saving and investing money for college education, most of them will continue having difficulty in meeting their children's college expenses. One obvious need is for parents to start saving fifteen years in advance of the first year of college.

How to pay for a college education

Any boy or girl with average ability should be able to secure a college education in this country. Few parents can afford to pay all the college bills out of savings and regular income. But there is no need for panic. There are many ways to secure the funds. At least some can come from income, since parents will no longer have their child at home. The normal cost of essentials for a child at home is around $1,000 during the nine-month school period. Another part can come from the student's part-time and summer jobs. And some can come from the college, a local or national organization, a loan, or other sources.

The student himself can work, save, borrow, and be sensible about his expenditures and the choice of a college. Student employment is an important source of financial aid. So are "room and board jobs" and cooperative houses where students may live and possibly prepare their own meals or eat meals prepared for them. Normally, a student should not work over fifteen hours per week when taking a normal college class load. Fifteen hours of work a week would pay a student $30 at $2 an hour.

The college work-study program

The program for work and study in college, established under the Economic Opportunity Act of 1964, will provide many new and educationally related

[1]Betty Lou Marple and Wesley W. Marple, "How Affluent Families Plan to Pay for College," *College Board Review*, Spring 1967.

student employment opportunities. Any student demonstrating financial need is presently eligible for this program.

Student loans for higher education are available up to about $1,400 a year, carrying a very low interest rate. The National Defense Student Loan Program, established in 1954, was one of the largest sources of student loans. There are also state loan programs under the Higher Education Act of 1965 to encourage states to establish guaranteed loan programs. There are also commercial loan programs through banks, insurance companies, and finance corporations.

Colleges are the first source to which students should apply for scholarships. Most scholarships are based on financial need as well as scholarship. There are also state scholarship programs which should be investigated.

The educational opportunity grants program

This program, established under the Higher Education Act of 1965, provides up to $800 annually to students who are admissible to college and who demonstrate "exceptional financial need." An additional $200 may be granted after the first college year if he ranks in the upper half of his college class.

GI benefits are presently available to some 3 million veterans whose service was after the Korean War. The major benefit to these veterans for financial aid for college is $130 per month, with added allowances for dependents.

Money management for college students

As a college student, you have the same reason as other individuals and families have for planning expenditures wisely. An intelligently planned budget will not deprive you of pleasure. On the contrary, it will help you to decide what to eliminate in order to have the things you need and really want.

If you are an unmarried college student, your family or guardian expects you—more or less—to manage your own expenditures during the college year. If you are a married college student, your budgeting problems will have to be centered around both family needs and college needs. The married college student has, in fact, a double problem. He has to take care of all or most of the regular family budgeting problems in addition to his central purpose for the time being—education.

A good reason for devoting some serious attention to money management now is that you are setting habits that will stay with you during your entire lifetime. Good money management habits established now will pay dividends many times during your life. Some will say, "I'll wait until I'm married to set up a good money management program." Others will wait until the car is paid for or until the next raise comes along, or until . . . *ad infinitum.* Somehow they never get around to doing the job because they are always waiting for the right time. The best way to become an expert at managing money is to begin practicing *now.*

You may be one of that group of college students who are spending money not directly earned by them. Perhaps there has been little opportunity for you to learn to manage money well. You may be, however, among the few who are good consumers. If you are a good consumer, you insist on receiving value for your money. If you stick to that principle, you will probably be successful in managing all your resources—time, money, and energy.

You may be facing, for the first time, the full responsibility of deciding for yourself how to plan and spend your money. If so, you belong to the large group of college students who need counseling in the management of personal finances.

"How," you ask, "do I know whether I'm successful in handling my personal finances?"

The answer to that question is not an easy one. It is possible to make ends meet and yet not be successful in money management. It is likewise possible to be a careful buyer of consumer goods and services and not be a successful money manager. The person who is successful in money management is one who plans, buys, and uses goods and services in such a manner that he gets what he most desires from those goods and services.

Test your money management IQ

The accompanying questionnaire, Money Management IQ, will help you discover your "dollar sense"—help you evaluate your skill in money management.

If your score is below 55, you really need to develop your skills in handling money. If your score embarrasses you, do not be discouraged. Remember the first time you drove a car or tried to hit a little ball with a golf club? Everything went wrong. Then, almost without knowing when, you began making the right moves without consciously thinking of them. The same results will happen as you learn to handle your money in a planned way. You may think it time-consuming and unrewarding at first. Soon you will be making your money achieve the major goals that you set up.

Define your goals

There are two fundamentals of money management for college students. the first is to plan your own budget. It is your money. Establish your own spending pattern and be sure that your money is going where you want it to go. The second fundamental is to set up your own goals. Knowing what you are aiming for will give a positive approach to budgeting. When you define your goals, you have taken the first step toward reaching them.

As a college student, you have certain financial obligations that can be classified as fixed expenses, such as tuition, board and room, and possibly transportation. As a rule you must meet these fixed expenses at a particular time. Then there are many flexible expenses, such as supplies, books, snacks, clothes, grooming items, recreation. The important thing is to be clear about your goals —aims, obligations, immediate and remote wants. Then make a definite plan for spending your dollars to meet your personal needs and wants. Use your spending plan to reach your goals.

A budgeted spending plan for college students

The first step in preparing a college budget is to get a true picture of your expenses by keeping a record of spending for two to four weeks. At the end of each week, total the amount spent for "fixed" or necessary expenses. These always must be paid. Other expenses are "flexible," that is, they can be cut out or cut down, depending on your needs and income. You are the one to decide which of your expenses are fixed and which are flexible. An accurate spending record and classification of expenses into fixed and flexible items will help you set up a spending plan that works.

Table 5-3, Budget Form for College Students, will help you differentiate between fixed and flexible expenses. Of course, you can add items or subtract any that you do not need to allow for in your own spending plan.

You will be one in a thousand if you can actually "balance the budget." But, like golf and tennis, even money management is a skill to be learned and practiced, and the attitude toward money management must be acquired. You

Money Management IQ

A SELF-TEST QUESTIONNAIRE ON PERSONAL SPENDING HABITS

This questionnaire, if filled out as accurately as your memory permits, will help you to discover your weaknesses in personal money management. Each "yes" answer rates 5 points. Add the points to find your money management IQ. If your score is

Over 75, consider yourself a *good* money manager.
Between 75 and 55, consider yourself *average.*
Between 55 and 35, you are *below average.*
Below 35, you are *very poor.*

1. Have you made a rough plan for your large expenses for the year?
2. Have you kept a written record of your expenditures for at least one month?
3. Have you examined your record of expenditures and made necessary changes?
4. Are you seldom "broke" before your next allowance or income is received?
5. When "broke" do you generally get along as best you can until your allowance is received?
6. Do you avoid making yourself miserable and unhappy by fretting about something you want but cannot afford?
7. Are you in the habit of spending moderately on personal grooming?
8. Can you generally be entertained without spending money?
9. Do you usually resist the spending pressures of friends?
10. Do you resist the spending of money according to your whim without regard to what you really need?
11. When "broke," do you tend to avoid getting an extra sum from your parents or guardian?
12. If you saw a clothing item in a store where you have a charge account, would you be likely to think about how to pay for it before you bought it?
13. Are you careful about not leaving cash in your room or carrying fairly large sums of money on your person?
14. Do you usually avoid buying clothes that you may wear only a few times?
15. Do you spend a moderate amount of money for food between meals?
16. Do you usually save ahead for something you want very much, such as a new dress or suit, a gift, a prom?
17. Do you make it a habit to go to more than one store to compare price and quality before deciding on a big purchase?
18. Would you say that about half your purchases are planned in advance and are not merely "impulse" buying?
19. Do you know whether your family carries personal belongings insurance, protecting such items as your luggage, clothes, jewelry, golf and tennis equipment?
20. Can you resist buying bargains just because they are advertised as bargains?
Your score: The number of checks ( ) $\times$ 5 = ( ).

can become quite efficient if you learn good management of your income while in college, and then continue using this skill in family income planning

MONEY MANAGEMENT FOR THE FAMILY

As we said, family money is the hardest in the world to manage. In the first place, more than half of American families, we are told, do not spend according to a plan. Most families, however, say they plan expenditures "after a fash-

TABLE 5-3   Budget Form for College Students

INCOME	ESTIMATED INCOME	ACTUAL INCOME
Balance on hand (including amounts owed to you)	$ _____	$ _____
Regular weekly income	_____	_____
Savings	_____	_____
Additions to allowance	_____	_____
Earnings	_____	_____
Gifts	_____	_____
Scholarship	_____	_____
Total	$ _____	$ _____

FIXED EXPENSES	ESTIMATED FIXED EXPENSE	ACTUAL AMOUNT SPENT
Food	$ _____	$ _____
Room	_____	_____
Tuition	_____	_____
Insurance	_____	_____
Transportation	_____	_____
Organization dues	_____	_____
Fees (laboratory, health, etc.)	_____	_____
Taxes	_____	_____
Other	_____	_____
Total fixed expenditures	$ _____	$ _____

FLEXIBLE EXPENSES	ESTIMATED EXPENSE	ACTUAL AMOUNT SPENT
Recreation	$ _____	$ _____
School supplies	_____	_____
Books	_____	_____
Clothing	_____	_____
Contributions	_____	_____
Grooming	_____	_____
Car—gas, oil, repairs	_____	_____
Snacks	_____	_____
Repairs (radio, watch, shoes, etc.)	_____	_____
Gifts	_____	_____
Laundry, dry cleaning	_____	_____
Cultural events	_____	_____
Health	_____	_____
Cigarettes	_____	_____
Beverages	_____	_____
Telephone	_____	_____
Other	_____	_____
Total flexible expenditures	$ _____	$ _____
Grand total	$ _____	$ _____

Actual income	$ _____
Actual amount spent	$ _____
Balance left	$ _____

ion"—a sort of unconscious planning. Many of these families feel "pinched" because they think that prices and taxes are too high and that all they need is more income! Maybe so. But there are indications that more dollars are not a cure-all. Between 1960 and 1970, for example, there was a 182 percent increase in the number of personal bankruptcy petitions, despite the fact that personal income increased 204 percent and per capita personal income increased 180 percent.

No doubt, sensible budgeting or better planning of family expenditures could have reduced the number of personal and family bankruptcy petitions and actual bankruptcies during that ten-year period. Underlying this upsurge of personal bankruptcies, however, are the familiar pillars of the American economy—materialism, easy credit, and changing attitudes toward spending.

The total outstanding consumer credit (home mortgages excluded) in 1971 reached a new peak of $137.2 billion. Debt repayment on this huge amount in the same year was equivalent to 14.8 percent of disposable personal income, up from 13.7 percent in 1970. Obviously, the use of credit makes it easier to buy. By the same token, however, many more families find it more difficult to repay.

For young families (head under 35), for example, current expenditures average more than current income. Debt averaged 81 percent of current income, while liquid assets and investments averaged 39 percent of debt owed. These families owed more installment debt than families in any other age group in 1970, and they lived on the edge of bankruptcy because they had only enough liquid assets and investments to maintain current expenditures for fifteen weeks! The probability of considerable irresponsibility of spending among many of the young marrieds with the head under age 35 is quite clear. This is even clearer when we find that in this family age group (25 to 34), 31.4 percent had incomes from $10,000 to $14,999 and 15.9 percent had incomes of $15,000 and over.[2] There is, no doubt, irresponsible spending on the part of many affluent families.

Irresponsible spending

There are any number of studies of families whose incomes are adequate and more but whose spending is reckless. Brenda Dervin,[3] in a careful study of sixty-eight families with adequate incomes, found a business executive, for example, who earned an annual income of $16,800, rented a house for $180 a month, drove a late-model car, dressed expensively, but ran up debts to 180 creditors totaling $18,000. A wife in another family, whose husband earned $9,000 a year, spent $800 a month more than the monthly income; a college professor and his wife earned $16,000, lived in a very modest $16,000 home that was poorly furnished and in need of repair, and owed bills of $5,500.

Even families in the top one-tenth income group report serious budget problems. A. C. Spectorsky made a study of wealthy families in Westchester County, New York, and found that many of them were spending about 40 percent over their annual income.

An interesting study by Mary E. Ryan and E. Scott Maynes[4] of 1,223 install-

[2] *Finance Facts Yearbook,* National Consumer Finance Association, Washington, 1972, p. 24.

[3] *The Spending Syndrome,* The University of Wisconsin Press, Madison, 1965.

[4] "The Excessively Indebted: Who and Why," *The Journal of Consumer Affairs,* Winter 1969, pp. 107–126.

ment debtor households selected from the Survey of Consumer Finances conducted by the University of Michigan Survey Research Center found that:

"The excessively indebted"

1.   Thirteen percent of installment debtors with incomes of $10,000 or more were in "some trouble." About 6 percent of the population of installment debtors are in this group.

2.   Eleven percent of the entire group were in "deep trouble," and 39 percent were in "some trouble" with respect to installment debt.

This study suggests that some segments of our population are "more prone to overextending their spending." These segments are likely to include the separated, divorced, widowed, and poor; those under age 25 and over age 65; and households headed by women and black households.

It appears, therefore, that debtor families who overspend, relative to their total incomes, place their budgets under pressure and hence may be expected to encounter trouble more frequently than debtor families who employ sensible management of their resources. In other words, management is the key to successful budgeting—not additional income, minus good management.

An exception to this generalization is the approximately 8 million families (1971) who receive less than $3,000 total family income. These families receive incomes *below* the minimum needed for bare necessities. Later in this chapter we shall discuss the special problems of families who are too poor to have the luxury of choosing how to spend their money.

The American life-style is product-centered

Even families in the top one-tenth income group report budget problems. What can the explanation for this be? Perhaps the American life-style is product-centered and materialistic and is reflected in consumer purchases and in the manner in which they are consumed. In general, most Americans spend money in order to meet the demands of their personal or family life-style, which is influenced by many forces such as culture, values, goals, resources, and communicative symbols. For example, the purchases of a single consumer could reflect the pattern of living of a neighbor. When a father with average income buys a bicycle just like his neighbor's, he is spending money to meet the demands of the life-styles which seem appropriate to him—usually for his own image.

Families, too, are concerned about making purchases that will reflect their current image as well as the image to which they aspire.

Cultural habits influence spending

Cultural patterns and habits of consumption influence our spending. Culture, for example, determines not only what food is eaten but also how it is prepared, and even the time of day it is consumed. Will it be grits and hot biscuits for breakfast or juice, eggs, bacon, toast, and coffee?

Cultural shopping patterns will often determine where one shops. Puerto Ricans and blacks in the urban ghettos are accustomed to shopping in their neighborhood from a market wagon, in small neighborhood stores, or from door-to-door salesmen. They also shop more frequently, and in some communities shopping is an important social activity.

Thus we see that the consumer isn't always as functionally oriented as he might be. Many things influence our spending: convenience, family pressures, economic factors, advertising, and feelings and wishes. Sometimes a consumer asks himself, "Do I need this?" More often he asks, "Do I want it?" or "Do I like it?" Less often he asks, "Can I afford it?"

At any rate, it appears that budgeting problems confront most American families regardless of age, income, life-style, and stage of family life cycle.

Budget demands during the family life cycle

In planning a budget, the family should try to predict or foresee its spending needs at different points in its life cycle. True, families vary in their life cycles, but much can be learned from consideration of typical life-cycle patterns.

Table 5-4 shows the life cycle for a moderate-income family. The age range for each stage of the family life cycle is shown in parentheses. The table does not give total dollar amounts consumed. For young singles the demand on the budget is usually light, but the tendency to spend is great. The recently married will have a heavy demand on the budget unless there are no children. Depending on the age of the parents, the primary-grade stage can be a period of considerable expenditure. With children in high school, the demands on the budget are heavy. When children are in college or at work, the budget demands can be very heavy (if in college) or light (if working on a job). During the preretirement and retirement period, the demand on the budget is generally light unless there are heavy medical bills not adequately covered by health and medical insurance.

Young single persons (44 million)

Young single adults, although less materialistic and pretentious than their parents, still are spenders. Business is quick to supply this group with what they want—like dungarees with a used, worn-out look. Barbers, losing business because of the "long-hair" trend, are promoting "stylists" at a high price. While the demand on a young single's budget need not be heavy, these young adults are spenders. Apparently, they prefer to "live rich rather than die rich."[5] They never lived through the terrible experience of the Great Depression (1929 to 1933), as most of their parents did, and so they think there will always be enough jobs and money. They have seen inflation at work, and they argue—with some merit—"why not buy now and pay later with cheaper dollars?"

The single person— "live rich rather than die rich"

Early marriage

Perhaps most young marrieds are living in their first apartment, in a trailer, or in communal housing with only a few personal items. The demands on the

[5] *U.S. News and World Report,* January 1972, p. 16.

TABLE 5-4 Family Life Cycle for a Moderate-Income Family

Family Life-Cycle Stage	Budget Demand
Young single (18–29 years)	Light
Early marriage (18–29 years)	Heavy (light if no children)
With children in primary grades (24–34 years)	Moderate
With children in high school (35–49 years)	Heavy
With children in college or at work (38–55 years)	Heavy (light)
Preretirement (50–64 years)	Light
Retirement (65 and over)	Light (if not ill)

budget need not be heavy unless they purchase new furniture and appliances or have children right away.

Marriage is like playing house

Incidentally, the Commission on Population Growth and the American Future estimated that it costs an American family about $90,000 to raise two children and to send them through four years of college.[6] This figure, based on current dollar values, represents both direct costs and the "opportunity" costs in lost earning power to the mother because she cannot work at a full-time job outside the home. The young wife, however, is apt to be working full time or part time outside the home for pay. In 1971, for example, the labor force included 41 percent of all married women. Even so, young marrieds tend to use credit cards, according to a University of Wisconsin study—73 percent of all couples under 35 years have installment credit. And many couples have a car on which they are making payments at the time of their marriage.

So many young couples who get married think marriage is like playing house—they're shocked when they find out how much it costs to play that game.

Children in primary grades

This is the time when the family may be trying to purchase a house in a neighborhood where there are better schools and a better environment. Studies of families in this stage of the life cycle indicate that they would prefer a house but that costs are usually too high. Consequently, they may satisfy their

Desire to own a home

desire for ownership by investing in a row house or other multifamily unit.

Health and medical costs can also be heavy unless the employer pays for good protection. Life insurance costs also enter the picture if inadequate coverage prevailed before.

Children in high school

This is a very expensive stage. Most parents of teen-agers find that they must spend a considerable amount of money for their recreation, clothes, and entertainment and for such items as television sets, record players, and records.

What shall we use for money?

At age 15 or 16 (depending on state laws), the teen-ager wants the family car or his own car. This puts a very heavy demand on the budget even if the teen-ager works summers or after school.

Major appliances may now be wearing out and require replacement. There may be a general increase in the standard of living, especially if the wife goes to work or the husband receives a few good increases in income.

This is the stage when even affluent families suddenly, if belatedly, realize that the youngsters are going to college! How can they manage this with inadequate savings?

Children in college or at work

The average costs for tuition and board and room rose 46 percent at public colleges and universities and 66 percent at private institutions between 1960 and 1970, according to the U.S. Department of Labor. In 1970, costs per year averaged $1,198 at public colleges and $2,520 at private colleges.[7]

Commuting students may require a car or money for traveling expenses. Money is needed for recreation and entertainment. Fortunately, brand-new wardrobes are not required for modern college students right now.

We know that many affluent families are not prepared for college expendi-

[6] *Finance Facts,* May 1972 (monthly).
[7] *Finance Facts,* January 1972 (monthly).

tures. Parents may be able to take money out of current income plus savings and pay for about half of the total college expenses. Some parents, however, can give their children only encouragement to continue their education. Going to college isn't an impossibility. We mentioned earlier that any student, with average grades or better, can complete his college or university education if he has good motivation and is in reasonably good health.

We didn't figure on inflation!

Besides the actual dollar costs of a college education, the family loses the unemployed student as a potential source of income. In the long run, however, the investment in a good college education or the equivalent in advanced vocational education produces a higher return in income and possibly satisfaction.

Preretirement

Income generally remains stable during this stage of the family life cycle unless the major breadwinner begins to work shorter hours. Usually, however, the demand on the budget is light. Many families increase their contributions to savings and investments at this time because the children are apt to be supporting themselves. And most major debts have been retired.

Family spending for entertainment, travel, and recreation, however, is apt to increase. There is also increased participation in community life, and more money is spent for books, clubs, and hobbies.

Retirement

Income during this stage is usually limited and fixed, coming from Social Security, savings, pensions, and perhaps investments.

Of the 22 million persons aged 65 and over in the United States, approximately 2 million live only on Social Security income. In fact, one out of four persons over age 65 is living a poverty existence (less than $3,000 a year for a two-person family).[8]

One in four over 65 lives in poverty

For most persons in the retirement stage, the demand on the budget is light unless chronic illness prevails and health insurance is inadequate.

This is the age, too, when many persons sell their home and move into an apartment or purchase a low-cost mobile home, which is easier to care for. Some aged persons are able to live in government-subsidized high-rise apartments.

Elderly people who sell their houses may choose to buy condominiums or cooperative apartments to avoid the capital gains tax on the income from the sale and to enjoy the advantages of ownership without the problems and cost of upkeep.

Some of the affluent retired population may be able to purchase a new car, travel, maintain seasonal residences, and engage in gardening, hunting, boating, and other activities.

In purchasing goods, older persons pay more attention to safety and comfort, and they spend a large amount on geriatric drugs and home and therapeutic remedies.

Considering the various stages of the family life cycle, then, it becomes obvious that intelligent budgeting, planning, and management have to take into account the changes that occur from one stage to another. And when retirement stares us in the face, most of us will look back over the years and say, "Family money *is* the hardest in the world to manage."

[8] *Finance Facts Yearbook,* 1972, p. 24.

RESPONSIBLE FAMILY SPENDING

Money management generally is mentioned as the most common cause, directly or indirectly, for marital discord. Family finance is often given as the most difficult problem in homemaking. It is one that causes much worry. The tendency of a young couple, very much in love, seems to be to expect that they will meet the financial problems *when they arise.* Such persons say, "When all is well, why plan?"

The tragedy among some families with this "meet it when it comes up" philosophy is that they refuse to meet or see the facts when the situation occurs. Other families, however, do meet the situation, but only by salvaging the results of their lack of planning beforehand. Such persons would not think of selecting a man to head a business or a surgeon to perform an operation unless he had had adequate training. Yet so many couples, deeply in love, are willing to go into marriage without knowing how to be wise managers of money.

People who cannot live within their income are, in general, poor managers. Money, like time and talent, can be wasted. Money has to be managed intelligently, or you will be on the losing side. And being on the losing side in money management is a serious matter, because you are playing a game for family happiness—for keeps.

How then do you prepare yourself for winning such an important game? The answer is training. Back of training, however, is attitude. The first prerequisite to wise management of money is attitude.

So much attention has been given to personality maladjustments as a cause of marital discord that we are likely to forget that normal people can achieve creative adjustments. A normal couple discover the facts, face them honestly, and seek an insight into their own pattern of behavior. We know from studies that happily married people are successful homemakers, not because they have no problems but because they face their problems and arrive at a working solution. An important attitude toward handling family finances successfully is the desire for joint planning, joint earning, and joint spending to the end that every member of the family gets the utmost satisfaction from the money spent.

Does it really pay to budget? In these days of inflated prices, why not put the salary in the bank and write checks as long as the money lasts?

Before answering this question, let's take a fresh look at two typical American families—the Johnsons and the Shaws. The names are fictitious, but the events are true.

A sad success story This is the story of Tom and Sue Johnson. Tom is a junior executive in a manufacturing plant. He believes that his future depends upon symbols—a fine house, a good social life, and an attractive wife to help him reach these objectives.

Tom believes he has a modern attitude toward marriage. Sue is a partner, not a semiservant. At the end of a short honeymoon, Tom announced quite firmly that he was turning the family money management job over to his wife. "My job," he said, "is to bring the checks home, and you're the one who buys the food and other things, so you pay the bills and keep the records."

Sue agreed. She knew next to nothing about family financial management, but she agreed to carry out her end of the deal.

Successful budgeting requires thought

In the ensuing months, Tom, freed from balancing the checkbook, went on spending sprees to improve the family image. This was the reason he bought a new hi-fi. No package deal for them—"We want the real components."

He got the stereo system, and Sue got the bill for $845!

Tom got a promotion, and then another promotion. His salary jumped from $8,500 to $13,000. Who couldn't move to the nice suburbs with that kind of money, and more to come later? So, to the suburbs they went.

Shortly after arriving in their new environment, Sue discovered that she was pregnant. "That settles it," said Tom. "We have to have a bigger place." A four-year-old house for $30,000 became a reality with no down payment (there were no savings) and VA mortgage payments of $165 a month for thirty years to cover principal, interest, taxes, and insurance.

During the next three years, they purchased new furnishings for the living room, den, and recreation room, all with small down payments and with the use of their "magic" credit cards.

The promotions didn't come as anticipated. One day the rugs and furniture were repossessed. In all, they racked up $8,462 in debts for twelve major items including $1,800 yet owed on a new car.

Sue tried to keep the bill collectors satisfied by paying a small amount to each of them. Her monthly fixed costs were $1,290, and Tom's take-home pay was $852!

Tom had no idea that he was almost insolvent. His future appeared promising at the company. But Sue was caught in the middle between pressing collectors and Tom, who thought she was doing fine.

"After all," she later confided to a family financial counselor, "Tom made $13,000 a year!"

Tom, an honorable person, refused to declare bankruptcy. Instead, he chose to sell the house, and they moved in with Sue's widowed mother. Tom took a "moonlighting" job to speed up the credit payments. Sue wanted a job, but her ulcers prohibited it. In the years that followed, Tom, a man who earned a good living, gave up his expensive spending sprees.

Senseless budgeting

This is the case of John and Ann Shaw, both just under 30 years of age and the parents of one child, a 4-year-old daughter. John earns $7,300 as a draftsman, and Ann does not work.

Ann announced one evening—without warning—that they were going on a budget. "Why?" John wanted to know. Because a nasty letter had come in the mail that morning from a bill collector's office, coupled with a telephone call from the credit manager of a department store, both demanding immediate payment. She said that all the bills were embarrassing and that they would be out on the street in a month or two.

A straitjacket budget is worse than no budget

Ann quite understandably sought security in a budget. She was determined to make her budget absolutely foolproof—no more worries about bills and more bills.

They did need a budget because John tended to go overboard in purchasing many little items for the home and taking Ann to expensive restaurants, often running up bills of $30 an evening plus baby-sitting expenses. They should have set up a savings program, they said many times, but that had low priority.

So, one evening, Ann said she was going to institute a tight budget for everyone. She doled out 25 cents here and 50 cents there (in keeping with a budget suggestion from a magazine). She cut her food bill down to $60 a month from $125, and limited cocktails to one each on Saturday nights.

In the following year, she relentlessly held the family down to the skimpy budget. It was touch and go. The car needed a $62 engine repair job, John had a dental bill for $35, and their daughter needed a larger bed—secondhand for $15.

There were other needs, and so John's haircut money went for gasoline. More juggling of the budget occurred. They fared even worse in their human relations. Their conversations soon centered on money and bills.

"Why do you have to have a big lunch downtown? Isn't a cup of coffee and sandwich enough? Don't I feed you at home?" And she would go off to sulk.

A few months of this, and John asked her whether they could reach some kind of compromise on the budget.

"You mean compromise on our lives," Ann said. "A compromise that will wreck us. Well, we don't need a compromise. We need a man who can live within the bounds of his own earning abilities."

There were more conversations like this in the months that followed. It was now clear to John that the budget was running the family. A bill collector came to the house one morning, and Ann hit the ceiling. She had made out the check a week ago! That evening when Tom came home, Ann screamed at him as he walked through the door, "Isn't it bad enough that you aren't able to support us? Couldn't you remember to mail the checks I gave you a week ago? Grant's called today for their money, and I felt like two cents. What did you do with the checks?"

John later told his lawyer, when arranging for a separation, that he had had it "up to here," pointing to his throat.

What lesson can we learn from these two rather typical cases? Were both families confused in the way they managed their finances? The Johnsons were in need of a monthly financial record, and the Shaws learned, the hard way, that a straitjacket budget can be worse than no budget at all.

The family that makes no plan for the financial future is asking for trouble, for no person can escape the shadow of a bill collector forever. At the other extreme, the family that sticks rigidly to a budget plan, come hell or high water, takes the zest out of living—and, worse, the love out of living, too.

Family budget plan (budgeting without bookkeeping)

There are a variety of ways of handling financial chores. What is best for one family may not be good for another. The success of any system depends on the personalities and abilities of the people involved.

For beginners, in particular, Table 5-5 suggests a reasonable distribution for a four-person family at three different income levels living in an urban community.

Consumption items came to only 81 percent of the total for the lower budget; and gifts, contributions, life insurance, social security, and personal income taxes accounted for 19 percent. In the intermediate budget, consumption items represented 79 percent; for the higher budget, these items represented 75 percent of the total.

TABLE 5-5   Three Budgets for a Four-Person Family, 1971*

	LOWER BUDGET	INTERMEDIATE BUDGET	HIGHER BUDGET
TOTAL BUDGET	*$7,214*	*$10,971*	*$15,905*
Total family consumption	5,841	8,626	11,935
Food	1,964	2,532	3,198
Housing	1,516	2,638	3,980
Transportation	536	964	1,250
Clothing, personal care	848	1,196	1,740
Medical care	609	612	638
Other consumption items	368	684	1,129
Other items	357	560	937
Taxes	1,016	1,785	3,033
Social Security and disability payments	387	419	419
Personal income taxes	629	1,366	2,614

* U.S. Department of Labor, Bureau of Labor Statistics, *Autumn 1971 Urban Family Budgets,* April 1972, pp. 1–3.

Budgeting is planning and management

The food budget (at home and restaurants) was 34 percent of the consumption budget at the lower level, 29 percent at the intermediate level, and 27 percent at the higher level. (For more details, see Taylor-Troelstrup Reading 14).

These allocations reflect a reasonable manner of living at each of these three levels at Autumn 1971 prices. Allowances, however, will have to be made for inflation since that time.

Those who are interested in consumption budgets for different family types—such as single persons under 35 years; husband and wife under 35 years with no children and with one and two children; husband and wife 65 years and older; and single persons 65 years and older—should consult the Taylor-Troelstrup Reading 24).

Beginning budgeters might find these figures and percentages useful as a general guide, making allowances, as we said, for inflation increases from year to year. Adjustments can be made on the basis of your experience, geographic location, and desires. The important thing to keep in mind is that budgeting is planning and management based upon realistic data—not bookkeeping.

Family budget plan: a divided responsibility

Changing Times magazine[9] recently invited some husbands and wives to sit down and talk about who paid the bills, who kept the records (if any), and who decided how much to spend on what. These couples had tried various budgeting plans and were quite satisfied with the systems they used because they worked for them. The most common plan for managing the income involved

Sharing budgeting tasks

"both spouses in a more or less equal sharing of the tasks." This system minimizes bookkeeping or eliminates it entirely. It meets the test of any good method of delegating financial responsibilities in a family in that it keeps the proper people informed about money matters. It is also convenient to use, and the couples interviewed were happy with it. Those are the elements that make any system work.

[9] "Divvying up the Family Money Chores," *Changing Times,* July 1972, pp. 36–38.

Budgeting by "divvying up"

A good budget expresses relative values

We said that family budgeting is planning and management—not book-keeping. Keeping accurate records of spending may be useful the first time you set up a plan, but it is not necessary after a family budget plan that "divvies up" responsibility is under way. Just keep the receipts and canceled checks for tax and reference purposes.

Dr. Carl F. Hawver prepared such a divided-responsibility *family budget plan* (FBP) for the National Consumer Finance Association. He offers these suggestions:[10]

1.   Figure your weekly cash needs and enter them in the proper column on the Worksheet for Family Spending. Follow normal pattern as to who spends what.

2.   Figure your "other" needs on a monthly basis and enter them in the "other monthly" columns. Don't forget to include bills such as insurance, taxes, etc., that come in less often than once a month. Divide their annual totals by 12 and place in "other monthly" column.

3.   Total "His" and "Hers" expenses together and compare average monthly income. Cut back expenses if necessary to stay within income, and still allow for regular savings programs.

After these three steps, no books need be kept. The plan will take some adjusting based on experience and goals, but soon it will fit a particular family. Then it will need no change until there is a change in income, age of children or in goals.

4.   It is easier to work this plan if all income is placed in a checking account. Cash needs will be met by cashing weekly checks in the amount determined in the plan. All other money will remain in the checking account so it will be available when monthly and less frequent bills are to be paid.

5.   Arrangements can be made at the bank for an automatic transfer of the planned amount from the checking account to the savings account. This guarantees that the savings amount as planned will be there, and will grow. This is far better than the old practice of putting into a savings account only what was left over after all bills are paid. Under that system, there never seemed to be anything left!

Now see the worksheet excerpts below.

EXPLANATION OF FAMILY BUDGET PLAN WORKSHEET ITEMS

CASH WEEKLY Some expenses are usually paid with cash. Such cash should be given out weekly. The husband and wife should each pick a regular day to write a check for HIS (and HER) regular cash needs for the week.

OTHER MONTHLY These columns include all other expense items and also savings and money being accumulated for bills that come in less often than once a month, like taxes, insurance, Christmas bills, etc.

HERS	**HIS**
LINE NO.	LINE NO.
1. *Food* is usually a "cash" item. The wife may choose to cash her check at the grocery store.	58. Add lines 52 through 57 and enter total also on line 88.
2. *Grocery store purchases* may	60. When payments on a car are finished, some families continue

[10] 1000 Sixteenth Street, N.W., Washington, D.C. 20036. Permission granted by the National Consumer Finance Association to use worksheets for family spending and explanations of worksheet items.

HERS

LINE NO.

include more than food (cigarets, soft drinks, paper goods, etc.).

3. Milk is usually much cheaper if purchased at the store with other groceries.

4. If the wife works, she may need to purchase lunches.

7. *Total:* Add both columns and put *food totals* on this line and on line 38 below.

8. *House operation:* These are costs faced by wife in keeping the house going.

9. *Electricity:* (if possible, average last twelve bills to get a realistic figure.)

10. *Gas:* (if possible, average last twelve bills to get a realistic figure.)

11. *Heating fuel:* (average over twelve months even though heat is only used six or eight months.)

12. *Telephone:* Establish a realistic average. Watch long distance charges for waste.

13. *Water:* Bills are frequently paid quarterly or semiannually. Establish a monthly average.

14. *Household help:* This included baby-sitters for working mothers, window washers, maids, lawn care, etc. Establish a realistic average.

15. *Furniture and equipment:* Repair and replacement of furniture and electrical appliances all over the home.

16. *Personal allowance:* The wife, like every member of the family, should have some money for personal items and gifts. This includes hair care, etc.

17. *Children's allowances:* Youngsters can frequently earn enough for their needs, and so will not have to take from family income. If not, they need enough allowance to cover school lunches, transportation to school and some entertainment.

18. *Newspapers and magazines:* This is in "HER" budget because the wife usually is home to pay the

HIS

LINE NO.

putting aside the same amount as savings toward the next car. This helps stabilize the budget.

61. This item covers public transportation necessary for work.

67. Add lines 60 through 66 and enter total also on line 89.

69. Each member of the family should have some personal allowance for his own needs and wishes. This is HIS.

72. This item includes education for all members of the family including the husband's training for a better job and special savings programs for college for the children.

73. Doctors, dentists, x-rays, etc., not covered by insurance.

74. All personal insurance, life, hospital, major medical, etc., not included in payroll deductions.

75. Dues and fees for unions, clubs, all organizations.

76. If you are self-employed or if your employer does not deduct enough to pay all your income tax, use this line to accumulate what you'll need for quarterly payments to the Internal Revenue Service.

77. This worksheet is intended to reflect *normal* expenditures for each item. If you have back debts when you *start* on the plan, figure how much you can pay on them each month and enter here. When they are paid off, this amount should be added to savings.

80. Add lines 69 through 79 and put total here and on line 90.

82. A single savings account can serve a family well until it gets so big that part can be invested to bring greater return. Savings for special things can be handled by percentages. For example, a family may agree to use 10 percent of all they save during a year for a vacation—20 percent may be deposited in a special account at the end of the year to build a fund for Johnny's college,

HERS

LINE NO.

paper boy and frequently sub-scribes to magazines.

20. See item 77 for explanation.

23. *Total:* Put totals in both columns of this line and on line 39 below.

28. Put totals on this line and on line 40 below.

36. Put totals on this line and on line 41 below.

42. Add lines 38, 39, 40 and 41 (both columns) and place totals in line 42.

43. Take total in "cash weekly" from line 42 and multiply by 4.33 to convert to a monthly figure. Put total in column 2.

44. In column 2 ("other monthly") add lines 42 and 43. Enter this also on line 95, in column 2.

45. Enter in column 1 the amount of your take-home pay and show how often you get paid (every seven days, fourteen days, fifteen days, thirty days, etc.). In column 2 show how much this will be per month: to convert, multiply weekly salary by 4.33. If you get paid every other week, divide check by 2 and multiply by 4.33. If you get paid twice a month (first and fifteenth), multiply by 2.

46. Enter here all "other" income of all members of the family from all sources if this is to be deposited in the family checking account. Do *not* include the pay check listed in 45. Show *monthly* total.

47. In column 2, add lines 45 and 46 and enter also on line 97, column 2.

HIS

LINE NO.

etc. *All* savings for whatever purpose go on this line.

83. Enter here any regular bond, mutual fund, employee stock option or other regular investment you make.

84. Enter here the cost of retirement income program you pay for except that deducted by your employer before you get your pay check.

86. Add lines 82 through 85 and put total here and on line 91.

92. Add lines 88 through 91 (both columns).

93. Multiply total of CASH WEEKLY (column 1, line 92) by 4.33 to get monthly figure. Put total in column 2.

94. Add lines 92 and 93 in column 2.

95. Transfer total from line 44 into column 2.

96. Add lines 94 and 95.

97. Transfer from line 47. This should be same figure as line 96. If 97 is larger put excess in savings—line 82. If expenses (line 96) are larger than income (line 97) cut expenses somewhere to bring down to income level.

WORKSHEET FOR FAMILY SPENDING DIVIDED-RESPONSIBILITY PLAN

See item-by-item explanation accompanying this worksheet. To convert weekly figures into monthly figures, multiply by 4.33.

Name: _____

Date: _____

LINE NO. HERS	COL. 1 CASH WEEKLY	COL. 2 OTHER MONTHLY	LINE NO. HIS	COL. 1 CASH WEEKLY	COL. 2 OTHER MONTHLY
1. FOOD			51. SHELTER		
2. Grocery store			52. Rent or mortgage		
3. Milk (if delivered)			53. Maintenance on home		
4. Lunches for working wife			54. Property taxes		
5.			55. Home insurance		
6.			56.		
7. Total			57.		
8. HOUSE OPERATION			58. Total		
9. Electricity			59. TRANSPORTATION		
10. Gas			60. Auto payments (or saving for new car)		
11. Heating fuel			61. Bus, taxi, or train		
12. Telephone			62. Gas & oil for car		
13. Water			63. Auto tires & repair		
14. Household help			64. Auto insurance		
15. Furniture & equipment			65.		
16. Personal allowance			66.		
17. Children's allowances			67. Total		
18. Newspapers & magazines			68. PERSONAL		
19. Dues & fees			69. Personal allowance		

	COL. 1	COL. 2		COL. 1	COL. 2
LINE NO. HERS	CASH WEEKLY	OTHER MONTHLY	LINE NO. HIS	CASH WEEKLY	OTHER MONTHLY
20. Payments on old bills			70. Family entertainment		
21.			71. Vacation fund		
22.			72. Education		
23. Total			73. Medicine & medical care		
24. CLOTHING			74. All insurance (health, life, etc.)		
25. Clothes for all family			75. Dues and fees		
26. Cleaning & laundry			76. Income taxes not deducted		
27.			77. Payments on old bills		
28. Total			78. Lunches for working husbands		
29. CONTRIBUTIONS			79.		
30. Churches			80. Total		
31. Christmas gifts			81. SAVINGS & INVESTMENTS		
32. Nonfamily gifts			82. Savings		
33. Family gifts			83. Regular investments		
34. Charities			84. Self-paid retirement plan		
35.			85.		
36. Total			86. Total		
37. SUMMARY: HER EXPENSES			87. SUMMARY: HIS EXPENSES		
38. Food			88. Shelter		
39. House operation			89. Transportation		
40. Clothing			90. Personal		
41. Contributions			91. Savings & Investment		
42. Total HER Expense			92. Total HIS Expense		

	COL. 1	COL. 2		COL. 1	COL. 2
LINE NO. HERS	CASH WEEKLY	OTHER MONTHLY	LINE NO. HIS	CASH WEEKLY	OTHER MONTHLY
43. Total cash × 4.33			93. Total cash × 4.33		
44. Total HER monthly expense			94. Total HIS monthly expense		
45. Pay check for ____ days			95. Plus HER monthly expense		
46. Other income			96. Average monthly expense		
47. Average monthly income			97. Average monthly income		

The family budget plan (FBP) worksheet is basic to successful family budgeting using the divided-responsibility plan. Most families will also use the paycheck control (PCC) sheet, which defines family goals on a monthly basis. This control sheet spells out the way each paycheck should be allocated to meet the planned expenditures shown on the worksheet.

The future goals control (FGC) sheet is designed to be used with the PCC sheet and the FBP worksheet. This control sheet helps the family achieve future goals by encouraging them (1) to establish such goals and (2) to develop a program to provide the money to pay for them.

(The detailed explanation of these two worksheets—the FGC and the PCC—appears in Taylor-Troelstrup Reading 25.)

Statement of net worth: annual inventory

Statements of net worth should be made annually so that the family will be aware of its financial progress. Net worth is the value of the family holdings (assets) minus current obligations (liabilities). Table 5-6 suggests typical kinds of assets and liabilities.

What valuations should you place on these holdings? Original cost is the easiest to determine, but may be too conservative during inflation years. Market sale value, however, is likely to be the most logical. Original cost usually does not reflect the true worth of goods because they generally lose value through obsolescence and depreciation. One can, of course, make allowances for depreciation as well as for increase in the value of goods. At any rate, it is obvious that valuation is not simple. Perhaps the wise thing to do is to keep an inventory of household furnishings and personal effects, indicating date of purchase and original cost.

Family assets are classified as *liquid* and *nonliquid*. Liquid assets, like stocks and savings accounts, can be converted to cash immediately. Nonliquid assets, like the market value of a house, the resale value of a car, or the cash value of a retirement fund, cannot be converted as easily to cash. For example, there may or may not be an active market for a used car. There may be a seller's market (high price) at one time and a buyer's market (low price) at another.

TABLE 5-6 Statement of Family Net Worth

Liquid assets:	
Cash on hand	$_____
Cash in checking account	_____
Savings account	_____
Market value of listed stocks	_____
Market value of listed bonds	_____
Life insurance cash surrender value	_____
Other	_____
Nonliquid assets:	
Market value of house	$_____
Market value of furniture, furnishings	_____
Car resale value	_____
Annuity cash value	_____
Retirement fund cash value	_____
Bid prices on unlisted stocks	_____
Bid prices on unlisted bonds	_____
Market value of buildings	_____
Market value of raw land	_____
Money loaned on mortgage	_____
Accounts receivable	_____
Other	_____
Total assets	_____
Liabilities:	
Bank loan	$_____
Loan on life insurance	_____
Mortgage on home	_____
Bills payable at stores	_____
Installment debt	_____
Other	_____
Total liabilities	_____
Net worth, December 31, 19_____	$_____

Most families are apt to have their major liability in the form of a mortgage on their home. Open charge accounts are usually due in thirty days. Installment contracts are quite common when the family purchases a car or new furniture for the house. These are all liabilities to the family.

We said that net worth is assets minus liabilities. The statement of net worth is often called a *balance sheet.*

Plans for use of net worth

Setting up an annual net-worth statement will enable a family to keep track of its financial progress from one year to the next. It serves as a sort of "save now and pay later" scheme. If successful, it can enable the family to reduce its use of expensive credit when the time comes to replace the car, pay for a vacation, repair the house, create an emergency fund, pay for a college education for the children, add to retirement income, or replace household appliances. Table 5-7 illustrates the use of "save now and pay later" in the case of replacing household equipment and appliances.

Save now and pay later
Planning in advance does it

Table 5-7 shows how the "buy now and pay later" and the "save now and buy later" plans would work in the purchase of five household items. Under the "buy now" plan, the items are purchased and paid for in monthly installments, as provided in a mail-order company's credit plan for the purchase of

TABLE 5-7 Save Now and Buy Later*

| | CASH PRICE | CREDIT CHARGE† | CASH PRICE PLUS CREDIT CHARGE | MONTHLY PAYMENT† | NUMBER OF MONTHS REQUIRED | |
					To Pay Credit Price	To Save the Cash Price at Monthly Payment Rate‡
Range	$ 224	$ 44	$ 268	$10.50	25.5	21.3
Refrigerator	250	49	299	11.00	27.2	22.7
Washing machine	242	49	291	11.00	26.5	22.0
Clothes dryer	183	35	218	9.00	24.2	20.3
Dishwasher	160	26	186	7.50	24.8	21.3
Total	1,059	203	1,262		128.2	107.6

*Family Economics Review, June 1964, p. 11.

†Based on the installment credit plan offered by a certain mail-order company for purchases of appliances. This plan allows 36 months to pay for a $500 purchase with shorter periods for smaller amounts.

‡Smaller final payments are represented by fractional months.

appliances. Under the "save now" plan, they are paid for in cash saved in monthly amounts equal to the installment payments.

The family that saved and bought for cash would have the five items (bought one after the other) in nine years. The family that used the installment credit plan would need twenty months more than nine years to pay for the same five items because there would be an extra $200 in credit charges. In this same twenty-month period the first family, by saving the amount of the installment payments, could accumulate cash enough to buy an item such as a television set or a room air conditioner in addition. "Save now and buy later" is a sort of "magic money" game that most of us have forgotten how to play. Perhaps more families will discover that they can be winners in the game of "save and invest" for future planned purchases. After all, credit cannot add dollars to income, but saving and investing can.

Inflation eats family budget

When planning a budget, it is necessary to keep in mind the decrease in purchasing power of the dollar, due largely to inflation in prices and increases in local, state, and federal taxes. These two substantial increases in the cost of living generally help to answer the budgeter's eternal complaint: Where does the money go?

To most consumers, such measures of living costs as the Consumer Price Index probably are too abstract to have much impact, but the dollars-and-cents figures for family budgets should give every family a jolt. The latest figures of the Bureau of Labor Statistics—lagging six months behind the date's costs—showed the following in Autumn 1971:

A decrease in purchasing power

1. The budget for an urban family of four, at an "intermediate" living standard of $10,971, is up from $9,076 4½ years earlier. This represents a 20 percent rise to maintain the same standard of living.

2. For a higher standard of living, $15,905 is needed, compared with the earlier figure of $13,050—up 22 percent. The Bureau's "lower-level" budget was up 22 percent also, rising from $5,915 to $7,214.

3. To put the matter of family costs in context, there have been accompanying gains in personal income. Otherwise, some of us would be in the poorhouse. Currently consumers are in the middle of a two-way squeeze: on one side rising prices, and on the other the fact that taxes have been absorbing increasing proportions of personal income.

4. To see what the combination of inflation and heavier taxes has done to family living costs in recent years, take a look at the Conference Board figures (Figure 5-1), showing that $18,570 was needed in 1972 to equal the purchasing power of $10,000 in 1949. During the intervening years, the bite taken out of that income by federal and Social Security taxes increased by $2,100. At the same time, inflation cut purchasing power by $6,470. Thus, $10,000 = $18,570, and you can add to the latter figure whatever state and local taxes you pay. They're so variable that the Conference Board left them out.

What inflation's squeeze is adding up to currently is a good deal more than the price "bulge" the federal government said would occur after the "freeze." There are likely to be increasing complaints that Phase IV isn't working and more demands for tougher policies and tougher enforcement.

FIGURE 5-1   Income in 1965 and 1972 necessary to equal 1949 purchasing power

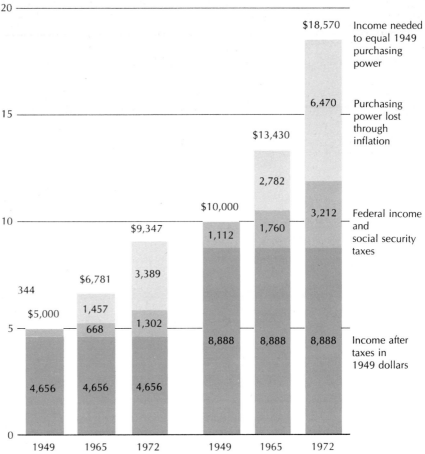

Thousands of dollars

SOURCE: The Conference Board. Reproduced in *Finance Facts,* June, 1972.

How some families cope
with inflation

Changing Times magazine (August 1971) received some twenty-five thousand letters from its readers on the subject of coping with recent inflationary costs. The accompanying table lists the items that families have cut down on the most.

What you can do
about inflation

ITEM	PERCENTAGE OF READERS
Recreation	59
Food away from home	52
Purchase of household appliances and furniture	48
Clothing	45
Purchase of car	30
Food at home	17
Operation of car	12
Homeownership	6
Medical care	5

The other categories in which families cut down included public transportation, 5 percent; education, 4 percent; fuel and utilities, 4 percent; and rent, 3 percent.

It is interesting that most people don't cut down on the items that have shown the highest price rise. Recreation, for example, has had only a moderate price rise, and yet most of the readers cited this cutback. Obviously, most people cut back in items which are discretionary in character—clothing, food away from home, and furniture. Items such as rent can hardly be cut at all. One reader went so far as to say he was living on roots, nuts, and berries!

When financial crises come

You may wonder why an account of family financial crises is included here. The most important reason is that no family can escape financial crises. Virtually all families, at one time or another, face one or more of the following family crises: loss of a child, orphanhood, hospitalization, widowhood, non-support, infidelity, illegitimacy, desertion, suicide, imprisonment, homicide, divorce, loss of job, sudden increase in income, and so forth. To the price paid in emotional stress are added always dollars-and-cents charges.

Death, the crisis perhaps least talked about, will normally come to the average family several times. Sudden impoverishment hovers constantly over all families except perhaps the wealthiest. Sudden and appreciable increases in income are difficult for many families to meet and too often become the focal point in family quarrels.

Many of these crises are financial blows when they come and should be a part of prudent money management planning. The sensible conclusion is to be prepared, as much as possible—to regard them as challenges. The main question, then, is not "How can family crises be avoided?" but rather "How can family crises be met?" Is it only a question of more income?

Would more money solve your problems?
Almost all families have financial crises

The fact remains that, for many families, wants seem to be one jump ahead of income no matter how high the income. Some years ago a Gallup poll asked this question: "What do you want most for your family?" The answer, in overwhelming numbers, was "Ten percent more income."

That was in 1956. Apparently our economy rubbed Aladdin's lamp, and the responding genie worked overtime. The real income of the average American family rose not a mere 10 percent, but over ten times that much. Measured in 1970 dollars, the average family that earned $100 a week in 1956 earned over $212 in 1970.

We are a lot better off financially. Most families have upgraded their standard of living. There is more money for homes, cars, appliances, color TV sets, new furniture, vacations, clothing, stereo, and motorboats. On the surface all is well. But probe a little deeper and you can see both boon and blight. Along with many material comforts have come financial woes of which our thrift-minded grandfathers never dreamed.

The astonishing contradiction of our time is the failure of a disturbingly large number of families to avoid financial stress in the face of continuously increasing real incomes. Money troubles beset many older families, but especially younger people just getting started.

At least half of our families owe money on possessions (not including homes). The nation's installment debt was over $109.5 billion in 1971. Add to this over $282.3 billion of home mortgage debts that still have to be paid off, and the outlines of the financial burden begin to become clear. All this affluence is by no stretch of the imagination bought and paid for.

A good part of the take-home pay is tagged for the bill collector even before it is received. Nationally, about $14 out of every $100 in take-home pay has a lien on it to pay installments due. Ten years ago, the figure was considerably lower. But creditors must be paid. If they are not, then a catastrophe like bankruptcy, accompanied by severe emotional reactions, is likely.

We find, however, that many families experience a sudden substantial loss in income. And contrary to general opinion, even sudden substantial increase in income does not automatically solve problems of people who still feel financially poor and insecure.

Sudden loss in family income

During economic depressions or recessions, more families experience serious income losses than at any other period. A major recession creates a crisis in family life, through loss of work and income, for which some families have no accustomed responses. The family may have to abandon certain plans, such as buying a home. It may not be able to continue membership in certain social clubs and thus no longer conforms to its social standards. It may not be able to pay bills on time, a standard in which it has always taken pride. It may experience the shifting of a dominant role from father to mother or to an older child. Not only is the entire family disorganized, but each member of the family may be personally disorganized over the loss of accustomed activities, over failure to meet financial responsibility, or over a feeling of lowered status.

The realization that the family cannot continue its past habits of social life usually causes severe emotional reactions. This period of acute emotional stress is terminated either by an adjustment to the situation or by the development of pathological reactions. If a family completely breaks or fails to adjust, the family life may disintegrate, or one member may be led to escape through mental illness, suicide, or running away.[11]

How can a family effectively meet a financial crisis? There are, say the experts, no pat answers. The following actions have aided some families.[12]

1. Face the facts as a family.
2. Agree on a temporary plan or procedure.
3. Clear the air of accusations with reference to "fixing the blame."
4. Cooperate in reducing expenses sufficiently.
5. Cooperate in pooling all family income for family use.
6. Discover together new cultural and psychological resources.
7. Look forward to reestablishing the business or profession.

Sudden increase in family income

There are no adequate studies of the effect of sudden prosperity on families and their members. But most of us know families that have had such an experience. Perhaps we also know, in a general way, that disintegration often takes place among such families. Apparently, family happiness is not automatically achieved by a sudden increase in family income.

It is not a simple case of saying, "Now we can get what we have always wanted and do the things we have always wanted to do." Foster and Wilson, in reporting on the case study of seventy-eight married women, concluded that

[11] Ruth S. Cavan and Katherine H. Ranck, *The Family and the Depression,* The University of Chicago Press, Chicago, 1938, pp. 6–7.

[12] Howard Becker and Reuben Hill (eds.), *Marriage and the Family,* D. C. Heath and Company, Boston, 1942, pp. 531–533.

"even when the income was increased, further obligations, a little exceeding the increase, were incurred."[13]

While we do not have sufficient accurate information on the effects of sudden prosperity, it may be that well-organized families remain organized, and disorganized families may tend to disintegrate further. Whether we agree with the above assumption or not, most of us will agree that any experience holds the potential of being either a destructive crisis experience or a constructive learning experience.

In the interest of reducing the chances of amily unhappiness, we need to learn how to meet family crises. Crises involving decreases or sudden increases in family income can disintegrate family life on the one hand or serve as the means of discovering or rediscovering a new and pleasant family relationship. Financial crises cannot be separated from other aspects of life. No problem is met in an isolated group of circumstances, but in relation to the total life of an individual.

The high cost of divorce

We are concerned here primarily with the dollar cost of divorce. This is not to suggest that the psychological, emotional, and personality costs are not as important as the financial price. Since all these aspects are interrelated, no single factor can be recognized as most important.

To the price paid in emotional stress in divorce must be added the dollar cost. Today, when one out of every three marriages ends in divorce and separation, we need to know about some of the less-known facts of the economic costs of divorce.

Some wit has called desertion a "poor man's divorce." The high dollar cost of divorce works in the other direction at times. Rather than desert, and unable to pay for a divorce, the couple may decide to remain married.

There is no such thing as a bargain divorce

We might as well try to answer: "How high is up?" as to attempt to give actual money costs of divorce. Every state has different divorce laws, and lawyers' fees are not standard. There are cut-rate divorces, but dangers are involved in these. Sometimes cases are handled dishonestly. Consequently, it is difficult to know whether one is legally divorced. Whatever the costs are, the final money arrangements will depend on the financial condition of the husband. If considerable money is spent seeking a divorce, less money is available afterward for the divorced couple.

A recent scale of bar association *minimum* fees for uncontested divorces showed that some New York counties have the highest figure—$500. The low of $75 was posted in some Texas counties. By region, the most expensive is New York–New Jersey–Pennsylvania, where minimums range from $150 to $500. Cheapest is the Southwest, with its range from $75 to $250. Of course, actual fees usually exceed the minimum. In a Midwestern city, for example, the legal fees for a contested divorce case of a family with a modest weekly take-home pay of $136.81 amounted to $1,800. Another uncontested case in New York for a couple with only average income cost $2,000 in legal fees. These two families are not alone, but are among some 1 million persons divorced annually in the United States in asking, "Why should a divorce be so costly?" Actually, many marriage counselors, clergymen, social workers, judges, and family service

---

[13] Robert G. Foster and Pauline Park Wilson, *Women after College,* Columbia University Press, New York, 1942, p. 52.

experts ask the same question. Men like Clark W. Blackburn, general director of the Family Service Association of America, believe that we need to reduce or eliminate the crushing financial burden on a couple dissolving marriage. These experts are not advocating "easy divorce," because they believe in thorough counseling to save the marriage. But once it becomes obvious that divorce is unavoidable, they recommend a quick, simple, and inexpensive termination.

Alimony plus support

The heaviest expenses in any divorce are alimony and the sum decreed for the support of children. In 1971 in the United States, there were over 3.8 million divorcees who received over $6 billion in alimony. The figures in Table 5-8 give a general picture of how much a divorce costs in alimony and support of children.

The amounts of alimony and support are usually based on the financial condition of the husband and wife; their earning capacity and property; the inheritance of either of them; the manner of living to which they are accustomed; the duration of their marriage; their age, health, and social position; and which of them is the guilty party and to what extent.

The real crux of how much a husband must pay, at least for the average-salaried person, is the time-honored phrase, "the manner of living to which they are accustomed." The courts generally will not let a wife improve her standard of living by getting a divorce. Most divorce lawyers have a form that provides them with fairly concrete proof of the standard of living to which a wife has been accustomed and of the money needed to support the children.

The ease of divorce in many states is an economic delusion to men of modest means. Some divorces are necessary, marriage experts say, no matter what the resultant hardships may be. But the impulsive divorce is not only a moral mistake but a financial one. Every available possibility for reconciliation should be thoroughly explored.

"No-fault" divorce cuts costs

A couple in Oregon ended their three-year marriage without the services of a lawyer. They paid $69 in court costs and saved the $250 that the Oregon State Bar lists as minimum attorney's fee in a divorce case.

A do-it-yourself divorce

The law trims red tape and eliminates the dogma that says that either the husband or wife must be to blame when a marriage fails. Like California's no-fault divorce law, it accepts "irreconcilable differences" as a basis for divorce. And, in cases where both parties agree and where neither children nor property is involved, it seems to bring divorce a step closer to the procedural technicality of a wedding.

TABLE 5-8   Alimony Plus Support

INCOME PER WEEK	ALIMONY (NO CHILDREN)	ALIMONY AND SUPPORT (CHILDREN)
$100	$ 40	$ 55 - 60
200	75	100 - 120
311	105	140 - 165

An enterprising person who has the time can do it without too much trouble, says an Oregon circuit judge. All the formal papers are available at about 10 cents each. Divorce kits are also available for about 25 cents.

These divorce kits can be dangerous, cautions the executive director of the Oregon State Bar. He said, "There are too many things a layman doesn't know that could cause difficulty." Apparently, a person should investigate the do-it-yourself divorce method carefully in states permitting no-fault divorce.

Ignorance of the law can be expensive

There hadn't been any domestic tranquility in the household for a long time, and Theresa J. had finally had enough. She packed up one evening and moved into a hotel for a few days until she could find an apartment and a divorce lawyer.

"Leaving the marital domicile" can be costly

The few days in the hotel cost her somewhere in the neighborhood of $208,000, actuarially speaking. By "leaving the marital domicile," she lost her claim on jointly held assets and to alimony. She actually had ample grounds for divorce and probably could have counted on an alimony award of $100 a week (which, over the course of her lifetime, would have come to a lot of money).

Women who've decided that divorce is the final solution are cautioned about moving out of the house by the Information Center on the Mature Woman —which evidently fears that even the mature woman is capable of immature behavior when she's emotionally upset.

Pause long enough to consult a lawyer, the information center counsels, citing a how-to handbook, *Compatible Divorce*, authored by divorce lawyer Robert Veit Sherwin. He points out that only when a woman's life is in danger or when she's threatened with physical harm may she decamp without forfeiting, under most state laws, claims on her husband for financial support.

If she cools it long enough to consult a lawyer who knows about such things, however, he'll probably arrange in writing, with the husband or his lawyer, an agreement that "the clients will temporarily separate without prejudice to the rights of either."

The wife can then move to a hotel or otherwise depart the scene with the prospect of long years of alimony to be collected.

In the case of the husband who is tempted to pack a bag and split, leaving the marital domicile makes him guilty of abandonment under most state laws. The penalty for that is not specified, but presumably a court might order him sent to jail or—even worse—make him move back with his wife.

Emotional cost of divorce

Divorce is never a clean break if children are involved. Every year, more than 225,000 children are affected by divorce in this country. If the mother and father fight for custody of the children, difficulty in visiting arrangements is inevitable.

The dollar costs, as well as emotional upsets, seldom end with the divorce. Young couples should be aware of these facts. It is unwise to assume that your case may be different. There is no such thing as an easy divorce. It costs more than emotional and psychological pain to all concerned, and especially to the children. It also costs more money than most people think. There is no such thing as a "bargain divorce."

SPEND FOR WHAT YOU REALLY WANT

A good budget should be your servant, never your master. The essence of successful money management is to get all the ideas you can from reliable sources but work out your own plan.

The important thing about your spending is the kind of life you are buying with your money and your savings. If you are buying family happiness and long-term security, your money management plan is a good one. If this is not the case, all the members of your family need to sit down together and work out another plan for spending the family income—a plan to fit your family and its income.

Some people spend their lives looking for the ideal place to invest money—where they can earn 5 to 10 percent or more. Few people realize that wise management of money in their day-to-day living and in their day-to-day purchasing decisions can net some of the best returns available. Each time the family spends nickels, dimes, and dollars, it is investing in a little piece of a way of living. Some find they have made a good investment, while others find they made their investment in such a haphazard, uninformed way that they have really made no gains in their way of life. The biggest investment that a person will ever make is in the way of life he purchases for his family.

We have concentrated our attention in this chapter on some 85 million Americans who make up the large group having sufficient incomes, education, and opportunities to maintain a decent standard of living, if they manage their resources. There are, however, about 25 million Americans who do not have the luxury of choosing how to spend their income. They try to meet basic needs with inadequate income.

CONSUMERS WITH SPECIAL NEEDS

Not all Americans share equally in the benefits afforded most consumers in our country. And they do not have the same choices about how their money is spent and where it is spent.

There is a growing concern for these consumers with special needs: the low-income—rural and urban—black, Spanish-speaking, Indian, and elderly people. There have been serious efforts to assist these people, but there remain great problems for them as consumers.

One in eight Americans lives in poverty

We are concerned here primarily with 25 million poor people—about one in every eight Americans lives in poverty. And the poorest of them are those who depend on public assistance.

The by-products of poverty include malnutrition, financial losses for those least able to afford them, ignorance, and broken homes. Consumer education will not cure poverty, but it can help the low-income group manage their small incomes better. It will also help give them a more effective influence in the marketplace.

Low-income consumers

Who are the poor? The Office of Economic Opportunity (OEO) poverty guidelines are $4,000 for a nonfarm family of four and $3,400 for a four-member farm family. The OEO guidelines range from $2,000 for a nonfarm family of one and $1,700 for a farm family of one to $5,900 for a nonfarm family of seven and $5,000 for a farm family of seven.[14]

Poverty estimates for ethnic groups in this country show that American Indian families are the poorest. Eighty percent of Indian families on reservations live in poverty. Among black families, 33.6 percent live in poverty, followed by 29.2 percent of Puerto Ricans and 28 percent of Mexican Americans. In glaring contrast, only 9.9 percent of whites live in poverty (Figure 5-2).

These comparative data answer the question: Who are the poor in the United States? They do not, however, give us ready answers to the very complex question: How can better management and planning of their very low incomes improve their standard of living?

How can 4 million low-income families meet basic needs with so little income, including welfare? Do most of these consumers have the opportunity of choosing how to spend their money?

In some poor families, decisions on spending the money are clear-cut—either powdered milk is substituted for fresh milk for a month or two, or one

[14]OEO Inst. 6004-1c, Nov. 19, 1971.

FIGURE 5-2 **Persons below the low-income level in 1970, by ethnic origin**

Population (in millions)

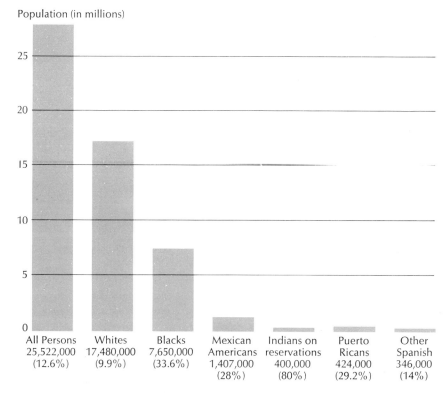

All Persons	Whites	Blacks	Mexican Americans	Indians on reservations	Puerto Ricans	Other Spanish
25,522,000	17,480,000	7,650,000	1,407,000	400,000	424,000	346,000
(12.6%)	(9.9%)	(33.6%)	(28%)	(80%)	(29.2%)	(14%)

SOURCE: U.S. Bureau of the Census, *Current Population Reports: Consumer Income,* ser. P-20, no. 224, March, 1971, table 6. *White House Conference on Children,* chart 13, p. 21 (Indians).

*The poor do not have the
luxury of choice*

of the children does not have a dress or shoes to wear to school. On the other hand, spending is done with little information on how to get the best value in the marketplace. For example, some will purchase flavored water with orange coloring and think it is orange juice or buy "investment" insurance which costs more and leaves them less protected than the same weekly sum placed in a local savings bank.

Even though a considerable amount of research has been done on the problems of the very poor, most of us do not really understand what makes them "tick." Research facts and observations are one thing, but understanding how the poor really feel and react is quite another.

Albert K. Cohen and Harold M. Hodges, for example, have observed the following attributes of people who live in poverty: [15]

1. They tend to live on a day-to-day basis.
2. They prefer the old and the familiar.
3. They do not trust the impersonal bureaucratic system.
4. They spend lots of time with relatives and neighbors.
5. They join few or no voluntary organizations.
6. They are anti-intellectual.
7. The males demonstrate masculinity and refuse to perform women's tasks.
8. They often use physical force to settle arguments.
9. They are fatalistic in their outlook.
10. The families are adult-centered, rather than child-centered.

Perhaps not all low-income consumers exhibit these characteristics, but they are relevant to the shopping behavior of many below the low-income level. For example, the desire to spend much time with relatives and neighbors leads to the neighborhood "demonstration party," which is a popular way to shop for goods even though they are usually overpriced, poorly made, and nonreturnable. Also, the tendency to live on a day-to-day basis is likely to lead to impulse buying. Few low-income families have long-range budget plans. They may buy a washing machine with a small cash down payment (this is all there is left), completely disregarding high interest costs. Then, too, the low-income person tends to use his money to satisfy immediate needs, without taking future needs or overall concerns into account. And the anti-intellectual person is not interested in learning how to get more for his dollar in a formal school setting.

Since most mothers in very poor families work outside the home, the shopping tasks are generally left to the children. And because the poor usually do not join voluntary organizations, they are unaware of local consumer agencies where they can register their complaints.

Much more could be said with regard to the many, many obstacles that prevent the poor from raising their purchasing power and from developing their management and planning abilities as consumers. But we should not forget that perhaps most poor people do not have the luxury of choice in spending

[15] *Characteristics of the Lower Blue Collar Class.*

their money that is enjoyed by those who have more education, and more income and who live in a healthier environment.

There are also many elderly (over age 65) poor in our country who are also consumers with special needs.

Elderly consumers

The typical elderly American consumer (20 million in 1972), 65 years and over, lives alone in a large city, receives about $135 a month from Social Security and $60 a month from a pension, rents a room for $18 a week, shops mostly at a small neighborhood store or from door-to-door salesmen, and often buys phony medicine.

One elderly person in four lives in poverty

One out of four persons 65 years and over—in contrast to one out of nine persons under age 65—lives in poverty. One-quarter of all elderly people (4.7 million) live in poverty. One-half of the 4.2 million elderly women live alone and in poverty. In 1970, half of the 7.2 million families with heads aged 65 or over had incomes of less than $5,053. One-quarter of these older families had incomes below $3,000. Of the 5.8 million older people living alone, half had incomes below $1,951, and one-third had incomes of less than $1,506. The median income (half below, half above) of families with heads over 65 was $5,053.[16]

Faced with such low incomes, these people need more than an effective consumer education program. Nevertheless, better planning and management of their small resources can help them secure more and better goods and services for each dollar spent.

Retired couple's budget

Most older Americans live on fixed incomes such as Social Security and small pensions, possibly supplemented by food stamps. Inflation presents a tragic problem for those in the low-income group. The 1972 Social Security amendment providing for an increase of 20 percent also provides for an automatic increase in Social Security to offset increased costs due to inflation.

Nearly two out of five aged couples have insufficient incomes to afford the intermediate budget established by the Bureau of Labor Statistics (Table 5-9). Approximately 38 percent have incomes below $4,000, and 12 percent have incomes from $4,000 to $5,000. The Social Security benefits for the typical retired couple are well below the amount necessary to maintain the moderate standard of living set by the Bureau of Labor Statistics in its intermediate budget, meeting less than three-fifths of the costs. Even the maximum benefits possible under Social Security would be more than $650 below this budget. The 20 percent increase voted by Congress in 1972 should help to provide a small portion of the minimum amount needed.

Comparable budgets for a retired single person, aged 65 or over, are not available at this time. Budget figures for such a person can be approximated by applying a factor of 55 percent of the consumption total for the retired couple. Autumn 1971 levels for a single person would then be $1,747, $2,466, and $3,626 for the consumption component of the lower, intermediate, and higher budgets, respectively.

Composition of the budgets for the elderly

The food budget (for food at home and away from home) was 30 percent of the consumption total in the lower budget, 28 percent in the intermediate budget, and 24 percent in the higher budget. Medical care, like food, represented a decreasing share of consumption as the budget level rose—13 percent

[16] Bureau of the Census.

TABLE 5-9   Budgets for a Retired Couple at Three Levels of Living, Urban United States, Autumn 1971

ITEM	LOWER BUDGET	INTERMEDIATE BUDGET	HIGHER BUDGET
Total budget	$3,319	$4,776	$7,443
Total family consumption	(96%) 3,176	(94%) 4,484	(88%) 6,592
Food	942	1,255	1,579
Housing	1,160	1,673	2,620
Transportation	225	438	797
Clothing and personal care	267	429	650
Medical care	424	427	429
Other family consumption	158	262	517
Other items	143	287	566
Personal income taxes	—	5	285

SOURCE: U.S. Department of Labor, Bureau of Labor Statistics, *News*, May 16, 1972.

in the lower budget, 10 percent in the intermediate budget, and 7 percent in the higher budget. Housing accounted for almost 40 percent of the three consumption totals. The constant share reflects the ownership of mortgage-free homes at all budget levels. Transportation stepped up from 7 percent of total consumption in the lower budget to 10 and 12 percent in the intermediate and higher budgets, respectively, the result of more automobile ownership at the highest budget level.

SUMMARY

The ability to use money efficiently does not come naturally. It has to be learned, just as we must learn to read and write. Most people do not really know how to use their money wisely. They probably never learned the basic principles of planning, managing, and spending their income.

What most of us need and want is a road map for financial maagement. First, think of financial management as organized spending and saving done ahead of time--not afterward. Second, remember that sensible planning is geared to your family's way of living. Third, bear in mind that it is reached by agreement between husband and wife. It really takes two to budget. Many families also do well to let the children participate in areas where their personal interest is involved, provided they can comprehend the issues. And fourth, remember that financial planning gives you a chance to think about alternative living plans and thus helps you clarify and appraise your goals and values.

QUESTIONS FOR DISCUSSION

1.   What are the characteristics of sensible family budgeting? Can the same budget be used for different families?

2.   Some family budget advocates believe that accounts must be kept if

budgeting is to succeed--a bookkeeping record of spending and balancing income and outgo, as in a business firm. Do you agree or disagree? Do you see advantages in the HIS and HER divided-responsibility system suggested in this chapter? Discuss.

3. Comment on the implications of the statement, "Not all Americans have the same choices about how their money is spent and where it is spent." How is this statement related to family budgeting?

4. How can inflation mess up your family budget planning? Be specific in pointing out what a family can do to counter inflationary forces.

5. How do separation and divorce affect the family budget? Discuss.

6. What do we mean when we say that a sudden appreciable increase in family income or a sudden appreciable decrease in family income can be a financial crisis to a family?

7. Fill in the Money Management IQ Test in this chapter. The score you give yourself is not as important as the thinking generated by the score. What do you propose doing about your personal management and planning of your income?

8. How do you account for irresponsible spending on the part of many affluent American families?

PROJECTS

1. Draw up a list of typical financial crises which might occur in the lives of students and their families and discuss their causes, possible solutions, and ways to avoid similar problems in the future.

2. If you are single, keep a personal budget for the duration of the semester or term as suggested in this chapter. Evaluate this experience. What are the advantages and disadvantages of keeping such a budget? What modifications would you make in the future?

3. If you are married, follow the divided-responsibility plan, suggested in this chapter, including making a statement of net worth toward the end of the term. Reflect on the changes that you both made during the semester or a shorter period. Where did you have to cut spending? Where did you add to expenditures? Why? Did your total net-worth value surprise you?

4. Refer to your own family budget. Figure the percentage spent on the consumption items only. (Use the latest Bureau of Labor Statistics data or the Autumn 1971 data given in this chapter, allowing some for inflation.) How do your percentage figures compare with the BLS figures which are most appropriate for your type of family, your age, the number and age of your children, your income, and the type of location in which you live (urban or rural)?

5. If you are living in a communal housing unit (whether single or married), try to obtain accurate data on comparable expenditures that you would make if you lived in an apartment or in a separate home. Compare the total consumption living expenses with your expenses in the communal housing unit. Compare the advantages and disadvantages of the two kinds of living arrangements.

6. "Money is all a poor person wants." "Personal satisfaction is more important than dollars and cents." "A poor person may stop trying to improve himself. Instead, he lives for today because today is enough of a challenge. Tomorrow is more than he can think about." "The poor live in their own world with its own set of values and attitudes."

Assuming there is an element of truth in these statements about families and individuals who are in the low-income group, is there any point in teaching them how to plan and manage their meager income? If you have never lived in a poor family, you may gain some insights by discussing this question with someone who has been a member of a low-income family as defined in this chapter.

SUGGESTED READINGS

A Pre-White House Conference on Aging: Summary of Development and Data, Report of the Special Senate Committee on Aging, November 1971.

Autumn 1971 Urban Family Budgets, U.S. Department of Labor, Bureau of Labor Statistics, April 1972

"Coping with Inflation: What Readers Report," *Changing Times,* August 1971, pp. 35–38.

Dervin, Brenda: *The Spending Syndrome,* The University of Wisconsin Press, Madison, 1965.

"Getting By on $20,000 a Year: Almost All of Them End up in the Red," *Life,* Dec. 20, 1968.

Morse, Richard L. D.: *Money Management Process,* Kansas State University, Manhattan, 1966.

Ryan, Mary E. and E. Scott Maynes: "The Excessively Indebted: Who and Why," *The Journal of Consumer Affairs,* Winter 1969, pp. 107–126.

Silverman, Charles: *Crisis in Black and White,* Random House, Inc., New York, 1964.

Taylor, Thayer C.: "In the Big Cities, Dig Black," *The Marketing Magazine,* Nov. 15, 1971.

The Nation's Youth: A Chart Book, Children's Bureau Publication no. 460, Washington, 1968.

"The Old in the Country of the Young," *Time,* Aug. 3, 1970.

Toffler, Alvin: *Future Shock,* Bantam Books, Inc., New York, 1970.

"When Folks Get Too Old or Ill to Manage Their Money," *Changing Times,* April 1972.

White Americans in Rural Poverty, USDA Agricultural Economic Report no. 124, November 1967.

CHAPTER 6
CONSUMER CREDIT AND BORROWING MONEY

Let the seller make full disclosure.
President L. B. Johnson

Consumer credit is joked about and glimpsed in ridiculing caricatures. These are some examples: "To make time fly just buy something on the installment plan." Or this one, "The people that economists used to say were underprivileged are now described as overfinanced." And *Life* magazine editorialized on "Is Thrift Un-American?" Said the multimillionaire Texan, Sid Richardson, "Out here in Texas, we judge a man's wealth by how much he owes." And Vance Packard calls us a "credit-card society." One magazine writer chose for his article the title, "Are You a Credit Drunk?" A symbolic case is that of the clerk earning $73 a week who went on a $10,000 binge with his credit card. After he was caught by the "credit detectives," he wrote, "All of a sudden the credit card was just like an Aladdin's lamp and you didn't even have to rub it."

Charles Dickens gave the world one of its most famous harried consumers, Mr. Micawber, David Copperfield's friend. Micawber always had a terrible time making ends meet. But despite his inability, he knew where the trouble lay: "Annual income twenty pounds, annual expenditure nineteen pounds six, result happiness. Annual income twenty pounds, annual expenditure twenty pounds ought and six, result misery."

But there are two sides to modern consumer credit—good and bad. Wisely used, it can lead to a higher standard of living. Unwisely used, it can lead to misery. Not too many decades ago we used to boast, "Pay as you go or stay home." Of course, few Americans can make such a boast today. At year-end 1971, consumer credit outstanding totaled $137.2 billion.

WHAT IS CONSUMER CREDIT?

The terms "consumer credit," "consumer debt," "short-term credit," "installment credit," and "mortage credit" have been bandied about so much that some clarification of their meaning is needed. Essentially, of course, credit is the asset side of the ledger, and debt the liability side. Thus, "consumer credit" is money or purchasing power extended by the lending agencies to consumers, and "consumer debt" is money owed the lending agencies by consumers.

Indebtedness of individuals can be broadly broken into two classes: mortgage debt (or real estate debt) and shorter-term debt, which includes a number of types of commitments, usually payable within a period of one to thirty-six months. In many publications, the term "consumer credit" is confined to a consideration of the shorter-term obligations. It is in this sense that consumer credit is used here.

Short-term or intermediate-term consumer credit may be further divided into two large groups: installment credit and noninstallment credit. Credit to be repaid in a series of installments is of various types, for example, automobile paper, other consumer-goods paper—such as loans on refrigerators or furniture—home repair and modernization loans, and personal installment loans. The term *paper* used in connection with consumer credit means installment sales notes held by banks, other financial institutions, or retail outlets. Personal installment loans, frequently made by banks, are for unspecified purposes, as distinguished from installment notes, which are frequently used for emergency medical care and other personal expenses but which also may be used for the purchase of a car, the modernization of a house, or the purchase of household equipment. They are also used for refinancing previous commitments, particularly in cases where a number of loans are being consolidated.

Noninstallment consumer credit consists of charge accounts, service credit—such as that extended by doctors, dentists, utility companies, and dry cleaners—and single payment loans, which are repaid in a single lump sum at the end of a specified time period.

Growth of consumer credit

At the end of 1971, consumer credit outstanding totaled $137.2 billion (Table 6-1). Noninstallment credit outstanding at the end of 1971 totaled $27.7 billion. Commercial banks had $10.3 billion outstanding in short-term single payment loans. The remaining $17.4 billion consisted of $7 billion in thirty-day accounts; $9.8 billion in charge accounts of retailers, service station credit, and miscellaneous credit cards; and $7.6 billion in service credit including medical, public utilities, and other bills of that type.

Installment credit of $109.5 billion was outstanding at the end of 1971. Of this, 42 percent was held by commercial banks, 29 percent by finance companies, 14 percent by retail outlets, 13 percent by credit unions, and 2 percent by savings banks and savings and loan associations combined.

USING CONSUMER CREDIT

Consumer ignorance about credit economics

"American consumers suffer from little knowledge of credit economics." So concluded economist Lewis Mandell after questioning a representative sample of American consumers about debt—what they knew about it and what their attitudes toward debt were.[1] The study reveals:

"Buddy you've been taken"

1.   There is great opposition to high interest rates—anything over 6 percent.
2.   Only one-third of those questioned believe installment debt to be a good thing, although about half of all Americans use it.
3.   Nearly all people want some kind of usury law which would put a ceiling of about a 10 percent interest charge on consumer credit.
4.   Most of the people interviewed recognized the bookkeeping expenses

[1] *Newsletter,* Institute for Social Research, Ann Arbor, Mich., Winter 1972, p. 6.

TABLE 6-1   Consumer Credit Outstanding, Year-End, 1960–1971 (in billions of dollars)

	1960	1965	1967	1968	1969	1970	1971
Total	56.1	90.3	102.1	113.2	122.5	126.8	137.2
Installment	42.9	71.3	80.9	89.9	98.2	101.2	109.5
Noninstallment	13.2	19.0	21.2	23.3	24.3	25.6	27.7
Single-payment loans	4.5	7.7	8.4	9.1	9.1	9.5	10.3
Charge accounts	5.3	6.4	7.0	7.8	8.2	8.8	9.8
Service credit	3.4	4.9	5.8	6.4	7.0	7.3	7.6

SOURCE: Federal Reserve Board.

NOTE: Parts may not add to totals due to rounding.

involved in maintaining credit accounts, but very few mentioned the risk factors to lenders.

5. Only 3 percent mentioned that the lender must borrow money—generally around prime interest rate—to finance a credit operation.

6. Most said that after the truth-in-lending law went into effect in 1969, their interest rates on car loans were on the average about one-half of the actual rates, both before and after the truth-in-lending law. In fact, only one borrower in ten can estimate the rate of interest being paid on a car loan with a 10 percent margin of error. Nearly one-half of all borrowers miss the mark by 50 percent or more.

Apparently, the federal law had little or no effect on consumer credit information. Merely disclosing the actual rate of interest, as required by the law, is not enough, since most consumers do not have any economic overview to make such facts intelligible to them.

Perhaps the most startling finding in the study is that personal characteristics don't have a bearing on knowledge about consumer credit. College graduates, for example, are no more knowledgeable than those who never attended college. "The only thing that distinguishes college graduates," said Dr. Mandell, "is their reluctance to admit ignorance—they are more likely to guess when in doubt."

Education for more effective use of consumer credit

Good credit laws are not an end in themselves. Education for personal economic competence is also needed. Intelligent preparation to cope with the economic facts of life will save many of us the headaches that come from living by trial and error. Nowhere is this more true than in the area of consumer credit. Young marrieds as well as older married people need the information and skill necessary to deal with advantages and dangers of consumer credit.

Practically everyone in this country uses credit in some form. In fact, four out of five young married couples with growing children are using installment credit for the purchase of durable goods.

Incidence of consumer credit usage

Studies by the Survey Research Center of the University of Michigan have revealed that some 52 percent of all families in 1971 owed no installment debt.

Repayment as a percent of disposable (after personal taxes) income varies by income level of the spending unit. Some 71 percent of the people in the low income levels, under $3,000, had no installment payments in 1971, and another 5 percent had payments of under 10 percent of disposable income (Figure 6-1). Among those having incomes of $15,000 and over, 54 percent had no installment payments, and 39 percent had payments of less than 10 percent of disposable income. Families with incomes of $10,000 to $14,999 seem most likely to be credit users, as shown by the fact that 60 percent of these families owed some installment credit in 1971. Families committed to installments over 20 percent or more of income (generally considered excessive) made up 10 percent or more of the three income groups below the $7,500 income level. This is in sharp contrast to 1970, when less than 10 percent of all groups of families had 20 percent or more of their incomes committed to installment payments.

Many families are committed to excessive installment repayment

The Michigan studies also show the level of commitment of debt repayment by age group (Figure 6-2). For example, 39 percent of the families in the under-25 age group, 27 percent in the 25- to 34-year age group, 19 percent in the 35- to 44-year age group, and 24 percent in the 45- to 54-year age group had 10 percent

FIGURE 6-1   Repayment of installment debt as a percent of disposable income, by income level, 1971

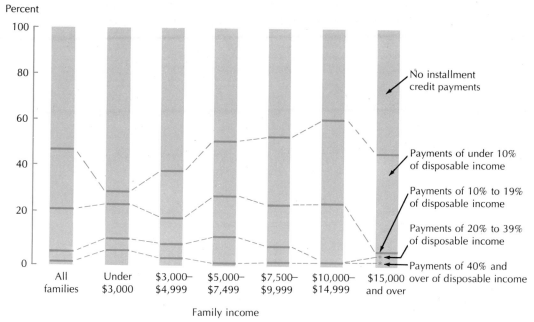

*Less than 0.5%

SOURCE: *1971 Survey of Consumer Finances,* Survey Research Center, University of Michigan, Ann Arbor.

FIGURE 6-2   Level of commitment of debt repayment, by age group, 1971

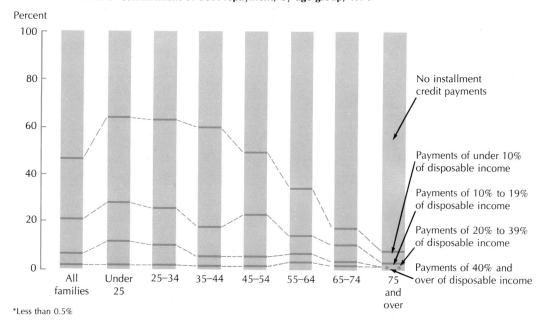

*Less than 0.5%

SOURCE: *1971 Survey of Consumer Finances,* Survey Research Center, University of Michigan, Ann Arbor.

or more of their disposable income committed to repayment of installment credit. By contrast, 15 percent of those in the 55- to 64-year age group, 11 percent in the 65- to 74-year age group, and 3 percent of those 75 and over had 10 percent or more of their 1971 disposable income committed to repayment of installment credit.

The amounts of monthly installment debt payments by income level and age of family head are shown in Table 6-2.

The trends in the use of consumer credit at the end of 1971 may be summarized as follows:

1. The total amount of consumer credit outstanding was the highest on record ($137.2 billion).

2. By type of credit, $38.3 billion, or about 35 percent of the installment debt outstanding at the end of 1971, was for the purchase of automobiles.

3. Debt repayments (installments) grew at a faster rate in 1971 than in 1970—up 8.1 percent—and were equivalent to 14.8 percent of disposable personal income.

4. About 48 percent of all families owed installment debt in 1971.

5. About 60 percent of families with incomes of $10,000 to $14,999 used installment credit in 1971.

6. Among low-income families (under $3,000) in 1971, 71 percent had no installment credit debt.

7. During the decade 1960–1970, noninstallment debt, which accounts for an average of 20 percent of total consumer credit debt, decreased at a slower pace than installment debt.

TABLE 6-2   Amount of Monthly Installment Debt Payments by Income and Age of Family Head (percentage distribution of families)

			EARLY 1971			EARLY 1970
	NONE	$1 $24	$25 $49	$50–$99	$100 OR OVER	$100 OR OVER
All families	52	9	8	15	16	16
Annual family income:						
Less than $3,000	71	12	11	3	3	1
$3,000–4,999	62	16	8	9	5	4
$5,000–7,499	49	10	11	17	13	10
$7,500–9,999	47	11	9	16	17	18
$10,000–14,999	40	6	9	23	22	24
$15,000 and over	54	3	5	17	21	26
Age of family head:						
Under age 25	34	9	15	24	18	22
25–34	34	8	10	28	20	27
35–44	38	13	9	18	22	19
45–54	49	7	12	12	20	16
55–64	64	10	6	11	9	8
65–74	82	8	5	4	1	2
75 and over	92	8	—	—	—	—

SOURCE: 1971 Survey of Consumer Finances, Survey Research Center, University of Michigan.
NOTE: Parts may not add to totals because of rounding.

8.   Users of installment credit were concentrated most heavily among young, middle-income families, especially those with children.

9.   Households with higher incomes were as likely to buy cars on credit as middle-income families.

10.   Black families were more likely to owe on installment debt than white families, although the average amount owed was less.[2]

11.   More white families owned bank and retail credit cards than black families.[3]

In the light of national trends in the use of consumer credit, is there a danger that debtors are a threat to their own well-being and that of their creditors?

The "excessively indebted"[4]

Excessively indebted consumers are those who have more installment debt than they can repay without difficulty. They are a threat to their own well-being and that of their creditors. These people, if they can be identified, are candidates for trouble as a result of excessive debt burdens. Mary E. Ryan and E. Scott Maynes made an excellent study of installment debts incurred primarily to finance the purchase of cars and other consumer durables, home repairs and improvements, travel, emergencies, and debt consolidation.

The data of the Ryan-Maynes study were taken from a survey of consumer finance by the University of Michigan Survey Research Center (SRC). The SRC sample represented 48 percent of the population, in forty-eight states, owing installment debt. According to this study:

1.   About 39 percent of all debtors were in "some trouble" because of too much credit.

2.   About 11 percent were in "deep trouble."

3.   The greatest proportion of "deep trouble" and "some trouble" debtors were found among the unmarried, the poor, those under 25, and those 65 and older.

4.   At least half of the debtor households headed by a woman and/or a black were in "some trouble."

5.   Laborers and service workers along with the unemployed and retired were marked by above-average likelihood of debt trouble.

6.   Underspenders as well as overspenders were more likely than others to be in deep trouble or some trouble.

The association of underspenders with debt trouble came as a surprise. This situation may have been due to "major shocks" and possibly to a low level of competence among some consumers, say these researchers.

For young marrieds (head under 35 years) current expenditures averaged a little more than current income. Debt averaged 81 percent of current income,

[2] *Family Economics Review,* December 1971, p. 9.

[3] Ibid.

[4] See Frederick E. Waddell, "A Borrowing, A Sorrowing," *The Journal of Consumer Affairs,* Summer 1970, pp. 31–45; see also Mary E. Ryan and E. Scott Maynes, "The Excessively Indebted: Who and Why," *The Journal of Consumer Affairs,* Winter 1969, pp. 107–126.

while liquid assets and investments averaged 39 percent of debt owed, according to recent Department of Agriculture studies.[5] As the age of the family head
increases, the ratio of debt to income declines from 81 percent for the young
family to 78 percent for the growing family (head 35 to 54 years) to 38 percent
for the retired family (head 65 and over).

WISE USE OF CREDIT

Up to this point we have been concerned with overuse or misuse of consumer
credit. There is, of course, a wise use of credit. Many people, particularly lenders, feel that there is legitimate use of credit by families and individuals. These
people point out, for example, that consumer credit is useful for families when
a purchase can be made at a lower-than-usual price, when a purchase cannot be
postponed without great hardship, or when the family does not wish to dip into
savings. Some claim that credit is useful for young families as a means of "forced
savings." This kind of thinking argues that when you buy on credit, you can enjoy the goods now—saving for them while you are using them. This argument neglects to mention that the so-called advantages of using credit should be
weighed against the "opportunity costs" of using credit because these may outweigh any of the above-mentioned advantages.

Opportunity costs

*Credit limits tomorrow's
purchasing power*

The use of credit does not increase one's purchasing power. It merely adds
to present purchasing power at the expense of tomorrow's. In other words, if the
amount of family purchasing power lost by way of interest payments were
placed in a savings account earning 5 percent compounded quarterly for forty-
five years (family life-span), this money would grow enormously. Let's assume
that interest payments over a forty-five-year span are about $17,000. This sum,
placed in a savings account earning 5 percent compounded quarterly for 45
years, would amount to some $66,000. This indicates that substantial "oppor-
tunity costs" are involved in the use of credit.[6]

It is apparent, then, that the use of credit, even the wise use of credit, results in erosion of purchasing power over the life-span of a family.

*Personal bankruptcy
and the wage-
earner plan*

Although financial failure is nothing new, recent trends in bankruptcy cases
have many people alarmed. During the unparalleled prosperity of the sixties,
the number of debtor-relief cases doubled, causing there to be more personal
bankruptcies per 1,000 households than there were during the depths of the
Great Depression.

Debtor relief is provided by the Federal Bankruptcy Act with a little help
from state statutes. Title 11 of the act provides for "straight bankruptcy" and a
"wage-earner plan."

Straight bankruptcy is a legal process whereby a debtor's assets are collected by the court, and sold for cash (except for certain assets which are exempt
and vary from state to state). The debtor is discharged from his unsatisfied debts
through the straight bankruptcy process. In 1970, more than 200,000 petitions
were filed for bankruptcy, and more than 180,000 involved personal bankruptcy.

[5] Quoted in *Finance Facts Yearbook,* National Consumer Finance Association, Washington, 1972, p. 38.
[6] Waddell, op. cit., p. 41.

The wage-earner plan, unlike straight bankruptcy, presents a blueprint to scale down a person's debts. The intent of this plan is to permit a wage earner to pay existing debts out of future earnings without being bothered by creditors. About thirty thousand people file these plans each year in the United States.

Straight bankruptcy has been a much more popular avenue of relief than the wage-earner plan. Since 1955, straight bankruptcy cases have accounted for over 90 percent of all personal petitions for financial relief of debts.

Causes for upsurge of bankruptcy cases

Perhaps underlying this upsurge are materialism and easy credit, according to some people. From the end of World War II until the mid-1960s, families loaded themselves with an unprecedented amount of debt, so that the "proportion of indebtedness to personal income increased from 14.2 percent in 1945 to 56.3 in 1965" and settled back slightly to about 50 percent in mid-1972.[7]

At any rate, the growth of bankruptcies can mean two different things—either a greater number of families are becoming insolvent (total liability exceeds total assets) or more insolvent families are choosing bankruptcy.

A trend toward more insolvency could arise because of an increase in fixed commitments and a decline in financial buffers against unexpected emergencies.

Drawn-out periods of prosperity may indeed breed greater commitments and thinner buffers. People convince themselves that tomorrow will be at least as good as today. They see no reason to forgo the good things in life today when tomorrow will take care of itself.

Since 1955, for example, families have been building up greater and greater consumer debt for each dollar of disposable income received. The ratio of consumer debt to disposable income increased from about 0.12 to 0.18 over the period 1955 to 1970.[8] The sad part of this accumulation of asset holdings is the fact that the spending goes largely for expensive durable goods. Durable goods generate no income under forced sale. Although economists long have noted that people purchase goods to maximize their utility (satisfaction), it is mighty hard to pay off the banker with a bag of utility!

Now, where do you attach the blame? Geraldine blames "the devil," but that seems too easy. There are many factors which lead people to face tomorrow on a thin string—keeping up with the Joneses and excessively generous credit, to name two. More than likely, both debtor and creditor have to share the responsibility for a family's slide into insolvency.

Or maybe, there are just more "bankrupt" insolvents? Not everyone, however, who is insolvent files a bankruptcy petition. It might be that more people *now* choose to declare bankruptcy. What could cause such a shift in behavior? Possibly the Puritan ethic is on its way out. With millions of credit cards, there is less need to deal with creditors face-to-face, which makes it easier to say "I want out from under."

Or it could be that the stigma associated with going bankrupt has diminished in recent years. We are more mobile today—a person can go bankrupt in Denver and start anew in Columbus. Or it may simply be that more people today know that bankruptcy is a feasible alternative to their problems.

[7] Reported in *The Washington Post,* March 1972, p. 71.

[8] *Business Review,* August 1971, p. 6.

Of course, there are costs to bankruptcy. Debtors pay through aggravation and loss of reputation. Creditors may recover very little. And society must bear a part of the burden to the extent that business passes on increased costs due to bad debt losses.

Credit management is important

Finally, it is likely that many people lack information about credit and proper budgeting. Creditors should take time to explain the terms of the agreement. Unfortunately, many credit managers lack the information needed to explain their own credit terms accurately.[9] Then, too, many consumers do not realize that using credit in itself isn't necessarily good or bad. It's the way you manage credit that counts. (Read the interesting story of a man who filed bankruptcy in Taylor-Troelstrup Reading 29.)

How to manage credit

Ask yourself these questions:

1. Shall I use credit for this purchase? To answer this question, you must consider other questions. Will the payments fit into your regular spending? Examine your budget for the answer. Will you, for example, have to skimp on necessities or other needed items?

2. How much will the credit cost? What's the difference between the cash price and the credit price? Would it be better to use your savings? You may be earning only 5 percent on your savings and paying 11 to 18 percent for credit.

3. Will the purchase last beyond the time of the final payment? Usually, it's no fun to pay for "dead horses"!

4. Will it mean better family living (better health, more satisfaction, a savings in time and energy)?

5. Can I afford it now?

Shopping for the best credit buy

There are various kinds of credit. Some kinds cost more than others, some are more convenient, and some are outright dangerous.

The main sources for credit are personal loan departments of commercial banks, small-loan companies, credit unions, and retail sales establishments. Before you use any of the credit sources, see how these plans compare with one another.

Secured loans

These loans you secure by pledging collateral such as stocks, savings accounts, or bonds. The least expensive of secured loans are passbook or savings account loans. Some banks and savings and loans associations will charge only 1 percent more than the account earns in interest or dividends.

Usually, however, loans secured by stocks and bonds cost more. Besides, you can't borrow on such security at full market value—possibly on only 60 percent of the market value. If the market value of your stock goes below the 60 or so percent level, you may have to sell your stocks or put up more collateral. Of course, the collateral is usually tied up until the loan is repaid.

[9]Marilyn M. Max and Richard L. D. Morse, *Retail Open End Credit Disclosures before and after Truth in Lending*, part I and part II, Kansas State University, Manhattan, July 1970.

Life insurance

If you have life insurance with cash-value accumulation, you can usually borrow up to 95 percent of the cash value at rates stated in the policy—presently around 5 to 6 percent a year. Of course, you depreciate your life insurance coverage by the amount you owe. Usually a life insurance company does not press you to repay the loan. For you, the interest is, at present, tax-deductible.

Charge accounts

This is about the cheapest kind of credit if you know how to manage it. The key to your success in charge accounts is to pay your bills *before* service charges are added. Commonly, you can get sixty days without a service charge, depending on when in the month you shopped. The trouble so many consumers have with charge accounts is in the different methods used to figure the interest. This problem is so important to consumers that a special effort will be made later in this chapter to explain it. Suffice it to say here that if you don't pay up by the close of the billing period, you may find yourself paying 18 percent a year or higher. Some retailers may no longer give you that sixty-day free period.

Personal loans

Personal loans at a credit union or a bank may cost 10 or 12 percent a year. These loans are usually easy to arrange at your credit union or bank and easy to fit into your budget because they are paid off in installments.

Retail installment sales contracts

This kind of credit has an advantage in that it is usually available in furniture and appliance stores and you sign the contract right there. This convenience, however, may be offset by high annual percentage rates of 24 to 36 percent— sometimes more.

Check-credit plans

First, you arrange with a bank or some other lender for a preapproved loan for up to a maximum amount. You don't use this credit until you write checks for more than the amount in the checking account. However, many banks cover your overdrafts by multiples of $100. In other words, if you use your line of credit for, say, $35, you would automatically get a loan of $100 with an annual percentage rate from 10 to 18 percent.

Credit cards

Credit cards are about the most convenient credit instruments yet devised. There are over 300 million credit cards in Americans' wallets. You can use them like charge accounts and get cost-free credit. But, as in the case of charge accounts, many people overuse them or fail to pay their bills before service charges are added. Most cards carry an annual 18 percent service charge.

The credit-card craze is just that. And there are so many ramifications wrapped up in the system that it deserves a separate analysis.

Credit cards

We are told that there are over 300 million credit cards in this country. Lewis Mandell, who directed the study[10] on credit-card use in 1970–1971 for the University of Michigan's Institute for Social Research, said that half of all families in this country have at least one card, that the average family has three cards, and that a sizable proportion use six cards or more.

Although credit cards are widely used, said Mandell, "few Americans tend to think of credit cards as a good thing whether they use them or not." He also said that "75 percent of all persons interviewed said that credit cards made it too easy to buy things that they may not really want or that they can't really afford." He also found that only the "highest income group treats the card primarily as a convenience."

There is also the danger of stolen and lost credit cards. Widespread credit-card thievery, often by syndicated gangsters, has cost consumers billions of dollars. About 100,000 credit cards are lost annually, and about 300,000 are stolen. To minimize the loss to owners of lost or stolen credit cards, the following changes have been initiated.

First, all credit cards issued after January 24, 1972, must provide some means of identification of the legitimate owner—signature, photo, or fingerprint. This was necessitated by an upsurge in the number of stolen credit cards and cards thrown away accidentally. Even organized crime got into the act, developing a sophisticated technique of forgery and setting up a thriving black market where the going rate for a credit card was anywhere from $100 up.

"Think of it as money!"

Secondly, there is a $50 liability ceiling for charges made with a lost or stolen card, and that liability exists only if the *card issuer* has furnished a self-addressed, postpaid envelope or card for notification of loss or theft. The stipulation that "holder agrees to pay for all purchases made by any user of this card until company has received notice of theft or loss" is now illegal.[11]

Some companies estimate that it will be to their advantage not to notify cardholders of the $50 ceiling or even to furnish the postpaid mailer. A Bank-Americard ad put it this way: "You can handle it. After all, it's your money."

Opportunities for misuse, however, still exist. A student recently described this "rip-off": He traveled to a Western state, using a friend's credit card. The friend remained in the clear by reporting the card as lost.

In such a case, however, if the company can prove that you gave the card to the person who ran up the bill, you could be fined, jailed, or both.

These new rules, then, help protect a credit-card owner from having to pay for charges made with his card by someone else. There are still ways of getting and using cards illegally, however. For example, dishonest store clerks can cheat you by entering false amounts on sales slips. You can protect yourself against this by checking your sales slip and by keeping track of what the clerk does with your credit card.[12]

Finally, if you lose a credit card, call the issuing company immediately and

10 *Newsletter,* Institute for Social Research, Ann Arbor, Mich., Summer 1972, p. 8.
11 Federal Trade Commission News, Apr. 13, 1972.
12 "Watch Out for the Credit Card Crooks," *Changing Times,* March 1971.

follow up the call with a written notice. Keep a copy of the notice. You can also buy credit-card insurance. Some homeowner's insurance policies cover credit cards.

CONTROLLING CONSUMER CREDIT

Consumer borrowers paid the enormous sum of $17.7 billion in interest on short-term loans during 1971.[13] Since July 1, 1969, American consumers have been getting a better break in their credit transactions. That's the date when most of the provisions of the Consumer Credit Protection Act became effective.

The Consumer Credit Protection Act (truth-in-lending law)

This important consumer protection act is primarily a law *requiring* disclosure. It does not limit finance charges. The following disclosures must be made by merchants, banks, and other credit grantors:

Cash price

Down payment

Total amount financed

Finance charge

Annual percentage rate of finance charge

Late charges

Total of payments

Amounts of payments

Certain other information

Disclosure must be made clearly in writing, and *before* credit is extended. Disclosure can also be made in a separate document given to the potential debtor *before* he signs the credit contract. Furthermore, premiums for credit life, accident, or health insurance may no longer be hidden. This insurance will repay the loan in the event the insured dies or becomes disabled. If obtaining such insurance is part of the transaction, the debtor must be fully informed of the requirement and the cost. If such insurance is offered but is not required to obtain the credit, the potential debtor, if he wants the insurance, must so indicate in writing. He must also state that a written disclosure of the cost has been made to him.

Revolving credit accounts are governed by different disclosure requirements. However, at the time such an account is opened, the customer must be told the details of the account's operation, how the finance charge is determined, and the annual percentage rate. Disclosures must also be made on the statements sent to customers. Among other things, this has the effect of requiring the disclosure that, for example, a 1½ percent a month charge is equal to an annual percentage rate of 18 percent.

Unfortunately, you should double-check your charge accounts (revolving credit) because the federal law *does* permit various methods of computing finance charges. We shall have more to say on this later.

[13] *Finance Facts Yearbook, 1972,* p. 33.

The truth-in-lending law also prohibits the use of misleading advertising that seems to promise different down-payment or installment amounts from those which are in fact available. If an ad contains any specific details of a credit plan other than the annual percentage rate, it must also include information on finance charges, rates, cash price, and down payment, as well as other information that may be required for the transaction. Such information is too often omitted in ads today.

The Consumer Credit Protection Act also limits garnishment of wages (the attachment by a creditor of part of an employee's wages). This attachment of wages was customarily abused by creditors. The act states that weekly garnishment cannot exceed the lesser of either (1) 25 percent of the after-tax pay or (2) the after-tax pay minus thirty times the federal minimum hourly wage. This provision took effect on July 1, 1970. The law also forbids an employer to fire an employee for one indebtedness. For willful violation of this section, an employer may be fined $1,000, be imprisoned up to one year, or both.

The act named the Board of Governors of the Federal Reserve System to issue Regulation Z for administering the law. Enforcement of the law is by other federal agencies—banks, the Bureau of Federal Credit Unions, the Federal Trade Commission, and others.

The act provides for fines up to $5,000, imprisonment for one year, or both. Violations also leave creditors open to civil suits by debtors. A debtor can sue for *twice* the amount of the finance charge (but no more than $1,000 or less than $106), and if he wins the suit, the creditor is required to pay attorney's fees and court costs.

A state that has its own truth-in-lending laws, with at least as good consumer protection as that provided by the federal act, may apply for certain exemptions. Possible exemptions are contained in the controversial Uniform Consumer Credit Code passed by several states at about the time the federal Consumer Credit Protection Act was passed.

The Uniform Consumer Credit Code (UCCC)

Students interested in analyzing this complex law, originally prepared to encourage uniformity in credit laws in the fifty states and to stall passage of the truth-in-lending law, can find a considerable body of information on the subject.[14] Suffice it to say that the objective of the UCCC was, on the whole, an improvement in the terms of consumer interest rates when compared with the higher interest rates permitted by most of the state consumer credit laws prior to the truth-in-lending law. Since the passage of the federal act, however, there appears to be little to gain and much to lose in adopting the UCCC model, although it contains several commendable features such as the prohibition of confession of judgment and the elimination of third-party agreements, referral selling, and wage assignments.

Credit bureaus: your credit rating

Is your credit "slip" showing? One way to find out is when you open your first credit account in a store. The store may open an account for you in less than an hour; sometimes it takes a day or longer. Behind the scenes of establishing credit is an elaborate national and international credit system. Your local credit

[14] See Richard L. D. Morse and William R. Fasse, "Where Is the Consumer in the Uniform Consumer Credit Code?" *Journal of Home Economics,* January 1970; Judge G. Brunn, *Critique of the Uniform Consumer Credit Code,* Consumer Research Foundation, 1969; and W. F. Willier, *Personal Finance Law Quarterly Report,* Fall 1969.

Credit bureaus know more about you than you do

bureau is at the center of the network. There are over 2,200 local credit bureaus in the United States. These bureaus are amassing data on everyone who uses credit. The facts come from many sources—banks, court and police records, press stories, directories, employers, other credit bureaus, personal references, other merchants, your neighbors and landlord, lending agencies, school and medical records, and legal records like judgments, bankruptcies, federal tax liens, and collections. In fact, you name it, and the bureau has it.

All this information is made available to all other credit bureaus through membership in the Associated Credit Bureaus of America. This means that your credit follows you wherever you go. You cannot clear your record, if it is not a good one, by moving to another town or state.

Are you a better credit risk when you make $10,000 rather than $8,000 a year? Not always. The right to credit must be earned. Stability of income counts for you. Table 6-3, How Your Credit Is Rated, shows the standards recommended for the use of bankers in a manual prepared by the American Bankers Association.

CREDIT ABUSES

Fair Credit Reporting Act, 1971

Does this man pay his bills on time? Has he always paid his debts in full? How much does he owe at this time, and to whom? Is his son a "hippie-type youth," active in antiestablishment concerns and suspected of using marijuana on occasion? Did his son or daughter organize protests against the war in Vietnam?

On the basis of answers to questions such as these, provided by a credit investigating agency, an automobile insurance company canceled the policy on a car despite the fact that the answers were entirely inaccurate. How do you correct such misinformation? Before passage of the Fair Credit Reporting Act by Congress on April 24, 1971, it was next to impossible to correct such errors. Although the new law does not protect consumers against misinformation and lies in every case, it does ensure consumer protection of some basic rights:

• When a credit reporting agency undertakes an investigation of a consumer's credit and character standing, a written notice must be sent to the consumer informing him that the investigation is under way and reminding him of his right to request a copy of the report.

• Upon written request to the credit bureau, consumers have the right at any time to see the information in their credit files and to be told the sources of the information.

• If a consumer disputes the accuracy or completeness of an item in his file, the reporting agency must make a reinvestigation within a reasonable time and insert the correct information in the record. If the reinvestigation does not resolve the dispute, the consumer can insert a brief (100 words or less) statement in his file.

When these new basic consumer rights are not complied with, the Federal Trade Commission (FTC) has the authority to proceed against those agencies

TABLE 6-3 How Your Credit Is Rated

	FAVORABLE	UNFAVORABLE
Employment	With good firm two years or more. Job involves skill, education.	Shifts jobs frequently. Employed in seasonal industry such as construction work. Unskilled labor.
Income	Steady, meets all normal needs.	Earnings fluctuate, depend on commissions, tips, one-shot deals. Amount barely covers requirements.
Residence	Owns own home or rents for long periods in good neighborhoods.	Lives in furnished rooms in poor neighborhoods. Changes address frequently.
Financial structure	Has savings account and checking account that requires minimum balance. Owns property, investments, life insurance.	No bank accounts. Few, if any, assets.
Debt record	Pays bills promptly. Usually makes large downpayment. Borrows infrequently and for constructive purpose.	Slow payer. Tries to put as much on credit as possible. Frequent loans for increasing amounts.
Litigation	No suits by creditors.	Record of suits and other legal action for nonpayment. Bankruptcy.
Personal characteristics	Family man. Not many dependents relative to income. Mature.	Large number of dependents. Marital difficulties. Young, impulsive.
Application behavior	Seeks loan from bank with which he regularly deals. Answers all questions fully and truthfully.	Applies for loan at banking office far removed from his residence or place of business. Makes misstatements on application. In great hurry to obtain cash.

which violate the law. In 1972, the FTC issued advisory guidelines intended to clarify the law. Failure to comply with them, however, may result in corrective action by the commission.

In essence, the five FTC interpretations:

1. Prohibit publication and distribution by credit bureaus of books containing consumers' credit ratings, called *credit guides.*

2. Allow the use of certain kinds of "protective bulletins" which identify check forgers, swindlers, and the like—provided no information in them is used in establishing the subjects' eligibility for credit, insurance, or employment.

3.   Require that consumers be informed when they are denied credit on the basis of information furnished by loan exchanges.

4.   Require that when an insurance company uses a state motor vehicle report to deny a consumer insurance or increase the cost, it inform him of the state agency's identity.

5.   Forbid consumer reporting agencies to prescreen prospects' names for credit worthiness for direct mail solicitations.

While most of the difficulties consumers still have are with enforcement, some critics believe the new law basically is flawed because it is aimed at correcting, rather than preventing, unfair credit reporting; some consumers may never even suspect that their files are inaccurate. The reporting agency still isn't prevented from reporting on a person's race, religion, or politics or from relaying neighborhood gossip about his sex life or drinking habits. (For more details, read *How to Find Out about Credit Reports,* in Taylor-Troelstrup Reading 33.)

Credit cards and tricky billing practices

The credit-card revolution has been a mixed blessing for the consumer. It is perhaps inevitable that our consumer protection laws have lagged behind the rapidly changing developments in the use of credit. The consumer has been harassed and intimidated by computer-written dunning letters; he has been shortchanged by tricky billing practices which result in interest rates far above the state legal usury ceilings; he is being given less and less time to pay his bills before incurring a finance charge; and he is forced to subsidize the credit-card system whenever he pays cash instead of using a credit card.

The most important terms to understand on open-end accounts—such as revolving charge accounts, credit cards, and check-credit plans—are the ones that tell you how the creditor figures interest.[15]

1.   *Previous balance*   This is the most common method creditors use to figure finance charges—and perhaps the costliest one. Your interest is figured on the balance outstanding at the start of the last billing cycle; payments, purchases, and returns that were made during that billing period aren't taken into account. You could be charged interest for amounts you have already paid.

Tricky finance charges can hurt you

If, for example, you charge $200 and pay $100 within twenty-five days, the next month you'll usually be charged $3 for the $200, a periodic rate of 1½ percent a month—but that's 3 percent of the $100 you really owe, which is an effective annual percentage rate of 36 percent, even though the stated rate is 18 percent.

2.   *Average daily balance*   In this method, the actual amounts outstanding each day during the billing are added up and divided by the number of days in the period. If, for example, the billing period starts on the first day of the month and if on that day your previous balance is $200, you pay half fifteen days later. Your average daily balance for the month is $150, and at 1½ percent a month you would be charged $2.25. Don't wait long before making payments in this plan, or it could be more expensive than the previous-balance plan.

---

[15] The *billing date* is the day *after* which no purchases are charged to that month's bill. The *closing date* is the day by which payment must be made to avoid additional finance charges. The *billing cycle* is the period from the billing date to the closing date.

3. *Adjusted balance*   Here the creditor computes the finance charge after payments are deducted. If, for example, you owe $200 on the first of the month and pay half of it fifteen days later, for a new or adjusted balance of $100, at 1½ percent a month you owe $1.50. This method is more advantageous to the customer than either of the other two methods.

4. *Past-due balance*   In this method there are no finance charges even if you do not make a payment during the billing cycle, *if* full payment is made within fifty-five days from the original cycle's closing date. This is the best method.

Some of the thousands of consumer complaints registered against these tricky billing systems are that (1) bills are sent too late for customers to pay without being assessed a finance charge, (2) a delay in processing a payment results in finance charges even when payment is prompt, and (3) the traditional thirty-day grace period has been reduced to twenty-five days by many stores— sometimes even to fifteen days—and at times the grace period ends a day or two *before* the closing date.

In recent years Sears and other retailers have been sued by state attorneys general and others for their practices, according to the *Wall Street Journal,* July 10, 1972. (See "Introduction of the Fair Credit Billing Act," Taylor-Troelstrup Reading 35. Senator Proxmire introduced a bill in the Senate, S.652, proposing a twelve-point program to strengthen the rights of consumers in credit-card and billing transactions.)

The annual percentage rate (APR)

Is your APR showing?

Suppose you need a car loan and decide to compare interest rates around town. You telephone various lenders. Most likely, some will tell you their interest rate is "5 percent add-on," "$6 per hundred," and "9 percent on $1,000." These creditors are not quoting the correct interest rates over the telephone or in person. Under the truth-in-lending act, all lenders must fully disclose the cost of credit in annual percentage rate (APR). This is the amount of interest charged for the loan, and it allows you to compare interest rates of different lenders. But all that is truth on paper is not always truth in conversation. So always ask what the APR is.

The Federal Trade Commission believes that the use of such terminology is confusing and is violative of the truth-in-lending act and Federal Reserve Regulation Z. The FTC said:

> No use should be made in advertising or in other communications with consumers of the add-on or discount rates, whether in percentages or dollars per hundred. Under the Truth-in-Lending Act and Regulation Z, only the annual percentage rate may be used in advertising the cost of consumer credit, and Truth-in-Lending contemplates that the annual percentage rate should be used in all oral or written communications to consumers rather than the previously popular add-on or discount rates. Continued use of such confusing terminology may be violative of both Truth-in-Lending and Section 5 of the Federal Trade Commission Act. [16]

Credit insurance: overcharging

When you borrow money, should you buy credit insurance—usually sold by banks, sales finance companies, and small-loan companies acting as selling agents for independent insurance companies—that will repay the loan if you

[16] *Federal Trade Commission News,* December 1971.

How to get soaked,
and good

die or become disabled? If you do buy this insurance today, you are apt to be overcharged. Senator William Proxmire claims that in 1970, buyers were overcharged at least $276 million. If the lending agency were buying this kind of insurance, it would shop around for the best buy. Consumers, however, are not familiar with this service and usually sign up for the protection wherever they borrow the money. They are unaware that the borrower pays and the lender takes a cut in the premium. The higher the premium, the higher the cut!

High premium rates represent only one aspect of the problem. The fine print in the contract may limit the protection that shows up front. For example, if you have a kidney condition and buy disability insurance, you won't be compensated for a kidney-caused disability unless it starts after six or twelve months, depending on the policy. Such practices can reduce anyone's coverage. There are several other hedges in most contracts.

Unlike regular life insurance, credit insurance is sold at a flat rate regardless of the age of the borrower. Most insurance companies, however, try to eliminate higher-risk groups—usually those 65 years and over.

The rates are probably too high because of the large commissions and dividends paid to lending agencies. Critics and others point out that the insurance companies return about 51 percent of credit life and disability premiums to policyholders in the form of real benefits. This is far below the payout ratios for standard group life and health insurance, the only types comparable to credit life and disability insurance.

The lower-cost insurers (Prudential Insurance of America and CUNA Mutual) manage to pay back about 75 percent in benefits. Higher-cost companies average only about 46 percent. Perhaps the solution is for the federal government to set fair rates, according to Senators William Proxmire and Philip Hart. It has also been suggested that the creditors be made to pay the premium. Many credit unions provide insurance at no extra charge. In any event, consumers should first decide whether they need this insurance, and second they should compare rates before buying. Rate studies indicate that a fair national average price for credit life is about 43 cents per $100 of initial debt. With disability insurance, be sure to check rates for various loan-payment periods. In some states if a lender stretches the loan period from twelve to thirteen months, he can charge 50 percent more for the thirty-day nonretroactive coverage. Why not insist on twelve months?[17]

Repossession of collateral
(writ of replevin)

This abuse of credit insurance needs to be remedied by the states, the federal government, or both.

This abuse is associated with installment selling and the conditional sales contract. For example, a buyer who purchased a $500 TV set, along with a service contract, made regular payments totaling $400 but failed to make the final $100 payment because he got into a dispute about servicing of the set. The seller began action in court for repossession of the TV and obtained a writ of replevin (repossession) which empowered the local sheriff to seize the TV set.

One-sided contracts

Historically, the law has been on the side of the creditor in such cases. Isn't it possible that some default debtors have perfectly valid defenses based on their creditors' failure to live up to their part of the original deal? Then, too, low-

---

[17] "How You Can Get Soaked," *Changing Times,* August 1972.

income debtors, in particular, generally face prohibitively extravagant legal expenses. The courts do not administer justice to these people, but rather act as collection agents of the creditors.

In 1972, the United States Supreme Court did strike down rights of creditors to repossess goods. What bothered the Court was that the plaintiffs received no prior notice and were allowed "no opportunity whatever to challenge the issuance of the writ of replevin" until after the property was actually seized. Justice Stewart stressed the rights for due process of law—"parties whose rights are to be affected are entitled to be heard; and in order that they may enjoy the right they must be notified."[18]

The Court made it clear that it did *not* question the power of the state to seize goods "before a final judgment to protect creditors so long as these creditors have tested their claim through the process of a prior hearing."

(For a more detailed story leading to the final Court decision, see Taylor-Troelstrup Reading 34.)

This court decision did not get to the heart of the real problem that debtor consumers experience when goods are repossessed. The Court did say that there must be a "prior hearing" *before* repossessing property. This does strike down the right to suddenly repossess goods before a hearing, but it does nothing for a debtor who cannot afford to go to court. Perhaps instituting neighborhood consumer courts, revising summons procedures, providing adequate free legal services in every community, and encouraging widespread consumer action to benefit low-income debtors who face extravagant legal expenses may be necessary to assure the debtor his day in court.

Holder-in-due-course doctrine

The holder-in-due-course doctrine, by which a bank or any financial institution that has purchased a promissory note from a retailer can collect from the customer even though the debt covers a refrigerator that didn't refrigerate or a car that didn't run, has outlived its usefulness, according to many critics.

"The mask behind which fraud hides"

When a customer threatens not to pay on the loan until the refrigerator or car is fixed, he learns that the store has sold the contract to another party. Since the new party, usually a bank or sales finance company, holds a valid promise to pay and has no legal responsibility for the merchandise, in most states the customer must pay without regard to the claim against the store.

A "deficiency judgment" can arise if you refuse to pay. The new holder of the loan agreement can usually repossess the merchandise and sell it to help pay off the loan. If the sum from the sale doesn't cover the entire balance owed, the lender can go to court and get a deficiency judgment that forces the customer to pay the remaining amount plus repossession costs, court costs, and attorneys' fees.

The Federal Trade Commission proposed a trade regulation that would make the third party (the one that buys the credit contract) subject to legitimate claims the consumer might make on the merchandise. A few states have imposed some limits on the "due-course" doctrine. Today, even though this doctrine has outlived its usefulness, it remains essentially a "mask behind which fraud hides."[19]

[18] *St. Louis Post-Dispatch,* Aug. 13, 1972, p. 10G.

[19] Warren G. Magnuson and Jean Carper, *The Dark Side of the Marketplace,* Prentice-Hall, Inc., Englewood Cliffs, N.J., 1968, p. 118.

Deceptive debt collectors

The Federal Trade Commission, in the fall of 1971, began public hearings to determine whether rule making or other action by it is warranted to correct unfair or deceptive debt collection practices. The FTC hearing produced considerable evidence of unfair and deceptive debt collection practices by creditors and collection agencies. Some of these practices included:

- Using fraudulent service of court summonses to obtain default judgments without notice
- Initiating suits against consumer debtors in distant locations resulting in default judgments because of their failure to defend
- Using collection notices containing false or misleading representations-- notices that simulate legal process, for example
- Using deceptive means to obtain confidential financial information from a debtor, such as offering a valuable gift or using the pretext that a "survey" is being conducted
- Notifying a debtor's employer of the debtor's past-due account or requesting the employer to help collect the debt, thus bringing undue pressure on the debtor
- Threatening to seize items which are, by law, exempt from legal collection processes and threatening to garnish, seize, attach, or sell any of the debtor's property or wages without a court order permitting such action
- Harassing the debtor by using profane or obscene language or by placing telephone calls continuously or at unusual times
- Using violence or threats of violence to collect debts
- Threatening to damage the debtor's credit status by referring his name to a bona fide credit reporting agency when no such action is contemplated

Many consumers permit debt collectors to scare them into silence regardless of the unfair, and at times illegal, methods used to collect debts. The attorney general's office, the Legal Aid Society, or any public legal aid group in the community may provide information or legal aid to a consumer who is harassed and threatened by debt collectors.

Women and Credit

"A cobweb of myths"

Women complain that they often can't get credit because of their sex. Estel Antell, a federal employee in Dallas, for example, would appear to be an ideal airline customer. Her income is $20,000 a year, and she flies about 100,000 miles annually. She moved from Dallas to Tulsa and applied to Continental Air Lines for a credit card in her own name.

"Back came a letter asking for my husband's signature," she says. "I called up and said, 'You must be kidding. How many men in my wage bracket do you ask for a wife's signature?'" She never received the card.

How common is Mrs. Antell's experience? Martha W. Griffiths, congresswoman from Michigan, testified in May, 1972, before the National Commission on Consumer Finances, a federal agency. She said, "Men and women today don't have equal access to credit. Banks, savings and loan associations, credit-card companies, finance companies, insurance companies, retail stores, and even the federal government discriminate against women in all stages of life--whether single, divorced, or widowed; with or without children; rich or poor; young or old."

Virginia Knauer, Special Assistant to the President for Consumer Affairs, told the International Consumer Credit Conference in Washington in May 1972 that "The reasoning used to deny women credit is often a cobweb of myths and suppositions unsupported by research on the statistical risks involved or on the individual's creditworthiness."

Ironically, working married women who established credit standing when they were single often appear to have the most difficulty. "You lose your credit when you marry," says Marsha King, president of the Texas division of Women's Equity Action League (WEAL), a national women's group. When she married and set about changing her name on her credit cards, she found Dallas retailers reluctant. She said she had an "excellent credit record." But "they told me I'd have to reapply in my husband's name."

Early in 1972, the St. Paul human rights agency sent a man and a woman separately to twenty-three area banks to borrow $600 for a used car. They both earned $12,000 annually and had almost identical financial and personal qualifications. About half of the banks "applied more stringent standards to the woman than to the man. These banks refused to lend the woman money without her husband's signature while waiving the cosignature requirement for the man."[20]

Loans are harder to get for women. Myths do, indeed, die the hard way.

NEW CONCEPTS OF CONSUMER CREDIT

Concept of collateral
has evaporated

Many people are unaware of the changes that have taken place in the practices of debt financing of consumer goods and services in the last decade or so. Dr. Colston Warne, professor of economics at Amherst College, pointed this out to the Senate Banking and Currency Committee when he said, "The most significant change has been the transmutation of this financial device into a merchandising tool."

In the first place, according to Dr. Warne, the concept of collateral has evaporated. Even in automobiles, thirty-six-month terms together with rapid new-car obsolescence, have rendered the goods small surety for the loan. The resale value of other durables (white goods, TV sets, furniture, and the like) is so low in today's market that no lender considers them as collateral. Their repossession on delinquency is almost universally accompanied by a deficiency-balance charge that becomes, of course, a lien on any income or property of the debtor. Hence, credit contracts for these goods constitute at bottom little more than a disguised wage, chattel, or mortage lien—often unrecognized by the borrower. Finally, the great increase in the use of credit to finance the purchase of soft goods and services is incontrovertible evidence of the divorcement of consumer credit from any concept of the goods financed serving as collateral for the debt.

In short, consumer credit extensions are made singly and solely against the lender's expectations of (1) the consumer's ability to maintain current income, or (2) the lender's ability to exercise command over the borrower's assets via the

[20] *The Wall Street Journal,* July 18, 1972, p. 1.

courts. To put it another way, in their extensions of credit for consumption, lenders are, first, looking to the federal government's ability to maintain nearly full employment for surety, and second, depending on the police power at their command to tap existing equities in homes and cars. Thus, the theorizing of the past about the functions of consumer credit, which was based on the concept of pacing time units of consumption with payments over the period of use of the durables that secured the debt, fails to fit reality.

Retailers acting as agents for lenders

A second concept of consumer credit that has evaporated, except in the case of a few of the largest retailers, says Dr. Warne, is the seller's responsibility for the loans disguised as sales. Although the courts and a good many state legislatures make a distinction between "carrying charges" and "interest," the practice that gave rise to that distinction is all but extinct. The retailer generally acts as an agent for a lender. Typically, the forms filled out by the consumer for the installment purchase of goods have been furnished the retailer by a lender. All conditions attending the loan, including a commission (kickback) for the retailer from a dealer reserve held out by the lender, have been set by a financing institution.

No longer does a retailer "carry the consumer" over a period of time, as the general store once carried the farmer between seeding and harvesting. As soon as the paper is signed, it is turned over to the lending agency. Only the old-style thirty-day charge account offered by department stores can in any sense be called a retailer-carrying service, and this is the only form of consumer credit that has failed to increase.

The new term—credit selling

The retail trade press has for a number of years been using a term that best expresses the present meaning of consumer credit. They speak repeatedly of "credit selling." Credit selling means two things: selling goods on credit, and selling credit as well as goods.

Credit selling is generally recognized as the core of present-day profitable retailing operations for four reasons. (1) The consumer buying on credit tends to buy higher-priced merchandise (he is easy to "trade up"), to buy more in volume, and to buy more frequently than the cash customer. (2) The credit customer does not shop around—he "marries" his seller-lender. (3) The amount of purchase per credit sale is typically enough larger than the cash sale to more than compensate for the extra overhead of credit selling. (4) Earnings on credit extensions frequently equal or better the net return from markups on merchandise. The National Automobile Dealers Association, for example, reported one year that the net profit from most dealers' operations was exactly equal to the small percentage return received by the dealers as a financing rebate from the lending agencies to whom they transferred their consumer paper.

Pressure to sell debt

Throughout retailing, therefore, there is a heavy and continuing pressure to sell debt. Salesmen in automobile showrooms and appliance stores are given larger commissions for credit sales. Department store employees are sometimes paid "spiffs" of $1 to $2 for each new credit customer signed up. Bank personnel are "spiffed" to bring in check credit, bank credit card or personal loan customers. And, as one after another seller-lender has placed increasing promotional emphasis on loans disguised as sales, as new lending schemes tied to sales have multiplied (credit cards and bank schemes), the traditional lender to consumers—the small-loan company—has accordingly been forced to greater promotional efforts. Thus, the advertising of debt as a way of life has expanded into a national propaganda effort of phenomenal proportions.

Overextension of credit   Installment selling has added another tool to the selling arsenal of salesmen. This rather new selling tool has enticed many unsuspecting and trusting consumers to incur more debt than they can afford. Thousands of families are forced into bankruptcy or on welfare because they are snared by deceptive sellers. To sellers it is simply business. They can tell you that it is legal; that it is necessary to keep the economy going; that after all, a salesman has to make a living; and that his employers have to meet quotas, budgets, and expenses. Large corporations are driven by the "growth" complex—if they do not grow rapidly, their stock will not be rated as a "growth stock." Most retailers do not carry their own paper. They sell it to banks and other big lenders at a discount price. This forces a consumer to deal with an institution, probably in another city, other than the original seller.

There is no accurate way of knowing the extent of overindebtedness. Morris Rabinowitch, president of Financial Counselors in San Francisco, at an annual meeting of the American Association of Credit Counselors on August 29, 1968, said that "More than one-third of all American families are overextended in their debts and are on the brink of serious trouble."[21] At the same meeting, Dr. William Regan, dean of the Business School, University of San Francisco, termed the American society one in which "everybody owes," and that there were 41,000 personal bankruptcies filed in California in 1967. Dean Regan felt that a "consumption ethic" has replaced the "work ethic."

Families that use installment credit comprise 65 percent of all American families. The *National Consumer Finance Association Yearbook for 1971* reported that on June 30, 1971, 182,851 personal (nonbusiness) bankruptcy petitions were filed in the United States—an increase of 45 percent over 1962.

The University of Michigan Survey Research Center found that 10 percent of families have installment obligations exceeding the 20 percent of income usually considered a danger point. Ten percent of our families in financial trouble adds up to about 6 million families.

Margolius pointed up a local example of overindebtedness at the large Washington, D.C., Naval Base. The commanding officer at the base found that 7 to 8 percent of the civilian staff was in debt to an extent requiring intervention with creditors.[22]

Many professional financial counselors blame our society's financial sickness on automobile loans and an ever-increasing number of personal loans. They recommend an intensive program of financial education for the consumer and the merchant. Young marrieds, in particular, are in need of financial education because this age group (ages 25 to 34) has the highest percent of disposable income committed to repayment of installment credit. This group, and most of us, must learn our credit limit, and the merchant must learn he can survive only with a healthy consumer.

[21] *U.S. News & World Report,* Sept. 16, 1968, p. 81.

[22] Sidney Margolius, *The Innocent Consumer vs. The Exploiters,* Trident Press, New York, 1967, p. 50.

Debt consolidation and debt adjusters

An ad in the paper reads, "Consolidate your debts; borrow $2,000 at 6 percent, pay back $14.33 a month." Sounds easy, but the 6 percent rate adds up to 15 to 40 percent when brokerage fees, closing costs, credit reports, insurance premium, and other costs are included. Such dishonest debt adjusters, and there are many, do not loan money. They try to keep their victims in bondage for many years. Abuses have been so bad that commercial debt adjusters have been banned in twenty-two states and regulated in twelve states.[23] Sixteen states have no regulation at all.

Most of the commercial debt pooling businesses are "just plain vultures," a credit manager said. A lawyer said, 'They can't do any more for you than you could do for yourself." A priest suggests, "You'd be better off going to a nonprofit consolidator."

More and more people in serious debt trouble consult honest debt consolidators or adjusters. This service is rendered usually without charge by some counseling groups and for a modest fee of about 10 to 12 percent of the indebtedness. Charles Neal, who has had much experience in private debt counseling, has doubts about creditors counseling debtors. In his book, *Sense with Dollars,* he wrote, "There is a serious conflict of interest. . . . It may be similar to asking the Tobacco Institute to help us curb our smoking. Those who helped you get into trouble in the first place qualify poorly as experts to help you get out."

Honest, nonprofit debt counseling ranges from the Michigan League Budget Service, which operates a chain of nonprofit counseling offices, to Family Debt Counselors of Phoenix, one of the oldest nonprofit counseling groups in the country. St. Paul, Minnesota, has the credit counseling service of the Credit Bureau and the Family Service Social Agency. The Legal Aid Society operates a financial counseling service in many cities (Chicago, Atlanta, Cleveland, Buffalo, and many more). A union member can go to his AFL-CIO Community Service Activities for free help.

Charles Neal and other critics of some consumer credit counseling services may be right in questioning whether extenders of credit (banks, insurance companies, consumer finance companies, etc.) can be objective in their debt counseling. The fact remains that the National Foundation for Consumer Credit, Inc. (NFCC), has been a leader in establishing some 120 consumer credit counseling services in about 36 states and Canada. These counseling services are sponsored by the NFCC but are locally owned and managed. Their credit counseling services must be free if sponsored by the NFCC. Also, counselors cannot be employed by any creditor of the family or individual being counseled.

According to the NFCC 1969 report of some 120 counseling services, over 60,000 American and Canadian families with debt problems were helped. The statistics concerning those interviewed in 1969 showed that only 38 percent needed counseling and financial advice, while over 50 percent needed the intervention of a neutral third party to develop a personal money management program. In the thirty-two operating offices which reported the number of

---

[23] *The New York Times,* Feb. 26, 1968.

families that elected bankruptcy, there was a decline from 1.5 percent in 1968 to 1.4 percent in 1969. [24]

Objectives of a good debt counseling program

A good consumer debt counseling program should (1) be honest in recommending bankruptcy to a client who is so deep in dept that relief via a wage-earner plan is impossible, (2) assist families or individuals in setting up a feasible money management program, (3) recognize when family members are in need of psychological or psychiatric counseling, (4) charge a fair and reasonable fee if counseling is not free, and (5) make the effort to get cooperation from the whole family to help carry out the program plan.

Easier credit for teen-agers

"Charge it" is a magic phrase to most adults. This magic phrase in the mouths of teen-agers is now an explosive buying weapon.

Along with the right to vote, many 18- and 19-year-olds are taking on serious legal responsibilities of adults: the right to enter into contracts, to sue or be sued, to borrow money, and to use credit. Seventeen states have already lowered the age of majority from 21 to 18 or 19.

"I want tomorrow today"

As legally full-fledged consumers, young adults will experience the dangers and advantages of wanting tomorrow today. More than ever, retailers will want their share from this group, numbering over 16 million and with an income of around $20 billion annually.

The right to enter into contracts means that young adults can be held to installment sales agreements, whereas previously the contract could be voided whether fraud could be proved or not.

Youths should be especially wary of eager salesmen who require little or no collateral. Credit jewelers, for example, have offered youngsters credit long before they became of legal age. Girls are pressured to buy flatware and stainless-steel pots and pans at exorbitant prices. Just prior to graduation, salesmen make a special drive to sell jewelry to boys to give to their girl friends. Teen-age married couples expecting their first baby are often pestered by door-to-door baby furniture salesmen who pass out credit to anyone gullible enough to sign on the dotted line. Encyclopedia salesmen sign up young marrieds and students for hundreds of dollars' worth of books. Business and dance schools have long been known to lure young applicants with pay-as-you learn advertisements.

According to a recent survey of the youth market, 19 percent of our youth (ages 14 to 18) possess department store credit cards. When retailers woo our teen-agers with come-ons such as charm courses, gift packs, free samples, or credit cards, they are giving them a taste of easy credit before most of them know how to use it. The president of the Bowery Savings Bank in New York City says that such credit is "something like teaching the young to use narcotics." Easy credit is a dangerous weapon in anybody's hand, let alone in the hands of inexperienced youth.

"Easy credit" hurts the poor

According to a massive study by the Federal Trade Commission (1966) of ninety-six retailers with sales of $226 million, which represented 85 percent of the sales of furniture, appliance, and department store retailers in the District of Columbia, the poor did pay more. [25] FTC found that low-income market retailers

[24] A full statistical report is available from the National Foundation for Consumer Credit, Inc., 18–19 H Street, N.W., Washington, D.C. 20006.

[25] *Economic Report on Installment Credit and Retail Sales Practices in the District of Columbia,* Washington, March 1968.

used installment credit in 93 percent of their sales, against 27 percent for general market retailers. On the average, goods purchased for $100 at wholesale sold for $255 in the low-income market stores, compared with $159 in general market stores. Furthermore, the poor paid, on the average, 24 percent for credit compared to an average of 20 percent for general market customers. This suggests that the marketing system for distribution of durable goods to low-income consumers is costly. Their markups are very much higher than those of general market retailers, as pointed out, but the low-income market retailers do not make particularly high net profits. Furthermore, the high prices charged by low-income market retailers suggest the absence of effective price competition. What competition there is takes the form of easier credit availability. Hence, the poor depend upon easy-credit merchants. And easy-credit merchants take "early action" against default rather than using such action as a last resort.

FTC recommends for the poor that (1) free financial, professional counseling be given in their neighborhood, (2) reasonable credit be made available, (3) legal rights of buyers and creditors be equalized, (4) chain stores be encouraged to enter the low-income area, and (5) consumer protection activities be intensified to eliminate fraud and deception in advertising and credit.

MANAGEMENT OF CREDIT

As you understand by now, consumer credit is intricate and deceptive. A few conclusions may be helpful.

1.   Use credit only when necessary or where benefits justify the cost and risk involved.
2.   Assume no more debt than you can safely repay out of current income.
3.   Shop for the best credit bargain. None of the credit terms are easy.
4.   Go to a bank or your credit union first to investigate the possibilities.
5.   Know your lender or dealer.
6.   Do not expect too much from creditors. After all, their main concern is to collect your debt.
7.   Use thirty-day charge accounts intelligently. Do not use them to spend next month's income, or charge accounts will become real debts.
8.   Do not let an installment debt run so long that the psychological enjoyment of "having it now" wears off before the debt is paid.
9.   When buying major items, such as a car and expensive appliances, it is not wise to sign up for terms that will have you owing more than the resale value of the article you bought. In some car deals, the buyer's debt exceeds the value of the car for fifteen or more months in the case of a small down payment and thirty-six months to pay.
10.   In general, make the down payment at large as possible and the repayment period as short as possible. The lower the down payment, the greater the percentage of cars that have had to be repossessed.
11.   Avoid *balloon notes,* in which the installments pay off only a part of the debt and after the last installment is paid, the balance is due in one payment. When you cannot handle the lump-sum payment, you are in difficulty.

12.   Let yourself be "sold down." The merchant or lender sells down when he believes that you are assuming too big a debt risk and suggests that you make a larger down payment, postpone the purchase, or use a layaway plan instead. The chances are that such businessmen, though rare in this day of selling credit as well as goods, know what they are talking about.

13.   Shop around for credit. Since July 1, 1969, consumers have had the advantage of knowing both the total dollar cost of credit and the total cost of credit in annual percentage rate on installment purchases. Take full advantage of this valuable information by shopping around for the best terms.

Whatever your reasons, using credit is not necessarily good or bad. It is the way you use it that counts. You have to manage credit. If you do not, your debts will manage you. Someone wisely said, "Credit is a good servant but a bad master."

A CASHLESS SOCIETY COMES CLOSER?

An article in the October 1967 issue of *Changing Times* magazine stated that "soon you'll never see money at all." Instead of money, "you'll see a plastic card and a telephone." Maybe so. This would be a convenience and it might be more efficient, but it could also be a booby trap for your budgeting.

The trends   There is no doubt about the trends. A cashless revolution is going on right now. There are over 300 million credit cards in this country today. Eight out of every ten adults have at least one card. In 1971, over 62 million people in this country held bank credit cards issued by nearly 10,000 banks.

The most popular bank credit cards are Master Charge and BankAmericard. Over one-fourth of our banks offer Master Charge cards, and close to a million retail stores accept them. BankAmericard is a close second to Master Charge in terms of number of holders and number of banks in the plan.

The public has accepted these and other credit cards at a fast rate. Sellers of goods and services—even many doctors, lawyers, and the Internal Revenue Service—have accepted credit cards.

The general acceptance of credit cards by the public and by retailers has led to technological experiments that may lead to a cashless society in the near future. The Bank of Delaware, for example, is using for each patron a plastic card with punched holes corresponding to his account number. Four cooperating retail stores are equipped with Touch-Tone telephones into which the plastic card is slipped. When a customer purchases an item, the clerk slips the card into a phone and dials instructions to a computer as to how payment is to be handled. The computer answers by voice, "yes" or "no" in regard to the customer's credit standing. If this system is successful, it is possible to extend it to over 60 million persons who presently have centralized credit files.

Preauthorized payment of bills has already been taken over by computers. This service can include mortgage payments, car payments, rent, insurance premiums, and many other kinds of regular payments.

A pilot test of a new credit-card system is presently set up in Upper Arlington, a suburb of Columbus, Ohio. Magnetized BankAmericards are used instead of ordinary credit cards. When you buy something, the salesclerk dials a bank's computer center, places the card in a special "terminal," reports the dollar amount of the sale, and gets an oral OK from the computer. The whole process takes about fifteen seconds and does away with most of the paper work. Meanwhile, the computer records the sale for billing to the customer and immediately credits the merchant's bank account for the transaction. That way, he doesn't have to wait for his money. An adjunct of the system is a twenty-four-hour-a-day automated teller, enabling customers to get a loan, make a deposit, transfer money between savings and checking accounts, or make loan payments—all with no human teller present. One of these days, say the sponsors, the total teller machine will be as commonplace as mailboxes.

Is this an invitation to trouble?

How you will manage under this checkless, cashless system will depend on your understanding of the system. You undoubtedly will find the new system more convenient, or you might find it an invitation to trouble. After all, credit doesn't add dollars to your income. And this system makes it too easy to spend and borrow. Some financial counseling experts believe that the easier it is to get credit, the more people will run into financial trouble. In the last ten years the average family income has increased about 50 percent, but family borrowing has gone up 100 percent. And personal bankruptcies went up 200 percent in the same period. In 1949 the average family paid out about 11 percent of its total income for debt repayment and interest charges, including mortgage installment, charge account cost, etc. Today it pays out over 22 percent. At this rate, what will it be by 1980? Perhaps by 1980 most of us will be in hock forever at 18 percent!

Discount for cash   So the cashless, checkless society may be here sooner than we think unless so many people get into a financial mess that somebody starts a 5 or 10 percent discount for the use of cash instead of credit. Perhaps some group could popularize cash instead of credit. Members could be issued official identification cards. The person with a card will patronize cooperating businesses, pay in cash, and get a discount for so doing. On the other hand, it may be too late to even dream about a cash-and-carry discount system. And it may also be too late to request credit cards to carry this warning: "Caution. Excessive use of credit cards may be hazardous to your economic health." Most of us can appreciate the advice of the *Lothian Mirror* (Texas): "It isn't buying on time that's difficult; it's paying on time."

QUESTIONS FOR DISCUSSION

1. Is it wise to buy on credit?
2. How can you tell a good credit risk from a poor credit risk?
3. Is consumer credit truly a vital part of today's America?
4. Can credit help stretch income?
5. What legal action is open to creditors when debtors fail to carry out the terms of credit contracts?

6.   Why did Congress pass the truth-in-lending law? The Fair Credit Reporting Act?

7.   What are the various methods of stating the cost of consumer credit?

8.   In the light of national trends in the use of consumer credit, is there a danger that debtors are a threat to their own well-being and that of their creditors?

9.   Why has personal bankruptcy been a more popular avenue of relief than the wage-earner plan?

10.   In what ways can the Consumer Credit Protection Act (the truth-in-lending law) help you in making a wiser decision when using credit in the marketplace?

11.   Should there be a law against the use of tricky methods for figuring finance charges?

12.   What is the meaning of APR?

13.   Why is it more difficult for women to get credit than it is for men?

PROJECTS

1.   Investigate the different methods used by local department stores or other retail businesses to compute finance charges. What different kinds of charge plans are available? Which one is best for the consumer?

2.   Shop around for a loan for a new car (know exactly the kind and model of car you want, the equipment you are going to buy, etc.). What credit source offers you the lowest interest rates? The best payment plans? Did each lender follow the information requirements spelled out in the truth-in-lending law?

3.   Interview people in your community or members of your family to find out what problems they have with their credit cards and charge accounts. Bring in billing statements and study them in class.

4.   Does your state have a consumer credit law providing for good consumer credit standards, practices, and policies? As a starter, send for the free pamphlet entitled *Consumer Credit Practices and Policies* published by Consumer Federation of America, 1012 Fourteenth Street, N.W., Washington, D.C. 20005.

5.   Prepare a report on the consumer credit promotional gimmicks and come-ons specifically directed at the youth market. Since older teen-agers are full-fledged legal consumers in over seventeen states, a whole new consumer credit market has opened up to them. How are they doing? Any pitfalls? Any advantages?

6.   Go to your local credit bureau to find out how it operates, the type of information recorded, and the ways in which an inaccurate record can be challenged and changed.

7.   Send for a copy of the Fair Credit Reporting Act or a summary of this federal law and discuss how it protects consumers from abuses. Work up a

couple of situations for role playing which show how consumers might use the Fair Credit Reporting Act.

8.   Discuss *(a)* problems low-income families face in obtaining credit from legitimate sources and *(b)* new experimental programs in making credit available to low-income consumers.

SUGGESTED READINGS

Annual Report to Congress on Truth in Lending, Board of Governors of the Federal Reserve System (see latest edition).

"Charge Account Bankers: The New Merchants." *Consumer Reports,* January 1971.

Consumer Credit Policy Statement No. 4, Federal Trade Commission news release, May 7, 1970.

"The Credit Card Trap," *Consumer Reports,* November 1971, pp. 1–2.

"Credit Insurance: How You Can Get Soaked," *Changing Times,* August 1972, pp.   6–9.

Credit Practices and Policies, Consumer Federation of America, Washington, 1972 (leaflet).

Finance Facts Yearbook, National Consumer Finance Association, Washington (see latest edition).

International Credit Union Yearbook, CUNA International, Madison, Wis. (see latest edition).

Kaplan, Lawrence J., and Salvatore Malteis: "The Economics of Loansharking," *American Journal of Economics and Sociology,* vol. 27, 1968.

NCFA Guide to the Fair Credit Reporting Act: What It Is, How to Comply, National Consumer Finance Association, Washington, 1971.

Neal, Charles: *Sense with Dollars,* Doubleday & Company, Inc., Garden City, N.Y., 1965.

What Truth in Lending Means to You, Board of Governors of the Federal Reserve System, 1970.

"Workshop on Consumer Credit," *Journal of Home Economics,* January 1968.

CHAPTER 7
BUYING FOOD

A first-class soup is more creative than a second-class poem.

D<sub>r. Jean Mayer, professor of nutrition at Harvard University, in a news release on June 15, 1971, said, "We are now in the midst of two food revolutions. First, our food habits are changing very rapidly. Second, the foods we are eating today are very different from what we consumed a few years ago. They can be expected to change even more in the coming decade."

Thus much of what we so recently knew has been turned upside down and inside out. Nearly all aspects of our lives are affected—the food we eat and the nutrition we think we obtain. Today, we are uncertain what our response should be.

PART 1   FOOD SHOPPING BEGINS AT HOME

Food habits are changing

Dr. Rodney Leonard, executive director of the Community Nutrition Institute in Washington, D.C., told the Food Labeling Conference on December 8 to 10, 1971, that the "food factory has more influence on nutritional intake than the family, displacing cultural practices and traditions which once transmitted nutritional skills from one generation to the next. Health experts tell us to count calories, but calories may be devoid of nutritional value other than energy." He said, "Consumers buy processed meat products and assume they are a primary source of protein; yet, they contain more fat now than even a generation ago." He goes on to say that "Today the American consumer is a functional illiterate in food and nutrition. The food processor and manufacturer insist the free market allows consumers to tell what products they want."[1] There is, however, no freedom in ignorance.

That, in a nutshell, is the problem confronting American consumers today. The need is to allow the consumer to communicate intelligently with those who will increasingly control the nutritional quality of our food supply.

Thus we have almost a whole new ball game today. This chapter will try to challenge consumers and inform them about the "food revolution" and the role they can play in securing the most nutritious and the safest food at a reasonable price in the marketplace.

Part I of this chapter will center on the fact that food shopping begins at home, and Part II will concentrate on food shopping in the marketplace.

We shall see that consumers need more specific information about food products—about quantity, type, and proportions of ingredients and about quality, nutrient value, wholesomeness, and relative price—to protect their economic interest and safeguard their health.

But first, we need to know the extent of hunger and malnutrition in the United States. We have been told that we even have "affluent malnutrition" as well as "low-income malnutrition."

QUALITY OF DIETS IN THE UNITED STATES

The U.S. Department of Agriculture made a nationwide survey of household food consumption in 1965. Diets that provided the recommended dietary allow-

[1] See Helen E. Nelson (ed.), *Consumer Policy on Food Labeling,* University of Wisconsin Extension Center for Consumer Affairs, Milwaukee, 1972.

ances set by the National Research Council's Food and Nutrition Board for seven nutrients—protein, calcium, iron, vitamin A value, thiamine, riboflavin, and ascorbic acid—were rated "good." Diets that furnished less than two-thirds of the allowance for one or more of these nutrients were rated "poor." The survey showed the following:

"You are what you eat"

1. One-half of the diets were good and one-fifth were poor in both urban and rural areas.
2. Diets were poor in more households in the North Central and Southern regions than in other regions.
3. More high- than low-income families had good diets, although there were poor diets at high-income levels.
4. Diets in 15 percent of the families were below allowances for three or more nutrients.
5. Diets were most often below allowances in calcium, vitamin A value, and ascorbic acid.
6. Relatively fewer families had good diets in 1965 than in 1955.
7. Calcium, vitamin A value, and ascorbic acid were the nutrients most often below allowances in both 1955 and 1965, but more often in 1965.

Increased consumption of milk or other good sources of calcium, vegetables, and fruit is needed to improve our diets. Awareness of the foods that make up a good diet, a desire to eat these foods, and enough money to buy adequate food are necessary if most families are to have good diets.

Teen-age nutrition

Dr. Evelyn B. Spindler, nutritionist with the U.S. Department of Agriculture, reported the startling and disturbing fact that "6 out of every 10 girls and 4 out of every 10 boys have poor diets."[2]

Why are America's teen-agers so poorly fed? Here, summarized by Dr. Spindler, are the main reasons: (1) They skip breakfast. A study of 2,000 Flint, Michigan, high school teen-agers found that nearly two-thirds regularly ate no breakfast. In an Illinois study, more than five times as many girls as boys ate no breakfast. Most of the girls missed breakfast for weight reasons. (2) They select snacks unwisely. One-fourth of teen-agers' calories come from snacks, according to an Iowa study. (3) They drink little or no milk, the important source for calcium. A major study in eight Western states found insufficient calcium intake in half of the girls and in one-fifth of the boys. (4) They are indifferent to meals. Why? Partly because of social pressures, their growing independence, and their hurried schedules. A study of Guilford, North Carolina, high school students found 15 percent missed at least one meal daily. A University of California study found a large percentage of teen-agers "who never really had one organized meal." (5) They fear fat. Many adolescent girls go on fad or crash diets. The result is they often deprive their bodies of much-needed nutrients. More teen-age girls than boys are overweight, according to studies of 15- and 16-year-olds in Oregon, Iowa, and Maine.

We like to feel that our youngsters are well fed in this country. But research on teen-age diets in this country confirms the ugly fact that many of them need improved eating habits.

[2] "Report on Teen-age Nutrition," *Clubwoman,* General Federation of Women's Clubs, March 1965.

What has happened since the last national nutritional survey was taken in 1965? In the fall of 1967, Congress directed the Department of Health, Education, and Welfare to survey and identify the prevalence, magnitude, and distribution of malnutrition and related health problems. The program selected ten states plus New York City as geographically representative of the major areas of the country. The evaluation of nutritional status involved about forty thousand individuals including representatives of the major races; the young and the old; low-, middle-, and high-income groups; and males and females. The results of this survey, the largest ever conducted in our country, should be of great value to Congress, health authorities, and consumers.

The major findings of the survey were as follows (Figure 7-1):

Malnutrition at all economic levels

1. A significant proportion of the population surveyed was malnourished or was showing a high risk of developing nutritional problems.
2. There was a high prevalence of low vitamin A among Mexican Americans in the low-income states, as contrasted to an absence of vitamin A problems among Puerto Ricans in the high-income states.
3. Malnutrition was found more commonly among blacks, less among Spanish Americans, and least among whites. Generally, there was increasing malnutrition as income level decreased.
4. Although income is a major determinant of nutritional status, other factors such as social, cultural, and geographic differences also have an effect on the level of nutrition of a group.
5. Adolescents, 10 to 16 years, had the highest prevalence of unsatisfactory nutritional status; male adolescents had more evidence of malnutrition than females. The elderly also had increased nutritional deficiencies; this finding was not restricted to the very poor or to any single ethnic group.
6. The higher the homemaker's educational level, the fewer the nutritional inadequacies in the children.
7. Many persons made poor food choices that led to inadequate diets and to poor use of money available for food—many households seldom used food rich in vitamin A. Also, there was heavy emphasis on meat, rather than use of less expensive but excellent protein sources, such as fish, poultry, or legumes. The data also showed that a substantial number of children and adolescents had caloric intakes below the dietary standards.
8. In adolescents it was found that between-meal snacks of high-carbohydrate foods such as candies, soft drinks, and pastries were associated with dental caries.
9. School lunch programs were found to be a very important part of good nourishment for many children, especially in the low-income states.
10. Evidence of retarded growth and development was more prevalent in the low-income states.
11. Obesity was found to be most prevalent in adult women. Men were less frequently obese, although white males had a relatively high prevalence of obesity when compared with black males.
12. With regard to specific nutrients, the following major points can be summarized:

FIGURE 7-1 Relative importance of nutritional problems in the ten-state nutritional survey, 1968 to 1970

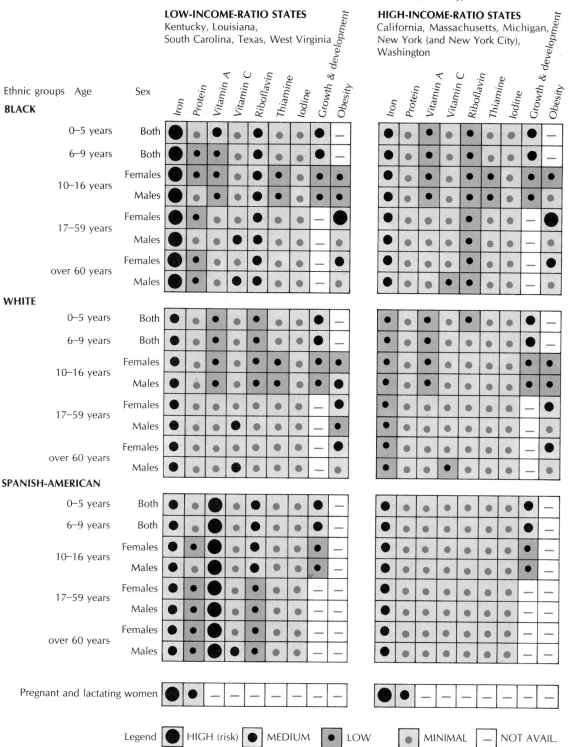

SOURCE: *Nutrition Today,* July–August, 1972, pp. 6–7.

a. Iron-deficiency anemia, as evidenced by a high prevalence of low levels of hemoglobin, was a widespread problem within the population surveyed.

b. A relatively large proportion of pregnant and lactating women had low serum albumin levels, suggesting marginal protein intake.

c. Vitamin A was a problem among many people, but especially among those in the low-income states.

d. Vitamin C was not a major problem except that males had a higher prevalence of lower vitamin C intake than females. The prevalence of low vitamin C intake increased with age.

e. Riboflavin and thiamine status was poor among blacks and young people.

f. There was no evidence of iodine deficiency.

These data are very important because for the first time, the scientific community has available to it a true picture (five volumes) of the nutritional health of a segment of the American people. Now one can study calmly the condition of some of our poor without being buffeted by the fiery oration that surrounded earlier discussions of the nutritional health of our people only a few years ago.

While it is difficult to compare the 1965 and the 1968–1970 nutritional surveys, it would appear that we have not made significant progress in terms of the prevalence, magnitude, and distribution of malnutrition and related health problems. However, health authorities are now aware of specific problem areas that need attention. Consumers, too, have sufficient evidence to make serious efforts to improve the qualitative feeding of the family at home.

BUYING NUTRITIOUS FOOD

American families spend about one-fifth of their income for food. Of course, they can spend much more, but they can be well nourished by spending much less than this amount. To get the most food value for your dollar, you must have knowledge about foods and stores and you must plan and buy carefully *The "basic four"* the food your family needs and likes. Everyone needs the same basic foods. How much each person needs depends largely on age, sex, occupation, and general health.

The first step toward buying nourishing foods is to learn the type of nutrients that are essential to the family's health and well-being. The second step is to learn which foods are good sources of these nutrients.

Nutritionists generally divide foods into groups to show how to select the right foods for good health. The U.S. Department of Agriculture Leaflet no. 424, *Food for Fitness*, suggests these four groups:

1. *Milk group.* Includes milk and dairy products like cheese and ice cream. This group gives calcium, protein, vitamin A, and riboflavin. These nutrients are so important that they should be supplied daily as follows:

Adults	2 or more cups
Teen-agers	1 quart at least
Children	3 to 4 cups
Pregnant and nursing mothers	1½ quarts at least

The alternatives and equivalents to milk on the basis of calcium furnished are:

1-inch cube cheese equals ⅔ cup milk
½ cup cottage cheese equals ⅓ cup milk
½ cup ice cream equals ¼ cup milk

2. *Meat group.* Includes meat, eggs, dry beans; provides protein, iron, and B vitamins. Two or more servings of beef, veal, pork, lamb, poultry, fish, or eggs should be provided daily. Alternates are cooked dry beans, peas or lentils, nuts, peanuts or peanut butter, soya flour, grits, and soybeans. The amount of one serving is two or three ounces of lean meat, poultry, fish, or lentils, four tablespoons of peanut butter, or two eggs.

3. *Vegetable and fruit group.* Provides chiefly vitamin A and vitamin C plus calcium, iron, and some of the B vitamins. Four or more servings should be provided daily for everyone. Serve at least every other day a citrus fruit or some other fruit or vegetable with lots of vitamin C and a dark green or deep yellow vegetable for vitamin A. But don't ignore potatoes and many other good vegetables and fruits.

4. *Bread and cereal group.* Four or more servings in any form that is either whole grain, enriched, or restored provide other B vitamins, iron, calories, and roughage. One serving equals one slice of bread, or a like amount in the form of crackers or baked goods, one ounce of dry cereal, or one-half to three-fourths cup of cooked cereal, cornmeal, grits, macaroni, noodles, rice, or spaghetti.

Well-balanced menus

Fats and sugars, added in cooking and at meals, provide calories for energy. Well-balanced menus can be planned at a reasonable cost using a large variety of foods, according to the Institute of Home Economics of the U.S. Department of Agriculture (Table 7-1).

A note of caution at this point, regarding the use of the basic four groups, is in order. Some nutritional experts, including Dr. Jean Mayer, mentioned earlier, believe that the basic-four classification is outdated. Traditional labeling, listing only some of the ingredients and supplemented by a system of education that just encourages people to eat more of the foods in the basic four groups, does not really do the job. For instance, in what food group is a pizza or a frozen spinach soufflé? Then, too, our food habits have changed much since 1941 or so.

The author is inclined to agree with Dr. Mayer and other nutritional authorities. Even with much-improved nutrient labeling in the works and more to come, the fact remains that the transitional period will not be over quickly. Until a good nutrient labeling program is completed, we will have to use the basic four groups. In other words, we will have to use both programs for some time.

We said earlier that we are now in the midst of two food revolutions. First, the foods we are eating are very different from those we consumed a few years ago. Second, our food habits are changing rapidly.

TABLE 7-1 Menu Patterns with Examples of Light and Heavy Meals

MENU PATTERN	LIGHT MEAL	FOOD GROUP	HEAVY MEAL	FOOD GROUP
		Breakfast		
fruit	orange juice	(3)	half grapefruit	(3)
cereal, milk	cereal, milk	(4, 1)		
egg or meat			bacon, eggs	(2)
bread, butter	cinnamon toast	(4)	toast, butter	(4)
milk (children)	hot chocolate	(1)	hot chocolate	(1)
coffee or tea	coffee		coffee	
		Lunch		
soup ⎫ Choose	chicken salad			
main dish ⎬ 1 or 2	sandwich	(2, 4)	broiled ground beef	(2)
salad ⎭	carrot sticks	(3)	green salad	(3)
fruit	apple	(3)	peach halves	
bread, butter			(canned)	(3)
			muffins, bread	(4)
beverage	milk	(1)	milk	(1)
		Dinner		
main dish	meat loaf	(2)	pork chops, gravy	(2, 1)
potato			baked potato	(3)
vegetable	broccoli, cheese			
	sauce	(3, 1)	spinach	(3)
salad	chef's salad,			
	French dressing	(3)	cabbage slaw	(3)
bread, butter	bread, butter	(4)	bread, butter	(4)
dessert	oatmeal cooky	(4)	frozen lemon	
			custard	(1)
beverage	milk (children)	(1)	milk (children)	(1)
	coffee		coffee	

Our rapidly changing food habits

Although we think we are eating the same foods we ate in the early 1940s, our food habits have changed since then, particularly among young people.

The veterans hospitals offer a good illustration. Hospital administrators are puzzled about how to cope with Vietnam veterans. They are different from other veterans. For example, World War I veterans didn't consider themselves fed unless they had meat and potatoes at every major meal. World War II veterans liked milk. Korean veterans were more interested in salads than their predecessors. Then came the Vietnam veterans, and the whole system broke down.

Vietnam veterans won't eat breakfast. When breakfast is brought in, they pull their blankets over their heads and refuse even to look at it. Then at 10 A.M. they go out to the hall and put their money in vending machines because they're hungry. And so it goes on all day long. They just will not eat their meals according to the patterns that satisfied their predecessors. Now, we could institute programs of nutritional education in the veterans hospitals in an effort to explain the importance of a good breakfast, but that would probably be, in military jargon, counterproductive.

For better or for worse, the pattern according to which people have fed themselves for many generations has broken down. People eat very differently today. Forty percent of all meals are now taken outside the home. The meals taken inside the home are very often a collection of snacks eaten on an individual or small-group basis. This is not the exception, but the rule. In many families, only the ritual meals, such as Christmas and Thanksgiving dinner, remain a symbol of the way families used to eat.

There have been similar changes in foods themselves. Some of these changes have been brought about by consumers; some have been brought about by industry. Many more women are working outside their homes now than was the case when people were primarily farmers and the job of the farm woman was right around the home. As a result, people have much less time to prepare meals. In addition, in many cases, the meal will not be enjoyed by the family as a group.

Industry has created new pressures. The food industry wants to take part in the growth of the economy, just as any other industry does. There are two hundred ten million people in this country, and the population is increasing relatively slowly—at the rate of a couple of million a year. People are becoming more and more inactive, and the amount of food consumed in the United States is basically going up very slowly. It is difficult to create a growing food industry *The food industry today* just by selling food, but you can if you start selling food *and services.* If you *sells food and services* can't sell more potatoes, you sell frozen french fried potatoes; instead of selling spinach, you sell frozen spinach soufflé. The combination of the industrial interests and the consumer's mode of living has had an impact, and instead of buying just food, the housewife buys food and a lot of services. Besides, we have replaced our nonunion labor with union labor, and there have been accompanying strictures in terms of food. In spite of the fact that prices to farmers are going up very slowly, prices of retail items are going up as fast as those of any manufactured product—which in turn means that industry has been looking not only for more efficient ways of doing things but also for cheaper raw materials as a way of keeping costs down. (Food costs rose twice as fast in 1972 as had been predicted—they were 5.5 percent higher than in 1971 the USDA told Congress recently.)

The combination of all this has led to a rapid transformation of the food supply, and this change is going to accelerate.

Textured proteins Some of us are interested, for many reasons, in the development of textured vegetable proteins as meat substitutes. One reason for this interest is that 1 acre can produce as much protein of this type as 10 acres can produce of conventional protein, which in a crowded world is an advantage. Obviously, the use of textured proteins could also keep prices down considerably. No one is sure how rapidly the market for these proteins is developing. The minimum estimate from the Stanford Research Institute is that it would be up to about $2 billion by 1980, replacing perhaps $5 billion worth of meat. From then on, it would develop extremely rapidly. Even now, factories in the United States are very impressive. Vats of dissolved vegetable protein from soybeans or wheat are pushed through what looks very much like a shower head. This produces filaments of protein, resembling nylon strands, which are immediately hardened and turned into nonwoven tissues. These roll out of the machinery like big sheets of newsprint and are dyed, flavored, and then cut into segments which become substitutes for corned beef, turkey, ham, and bacon. These products can be produced at the same rate at which textiles and newsprint are produced—hundreds of feet a minute. They taste pretty good. It is possible to introduce all sorts of nutritional components into them—vitamin B_{12}, other B vitamins, trace elements, and so on—and this will have to be done, by law.

The basic four did not do the job

The point is that developments along these lines will be very rapid as time goes on. It is obvious, however, that traditional labeling, listing only some ingredients and supplemented by a system of education that just encourages people to eat more of the foods in the basic groups, will not really do the job. We must realize that we have very few options if people are to be well fed after the disappearance of traditional food habits and, in many cases, traditional foods. The options are really only two.

First, we could try to enrich and fortify every food with every type of nutrient needed. (It's not an absurd suggestion; it's a possibility.) At present this is undesirable because too much regulation would be involved. We don't have the machinery to do it on a large scale because we don't know enough yet. However, we are doing it at present for foods which constitute a whole meal, such as Metrecal or baby formula. This option, then, is a realistic one.

The other option is to educate people in nutrition so that they can construct a decent diet for themselves. Admittedly, there will still be a need for regulation—for instance, in the case of textured vegetable proteins because they are meat substitutes. We probably will look at them very carefully because of what they need to contain in order to qualify as meat substitutes. This option would not involve regulating every food; rather, there would be an opportunity for choice based on sound nutritional education.

Even a nutritionist can't tell

At present, no matter how much you know about nutrition, you can't deal with most of the processed foods. Consider frozen spinach soufflé, for example, mentioned earlier. What does it contain? Spinach, for one thing, since it says so on the label and it's green. The second ingredient listed is vegetable fat. Who knows whether that means that the soufflé has a high or a low fat content, whether the fat is saturated or not, or whether it is high or low in calories. Eggs are also listed as an ingredient, but you can't really tell whether egg yolk or egg white is meant; whether the product is high in cholesterol, in which case some people should avoid it; or whether mostly egg white is used to give it texture, in which case it is fine. The point is that until labels provide more specific information, all the nutritional knowledge in the world is really not going to help you when you eat something other than the food in the basic four groups. And most of the foods we eat today don't fit in those four groups.

FOOD EXPENDITURES

The purchase of food is one of the most important expenditures families make. In 1971 personal expenditures for food at home totaled $118.4 billion, about $4.4 billion more than in 1970. Including spending for food away from home, personal expenditures for food totaled over $125 billion in 1971.

Food at home accounted for about 15.8 percent of per capita disposable income (after taxes) in 1972, in contrast to about 20 percent in 1960 (Table 7-2).

TABLE 7-2 **Expenditures for Food in Relation to Disposable Income, 1960 and 1965–1972** [a]

YEAR	DISPOSABLE PERSONAL INCOME, BILLIONS OF DOLLARS	PERSONAL COMSUMPTION EXPENDITURES FOR FOOD [b]					
		For use at home [c]		Away from home [d]		Total	
		Amount billions of dollars	Percentage of income	Amount billions of dollars	Percentage of income	Amount billions of dollars	Percentage of income
1960	350.0	56.8	16.2	13.3	3.8	70.1	20.0
1965	473.2	69.3	14.6	16.5	3.5	85.8	18.1
1966	511.9	73.8	14.4	18.2	3.6	92.0	18.0
1967	546.3	74.5	13.6	19.4	3.6	93.9	17.2
1968	591.0	79.0	13.4	20.7	3.5	99.7	16.9
1969	634.2	84.2	13.3	21.9	3.4	106.1	16.7
1970	687.8	90.6	13.2	23.4	3.4	114.0	16.6
1971	741.3	93.8	12.7	24.5	3.3	118.3	16.0
1972 [e]	765.7	95.4	12.5	25.6	3.3	121.0	15.8

[a] Quarterly data are seasonally adjusted annual rates.

[b] Derived from data of the Department of Commerce, *Survey of Current Business,* and *The National Income and Product Accounts of the United States, 1929–65,* assuming one-fourth of purchased meals and beverages is alcoholic beverages and the balance of reported alcoholic beverages is for off-premise use (consistent with 1963 Census of Business merchandise line sales). Omits alcoholic beverages, food donated by government agencies to schools and needy persons, and nonpersonal spending for food such as business purchases of meals, food furnished inmates of hospitals and institutions, and food included with transportation tickets and camp fees.

[c] Includes food consumed on farms where produced.

[d] Includes food served to the military and employees of hospitals, prisons, and food service establishments.

[e] Preliminary.

Food is purchased more frequently than any other major item; it is nondurable; and it is one of the few items for which families usually pay cash. Furthermore, the health of the family members depends on the income available and the skill used in managing the food budget and preparing the meals.

Retail food prices higher today

Families have been very concerned over the increase in food prices at home and away from home, especially since 1970. Between August, 1971, when wage-price ceilings were imposed, and May, 1972, prices of retail food at home advanced 2 percent. Expenditures for food at home in 1972 were about 5½ percent above those in 1971. Retail prices of beef and veal averaged 12 percent higher in 1972 than in 1971, prices of fruits and vegetables were about 8 percent higher, and prices of pork were about 11 percent higher. [3]

The Consumer Price Index for Urban Wage Earners and Clerical Workers prepared by the Bureau of Labor Statistics reported that retail food prices (1967 = 100) increased 4.6 points between April, 1971, and April, 1972.

Federal controls on food prices

There are a number of reasons for the substantial increase in retail food prices as compared with prices of other consumer goods. First, the Federal Price Commission controls are based upon a "voluntary system which needs [consumer] help if Americans are to win the fight against inflation." [4] Second, the

[3] *The National Food Situation,* U.S. Department of Agriculture, May, 1972, pp. 4, 6.

[4] *Retail Price Controls,* Internal Revenue Service, Publication S-3021, 1972.

Cost of Living Council decided to exempt unprocessed agricultural products and raw seafood, which means that there are no price controls on fresh products such as vegetables, fruit, and fish. Live animals are unprocessed agricultural products and thus are exempt from controls, and the increased costs of animals are reflected in the retail prices of meat. [5]

Ralph Nader, consumer advocate and critic of the Nixon administration's price-control program, says that there is no consumer participation in the Price Commission's work. He said, "Only companies participate, and when they make contacts with commission staff . . . the public doesn't know about it." In addition, he said, "There is no disclosure of price increases made in violation of the law." So, despite "nearly 20,000 cited violations, consumers don't have specific information on which to base demands for rebates, which altogether might total millions of dollars." [6]

The causes of ballooning food prices are complex. (For a brief explanation of the complexity of food price control, see the *Wall Street Journal* (Apr.3, 1972) article "Difficult Recipe," in Taylor-Troelstrup Reading 49.)

Disposable personal income and food expenditures

Food expenditures accounted for about 15.8 percent of disposable personal income in 1972, according to preliminary estimates (Table 7-2), which represents a decrease of 4.2 percent of income from 1960. In other words, as disposable income rose more rapidly than food expenditures, the share of the nation's income allocated to food declined to about 15.8 percent in 1972, down from 16.0 percent in 1971. This decrease in percentage figures can be deceiving. Actually, the increase in the dollar costs of food since 1960 has been very high, according to the federal government's cost-of-living index.

When the food industry points to the 15.8 percent of personal disposable income spent for food and says, "Consumers never had it so good," it really needs to be reminded that the decline was due, in part, to the nearly universal principle that as personal income rises, people tend to spend a smaller percentage of it for food. Some credit is therefore due to increased earnings of husband and wife in the last twelve years. Furthermore, the 15.8 percent figure includes expenditures of nonprofit institutions and single persons as well as families.

More realistic figures on the cost of food are those of the Bureau of Labor Statistics for three budget levels for a four-person family in the fall of 1971, mentioned in Chapter 5. In this study the recommended cost of food for the lower budget ($7,214) was $1,964, or 34 percent of the consumption total; for the intermediate budget ($10,971), the recommended cost of food was $2,532, or 29 percent of the consumption total; and for the higher budget ($15,905), the recommended cost of food was $3,198, or 27 percent of the consumption total.

The average worker

The Labor Department released figures in April, 1972, showing that the average worker in the United States made less than the minimum budget figure ($7,214). On the basis of these data, the average American worker is spending more than one out of every three dollars to buy food for his family, both at home and away from home. [7]

For retired couples the Bureau of Labor Statistics (Autumn, 1971, prices)

[5] Ibid.

[6] *The New Republic,* Apr. 15, 1972, p. 12.

[7] Reported in *Community Nutrition Institute Weekly Report,* May 4, 1972, p. 4.

Retired couples recommended for the lower ($3,319), intermediate ($4,776), and higher ($7,443) budgets food costs of 30 percent, 28 percent, and 24 percent, respectively. There has, of course, been increased inflation since late 1971.

As we said earlier, the Bureau of Labor Statistics figures are more realistic than the disposable personal income data in terms of the cost of food at home. A glance at Table 7-3, The Cost of Food at Home, will reveal instantly the high dollar cost of food.

TABLE 7-3   Cost of Food at Home Estimated for Food Plans at Three Cost Levels, June, 1972, United States Average [a]

SEX-AGE GROUP [b]	COST FOR ONE WEEK			COST FOR ONE MONTH		
	Low-cost plan	Moderate-cost plan	Liberal plan	Low-cost plan	Moderate-cost plan	Liberal plan
Families:						
Family of two:						
Head 20–35 years [c]	$19.40	$24.60	$30.50	$83.70	$107.00	$132.00
Head 55–75 years [c]	15.80	20.60	24.90	68.50	89.30	107.70
Family of four:						
Preschool children [d]	28.10	35.70	43.70	121.30	155.10	189.40
Schoolchildren [e]	32.60	41.70	51.40	141.10	181.10	223.00
Individuals: [f]						
Children, under 1 year	3.70	4.70	5.20	16.10	20.30	22.70
1–3 years	4.80	6.00	7.20	20.60	26.00	31.20
3–6 years	5.70	7.30	8.80	24.60	31.80	38.20
6–9 years	6.90	8.90	11.10	30.00	38.60	48.30
Girls, 9–12 years	7.90	10.20	12.00	34.10	44.30	52.00
12–15 years	8.70	11.30	13.70	37.60	49.10	59.60
15–20 years	8.90	11.30	13.40	38.40	48.80	58.10
Boys, 9–12 years	8.10	10.40	12.60	35.00	45.20	54.70
12–15 years	9.40	12.50	14.90	40.90	54.00	64.60
15–20 years	10.90	13.90	16.80	47.20	60.20	72.90
Women, 20–35 years	8.20	10.40	12.60	35.30	45.20	54.70
35–55 years	7.80	10.00	12.20	33.90	43.50	52.60
55–75 years	6.60	8.60	10.30	28.70	37.40	44.80
75 years and over	6.00	7.70	9.40	26.10	33.20	40.80
Pregnant	9.70	12.20	14.40	42.10	52.80	62.60
Nursing	11.20	14.00	16.40	48.70	60.70	71.20
Men, 20–35 years	9.40	12.00	15.10	40.80	52.10	65.30
35–55 years	8.70	11.20	13.70	37.90	48.50	59.40
55–75 years	7.80	10.10	12.30	33.60	43.80	53.10
75 years and over	7.20	9.70	11.80	31.40	42.20	51.10

[a] Estimates computed from quantities in food plans published in *Family Economics Review*, October, 1964. Costs of the plans were first estimated by using average price per pound of each food group paid by urban survey families at three income levels in 1965. These prices were adjusted to current levels by use of *Retail Food Prices by Cities* released by the Bureau of Labor Statistics.

[b] Persons of the first age listed up to but not including the second age.

[c] Ten percent added for family-size adjustment.

[d] Man and woman, 20 to 35 years; children 1 to 3 and 3 to 6 years.

[e] Man and woman, 20 to 35 years; child, 6 to 9; and boy, 9 to 12 years.

[f] Costs given for persons in families of four. For families of other sizes, adjust thus: one-person family, add 20 percent; two-person family, add 10 percent; three-person family, add 5 percent; five-person family, subtract 5 percent; six-person family or more, subtract 10 percent.

SOURCE: *Family Economics Review*, September, 1972.

What, then, can we conclude from the above data? First, the average American worker's family with an income of $7,214 spends about one-third of its income for food; second, the average retired couple spends from 24 to 30 percent of their income for food; and third, the family of four with an average income of about $10,971 will spend about 29 percent of its income for food.

The low-income consumer: food costs in the ghettos

In the United States about 25 million people—almost one in every eight Americans—live in poverty. In 1971 about 14.2 million persons, or 6.9 percent of our population, received public assistance to purchase basic supplies of food and clothing and to obtain shelter. In the twenty-six largest cities, one in every ten persons (10.3 percent) received public assistance.

In the ghettos

Many low-income consumers would not be able to meet even basic nutritional needs without food stamps. Eligible persons can get food stamps each month, paying less than the stamps are worth, or if they are very poor, they can get the stamps free. When they purchase food at the grocery store, they pay with stamps.

The theory behind food-stamp subsidy is a good one, but there are problems in implementation.

For most American families, then, the largest percentage of consumption expenditures is for food at home or away from home.

There is also the increasing problem of health hazards in many foods— additives, food coloring, feed hormones, "empty calories," vitamin poisoning, snacks with little nutrition, and overacceptance of heavily advertised foods as a fetish in diet, to mention a few. In addition to health hazards in food, there are financial waste in trading stamps and other promotional gimmicks, short-weighting, nonprice competition, freezer-meat frauds, and other deceptions in the marketplace.

Shopping skills eroded

Technological progress has also widened the information gap. Many consumers are finding their shopping skills eroded by scientific marketing, irresponsible advertising, clever packaging, and new kinds of processing. Who, for example, can pinch a cyclamate or tell the amount of meat contained in a frozen dinner? Again, the food industry has been less than enlightening.

The stakes in this game are not peanuts. After all, we spent no less than $118.3 billion dollars for food at home in 1971. Most families spend more dollars for food than for any other major purchase. More important, perhaps, is the increasing threat of unsafe, untested, and unnecessary chemicals in food products.

CHEMICALS IN FOOD

Food additives are a controversial subject today as the FDA and its critics argue over the safety of various additives, their effectiveness, and their necessity.

The "chemical feast"

One thing, however, is certain about food additives: A lot of them are used. They constitute a $500-million market. Dr. Ben Feingold, an authority on chemicals in food, lists more than 2,200 different substances added to food. Among them are 33 different types of preservatives, 112 thickeners and stabilizers, 28 antioxidants, and over 1,600 artificial flavorings.

During the 1950s many people became concerned about the increasing use of additives. One result of this was a series of federal laws.

In 1958, Congress passed the Food Additives Amendment to the 1938 Food, Drug, and Cosmetic Act. The amendment's basic purpose was to protect public health by requiring proof of a substance's safety before it could be added to food. The Food and Drug Administration was made responsible for determining additive safety.

The Delaney Clause of the 1958 amendment provided further protection against dangerous additives. It required the FDA to ban any additive which induces cancer in laboratory animals.

A third protection, the Color Additives Amendment, was passed by Congress in 1960. Under its provisions, the FDA must certify the safety of color additives. Since 1960 several color additives have been removed from the market because tests showed they were possible cancer-causing agents.

However, despite these laws, consumer protection against the dangers of numerous additives is far from complete. Some additives do not come under the 1958 amendment's provisions because they were in use and were considered safe when the law went into effect. These make up the GRAS (Generally Recognized As Safe) List.

Many critics have charged the FDA with being lax in its testing of food additives. One recent controversy involving cyclamates illustrates the critics' charges. Only after private tests had shown their danger did the FDA order cyclamates removed from the market.

And that's only one example. Other widely used additives are under attack from several sources, among them BHA and BHT, preservatives used in cereals and many other foods; the synthetic color used for oranges; and nitrites and nitrates, used in meats. In August, 1972, the USDA ruled that nitrites and nitrates would have to be listed on packages of cured meats after February 19, 1973. Food additives today are embroiled in a controversy, with no end in sight.

In late 1972, two more bills were introduced but had not passed at this writing. One bill, the Food Protective Act, would seek to broaden the authority of the Food and Drug Administration to regulate food additives and would require the government to set nutritional standards for food. The other bill would seek to broaden coverage of the Delaney section of the present law banning the use of additives which have been shown to cause cancer in animals or humans. This bill would also ban additives linked to hereditary changes and birth defects, says Dr. Dee Graham, chairman of the food science and nutrition department of the University of Missouri.

Food additives are used mainly because they serve a useful purpose without posing a significant threat to human health. However, the overall impact, some scientists say, can be nothing but alarming. The combination of known facts about additive hazards, the huge volume of their use, and the great voids in knowledge about their effects on people outweigh all the reassuring arguments.

Michael F. Jacobson, presently with the Center for Science in the Public Interest, points out in his recent book, *Eater's Digest,* that the main reason for the use of additives is to increase the profitability of food manufacturers. He says that chemicals are often less expensive than the natural substances they replace, and they make for greater efficiency in the processing, storage, distribution, and marketing of food products. He said, "All food additives help companies make money, and that, in a nutshell, is why additives are usually used."[8]

Many scientists say that one of the chief reasons for adding chemicals to foods is to keep them from spoiling in transit. And some additives keep foods as close to their original form as possible.

Our change in life-style—more women working, less time for food preparation, more demand for convenience foods, and more attractive food—has helped speed up the acceptance of added chemicals in our food.

Dangers in additives: vitamin poisoning

Perhaps Dr. Dee Graham best summed up the dangers in the use of additives when he said, "There is no such thing as a safe additive, only safe uses for food additives under definite circumstances."

The "sugar-coated children's hour"—TV

Children's vitamins, heavily advertised on television and through other media, are of special concern. Dr. Albert Rauber, Emory University pediatrics professor, says that the candy-flavored children's vitamins advertised on television are usually unnecessary and sometimes dangerous. Dr. Rauber, also director of the Poison Control Center in Atlanta, Georgia, said that he "linked television advertising to 34 cases of vitamin poisoning . . . handled by the control center during the first months of 1972."[9] Each year more than 3,400 cases of vitamin poisoning among children under 5 are reported. An additional 370 children suffer from the more serious iron poisoning.[10] (The interesting case of a 5-year-old child who ate forty Pals vitamins containing iron on September 10, 1972, is reported in Taylor-Troelstrup Reading 43.)

Dr. Jean Mayer, professor of nutrition at Harvard University, said, "Every day, Americans are inundated with vitamin advertising, some of which is outrageous."[11]

Sometimes buck-passing kills

On November 10, 1972, Action for Children's Television, a group of concerned parents, asked the Federal Trade Commission to ban vitamin ads on children's TV shows. The FTC staff has not acted on the request. As of this writing, the FDA has not taken action either. And the Federal Communications Commission, which could ban the ads, is waiting for reactions from the FDA and the FTC. So the buck-passing continues, and each day children are rushed to hospitals to be treated for vitamin poisoning.

What is the consumer to do?

First, if you eat a well-balanced daily diet, including plenty of fruits, vegetables, whole-grain or enriched grain products, vitamin D-enriched milk, and other animal products, you don't need vitamin supplements, says Dr. Jean Mayer, noted professor of nutrition at Harvard University. The "if," however, is a big one, as shown by the findings of the latest nutritional survey, 1969 to 1970.

Second, we have not been successful in educating the consumer to read food labels and stop buying foods containing *extra* additives. However, the consumer cannot very well do this until the FDA and the food manufacturers become convinced that labels should provide nutritional information. The labels

[8] *Eater's Digest: The Consumer's Factbook of Food Additives,* Doubleday & Company, Inc., Garden City, N.Y., 1972.

[9] Associated Press report, Apr. 15, 1972.

[10] Chicago *Daily News* syndicated article reported in the *St. Louis Post-Dispatch,* Apr. 16, 1972, p. 12G.

[11] *St. Louis Post-Dispatch,* Sept. 13, 1972, p. 5E.

of many food products will supply such information in the near future, as we shall see in Part II of this chapter.

Third, consumers can try to persuade the FDA to require that nutritional information, in easily understandable units, appear on food labels. There is a *recommended dietary allowance* (RDA) for each nutrient—that is, the amount of that nutrient that you need each day. This is the amount that you should seek to get from your vitamin supplement—any more would be a waste of money, unnecessary, and possibly dangerous, as we have already noted.

Your RDA may be showing

Fourth, Citrus Red No. 2, an artificial coloring additive used in meats and on oranges, has not been banned by the FDA. Many experts consider it unsafe, however. Make your views know to the FDA, to your representatives in Congress, and to food processors.

Finally, the problem of food additives is a complex one offering no simple solution. Undoubtedly, it may be impractical and unsafe to remove all additives. Some are needed to prevent spoilage. But the value of others is questionable.

The long-term effects of additives on the human body are as yet unknown, but researchers continually find dangers in many of them. (See Taylor-Troelstrup Reading 47.)

HEALTH FOODS: ORGANIC FOOD

Organic food hoax

What are organic foods? The Federal Drug Administration is reluctant to define the term "organic." The Federal Trade Commission is also supposed to be drawing up definitions of health foods. Recently the FTC ruled that Sugar in the Raw, a health food favorite, couldn't be advertised as higher in nutrition than other sugar. The nutritional superiority of health foods is a popular claim today. Food scientists disagree that health foods provide more nutrition than conventional foods. Organic foods are grown without the use of manufactured chemical fertilizers or pesticides. Natural foods are those which aren't treated with preservatives, emulsifiers, artificial flavorings, or colorings. Not all organic foods are natural foods, and vice versa.

Health foods: big business

Nearly two thousand specialty stores and many supermarkets have organic food departments, and some food stores boast of products without "unnatural" preservatives. Sales in health food stores and retail outlets are estimated to have exceeded $5 billion in 1972, which is proof that the number of converts to organic eating is growing rapidly.

This rapid growth in sales of health foods is going on despite the fact that "research done so far has not been able to demonstrate any difference" between commercially and organically grown foods. [12]

High prices for organic foods?

A *Changing Times* article (June, 1972) warned consumers not only about the untruthfulness of nutritional claims and production claims but also about the difficulty in finding a store that won't rook you if you happen to be an organic food fan. Organic foods and health foods have always been "high-margin" products with markups as high as 75 percent, as against about 30 percent for comparable conventional foods. And then you can't be sure that you are getting na-

Organic foods need certification

[12] "Health Foods: Fact or Fakery?" *Everybody's Money*, Autumn, 1972, p. 4.

tural foods because there is practically no certification program. In 1972, a bill was introduced in Congress aimed at providing "safeguards for consumers of organically grown food." This proposal, the Organic Food Inspection Certification Act, would provide for federal inspection and certification of farms producing organically grown food. Today the consumer and the bona fide organic farmer have no protection against fraud and deception in the marketplace. [13] Unfortunately, the only way to know what you are eating is to grow your own "health foods." And, if you grow your own, the cost should be much less. (See Taylor-Troelstrup Reading 44, for an interesting article on health foods facts.)

HOW FOOD MONEY CAN BE WASTED

Impulse buying

The first rule is to avoid impulse buying. Careful surveys of consumer buying habits in food supermarkets reveal that well over one-half of all food purchases are impulse buying. The National Commission on Food Marketing reported: "Impulse-buying is common." Some experts claim that you can save as much as 25 percent of your food costs if you purchase only the food on your buying list.

If we buy with a child in a food supermarket, we may reach the check-out counter with cookies, gum, and candy. We start for bread and end up buying cookies and doughnuts because the fragrance proves overwhelming. Solution—stick to your marketing list.

Convenience food: economy or extravagance?

The food industry is succeeding in converting inexpensive ingredients into costly processed foods or providing them in a new convenience form, such as prebuttered vegetables and cheese slices, and marketing them at higher prices. Most partially prepared items—frozen corn on the cob, stuffed baked potatoes, cheese in a spray can, and frozen dinners—will cost more than the fresh. Some convenience foods, like frozen concentrated orange juice, frozen green peas, canned orange juice, fruit cocktail, and some cake mixes, are often cheaper than their fresh counterparts.

Built-in maid service

Many of the convenience or "built-in maid service" items have startling prices if you figure the real value. The innocent consumer, for example, pays $1.07 a pound for sugar in some presweetened breakfast foods; about 15 cents a pound more for sliced cold cuts of meat—and even more for cheeses sliced, grated, or wrapped in foil; over twice as much per pound for frozen beef patties; broccoli spears in butter sauce at 3.9 cents an ounce in contrast to frozen broccoli spears at about 1.8 cents an ounce; about twice as much per ounce for peas in butter sauce as for frozen peas in polyethylene bags. The same doubling or further multiplication in price occurs in many other convenience foods. It is strange that many consumers buy "diet" margarine at a price about three times that of ordinary margarine, though the leading ingredient in the "diet" version is

[13] *Community Nutrition Institute Weekly Report,* June 8, 1972, p. 3.

water. The fairly recent twist of corn flakes with strawberries or some other fruit is an expensive food. At 55 cents for an 8-ounce package, you get about 20 cents worth of cornflakes and about fifteen freeze-dried strawberries worth about 20 cents. The price is approximately $1.10 a pound for cereal with dried fruit. [14]

Some nutritional value lost

A matter of as much concern as increased cost of most convenience foods is the reduced nutritional value of many prepared and processed foods. Many of the processed food and meat products have cheap fillers, extenders, and a considerable amount of water. Consumers Union, for example, tested twenty-five brands of frankfurters in New York City and found excessive use of extenders, the misuse of coloring agents, and mislabeling. One of the most widely used convenience foods—dehydrated mashed potatoes—costs about twice as much per serving and has only approximately 50 percent as much vitamin C as fresh mashed potatoes. Some of the vitamin B also is lost in dehydrated potatoes. Likewise, a slice or two of "balloon" bread (air added when baking in larger pans) provides considerably less nutritional value than fine-grained bread for youngsters' sandwiches. Many other examples of loss of nutritional value can be found in other convenience foods, notably TV dinners, frozen meat and poultry pies (need have no more than 25 percent meat), frozen and canned chow meins (need have only 4 to 6 percent deboned meat), and chopped poultry "with broth" (which can have as much as 50 percent added liquid without specifying the amount of water). In 1967 the USDA regulation required that canned and dry soups may not be labeled "chicken" or "turkey" unless they contain at least 2 percent of these poultry meats when ready to serve. This was not a very impressive nutritional victory for consumers. One wonders why frozen breaded shrimp need be only 50 percent shrimp, and frozen deviled crab only 22 percent crabmeat. The popular 11-ounce TV dinner package of "meat loaf with potatoes and peas" costs about $1 a pound for meat loaf that is more loaf than meat.

Time saved versus money lost

Unfortunately, the USDA has not been very helpful in exposing the truth of the high cost of most processed and convenience foods and the loss in nutritional value. THE USDA literature has emphasized the amount of "time" saved when using convenience foods. And time is saved because they reduce the amount of preparation required at home. Consumers, however, need more information than the "time" saved. Consumers cannot make intelligent decisions in the marketplace unless they have information on exact amounts of all ingredients in processed or convenience foods. This kind of information is more important today than it was a decade ago. Dr. Gordon Bivens, professor of family economics at the University of Missouri, pointed out the fact that in 1965 the expenditures for thirty-two convenience foods averaged 30 percent of the total amount spent for food at home in one week in United States homes, in contrast

[14] Sidney Margolius, *The Great American Food Hoax,* Walker Publishing Company, Inc., New York, 1971.

to about 27 percent in 1955; and that families with low incomes "increased their expenditures for the 32 convenience foods more than higher income families."[15]

The question about the use of convenience foods boils down to this: Is the time saved in preparation of the meal or the package lunch worth the extra cost (sometimes 100 to 200 percent more) and the possible loss in nutritional value?

The future: mechanized meals

What! No kitchen in the home?

Some exciting things are happening in the world of food. In the near future, home kitchens will be obsolete, meal selection will be made from computerized menus, and food will be delivered into homes through chutes from a central kitchen. Shades of George Orwell!

They tell us that more and more of the food we consume will be partially or completely prepared outside the home. Already, 40 percent of the food we eat is in this category, and in ten years the proportion will increase to 80 percent. This includes products that are frozen, dehydrated, and instantly prepared as well as baked goods, take-out pizzas, fried chicken, chow mein, and you name it.

Even more convenience will be built into the foods we prepare at home, making the cooking of what used to be complex dishes easier. Dr. Jack Krum, assistant research director of the R. T. French Company, says that "84 percent of all food companies are planning to introduce new products this year [1972] and 62 percent of these will be convenience foods."

Is it possible to overconvenience a food supply? Probably not. There are, however, some questions we should raise: (1) Are some convenience foods really pseudo convenience foods, with higher prices and added cheap fillers? (2) Will you be satisfied if a company adds a little flavoring and doubles the price? (3) Will you continue to accept noncompetitive pricing such as increased brand advertising? (4) How can you check the nutritional content and value of convenience foods? As consumers, all of us have to get answers to these questions and do something about the problems they pose. Food manufacturers will not change their policies as long as they make more profits under the present system of inadequate labeling of foods.

National brands versus store or private labels

National brands of food are products sold under manufacturers' advertised brands. Similar food products sold under retailers' or other distributors' brands are called "private" or "store" labels. In a research study of 174 large food retailers, conducted by the National Commission on Food Marketing in 1966, private labels had been adopted by practically all the major food retailers. David Call, professor of food economics at Cornell University, concluded that there were very few consumers who did not have an opportunity to shop in retail stores where private food-label programs were offered.[16] Yet, some 50 percent of consumers do not understand the basic concept of private label programs, according to the findings of the Food Commission. This unfamiliarity with private labels is unfortunate because their economic advantages to the consumer are considerable. Table 7-4 clearly shows lower prices for store brands than for advertised national brands. Foods of equal quality, to the extent possible, were compared in this study. On the average, the advertised national

---

[15] *Family Economics Review,* December, 1967.

[16] "Private Label and Consumer Choice in the Food Industry," *Journal of Consumer Affairs,* Winter, 1967, pp. 149–160.

TABLE 7-4 Average Retail Prices per Case for Selected Products

PRODUCT	PRIVATE LABEL	ADVERTISED NATIONAL BRANDS	PERCENT DIFFERENCES
Frozen orange concentrate	$ 8.74	$11.57	32.4
Frozen green beans	4.84	6.42	30.0
Canned green beans	4.57	6.46	41.3
Canned green peas	4.76	5.54	16.4
Canned cling peaches	6.24	6.54	4.8
Canned Bartlett pears	10.86	13.00	19.7
Canned applesauce	3.29	3.65	10.8
Catsup	4.46	5.51	23.5
Evaporated milk	6.52	7.49	14.9
Tuna fish	12.72	15.46	21.5
Average, 10 foods	6.71	8.16	21.6

brand was priced 21.6 percent higher than the private-store brands. Private-store brands are frequently used as "specials" on weekend sales. These "specials" should attract a sizable share of the consumer's dollar to their brand. The Food Commission study showed that the retailers' gross margins on thirteen private-store brands of foods were reduced by 50 percent, on the average, when on "special" sale at retail stores. In addition to definite price advantage of store brands of similar-quality food compared to nationally advertised food brands, store brands have provided a competitive limitation on unnecessary advertising and premature cost raising of nationally advertised brands. This is a healthy situation in the food industry, where great efforts are made by nationally advertised brands to eliminate price and quality competition.

Vitamin and dietary supplements

Americans spend over half a billion dollars annually on vitamins, minerals, and other types of food supplements. All the nutrients essential to the maintenance of health in a normal individual are supplied by an adequate diet, according to the Council on Foods and Nutrition. Food is the best source for vitamins.

In his talk to the National Congress of Medical Quackery, the Food and Drug Commissioner said:

> The most widespread and expensive type of quackery today is the promotion of vitamin products, special dietary foods, and food supplements. Millions of consumers are being misled concerning their need for such products. Complicating this problem is a vast and growing "folklore" or "mythology" of nutrition which is being built up by pseudo-scientific literature. Especially disturbing is the tendency shown by some big and hitherto respected food concerns to use quackery in their sales material.

On June 20, 1968, the FDA began holding hearings on a labeling proposal aimed at reducing the excessive promotion and sale of certain vitamin, mineral, and special dietary food products. The FDA wants to require the following words to be added to most of these products: "Vitamins and minerals are supplied in abundant amounts by commonly available foods. Except for persons with special medical needs, there is no scientific basis for recommending routine use of dietary supplements." The FDA argued that many consumers spend large sums of money needlessly, and excessive amounts of certain items can be harmful. More than one hundred leading drug and food firms attacked the proposed label regulations. Behind their objections was a well-founded fear of loss of sales.

Diets to lose weight

In connection with taking vitamin preparations without a prescription or taking a pill to help lose weight, Dr. Milford O. Rouse, president of the American Medical Association in 1967, said, and most authorities agree, that there is no way for a normal person to lose weight except by eating fewer calories than he uses up expending energy. He said, "There is no tablet . . . no pill . . . no chewing gum . . . no tonic . . . that will reduce you while you eat all you want." He said that "crash diets . . . can be dangerous to your health."[17] Two of the better-known crash diets, the Air Force and the Mayo Clinic diets, are not authorized by the organizations named. Dr. Frederick Wolff, director of research at the Washington Hospital Center, said at a Senate subcommittee hearing that "diet pills do more harm than good." He explained that they may cause some people to become addicted to them, since most of them are simply pep pills made up of amphetamine compounds.

Trading stamps and other gimmicks   Trading stamps, after taking a licking, may be ready for a resurgence. The volume was nearly $700 million in 1972, compared with $900 million in 1968, estimates the Trading Stamp Institute of America.

There is an increasing controversy over the effects of trading stamps on consumers, on retailers, and on the prices that stamp-giving retailers charge customers. The consumer, however, is primarily interested in this question: "Do stamps really save money?"

Sperry and Hutchinson concedes that stamps must produce at least 12 percent increase in sales for stamps to pay their way. Retailers unable to increase their sales by at least 12 percent must operate at a loss until the stamp contract expires or raise their prices. Grocers operate on a narrow net profit margin of about 1¾ percent of sales. In a national survey in 1966 by the USDA Agriculture Marketing Service, 75 percent of supermarket operators reported increased operating expenses after introducing stamps. Fewer than 10 percent of the store managers were able to absorb the increase; 26 percent raised their prices; 44 percent used fewer specials; and 38 percent reduced their expenditures on advertising.

The Supermarket Institute claims that the use of stamps "costs a supermarket between $25,000 and $35,000 a year, a price roughly double the profit margin that it hopes to wring from its sales." Promotion, too, has lost its competitive edge because it just doesn't pay if everyone gives stamps. Until 1967, S & H did well on investment—35 percent after taxes, which was about three times that of a food chain.[18] It would appear that stamp companies are practically the only ones who gain in this game of entrapment. Retailers are beginning to resent being in the middle between increasing operating costs (partly from trading stamps) and growing consumer resentment of higher and higher food prices.

---

[17] Reported in *U.S. Consumer,* Sept. 20, 1967.

[18] After 1967, S & H's financial picture was complicated by the acquisition of the carpet company Bigelow-Sanford.

Mrs. Marlene Chapla, spokesman for the Denver, Colorado, supermarket boycotts, said, "We're sick and tired of excuses, and we're fed up with free dishes, bingo games, and trading stamps. All we want is lower prices." A Denver food chain responded with this advertisement: "Trading stamps and Gimmicks, No? Lower prices, Yes? But you can't have both."

The attitude of most supermarket managers was summed up by President Clarence Adamy of the National Association of Food Chains in 1966 when he said, "There is not a retailer who likes the games or stamps."

Consumers may also feel like Mr. Adamy when they realize that "trading stamps raise the price of groceries about 2 percent," according to Super Market Institute executive director, Michael O'Connor.[19]

Short weights are common in many prepackaged foods. Before the days of prepackaged foods (now 85 percent of family food), the consumer had to watch the "butcher's thumb" or worry about inaccurate store scales. That old problem is still with us, but supermarkets today need to weigh only about 15 percent of their food products.

Shortages in packaged meats in one state cost its residents an estimated $16 million annually, says *Consumer Reports* in its April 16, 1970, issue.

Meat shortages were detected by Tennessee officials in 58 percent of the stores selling to moderate-income families and in 75 percent of those serving low-income consumers.

New York State inspectors found meat shortages in 28 percent of the twenty-three stores they checked in fourteen cities and suburbs in December, 1969.

"Los Angeles inspectors at about the same time ran a concentrated check on fresh meat, fish, poultry and delicatessen items, and found shortages in more than 32 percent of prepackaged or cut-to-order purchases," says *Consumer Reports.*

The likelihood of honest weights and counts depends heavily on the vigor of state inspectors. *Consumer Reports* cites the efforts of one New Jersey county department which obtained convictions for short weight or short measure of two bread makers and of other firms selling grass seed, sugar, hard candy, bread stuffing, and extension cords.

"Don't rock the boat" attitudes

"The fact is," concludes *Consumer Reports,* "that in too many localities the weights-and-measures officials rely all too heavily on the public to detect suspected shortages, and only then make an investigation."

Most state and county officials say that at best they cannot run periodic checks on anywhere near all the thousands of packaged items sold in an average supermarket. Thus *Consumer Reports* recommends that if a purchaser finds more than one instance of a short weight or count, he return the items to the store for a refund and consider notifying the local, county, or state weights-and-measures department. A jail sentence for conviction of short-weighting may be more effective than a fine or a mere tap on the wrist. This is what happened in Fairfax County, Virginia, when the president of the Just Good Meats and a salesman at the store were fined $2,000 and sentenced to a year in jail for short-weight sales.[20]

[19]*Marketing Insights,* Oct. 31, 1966, p. 3.
[20]*The Washington Post,* June 10, 1970, p. A1.

Non-price competition

Consumers have a large stake in effective competition in the food industry. Price competition, or lack of it, affects the consumers' real income. The National Commission on Food Marketing was sufficiently concerned about non-price competition in the food industry to investigate this area. Dr. G. E. Brandow, of Pennsylvania State University, was executive director of the National Commission on Food Marketing. According to Dr. Brandow, the commission found much that was favorable about the food industry but that there were areas of poor performance, notably in price competition.[21]

The commission study found that competition in the food industry produces excessive emphasis on efforts to sell products and services. This excessive cost takes the form of high advertising and other promotional costs and extensive use of salesmen or brokers to push retail sales. Retailers use trading stamps, games, and other selling devices. It all costs money, and the consumer pays for it.

The cereal manufacturers, for example, spend more for promotion, packaging, and color than they do for ingredients. About 20 percent of the price the consumer pays for breakfast cereals goes to persuade her to buy a particular brand. The cost of advertising and promotion is 36.5 percent of the retail price of breakfast cereals. Net profits before taxes average 14.1 percent of the retail price of the cereal.[22] Brandow concludes that "It is not conceivable that information or other value to consumers justifies this cost." The great increase in advertising and promotion costs of food manufacturers was estimated to be $2.9 billion in 1968, in contrast to $560 million in 1950, according to *Advertising Age,* August 25, 1969. Four of the ten largest advertisers now are manufacturers of supermarket products. *Advertising Age,* August 25, 1969, stated that in 1968, General Foods spent $154 million on advertising; Kellogg, $47 million; Standard Brands, $65 million; General Mills, $58 million; and Kraftco, $58 million. The 1968 net profit on invested capital was high on the whole for food manufacturers—General Foods had 16.3 percent, Kraftco, 11.9 percent; A & P, 7.06 percent; and Kroger, 12.07 percent, to mention a few.

Antitrust and monopoly prices

It is difficult for government to break monopoly prices in the food industry because a few national chains do over one-half of the retail food business, and only a few very large food manufacturers produce most of the basic food sold at retail stores. The market power of these giants is apparently so great that they dominate the price of many food commodities. Evidence of their dominance can be seen by reviewing antitrust cases against such giants as Swift and Company, Kraftco, Borden's, Foremost, and Ward Bakery Products (to mention a few) and food chain stores such as Safeway and A & P.[23]

The lack of price competition in some foods is blamed on "leadership" prices—if one chain lowers or increases prices, they all lower or raise prices,

[21] See Brandow's article in *The Journal of Consumer Affairs,* Winter, 1967, pp. 139–147.

[22] *Hearings on Fair Packaging and Labeling,* Government Printing Office, Washington, 1966, part 2, p. 1035.

[23] Ibid., pp. 1037–1043.

says the Federal Trade Commission. Brandow recommends "vigorous antitrust policies . . . to maintain a structure of the industry conducive to effective competition." The Food Commission emphasized antimerger policy—a mild form of antitrust restraint—as one means of maintaining price competition. The Federal Trade Commission has recently laid down guidelines on mergers by large food retailers. Consumers could help themselves, within limitations, if they became expert buyers of food. It is difficult, however, to become an effective buyer of food unless there are quality standards of food products at the point of sale to the consumer.

Imitation foods
Most of us are familiar with imitation foods on the market—margarine, saccharine, orange-flavored breakfast drinks, coffee whiteners, nondairy whipped toppings, and imitation meats and milk. And many more imitation products are on the way because of their competitive and cost advantages.

Questions about the nutritional content, dietary impact, safety, labeling, and advertising of imitation foods have been raised by nutritionists and other professionals. There is little information and knowledge about imitation foods, especially in terms of caloric, vitamin, and mineral content, according to Dr. Robert O. Herrmann and Dr. Rex H. Warland.[24] For example, these authors say that imitation meat products constituted from isolated soy-bean protein compare favorably with cooked beef in amino acid content. But they "lack appreciable amounts of the vitamins and minerals found in meat."

Many imitation-food product labels offer little meaningful information. It is suggested, for example, that labels should indicate the function of all additives, such as "emulsifier" instead of "sorbitan monostearate," and the percentage by weight of each additive. It would also be useful if labels specified the origin of the ingredients more completely . Labeling the source of vegetable oils, for example, would help those concerned with their intake of saturated fatty acids to identify products containing coconut oil.

The solution to the problem may be enlightened federal regulation of labeling and advertising and effective consumer education.

TRUTH-IN-PACKAGING

For five years Senator Philip A. Hart of Michigan had been urging a law to make it easier for consumers to see how much they were getting for their money. Before deceptive packaging became common, consumers could depend upon our weights-and-measures laws. At that time many foods were sold from bins and weighed out at the store, usually in ½- and 1-pound amounts. Implicit in this basic assumption was recognition also of the consumer's right to examine the product and compare it to other similar products, her right to name the quantity she chose to buy, and her right to compare prices. The consumer could recognize these rights when she bought in bulk. Modern packaging has eroded the consumer's right to examine the product and compare prices. The consumer's inability to compare prices of the same or similar products means that she cannot achieve rational choice.

[24] "The New Wave of Imitation Foods: Problems Ahead," *The Journal of Consumer Affairs*, Summer, 1971, pp. 56–69.

Packaging deceptions

The consumer testimony at the Hart hearings came as a surprise to the industry. Sellers had ignored the effect of their conduct on consumers. However, as one witness after another cited packaging malpractices in baby foods, cereals, cooking oils, canned goods, cake mixes, frozen foods, cookies, candy, crackers, fruit juices, bread, bacon, and many other foods, the point got across.[25] Even *Advertising Age* was moved to comment:

> We must confess that, as consumers, our sympathy lies with the statements of Senator Hart's subcommittee which concern deception, and particularly deceptive packaging. It would be nicer to live in a simple world in which "pound" packages contained 16 oz., and not 15 or 14½; which "quart" bottles were actually quarts, not fifths, or even 25 oz., in which packages containing the same weight or volume didn't look as though one were twice as big as another . . . and so on. . . . A little standardization might help everyone.

Other trade papers were also impressed. *Food and Drug Packaging,* for example, described the testimony as the "rumblings of consumer discontent erupting into a full-blown packaging controversy." But it was not the trade comment that jolted the $100 billion industry. It was what occurred in the public press and on television and on radio.

"A story for our times,"[26]

Consumer issues seldom receive much attention in the mass media. This time the media did report the issue. Deceptive packaging made good pictures. So deceptive practices were shown on a few television screens, and headlines like "The grocery cart is being used to take shoppers for a ride" topped news stories.

Many newspaper editorials called Senator Hart silly ("our housewives are too smart to be fooled") or ("regulation will curb the freedom of enterprising packagers"). But the food industry, so accustomed to a docile press, was not looking for a dialog. The trade paper *Packaging* pointed out in its August, 1962, issue, "If we don't smother all this talk about how the consumer is being deceived and cheated our whole economy will emerge 'sell' shocked."

Food industry fought packaging law

By this time, after the second year of Senate hearings, the food industry decided to oppose *any* packaging law. And it certainly did not want any more exposure of its misdoings. Yet, a few months before the second set of hearings in early 1963, Paul Willis, president of the Grocery Manufacturers Association, was given the job to make the food industry's position clear to the nation's news media. He told his audience at the Television Bureau of Advertising's annual meeting that he had met with sixteen top management people from national magazines. He suggested to the publishers "that the day was here when their editorial department and business department might better understand their interdependency relationships as they affect the operating results of their company; and as their operations affect the advertiser—their bread and butter."

[25] See the five volumes on the hearings held by the Senate and the House for specific details.

[26] For full report, see *Consumer Reports,* March, 1965.

FIGURE 7-2 Readers taken in by this gimmick told CU that they had reached for Birds Eye beans, a General Foods product, as they wheeled by, thinking the big "17¢" (see package at right) was a lower price, only to find at the check-out counter that it referred to coupons, not beans. The beans in this carton actually cost more than those in the regular one, left.

SOURCE: *Consumer Reports,* Mar. 25, 1965. Consumers Union, Inc.

The magazine people, he said, had understood. They had begun to run articles to create "a favorable public attitude" toward food advertisers. He regretted, however, that he could not say "similar nice things about the relationship of our advertisers with television." He said television received about "65 percent of their advertising revenue from GMA members." "These advertisers," he said, "have seen some television newscasts where they seemingly took great delight in bellowing out stories that were critical of this industry." He closed his speech with a question: "What can you do additionally that will influence your advertiser to spend more of his advertising dollar with you?"

The broadcasters, with one or two exceptions, got the message. On radio only Edward P. Morgan (ABC) gave news about the hearings. Since the speech, several scheduled television appearances of Senator Hart were canceled. So the food industry entered the 1965 legislative year with its trade groups coordinated and the news media under control.

Let's keep politics out of the pantry

In the January 26, 1965, issue of *Look,* the editorial pages displayed the by-line of an advertiser: Charles C. Mortimer, chairman of General Foods, as author of an article, "Let's Keep Politics Out of the Pantry." In the article he salutes the American housewife as a shrewd and happy woman—shrewd because "when it comes to clever buying," she "can give lessons to a Yankee horse trader," and happy because "she takes it for granted that what she has bought is the purest, most nutritious, easiest-to-prepare food the world has ever seen." (Recorded against his own food company are twenty-eight violations in the last twenty-five years against one of our regulatory laws, the Federal Food, Drug, and Cosmetic Act.)

What further disturbed Mr. Mortimer is that American housewives probably do *not* know that their good fortune as a food shopper results from "the machinery of free competition." The informed reader will find his eulogies of competition even more interesting than his protestations on behalf of existing government regulations over food. For he is chairman of a food combine that is the nation's largest and prime example of what the Federal Trade Commission called "economic power and market concentration created by the great merger movement." It markets 250 products, and has challenged an FTC order to dissolve a more recent merger; and the earnings from its many merger-acquired companies are such that it commands over $100 million worth of advertising power a year.

Since there was another side to the packaging issue than the one Mr. Mortimer presented, Senator Hart asked whether he might not be given an opportunity to clarify some of these matters for readers of *Look*. Gardner Cowles, editorial chairman of *Look,* answered by taking full-page ads in other magazines, to publicize its sponsorship of Mr. Mortimer's article.

This has to be one of the great stories of our time on the freedom of the press when pressure is brought to bear on the big advertising revenue of mass media. And, because of this all-out, no-holds-barred drive to defeat the Fair Packaging and Labeling Act, the FPLA was a weak compromise when finally passed in 1966. This act, like most proposed consumer laws, is largely defensive. Even *Advertising Age* commented that it would be nice to be able to buy something in an even pound again.

THE FAIR PACKAGING AND LABELING ACT, 1966

The FPLA, passed by Congress on October 4, 1966, became effective in July, 1967. Unfortunately, the act is inadequate to protect shoppers from deception and confusion, and it also lacks the power to give consumers sufficient information to shop rationally.

First to go was required listing of all ingredients on food labels. Next was the federal government's right to compel standardization of package sizes. Manufacturers are required to print their names and addresses and to display the net weight prominently, both in ounces and in fractions of pounds, pints, quarts, and so on. They also have to define a serving, if these are listed, and drop misleading weight descriptions like "giant" and "jumbo."

Promises, promises

The FPLA was never seriously intended to be enforced. First, Congress voted insufficient funds, and its enforcement was parceled out to three federal agencies. The FDA is responsible for foods, drugs, and cosmetics; the FTC is responsible for other consumer products; and the Office of Weights and Measures (Commerce Department) was asked to obtain the voluntary agreement of manufacturers to reduce the number of different-sized packages. Division of responsibilities is likely to end in inadequate enforcement of a law.

Funding the FPLA
No budget for enforcement

In 1968, when congressional funding was at its most generous, these three agencies were given only $1.08 million. By 1969 the FDA's $115,300 had been slashed in half, and in 1970 it was deleted entirely. This left the agency with no resources to police the $125-billion food industry, quite apart from the drug and cosmetic manufacturers. According to Stanley E. Cohen, of *Advertising*

Age, the House Appropriations Committee told the FDA: "If you are pinched for funds, give truth-in-packaging a low priority."[27]

Food industries hit back: few package changes

Too many exemptions

The federal agencies were also hit by the same giant food industries which had stunted the FPLA on the vine. Some of the giants initiated lawsuits to establish exemptions. The FDA then exempted the following products from all or part of the regulations: soft drinks, ice cream, milk, butter, margarine, cream, wheat, flour, corn flour, eggs in cartons, all random-weight packages, and penny candy. Some companies, such as those in the baking industry, made no serious effort to conform to the FPLA.

Self-regulation fails

There was little effort to reduce the number of different-sized packages and thus little cut back in the 8,000 or more packages on an average supermarket's shelves. The Commerce Department did succeed in reducing 267 package sizes of twenty-five staples. Some of these reductions were spectacular—toothpaste was cut down to five sizes from fifty-seven, but sixteen package sizes of breakfast cereals and fifty-six package sizes of crackers and cookies are still available.

In a check of food product labels the FDA found that food was sold in 5-, 7-, 8-, 9-, 10-, 11-, 12-, 13-, 15-, 16-, 18-, 20-, and 42-ounce packages and that all were described as "large size." Other size designations were more imaginative and informative. Among these were "jug size," "ketchup-lover's size," "coffee-lover's size," "tribe size," "pass-around size," "patio size," and "fun size." Probably some 60 percent of all food products continue to come in nonstandard packages.[28]

Packaging to price

Concealed price rise

Allied to the fractional ounce is the slippage in quantity, concealed by the fact that the price and the container size remain the same. In May, 1969, the House Special Studies Subcommittee, headed by Congressman Benjamin S. Rosenthal, turned up 600 food and drug items which had dwindled in quantity since 1965 without an equivalent decrease in price. This practice conceals a price rise. And once one company starts the slippage, competitors are almost forced to follow suit.

Gimmicks—on the way out

The regulations on "cents-off" offers, introductory offers, economy sizes, and coupon offers became effective on December 31, 1972. It took the Federal Trade Commission and the Food and Drug Administration, who share authority for enforcing the Fair Packaging and Labeling Act, more than four years to draft them. These regulations will govern the use of such gimmicks for food, drugs, cosmetics, and other household products. Here's a rundown of the regulations:

Look, Ma, no gimmicks!

1. *Cents-off offers.* They will be valid only if the label reads like this: "Regular price—50 cents; cents off—6 cents; you pay 44 cents." Only three such cents-off deals are allowed each year in any given area for each size of a specific item, with the offer limited to a maximum six-month period during any twelve-month interval.

Who will watch the regulators?

2. *Introductory offers.* The product must be new, significantly changed, or newly introduced in the geographic area in which the special is offered. The duration of the promotion is six months. After that, the distributor must sell the product at the regular or a higher price.

3. *Economy size.* The packer must sell the same brand in at least one

[27] *Fair Packaging and Labeling—When?* Consumers Union, Inc., Mount Vernon, N.Y., July 15, 1968, pp. 20–21.

[28] *FDA Papers,* September, 1971, p. 15.

other size, and the economy-size package must be sold at a price at least 5 percent lower than the prices of other packages of the same product.

4. *Coupon offers.* The consumer must be told what the coupon is worth in cash or goods so that there will be no confusion at the check-out counter.

These rules should help people compare one cut-price bargain with another. Furthermore, it is hoped that they will bring an end to deceptive promotions that were 100 percent phony.

Thus there has been some progress in reducing deceptive promotions— a plus for the Fair Packaging and Labeling Act. But what has happened to package sizes? How has the FPLA changed food packaging and labeling since its passage in 1966? On the plus side, consumers stand to gain in the following ways:

1. The predominant ingredient must be used first in the name of mixed products. For example, banana-nut bread cannot be called nut-banana bread if it contains more bananas than nuts.

2. The statement telling what is in the product must be in boldface print.

3. Net contents must be listed in order of predominance in the product.

4. Effective January 1, 1972, a product labeled "economy size" must offer at least a 5 percent better value than other sizes of the same product; also, cents-off offers must show the regular price, the amount of cents off, and the net price.

And more promises   Most of the improvements in packaging and labeling anticipated to come out of the FPLA have not been realized. Furthermore, consumer groups presently favor measures that will provide more information, such as nutrient labeling, open dating, percentage-ingredient labeling, unit pricing, more grades, and "drained weight" replacing the useless "net weight," especially for canned goods. Meantime, the FDA offers this advice: "Fulfillment of the promises of the FPLA will depend on the continued active participation and cooperation of the regulated industries, label designers and manufacturers, State and Federal officials and consumers."[29] Dr. Leland Gordon, a leading authority on weights and measures, made this statement in reference to the FPLA: "Never in this century has so complicated a law been enacted, with administrative responsibility divided among several agencies. It will take years to achieve full implementation."[30]

PART 2   FOOD SHOPPING IN THE MARKETPLACE

Shopping for food is a complex problem. A consumer who has done a good job of mental food planning at home does not want to lose that benefit by poor buying in the marketplace. In order to serve tasty, nutritious, economical food

[29] *FDA Papers,* October, 1969, p. 27.
[30] *Fair Packaging and Labeling—When?* op. cit. p. 21.

at all times and to win the "battle of the budget," one must give constant attention to food costs.

The right quality and quantity of food for the family depend mainly on the buying practices of the homemaker, on the information she has and her skill in choosing food, on her willingness to shop at stores where the best buys are available, and on her actual selection of food. She must decide:

1. What to buy
2. Where to buy
3. When to buy
4. How much to buy
5. Whether to buy bulk or packaged, canned or fresh, or frozen or dehydrated foods
6. How to pay
7. What quality or grade to use for specific purposes
8. Who will buy
9. How to use nutrient labeling information

Soon the food manager in the home will have the advantage of vastly improved labeling information: open dating and unit pricing (in many food stores now), nutrient and percentage-ingredient labeling (experimentally available in some food stores as early as 1972–1973), and "drained weight" replacing "net weight" on labels of canned foods. These revolutionary changes on many food labels will be advantageous as a tool for choosing a good diet. Some nutrition specialists have suggested that we abandon the daily food guide with its basic four groups, referred to earlier, in favor of using nutrient labeling. Regardless of whether the home food manager chooses to use nutritional information or the basic four groups as a guide, there will be a need for supplemental information and aids.

But why this revolutionary change in food labeling?

WORKING WIVES CHANGE FOOD-BUYING PATTERNS

The saying that "woman's work is never done" appears more true today than ever before, and this despite all the laborsaving devices and convenience that technology has provided to ease the load. But consider the 31.5 million women between the ages of 18 and 64 presently holding jobs (U.S. Labor Department estimates for 1972). Most of them run households. And this big job, by and large, has not been delegated. What influence, then, does the working wife have on food-buying patterns?

Food-buying patterns change

In 1972 the Bureau of Advertising hired Response Analysis, Inc., of Princeton, New Jersey, to do a national probability sample of food-buying patterns of about one thousand women. These were some of the findings:

1. The responsibility for food shopping is firmly established among women in middle- and upper-income families. In lower-income households men are most likely to share the food-buying chores.

2.   Some 77 percent of all working wives do the food shopping, as compared with 83 percent of wives who do not work.

3.   About one out of three husbands usually go along on the food-buying trips.

4.   Nine out of ten women shop mainly in supermarkets.

5.   About 70 percent of working women do major shopping only once a week.

6.   Among full-time housewives, 41 percent reported that Friday is their usual shopping day, and 21 percent named Saturday.

7.   Working housewives are likely to shop in the late afternoons or evenings.

8.   Two-thirds of all the women interviewed said that they go to the food store with a complete shopping list. They said that they check their supplies on hand (86 percent), check advertised specials (79 percent), and discuss their food purchases with their families (58 percent). Those who consult advertising (83 percent) look at newspaper ads.

CHANGING FOOD HABITS

Costly food habits

The national nutritional survey taken in 1968–1970, you may recall, revealed that a significant proportion of our population was malnourished or at a high risk of developing nutritional problems. One of the problems of poor American diets is lack of balance arising from voluntary changes in food habits. Some of these changing food habits are (1) a decline in family-group eating, (2) greater use of limited-variety convenience foods, (3) more selection of food on the basis of taste rather than nutritional content, (4) more snacking on limited-variety convenience foods, (5) meal skipping, (6) more eating away from home at limited-variety fast-service restaurants, (7) declining nutritional knowledge and awareness in an urbanizing society, (8) earlier determination of food choices by youth based on the limited-variety habits of a youth culture, (9) a declining priority of food in family budgets, and (10) a rise in the popularity of health food fads and limited-variety diets such as the Zen macrobiotic.

Given the fairly serious evidence of malnutrition among all income groups today, the changing food habits of our people, and our general ignorance about such health matters as vitamins and nutrition,[31] how can people better ensure that they are eating a well-balanced, healthful diet at a price they can afford? Perhaps we should begin with a discussion of how to get more for our food dollar and then investigate the proposals for a comprehensive national food marketing program.

HOW TO GET MORE FOR YOUR FOOD DOLLAR

Use the food ads

Food shopping begins at home. Studying the food ads in the local papers and listening to local radio food programs will often suggest the best daily or

---

[31] *A Study of Health Practices and Opinions,* National Technical Information Services, Springfield, Va., 1972. (Commissioned by the FDA.)

weekly buys. Comparing food costs *before* marketing is both economical and time-saving.

Place all the desired ads before you, with your grocery list handy. When comparing the price of veal shoulder roast, for example, circle the best buy and double-circle the next-best buy. Jot down the name of the retail store opposite the particular food on your list.

After an experience or two in comparing prices and knowing what you want before you leave home to shop for food, you will find that you have saved as much as half an hour or more in the marketplace—and been much easier on your pocketbook.

Weekend food shopping: does it pay?

Generally, it pays to market for food on weekends. In national food chain stores, most price reductions occur on Thursday, Friday, and Saturday. On Monday, prices frequently increase. In one survey of retail national food chain stores, about 86 percent of the fresh fruits and vegetables were reduced on Thursday, Friday, and Saturday. Spot surveys also indicate that some food prices are increased in the latter part of the week.

Independent food stores seem to have a more flexible price policy than many national food chain stores. There is evidence to support the conclusion that food prices are also reduced in many independent stores during the weekend. Like the national chain food stores, independent stores tend to increase some prices on Monday. One may conclude, therefore, that shoppers can make their best buys in the latter part of the week.

One result of weekend price reductions is the heavy concentration of shoppers and consequent crowding, particularly in afternoons and evenings. Some competent marketing observers have concluded that marketing costs could be reduced if sales were more evenly distributed throughout the week. In view of the pressure of retail competition and force of habit on the part of the retailers themselves, any corrective measure is likely to make slow progress.

The Stanford University Food Research Institute, a few years ago, in Palo Alto, California, compared 1,546 price observations of 225 food items advertised as specials. They found that in 96 food items (1) the consumer could have saved over 20 percent if he had purchased all the specials; (2) most of the specials offered were standard foods commonly purchased weekly; (3) the stores with the lowest-priced specials generally maintained higher prices on other food products than their competitors.

Buy by the calendar

Food prices go through seasonal cycles that can be plotted by the calendar. Use Table 7-5, worked out by *Changing Times,* as a general guide, subject to the changes that can be brought on by an unexpected freeze or a prolonged drought.

Shopper's guide to common can sizes

The information now provided on can labels does not always make it easy to judge how far the food will go. Sometimes the label indicates the number of servings, and an article in *Changing Times* magazine (July, 1972) suggests that a better idea would be to convert weights into cups and servings. This is especially important in the case of canned meats, poultry, fish, and seafood because these products are usually advertised and sold by weight.

Labels on cans don't tell you enough

Figure 7-3 lists popular sizes of containers, along with the number of cups and servings you can expect from each. One-half cup is usually recommended as a single adult serving of most canned foods except possibly whole fruits.

TABLE 7-5 **Calendar of the Best Food Buys**

MONTH	MEAT, FISH, ETC.	DAIRY PRODUCTS	VEGETABLES	FRUIT	MISCELLANEOUS
January	Chicken (broilers & fryers), pork and pork products, eggs		Potatoes, cabbage, onions, lettuce	Oranges, apples, tangerines, grapefruit	Tree nuts, raisins, honey
February	Eggs, better-grade beef		Lettuce, celery, potatoes, cabbage	Oranges, grapefruit	Tree nuts, raisins, honey
March	Chicken (broilers & fryers), frozen fish, eggs		Dried beans, potatoes	Canned & frozen citrus fruit, juices	Raisins, prunes
April	Chicken (broilers & fryers), pork and pork products, eggs	Cottage cheese	Cabbage, carrots, potatoes, spring greens, celery	Apples, oranges	Raisins, prunes
May	Chicken (broilers & fryers), eggs	Butter, milk, cheese, cottage cheese	Asparagus, onions, lettuce, cabbage, spring greens	Strawberries	
June	Chicken (broilers & fryers), fresh fish	Butter, milk, cheese, ice cream	Potatoes, onions, lettuce, snap beans	Berries, cantaloupe	
July	Chicken (broilers & fryers), turkey (fryers & roasters)	Cheese, ice cream, cottage cheese	Cabbage, tomatoes, potatoes, local vegetables	Lemons, peaches, watermelons, cantaloupe, limes, plums, apricots	

	Fresh fish	Ice cream	Local vegetables		
August		Ice cream		Grapes, pears, watermelons, peaches, plums	
September	Stewing chicken, lamb	Cottage cheese	Onions, carrots, cabbages, tomatoes, corn	Grapes, pears	Rice
October	Stewing chicken, turkey, lamb, pork	Cheese	Potatoes, onions, sweet potatoes, cauliflower, dried beans, pumpkins, cabbage	Apples, pears	Honey
November	Turkey, pork and pork products		Potatoes, onions, sweet potatoes, cauliflower, cabbage, pumpkins	Cranberries, apples	Tree nuts, raisins, honey
December	Turkey, pork		Onions, sweet potatoes, potatoes	Grapefruit, cranberries, oranges, dried fruit	Honey, tree nuts

FIGURE 7-3   Shopper's guide to common can sizes

Common net weight or liquid measurement	Frequent use	Number of cups and servings (approx.)
6 fl. oz	For individual servings of single-strength fruit juices and frozen concentrated juices	$3/4$ cup 1 + serving 5 − 6 *(concentrated)
8 to $8^3/_4$ oz	For most fruits, vegetables and specialty foods, such as macaroni and spaghetti	1 cup 2 servings
$10^1/_2$ to 12 oz	Mainly for condensed soups, but also for some fruits, vegetables, meat, fish and specialty products	$1^1/_4$ cups 2 − 3 servings
14 to 16 oz	For specialty items like baked beans, chili con carne, date and nut bread; also for various fruits, including cranberry sauce and blueberries	$1^3/_4$ cups 3 − 4 servings
16 to 17 oz	For most vegetables and fruits, some meat products, ready-to-serve soups, specialties	2 cups 4 servings
20 to $20^1/_2$ oz 18 fl. oz	For juices, ready-to-serve soups, pineapple, apple slices	$2^1/_2$ cups 5 servings
27 to 29 oz	Primarily for fruits, such as peaches, pears, plums and fruit cocktail, and for some vegetables (pumpkin, tomatoes, spinach and other greens)	$3^1/_2$ cups 5 − 7 servings
49 to 51 oz 46 fl. oz	For fruit and vegetable juices and some vegetables	$5^3/_4$ cups 10−12 servings

SOURCE: *Changing Times,* The Kiplinger magazine, July, 1972. Permission granted to reproduce the table by the USDA, Consumer and Marketing Service.

There are many other ways to get more satisfaction as well as more food for your dollar. Here are some ideas from home economists.

Secrets of a smart shopper

This excellent list of ideas for smart food shopping came from the Consumers Cooperative of Berkeley, Inc., in California:[32]

Before You Go to the Food Store:

- Establish a rough limit on what a certain type of food should cost for your family. For example, not more than one dollar (or whatever you decide) for the main dish for dinner; 25¢ to 30¢ for breakfast fruit, or vegetables for dinner or dessert, etc.

- Certain foods are good buys all year 'round. Use them frequently. For example, your list might include frozen orange juice, canned tomatoes, concentrated milk and/or nonfat dry milk, rolled oats in 5 lb. bag or wheat shreds. Each family will have its own favorites.

- Keep a shopping list in your kitchen. As you finish an item that you use regularly, put it on the list. As you think of ideas for upcoming meals, put the needed items on the list.

- Plan to do a major shopping once a week. Plan your menus ahead for one week, if possible. Check supplies on hand and complete your shopping list accordingly. The less often you go to the store, the fewer opportunities you will have for impulse buying, although you may want to pick up fresh food at least twice a week.

- When planning menus, consider the cost of convenience foods. If you buy "built-in maid service," you usually pay for it. There are exceptions (frozen orange juice, frozen peas) but they are rare. While a convenience food can be a blessing on occasion, regular use can skyrocket the budget. For instance, macaroni and cheese "made from scratch" is much less expensive, almost as easy to prepare, and usually more nutritious than the package of frozen products.

- Plan to buy "store" brands of canned and frozen foods, paper products, health and beauty aids, cleaning aids, etc. Usually the quality is comparable to nationally advertised brands while the cost is less.

- Check ads for seasonal low prices on meat, poultry, fish, fresh produce and grocery items. Alter your menu when you find a good buy. Compare prices of fresh, frozen and canned versions of the same item. Sometimes there is considerable price difference, while the nutritive value may be the same. Flavor, of course, may differ considerably.

- Save shopping time by organizing your shopping list according to categories as stocked in the store so that you do not retrace your steps. Plan to buy frozen and refrigerated items last so that they will not warm up too much.

In the Store:

- Eat before you shop! Research has shown that a hungry shopper is more likely to indulge in impulse buying.

- Leave the kids home if you can't say "NO" and mean it.

- Buying larger sizes? Use the unit prices on label or a Budget Gadget to figure the cost per pound or pint. Beware of optical illusions in packaging. Sometimes a larger bottle, for example a salad oil bottle, contains fewer ounces than one that looks smaller.

- Avoid or choose with care most items displayed in center aisle or at the front of

[32]Permission to reproduce granted by the Consumers Cooperative of Berkeley, Inc., 4805 Central Avenue, Richmond, Calif. 94804.

the store. These are often "impulse purchases" and may be poor values. Sometimes they are "in and outs"—products not regularly stocked which may or may not be poor buys.

- Don't buy a product just because a demonstrator offers you a sample. Consider if this is really something you want at a price you can afford.
- Ask the checker to call the prices as he rings up your order. No one can remember all prices accurately. Special prices may not be marked on the package; clerks may ring up the regular price.

After You Shop:
- Don't stop on the way home to do errands. Many foods deteriorate rapidly in quality if unrefrigerated for an hour or more.
- Check your purchases against the cash register tag to see that you paid only for what you received and that the prices charged were correct. If you find inaccuracies or discrepancies, report them to the manager the next time you shop.
- Keep track of your food costs. Separate costs of non-foods and pet foods from "people foods." Compare what you are spending with the guidelines [Table 7-6] below:

TABLE 7-6 Weekly Food Budget Guidelines

	LOW-COST PLAN	MODERATE-COST PLAN	LIBERAL PLAN
Family of two, head 20–35 years	$19.40	$24.60	$30.50
Family of two, head 55–75 years	15.80	20.60	24.90
Family of four, preschool children	28.20	35.70	43.70
Family of four, schoolchildren	32.60	41.70	51.40

SOURCE: U.S. Department of Agriculture cost-of-food-at-home figures for June, 1972; United States average. Use the latest monthly figures.

- Check if you are wasting food by preparing too much or serving foods your family doesn't like. Either prepare quantities that will just feed your family for one meal without leftovers or plan to have enough leftovers for another meal.

BUDGETING BY FOOD GROUPS (THE BASIC FOUR)

Some family food managers may still prefer to budget their food money by food groups (the basic-four system), although the nutrient labeling program recently proposed by the FDA and several other organizations is likely to modify the basic-four system. Many food managers are likely to adopt the nutritional information system when fully implemented by the FDA and the food industry. The basic-four system is still useful, however, and some food managers like to budget their money according to the four groups.

Families may be willing to use economical choices from one group if they can splurge on foods in another. Table 7-7 shows the average share of each food dollar that families spend for foods in the major groups, and also expenditures under a low-cost plan.

The average American shopper could get a good diet at a lower cost by using *more* of each food dollar for milk and milk products, vegetables and fruit,

TABLE 7-7   Budgeting by Food Groups: The Basic Four*

	AVERAGE EXPENDITURE	LOW-COST PLAN
Milk, cheese, ice cream	$0.13	$0.18
Meat, poultry, fish, eggs, legumes	0.40	0.30
Vegetables and fruit	0.20	0.25
Cereals, bakery products	0.13	0.16
Other food	0.14	0.11
	$1.00	$1.00

* The cost of commercially prepared mixtures included with the food group of the main ingredient.
SOURCE: "Budgeting by Food Groups," *Family Economics Review,* September, 1972, p. 21.

and cereals and bakery goods and *less* of each food dollar for foods in the meat group and other foods such as fats, oils, sugar, sweets, coffee, tea, and soft drinks.

Cost of food at home   Some families may find the "cost of food at home" estimated for food plans at three cost levels by the Consumer and Food Economics Institute of the USDA a help in budgeting. See Table 7-4 on page 219. The cost-of-food-at-home data are revised each month and can be found in newspapers. The monthly issues of *Family Economics Review* also present the latest cost data..

LABELS THAT TELL YOU SOMETHING

The Truth-in-Food-Labeling Act (TFLA), introduced in Congress in early 1972, could provide one of the "most fundamental changes in the history of food labeling in this country." So said FDA Commissioner Charles C. Edwards. When the FDA came up with its own food labeling program in the summer of 1972, the recommendations appeared to have been designed to pacify consumers rather than doing something meaningful about truth-in-labeling. The FDA proposals were originally concerned primarily with voluntary guidelines for the nutrient labeling of packaged foods under its jurisdiction, whereas the TFLA, as written, would require that labels on food products include a quality grade, a complete list of ingredients, a statement of nutritional values, and the "pull date" after which the food cannot be sold as fresh.

The basic issues   The basic question is this: Do consumers have the right to know exactly what they are eating? If the answer is "Yes," then labels must (1) give consumers understandable information on the quality of the food product by means of a simple grading system, (2) list all ingredients by percentage and also indicate their nutritive value, and (3) show the pull date, unit price, and drained weight.

Getting full value for your food dollar   Labels that really tell you something are also a powerful economic tool for fighting inflation in the supermarket. Honest, complete, and accurate labeling is the consumer's greatest weapon in making sure he gets full value for his food dollar. Finally, consumer health and safety come first. The following labeling information on most food cans and packages will go a long way toward helping consumers get full value for their food dollars:

Open dating

The vocabulary of food dating has not been universally agreed on, but most experts believe that the pull date (most commonly used voluntarily today)—the last day a retail store should offer the food for sale—is the best system to use. (See Taylor-Troelstrup Reading 45 for other definitions of open dating.) Supermarkets and some food packers have dropped their opposition to open dating now that most consumers know that an open date (in code) has been on packages of food products needing freshness dates for a long time. About 60 percent of this nation's chain supermarkets already are voluntarily marking their store brands, and some manufacturers are marking their national brands—Pillsbury's and Borden's refrigerated dough, all major dry and liquid baby formulas, and Hellman's mayonnaise and Skippy peanut butter, for example.

Is the food fresh?

Studies by the U.S. Department of Agriculture[33] have confirmed that open dating benefits supermarkets because it builds up customer confidence in the store. It does *not* cause any increase in outdated food as a result of customers' selecting the freshest items first. Store managers interviewed in Jewel supermarkets in Chicago were generally pleased with customer reactions and improvements in stock rotation after Jewel began open dating on about 150 of its store brands. Kroger supermarkets were also pleased because stocks of outdated food began declining as soon as store personnel became aware of the test. So, with open dating, industry self-regulation appeared to be getting somewhere. Yet the food industry in this case seems to be leaning toward some form of federal regulation because many states are considering instituting their own open-dating definitions or tools to use in their regulatory laws. The only way out of this dilemma is uniformity of legislation.

The key to freshness is good handling and proper refrigeration practices from processor to the retail store. The pull date and optimum storage conditions should be explained clearly on the label, and the label should also tell how long the food may be stored at home.

Unit pricing

Unit pricing is a system designed to help shoppers compare prices on grocery items and other products. Two prices are shown on each product—the price per package and the price per unit of measure (pound, ounce, quart, etc.).

For example, the price information on two cans of tomatoes—a 12-ounce can selling for 21 cents and an 8-ounce can selling for 15 cents—might read:

Brand X tomatoes—12-ounce can, 21 cents. Price per pound, 28 cents.

Brand Y tomatoes—8-ounce can, 15 cents. Price per pound, 30 cents.

$1.20 divided by 14 ounces is what? Goodbye, slide rule

Using that information, one can see that brand X costs 2 cents a pound less than brand Y. In addition, it permits shoppers to compare unit prices of small, medium, and large packages of the same brand to determine how much, if anything, they can save by purchasing larger sizes.

[33] Reported in *Consumer Reports*, June 1972, p. 391.

Shoppers have always purchased meat, fresh fruits, and vegetables by the pound or ounce, and prices are usually stamped on these items now.

With unit pricing, a housewife can tell at a glance whether she can save a few cents by buying a large jar of peanut butter at 40 cents a pound, as compared with a smaller jar of the same brand priced at 44 cents a pound.

Unit pricing does not, however, give customers information on the quality of the items, but it does say which costs less on a unit basis.

Many supermarkets are using unit pricing. Mrs. Virginia Knauer, who heads the President's Committee on Consumer Interest, supports unit pricing. So does Clarence G. Adamy, president of the National Association of Food Chains.

But will shoppers make use of this information? Two tests, one sponsored by the National Association of Food Chains and Safeway Stores and the other by the Consumer Research Institute, a business-supported foundation, concluded that at least 30 percent of shoppers make use of unit-pricing information. The tests also showed that most shoppers, including many who did not use the information, felt it should be available to those who want it. Grand Union, A&P, Jewel, Giant, National Tea, and First National were among the first chains to use unit pricing. Among the large cooperative food stores to use unit pricing were the nine stores (60,000 members) of Consumers Cooperative of Berkeley and the Consumers Cooperative Society of Palo Alto.

The cost of unit pricing for small and large food chains is "negligible" because they use computers. Single, small grocery stores, however, may find this information service costly unless several of them contract for the use of computer time as a group. This is entirely feasible. However, the Benner Tea Company of Burlington, Iowa, a small food chain, has installed the system at its twenty-one stores at an installation cost of only $200 and a weekly maintenance cost of $4 per store, says Philip Neally, executive vice president in charge of sales for the company. Neally says that the use of a computer, which Benner employs for many other purposes, has made the cost per unit almost negligible. He said that sales increased 4 percent during the first six weeks of unit pricing, but that there was a 10 percent increase in the number of customers going through the check-out counters. [34]

Unit-price comparisons, however, have some limitations. For example, unit-price comparisons between "net-weight" cans and packages of frozen foods are impossible. Consumers Union made such a comparison showing that it would be possible for canned green beans selling for 28 cents a pound actually to cost 7 percent more than the frozen variety selling for 44 cents a pound. [35]

Some weights-and-measures men fear unit pricing because it will take a great deal of time. Nevertheless, the 1971 National Weights and Measures Conference recommended a model unit-pricing regulation for adoption by the states. Henry Stern, deputy director of New York City's Office of Consumer Affairs, which incorporates the Office of Weights and Measures, said that unit pricing does tend to encourage preprinted unit price and selling price on labels of certain products, such as bread, but he is inclined to look favorably on this practice. [36]

[34] *The New York Times News Service,* Aug. 28, 1970.
[35] *Consumer Reports,* October 1972, pp. 665–669.
[36] *Of Consuming Interest,* July 25, 1972, p. 3.

Net weight versus minimum drained weight

The chances are that no one can make a rational price choice among canned foods at this time. Not even a computer or unit-price posting could help.

Net weight disclosures on canned food labels are "virtually useless as a buying yardstick"

It's not the shopper's fault, though. The problem, says Consumers Union, is that net-weight disclosures on canned food labels are "virtually useless as a buying yardstick."

The reason for this is simply that net weight refers not only to the food in the can but also to the liquid in which it is packed. Thus a 16-ounce "net-weight" can of peach slices might provide only 11 or fewer ounces of peaches.

Peaches, as well as most other fruits and vegetables, are among foods packed under a Food and Drug Administration rule requiring that a container be filled with the most that can be sealed into it and heat-treated without crushing the food.

"It's another fact of life," the consumer organization adds, "that the present net-weight labeling masks the considerable chunk of the consumer food dollar that goes toward paying for salt water or sugar syrup."

But, says Consumers Union, "some brands seem to be able to provide consumers as much as 1½ to 2 ounces more uncrushed fruit than other brands packed in a can of the same size." That, says CU, is an average finding. In random findings the differences were as high as 3 ounces.

The nonprofit consumer advisory organization says its study also shows that "the lowest-priced brand of a canned food often costs more per pound than higher-priced brands when the liquid is drained away."

The October, 1972, issue of *Consumer Reports,* CU's monthly, carries a table showing, for example, that 16 ounces of whole apricots of one brand costing 25 cents could actually mean 53 cents per pound of apricots, while another brand with the same labeled weight costing 29 cents could cost less per pound of apricots it provides.

In another example, the same 42-cent outlay for 16 ounces of two brands of citrus-fruit salad may really mean either 61 cents or 71 cents for a drained pound of food. Obviously, food-processing interests do not greet with gladness the suggestion that drained weights be disclosed.

Consumers Union advocates that labels on canned and bottled foodstuffs should reveal drained weights. While noting the contention of the National Canners Association that the liquid contents of a can may contain some of the food's nutrients, CU says it is a fact of life that many consumers do not make use of the liquid.

Shoppers will continue to buy in the dark until drained-weight disclosures are made for all canned, bottled, and frozen vegetables. That disclosure could then be used as a basis on which retail stores could make a realistic calculation of unit prices for consumers.

Ingredient labeling by percentage

About 2,500 years ago, a Scythian philosopher named Anarharsis complained about the evils of the Scythian marketplace. "The market," he said, "is the place set apart where men may deceive the public."

There is the tale of an inspector who visited a factory producing tins of nightingale meat after receiving complaints from customers that the contents tasted suspiciously like beef. He was quickly assured that although there was of course some beef in the product, the company still guaranteed the respectable ratio of one to one: one nightingale to one ox! [37]

Caveat emptor

Playing blindman's bluff

For many years percentage ingredient listing was fought on the grounds that it would give away secrets. Most processors, however, know what is inside a competitor's can. Secrets involve mainly spicing and blending. Consumers would gladly forgo this information if they could be sure of how much meat and other principal ingredients they were getting.

A more important reason behind some food processors' attitudes is that they don't want FDA inspectors examining plant records and making their own tests to see whether the label information is true. FDA records show that a common trick is to skimp on the good ingredients and add cheap fillers. Enforced percentage-ingredient labeling would increase the chance of getting caught by the FDA or by the shopper.

Faced with invitations to cooperate in percentage-ingredient labeling experiments recently, some food manufacturers balked. The Berkeley Co-op, for example, had difficulty in persuading its suppliers to go along, and it was refused by Foell (a meat-packer), Boston Bonnie, and Ralston Purina.

Esther Peterson, formerly President Johnson's Special Assistant for Consumer Affairs and presently with Giant Foods, had a similar experience. Only after months of bargaining could she induce Giant to persuade some of its suppliers to provide even a modest amount of ingredient information. Today, Giant's and Berkeley Co-op's new ingredient programs tell shoppers how much chicken is contained in chicken soup. Today, both Giant and the Berkeley Co-op have relabeled all their house brands with experimental ingredient labeling. These stores plan to do their own evaluation in addition to that done by outside researchers and the FDA. Other large food chains—the First National Stores, the Kroger Company, and Jewel Food Stores—planned and carried out their own experiments with ingredient labeling programs. An independent team of researchers under the direction of Dr. Daniel I. Padberg, associate professor of marketing at Cornell University, was contracted by the FDA to evaluate the programs. More details will be presented later when we take up the FDA's proposed criteria for nutrient labeling.

Today, however, consumers want and need more information in order to buy intelligently. They are not willing to buy products primarily on the basis of advertisements and claims. Representative Mark Andrews (Republican from North Dakota) in the House debate on improving food labeling said, "It is long past due that the Food and Drug Administration puts on the label not only what is in the food but the percentage of the individual ingredients, because the consuming public has the right to know." [38]

Given the selfish facts of the food industry's marketing, will the FDA be too timid to push the giants faster than they want to go? In 1972, the FDA turned down a petition by LABEL, Inc., a group of George Washington University students, requesting the listing of all ingredients on food packages.

[37] *Consumer Affairs,* no. 3, 1970, p. 5.
[38] *Of Consuming Interest,* July 25, 1972, p. 2.

One of the most forthright recommendations relative to ingredient labeling came out of a national seminar held from December 8 to 10, 1971, sponsored by the Community Nutrition Institute and the Center for Consumer Affairs, University of Wisconsin Extension. Some one hundred representatives of the food industry, government, and academia made the following recommendations to the FDA:

1.   The labels of all food products, including those for which a Standard of Identity has been set, list the common or usual names of all ingredients, including food additives, and their function. Where deemed helpful to consumers, it is urgent that product labels should list ingredients by percentage to aid consumers in assessing economic value and food quality.

2.   Food ingredients to be identified in terms of their source, such as "wheat protein-hydrolysate" (rather than just "protein hydrolysate"), "potato starch" (rather than just "starch"), and "peanut oil" (rather than just "vegetable oil").

3.   We call for immediate revision and standardization of the presently complex and deceitful terminology used by the food industry and the Department of Agriculture in the grading of fruits, vegetables, eggs, dairy and similar products. [39]

Many food giants may adopt the FDA's nutrient labeling guidelines. The larger food processors already have most of the needed information in their files. They are bracing themselves to use it in the hope of satisfying consumers' growing demand for more useful information on the labels.

Ingredient labeling, food scientists say, is a technically more difficult problem than nutrient labeling. We have the technology to determine how much protein there is in a can of stew, but it is not always easy to find out how much meat or carrots the can contains because processing does all sorts of things to components. For example, dehydrated carrots are a different ingredient from nondehydrated carrots. Some components shrink, some swell, and some dissolve. One ends up, therefore, agreeing on a recipe rather than a description. Food technologists are working hard on this problem in order to be able to tell shoppers, via the label, what they can't see for themselves.

Nutrient labeling

Prior to the FDA's proposed food labeling system announced on March 30, 1972, most labels for processed or formulated foods carried only the name of the product and, in most instances, a list of the ingredients in order of predominance (as required under Standards of Identity for foods containing two or more ingredients), but no percentages of ingredients.

Nutrient labeling advocates contend that the present labels discourage the food industry from producing food with higher nutritional values. Without some method of transmitting meaningful nutritional information, companies in the food industry must compete on a basis of cost of ingredients rather than their nutritional value, or quality.

Even under the present Standards of Identity system, a nutritionist could

[39] Helen E. Nelson (ed.), *Consumer Policy on Food Labeling*, University of Wisconsin Extension, Center for Consumer Affairs, Milwaukee, 1972.

not be certain of the exact amount of nutrients, carbohydrates, and fat in a certain food product. For health and dietary reasons, consumers must know exactly what is in the foods they buy. The lack of exact information in the case of processed foods poses a particular problem today because these foods do not fall into traditional food categories—the basic four. For example, what food group do frozen dinners and snacks fall into?

According to Dr. Jean Mayer, chairman of the 1969 White House Conference on Food, Nutrition, and Health, the public's nutritional status can be protected either through compulsory enrichment and fortification of foods, which he thinks is undesirable because it would require too much regulation, or through education of the public, enabling consumers to know what is in the foods they buy. The latter choice—which would involve nutrient labeling of packaged food—was recommended by the 1969 White House Conference on Food, Nutrition, and Health.

Accordingly, an ad hoc nutrient labeling advisory committee headed by Dr. Mayer, and made up of nutritional experts and representatives of consumer groups, government, and industry, was set up. This committee worked closely with the FDA to develop an easy-to-understand nutrient labeling system that consumers could use when selecting food in retail stores. Four large food chains and one large retail food cooperative agreed to cooperate with the FDA by experimenting with nutrient labeling in their own stores. These were Consumers Cooperative of Berkeley (nine supermarkets and 60,000 members), First National Stores, Giant Food Stores, the Kroger Company, and Jewel Food Stores. Each of these carried out its own nutrient labeling experiment and educational program. An independent team of researchers under the direction of Dr. Daniel I. Padberg, associate professor of marketing at Cornell University, evaluated the experimental nutrient labeling programs undertaken by Kroger, Giant, Jewel, and First National in cooperation with the FDA.

New facts revealed by the nutrient labeling study
The Padberg study

The Padberg study showed that about one-fourth of the consumers interviewed were aware of labeling at these cooperating food chains, 15 percent understood the labels, and 10 percent used them; however, 59 percent of those who saw and understood the labels used them. Understanding and use of the information increased with the duration of the program, and there was evidence of increases in nutritional knowledge and sensitivity. The final survey showed 16 percent using the labels in a purchase decision.

Consumers have the right to know

In answers to specific questions, 98.3 percent of Kroger shoppers said that they felt "consumers have the right to know the nutritional value of food products." The experts see nutrient labeling of food products as a direct input to the food-buying decision. Consumers, however, tend to see its value in a more general way. They see themselves benefiting from it because it affects the advertising and accountability of food manufacturers. Customers also found it easier to have confidence in an industry which makes open disclosure of some of the basic facts about nutrient labeling along with open dating and unit pricing. The study also noted that nutrient labeling might create a whole new basis of product competition, with the most nutritious product carrying off the honors, providing the price is right.

The FDA felt that the Padberg study had "provided the answers to the basic questions. The strong consumer interest in nutritional labeling and the evidence that consumers are able to understand and use nutritional labeling indicate that such a proposal is timely." (More details of the evaluation of the nutrient labeling programs are reproduced from the *Federal Register,* vol. 37, no. 62, Mar. 20, 1972,—Taylor-Troelstrup Reading 46.)

New FDA food label rules: a step in the right direction [40]
A major first step

On January 17, 1973, the FDA announced a twelve-part program intended to bring about far-reaching changes in the labeling and promotion of food products in this country.

The new program, culminating several years of study and discussion, is designed to provide the American consumer with specific and meaningful new information on the identity, quality, and nutritional value of a wide variety of general and special foods available in the nation's marketplace.

The "actions we are announcing . . . will result in the most significant change in food labeling practices since food labeling began," said Dr. Charles C. Edwards, FDA commissioner. He said, "They mark the beginning of a new era in providing consumers with complete, concise and informative food labeling." At General Mills, a spokesman expressed "strong approval" of the new labeling program, as did Virginia Knauer, Special Assistant to President Nixon for Consumer Affairs. Mrs. Esther Peterson, former Special Assistant to President Johnson for Consumer Affairs and now consumer consultant to Giant Foods, a food chain store system, in a more cautious tone called the new program "a great step ahead."

One of the loudest critics of the FDA rules, Representative Benjamin Rosenthal (New York), complained that "this proposal is based on the quicksand of those two oft-credited concepts—*voluntary* compliance and self-regulation." Said Rosenthal, "It has no teeth, no incentive, and no guts." At this time, perhaps we can go along with Dr. Jean Mayer, of Harvard, a leading nutritionist, who called the program "a major first step."

The following is a brief description of each of the twelve new proposals.

NUTRIENT LABELING [41]

On January 19, 1973, the FDA unveiled a new set of regulations on food labeling that are going to mean a great deal to consumers. The impetus for consideration of nutrient labeling came about because influential consumer groups have quietly been demanding the nutritional facts about a food product on the label. In 1969 the White House Conference on Food, Nutrition, and Health focused on poverty, hunger, and malnutrition. One of its recommendations for correcting the latter malady was increased information on food labels.

Simply stated, nutrient labeling provides an indication of the amount of certain major nutrients in an average serving of food. This seems to be a simple concept, but in fact it is a rather complex problem.

Need for new labeling regulations

Earlier in this chapter we presented the reasons for giving the consumer important information on food labels. The minimum requirements for good food labeling, it was stated, include open dating, unit pricing, net drained weight,

[40] For details, see the *Federal Register,* vol. 38, no. 13, part III, Jan. 19, 1973.
[41] Ibid.

*Consumers demand
nutrient labeling* percentage-ingredient labeling, and nutrient labeling. At present there are no federal regulations concerning these, although there are three kinds of regulatory standards for food products being shipped across state lines—standards of identity, standards of minimum quality, and standards of fill of container. Thus we have a long way to go in securing adequate information on food labels.

Some food chains and the Berkeley Food Cooperatives are using open dating and unit pricing on a voluntary basis. There is also some voluntary ingredient labeling in addition to the present federal required regulations which must meet the established "standard of identity" or list the ingredients in the order of predominance. These standards are good as far as they go. The next step forward is to require percentage-ingredient labeling. Net-weight disclosures on canned food labels are "virtually useless as a buying yardstick," according to Consumers Union (*Consumer Reports,* March, 1973). The drained weight— what's left after the liquid is drained off—should also be on the label. According to the CU study, a can of peaches listed as having a net weight of 16 ounces might contain only 11 or fewer ounces of peaches. Drained weight should be on labels for all processed fruits and vegetables packed in syrup, brine, water, or natural juice.

**Nutrient labeling rules
on a voluntary basis** On January 19, 1973, the FDA announced an extensive revamped food labeling program to help consumers more accurately identify the nutritional content of a wide variety of foods. These rules, however, will not go into effect until December 31, 1974.

The FDA rules are essentially in three parts:

New FDA labeling rules 1.   The first set of rules covers labeling of processed foods. Food packages must show the number of calories in an average portion, the number of grams of protein, the carbohydrate and fat content, and the proportion of the daily needs of key vitamins and minerals contained in each serving.

2.   The second set of rules covers the labeling of the type of fat that is contained in certain foods. This is of special importance to people who have been advised by their doctors—or who have decided for themselves—to watch their intake of cholesterol. This new type of labeling will indicate the amount of cholesterol, of saturated fat, and of polyunsaturated fat in all edible fats, oils, and shortenings.

3.   The third group of regulations sets the standards for vitamins and minerals sold as dietary supplements. These rules are intended to deter the unsuspecting buyer from spending needless sums of money for unnecessary, and sometimes potentially dangerous, amounts of certain vitamins. By the same token, the regulations will prevent certain foods, especially breakfast cereals, from being overfortified with nutrients.

The FDA rules, even though cast as a voluntary program, are really giving food manufacturers a clear choice—put the proof on the package and can, or take the lard out of the advertising. In other words, when a food processor says that his product is "enriched" or "fortified," he'll have to *put up* or *shut up*— *"Put up or shut up"* back up his claim—and list, in addition to ingredients, the amount of calories, carbohydrates, fats, and vitamins.

Imitation foods The rules will at last make some sense of the term "imitation." This term will not have to be prominently shown on the labels of foods which are like the real thing but which are not as nutritious. Imitation foods that are as nutritious as the real article will no longer have to be labeled. They can be sold under their own distinctive names.

Recommended daily allowance (RDA)

You can forget the minimum daily requirement (MDR) and remember its successor—recommended daily allowance (RDA), which is nearly double the suggested daily intake of various vitamins and minerals for children and adults. Depending on the amount of vitamins and minerals a food product contains over and above the RDA, the FDA can classify it as an ordinary food, a special dietary food, or a drug intended for treating a disease.

The FDA rules also include stringent prohibitions on food designated for special dietary use, including a prohibition on claims that the product can by itself prevent, treat, or cure disease. The label may not imply that a diet of ordinary foods cannot supply adequate nutrients, and claims that transportation, storage, or cooking of foods may result in an inadequate or deficient diet are forbidden. Also disallowed are claims that such nonnutritive ingredients as rutin and other similar ingredients have nutritional value. (Those who are desirous of more details about the FDA regulations should consult Taylor-Troelstrup Reading 46.)

What do all these regulations add up to?
We eat to remain healthy

What all these regulations add up to is a detailed inventory of the variety of nutrients we need to remain healthy—which is, after all, the basic reason why we eat. At the present moment, consumers have only the most general idea of what is in a particular box or can. This is especially so in the case of unidentifiable snacks and mixtures, as well as new, unfamiliar products.

At present, food labels show only a list of ingredients in the order of greatest proportion. For example, if the label says "water, sugar, peaches," it means that there's more water than sugar and more sugar than peaches. But there is no way to know whether there is just a little more water than sugar or whether the food contains 90 percent water, 8 percent sugar, and 2 percent peaches.

Label requirements not costly to food processors

Are all the new labeling requirements costly to food manufacturers? Rumors circulated by opponents of labeling suggest that all these new labeling requirements are going to cost the food producers so much money that the prices of food will go up. Don't worry. All the serious studies disprove the claim. Moreover, the Food and Drug Administration is giving the food companies plenty of time to make the change so that they can use up old labels and will not have to throw away costly supplies.

It is true that manufacturers who do not know the nutrient content of the foods they sell will have to have them analyzed. But the cost of such analyses, even of samples large enough to be representative, is very small indeed in relation to the profits earned by the enormous amounts of foods produced.

Many conscientious manufacturers already routinely do such analyses as part of their quality control. Admittedly, the problem is more difficult when dealing with natural products, like fruit and vegetables, than with fabricated foods.

How the new food label may look

Under the FDA guidelines, a food concern that makes a nutritional claim must follow the FDA regulations just summarized. The label on a package or can could look like the following example:

NUTRITIONAL INFORMATION

1 cup	255 calories
Protein	8 grams
Fat	5 grams
Carbohydrates	45 grams

Percent of Recommended Daily Allowance
(RDA) in This Order

Protein	10
Vitamin A	10
Vitamin C	30
Thiamine	5
Riboflavin	15
Niacin	20
Calcium	0
Iron	5

The label above shows that 1 cup of this food product provides 10 percent of the daily protein need, 30 percent of the daily need for vitamin C, and so on. The above model shows all seven key vitamins on the information panel. The FDA regulation says that the processor *may* choose to list only those nutrients present in amounts constituting 2 percent or more of the RDA.

A critical look at FDA nutrient labeling

Dr. Jean Mayer, Harvard nutritionist, called the FDA program a "major first step." As soon as possible, we need to add to labels (1) the percentage of major or all ingredients (the FDA feels it does not have the authority to enforce percentage-ingredient labeling), (2) open dating, (3) unit pricing, and (4) net *drained* weight. This additional information, where appropriate, should be mandatory and uniform in every state. Currently, several states are mulling legislation for open dating and nutrient labeling. Imagine the confusion if there were

More information needed

fifty more or less different sets of regulations! Additional information is needed, and uniformity can best be achieved through federal legislation and authority.

Labeling the nutrients only, without showing percentages of ingredients, could be a trap for consumers, who would be buying a lot of water, fortified gravy, and sugar because, as of now, net drained weight is not required information.

Ingredient percentages should be on label

The point that needs emphasis is that most consumers will eventually accept food substitutes and synthetic vitamins if the price is reasonable, but they do want and should have the ingredients listed on the label in the order of percentage amounts. Consumers Cooperative (Berkeley, California) and Giant Foods (a southeastern food chain) are already experimenting with percentage-ingredient and nutrient information on their own labels. Co-op beef stew, for example, lists 60 percent gravy (water, flour, tomato paste, salt, onion powder, caramel coloring, and pepper), 25 percent beef, 10 percent potatoes, and 5 percent carrots.

Sidney Margolius,[42] a well-known consumer advocate and journalist, is of the opinion that unless labels show the actual amounts of the various ingredients, processors could add protein from such low-cost sources as soybeans, nonfat milk, cereals, and synthetic vitamins. This is what happened when the manu-

---

[42]"Nutritional Labeling," *The Machinist,* May 11, 1972, p. 6.

facturers of dry cereals and diluted fruit-flavored beverages added low-cost synthetic vitamins and advertised their products as having "100 percent of your daily needs" or "more vitamin C than orange juice." There is nothing nutritionally wrong in using low-cost synthetic vitamins. Actually, the economic cost is lowered because synthetic vitamins are cheap. A processor, for example, can add a whole day's supply of all vitamins (except D) to a 4-ounce box of corn-flakes for only ¼ of 1 cent. The issue arises when the processor charges you 15 to 20 cents more for adding ¼ of 1 cent's worth of synthetic vitamins.

Synthetic vitamins—the
problem is fair prices

Michael Jacobson, of the Center for Science in the Public Interest, has cited the example of Wheaties and Total, both made by General Mills. Both cereals have identical ingredients, except that Total contains 100 percent of the minimum daily requirement of nine vitamins and one mineral. Wheaties are also enriched with added vitamins, but only about one-third as much as is added to Total. The added synthetic vitamins in Total cost General Mills only about ½ of 1 cent, according to Jacobson, and yet the consumer pays 18 cents more for a box of Total than for a box of Wheaties. Such a situation will not be permitted after January 1, 1975, the date when the new requirements will go into effect.

Nutrient labeling of the type proposed by the FDA is not entirely precise. Using such information, the consumer might underestimate the nutritional quality of his day's food because the standard RDA is higher than the recommended allowance for most of the twenty-four age-sex categories. Also, contributions of less than 5 percent of the standard in a diet could be substantial in some cases. For the person who wants to estimate the nutritive value of his diet and compare results with the RDA for his age-sex category, more precise information is available in the USDA publication *Nutritive Value of Foods*, H.G.-72. (See Taylor-Troelstrup Reading 46 for more about nutrient labeling suggestions.)

The following would further strengthen the FDA nutrient label regulation:

1. Switching from a voluntary to a mandatory system of labeling.
2. Requiring a list of *all* seven key vitamins on the information panel. A standardized list is essential, advises the Berkeley Cooperative, to *(a)* facilitate nutrient comparisons of the same or varied foods, *(b)* prevent consumers from mistaking a product listing three or fewer nutrients as a good nutrient source, and *(c)* emphasize the necessity of eating a wide variety of foods to meet daily nutritional requirements.
3. Revising the ground rules to reduce the number of exceptions food packagers can seek for small or irregularly sized packages.
4. Where cholesterol labeling is used, a requirement that *(a)* fat labeling also be used, *(b)* the ratio of polyunsaturated to saturated fats be included on the label, and *(c)* the source of vegetable fat be identified.
5. Development of more reasonable procedures by which nutritional claims for "health foods" can be challenged and either validated or proved false.
6. Standardization of "serving size." Presently, the FDA defines serving size as a "reasonable quantity of food suited for, or practicable of, consumption as part of a meal by an adult male engaged in light physical activity, or by an infant or child under 4 years of age when the article purports or is represented

to be for consumption by an infant or child under 4 years of age." To consumers, 1- or ½-cup terms are understandable.

New FDA ingredient and nutrient labeling—a step in the right direction

Changes in advertising coming

The FDA is giving food manufacturers a clear choice—put the proof on the package and can, or take the lard out of the advertising. Any food processor adding nutrients to a product or advertising caloric or nutritional values will have to list, in addition to ingredients, the amount of calories, carbohydrates, fats, and vitamins. The changes will mean new labels and changes in advertising.

The FDA's proposal set December 31, 1974, as the date on which food products that are shipped will be required to conform to all new requirements unless there are modifications prior to that date.

THE PRINCIPLE OF "AFFIRMATIVE DECLARATION"

The new nutrient labeling program is a rare example of a federal agency's telling food manufacturers that under certain circumstances, they *must* give certain kinds of information about the contents of a can or package. In other words, the food processors must make an affirmative declaration of the nutrients contained in a given amount of food.

The Federal Trade Commission has already used this affirmative-declaration approach in regard to electric light bulbs and is trying to get its way in declaring "octane rating" on all gasoline pumps. In other words, the affirmative declaration is giving consumers the opportunity to say, "Give me the basic information I need to make an intelligent decision for myself. Enough of protecting me and not telling me anything."

IS THE BASIC-FOUR GUIDELINE OBSOLETE?

The basic four are still useful

The basic-four guideline focuses on food guides—the kinds and amounts of foods to eat—rather than on the nutritive value of foods. Consumers have been urged to be concerned about how much milk, etc., they need each day rather than about how much calcium or riboflavin they need. Does this mean that the basic four groups—milk, meat, vegetables and fruit, and breads and cereals—will be abandoned in favor of nutrient labeling as a tool for choosing a good diet?

Nutrient labeling is a sharper tool

Probably not. Some people are likely to use the basic-four guide because it appears to be easier to understand. This is not necessarily a good reason; a glance at our health records—obesity, heart ailments, food allergies, overconsumption of overprocessed foods, and so on—shows that after many years of basic-four education, a higher percentage of Americans are undernourished today than fifteen years ago! We failed rather miserably in educating people to use the basic-four guidelines effectively. So, maybe the time is ripe for a nutrient labeling program. If we fail to use nutrient information effectively, we may have to try something else. Those of us who used the basic-four guidelines did not have available to us labels giving basic nutritional information to use as a guide in our food shopping. Nutrient labeling and the basic-four body-builder guideline complement each other. Nutrient labeling is merely a sharper tool to use in achieving better health for better living.

FEDERAL FOOD STANDARDS

"A standard is a physical, written, graphic, or other representation of a product or a procedure established by authority, custom, or general consent with which other products or procedures of a like nature are compared for identification, or measurement or to which they are made to conform."[43]

The need for quality standards

The basic role of standards is simply to supply a common language understood and respected by both seller and buyer. Standards function as the language of careful description in the production and exchange of goods in somewhat the same way that mathematics is the language of the sciences. It is unfortunate that when it comes to most consumer goods, foods included, we have few standards available to the ultimate consumer. We seem to be caught up in a social time lag.

Standards of identity are limited only to "minimum quality," as we learned earlier. The next step is to take minimum standards the rest of the way and establish additional grades of quality. With some education on the meaning of grades, it would seem that all our needs would be met by grade labeling. All the products of the same grade would have virtually the same quality, and our purchase could then be made on the basis of style, cost, availability, brand name even, and other factors easy to determine.

A recent law requires the federal government to set quality grades for automobile tires, an exciting development we are watching with interest. During World War II, when food was scarce, the federal government established quality grade standards for food at the consumer level. If quality grade standards were useful then, why not now? Our neighbor to the north, Canada, has for several years required quality grades on food. Many other countries have quality grades placed on the label of the food product.

In our country, there are now standardized and recognized quality grades in use. Private-branders often specify them to suppliers. But these quality grades rarely get on the labels of foods. In 1966, the National Commission on Food Marketing, established by Congress, recommended wider use of grade labeling. Thus far, Congress has not heeded the recommendation of that commission, nor has private industry.

Grade labeling versus descriptive labeling

Standardized descriptive labeling, endorsed by the National Canners Association, is not a complete alternative to grade labeling. Both kinds of labeling can be used on the same food label. This is evident from the practice of private brand-grade labeling by the canning industry, which has opposed A, B, C grade labeling. Dr. Richard L. D. Morse, an authority on grade labeling, favors A, B,

[43] Jessie V. Coles, *Standards and Labels for Consumers' Goods,* The Ronald Press Company, New York, 1949, p. 107.

C or 1, 2, 3 grade terms on labels for products in which an ordinal or successive arrangement of product quality is possible.[44] Morse is of the opinion that consumer grades are of primary concern to those who wish to improve the efficiency of the marketing system and to improve the effectiveness of the price mechanism for communicating consumer preferences to producers of products. Grading can also assist consumers in buying more intelligently in the marketplace.

Federal food standards [45]

All food standards established by the federal government fall into two general classes: voluntary and regulatory. Here is a brief listing of the principal kinds of voluntary and regulatory federal standards for food.

VOLUNTARY STANDARDS

U.S. Department of Agriculture grade standards

Under authority of the Agricultural Marketing Act of 1946 and related statutes, USDA has issued grade standards for some three hundred food and farm products.

Food products for which grade standards have been established are beef, veal, and calf; lamb and mutton; poultry, including turkey, chicken, duck, goose, guinea hen, and squab; eggs; manufactured dairy products, including butter, Cheddar cheese, and instant nonfat dry milk; fresh fruits, vegetables, and nuts; canned, frozen, and dried fruits and vegetables and related products such as preserves; and rice, dry beans, and peas. U.S. grade standards are also available for grains but not for the food products, such as flour and cereal, into which grain is processed.

The USDA provides official grading services, often in cooperation with state departments of agriculture, to packers, processors, distributors, and others who wish official certification of the grade of a product. The grade standards also are often used by packers and processors as a quality-control tool.

Federal law does not require use of the U.S. grade standards or the official grading services. Official grading is required under some state and local ordinances and some industry marketing programs.

Grade labeling not required by federal law

Products which have been officially graded may carry the USDA grade name or grade shield, such as the familiar purple "USDA Choice" shield seen on cuts of beef or the "U.S. Grade A" on cartons of eggs. Grade labeling, however, is not required by federal law, even though a product has been officially graded. On the other hand, a packer or processor may not label his product with an official grade name such as Grade A (even without the "U.S." prefix) unless it actually measures up to the federal standard for that grade. Mislabeling of this sort would be deemed a violation of the Food, Drug, and Cosmetic Act.

---

[44] Unpublished paper entitled "Need for Consumer Grades," presented at the National Marketing Service Workshop in Louisville, Nov. 11, 1964.
[45] *U.S.D.A. Standards for Food and Farm Products*, AH-341, U.S. Office of Information, April, 1972.

National Marine Fisheries
Service grade standards

The U.S. Department of Commerce's National Marine and Fisheries Service provides grade standards and grading services for fishery products similar to those provided by the USDA for other foods. To date, fifteen U.S. grade standards have been developed for frozen processed fishery products, covering such products as semiprocessed raw whole fish, fish blocks, cut fish portions, steaks, and fillets; breaded raw and precooked fish portions and sticks; raw headless and breaded shrimp; and raw and fried scallops. Such products when produced and graded under the U.S. Department of Commerce inspection program may carry the USDA "Federally Inspected" mark and/or the U.S. grade shield. However, as under the USDA grading programs, grade labeling is *not* required by federal law, even though products are officially inspected and graded.

REGULATORY STANDARDS

U.S. Department of
Agriculture standards of
composition and identity

The USDA has established minimum content requirements for federally inspected meat and poultry products (usually canned or frozen) under the Federal Meat Inspection Act and the Poultry Products Inspection Act.

To be labeled with a particular name—such as "beef stew"—a federally inspected meat or poultry product must meet specified content requirements. These requirements assure the consumer that he's getting what the label says he's getting. They do not, however, keep different companies from making distinctive recipes. The USDA minimum content requirement for beef stew specifies the minimum percentage of *beef only* (25 percent) that the stew must contain. It doesn't keep the manufacturer from using combinations of seasonings or increasing the amount of beef to make his product unique.

The USDA has also established complete standards of identity for these products: chopped ham, corned beef hash, and oleomargarine. They go further than the composition standards, setting specific and optional ingredients.

Food and Drug
Administration standards

The Federal Food, Drug, and Cosmetic Act provides for three kinds of regulatory standards for products being shipped across state lines: standards of identity, standards of minimum quality, and standards of fill of container. All these standards are administered by the Food and Drug Administration of the U.S. Department of Health, Education, and Welfare. The law sets forth penalties for noncompliance.

Standards of Identity

The FDA standards of identity (like the USDA's) establish what a given food product is—for example, what a food must be to be labeled "preserves." The FDA standards of identity also provide for use of optional ingredients in addition to the mandatory ingredients that make the product what it is. Standards of identity have eliminated from the market such things as "raspberry spread" —made from a little fruit; a lot of water; pectin, sugar, and artificial coloring and flavoring; and a few grass seeds to suggest a fruit product.

The FDA has standards of identity for a large number of food products (excluding meat and poultry products, which are covered by the USDA.).

Types of products for which standards of identity have been formulated by the FDA include cacao products; cereal flour and related products; macaroni and noodle products; frozen desserts; food flavoring; dressings for food; canned fruits and fruit juices; fruit butters, jellies, preserves, and related products; non-alcoholic beverages; canned and frozen shellfish; eggs and egg products; oleo-margarine and margarine; nut products; canned vegetables; and tomato products.

Minimum standards of quality

FDA standards of quality have been set for a number of canned fruits and vegetables to supplement standards of identity. These are minimum standards for such factors as tenderness, color, and freedom from defects. They are regulatory, as opposed to USDA grade standards of quality, which are for voluntary use.

If a food does not meet the FDA quality standards, it must be labeled "Below Standard in Quality; Good Food--Not High Grade." Other words may be substituted for the second part of the statement to show in what respect the product is substandard. The label could read, "Below Standard in Quality; Excessively Broken" or "Below Standard in Quality; Excessive Peel." The consumer seldom, if ever, sees a product with a substandard label.

(When USDA grade standards are developed for a product for which the FDA has a minimum standard of quality, the requirements for the lowest grade level the USDA sets are at least as high as the FDA minimum. USDA grade standards for canned tomatoes, for example, are U.S. Grades A, B, and C. U.S. Grade C is comparable to the FDA's minimum standard of quality.)

Standards of fill of container

These standards tell the packer how full a container must be to avoid deception. They reduce the selling of air or water in place of food.

Public Health Service food standards

Under the Public Health Service Act, the Public Health Service has formulated food standards to help fight infectious diseases. The PHS, an agency of the U.S. Department of Health, Education, and Welfare, advises state and local governments on safety standards for milk and milk products, drinking water, shellfish, and some other foods. The PHS also has standards for the safety and wholesomeness of foods and drinking water aboard all interstate passenger carriers.

The most familiar PHS standard is for Grade A milk. In contrast to USDA quality grade standards for food, the PHS standard for Grade A milk is largely a standard of wholesomeness.

To promote uniform and effective controls, the PHS developed a milk ordinance which now serves as the basis of Grade A milk sanitation laws in many states. Its provisions may be adopted voluntarily—in whole or in part—by states. Under the ordinance, procedures for inspection of milk and milk products are used to determine whether milk is Grade A.

U.S. GOVERNMENT INSPECTION AND GRADING: MEAT, POULTRY, AND FISH

It is not enough for consumers to know the principal kinds of voluntary and regulatory federal standards for food. We should also be able to recognize and know the difference between USDA inspection label and the grade label. A joint study by the USDA and the National Livestock Meat Board in 1967 pointed out that most consumers are confused about the meaning of federal inspection marks and grade marks. The inspection mark tells the buyer that the meat or meat product is wholesome. The grade mark indicates the quality of the meat. In other words, nutrient information and grades are *not* the same.

The Wholesome Meat Act of 1967 created a big moral crisis among the USDA's meat and poultry inspectors because the inspectors felt intimidated by industry, according to several investigations. Ralph Nader, following a two-year investigation of federal meat inspection ending in early 1971, said that the USDA has favored the interests of the agricultural and chemical industries at the expense of the American consumer.

Meat inspectors intimidated

The report says further that corruption, ineptness, and general laxity of meat inspection have rendered the Wholesome Meat Act of 1967 all but ineffective. Nader adds that the USDA is torn between consumer interests on the one hand and the interests of food producers and processors on the other. As an example, the report details the case of a chicken processing plant in North Carolina owned by Central Soya, Inc.; 40 percent of the chickens leaving the plant for sale in East coast supermarkets were unfit to eat by USDA standards. When the federal inspector suspended operations of the plant, Central Soya resisted enforcement. Eventually, the USDA office responded by transferring the plant inspector!

Another federal inspector at a poultry processing plant in Morton, Mississippi, was fired eight days after writing the General Accounting Office in Washington complaining about the lack of support he had received from the USDA in enforcing meat inspection regulations.

The Director of New Jersey Consumer Health Services cited studies showing that up to one-half of all USDA-inspected poultry contains salmonella and other harmful bacteria. [46]

In midsummer, 1972, forty federal meat inspectors, three meat processing companies, and six company officials were indicted by a federal grand jury on charges of bribery, perjury, and conspiracy; the meat processors were charged with bribing federal meat inspectors to influence the latter in performance of their inspection duties. The USDA sent new staff inspectors to the Boston area to replace those indicted.

Poultry grade and inspection marks

Poultry is an expensive meat to purchase, as a rule, because there is only a small percentage of meat in a dressed bird. The Department of Agriculture has compiled the percentage of meat in six kinds of dressed bird. To figure cost per pound, divide the price per pound for a dressed bird by the percentage given here.

[46] *The Washington Post,* Mar. 28, 1972.

	PERCENTAGE		PERCENTAGE
Fattened roasting chickens	63	Unfattened broilers	54
Unfattened roasting chickens	57	Fattened hens	64
Fattened broilers	61	Turkeys	68

Graded
ready-to-cook   Graded and inspected
ready-to-cook   Inspected for
wholesomeness
ready-to-cook   Graded dressed

FIGURE 7-4   Poultry grade levels and inspection marks

If you need only a few pieces of chicken, it may be cheaper to buy just those you want. Breasts from roasters contain about 72 percent edible meat; drumsticks yield about 75 percent. If you want a turkey meal without eating turkey all week, buy turkey cuts.

On January 1, 1950, a revised program of the U.S. Department of Agriculture for the grading and inspection of poultry went into effect. Although a voluntary program, the regulations apply to those members of the poultry industry who request inspection and grading services of the department.

An important part of the program deals with the requirements for the sanitation of dressing plants. Since January 1, 1951, all ready-to-cook poultry prepared in official plants approved by the Department of Agriculture have been processed under the same sanitary standards.

Broiling and frying chickens are now one class and may be termed *broilers* or *fryers.* Stewing chickens may be described as *hens, stewing chickens,* or *fowl.* The term *dressed* is used for birds that have been bled and picked, but not drawn. *Ready-to-cook* describes poultry that has been fully drawn, or eviscerated.

The official grade label, in the form of a shield, states the quality (U.S. Grade A or U.S. Grade B), the style of processing (dressed or ready-to-cook), and the class (stewing chicken). The label also states that the product is government graded.

Ready-to-cook poultry that has been inspected for wholesomeness by a federal veterinarian but not graded for quality carries an inspection mark in the form of a circle. Ready-to-cook poultry that has been both graded and inspected carries a combination label, a shield within a circle.

Inadequate poultry labeling

The USDA declines to require separate weights for the poultry and the stuffing in each package. The stuffing weight often exceeds 25 percent of the total weight of the bird and the stuffing. Is the consumer not entitled to know the true quantity of the product he is buying? The label should show the net weight of the turkey unstuffed and the combined weight of poultry and stuffing.

Present grading standards of USDA consider the birds' conformation, fleshing, fat covering, and defeathering; cuts, tears, and gouges; broken bones and missing parts; discoloration of the skin and flesh; and freezer burns. On the basis of these largely visual factors, the birds are graded A, B, or C. Most of these factors indicate only marketability, not flavor and tenderness. It is true that the label must show whether the bird is young, old, or, mature, which is a factor in tenderness. But processing techniques also affect tenderness, and judging by Consumers Union test results, there are "clear differences in quality among birds labeled Grade A."

The Wholesome Poultry Products Act of 1968

This law amends the poultry products inspection law. The amendments provide for extension of federal jurisdiction to state poultry inspection programs that do not measure up to federal standards within two years. The new measure will affect an estimated 1.6 billion pounds of poultry, or about 13 percent of the nation's output. That portion is not federally inspected because it is not shipped across state lines. Congress was told that a spot check of retail markets in sixteen states had shown that one out of five chickens not federally inspected was unfit for human consumption, according to Dr. Mehren, Assistant Secretary of Agriculture. Thirty-two states had no poultry inspection in 1968, eleven states had voluntary inspection, and seven states had some mandatory features in their inspection laws.

In 1968 the Wholesome Poultry Products Act became effective. In 1971, the General Accounting Office said that staff investigators observed contaminated poultry products—some tainted by fecal matter, digestive-tract contents, bile, and feathers—in thirty-five of the sixty-eight federally inspected plants surveyed. In most of the sixty-eight plants, the GAO added, investigators also found other unacceptable conditions including dirty equipment, inadequate *Food industry influence is powerful* pest control, and dirty floors, walls, and overhead structures. The sixty-eight plants surveyed accounted for about 19 percent of United States poultry slaughter in 1970, the GAO report said, adding that the evidence demonstrated that the USDA was "not adequately enforcing its sanitation standards at poultry plants."[47] This is the GAO's function as a congressional watchdog.

In 1972 the USDA, under extreme pressure to create a new and separate department for inspection of poultry and meat plants, established the Animal and Plant Health Inspection Service. It remains to be seen whether changing the name of a department (it was formerly called the Consumer and Marketing Service) that is still run by the USDA will improve the intolerable inspection and accrediting record of the USDA meat inspection agency.

The USDA claims that the meat inspection agency does not have the budget to make an adequate investigation of meat and poultry plants. If the meat and poultry lobbies continue to keep the federal meat and poultry agencies understaffed and incapable of dealing properly with inspection activities, creating a new agency in name only is not apt to improve the present intolerable inspection system.

[47] *Community Nutrition Institute Weekly Report*, Dec. 2. 1971, p. 7.

Fish product inspection

There is much misunderstanding about fish product inspection. Few people realize that there is no mandatory federal inspection program for fishery products yet. There is a voluntary program run by the Bureau of Commercial Fisheries, but it covers only about 20 percent of all fish products sold. The FDA spot-checks imported products and domestic plants, and the Public Health Service conducts a certification program to ensure cleanliness of shellfish. There is need for required inspection of all fish products.

In 1966 there were more recalls of contaminated fish products than in most recent years. Inspection of smoked fish processing plants by FDA, for example, showed that all but two were operating under conditions described as dangerously unsanitary. As a result Senator Philip Hart introduced a bill in 1968 to set up broad inspection of fish products, but the bill met so much opposition that it did not get out of committee. And yet, preliminary studies show that the 2,200 fish processing plants in the United States are inspected "an average of less than once a year," that "virtually no fishing vessels are inspected," and that imported fish, which constitute about 50 percent of the total fish consumption here, enter the country almost entirely uninspected.

MILK AND MILK PRODUCTS

Grades and kinds of milk

The U.S. Public Health Service Milk Ordinance standards have been adopted by most American cities. This ordinance provides for three grades of fluid milk.

1. *Certified milk.* Very rigid sanitary requirements; sold only by licensed dealers; expensive.
2. *Grade A, pasteurized.* Must not contain more than 30,000 bacteria per cubic centimeter; must have hooded caps; must be kept below 50 degrees at all times.
3. *Grade B, pasteurized.* May contain as many as 50,000 bacteria per cubic centimeter when delivered to the consumer; need not have hooded caps.
4. *Grade C, pasteurized.* Is below Grade B requirements.

The ordinance also provides for three grades of raw milk, A, B, and C. Grade A pasteurized milk is the most common form of milk for table use. Milk delivered to the home costs from 2 to 4 cents a quart more than when purchased at milk stores in gallon and half-gallon quantities.

Homogenized milk is processed so that the fat does not separate and rise to the top of the bottle. It is thought to be more digestible, but authorities are still battling over this assumption. Some pediatricians believe that only in the case of infants is there value in homogenization, since it softens the curd of milk. There are no extra food values in homogenized milk, but the consumer pays 1 to 2 cents a quart more for it, though the process costs are very low.

As yet, science has discovered no milk substitute. It is possible, however, to reduce the cost of milk without decreasing the food value. This can be done by using evaporated milk.

Evaporated milk mixed with an equal volume of water is whole milk slightly above the average for the composition of bottled milk. Some evaporated milk is enriched with vitamin D. One pint of evaporated milk (before water is added) is equal in food value to a quart of fresh milk, at a little more than half the price.

Many homemakers prefer evaporated milk for cooking, and it is recommended for cream sauces, gravies, cream soup, chowder, scalloped vegetables, custards, puddings, dessert sauces, cakes, cookies, breads, frozen desserts, and candy. Undiluted evaporated milk is used by many families in coffee, candy, and frozen desserts, and as an emulsifier in mayonnaise. When thoroughly chilled, it can be whipped like cream.

Dried milk (powdered milk) is used largely for cooking purposes, in the proportion of ¾ cup of dried milk to 1 quart of water.

Skim milk (nonfat milk) can also be used for cooking purposes. The cost of this product may be from 22 to 25 cents a quart.

Milk equivalents in the diet

Here are some substitutes for fresh whole milk in mathematical terms, which will help in calculating food values.

1 quart of skim milk plus 1½ ounces of butter equals 1 quart of fluid milk.

1 pint of undiluted evaporated milk equals 1 quart of fluid milk.

⅓ pound of Cheddar cheese equals 1 quart of fluid milk.

¼ pound of dried whole milk equals 1 quart of fluid milk.

Filled milk is a combination of dairy and nondairy products. It is presently made from either skim or nonfat dry milk, but the butterfat has been replaced by less expensive vegetable fat. The true synthetic milks replace both the butterfat and the nonfat milk solids with soybeans or soya protein combined with sodium caseinate, which is derived from real milk.

Filled milk under federal law cannot be shipped from one state to another. Synthetic milk can be if it meets legal labeling standards.

Are these so-called fake milks as good as real milk? Some experts say that filled milk is, if vitamin A has been added to it. There is some disagreement about synthetic milk. Apparently, it is not yet nutritionally equivalent to real milk. Some scientists say there is no reason why synthetic milk cannot be as nutritious as real milk.

How to buy cheese The most food value for the money is in *American Cheddar* cheese. About 5 quarts of milk are required to make 1 pound. Thus all the proteins, fats, minerals, and vitamins found in whole milk are found in Cheddar cheese.

There are over four hundred varieties of cheese made in this country. The fancy processed cheese is generally Cheddar, processed with inexpensive fillers and water.

Sharp cheese costs more than mild cheese because it is aged.

Cheese is not a complete substitute for meat or eggs because it is low in protein, although high in butterfat.

The federal government has established the following quality grades for American Cheddar cheese, and some manufacturers use them.

	QUALITY SCORE
U.S. Extra Fancy	95 and above
U.S. Fancy	92-94
U.S. No. 1	89-91
U.S. No. 2	86-88
U.S. No. 3	83-85
Culls	Below 83

Cottage cheese is usually the next best buy in food value. It is made from skim milk, and therefore has no butterfat or vitamin A. It cannot replace whole milk in the diet. No U.S. grades have as yet been produced for cottage cheese, but rigid specifications have been set to cover its manufacture and quality. Cottage cheese may carry a shield stating that it is "Quality Approved" by the U.S. Department of Agriculture.

Grades of butter

Butter is the dairy product most widely sold on the basis of U.S. grades. The letters "U.S." before the grade mark on the carton or wrapper indicate that the butter has been graded by an authorized grader of the U.S. Department of Agriculture.

The letters AA, A, B, or the numerical score, 93, 92, 90, without the prefix "U.S." on the package indicate that the butter has not been certified by a federal butter grader.

Some states have enacted a law requiring that butter be grade labeled, and in these localities the letters or grade names on butter cartons denote state standards, applied by state graders. Such state grades do not carry the prefix "U.S.", but may show the state name or seal.

A grade mark on the package without the prefix "U.S." or state identification reflects the manufacturer's or distributor's own standard of quality. This butter may be of good quality, but since it is not federally graded the consumer must necessarily rely on the distributor's statement that it meets the quality designation on the package.

U.S. grades for butter include U.S. Grade AA (U.S. 93 score), U.S. Grade A (U.S. 92 score), and U.S. Grade B (U.S. 90 score). "Score" refers to the total number of points allotted a sample on the basis of the quality of several factors —chiefly flavor, but also including body, texture, color, and salt.

To be rated U.S. Grade AA, butter must have a fine, highly pleasing aroma and a delicate, sweet taste. Americans like butter, though it is comparatively expensive. It takes from 10½ to 11 quarts of milk to produce 1 pound of butter.

Standards for margarine

Oleomargarine, or margarine, as it is more generally called, when fortified with vitamin A has as much food value as butter, according to the American Medical Association. In addition, margarine does not become rancid as quickly as butter. Margarine is a genuine food, made from refined food fats, such as cottonseed oil, soybean oil, peanut oil, and meat fats. These oils are blended with pasteurized cultured skim milk and salt for flavor. The retail price of margarine is often less than half the price for the same weight of 92-score butter.

Many laws, both state and federal, have been passed in the last 50 years to protect the butter interests. Congress finally repealed the 64-year-old antimargarine taxes and license fees and permitted the sale of yellow margarine in interstate commerce on July 1, 1950.

The quality and purity of margarine that enters interstate commerce are guarded by two federal agencies. For instance, margarine that contains animal fats is inspected by the Federal Meat Inspection Service. Margarine that contains only vegetable oils comes under the supervision of the Federal Food, Drug, and Cosmetic Act. Margarine must contain 80 percent fat, which corresponds to the 80 percent fat requirement for butter.

EGGS

Know the eggs you buy

The alert consumer always considers value in purchases more than price. When prices are high, it is especially important to know where and how to get the most for your egg money. To get the best buy, know quality or grade, know size or weight, know about shell color, and know their food values.

In many places, eggs are sold by grade, and the quality is stated in terms of grade on the label of the egg carton. An egg in one of the top grades, AA or A, should have a large amount of firm white and a round, upstanding yolk. Eggs of such quality are preferred for poaching, frying, and cooking in the shell.

Grade B eggs, just as satisfactory for scrambling and for baking and cooking, have thinner whites and somewhat flatter yolks. They offer the same food values as the top grades. Grade B eggs may cost as much as 10 or 12 cents a dozen less than Grade A eggs of the same weight.

In terms of value on a scale, the size of eggs means the same as weight. A dozen jumbo eggs weigh not less than 30 ounces. A dozen eggs labeled "Extra Large" must weigh at least 27 ounces, and eggs of the more common size, Large, weigh not less than 24 ounces to the dozen.

Let us stop here a minute: 24 ounces equals 1½ pounds. That is worth remembering when you consider relative prices of eggs, meat, fish, cheese, and other protein foods that are purchased by the pound. It takes only eight large eggs, two-thirds of a dozen, to make a pound, and they cost two-thirds the price of a dozen. But you buy eggs by the dozen unit, and you get 1½ pounds of a meat alternative food in twelve large eggs.

If you pay 60 cents for a dozen large eggs (weighing 24 ounces or more), you are actually paying only at the rate of around 40 cents a pound, because the shells, the only waste, weigh very little. This waste is especially small when compared with that of many other protein foods.

Medium eggs run 21 ounces or more per dozen eggs, and small or pullet eggs weigh 18 or more ounces per dozen. The small eggs are seldom on the market except in late summer and fall, when they are usually good buys. Any time of year, it pays to figure the relation between the price of eggs and their weight or size. Table 7-8, Comparative Values in Grade A Eggs Based on Weight, will help you to compare egg-weight values.

Comparing the prices of eggs of the same size (large, for example) but of different qualities (Grades AA, A, B) is also worthwhile. For instance, such a

TABLE 7-8   Comparative Values in Grade A Eggs Based on Weight

When Large Grade A Eggs, at Least 24 Ounces per Dozen, Cost	Medium-sized Grade A Eggs, at Least 21 Ounces per Dozen, Are as Good a Buy or Better at	And Small Grade A Eggs, at Least 18 Ounces per Dozen, Are as Good a Buy or Better at
$.46 - $.50	$.40 - $.44	$.34 - $.38
.51 - .55	.45 - .48	.39 - .41
.56 - .60	.49 - .52	.42 - .45
.61 - .65	.53 - .57	.46 - .49
.66 - .70	.58 - .61	.50 - .52
.71 - .75	.62 - .66	.53 - .56
.76 - .80	.67 - .70	.57 - .60
.81 - .85	.71 - .74	.61 - .64
.86 - .90	.75 - .79	.64 - .68
.91 - .95	.80 - .83	.69 - .71

comparison may show that Grade B and Grade C eggs are priced from 10 to 15 cents a dozen lower than higher-quality eggs of the same weight.

Finally, know the food values that eggs have to offer: high-quality protein, iron, vitamin A, riboflavin, thiamine, and some vitamin D, all stored inside an eggshell. Eggs rate as a protective food along with meat, poultry, fish, dry peas, and beans. And of them all, none of these protein foods is so versatile as eggs. They fill the bill for young and old alike at any meal—as a main dish, in soup and salad, or in the beverage or dessert.

FRUITS AND VEGETABLES

Increase family use of fruits and vegetables

Nutrition experts figure that about 21 percent of the family food costs should go into the purchase of fruits and vegetables. This is probably far above typical family expenditures, because most families usually do not have enough of these foods in their diets.

The average family should eat more fruits and vegetables

Modern science has discovered that fruits and vegetables are valuable to the diet in many ways. First, leafy vegetables, skins, and fibers provide needed roughage. Second, fruits and vegetables are rich in vitamins that are essential to good health. Third, some fruits and vegetables are good sources of minerals. And finally, some fruits and vegetables are rich in fuel content.

Generally, green and yellow vegetables, such as green lettuce, sweet potatoes and tomatoes, peaches, and apricots, are rich in vitamin A.

Oranges, lemons, grapefruit, tomatoes, limes, and tangerines are rich in vitamin C. Since vitamin C cannot be stored in the body, we need a fresh supply every day.

The B family of vitamins (thiamine, riboflavin, niacin) are found in apples, apricots, bananas, cabbage, kale, and dried peas. Iron is supplied by the green leafy vegetables, such a broccoli, chard, spinach, and lettuce.

How to buy fresh fruits and vegetables

There are many ways in which you can get more for your money when purchasing fresh fruits and vegetables. The following suggestions are used by wise shoppers:

1. Select fruit and vegetables the family likes.
2. Select fruit and vegetables that are most plentiful in the market.
3. Use fruit and vegetables that are in season.
4. By using a variety of fruit and vegetables, it is easier to keep costs down.
5. Purchase in as large quantities as use and storage without loss permit.
6. If possible, shop personally and as early in the day as demands on your time permit.
7. When handling fruit (the touch system), be careful, because careless handling increases spoilage and adds to the price that consumers pay.
8. Low price is not necessarily an indication of poor quality. There may be an oversupply of that particular product.
9. The most expensive quality may not be the best buy for a particular use. For example, topless carrots sold by the pound are just as good for stews and soups or served raw, and they are cheaper than bunch carrots.
10. Blemishes on fruit may affect the looks but not the eating quality. Shriveled, wilted, and discolored vegetables, however, are usually poor buys.
11. Buy by weight rather than measure whenever possible, because numbers, pints, or quarts do not have consistent meaning. Cauliflower heads, for instance, may vary from 25 to 50 ounces.
12. Sometimes packaged fruits have poor-quality specimens in the lower layers, and fruit or vegetables in bags are not always all of the same quality.
13. Carrots, kale, collards, spinach, and green cabbage are often the least expensive vegetables, but they have high food value.
14. Compare prices in the food advertisements and in the stores.
15. Compare the costs of fresh, canned, frozen, and dried fruit and vegetables.

Grading is permissive

The U.S. Department of Agriculture has established standards at the wholesale level for some seventy fresh fruits and vegetables. There are twelve consumer-level standards at retail stores. All federal inspection is based on these standards, but their use is permissive.

Each fruit and vegetable has its own set of quality grades. The principal United States grades are U.S. Fancy, U.S. No. 1, U.S. No. 2, U.S. Commercial, and U.S. Combination. The quality grade is marked on the container, which speeds the handling of the produce. Some use has been made by homemakers of standard grades in the purchase of apples, grapefruit, oranges, peaches, and potatoes in quantity.

One reason that consumers do not see the grade quality is the fact that by the time the consumer gets the fruit, a lot graded U.S. No. 1 may have deteriorated to U.S. No. 2. This is, of course, no argument in support of keeping the consumer ignorant of grade classifications. It is merely a reason given by many retailers.

Sizes of apples and citrus fruits

Boxes of apples are usually stamped with numbers to represent the count per standard box. Here are the sizes that are found in the market.

48	80	100	125	163	210
56	88	104	138	165	232
64	96	113	150	180	252
72					

Likewise, the size of citrus fruit is indicated by the count of fruit in a box. Fruit packed in a California box will be a little smaller than that packed in Florida or Texas because the California box capacity is 1⅗ bushels and the Texas and Florida box capacity is 1⅗ bushels. The following sizes are found in the market.

GRAPEFRUIT		LEMONS		ORANGES		TANGERINES	
28	80	180	420	64	220	48	150
36	96	210	432	80	226	60	168
46	112	240	442	96	250	76	176
54	126	252	490	100	252	90	192
64	150	270	540	112	288	96	200
70		300	588	126	324	100	210
		360		150	344	120	246
				176	360	144	294
				200	392		
				216	420		

Processed fruits and vegetables

Processed foods may be canned, frozen, dehydrated, or dried. Each of these processes has an effect on food values and on the price paid by the consumer. Generally, the most food value in relation to the cost is found in fresh fruits and vegetables in season and properly cared for; then, in the following order: dried and dehydrated foods, canned foods, and frozen foods. This generalization needs to be checked from time to time, because processes improve and consumer demand is an uncertain factor at best.

Dried and dehydrated foods

Dried foods are usually more economical buys, because they are the least expensive to handle and ship. The Food and Drug Administration standard for dried fruits does not permit more than 24 to 26 percent moisture in fruits that are dried in a dehydrator. When not more than 5 or 6 percent moisture remains in the fruit they are called "dehydrated" foods.

The food value in dehydrated foods varies, but generally the minerals and calories do not vanish in the water. Some vitamins, however, are lost. As yet, dehydrated foods are not very popular because the process needs improvement.

The process of drying fruits changes the food values to a considerable extent. Fuel value is greatly increased, and mineral value is increased to a less extent. In some cases, vitamin value is also increased. Nearly all dried fruits are excellent sources of vitamin A. Dry beans are often used as a substitute for meat, but they need to be supplemented by animal proteins, such as milk, eggs, fish, or cheese.

The federal standards for dry edible beans and peas are widely used by the trade, but the grades rarely appear on consumer packages.

Grades for beans and peas are based on such factors as color, presence or absence of defects, foreign material, and beans or peas of other classes. Defects may be those caused by weather, disease, insects, or mechanical means.

There are special "handpicked" grades for beans, which are well adapted for consumer sales. The top grade is U.S. Choice Handpicked, followed by U.S. No. 1 Handpicked, U.S. No. 2 Handpicked, and U.S. No. 3 Handpicked. In other than the handpicked grades, grades for beans are simply numerical. Grades for dry peas, both whole and split, are also numerical.

Frozen fruits, juices, and vegetables and precooked frozen foods

One of the major problems is in the mishandling of frozen foods before they reach the consumer. During the past decade, food and drug officials and the frozen food industry have become increasingly disturbed over the mishandling of frozen foods. There has been little effort to alert consumers to this problem, despite their need to know about damage to the quality of frozen food by temperatures above 0 degrees Fahrenheit.

Freeze-dried foods

Freeze drying is one of the greatest techniques known for drying foodstuffs, causing far less damage to flavor, texture, and color than conventional heat drying. In freeze drying, food is first frozen; then, in a partial vacuum, the ice crystals thus formed in it are transformed directly into vapor without melting. When processing is done carefully, the cellular structure of the food remains intact, little shrinkage or shriveling results, and nutritive values are fairly well preserved. Because the dried product is nearly full size and is porous, reconstitution is quite easy.

The advantages are obvious. Food does not have to be refrigerated, and weight is reduced. It is claimed that products resume the taste, texture, and appearance of fresh foods when they are reconstituted.

This is a promising new process. The process has worked only on fairly thin pieces of food, half an inch or so thick. Some foods (broccoli) do not freeze-dry well, and others (carrots) are better dried by conventional methods. The process is still quite expensive, and packaging problems are keeping prices up.

The first of such foods to be widely distributed for retail stores was Lipton's chicken-rice soup and meats in some of Campbell's Red Kettle soups and in Armour Star Lite outdoor foods. There are others entering this market, a market that the Reader's Digest billed as "the greatest breakthrough in food preservation since the invention of the tin can." Time will tell. In 1968, freeze-dried coffee became quite popular although expensive.

Canned fruits and vegetables

Canned fruits and vegetables are very popular with the homemaker. In canning there are, however, minor losses of minerals. Water-soluble nutrients are dissolved in the liquid in which the food is canned. Thus, it is wise to use all the liquid in the can.

Vitamin A is only slightly affected in canning. There is some loss of thiamine and riboflavin. The retention of vitamin C is higher in citrus products than in tomato juice and canned vegetables. In some cases, food analysts have found canned vegetables superior in nutrients to fresh produce that has been allowed to stand in a market, especially in sunlight or warmth, or that has been washed.

Brand identifications and grade labeling

Brand identifications do not give consumers the information needed to make an intelligent selection. Adequate label information should accompany brand names. The permissive standardized labeling program promoted by the National Canners Association is an attempt to "describe" the contents in addition to the statements required by law under the Federal Food, Drug, and Cosmetic Act.

Descriptive labels do not give information about quality, except in general terms not based on accepted standards. To select canned foods wisely, consumers need, in addition to brand names and standard descriptions, standard quality grades. Some canneries and large chain stores and consumer cooperatives have included standard graded canned fruits and vegetables.

Grade-labeling facts for the wise shopper

For the wise shopper who wants to buy by standard grade rather than by guess and by grab, here are the necessary facts:

> Grade A or Fancy stands for "excellent." Use it for special occasions.
> Grade B, Choice or Extra Standard, is for "good." Use it for every day.
> Grade C or Standard is for "fair." Use it for thrift.

FIGURE 7-5

SOURCE: U.S. Department of Agriculture, Production and Marketing Administration.

FIGURE 7-6

HALVES
BARTLETT PEARS
In Water   Slightly Sweetened
BELOW STANDARD IN QUALITY
Mixed Sizes—Unevenly Trimmed

SOURCE: U.S. Department of Agriculture, Production and Marketing Administration.

All grades have the same food value, but each serves a different purpose and has a different price. Over forty fruits and vegetables now have standards worked out by the cooperative efforts of the U.S. Department of Agriculture and private canners.

The U.S. Department of Agriculture inspects and certifies these products as to quality and condition on requests of processors, buyers, federal and state purchasing departments, or other interested parties. These applicants pay the cost of inspection.

Some canners, freezers, and distributors use grade designations on their labels. Labels may also carry additional information descriptive of the product, such as the number of halves in canned peaches or pears, the sieve size of peas, cooking instructions for frozen vegetables, or special statements for dietetic foods.

Any processor or distributor may use the terms "Grade A," "Grade B," and "Grade C" on labels to describe the quality of his products, whether or not they have been inspected. However, products thus labeled must meet the specifications of the Department's standards for the grade claimed; otherwise, the products may be considered mislabeled.

Some processing plants operate voluntarily under continuous inspection— a service offered by the U.S. Department of Agriculture at a nominal fee to packers. These plants have been carefully selected and thoroughly inspected to make sure that they meet strict sanitary requirements. Processors who operate their plants under U.S. Department of Agriculture continuous inspection may use the prefix "U.S." before their grade designation on their label (such as U.S. Grade A), as well as the statement "Packed under continuous inspection of the U.S. Department of Agriculture."

A wise shopper will look for the brand and a reliable standard grade. Grade labels are not common in food stores because they are generally opposed by food processors. Consumers can cast an economic vote for grading by patronizing the stores that stock graded foods. Let your store know that you appreciate graded foods, because this is the best way of convincing the producers and the food store owners of the importance of graded labels.

Some hints for buying canned fruits and vegetables are:

1. Compare different brand prices for the same grade.
2. Find the brands and the grades best suited to your family uses.
3. Buy the largest size of can that you can economically use.
4. Purchasing in quantity—case lots—saves from 5 to 10 percent.
5. Look for the special sales just prior to the appearance of the new crop in cans.
6. Buy by grades according to intended use of the food.
7. Also buy according to Nutrient labeling information whenever available. The label should show approximate Nutrients per cup and the percentages of all ingredients on the principal ones, drained weight, unit pricing, and the pull date if it is a perishable product.

CONFUSING FOOD STANDARDS

The food standards now in use in this country are necessary and useful to growers, brokers, shippers, and wholesalers, but they are less useful to consumers. Labels do not provide the information needed to compare values and thus *What you don't know* make the best buys. At present, nutrient information appears on some labels. *can hurt you* Meat grades (prime, choice and three lower grades—choice is usually the only grade offered in retail stores) are not a guide to food value, which is more or less the same whatever the grade because the main factors involved in grades of meat are tenderness, juiciness, and taste. In other words, lower grades of fresh meat have about the same food value (nutrients) as choice or prime grades.

A list of standards in the publication *Standards for Meat and Poultry Products* points up the "ingredient mysteries" of these products. The following are a few examples:

Beef with barbecue sauce must contain at least 50 percent beef (cooked basis).

Brunswick stew must contain at least 25 percent meat.

Ingredient mysteries of Beans with ham in sauce must contain at least 12 percent ham (cooked *meat and poultry* basis).
products Chili macaroni must contain at least 16 percent meat.

Frozen dinners must contain at least 25 percent meat or meat food product (cooked basis).

Poultry dinners must contain at least 18 percent meat.

Poultry stew must contain at least 12 percent poultry meat.

Information concerning meat content, unfortunately for consumers, is not yet on labels. Informative labeling should tell people what they can't see for themselves. (See Taylor-Troelstrup Reading 40 for a detailed list of many canned or packaged meat and poultry products the labels of which do not show the percentage of meat or poultry contained.)

Also not generally known is the fact that the ingredients in a "nonstandard" food product must be listed on the label in order of weight predominance, starting with the most prominent ingredient. However, the label doesn't always tell you the percentage of nutrients in the food.

Present food standards can fool you in other ways. The labels of most packages and cans are required, under standards of fill, to show net weight. At the request of the House Committee on Government Operations (Special Consumer Inquiry), the USDA tested 148 cans of fruit and vegetables marked under standards of fill.[48] The following results were typical. The cans were tested for net contents versus drained weight (percentage of fruit or vegetable to syrup):

One pound (16 ounces) of canned food may provide only 11 ounces of edible food

Pear halves, vacuum-packed, 8-ounce can: Heinz, 54.5 percent; Zippy, 69.5 percent

Peach halves, 16-ounce can—Town House, 66.5 percent; Del Monte, 64.8 percent

Whole-kernel corn, brine-packed, 12-ounce can: Del Monte, 82.3 percent; Green Giant, 84.3 percent

Thus we can conclude that net weight is not a reliable standard for comparison purposes. Drained-weight disclosures give the consumer accurate information about the edible portion of food contained in the can.

Making value comparisons can also be tricky under the present labeling system. At the same House hearings, for example, two cans of Del Monte whole-kernel corn, each priced at two for 53 cents, were opened. One was labeled "12-ounce, vacuum-packed," and the other was labeled "17-ounce, brine-packed." When the liquid was drained off, the corn in the larger can weighed 11.3 ounces, only ½ ounce more than the corn in the smaller can. The USDA rated both as about equal nutritionally, although one appeared to offer about 50 percent more edible product for the same price. Thus net-weight disclosures are almost useless as a buying yardstick.

Drained-weight disclosures needed

The present net-weight labeling masks the considerable chunk of the consumer food dollar that goes toward paying for salt water or sugar syrup. Shoppers will continue to buy in the dark until drained-weight disclosures are made mandatory for all canned and bottled foods.

MEAT LABELING

We learned earlier that the USDA has issued voluntary grade standards for over thirty food and farm products, including meat and poultry. Frankfurters and hamburgers are probably the most popular meat products consumed by Americans. We eat over 15 billion "franks" a year. What is in a frankfurter? What does the label tell you? Between 1937 and 1967, the fat content of franks

[48] Reported in *U.S. Consumer*, June 11, 1969. (Name changed to *Consumer Newsweek*.) See also *Consumer Newsweek*, June 26, 1972.

"No guide other than her own instinct"

increased from 18.6 to 31.2 percent, and the protein content decreased from 19.6 to 11.8 percent, according to the American Meat Institute. Since 1967, the fat content of franks has been in the 33 to 35 percent range, said the American Meat Institute when testifying before the House Special Consumer Inquiry in 1969. The USDA, however, said that their tests showed brands exceeding 40 percent fat, with one brand reaching 51 percent. Other allowable ingredients in franks include pork lips, snouts, and stomachs; goat lungs, spleen, and tripe; veal (for flavor); up to 3 percent cereal or other extender; up to 10 percent added water; and up to 15 percent poultry.

Success versus standards

The primary issue at the House hearings was the amount of fat to be permitted in franks. The American Meat Institute said at this hearing: "We question the need to establish a fat limit for franks. We think the success of the product speaks for itself." Virginia Knauer, President Nixon's consumer counsel, disagreed. She said the fat content should be limited to 30 percent. Mrs. Knauer also stated that a consumer has "no guide other than her own instinct" at the present time when selecting meat and poultry products not subject to standards of identity. Fortunately, frankfurters are presently limited to 30 percent fat content. This is progress. But even now, a physician could not tell his heart and coronary patients whether to eat franks or not because the labels do not give the percentage of ingredients. The aim of good labeling is, after all, to tell people what they can't see for themselves.

Forces working against better food labeling

The food industry, consisting of hundreds of separate organizations representing farmers, producers, manufacturers, canners, freezers, and packagers, has very strong lobbies in Washington. The food industry also has many close unofficial ties with the USDA and the FDA. It is strong politically, and it has an influence on the media. G. A. Willis, president of the Grocery Manufacturers of America, on one occasion reminded the media of the interdependence of the $110-billion food industry and their own "bread and butter." Fear of advertiser retaliation still lingers.

The food industry has consistently balked at providing consumers with certain basic shopping information. For example, it has criticized the idea of grade labeling—quality grades which would tell shoppers what they can't see for themselves.

On the grounds that it must keep product secrets, the food industry has refused to list all ingredients in food products except pet foods. Since 1962, the industry has even opposed the FDA's attempt to draw up some regulations concerning special dietary foods and supplements.

Millions of Skippy eaters can't be wrong!

Where food standards are concerned, the industry usually puts its concern for sales ahead of quality, or even safety. The classic case of peanut butter dragged on for a decade. Manufacturers suggested that kids actually did not like peanut butter containing 90 percent peanuts, the FDA minimum. After all, millions of Skippy eaters can't be wrong.

Even the dairy industry engineered punitive legislation against the sale of margarine and the sale of filled milk in interstate commerce, as well as other measures that cost consumers many millions of dollars annually.

The USDA and the FDA are responsible chiefly for monitoring our food supply. Unfortunately, their responsibilities do not specifically include the maintenance of quality and nutritional levels. They are more concerned about safety than about the nutritional value of foods. The rule of thumb that the FDA is now applying to drugs—that they must do positive good, not just be harmless—has not been applied generally to foods. Only recently (1971) has the FDA seen fit to be concerned with the nutritional value of foods as well as their potential ill effects. Consumers, of course, are partially to blame because they have been relatively inactive in supporting FDA suggestions for improving information on food labels.

Historically, the USDA has assisted farmers and agribusinesses in producing more and more food and has taken much less interest in what happens to that food en route from farmer to processor to consumer. Its procedure for setting food standards has accommodated industry practice more than nutritional needs. The recent hearings on frankfurters are a clear indication of that. The department admitted that its recommendation on the fat content, and indirectly the protein content, of frankfurters was based primarily on the prevailing practice of the industry. It also admitted that it had not consulted with any recognized nutritional authorities, in government or out, as to what would be the ideal standard from a nutritional point of view. The standard for hamburger was set so long ago, and in such an apparently informal way, that nobody in the department is quite sure how it came about or on what grounds the fat limit was chosen. It is highly likely that neither nutritional nor consumer representatives were consulted.

The problem of outdated, perhaps irrelevant, standards is most acute, however, with the Food and Drug Administration. Most of our important standards for fortification were the product of a national need to maximize nutrition in the population during World War II. The standard for the fortification of bread, for instance, was set during that period and is unchanged today. The fact that it has remained unchanged immediately calls into question its relevance. Bread is no longer consumed as widely or in as much quantity. It is being cut out of diets by a weight-conscious population or is being replaced by a variety of other baked items, few of which, if any, are fortified. Even if the consumption of bread was not unchanged, the kind of fortification in it would still be outdated. The National Research Council's Food and Nutrition Board has published minimum requirements for a number of nutrients which were undiscussed during the period of World War II. These new nutrients have not yet been translated by the FDA into standards for foods now being marketed. The FDA knows that many of its standards are badly outdated from a nutritional point of view. It knows that it should review all standards that have been set since the post-World War II period. Yet it did little about standards until the nutrient labeling issue in 1971 forced it into action.

Over the years, according to competent evaluators, the attitude of our major food regulatory agencies—the USDA and the FDA—has been one of "don't rock the boat." They have adopted a comfortable, do-nothing policy. The USDA has, for example, on more than one occasion, quietly and securely filed away critical reports on processed food products which deserved to see the light of day. Only a Ralph Nader was able to locate one such report on excessive bacteria in some food products, forcing a reluctant Secretary of Agriculture to make the report public.

"Don't rock the boat"   This "don't rock the boat" attitude also came out in the recent House hear-

ings when the committee chairman asked Dr. Ley, then FDA commissioner, whether it would not be a good idea to have grades for food products and to place specific information concerning grade and ingredients on packages and cans. Dr. Ley avoided a direct answer when he said, "I don't know whether I have authority to do this." The USDA witness, however, admitted that "this would be helpful." The canning industry witness said, "There is already enough information on the label."

Canada has grade labeling on many canned goods. Some of our processors distribute their canned products there. If they are willing to meet the requirements of the Canadian quality grading law, why aren't they willing to tell consumers on this side of the border what they have to tell Canadians?

The National Commission on Food Marketing felt so strongly concerning the need for better food standards and for grading that it incorporated into its final report the following recommendation: (1) Consumer grades should be developed and required to appear on all foods for which such grades are feasible, and (2) the FDA should establish standards of identity for all foods for which standards are practicable. [49]

Most of our federal regulatory agencies are presently going through a "bloodbath," a no-holds-barred evaluation. First, Ralph Nader's Raiders rode roughly over the FDA and USDA. Presently, congressional hearings are trying to spot inefficiences in these two agencies.

There will always be some unknown variables in the area of food standards. No informed person would deny that we do not utilize some of the standards and good practices already known. But we seem to be caught in a social time lag. It seems to us, who view the matter from the consumer's viewpoint, that standards and specifications should function as a language of careful description in the production and exchange of products in somewhat the same way that mathematics is the language of the sciences. We should do all in our power at least to use our present knowledge about food standards and develop a common language that the seller and the ultimate consumer can understand. These tasks are not beyond our technical capabilities.

And all the tired arguments—the stifling of initiative, the loss of variety with consequent restrictions on freedom of consumer choice, the problems of enforcement—can also be answered, given the will to restore true consumer sovereignty to the marketplace. For with a system of effective standards, competition becomes true price competition, the most efficient producer-distributor relationship prevails, meaningless product differentiation disappears, advertising is restored to its legitimate function of conveying information, and we reap all the benefits of an orderly production-distribution system.

Why aren't we living in this marketplace paradise? Because too many important interests are vested in the present inefficient system. Perhaps when it is recognized that the general welfare and consumer welfare are virtually synonymous, some system will be devised to restore consumer sovereignty. Why not *help* restore some consumer sovereignty in the marketplace by improving and extending food standards and by conveying all essential information on the label? The aim of food labeling is to tell people what they cannot see for

[49] National Commission on Food Marketing: *Food from Farmer to Consumer,* p. 109. U.S. Government Publication, 1966.

themselves. But too often in the past, as Senator Charles Percy of Illinois said, "These agencies established as watchdogs for the public interest have become lapdogs for private interests."

YOUR MONEY'S WORTH IN FOOD: A RECAP

If your family is typical, very likely 40 to 50 percent of your money for food goes for meat, dairy products, and eggs. About one-fifth of this is spent for vegetables and fruit. The rest is nearly equally divided among the grain products; the fats, oils, sugar, and sweets; and such items as vinegar, spices, leavening agents, coffee, tea, and other beverages.

Question: "Do you wonder whether your money for food is spent to the best advantage?" A good way to determine this is to compare foods in each of the groups by their yield in nutrients as well as by their price. A few examples will point this up.

Meat, poultry, fish, and eggs are important for their high-quality protein, iron, and the B vitamins. To make worthwhile savings, judge them on a comparative basis. Some meat has bone and gristle. Buying the less expensive cuts of meat can save money with no loss in food value, provided the cuts do not have large amounts of bone, fat, and gristle. Dry beans or peas as a main dish are an economical substitute for meat. Buy lower-grade eggs for scrambling or baking. Small eggs are as economical as large ones when they are at least one-fourth cheaper.

As for the dairy products, everybody needs milk in some form because it is the best source for calcium and an important source of protein and riboflavin. One serving of fluid whole milk, evaporated milk, buttermilk, skim milk, or dry milk furnishes about the same amount of nutrients but at widely different costs. Dry milk generally costs least and fluid milk the most per serving. Cream cheese is more expensive for the value received than most other milk products, except butter and cream. Cottage cheese is a bargain for protein and riboflavin. Cheddar cheese is a more economical source of calcium than cottage cheese.

Vegetables and fruits furnish a large share of the vitamin A value and most of the vitamin C. Certain vegetables and fruits, however, are better buys than others, although prices vary with locality, season, and form or processing. Usually, the best buys for vitamin A—dark green or deep yellow vegetables—are carrots, collards, kale, spinach, sweet potatoes, and winter squash. Most other common fruits and vegetables, including light green and pale yellow ones, are usually more expensive sources of vitamin A because they contain only small amounts. It would take about 7 cups of corn to give as much vitamin A value as $\frac{1}{4}$ cup of carrots, and would cost about ten times more than the carrots.

Oranges, grapefruit, and raw cabbage generally supply the most vitamin C for the money. Some dark green leaves, potatoes, sweet potatoes—properly cooked—also give vitamin C at moderately low cost. Tomato juice and canned tomatoes usually are cheaper sources for vitamin C, except possibly fresh tomatoes in season. Most other common fruits and vegetables furnish less vitamin

C and cost more. Some vegetables and fruits have both vitamins A and C—tomatoes and sweet potatoes—and may be good buys.

Canned, frozen, dried, and fresh fruits and vegetables vary considerably in price per serving. As a rule, these foods in canned and dried form are cheaper. The safest way, however, is to make a comparison of price per serving.

Whole-grain, restored, or enriched cereals and bread can mean extra food value for the money. Natural whole grains are significant sources of iron, thiamine, riboflavin, and niacin. Many breakfast foods have nutrients, lost in milling, "restored." There is no federal standard for restored cereals. It is, therefore, safer to purchase enriched bread or flour, because the federal standards require a minimum amount of iron, thiamine, riboflavin, and niacin for enrichment. If breads of various types cost the same or a few cents more per pound of bread, the whole-grain or enriched kinds are the best nutrient buys for the money. The same is true of cereals. Cold cereals are not as good nutrient buys as cereals that have to be cooked. Since 1972, however, some cold cereals have added nutrients.

It is well to remember that many convenience foods are still more expensive, if you discount the time element, than those prepared at home from the ingredients. Canned and frozen fruits and vegetables are often best buys, because they are canned and frozen when supplies are large and prices low. There is also none of the waste that occurs in the handling and storage of perishable produce.

Pay cash for food. Credit costs money, and you will pay for the extra cost. In selecting supermarkets, compare prices for food value. Remember that gimmicks like trading stamps, premiums, and the forms of lottery or games of chance increase the cost of food. When you spend almost one-fifth of your income for food, it pays to get the most value per dollar for your family.

YOUR HEALTH'S WORTH IN FOOD: A RECAP

The aim of good food labeling is to tell shoppers what they can't see for themselves. The basic-four system for planning balanced meals for good eating was, and still is, a useful tool, but it just isn't good enough.

The day has now come when the traditional symbols of the food marketing system are irrelevant at best and harmful at worst. Quality designations for beef, for example, are measures of fat. The beef grade under the old system that consumers believe to be best is the highest in fat content, hardly a nutritional quality in a society which already consumes too much fat. Grades for fruit and vegetables are based on color, size, consistency, and configuration, all attributes which may once have borne some relation to nutrition but which have little such relevance today. Such quality grades are meaningless for a fully prepared frozen dinner or dozens of other processed convenience foods.

Food scientists are now evolving new symbols for transmitting more vital information. These include such concepts as unit pricing, open dating, drained-weight labeling, nutrient labeling, and percentage-ingredient labeling. These are the elements of a new common language for commerce and consumers.

These concepts anticipate the development by the FDA of nutritional standards for frozen dinners and many other processed food products.

The aim of meaningful labeling is to enable consumers to compare values and make their choices intelligently. Legislation which does this will serve all who use the marketing system. And as Rodney Leonard, managing editor of *Community Nutrition Institute Weekly Report,* said: "It is hardly less necessary in the marketing of today's processed foods than having a single common currency."

QUESTIONS FOR DISCUSSION

1. Is it possible to overconvenience our food supply?

2. What's all the fuss about health foods? Out of the worry over additives and pesticides has emerged the boom in "organic" foods. It may be true that they are safer, but are they really more nutritious or worth the extra cost?

3. It is very important to show federal grades on the labels of food packages, but grades are *not* a measure of nutritive value or wholesomeness. Explain.

4. "A vitamin is a vitamin is a vitamin, no matter what raw material it comes from." What does this statement mean?

5. A number of vitamin preparations are promoted on the supposition that if the RDA is good for you, then ten times the RDA should be ten times as good. Discuss this with a medical doctor or a nutritionist or read a reliable medical source. What are the scientific facts?

6. What is the RDA? What is the recommended allowance of each of the seven or eight most important nutrients that the average person needs every day? Finally, do cans and packages show the percentage of each important ingredient?

7. What evidence is there of "affluent malnutrition" in the most recent health surveys in this country?

PROJECTS

1. Survey your college cafeteria to determine the cost and variety of foods available. Develop plans for the "best buy" and for low- and moderate-cost lunches, all nutritionally sound.

2. Make a list of food products that teen-agers purchase regularly. Study the advertising appeals made for these foods on television. How nutritious are these food products?

3. Compare cost variation in foods available in different forms (fresh, frozen, canned). Then compare the net weight stated on the label with the drained weight and figure the actual cost of edible food.

4. Make a list of the foods advertised on children's television programs (gum, snacks, pastry, candy, cookies, vitamins, soft drinks, dry cereals, etc.).

Do the ads reveal advocacy of nutritionally inferior foods? What percentage of these foods are promoted on the basis of their sugared, sweetened, or fried qualities? What percentage of these ads establish food habits which dentists and doctors generally deplore? List ads promoting children's vitamins in pill form and evaluate this kind of advertising appeal to children. Do some of the ads teach poor nutrition habits? If they do, cite the specific errors. Can you write counterads?

5. Form a committee and study the information given on the label of a convenience food. How does the name of the product compare with the ingredients listed on the package in descending order of quantity? (Many students are surprised to learn, for example, that the main ingredient in some turkey pot pies is not turkey, but chicken and turkey broth; that creamed chicken contains no cream, just milk; and that some lemon cream pies contain no lemon, cream, or eggs.) The product or products chosen can then be separated by ingredient, and each ingredient weighed. Students can thus determine, for instance, what percentage of the TV beef dinner is beef, what percentage is gravy, and what percentage is vegetable. Is the photograph on the package a fair representation of the product itself? After weighing the individual ingredients and figuring out the percentages, some students could calculate exactly how much the meat would cost per pound. The results may be quite startling.

6. Make a weekly "specials" survey of the major food stores in your marketing area or in your town if it is a small one. Include national chains, regional chains, and independents if possible. Students working in pairs could be assigned to each store. The purpose of the survey is to learn to what extent *advertised* items are *(a)* available, *(b)* marked at sale prices, *(c)* restricted in their availability, and *(d)* priced lower than the regular price.

Take the "Thursday special" advertisement to the store within forty-eight hours of issue and note the availability of items and price-making practices. Return two and four weeks later to reprice the items appearing in the original advertisement. Tabulate the results of the survey.

SUGGESTED READINGS

Anderson, W. Thomas, Jr.: *The Convenience-oriented Consumer,* University of Texas, Graduate School of Business, Bureau of Business Research, Austin, 1971.

Baker, Allen J., and William W. Gallimore: "Substitute and Synthetic Foods with Emphasis on Soy Protein," *Marketing and Transportation Situation,* USDA Economic Research Service, February, 1972, pp. 12–14.

"Food Dating: Now You See It, Now You Don't," *Consumer Reports,* June, 1972, pp. 391–394.

"Frankfurters," *Consumer Reports,* February, 1972, pp. 73–79.

Harmer, Ruth Mulvey: *Unfit for Human Consumption,* Prentice-Hall, Inc., Englewood Cliffs, N.J., 1971.

Margolius, Sidney: *The Great American Food Hoax,* Walker Publishing Company, Inc., New York, 1971.

Morse, Richard L. D.: "Labels That Tell You Something," *Journal of Home Economics,* April, 1972, pp. 28–33.

Padberg, D. I.: *Study on Evaluation of Consumer Attitude towards F.D.A. Nutritional Labeling,* Cornell University, Ithaca, N.Y., 1972.

Price Control Programs, 1917–71, USDA Economic Research Service, April, 1972.

Schuck, Peter: "The Curious Case of the Indicted Meat Inspectors," *Harper's,* September, 1972.

Van de Mark, Mildred S., and Virginia Ruth Sherman Underwood: "Dietary Habits and Food Consumption Patterns of Teenage Families," *Nutrition Today,* October, 1971, p. 540.

Winter, Ruth: *Beware of the Food You Eat,* Crown Publishers, Inc., New York, 1971.

CHAPTER 8

CHAPTER 8
FAMILY CLOTHING MANAGEMENT

There are no norms for choice in clothing as there are in the nutritional needs of the body. Clothing problems in a family must be analyzed in terms of the individual in a group setting. Style, fashion, and fad need to be adapted to individual differences within the financial limits of the family.

In addition, the way we wear our clothes is as important as what we wear. Being well dressed for the occasion, and being aware of it, benefits all members of the family psychologically, physically, and socially. It helps a person to be self-confident, to act and speak more effectively in public. People who are well dressed in the sense of having used good taste in the selection of their clothes are more readily accepted in most social situations.

But the managerial problems of clothing the family so that all members are properly dressed for all occasions are numerous and often difficult. Adequate income does not always solve clothing problems. Even families with luxury incomes are not necessarily style conscious and may not use good sense and taste in costume coordination.

For moderate-income and low-income families, clothing expenditures are not regular. Seasonal demands and sudden disintegration of garments make it difficult for every member to have an adequate wardrobe at all times. And even the best-planned clothing budget can be ruined by unexpected expenses, such as medical and housing bills.

THE PROBLEM OF FAMILY CLOTHING

The right clothes are a mental stimulant

You are what you wear?

Whether we like it or not, a girl gets more flattering masculine attention if she is attractive and knows how to wear clothes than if she has a Phi Beta Kappa key. A lady's looks and general grooming are a powerful magnet, and, no doubt, women appraise men in the same way. We hasten to add that attractive dress is not enough in the long run to hold the attention of others, but the right clothes, worn well, give a mental stimulus to the wearer, to the family, and to personal friends and promote an air of confidence.

If there is truth in the assumption that our innermost life tends to become evident in the choices we make, it might follow that a glance at a family's wardrobe may be more revealing than a composite diary of its members.

Some women, especially mothers devoted to their children, seem to stand still in the matter of dress when the world about them moves forward. Often a wife allows herself to look dowdy and perhaps, as a result, considerably older than her husband, because she has let household duties absorb all her interest. But the husband's contacts with the business and professional world may have kept him alert and well groomed in keeping with his position and associates. On the other hand, a man who allows himself to slip in his grooming may be slipping in his business and social life.

Other women of a retiring nature are perhaps too conservative in their dress. Still others wear too youthful or extreme clothes or makeup in a conspicuous manner. Generally, conspicuous dress emphasizes rather than conceals age in either sex. If a woman's dress or hat, or a man's suit or tie, dominates the picture, that person is not well dressed in spite of the fact that those items originally may have worn a high price tag.

Family happiness is involved

The family attitudes toward dress, especially on the part of the mother, are important to the good mental health of each member of the family. Good grooming, good taste in dress, and an active interest in style, fashion, and even fads are assets to family happiness.

The clothing one wears plays an important part in adjusting to the social group. Clothing management, as such, is largely a psychological problem, because it affects the personality development and happiness of each member of the family. No one but the family or close friends may observe our eating manners and food standards, but as soon as we step outside the door, our clothes and how we wear them are appraised by those we meet. Much of this appraisal is unconscious. Perhaps we need to build a consciousness of good dress without creating the value that good dress is everything.

Parents who allow their children to feel unhappy about their methods of dress may be responsible for personality maladjustments later in their lives. The clothing needs of children differ because of individual differences in personality and in physique. A study made by the Bureau of Home Economics on measurements of children shows that many children of like age have entirely different body proportions and dimensions.[1] Ignorance of this fact often results in unhappy relationships between mother and children. It is of utmost importance to help a child to feel no different from others, even when the body is developing in a different way.

Considerable unhappiness can be needlessly generated if, for example, a mother insists on dressing a rather tall, early-teen-age daughter in below-knee-length dresses, with hair in long braids, when the girls in her set are wearing shorter skirts, sweaters, and long hair. Insistence on "bucking the crowd" usually produces a weepy, irritable, unhappy youngster. At the same time, parents need to help youngsters understand that there is not an unlimited amount of money for clothing.

It is wise to let children gradually assume responsibility in selecting their clothes. By intelligent discussion of their personal assets and liabilities, children can develop skill in self-analysis and in selecting or creating clothes that are acceptable to others and that at the same time accentuate their individual personalities.

Training children to select and care for clothing

Children who are accustomed to an environment of good grooming and common sense in dressing are not likely to fail to acquire these good habits. They may go through certain stages of refusing to wear suitable footwear, for instance, or adequate clothes on the pretext that such things are not "in style." At times, they may wear the most illogical clothes because these happen to be the fad. High school and college-age youngsters are usually the worst offenders in this respect. In time, sense and intelligence in dressing will return, plus an individual style and air—the reverse of the herd instinct.

Even preschool children can be taught how to select, wear, and care for their own clothing. If a young child is going to attend a birthday party, let him select what he will wear. Let him choose from among several around-home garments. Then, let him select from two pairs of shoes that are acceptable for

[1]Ruth O'Brien and Meyer A. Girshick, *Children's Body Measurements for Size in Garments and Patterns,* U.S. Department of Agriculture, Bureau of Home Economics, Miscellaneous Publication 365, 1939.

the occasion but quite different in appearance. At a store, let him select from two or three garments first picked out by the parent.

As the child grows in responsibility, allow him to plan his clothing needs for six months, then perhaps for the next twelve months. Follow this by allowing absolute independent action with parents as permissive consultants only. By this time, the child should have a monthly or annual clothes allowance; so make him responsible for living within his clothing budget and for selecting and caring for his personal clothing.

No one child should be favored above some other member of the family in sharing the family clothing budget. This is almost a certain invitation to family squabbles and possible maladjustments. The manner in which these group problems are handled reveals the kind of spirit that exists in the family. If the family has succeeded in creating individual responsibility in budgeting the family income, the stage is set for continuance of this frank and friendly policy in determining individual clothing expenditures and responsibility for care and upkeep of clothes.

In some homes, proper family attitudes toward sharing space for clothing must also be developed.

Developing skills in clothing management

For a vast majority of families, an adequate wardrobe for every member is possible only by intelligent management. Here is the most practical way to plan and carry out a clothing budget:

1. Know the maximum amount of money available for the family clothing.
2. Analyze the characteristics of each member of the family as applied to clothing needs.
3. Plan, even two and three years in advance, the wardrobe needs of the family.
4. Select the best stores for values, and shop the sales.
5. Select the right garments for specific uses.
6. Use all available information concerning quality, workmanship, shrinkage, colorfastness, suitability, care, and upkeep of clothes.
7. Teach children good clothing habits in terms of care and upkeep.
8. Teach teen-age budgeting for clothes.
9. Discover family resources for home production of clothing items.

All these problems involve information, correct family attitudes, some skills, and time and energy, particularly when the family income is inadequate. But a limited income can be offset by skill in planning (1) how to buy, (2) when to buy, (3) where to buy, (4) care and upkeep, and (5) home production.

How much to spend for family clothing

Everyone wants to be well dressed, but it is difficult to agree on what it should cost to achieve this objective. This is a good time to turn to the figures compiled by budget experts. It is well to keep in mind, however, that no family is "average" in its expenditures. The amount of money spent for clothing depends on the age, sex, and number of persons in the family; on the climate; on personal taste, social needs, and occupations; and, importantly, on the family income.

After food, housing, and transportation, the largest expenditure in the average American family's budget is for clothing. Clothes cost about $275 per person per year on the average.

You can't force your own budget, however, to match a statistical average. Each family is different. But averages can give you an idea of whether your own spending may be out of line.

The Bureau of Labor Statistics (BLS) creates model budgets at three standards of living—lower, moderate, and higher. These budgets cover only consumption of goods and services—usually around 81 to 85 percent of the total income of a family. Also, keep in mind that the BLS model budget is for a moderate-income family living in an urban community (husband 38, wife at home, full time, a boy 13, and a girl 8) and having a moderate budget of $10,971 in 1971. The BLS surveys report that the average 1971 income of such a family was slightly under $14,000.

Table 8-1 shows the 1971 BLS clothing budget for the moderate-level urban family of four in 1971. Keep in mind that in the case of clothing, established families have a stock of basic items, and so this budget represents only replacement costs.

Despite the sizable differences between the amounts of the BLS budgets for higher and lower living standards, the proportion of money spent for clothes is about the same because the same kinds of articles are bought at each level—suits, shoes, and so on. The amount spent, however, at the three different standards of living differs with the quality and quantity of things purchased. How much a family spends for clothing depends also on how much education the head of the family household has had; the higher the educational level, the greater the clothing expenditure.

The USDA recently figured that the average family's total cost of clothing a child from birth to age 17 is $3,500 to $3,700. The peak clothing-expense years come when the youngsters are in their midteens. Also, at age 25 clothing costs begin to taper off for both sexes.

The effects of age and sex on clothing expenditures are hard to determine

It is difficult to know how age and sex affect clothing expenditures because recent data are hard to come by at this time. Generalizations on clothing expenditures of urban families may prove to be out of kilter because of drastic changes in current life-styles, social mores, and fashions. The following generalizations, however, may be fairly accurate:

1.   Average clothing expenditures increase as a child grows older, peak in his midteens, and then decline with advancing age.

2.   Clothing expenditures for adults 18 to 64 years old differ with family status, interests, and financial pressures.

3.   Clothing expenditures increase as family income increases, but at a slower pace, except the portion going to wives.

TABLE 8-1 Clothing Budget of Moderate-Level Urban Family of Four (1971)

Husband	$222
Wife	234
Boy (age 13)	215
Girl (age 8)	187
Clothing materials and services	83
Total family clothing costs	$941

4. If there is an increase in income, women and girls increase their clothing expenditures more than men and boys increase theirs.

5. At all income levels, clothing for a child 2 to 5 years old costs the family about half as much as that for a man.

6. The average clothing expenditure is generally highest in the Northeast and lowest in the South.

7. For females, the average price paid per garment increases with the age of the person and is highest for the oldest group.

8. The proportion of the clothing budget spent for clothing services— such as cleaning and shoe repairs—increases for everybody as living standards increase.

PLANNING AND BUYING THE FAMILY'S CLOTHING

Pay cash for clothing

When buying clothing, you have the choice of paying cash or using credit. Generally, it is best to pay cash. The best method, however, depends in part on your situation. Families with irregular incomes have more of a payment problem than families with regular weekly or monthly income. Regardless of the nature of the income, there is a compelling principle related to the decision of how to pay for clothing. It is this: clothes are consumer goods that do not earn income for the buyer and therefore should be paid for in cash. Credit can be used with some justification, other things being equal, for clothing that outlasts credit payments. Credit costs, however, are high for typical credit plans.

Ideally, a family should allocate some percentage of its income for clothing, thus making cash more readily available for clothing. The percentage of cash set aside for clothing will vary with different families, but 10 to 12 percent is a reasonable allocation in terms of the most recent studies on clothing expenditures.

The power of fashion

Fashion, style, fad, craze, and good taste have various meanings to various people. Paul H. Nystrom, in his classic *Economics of Fashion,*[2] defines these terms as follows:

"Style is a characteristic or distinctive mode or method of expression, presentation or conception in the field of some art."

"Fashion is nothing more or less than the prevailing style at any given time." Whenever a style is accepted or followed it is the fashion.

"A fad is merely a miniature fashion in some unimportant matter or detail."

"A craze is a fad or fashion accompanied by much crowd excitement or emotion."

"Taste . . . is the ability to discern or appreciate what is beautiful or appropriate." Good taste is present when one makes the most artistic use of current fashions.

[2] Paul H. Nystrom, *Economics of Fashion.* Copyright 1928 by The Ronald Press Company, New York, pp. 3–7. Reprinted with permission.

Fashion, says Nystrom, seems to be the result of powerful forces in human nature. We laugh, sometimes, at fashion, but generally we accept it. Strangely enough, the influence of fashion is such as to make a style, when accepted, seem beautiful, no matter how hideous it might have appeared at other times.

Fashion is perhaps the most extravagant force in clothing selection, for imitation and conspicuous consumption play important roles. As fashion changes, garments become socially obsolete. And conformity tends to become so important, if you want that well-dressed appearance, that all other values are rejected. This is especially important during the teen-age period. If necessary, teen-agers will sacrifice health, comfort, economy, and even becomingness to achieve conformity and social acceptance.

The following account of a shopping expedition of a college freshman girl exemplifies the force of fashion:

I have been contemplating the purchase of a brown cardigan sweater for almost a year now (sounds impossible but very true), since that's the general procedure I have to go through before coming through with a major purchase. My indecision came when trying to decide between a cashmere, which was more durable but far more expensive, and a good-quality wool sweater. Before coming to college there would have been no question. I would have simply purchased a wool sweater, since I hadn't come into contact with the cashmere-conscious students. Well, I made the rounds of all the stores comparing the different cashmere and wool sweaters and trying desperately to decide, or rationalize, which would be the more satisfying for the amount of money in the long run.

I couldn't decide! Was a cashmere worth three times more than a wool one? If I got one cashmere, would it go well with my wool pull-overs? If I got one, would I ever be satisfied with anything else but cashmere? Yet, I figured—everyone has cashmere and admires it and would comment on mine, if I got one. I could wear it on a casual date and be much more in style and would possibly make a better impression. But would it be a false impression? Could I afford to continue buying sweaters of that quality?

Time was short! I had to decide. My eyes wandered and suddenly landed on a cashmere sweater in a shade of green that I just loved. It was deep and striking. I asked to see the sweater. It happened to be a turtle-neck. I shouldn't wear such high-necked things but, on the other hand, many people did, and it was different from anything else I had. Well, I was all keyed up to the point where I had to buy something, preferably a sweater, and since I couldn't decide about the brown cardigan, I bought the green one that I had no intention of buying.

The final factor in determining this purchase was the girl's feeling of conformity and of social acceptance by her group.

Wardrobe planning by inventory

An adequate wardrobe is not dependent on how much money you spend. It depends as much or more on careful planning and good management of the clothing dollar. The first step in having an adequate wardrobe on a modest income is in knowing what you have and what you need—in short, a common-sense clothing inventory. To dress each family properly, there must be no last-minute hasty buying and needless mistakes.

There is really no average family. Each individual and each family lives a slightly different life from other families, and their clothing requirements are bound to differ. Income, occupations, social life, climate, vacations, and travel plans must be taken into account. For most families, the clothing dollar needs to be spent for comfort, usefulness, good style, and quality, rather than for quantity. It is necessary to buy with foresight and not fall into temptations of the moment or be led astray by whims—purchasing a dress, for instance, because "it looked so lovely in the window."

Each purchase should be backed by reason rather than rationalization, although the latter may be fun for the moment. Everyone enjoys a nonsensical fling once in a while, but it is wise to control such flings by channeling them into the inexpensive and less basic clothing items.

Buying new clothes without first knowing what is in the clothes closet is like buying food without knowing what is in the pantry. For good wardrobe planning, it is necessary to be on spending terms with the six clothing inventory principles given on page 287. Accompanying this list of principles are two clothing replacement inventories, one for the husband and one for the wife. Similar inventory lists can be prepared for each child in the family.

Analyzing flops and successes

The value of analyzing the flops and successes in your clothes closet depends, to a great extent, on the insight gained from the analysis. One mother, on analyzing the items and cost, found that she had spent five times as much for little-used garments that hung in the closet as for those she used regularly. She decided to spend more of her share of the family clothing money for good suits, versatile dresses, and semiformal or informal dresses, and less on vacation and formal clothes that she seldom wore. With the money saved, she could afford accessories for each costume and a much-needed casual coat.

Another mother, analyzing the clothing inventory of her two grade-school boys, discovered that one child was spending twice as much for clothes as his brother, because he was careless and destructive. This mother had a job outside the home. In checking on her own clothing expenditures, she decided that too large a percentage was being spent on luxury underwear and hose. She switched to simple types of underwear and daytime sheer hose for general wear, and transferred the difference to good dresses and suits.

A third family had two fashion-conscious girls whose associates had much more money than they had to spend for clothes. When the mother and the girls studied their clothing inventory, they realized that they obtained pleasure and use from a wide variety of garments. They decided to buy jackets, sweaters, skirts, and blouses that could be alternated and changed by scarves, costume jewelry, and similar accessories. They could double the value of their dress allowances by making each garment serve a double duty wherever possible. They learned to use many style-right ideas that took little time and money.

Teen-age clothing budget

If there are teen-agers in the family, the mere fact that a family clothing inventory has been made does not necessarily mean that the family has solved its clothing problems. The subject of clothes can be one of the greatest little peace

Clothing Replacement Inventory—Husband

ANNUAL REPLACEMENT COST $___   TOTAL COST $___

Present Items	Stock	Annual Replacement	Unit Price	Annual Cost
Hats:				
felt	___	1	$10.00	$10.00
sport	___	___	___	___
straw	___	___	___	___
Overcoats	___	⅓	60.00	20.00
Sweaters	___			
Suits:				
business	___	___	___	___
tuxedo	___	___	___	___
Slacks	___	___	___	___
Shirts:				
dress	___	___	___	___
collar attached	___	___	___	___
Socks	___	___	___	___
Underwear:				
shirts	___	___	___	___
shorts	___	___	___	___
Bathrobes	___	___	___	___
Pajamas	___	___	___	___
Shoes:				
dress	___	___	___	___
sport	___	___	___	___
business	___	___	___	___
House slippers	___	___	___	___
Ties:				
bow	___	___	___	___
other	___	___	___	___
Gloves	___	___	___	___
Bathing trunks	___	___	___	___
Emergency	___	___	___	___
Annual upkeep cost:				
Cleaning overcoat	___	___	___	___
Cleaning suits	___	___	___	___
Pressing suits	___	___	___	___
Blocking hats	___	___	___	___
Repairing shoes	___	___	___	___

1. All usable clothes are listed. Discarded clothes are made wearable. Individual replacement needs are made known, and their approximate costs are listed.
2. The total clothing allotment is subdivided to suit the needs of each individual member of the family.
3. Purchases are made in the order of urgency before desirability.
4. Purchases may be made with a long view for coordination and economy, and may even be based on a 3-year plan for the most expensive items, such as a winter overcoat or a fur coat.
5. Plans are made for upkeep and general care of clothing.
6. A flexible balance is left, even if small, for unforeseen emergency requirements.

Clothing Replacement Inventory—Wife

ANNUAL REPLACEMENT COST $____   TOTAL COST $____

Present Items	Stock	Annual Replacement	Unit Price	Annual Cost
Hats:				
winter	_____	_____	$_____	$_____
summer	_____	_____	_____	_____
casual	_____	_____		
Coats:				
fur	_____	_____	_____	_____
winter cloth	_____	_____	_____	_____
casual	_____	_____	_____	_____
Suits:				
wool	_____	_____	_____	_____
other fibers	_____	_____	_____	_____
Blouses:				
cotton	_____	_____	_____	_____
other fibers	_____	_____	_____	_____
Sweaters	_____	_____	_____	_____
Dresses:				
evening	_____	_____	_____	_____
dinner	_____	_____	_____	_____
afternoon	_____	_____	_____	_____
casual	_____	_____	_____	_____
house	_____	_____	_____	_____
Slacks	_____	_____	_____	_____
Lingerie	_____	_____	_____	_____
Foundation garments	_____	_____	_____	_____
Bathrobes	_____	_____	_____	_____
Housecoats	_____	_____	_____	_____
Nightgowns	_____	_____	_____	_____
Stockings:				
sheer	_____	_____	_____	_____
semisheer	_____	_____	_____	_____
Shoes:				
evening	_____	_____	_____	_____
dress	_____	_____	_____	_____
sports	_____	_____	_____	_____
Slippers	_____	_____	_____	_____
Rainwear	_____	_____	_____	_____
Bathing suits and beachwear	_____	_____	_____	_____
Gloves:				
leather	_____	_____	_____	_____
fabric	_____	_____	_____	_____
Handbags:				
evening	_____	_____	_____	_____
street	_____	_____	_____	_____
Emergency	_____	_____	_____	_____
Annual upkeep cost:				
Cleaning and glazing fur coat	_____	_____	_____	_____
Cleaning and pressing garments	_____	_____	_____	_____
Repairing shoes	_____	_____	_____	_____

wreckers in any modest-income household. Teen-agers believe that clothes are about the most important things in the world. They are at the age when classmates are playing the game of trying to outdress each other. This game usually results in tears and much unhappiness for parents and children. When this happens, a family meeting is in order.

If children have not been brought up on a family budget based on increasing consumer responsibilities as they grow older, it may not be too late to lay the problem wide open and honestly face it. Let them know how much money is available for clothes for each youngster, and why. If everybody agrees, for example, that the teen-agers may each have $175 to $210 a year for their clothes, including repairs and cleaning bills, the chances are good that they will jump at the opportunity of making their own decisions. The clothing budget will have a personal meaning because they have a voice in deciding on what they need.

Fathers still wonder, "Why so much money?"

For inexperienced youngsters, it is better to give the clothing allowance in quarterly payments, because they are likely to go wild at first. It is also wise to insist that they (1) buy sturdy shoes for school wear, (2) keep supplied with rainy-weather equipment, (3) do not wear ragged underwear and socks to save money, and (4) do not expect that the next quarterly allowance will be advanced if they have spent their money unwisely.

Many youngsters under such a clothing budget have tracked down bargains like hunting dogs. The girls think twice before buying junk jewelry, a scarf that will not launder, a blouse that might require dry cleaning. They learn that a cheap sweater that will not launder is no economy even if it costs only half as much as a good sweater. Boys are likely to develop amazing caution about buying a sports jacket that does not look well with more than one pair of slacks.

Both boys and girls are more likely to keep their best clothes for dress occasions and to take better care of all their clothing. Shoes are taken to the repair shop before it is too late; girls take better care of blouses and sweaters. The lost-clothing problem will probably end abruptly. And, perhaps best of all, in some families the youngsters will forget to remind parents "what the other kids get." This, indeed, would be welcome in many homes.

Whatever the total annual expenditure of teen-agers, especially daughters, fathers still wonder why the young ladies of the house complain that they don't have "a thing to wear." Ah, women!

Combine buying skill with care of clothing

There is no satisfactory substitute for the feeling of being properly dressed for the occasion. This, in turn, contributes to personal happiness. It is not necessary to spend a lot of money to have an adequate wardrobe for the family. How well the homemaker plans and how skillfully she buys and oversees the buying of all members of the family are as important as the amount of money spent.

The first requirement for a satisfactory wardrobe is to take stock of what you have and make a list of what you need for the year. Be sure they are necessary items. Extras can follow the essentials. One hundred dollars well planned can bring more satisfactions than $200 unplanned.

Your money interest, however, does not cease with a well-planned wardrobe. Proper care of clothes can prolong their life. Managing the care of clothing, however, is more successful and costs less money if skill and all possible information are used in the selection of clothing in the market.

Gains that may come from wise planning of the family wardrobe can be easily lost through careless shopping in the stores. Getting your money's worth depends on intelligent shopping for the wardrobe you planned at the prices you expect to pay.

The following seven shopping principles can help you save money and get lasting satisfaction from the purchases that not only are necessary to clothe the family but actually keep its members happy and contented.

Compare values

Clothing stores vary in price, even on similar items. Some stores change some of their prices daily and weekly. The higher-priced suit, for example, is not always the best buy in terms of value and style. No two stores have identical operating costs; therefore, their margins of profit are different. The more efficient stores often sell goods of equal quality and style at lower prices. Experienced professional comparative shoppers say that it is necessary to shop at least five stores before purchasing expensive clothing items, such as a coat, suit, or good-quality dress.

Select basic or classic styles

Classic styles almost always mean simple styling, which can mean better-quality fabric and finish. Many stores now feature such styles with the suggestion that they do not become dated. In addition, their appearance can be changed by different accessories. Simple lines also mean lower cleaning costs. One manufacturer of women's clothing put a date on his labels so that purchasers could see how long a particular line remained in fashion.

Buying clothes that fit your needs

Do not develop a case of "bargainitis." Do not buy an article merely because you like the color or because the price has been reduced. It is difficult to resist a bargain, but no garment is a bargain unless it fits your needs. The color that you found irresistible in the store will soon cease to delight you if it does not harmonize with your wardrobe.

Purchase middle-price items

Most stores have several price ranges for all types of clothing. Salespersons, especially those on commission, may attempt to "trade up" customers to the highest-priced group, but this group may not have enough additional value and style to offset its high price. The lowest-priced goods usually cut costs by using cheaper-quality raw materials, resulting in unsatisfactory wear. The middle-price lines are usually safest to buy because good-quality materials may be used, and costs saved by eliminating nonessentials do not affect good styling and wear.

Shop store brands

It is possible to save up to 25 percent on many clothing items of the same quality and style as the nationally advertised brands. Some manufacturers make identical clothes that are sold under several brand names at different price levels. Large retailers, such as department stores and mail-order houses, have their own store brands. They can often sell clothes more cheaply than smaller competitors who handle nationally known brands, because costs of a wholesaler and of national advertising are eliminated. Store brands exist because prices for nationally advertised clothing are seldom reduced after the items have won public acceptance. Money-saving store or private brands have made considerable headway, especially in the staple clothing, hosiery, and shoe lines.

Shop regular store sales

When you know your clothing needs in advance and plan for cash purchases at reliable sales, it is possible to save up to 50 percent on some clothing purchases. Get acquainted with the months for such sales in your locality, as suggested later in this chapter.

Pay cash

You get more for your money at stores that have strictly cash terms, unless the customer buys on the installment plan and pays a reasonable interest rate. Installment buying is expensive and should be avoided if possible. Some credit stores mark up clothing prices considerably to pay for the cost of credit and, in some cases, for their delivery costs. Some cash clothing stores can sell an identical dress, for example, for 25 percent less than a competitor who offers credit.

Who gets what and when
The accompanying table lists some of the major items that the typical urban family buys with its clothing money, according to *Changing Times* magazine (August, 1972), and how often it buys them. The figures correspond to BLS estimates for a family on a moderate-level budget.

HUSBAND	BOY
Topcoats, one every eight years	Topcoats, one every four years
Sweaters, one every four years	Sweaters, one a year
Suits, one every three years	Jackets, sport coats, one a year
Slacks, three a year	Slacks, jeans, six a year
Shirts, four to five a year	Shirts, six a year
Footwear, two pairs a year	Footwear, four pairs a year
WIFE	**GIRL**
Coats, one a year	Coats, one a year
Sweaters, one a year	Sweaters, one a year
Dresses and suits, two a year	Dresses, skirts, three to four a year
Blouses, shirts, one to two a year	Blouses, one a year
Slacks, jeans, shorts, two a year	Slacks, jeans, shorts, playsuits, three to four a year
Footwear, three pairs a year	Footwear, five pairs a year

Shopping calendar

Table 8-2 shows the pattern that stores generally follow in setting up promotions throughout the year. Some are sales; others are special promotions that sometimes, but not always, include a sale on merchandise being promoted.

How to select clothing stores

There are many kinds of clothing stores to serve the variety of tastes of consumers. Since methods of merchandising vary, the problem is to discover the stores that serve your purposes most satisfactorily.[3] The general answer is found in the answers to these five questions.

Does the store stock a fairly wide range of qualities at different prices?

Some retail stores cater only to one class of customers. Thus, an exclusive women's apparel store may offer dresses at $50 and up. Or a men's clothing store may offer suits at a top price of $49.50. Neither store is seeking to interest all consumers. In addition, a good store will have a wide variety of styles, color, and sizes.

[3] For an excellent source on the subject of selecting clothing stores, see Sidney Margolius, *The Consumers' Guide to Better Buying,* New American Library of World Literature, Inc., New York, 1963.

TABLE 8-2   Shopping Calendar

JANUARY	FEBRUARY	MARCH
White sales, storewide clearance, resort wear, fur sales, furniture sales (third week)	Furniture and home furnishings sales, Valentine's Day gifts, Washington's Birthday sales, housewares	Housewares, china, silver, garden supplies, spring and Easter promotions
APRIL	MAY	JUNE
Spring-cleaning supplies, moth preventives, paints, housewares, fur storage campaigns, outdoor furniture	Mother's Day gifts, summer sportswear, air conditioning, fans, bridal fashions, garden supplies, outdoor furniture	Graduation, Father's Day, and bridal gifts, sportswear; camp clothes and supplies; vacation needs
JULY	AUGUST	SEPTEMBER
Fourth of July clearances, sporting goods, sportswear, furniture sales (fourth week)	Furniture sales, fur sales, back-to-school items, fall fashions, fall fabrics	Back-to-school items, fall fashions, men's and boys' sportswear, home furnishings, china and glassware, accessories
OCTOBER	NOVEMBER	DECEMBER
Women's coats, suits, and furs; men's and boys' outerwear; millinery and accessories; Columbus Day sales; home furnishings	Christmas toys, pre-Christmas value promotions, Thanksgiving weekend sales, china, glassware, table linens, home furnishings	Christmas campaigns, gift promotions, resort wear—North and South (fourth week)

SOURCE: National Retail Merchants' Association.

Does the store give good value for the money?

Intelligent consumers are price-conscious. Some consumers like an expensive atmosphere and settings and are willing to pay more for such a shopping environment. This factor constitutes value for them. Others prefer to have the value in goods rather than in atmosphere. Nevertheless, almost everyone tends to shop around for the stores that give the most value for the money spent.

The store that charges the highest price does not necessarily offer the best goods. The outlet with low prices may not be sacrificing quality. Some stores have low prices but offer poor-quality merchandise. The consumer needs to develop skill in buying to see through the camouflage of atmosphere or of too persuasive selling.

Is the store conveniently located?

Choose the clothing stores that meet your needs best

Most people are willing to accept some inconvenience in terms of distance and accessibility when shopping for the more expensive clothing items, because this occurs only a few times a year. They are willing to drive to a larger city or to shopping centers where there are branches of large city department stores.

Mail-order houses offer a convenience that appeals to consumers who want good-quality merchandise at medium prices. The catalogs are attractive and, on the whole, carry accurate descriptive information.

What kinds of service are offered by the store?

Besides convenience in terms of distance a store should have enough salespeople to serve customers promptly. Some stores reduce their sales force, but pass on the savings to the consumer. The appeal in such stores is based on price rather than on quick service. Other stores emphasize delivery service, charge accounts, liberal policy on returned goods, comfortable lounges, and even nurseries for the children. These services cost money. But some people are willing and can afford to shop such retail establishments.

When shopping in such stores, remember that you are paying for service in addition to your actual purchases. But also remember that you can save money by shopping around and comparing price and quality values.

These four considerations—quality level, price level, convenience, and service—are the most important economic factors in selecting clothing markets. There remains another quality that may be just as important when selecting a store—fair business ethics.

Does the store practice honesty and fair business ethics?[4]

The best merchants are not satisfied unless they can help their customers get their money's worth. Shrewdness and trickery have no place in a good store.

The merchant who serves you best gives expert guidance concerning all important information about clothing items. Examine his advertising. Is it accu-

[4] See your Better Business Bureau, financed by business in most cities of the country, for investigations of sharp and tricky practices.

TABLE 8-3 Shopping Facilities

OUTLETS	DESCRIPTION	ADVANTAGES	DISADVANTAGES
Retail stores: Business establishments engaged in selling merchandise to consumers	Department: Chain or independent store merchandising a large variety of goods, divided into departments for purchasing, promoting, and selling	Many services are usually offered. One-stop shopping is possible. A wide selection of goods is provided in every price range. Merchandise may be returned.	The size of the store and location of departments may make it difficult to find what you want. Department stores are often located in areas beyond your neighborhood. One-stop shopping is not possible. Prices may be higher than in larger stores.
Chain: Member of a group of stores with similar goods and policies	Specialty: Chain or independent store specializing in a limited type of merchandise, such as children's wear, shoes, clothing, books, furnishings, or groceres	There is greater variety within the area of specialty than in general stores. A wide range of prices is available in the specialty items. Salespersons are usually trained, and their knowledge of the specialty results in good service and advice.	
True chain: Owned and operated by one company			
Voluntary chain: Independent stores associated for common buying and promotional activities	Variety: Chain or independent store selling a variety of consumer goods usually in a low price range and with a high amount of self-service and open counter display	Merchandise is openly displayed. Self-service is speedy. The price range is low. Great variety is available.	Salespeople may not be well trained. Shopping traffic may be heavy. Few services are provided.
Independent: Operated by the owner	Discount: Chain or independent store selling some known lines of merchandise at low prices	Parking is convenient. Self-service is speedy. Prices may be lower than other retailers. Stores are usually open for night shopping.	Usually little effort is made to display merchandise attractively. Service is limited. Return privileges are limited. Little or no home service on appliances or equipment is provided. Location may be inconvenient. There are usually few salespeople.

Type	Advantages	Disadvantages
Nonstore retailers: Businesses established to sell goods to consumers on a nonstore basis		
Direct door-to-door: Selling in the consumer's home	Shopping at home is convenient. Often the product is demonstrated for you. Offers the opportunity to see or use items in your home before purchasing them.	There is little opportunity for comparisons of products and prices. Investigating the qualifications of the salesman is up to you. Salesman may come at an inconvenient time. There is limited selection and price range.
Mail order: Selling through orders received and delivered by mail	Armchair shopping is convenient. Saves time and energy. Return privileges are offered. Prices are usually reasonable. Catalog descriptions are usually accurate and helpful.	There is no opportunity to see and inspect merchandise before buying. You pay the cost of delivery. The time lapse between ordering and delivery may be inconvenient.
Vending machines: Providing goods through a coin-operated machine on a self-service basis	It is quick and easy. It offers 24-hour service.	There is limited opportunity to inspect products. Machines are impersonal. No returns or services are possible.
Cooperatives: Associations created and jointly owned by their members, operated for their mutual benefit — **Consumers' cooperatives:** Formed by private consumers to buy products and services jointly at favorable prices for selling to members	Profit is divided among members. Prices compare with and are often lower than those in retail stores.	The amount and variety of merchandise may be limited. There may be a lack of professional retailer know-how. Services may be limited. Location may be inconvenient.

SOURCE: Reproduced with permission from Household Finance Corporation, *Money Management: Your Shopping Dollar,* Chicago.

rate and sufficiently informative? Read the labels. Do they tell you everything you want to know? Observe the salespeople. Are they well informed and competent, and do they show a desire to serve you?

Know the adjustment policy of the store. Are they reasonably fair in making adjustments? If they hide behind every legal right, or if they are evasive, give some other store your business and economic vote.

Some consumers are interested in the way stores treat their help and in other personnel policies. Union members, in particular, prefer to buy in stores that sell merchandise produced and sold by union labor.

All other things being equal, an honest, informative merchant is your best bet in the continuous struggle to get the most value for your money.

Shopping facilities Table 8-3, Shopping Facilities, describes the various kinds of available shopping facilities, comparing their advantages and disadvantages. You have probably noticed also the following trends in retail business.

1. Variety stores, supermarkets, and drugstores carry clothing items, usually the lower-priced goods.

2. Drive-in stores sell shoes and clothing.

3. Some stores are now self-service, and there are self-service departments in regular department stores.

4. Door-to-door selling is used by some department stores.

5. Shopping centers are established within easy distance of residential centers.

6. Discount stores have been established, and there is discount selling in regular department stores to meet this competition.

7. Vending machines are set up in convenient places for quick and easy service and round-the-clock selling.

Typical margins of department stores You may be a better shopper by knowing approximate markups of important clothing items. The margin or markup percentage varies from store to store and from item to item. For example, *Changing Times* magazine published margins used by department stores with annual sales of $2 million to $5 million. The percentages came from a report of the National Retail Merchants Association.

Only part of this margin is profit because the markup has to cover the expenses of the store. Nevertheless, the margins help you figure approximate price reductions. For example, a 15 percent cut on an item with a 25 percent margin is better than a 15 percent cut on an item with a 77 percent margin.

Usually, stores figure markups on a percentage of the retail price rather than on the wholesale cost. An item that costs 40 cents and sells for 60 cents may have a margin of 33⅓ percent (20 cents divided by 60 cents).

Discount stores Legitimate discount stores have forced a change in prices and in merchandising goods. Some large department stores have reduced personnel and expensive services, and have cut prices to meet this new competition. A few department stores have rented space in their own stores to regular discount chains. Others have set up their own discount units or stores.

Do you usually get lower prices for comparable quality in discount stores? Studies indicate that, on the whole, prices in discount houses are lower than

ITEM	AMOUNT ADDED ON AS PERCENT OF WHOLESALE COST
Costume jewelry	81.8
Handbags, small leather goods	70.9
Women's, children's gloves	72.1
Women's shoes	77.6
Children's shoes	70.0
Women's, misses' coats and suits	67.5
Men's clothing	71.8
Boys' clothing	61.0
Men's, boys' shoes	69.2

prices in standard department stores and independent specialty stores. But in highly competitive areas, the specialty and department stores often meet discount prices. Some discount stores may have a few items marked higher than those in other competing stores. Successful discount stores usually sell fast-moving items and may offer less variety in size, color, style, and quality. A few manufacturers will not sell to a discount house or will sell the same item under a different label. Often, discount stores make a "special purchase" deal with a manufacturer and then offer an exceptional bargain to consumers.

Nondiscount stores are increasing their "private label" brands. These retailers also purchase "distress goods—surplus stocks of manufacturers, wholesalers, and other stores—and offer them at much lower prices built around a "special purchase." However, some of these "sales" are fictitious.

Textile Fiber Products Identification Act Consumers have a new shopping aid when buying clothing, rugs, curtains, slipcovers, and various household textiles. This federal law, which became effective March 3, 1960, requires that all textile products carry a label stating the exact percentage of each fiber in the fabric. Furthermore, when trademarks and trade names are used on labels, the generic name [chemical family category] must also appear "in immediate conjunction therewith and such trademark and generic names must appear in type or lettering of equal size and conspicuousness." If it is a two-sided label, the front side must show clearly the words "fiber content on reverse side."

Consumers must become acquainted with the generic names that are on textile labels. Most consumers know the properties and characteristics of the natural textile fibers—cotton, wool, silk, and linen—but many of the synthetic fibers were known only by their trademarks or trade names. Now the more than seven hundred trade names for man-made fibers are classified within one or more of the sixteen generic groups that have been defined by the Federal Trade Commission. The qualities of these generic groups, when understood, serve as guides to proper washing, drying, pressing temperatures, and the durability of the fabrics.

To aid consumers in understanding the generic groups of man-made textile fibers, a list of properties, trade names, and use is presented in Table 8-4, A Quick Guide to Synthetic Fibers.

TABLE 8-4 A Quick Guide to Synthetic Fibers

CHEMICAL GENERIC NAME	SOME TRADE NAMES	PROPERTIES
Acrylics	Acrilan, Vyleran, Orlon, Zefran, Creslan	Soft hand, lightweight, bulk (warmth without weight); resistant to sunlight; wrinkle-resistant; good dimensional stability; dries fast; pleats and creases can be heat-set permanently.
Modacrylics (modified acrylic)	Dynel, Verel	Similar to acrylics but nonflammable; very sensitive to heat; subject to pilling.
Polyesters	Dacron, Kodel, Vycron	Wrinkle-resistant; pleats and creases can be permanently set by heat; dimensionally stable; good body, drape, and hand; little or no ironing necessary, so adds easy-care qualities; favored for its worsted hand.
Nylon	Nylenka, Banlon, Chemstrand, Agilon, Du Pont, IRC	Strongest of all fibers even when wet, yet lightweight; resists abrasion; wrinkle-resistant; dries fast; dimensionally stable; resists perspiration damage; good elasticity; wear and tear resistance; easy care; pleat retention in a multiplicity of fabrics.
Olefin	Olane, Prolene, Reevon	Auto seat covers; outdoor furniture; marine rope, belts; handbags. Strong and lightweight; highly resistant to rubbing and stretching; easily cleaned.
Nytril	Darvan	Deep-pile women's coats; soft, resilient quality; used in sweaters.
Saran	Dawbarn, Velon	Excellent resistance to soiling and staining; resistant to acids and alkalies and to attack by bacteria and insects. Principally used in screens, upholstery, fabrics, and carpets, and in blends with other fibers for drapery and casement cloth.
Spandex	Tycron, Vyrene	Elasticity; softer than rubber but having many of the same properties; extremely lightweight; used in foundation garments and swimwear.
Vinal	Vinylon	Reported to be useful in a wide variety of textile applications, including all forms of wearing apparel, blankets, curtains, sheets, carpets, tire cord, fish nettings, tents, and ropes. High softening temperature; high dry strength.
Vinyon	Vinyon, Rhovyl T	Resistant to moths and mildew; nonflammability (melts but does not flame); low melting point, can be easily molded.
Rayon	Tyrex, rayon, Fortisan, Super L, Corval, Topel	Absorbency; washability; will shrink unless treated for shrinkage; easy ironing with a fairly hot iron. No resistance to wrinkling; special finish required if resistance is desired. Flammability if napped; fabric should be treated for flame resistance.
Acetate	Arnel, Avisco, Celanese, Estron	Little absorbency, so dries rather quickly. Heat sensitivity, so fabric must be pressed with a cool iron to prevent fusing at thick places. Triacetates will stand higher iron-

TABLE 8-4 (Continued)

CHEMICAL GENERIC NAME	SOME TRADE NAMES	PROPERTIES
		ing temperatures. Some wrinkle resistance. Poor resistance to fume or gas fading (color change due to atmospheric conditions). Spun or dope dyeing developed to overcome this problem. Tendency to accumulate static electricity.
Azlon		Fabrics made from protein fibers. Following properties are usually contributed by these fibers: softness, elasticity, absorbency, dimensional stability.
Glass	Fiberglas, PPG, Uniformat	Little absorbency, so can be washed easily and dried quickly. Flame-resistant; resistant to fungi, microorganisms, moths, acid, and rot. Little resistance to flexing, having tendency to break along crease lines. Freedom from odor.
Metallic	Lurex, Reymet, Fairtex, Mallora, Lame, Metlon	Metallic fibers coated with plastic; widely used as ornamental fibers in clothing and household textiles; do not tarnish with wear or use. Plastic coating has tendency to stick to iron if too high heat is used.
Rubber	Polyisoprene	Core for covered yarns used in a wide variety of fabrics; foundation garments, suspenders, garters, and similar garments. Yarns vary greatly in tensile strength but have great elongation and 100 percent elastic recovery. Do not absorb moisture and are moderately resistant to heat. Should not be exposed to excessive sunlight or heat, or to oils, fats, or greases (lotions or creams).

PROBLEMS CONSUMERS FACE IN CLOTHING AND TEXTILE STANDARDS AND LABELING[5]

Much of the information presented in this chapter in regard to planning, buying, care of, and paying for clothing and shoes could be even more useful to the consumer if there were better standards of labeling. The contemporary revolution in textiles and clothing, with all its salient benefits, brings problems, too. First came rayon, and then nylon, followed by dozens of other man-made fibers and yarns. Chemical manipulation also modified familiar natural fibers into substantially new products—cotton that has some of the characteristics of synthetics, and wool that does not shrink and retains a crease. New finishes have been created. New ways have been discovered to weave fabrics and to

[5] For details, see Consumer Advisory Council, *Consumer Issue, 66,* Government Printing Office, Washington, 1966; *Consumers Union Report for the President's Committee on Consumer Interests,* April, 1966.

manufacture garments using almost every combination of these components. And the revolution is still going on.

Complexity of modern textiles

Consumers have fallen hopelessly behind in their understanding of modern textiles. Even the most knowledgeable people have trouble identifying the fabric of which a garment is made, and even when given this information they cannot adequately predict the garment's performance. Fiber and fabrics producers often publish information about their products, but it tends to be highly promotional or technical, beyond the comprehension of the average customer, salesperson, and merchant alike.

One special problem in textiles is premature marketing of innovations by which the consumer does the testing. Prematurity often involves exaggerated claims. The classic example was wash-and-wear a few years ago. A similar situation seems to exist with the new "durable press" or "permanent press" garments. There is also a considerable amount of fabric failure in washing and dry cleaning.

Some of these problems stem straight from the new materials and processes. Others are the same old problems that we failed to solve before the revolution and that have now become more acute as a result of it.

We need to give more serious attention to safety, size, dimensional stability (shrinkage), colorfastness, performance claims, care and maintenance, and durability and workmanship.

Permanent care labeling for wearing apparel

Permanently attached care labels will appear on most articles of wearing apparel as a result of a new rule issued by the Federal Trade Commission. The rule is intended to help consumers select apparel according to the type of care necessary and avoid damage to items through improper care. The care instructions, which apply to articles leaving manufacturing plants after July 3, 1972, must (1) fully inform the purchaser about regular care and maintenance procedures, (2) warn the purchaser of any care methods usually applicable to similar articles that should not be used, (3) remain legible for the useful life of the articles, and (4) be made readily accessible to the user.

Garment labels end washday worries

All domestic and imported garments and hosiery are covered by the rule. In addition, fabrics sold to consumers for home sewing of wearing apparel must be accompanied by care labels that can be attached permanently by sewing, ironing, or other household methods. Footwear, other than hosiery, and articles used exclusively as covering for the hands are excluded from the rule.

The care instructions must apply to the entire item, including nondetachable linings, trim, and other details. Any exceptions must be indicated on the label. An intentionally removable part, such as a zip-out lining, must be labeled separately when it requires a different care procedure from that used for the main garment. With approval from the FTC, nonpermanent labeling, such as a hangtag, will be allowed on items that would be substantially impaired by a permanent label, and (with approval) items priced at $3 or less that are completely washable will be exempted from any labeling.

British care labels

In Britain, an organization composed of firms interested in various aspects of laundering, textiles, domestic appliances, washing products, and allied matters, including retailing, introduced a care-labeling scheme according to which all washable textiles are classified into eight groups. Each garment has attached to it a label identifying the specific laundering group to which it belongs. The

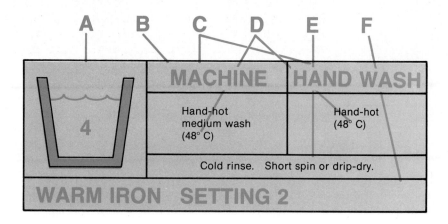

A. Wash code number   D. Washing temperature
B. Machine agitation   E. Spinning and wringing
C. Washing method   F. Finishing and cautionary instructions

FIGURE 8-1 British care labels

complete eight-process chart appears on detergent packages and washing machines. Figure 8-1 shows British care labels.

Flammable fabrics: progress or more deaths?

"There are annually 3,000 to 5,000 deaths and 150,000 to 250,000 injuries from burns associated with flammable fabrics," says HEW in a 1972 report. And nobody knows how many deaths and injuries there have been since the Flammable Fabrics Act in 1953. This act aimed to remove only "explosive" textiles from the market—mostly "fiery sweaters."

The 1967 Flammable Fabrics Act Amendment was broadened to include all wearing apparel and interior furnishing items which present "unreasonable risk of the occurrence of fire leading to death, injury, or significant property damage." The Secretary of Commerce was responsible for development of new-product standards.

"Negative labeling"

A standard covering flammability of carpets and rugs over 24 square feet was developed in 1970 and made effective in April, 1971. An amendment to this standard, made in December, 1971, includes rugs smaller than 4 by 6 feet. According to the FTC, the agency that enforces flammability standards, any small rug that does not pass the "pill" test must bear a readable label: "Flammable; should not be used near sources of ignition."

On November 17, 1970, a proposed flammability standard for children's sleepwear was published. Children's sleepwear (such as nightgowns, pajamas, and robes in sizes up to and including 6X) and fabrics intended or promoted for use in these items are covered in this standard. For this standard, as first announced, there could be no failures during testing. However, the pressures of manufacturers were so great that the Department of Commerce amended the requirement to allow a statistical sampling plan.

The November, 1970, proposal affects sleepwear up to size 6X, which is what a big 5-year-old might wear. For another thing, sleepwear didn't have to meet the flammability test until July, 1973 (1½ years later). And even then, sleepwear could continue to be sold, just as long as it was manufactured before July 28, 1973. The labels on such sleepwear must carry the warning that it is flammable. As of July 28, 1973, all garments must be "flame-retardant." (Read "What's in a Label?" Taylor-Troelstrup Reading 54.)

In October, 1972, the Flammable Fabrics Act Funds bill authorized $4 million for administering the present law and directed the federal government to set standards of flammability for children's sleepwear.

Why the shameful delays?

Children die and government yawns

It took five years after Congress called for action in its 1967 amendment to the Flammable Fabrics Act and two years or longer after a standard was promulgated before the public was protected. That's a long delay; in the meantime, tens of thousands of children and elderly persons died, and countless thousands of others were injured.

There are many problems to overcome. First, how can you tell the Department of Commerce, which is supposed to promote business, to regulate it at the same time? The result has been that Commerce has been ridiculously weak. It's a "no-law" law, one of those laws that Congress passes right into regulatory oblivion. Second, there have been multiple technical problems: the fact that fabrics and garments may burn differently, difficulties in achieving fire-resistant blends, variability in laundering results, and possible impairment of aesthetic properties —color and texture.

Is there no social conscience?

Yet in its February, 1972, issue, *Consumer Reports* cited "intolerable delay in making the new children's sleepwear flammability standard effective." The CU editorial also said, "We would not be so concerned were it not for the poor job of the sleepwear manufacturers in complying with the standard. Even before the standard was finally issued, one firm, Sears, had a product on the market that could meet the flammability standard."

In July, 1971, when the Commerce Department finally published the standard for children's sleepwear, it said the standard was "reasonable, technologically practicable and appropriate." Yet for years, segments of the apparel industry have been fighting the standard. And year after year, some 3,000 persons are burned to death by fires associated with the clothing they wear, while another 150,000 or more are injured. A more likely explanation for industry wailing may be that with clothing, as with automobiles, there's no big sales pitch to be made with safety, and so there's little commercial incentive to run ahead of government pressure. (Read the article published in the *Washington Post*, Feb. 25, 1972, on hearings on children's flammable sleepwear, in Taylor-Troelstrup Reading 55.)

Is the size tag reliable?

You buy a size 8 dress for your daughter. You get it home and it doesn't fit like the last size 8 dress you bought. You see red.

The dress in the size your daughter usually takes is either too large or too small. As the anger subsides, you ask yourself, "Why can't all size 8 dresses be cut the same?" Put another way, "Why can't standards be set for sizes so that we know what we're buying?"

The National Bureau of Standards is working on the problem. Specifications for sizes of girls' clothing are undergoing their first review since 1948 at the request of the Mail Order Association of America.

C. Warren Devereux, technical standards coordinator of the bureau's Office of Engineering Standards Services, said that the new standards probably will be effective in 1973 or 1974.

Under the proposed new standards for girls' clothing, slims will be identified by the size number plus the designation "S." Regulars will be identified by the size number plus the designation "R." Chubbies will be identified by the size number plus the designation "½."

The numbers refer to height. A size 10 girl, for example, whether slim, regular, or chubby, will always be 55 inches in height—with corresponding body measurements shown in Bureau of Standards tables. A size 8 girl will be 53 inches tall; a size 16 girl, 62½ inches tall; a size 7 girl, 51 inches tall; a size 12 girl, 57½ inches tall; and a size 14 girl, 60 inches tall.

The body measurements in each size include bust, waist, hips, vertical trunk, neck base, upper arm, thigh, calf, knee, and shoulder length. According to Devereux, the measurements are based on a U.S. Department of Agriculture survey.

Recommended new standards for women went into effect in 1971 and will be remembered for bruising the ego of the fully grown American female. Devereux recalled that the new standards for women include broader seat measurement than was cited in earlier standards. Body measurements also show that the contemporary American woman is larger through the hips than her ancestors were.

In 1971, standards for boys' clothing were also accepted. These brought about the change from just regular pants to three kinds—slim, husky, and regular. According to measurements, boys today tend to be from 1 inch to 1½ inches taller than boys a generation ago.

The boys' and girls' standards cover from postinfant to preteen ages.

All these new standards for body-size measurements are voluntary on the part of manufacturers. The history of voluntary standards in this country has not been encouraging from the consumer's point of view.

What about standards for men's clothing? To date, they have been set largely by the armed services.

Dimensional stability

Shrinkage is a perennial problem with textiles. But great strides have been made in solving it. Preshrinking of woven textile products is widely practiced. Wool can now be stabilized somewhat. There is very little shrinkage in synthetic-fiber fabrics. Even some knit goods are now advertised as maintaining their size after proper laundering.

The consumer's problem in the midst of these advances is that he must learn how to distinguish the garments that are stable from those that are not. Shrinkage behavior of garments with no shrinkage designation is completely unpredictable. Some processes, such as Sanforizing, are fairly reliable. Some manufacturers, while using fabric that is properly stabilized, will use thread or other components that shrink, causing seams to pucker. But how is a consumer to tell what the shrinkage will be in a product that merely says "preshrunk"? In the absence of standards, "preshrunk" can mean anything.

In the case of stretchy knit fabrics and garments, the shopper faces a chaos of meaningless claims. Even the new synthetic-fiber stretch fabrics pose many problems. Neither industry standards nor consumer standards exist to define the stretch in stretch fabrics.

Standards for dimensional stability are essential to consumer satisfaction. If voluntary standards cannot be agreed upon by industry, consumers, and the federal government, the FTC ought to ask the National Bureau of Standards to develop standards. After standards have been established and agreed upon, the label should be required to state the type of care and maintenance necessary to maintain the dimensional stability of the product.

Colorfastness

In the present market there is no way for a consumer to know the degree of colorfastness of any item or textile. Technology exists by which the consumer could be given full information. American Standard L-22 (performance requirements for textiles) defines a minimum degree of colorfastness and a standard test procedure for about seventy-five basic end uses for fabrics. A majority of the industry agreed to use these important standards. Today, however, L-22 remains unknown to the consumer.

In the fall of 1969, by order of the FTC, the United States of America Standards Institute, Inc., name was changed to the American National Standards Institute, Inc. (ANSI). The chief function of the ANSI is not development of standards, but the adoption of standards formulated by its member organizations. The ANSI is presently making efforts to get its members to adopt a revision of L-22 standards. This information certainly could and should be given to consumers.

Performance claims

The performance of textile products is their basic claim to utility. But when manufacturers write about performance in ads and on labels, they usually use the same superlatives. It would be rare to see a manufacturer state that his product performs less well than that of his competitors. Nevertheless, product performance often does differ among competing products. It must mean that similar words have different meanings from one manufacturer to the next. Consumers Union, for example, tested water-repellent topcoats reported in *Consumer Reports,* April, 1966. Standard tests showed clear differences among the coats tested. But the manufacturer does not put this important information on the label. There are many other examples. How permanent are the new "permanent press" finishes? How warm are "winter-weight" blankets? How resistant is "stain-resistant" finish?

Words should have clearly defined meanings, and ways should be found to get this information to the purchaser.

Durability and workmanship

Before the advent of the new finishes, synthetic interlinings, and other hidden components of contemporary clothing, a knowledgeable consumer could make a fairly intelligent judgment on tailoring and workmanship. He could also recognize the fabric as wool, cotton, linen, or silk, and thus estimate its durability pretty well. Today, however, it is difficult even for an expert with laboratory facilities to evaluate textile products. The advertisements proclaim the new miracles. In the absence of experience or expertise, the consumer is bewildered by all the claims and counterclaims. In the ready-to-wear shop, how can he know whether a suit will lose its shape after a few dry cleanings, or whether an attractively woven fabric of some unpronounceable fiber is going to pill? Such information on estimated service is nowhere available on the labels and tags. Quite obviously, people need this information.

Development in knitted products
Growing popularity of knitted fabrics

The knitting industry estimates that knits accounted for more than one-third of all apparel fabrics in 1970 and that their use will continue to increase. In addition to the special properties of knits, rapid fashion changes, approximating six to eight seasons a year, have played a part in their growth. Manufacturers of knitted fabrics are able to respond quickly to fashion changes because of the flexibility of the knitting process and the relative profitability of short production runs as compared with production runs of woven fabrics.

To compete with knits, stretch is being added to woven fabrics by using textured polyester filament, by blending Spandex with polyester-rayon and polyester-cotton, by adding Anidex (a stretch fiber), by mechanical shrinkage, and by chemical treatment. It seems likely that woven fabrics will continue to be used for durable staples such as jeans, as well as for tailored suits and other garments that are highly constructed.

Knitted fabrics, providing stretch and wrinkle resistance, have long been used for underwear and nightwear. In recent years they have become popular for women's dresses, slacks, and suits and are increasingly used for men's slacks, sport jackets, shirts and suits.

Double-weft knits (sold mostly for women's clothing) have been the fastest-growing segment of the industry, but there have been some recent slowdowns and clearance sales. Modified raschel and tricot knits are expected to become increasingly important for men's suits in wool blends and cotton blends during the coming years. These warp knits are more stable than double-weft knits and present fewer tailoring problems.

WHAT NEEDS TO BE DONE IN STANDARDS AND LABELING?

What needs to be done, then, to help the consumer? All the other problems discussed, except safety, may be considered to stem from inadequate communication between seller and buyer. Communication implies language, and language implies definition. Thus, when the consumer asks about sizes, a reply should be possible in universally accepted terms; when he asks about colorfastness to light, a reply should be possible on the basis of a definition of "colorfastness to light" adhered to by every manufacturer.

Standards   In some circles these definitions are called "standards" and the process of developing them is called "standardization." Critics of standards falsely equate them with potentially rigid uniformity of manufacture or product design. What standardization does connote is uniformity of meaning, or, simply, a definition. The more complicated concepts must often be defined in terms of test methods. For example, the flammability of a textile product can be described meaningfully only by specifying the kind of flame to which it will be exposed, the duration of exposure, the condition of the product at the time of exposure (dry, brushed, etc.), and so on. The item that fails to sustain a flame under these conditions meets the definition for nonflammability.

It would be immensely helpful to consumers if the textile industry would agree on sets of definitions for all the important properties of textile products and would use the defined property characterizations in describing their products. There is no good reason why industry, together with government and consumer representatives, should not be able to take such a step voluntarily rather than under compulsion. Only those properties affecting the safety of the user clearly need to be set by law. But if industry proves itself unwilling or unable to agree on some voluntary definitions, compulsory ones should then be imposed.

Actually, a reasonably good start has been made toward formulating standards for the characteristics of many textile products. There are some products, however, for which research remains to be done on the technical background upon which standards should be built. But this should present no obstacle. In the 1930s, the National Bureau of Standards performed exemplary work of this kind. It developed standards and specifications (groups of standards, sometimes including required levels of performance for each characteristic) for blankets, women's hosiery, carpets and rugs, and other products. This kind of work should be resumed by the Institute of Applied Technology of the Bureau of Standards.

Voluntary standards

Like the "no-law" law, standards which are not used are "no-standards." There is a long history of commercial standards (on size, for example) that are not used, even by those who have signed them. ANSI standard L-22 (Performance Requirements for Textiles) has lain dormant since its adoption several years ago; it might have laid the basis for a system of informatve end-use labeling. Some people argue that these standards are not dormant but are used by the industry internally, even though the consumer never knows it. But what the consumer does not know will not help him. As we have pointed out, the problem is to tell him what he needs to know. What does it matter that one producer's product conforms to L-22 specifications and another's does not, if the consumer cannot single out the conforming product? It does no good to assure him that "a large part of the industry conforms to L-22." Nor does it help to say that many producers are using the sizing standards of Commercial Standard CS 215-58, without telling the consumer exactly what producers are so doing.

Solving the consumer's textile problems means not merely establishing definitions or standards. Equally important, it means letting him in on the secret of product characteristics. Various methods for conveying this information have been proposed.

Standards definitions

One proposal—the most modest—would require that any descriptions of properties of textiles on labels or in advertisements must be in terms of the agreed-upon definitions. Policing would have to be provided. Perhaps, if their procedures could be speeded up, it could fall under the normal jurisdiction of the FTC, which would at last be given firm criteria for determining when advertising is deceptive. But such a proposal, while quieting fake or meaningless claims, would fall far short of full disclosure. It would leave each producer free to decide which properties if any he would publicize. Some manufacturers would probably decide to remain mute on the most important properties of a product, promoting some other about which his competitor was silent. The consumer would then be left with his present inability to compare the quality of competing products.

Informative labeling in Sweden and England

A more effective approach is the Swedish Varudeklarationsnamnden (VDN) labeling system, established in 1951 and still going strong. The VDN is financed and administered by government, business, and consumer groups, whose representatives meet to agree on the essential information needed by the consumer. Each product characteristic is defined and, when necessary, made verifiable by reference to a standard test method devised by a standards-making agency. Labels of quality are also established, when appropriate, for each characteristic. Once all this has been done, a manufacturer may apply for use of the standardized label on his product. He pays a small fee for the right to do so, but his expense is offset by the value of the label in attracting buyers. The VDN authority, on its part, publicizes its labels as a trustworthy source of consumer information. Although the manufacturer must put on the label only a required minimum of information, all characteristics of his product he chooses to label must conform to the standard terminology.

The British Tell-Tag System is modeled on Sweden's system. But in England the manufacturer must include all the defined characteristics on his labels, using the standard terminology and grade levels. In each country, the labeling agency itself polices the system.

The consumer in Sweden and England is thus in the enviable position of being able to get reliable information at the point of sale on the essential characteristics of the product he wants, and to get it in a form that makes direct comparison easy and accurate. He can translate price differences into precise quality differences, and he can make an intelligent decision about whether to pay more or less, depending on his own particular needs.

The consumer selects

Under the Swedish and British systems, the consumer is required to evaluate the level of quality of each characteristic on the label of one brand of product against the comparable information on another. For example, in shopping for a blanket, he might find one labeled as follows:

"Colorfastness to laundering, excellent; dimensional stability, fair; durability, good; piling, poor."

Another blanket might state:

"Colorfastness to laundering, fair; dimensional stability, excellent; durability, fair; piling, good."

Manufacturers who adopt the VDN label must include all the information required in the specification. A Swedish VDN informative label on curtain fabric might have the following characteristics:

VDN
CURTAIN MATERIAL

Width:
  See separate label.
Material:
  100% cotton.

Colorfastness:
   To light, 6-8
   To washing, 4-5
   (Highest rating is 4-5, except for fastness
      to light, where it is 6-8.)
Shrinkage:
   0% in length.
Washing:
   Method—Colored fabrics, 60° C.
   (Manufacturer's name and address here.)

Assuming that all the blankets or curtain fabrics are the same in other important characteristics, and assuming that the consumer knows and understands the labeling definitions, his chances of making a wise decision are definitely better than they would have been if all he had to go on were store claims such as "The best blanket ever sold" or manufacturer claims such as "Gorgeous colors . . . heavenly . . . Zephyrlike." But the decision on which blanket or curtain to buy is still a difficult one.

Standards of quality

If the L-22 standard were used as a basis for certification, we would, in fact, right now have a "minimum standard of grade" scheme.

Many manufacturers, in opposing the use of L-22, argue that the minimum tends to become the maximum, and that, anyway, their products are well above the minimum and would be competing with others at the minimum, both carrying the L-22 certification, so that the consumer could make no distinction.

These arguments have some validity. The answer to them would be a multiple "standards of grade" system. True, it would be most complex to devise, but it would also be the easiest for the the consumer to use. Again, we have a prototype in wide use—the USDA food grading scheme. The Department of Agriculture says: "USDA grades for food are a dependable, nationally uniform guide to quality and a means of making valid comparisons of quality and price." USDA grading schemes have been established for more than 300 farm products—meat, poultry, eggs, dairy products, and fruits and vegetables, among other foods. They are voluntary grades "unless required under State or local law or an industry program."

Textile grading, like food grading, would define several grades of overall quality for each product. A product could not receive a top-grade designation unless it met the requirements for top grade for each characteristic entering into the overall quality definition for that product. The consumer, having learned the meaning of the grades, could make selections far more easily than under any other scheme. Once he knew that two products were of the same grade, he could limit his comparison to color, style, special features, and price. How much easier and more rewarding shopping would become under such conditions!

Why oppose standards?

Why, then, do we not have such schemes for some kinds of textile products, at least? P. G. Agnew, that giant figure in the standards movement, probably puts his finger on the right answer when he says:

> Perhaps [the manufacturers] attitude may be fairly summarized by saying that insofar as they are aware of the movement they see it simply as a feeble and ill-advised attack upon the institution of trade brands. Because trade brands and the tremendous volume of advertising based upon them constitute the very citadel of modern merchandising, the attitude is that the movement for consumer standards is to be ignored if possible; but if it cannot be ignored, it must be fought.

And Jessie Coles sees it this way: "Their real reason is that they fear the effects of standards . . . upon the quasi-monopolistic positions they have developed through advertising and use of brands. Many apparently fear the effect which public knowledge of qualities of their goods would have upon their sales."

There are, to be sure, difficult technical problems to be solved. Standards need to be developed; overall quality and grade levels must be defined. Says Jessie Coles: "The development of such information may require much spe-

What Is My Clothing IQ?

1. Have you any costly clothing mistakes hanging in your closet?
2. Do you make an annual or periodical replacement inventory of all your clothing?
3. Do you set aside a certain amount of your income for clothes and keep within that limit?
4. Do you save money in advance and shop the genuine clothing sales?
5. Do you generally buy clothing that fits your needs?
6. Do you shop several stores and compare quality, value, style, and fit?
7. Do you generally compare the store brands and the nationally advertised brands?
8. Do you know what to check when shopping the more expensive clothing items?
9. Do you avoid "bargains" when you have no immediate need for the merchandise?
10. Do you know how to combine friendliness, courtesy, and good buying techniques when consulting a salesperson?
11. Do you always read the clothing tags and labels that are available?
12. Do you take the time to tell a salesperson who is helping you that it would be a good idea to have more informative labels?
13. Do you handle clothing in a store carefully to prevent damage and to minimize waste?
14. Do you realize that credit and delivery add to the cost of clothing purchased in stores that offer these services?
15. Do you always purchase clothing with the intention of keeping it and return goods only if they have material defects?
16. Do you buy clothing when you are bored or when you are angry or upset about something?
17. Do you think about the upkeep cost when buying clothing?
18. Do you build your wardrobe around two or three color schemes or around many colors?
19. Can you clearly describe to a salesperson exactly what you want?
20. Do you ask to see more than one quality level for comparison to get the best value for the money or possibly save money?
21. Do you avoid buying clothing in chain stores and department stores?
22. Do you generally buy clothing at the highest price level that your budget can stand?
23. Do you file for later reference valuable information that teaches better buymanship?
24. Do you read hangtags and permanent labels that explain how to care for garments that you purchase?

cialized research and considerable time and effort. However, the absence of adequate information does not constitute a serious or permanent obstacle, since its development can be accomplished if such a program is consciously planned and seriously pursued."

The fact is that on an industry level in some cases such standards of quality already exist. Manufacturers make and sell different quality lines, using their own definitions of quality. As in other standards endeavors, obstacles to agreement among different interests will crumble in the face of determined effort. If many foods can be graded, textile products can also be graded.

Certification list

The government, through the General Services Administration, buys many consumer products, and these are tested for conformance to GSA purchase specifications. It has been proposed that conforming products should be certified by the GSA. Such certification lists could give standing to many otherwise unknown brands, bringing small manufacturers into effective competition with highly advertised brands. Thus the work of governmental technical efforts would be used doubly—for its own purchasing and for the benefit of the consumer.

QUESTIONS FOR DISCUSSION

1. The higher the educational level of the head of the family, the greater the family's clothing expenditure.

2. Do you think that British care labels are more informative than American care labels on washable textile garments?

3. How do you account for the twenty-year delay in a federal law that requires all garments to meet flame-retardant standards?

4. What are some of the difficulties in creating specifications for standard size tags for girls' clothing, women's clothing, and boys' clothing? Why are there no recent standards for sizing men's clothing?

5. Do you know what your clothing IQ is? Why not test yourself?

6. Using the Clothing Replacement Inventory suggested in this chapter, how much will it cost to replace or add to your present wardrobe for the next twelve months?

PROJECTS

1. The following are examples of instructions which may or may not be acceptable for permanent care labeling of textile wearing apparel: *(a)* Machine-wash in sudsy water at medium temperature, rinse well, tumble dry thoroughly, hang immediately. Garment may be drip-dried and steam-pressed. *(b)* Machine-wash warm. Gentle cycle. Do not use chlorine bleach. *(c)* Hand-wash cold. Do not twist or wring. Reshape. Dry flat. Do not dry-clean. *(d)* Dry-clean only. Do not use petroleum solvents or the coin-operated method of dry cleaning. Do

you think these examples of instructions are adequate? In answering this question, name a particular garment which would be adequately cared for by following each of the four kinds of care instructions.

2. Study the British care label (Figure 8-1). Do you prefer this care label to an American care label on one of your own garments?

3. Study the Swedish VDN information label on curtain material (page 307). Is this information completely satisfactory? Why or why not?

4. If you live in or near a city large enough to have several stores owned by the same firm in the same area (include suburbs and a ghetto area if possible), compare the price of the same garment in two or more of these stores. If the prices are different, try to determine the reasons for this difference. Are the reasons valid in your opinion?

5. Clothing, fashion, and merchandising majors may enjoy staging a class demonstration of how to select several basic clothing items (for men and women). Include illustrations of poor and better clothing choices by pointing to weaknesses and strengths.

6. Sleepwear manufactured after July 29, 1973, must be flame-retardant. Shop several stores to see whether sleepwear items carrying the cautionary label "Should not be worn near sources of fire" are still in stock. Both domestic and imported garments are covered by this rule. Go the next step—talk to the store owner or manager.

SUGGESTED READINGS

Buck, George S.: *Flammability Report,* Textile Industries, November 1971.

Care Labeling of Textile Wearing Apparel, Federal Trade Commission, 1970.

"Children's Flammable Sleepwear," *Consumer Reports,* February, 1972, p. 106.

"Flammable Fabrics," *Consumer Close-Ups,* Cornell University, Ithaca, N.Y., May 22, 1972, pp. 1–4.

"Flammable Fabrics Hot Line, . . ." *Consumer Newsweek,* Dec. 13, 1972.

Furness, Betty: Statement inserted in *Congressional Record,* Jan. 27, 1972, p. 620, on flammable fabrics.

Textile Handbook, American Home Economics Association, Washington, 1970.

Wagner, Mary, and Rachel Dardis: "Does the Consumer Gain from White Sales?" *The Journal of Consumer Affairs,* Winter, 1971.

Wingate, Isable B.: *Textile Fibers and Their Selection,* 6th Ed., Prentice-Hall, Inc., Englewood Cliffs, N.J., 1970.

CHAPTER 9
A HOME FOR YOUR FAMILY

What do young married couples want most after they are married? Their own home. But the shelter problem is not a simple one. There are many complex factors in the economics and sociology of housing. Modern fixtures and hidden costs present technically subtle and expensive options. Schools, neighborhood, and other environmental factors in the urban centers present complicated and future mobile risks for the family that is tied to an owned home.

High carrying charges and unexpected tax assessments for modern municipal developments put a premium on foresight about ability to pay for a house out of regular income. Mortgage companies and other links of the modern corporate housing industry involve technicalities with which few persons are prepared to deal intelligently and safely. Dozens of risks, big and little, are smothered under sales talks. One of the major risks is deciding how much to budget for shelter. One thing is certain today: The average family can't afford an average conventionally financed new house today because it sells for about $36,000!

INTRODUCTION

Problems facing young married

The following questions represent the problems that must be decided and overcome by young couples who wonder whether it is wiser to keep renting the family shelter or to begin planning for ultimate purchase of a home.

Should we buy or rent quarters?

How much can we afford to spend on housing?

If we purchase a house, how can we finance it at the least cost?

What are the legal pitfalls and problems?

How do we go about selecting a good site or location?

How difficult is it to rent if you have small children?

What are the advantages and disadvantages in owning or renting a home?

Is it cheaper to own than to rent?

Where can we get reliable information in settling these problems?

Are there many unexpected expenses when moving into a new home?

How much will hazard insurance cost on a home?

What is involved when working through a real estate broker?

Is the home that is being considered in keeping with future family needs?

There is an almost universal prejudice against children on the part of landlords. Some young married couples postpone having children because they are unwilling to subject themselves to the indignities often encountered in searching for adequate living quarters for a growing family. In the first place, rental charges are too high. And in the second place, even with sufficient income to rent modern quarters in a good neighborhood, landlord prejudice against young children limits the rental possibilities.

Families that are forced to buy or build homes under these two pressures are likely to find it difficult to regain the flexibility of rental status without inconvenience, loss of equity, or both, if they cannot carry the expense of their purchase.

Your housing goals

Finding the best place to live is one of the most important decisions an individual or family makes. The values responsible for choices in housing vary from family to family and for one family for different periods in its life cycle. Even though few families can achieve all their housing goals, a more satisfying decision can be made if a family is aware of the goals it desires the most.

Many families want reasonable privacy, comfort, health and safety, facilities for leisure-time activities, convenient and accessible stores and good schools, prestige (good address and the right playmates for the children), congenial neighbors, churches, good playgrounds, and other goals.

When thinking about your housing goals, picture your family's daily needs and activities. Children need play and study space, breadwinners need to relax, and the family needs space and facilities to live together as a unit. The more you plan how you want to live, the more likely are the prospects of knowing what kind of living space to rent, buy, or build.

Housing and the family life cycle

The requirements of a family home change during the life of the family. These changes, moreover, parallel changes in the family life pattern. Also, family members undergo many changes: financial; physical and mental; culture interests; children growing up, then leaving home for schooling, then getting married. These and other changes affect family life from beginning to end, dividing the family cycle into the (1) beginning family, (2) expanding family, (3) launching family, (4) middle-age family, and (5) old-age family.

The modern home, in whatever form, is often the core of family life. There have been changes in the functions of the home, but basically most American homes provide space for cooking, eating, sleeping, recreation—play, hobbies, listening—carport or garage, personal hygiene, laundering, and storage. Most people never own a home in which they live out the entire family cycle from early marriage to death. Why? For one reason, we are a "mobile people." The United States Chamber of Commerce has reported that in one year 35 million people, 21 percent of the population, moved to different homes—23 million to different homes in the same county, 7 million to a different county in the same state, and 5 million to a different state or out of the country. Also, about 6½ million people live in mobile homes today. For another reason, American families strive to become more affluent, and their wants and desires include better or more expensive housing when there is increased ability to pay for it. All in all, selecting housing for a family is a highly complex problem.

Will life-style outdate today's homes?

The influence of the long-haired culture

In Chapter 4 we said that the trend toward communal living may bring changes in house design the likes of which the traditionalist never dreamed of. The "upper middle-class family's wealth and mobility have set a standard of house design to date, but the long-haired culture is making itself heard," report three experts in the field of housing and marketing.[1] They see large central meeting rooms, dormitory wings, communal nurseries, large rooms for recreation and group therapy, and big kitchens to accommodate large-scale meal

---

[1]Mary Jo Weale, James Croake, and W. Bruce Weale. "What Happened to the Parlor?" *The Journal of Home Economics*, April, 1972, pp. 26–27.

preparation. In time, the dining room and kitchen may be replaced by computer-programmed delivery of ready-to-eat foods; this will decrease dependence on a car. Ultimately, these three experts see a "self-sufficient home" with its own power source.

Other housing experts say that conventional housing is on the way out. By the year 2000, they say, the house you live in now will be as antique as the bustle or the front parlor. Meantime, most of us will probably live in housing pretty much as we see it today.

Basic concepts in housing

When considering the various alternatives in family housing, use the following basic concepts as guidelines:

1. The choice of a home is related to family goals.
2. The consumer considers alternative ways of securing shelter.
3. Housing requires large amounts of capital.
4. Homeownership is ordinarily a long-term investment.
5. Housing investment is sensitive to future trends.
6. Fixed charges and operating expenses are significant factors of homeownership.
7. Houses are relatively immobile (6.5 million people live in 2 million mobile homes).
8. Housing is beginning to benefit from mass-production techniques.
9. Construction materials are in shortest supply when demand is greatest.
10. Restrictive practices sometimes prevent use of new and economical designs, materials, and construction methods.
11. Housing may involve a "do-it-yourself" program.

RENTING, BUYING, OR BUILDING

In 1890 almost half of the families in the United States owned their own homes. The Great Depression of the early 1930s reversed this trend, causing homeownership to fall to an all-time low of 43.6 percent in 1940. By 1960 the homeownership rate had increased to 61.9 percent. By 1970, homes were owned by 64 percent of all families, according to the 1970 census survey. Data from the 1970 and 1969 surveys show that the rate of ownership varies from about 50 percent for households with incomes under $3,000 to nearly 85 percent for those with incomes of $15,000 and over. About 42 percent of families with the head under 35 years of age own their own home; the ownership rate for the above-35 age group is over 70 percent.

Black homeownership

The 1970 housing census revealed that homeownership among blacks is much more extensive than many people might believe. Nearly 2.6 million blacks, or 41.5 percent, own the homes they occupy.

During the 1960s the increase in the percentage of homeowning blacks outpaced that in the percentage of homeowning whites. For whites, the increase was from 61.9 to 62.9 percent, while for blacks, ownership rates moved from 38.4 to 41.5 percent. The homeownership rate among blacks was highest in the South, at 46.9 percent, and lowest in the Northeast, where it was 28.6 percent. The rates for the North Central and Western regions were 42.1 and 40 percent, respectively.

Ownership of second homes

A study published by the Bureau of the Census in 1969 reported upon second, or vacation, homes owned by American families. The study found that 1.7 million of the 58.8 million families in the nation own a second home which they use for vacations during some part of the year. About 21 percent of the heads of household owning a second home are 65 years of age or over. The largest group of owners of second homes is composed of persons between the ages of 35 and 64. This age group accounted for 71 percent of all owners of vacation homes.

The fact that about 64 percent of all homes are owned by those who live in them, or that about 41.5 percent of blacks own the homes they occupy, is not a valid reason for you and your family to own a home. Before making the important decision to rent, buy, or build a home, the husband and wife should sit down with a pencil and paper and take a look at (1) the advantages and disadvantages of renting, buying, and building a home and (2) whether they can afford to buy or build.

Buying or building

You may prefer to buy or build when:

Decision, decisions!

1.   You have enough money saved.
2.   You feel up to the responsibilities of ownership.
3.   You can predict your family needs far enough into the future.
4.   You know how many years you are likely to be satisfied with a particular house.
5.   You find favorable housing marketing conditions with regard to costs and vacancies in a particular area.

You may prefer to rent when:
1.   You really feel that there are too many responsibilities involved in homeownership.
2.   You expect to move in a few years.
3.   You cannot evaluate your future housing needs.
4.   You are not sure about the new community.
5.   You do not have the financing needed to build or buy a house.

Buying choices

There are numerous buying decisions available in most communities— older homes, modular homes, condominiums, cooperative apartments, row houses, mobile homes, and new homes:

Home, sweet older homes

1.   Older homes come in many varieties. Generally, they are in older neighborhoods and possibly near public libraries, older schools, and markets. They are likely to provide more space at a lower cost and possibly are in need of repairs and paint.

2.   Modular homes are quite popular now as they usually cost less per square foot because they are factory-manufactured to standard living-unit sections which can be arranged in several ways to change the design of the house. Economy is one important advantage. Furthermore, the units of the house can be assembled into a finished product on the site in a remarkably short time.

A sudden surge of interest

3.   Condominiums and cooperatives are similar in that they involve a form of ownership in which certain expenses in relation to maintenance, equipment, and grounds are shared. There are differences which will be taken up shortly.

4. Townhouses are also individually owned, each with its own front and back but with common sidewalls. Generally, each family has a ground level and a second-story level. Their main advantage is economy because savings in building costs are possible.

Home, sweet mobile homes

5. Mobile homes are factory-built and portable and are without a permanent foundation; they are connected to utilities. Usually the home is fully equipped, and movable panels make it possible to expand bedrooms, the living room, or a study. The main advantages of this kind of housing are economy and lower maintenance costs.

6. Building a new house is the best way to get housing tailored to your needs. You can buy blueprints and hire a builder to construct the house, or you can choose one of several house plans offered by a contractor. There usually are several ways to modify any house plan. You also can buy a prefabricated house and hire a contractor to erect it from sections shipped to the site. Non-factory parts are built on the site. Some people with building skills and patience can purchase a "shell house" and complete it or hire someone to finish it. You should be sure about the financing of such a house before signing the contract.

An average middle-income family can't afford an average new house today

7. You can also hire an architect to design a house for you. His services usually include preliminary sketches, final blueprints, and supervision of the construction. His fees may seem large, but if he is a good architect, your house will be built according to the blueprint plans and specifications. It is likely to be more expensive than other kinds of housing.

Renting choices

You can rent almost any kind of housing—apartments, duplexes, townhouses, individual homes, and mobile homes.

In apartment living, there will be a landlord or manager who collects the rent; takes care of the grounds, heating, and maintenance; and perhaps furnishes laundry equipment and major appliances. Sometimes all utilities are included in the rent. There is usually limited private yard space and storage room. There are renter rights as well as landlord rights, and it will pay you to know what these are.

A rented house usually provides more space in every way. The tenant is likely to be responsible for routine maintenance, the sidewalks, and the yard and perhaps for some decorating. Utilities are almost always paid by the tenant.

Duplexes and townhouses usually offer more space and private yard area than most apartments. Utility costs are likely to be assumed by the tenant.

FINANCING THE PURCHASE OF YOUR HOME

The cheapest and safest way to purchase a home is to pay cash. If a mortgage is placed on a house, you may lose both the house and past payments in the event you cannot make the payments on time. However, most families, particularly younger families, purchase a home with a minimum down payment and a long-term mortgage of twenty-five to thirty years.

Mortgaging a home

To finance your house, you will need a mortgage loan. A *mortgage* is a conditional assignment of the property to the lender, which can be put into effect if the borrower fails in the terms of the contract. Most home loans are made by savings and loan associations, savings banks, commercial banks, insurance companies, and individuals. More than 90 percent of the families who buy homes do so with a mortgage loan. Of the three types of institutions, only the savings and loan associations specialize in making home loans exclusively. Currently they finance about 44 percent of all homes in the United States.

If you wish to do business with an insurance company, you will have to deal with a local real estate broker or an insurance agent. A loan may be secured from an individual, but it may cost more than from a financial institution.

An *amortized loan* requires the borrower to make a fixed monthly payment that not only includes the interest (and possibly taxes and insurance) but also reduces the principal of the mortgage debt after each month's payment. The earlier monthly payments include mostly interest. It is possible, therefore, to make payments for several years with only a small proportion going into your equity in the house.

In a $7\frac{1}{2}$ percent twenty-year amortized loan, more than 63 percent of the first payment is interest. In the seventh year, payments are split about fifty-fifty between interest and principal. While you may think you are paying yourself instead of a landlord as in the case of renting, this is not quite true during the first few years of an amortized loan.

Accessories to the mortgage

Before shopping for a mortgage loan, it is wise to know the terms, or language, of the lending trade.

An *open-end mortgage* allows you to borrow more money in the future without rewriting the mortgage in case you want to repair or enlarge the house.

A *prepayment privilege* grants you the opportunity to prepay the mortgage before maturity without penalty. You may wish to refinance at lower rates or to pay it off completely.

A *packaged mortgage* covers the cost of household equipment as well as the house itself.

A *deed* is the written instrument that transfers the title of property from one party to another. There are two principal kinds of deeds.

A *quitclaim deed* conveys to the grantee whatever title the grantor may have had and throws the risk on the grantee.

A *warranty deed* conveys title, and the grantor warrants that his title to the property and his right to transfer it are not defective. The grantee can go to court to recover from the seller in the event of breach of the warranty.

An *abstract* is one of four methods of checking the safety of a title to property. This involves a history of the ownership of the property. Most or all liens, legal transactions, deeds, mortgages, sales, etc., are recorded in the abstract. It provides reassurance for the buyer.

Title insurance is a guarantee for a fee against any defects. *Certificate of title* is a certification by an attorney that he has examined the records of the property and in his opinion there are no unsettled or prior liens or claims.

The *Torrence certificate,* used largely in big cities, is issued by a governmental unit evidencing and registering title to real property.

Kinds of mortgage loans

There are three possible choices for a mortgage loan: conventional loan, VA (Veterans Administration) loan, and FHA (Federal Housing Administration) guarantee loan. All three types are available from the same sources—savings and loan associations, commercial banks, savings banks, insurance companies, and mortgage bankers.

In a *conventional loan,* you offer only two kinds of security: the mortgaged property and your own credit and investment worth. There is no third party to back the loan, which explains why such loans are more conservative. Most mortgage loans are conventional loans, which represent the basic forms of wholly private financing. But these loans vary widely in form.

In a *VA loan,* the federal government guarantees payment of a large portion of the loan. This means extra safety to the lender, so the cost is generally less than for the other kinds of loans. Only qualified veterans can apply for VA loans.

There is an important difference between VA and FHA guarantee loans and conventional loans. The object of the VA loan guarantee is to help veterans buy homes. VA appraisals are usually very strict, because the federal government does not want a veteran to be overcharged. VA appraisal, therefore, serves as a good guide to a fair price for a home.

FHA-insured mortgage

The Federal Housing Administration does not actually make loans. It agrees to insure the lender against loss in case of default. It insures mortgage loans made by banks, savings and loan associations, mortgage companies, and other lending institutions approved by the FHA.

The borrower pays ½ percent premium for this insurance on the unpaid balance of the loan. This added security usually makes it possible for a buyer to finance a home on more liberal terms than would otherwise be available—a larger loan with longer time to pay, probably at a lower interest rate.

You can apply for an FHA-insured mortgage loan to any approved lending institution. The lender will supply the necessary forms, help you to complete them, and, if willing to make the loan, will submit your application to the FHA insuring office.

When your application reaches the FHA office, the staff must process it. FHA processing involves a thorough analysis of the entire transaction—your qualifications as a mortgagor; the property's estimated value and conformance to FHA minimum property standards for location, design, and construction; and the suitability of the mortgage terms for you and for the FHA.

After the lending institution notifies you that the FHA has approved the application, it arranges with you for the closing of the loan. At the closing, the FHA endorses the mortgage for insurance. Closing costs consist of such items as the lender's service charge, the cost of title search and insurance, and charges for preparing, recording, and notarizing the deed and mortgage.

The borrower must meet certain requirements

The chief requirements for the borrower are a good credit record, the cash required for down payment and closing costs, and a steady income that will enable him to make the monthly mortgage payments without difficulty.

The FHA has no arbitrary rules with respect to age or income. It does consider these factors, but only in relation to ability to repay the loan over the period of the mortgage. Each application received by the FHA is considered individually on its own merits. There are guidelines, but they are not rigid. No two families have exactly the same circumstances. Family obligations, responsibilities, future prospects, and ideas on spending all differ widely.

The FHA also sponsors a subsidy program, known as 235, for low- and moderate-income families who would not be able to purchase a house under an unsubsidized program. Down payments can be as low as $200, and interest as low as 1 percent. Although the program has enabled many families to become homeowners, there have been some problems. For example, some owners of 235 homes have complained about shoddy construction of their houses. Also, some lenders have sold houses for more than they are worth, forcing families to vacate their houses because they couldn't meet payments.

Home mortgage costs

Buying a house is expensive any way you look at it. Installment purchase plans, despite high costs, have made it possible for many people to own their own homes today. For example, on a thirty-year mortgage at 8½ percent, the cost per $1,000 is $7.69 per month (Table 9-1).

Table 9-2 shows you how to reduce mortgage costs. On a twenty-five year 9 percent loan, every $1,000 of down payment decreases the amount of total interest paid by approximately $1,510. If you repay a loan in twenty-five years instead of thirty years, you will pay about $7,420 less in interest.

How much interest would you pay for a given number of years? The answers depend on the number of years a mortgage runs and on the interest rate. Table 9-3 shows the cost of a $20,000 mortgage loan at varying interest rates over a twenty-five-year period. If, for example, you can get a $20,000 loan for a twenty-five-year period at 7½ percent rather than at 9 percent, there would be a saving of $5,890.

TABLE 9-1   Monthly Payments for Each $1,000 Borrowed*

INTEREST RATE (PERCENT)	PAYMENT PERIOD, years			
	15	20	25	30
7	$8.99	$7.76	$7.07	$6.66
7½	9.28	8.06	7.39	7.00
8	9.56	8.37	7.72	7.34
8½	9.85	8.68	8.06	7.69
9	10.15	9.00	8.40	8.05
9½	10.45	9.33	8.74	8.41
10	10.75	9.66	9.09	8.78

* *Selecting and Financing a Home,* Home and Garden Bulletin no. 182, Agricultural Research Service, December, 1970, p. 15.

TABLE 9-2 Effect on Size of Down Payment on Cost of a $20,000 Home, with Interest at 9 percent

DOWN PAYMENT	MONTHLY PAYMENT (PRINCIPAL AND INTEREST)			TOTAL INTEREST		
	Twenty years	Twenty-five years	Thirty years	Twenty years	Twenty-five years	Thirty years
$0	$180	$168	$161	$23,160	$30,220	$37,820
500	176	164	157	22,580	29,460	36,880
1,000	171	160	153	22,000	28,710	35,930
2,000	162	151	145	20,850	27,200	34,040
3,000	153	143	137	19,690	25,690	32,150
4,000	144	134	129	18,530	24,180	30,260
5,000	135	126	121	17,370	22,670	28,370

NOTE: Monthly payment rounded to nearest $1; total interest rounded to nearest $10.
SOURCE: *Selecting and Financing a Home,* Home and Garden Bulletin no. 182, Agricultural Research Service, December, 1970, p. 22

TABLE 9-3 Monthly Payment and Interest Cost on a $20,000 Loan at Varying Interest Rates over a Twenty-five-year Period

INTEREST RATE (PERCENT)	MONTHLY PAYMENT (PRINCIPAL AND INTEREST)	TOTAL INTEREST OVER TWENTY-FIVE YEARS
7	$141	$22,390
7½	148	24,330
8	154	26,280
8½	161	28,200
9	168	30,220
9½	175	32,270
10	182	34,460

SOURCE: *Selecting and Financing a Home,* Home and Garden Bulletin no. 182, Agricultural Research Service, December, 1970, p. 22.

Whenever possible, you should try to (1) maximize the down payment, (2) shop for the lowest interest rate, (3) reduce the maturity, or (4) do all three.

Variable rates on home mortgages

Theoretically, under the variable-rate concept the interest on a home mortgage would move up or down periodically to reflect changes in interest rates in the money and capital markets generally. Such an instrument will protect lenders against an increase in interest rates, under the fixed-rate system, and will lower the value of the mortgage note. If the mortgage rates go down, the borrower will stand to gain, providing his mortgage rate is above the going rate at any given time.

Can you have your cake and eat it too?

This idea is being discussed actively at the present time. The question is: Could this be a way out? To many homeowners with a mortgage, this is a shocker, and yet it is not a radical notion. In commercial banking, rates on corporate loans often are tied to the prime lending rate. Nor are variable rates unknown in home loans. A 1969 survey by the U.S. Savings and Loan League of 766 savings and loan associations revealed that 10 percent of them had interest adjustment clauses in all or some of their home mortgages. Variable mortgage rates are used also in New England. Elsewhere in the country, variable rates are used less frequently.

It is easy to see why lenders would have liked mortgage-rate flexibility from 1965 to 1970—home mortgage rates on conventional new-home mortgages increased from 5.8 percent in 1965 to about 8.55 percent in 1970. However, the lenders might have had second thoughts during the period from 1960 to 1965, when the rates went down from 6.21 to about 5.81 percent.

The real hitch is how to work it. Several proposals, some quite technical, have been described in *Changing Times* magazine (December, 1970). Some of the schemes favor lenders, and a couple of them hold attractions for borrowers. What is the best advice for borrowers at this time? *Changing Times* magazine offered the following sane recommendations:

1. Secure an amortized loan (it builds equity and reduces the debt).
2. A fixed interest rate protects you against future rises in the cost of money.
3. If the cost of money falls below your home mortgage rate, be sure you have a no-penalty or a minimum-penalty clause on paying off the loan before maturity. Then you can refinance to take advantage of cheaper money.
4. Without a no-penalty clause, paying off the mortgage before maturity usually involves a penalty. Under an FHA loan, it is a maximum of 1 percent of the original loan if you settle up within the first ten years. VA financing has no penalty. Conventional loans may call for the payment of 3 percent during the first year, 2 percent during the second year, and 1 percent during the third year. Refinancing may involve new settlement charges also.

Taking over an old mortgage

How would you like to buy a house and pay less than the current rate of about 7¾ to 8¼ percent interest for a home loan? You may be able to assume an existing mortgage at around 6 percent interest. This rate was available prior to about 1965.

It could be a good deal

Transferring a mortgage can be advantageous to the seller too because he may avoid some costs that might be involved in a regular sale—discount points, prepayment penalties, and certain settlement charges.

If you like the house, expect to make a sizable down payment. For example, assume that the owner of the house you are interested in purchased it new for $20,000 in 1963 under a thirty-year no-money-down 5¼ percent VA loan. He now has an equity of $2,750 in the house. Over an eight-year period, its value appreciated about 30 percent, to $26,000. If this is the price you agree to, your down payment might be around $8,750 plus settlement fees. By taking over his remaining mortgage at a low 5¼ percent for the next twenty-two years, you would pay about $110 per month. Under current conventional rates, a $26,000 house with the same down payment would cost about $140 per month.

The mechanics of transferring a mortgage are quite simple, but there are legalities to observe and pitfalls to avoid:

1.   The new owner does not automatically erase the present owner's responsibility for repaying the loan unless the original owner releases him from this responsibility.

2.   The seller is apt to jack up the price unrealistically because he has a low-interest plum to dangle.

3.   Get a copy of the original mortgage document.

4.   Lenders often have the power to use "acceleration clauses" to block assumptions they regard as risky by demanding repayment in full.

5.   Some lenders view a transfer as an opportunity to raise the interest rate.

The cost of closing a house-buying deal

When you purchase a house, there will be a number of fees called *closing costs*. These costs may add up to $1,000 or so, and they are paid in cash. These charges vary depending on local practices and house costs. The most common charges (based on FHA financing) are for:

1.   The application fee (to ensure the mortgage and property appraisal)
2.   A credit report
3.   A survey of the property
4.   A title search and examination
5.   Title insurance
6.   Attorney fees
7.   Origination fees (limited by the FHA and VA to 1 percent of the mortgage-lender's charge for arranging loan)
8.   Preparation documents (drawing up mortgage, deed, or note)

Take your lawyer with you when you close the deal

9.   The closing fee (paid to the attorney handling the settlement transaction)
10.   Recording fees (entering documents in the registry books of the county)
11.   Transfer taxes (levied when property changes ownership)
12.   Escrow fees (the sum paid a third party who acts as the custodian of money and documents to be held until the transactions are completed)

There are a few other costs such as paying the seller for taxes he paid in advance, hazard insurance paid by the seller to cover real estate taxes, interest due on the loan between the closing and the date of the first payment, and (under FHA) a deposit for the initial insurance.

Some of these charges are questionable today. In time, the government may regulate some of them. You can't do much about closing costs now, but you can get all the fees and charges itemized and added before the settlement. You can probably get your own hazard insurance more cheaply, hire your own lawyer for the title search, and possibly arrange to save in other ways. You might also try to shift as many of these expenses as possible to the seller or lender. If you have your own lawyer, it is his responsibility to see that you do not pay charges or fees that should be paid by others. An attorney can usually save you more than he costs.

Meanwhile, the Department of Housing and Urban Development and the Veterans Administration are jointly investigating closing costs.

The fine print in home mortgages

A little-publicized battle between Ralph Nader's Public Interest Research Group and the home mortgage industry is receiving increased public attention as a result of public statements from some members of Congress after hearings which the consumer protection group pressured the industry into holding in Washington.

The dispute is over the fine print of a model mortgage contract prepared by the Federal National Mortgage Association and the Federal Home Loan Mortgage Corporation after consulting with lending institutions, but without consulting consumer groups. Critics contend that the document is weighted heavily in favor of lending institutions and offers little protection to home buyers.

The "fine print" taketh away

Mr. Nader's group has found thirty-three parts of the contract which it believes should be modified so that the interests of both parties are protected.

Among the provisions to which the critics take exception is one that would require the home buyer to pay his taxes in advance to the lenders as part of his monthly payment. The lender would not have to put the money in escrow, as is required for federally insured mortgages, but would have the use of the money, interest-free, until the annual tax bill is due, usually toward the end of the year. The Nader study has calculated that home buyers would lose between $70 million and $100 million in interest each year. That is quite a windfall for some banks and loan companies.

The Nader efforts halted the original industry plan to put the new model mortgage contract into effect in January, 1973. In the interest of home buyers, a more equitable model mortgage should be prepared.

Other mortgage lending practices

Most borrowers are not aware of certain other mortgage lending practices which may be distasteful if not actually an abuse. Here are a few examples:

1. Sometimes mortgage companies require borrowers to purchase insurance coverage at premium rates higher than market rates.

What you don't know can hurt you

2. In passing the conditional title to the lender, the new homeowner has actually signed a personal note. In the event of default, the mortgagee can hold the mortgagor personally liable if the forced sale does not yield enough money to pay the loan.

3. Many buyers are not aware of a clause denying the borrower the right to pay off his loan prior to maturity of the mortgage. It is doubtful that a lender would permit a borrower to pay off the loan earlier or to reduce his loan in the event the borrower were paying a high interest rate. Few borrowers take the time to read a mortgage contract. When all goes well, everybody is happy. But what you don't know *can* hurt you. When a borrower defaults, the lender can then point out the many clauses which favor *him.*

4. Some borrowers are surprised to discover that after they have the FHA loan approved, lenders will not make a loan because the FHA rates are too low. Interest rates on all types of loans increase in response to tight money. For example, interest rates on conventional new homes increased on the average from 5.81 percent in 1965 to 8.55 percent in mid-1970. These were exceptionally high interest rates. The FHA guaranteed loan rates were well below these market rates. Consequently, lenders could not afford to lend at below-market rates. To get around this situation, lenders would "discount" FHA mortgages. In other

words, the borrower would pay the lender a commission, commonly called a *discount* or *points*. One point is a charge of 1 percent of the amount loaned. This could be assessed against the buyer or the seller. If you have to pay four points on a $20,000 loan, you get $19,200 ($20,000 × 0.04% = $800). You pay interest on the full $20,000. The $800 additional interest brings the interest yield desired by lenders in the market. Incidentally, the points you pay are not tax-deductible at this time.

HOW MUCH HOUSING CAN YOU AFFORD?

You can say one thing about the average house being built today: The average man can't afford it. The average conventionally financed new house sells for about $36,000. It will take about $10,000 for a down payment and around $200 a month to carry the loan of $26,000. Then you add outlays for taxes, insurance, furnishings, and upkeep. How many average families can afford an average house? Very few, because the average family income is about $10,000 a year.

Before getting down to the "facts" of real housing costs, let's shoot holes in the so-called rule of thumb that a family can afford a house costing 2½ times its annual gross income. While the theory might have had some small merit twenty or thirty years ago, it has become less and less reliable as an indicator, and today it is worthless.

Banks and other lending institutions are well aware of this and, consequently, want to know a lot more about a family's financial position than its annual income. One family, for example, with a gross income of $12,000 might be able to afford a house costing $30,000, while another with an identical income might be a poor mortgage risk in the purchase of a $20,000 house. Why? We are living in a credit economy. Whereas a homeowner once owed money only on a house—and later also on a car—he now is trailed by a string of debts that figuratively keeps a close eye on everything he does.

Don't be led astray by a formula

Therefore, the big question in appraising his ability to maintain regular monthly mortgage payments on his house is: How much is he putting out for other things? And since this varies so greatly among families, it is impossible to say that he can afford a house costing 2½ times his annual gross income. This would be true even if every family had the same income, owed the same amount, and spent equal sums for necessities and luxuries. Smith might have $10,000 in the bank after making a down payment of $10,000, whereas Johnson might have to struggle to produce a $5,000 down payment and have nothing left to pay the many extra costs and provide for emergencies. Thus Smith would be in a much better position to handle a $30,000 house than Johnson would be to handle a $20,000 house. Therefore, it should be clear that no formula that is based primarily on income can be followed.

If you are interested in homeownership, it is very important to be realistic about whether you can afford to buy a house without jeopardizing your ability to make other important expenditures.

The real costs of homeownership

The cost of a house is apt to be the largest sum you contract for during your lifetime. It will cost much more than your rent or the mortgage payment.

Dream or reality?   The practical method of figuring the cost of homeownership is to have a specific house in mind. Let's assume you have a specific single house in mind that costs $35,000, with $10,000 down and a $25,000 first mortgage at 7¾ percent interest for twenty years. The economic expenses incurred in owning this single home are shown in Table 9 4:

TABLE 9-4   Estimated Annual Expenses Incurred by Owner of a $35,000 House

EXPENSE ITEMS	BUDGET	
	Per Month*	Annual
7¾% interest, $25,000, first mortgage	$205	$2,460
Taxes (1%)	29	350
Insurance (homeowner's) (½%)	14.50	175
Repairs and maintenance (2%)	58	700
Depreciation (2%)	58	700
Heating fuel	20	240
Electricity	15	180
Water	12	144
Garbage collection	5	60
Telephone	12	144
Loss of interest at 6% on $10,000		
down payment	50	600
Totals	$478.50	$5,753

*Monthly estimated to closest dollar.

The economic cost of owning this particular house is approximately $5,753 annually, or about $478.50 monthly. Obviously, many unknown variables such as taxes, location, climate, cost of living, neighborhood, and many other incomparables would come into play if one applied the same percentages (1 percent for taxes, etc.) to a $35,000 house almost anywhere else. The point is, however, that it is important to find out *all* the essential costs of a particular house in a particular locality before deciding whether to buy it.

Then, there are the other regular family expenses—food, clothing, transportation, and so on, mentioned in Chapter 5—to be considered before the final decision is made. Be sure the other regular expenses and payments fit into your total spending plan.

The common point of view that anyone who can afford to pay rent can afford to own a home is naïve. If one took the conservative point of view, held by some bankers, that not more than 1¾ times annual income should be invested in a house, then a prospective buyer should have an annual net income of $17,000 to $19,000 in order to buy a $35,000 house. How many families have that kind of income?

Other costs are incurred in single-home ownership besides those listed above. According to housing appraisers, house buyers frequently run into trouble because of the following:

1. They fail to realize that the down payment is a cost. A buyer who makes a $10,000 down payment cannot invest this sum safely at 6 percent, and therefore this loss in income becomes an added cost of homeownership.

2. They don't realize that every house depreciates as soon as it is built and continues to depreciate as long as it is occupied.

3. They tend to underestimate commuting costs to jobs and shopping places.

4. They select the wrong neighborhood and become unhappy.

5. They choose houses which become too small in a short time and are apt to build or purchase a larger house.

6. They select a house with bad features such as poor floor plans.

7. They are unaware that used homes cost more to maintain and repair than new ones.

8. They discover zoning restrictions only after it is too late.

9. They don't know that builders of new houses put in inexpensive gimmicks that give the illusion of more space and hide defects that show up later.

10. They don't realize that American families move often. Six or seven years is about the limit for a family to live in one house.

However, if you can afford the house your family really wants, go ahead and buy it. But don't make the mistake of thinking that you are saving money. Rather, enjoy your house fully. Psychological happiness has no price tag.

MOVING: COSTLY AND OFTEN A NIGHTMARE

According to the Bureau of the Census, nearly one-fifth of our population moves from one living unit to another unit each year. For many of these Americans, the experience itself and the economic cost involved make the move a nightmare. This is so despite new Interstate Commerce Commission regulations designed to curb abuses by household movers. The new rules took effect in 1970. Nonetheless, complaints continue to pour into the ICC at about the same rate as before—some 350 a week during the peak season. The agency continues to get more than 10,000 complaints a year, ICC officials say.

Major complaints [2]

In 1972, the ICC opened an investigation into consumer complaints. Most of the complaints were directed against four of the largest household goods movers—Aero Mayflower, Allied Van Lines, United Van Lines, and North American Van Lines.

*The moving man cometh
—beware!*

The investigation of Aero Mayflower was completed in August, 1972. The evidence against this company was so bad that ICC Chairman Rupert L. Murphy filed a cease-and-desist order against the company revoking for fifteen days its authority to carry certain types of goods. Mr. Murphy says that if the firm fails to comply with ICC regulations in the future, it will be threatened with the ICC's ultimate weapon—loss of its authorization to carry household goods.

The ICC has never used its revocation authority since it assumed the power

[2] United Press International story, Nov. 8, 1972.

to regulate interstate movers in 1935. One wonders about this regulatory neglect in the light of decades of complaints from thousands of frustrated consumers.

The major complaints against interstate movers concern (1) loss and damage claims, (2) inordinate delays in settlement of claims, (3) inadequate compensation, (4) underestimates of moving costs, (5) failure to meet delivery dates, (6) carelessness and indifference of personnel in packing, handling, and storing expensive furniture, (7) too many incompetent personnel, and (8) abuse of those whose belongings are being moved.

The 1967 ICC rules

Under the ICC rules that took effect in 1967, moving companies must:

1.   Give at least twenty-four hours' notice when charges are going to be 10 percent or $25 more than the estimate, whichever is greater.
2.   Pay a minimum of 60 cents a pound for lost or damaged articles rather than the former rate of 30 cents a pound.
3.   Notify the customer, at company expense, at least twenty-four hours in advance if delivery is going to be a day or more late.
4.   Acknowledge damage or loss claims within thirty days and pay up or otherwise respond within 120 days.
5.   Bear liability for the declared value of the shipment if the customer requests it and pay 50 cents per $100 of estimated value, which must equal at least $1.25 per pound shipped. A 4,000-pound load, for example, must be valued at $5,000, and the charge would be $25.
6.   Give the customer a copy of "General Information for Shippers of Household Goods," a leaflet explaining consumer rights.
7.   Reweigh the load if there is reason to question the actual weight; however, this may incur an extra charge if the difference does not exceed 100 pounds or 2 percent of the lower net weight.

The moving industry   There are only 2,500 household goods movers to service the 1 million American families that move across state lines annually, says ICC chairman, Rupert L. Murphy. In practice, the ICC usually follows the decisions of the American Movers Conference, the chief industry association, which is controlled by the largest movers. Since the AMC is a subsidiary of the powerful American Trucking Association, the ICC has not been in the habit of lifting an interstate license from a large mover because of a violation. An illustration of the attitude of the ICC can be seen in the agency's effort to pass long-needed new regulations in 1960. The big trucking firms fought these mild proposals bitterly, even through court suits, and in the end the ICC backed down until the final regulations were a mere shadow of the original mild proposals.

ICC's jurisdiction also has declined. The biggest loophole, for example, has to do with the "commercial zone." Any community is entitled to set up such a zone, usually corresponding to metropolitan areas and at times including parts of two or more states. Movers are exempt from ICC regulation in such zones. Consequently, in these places movers can charge what the traffic will bear in contrast to regulated rates.

Estimates and costs of moving

Once a family has decided to move and has contacted several movers, each moving company will send a representative to the home to make an estimate of the cost. According to the American Movers Conference, every effort is made to keep the final bill within 5 to 10 percent of the estimate.

There are several factors involved in making an estimate of costs—distance, intrastate or interstate, special handling needs, value protection, timing, and scheduling—and other factors. Charges for intrastate are usually regulated by a public service commission in each state. Interstate rates are under the jurisdiction of the ICC and are based on distance and weight. Whatever the charges for moving, the mover usually insists on being paid before he unloads your goods. He can accept only cash, traveler's or certified checks, and money orders, unless some other method of payment has been prearranged.

Insurance

According to the AMC, one in every four shipments involves a claim of some kind. Twenty-five percent of shipments suffer some damage. The average claim is probably around $42. The losses are probably much higher than settlements because the interstate mover is liable for only 60 cents per pound! It may pay to take out additional insurance.

The ICC has no authority to compel movers to settle claims for loss or damage, but it will provide names of insurance companies. Thus, there is no machinery for the settling of disputes except the long, involved court procedures. But there may be an answer to this problem if Senator Warren Magnuson, chairman of the Senate Commerce Committee, has his way. He plans to hold public hearings and may introduce legislation to give consumers better protection.

A few moving pointers

Before contracting for moving, check with your own insurance agent concerning your household insurance. It is likely to give some coverage in case of moving. Then consider the following precautionary measures:

1. Before moving, sell as many goods as possible—especially heavy, outdated items.
2. Very low bids are likely to be unrealistic.
3. When awarding the job, get a copy of the contract stating the rate to be charged, liability, and dates of pickup and delivery.
4. Choose insurance from other sources than the van company. Insure against major damage or loss. Check your present coverage first.
5. Keep a list of what is in each box or package.
6. Make a complete inventory of all items.
7. When loading, challenge any written statement by the van mover that a piece is already "marred and scarred" if it is not.
8. Count all crates, boxes, and barrels as they leave the house.
9. Get from the local agent the name and address of the destination agent, the file number and van number of your shipment, and the driver's name.
10. Request advance notice of lateness and immediate notice of actual charges. Better have a certified check for 50 percent more than the estimate of the costs.
11. If the van is overdue, contact the local agent and keep a record of all resultant expenses.

12. After the van arrives, examine the bill of lading carefully. Note weight before paying.

13. When unloading, tell where to put the various items. Insist that all disassembled pieces be put together.

14. When unloading is over, indicate any damage or lost articles before signing. You may write in: "Accepted subject to concealed loss or damage." Later, when damaged goods or lost articles are identified, file damage and loss claims. State the original value, because the company will depreciate the value. If you do not get action, report the matter to the Interstate Commerce Commission, Washington, D.C. 20423. As a last resort, a letter from your lawyer to the van line's headquarters may help.

First-year expenses of homeownership

Outfitting a new house or moving from one home to another costs money. Besides moving expenses, you are likely to need several items for making the home livable. Few people budget enough money for these purposes. The University of Houston surveyed 218 new homeowners and found they spent an average of $1,580 on new furniture and equipment the first year. The main items are shown in Table 9-5, First-Year Expenses of Homeownership, in relation to the value of the house.

Some of this spending may not be necessary immediately or at all. The fact remains that there will be costly items to buy other than air conditioner, kitchen appliances, and laundry equipment that you normally foresee and plan for. Watch out for these budget busters. If you are moving from a rented apartment, chances are that you will need yard tools, grass seed, fertilizer, and other such items not in your budget. It may, therefore, be wise to provide about 10 percent of the cost of the house for planned and unplanned expenditures the first year.

TABLE 9-5   First-Year Expenses of Homeownership

	VALUE OF HOUSE	
ITEMS	$15,000 to $20,000	Over $20,000
Power lawn mower	$ 55.00	$ 93.00
Fencing	197.00	257.00
Carpets, carpeting	186.00	1,085.00
Draperies, curtains	105.00	432.00
Furniture, living room	173.00	780.00
Furniture, bedrooms	133.00	579.00
Furniture, dining room	250.00	—
Furniture, den	116.00	566.00
Shrubbery	78.00	266.00
Patio	—	217.00
Furniture, outdoor	57.00	83.00

Budget busters

OTHER KINDS OF HOUSING

Homeownership is usually identified with a single-family house. There are other choices. What shall it be? A cooperative apartment? A condominium? A mobile home?

Cooperative housing   Under the cooperative-apartment type of ownership the apartment dweller owns shares in a nonprofit corporation which holds title to the building, and he has a long-term proprietary lease on his individual apartment. The real estate taxes and operating costs are prorated among the owners, and the cooperative makes all disbursements and assessments. The transfer of the apartment unit is accomplished by a transfer of shares in the corporation.

While the cooperative idea in housing has been around a long time, it didn't take off in this country until 1950, after legislation was passed permitting the Federal Housing Administration to insure the mortgages of cooperative housing. Technical organizations have been set up to design the housing, get the financing, contract for construction, and then sell the project to prospective member-residents. After the project is completed and the cooperative is set up, a service organization, like the United Housing Foundation in New York, can be brought in on a fee basis to act as managing agent.

The FHA has insured over $2 billion in cooperative-housing mortgages for some 1 million middle-income families. Another program provides low-cost housing for low- or moderate-income families, the elderly and disabled, and people in rural communities.

There is also a state mortgage plan in New York. Through this program, the UHF has built Co-op City in the Bronx to accommodate 15,000 families of moderate income. Another new cooperative-housing project in Brooklyn, Twin Pines Village, houses about 6,000 persons.

All cooperatives are nonprofit corporations owned and operated for the benefit of the members. As a member, you own a share that gives you a vote and the right to occupy one apartment unit at considerable savings. There are no definite figures on how much you will save by living in a co-op apartment, but the FHA estimates that the costs are about 20 percent less than the rent for comparable apartments.

The savings come about for several reasons:

1. Building costs are lower.
2. Administrative and maintenance costs are lower because owners take better care of their apartments than renters.
3. Long-term, low-cost financing keeps costs down.
4. There is fuller occupancy and less turnover.
5. Owners can claim income tax deductions that are not available to renters.

All cooperatives with FHA-insured mortgages permit equity. The equity or transfer value is made up of the down payment (modest), the occupancy fee, the value of any board-approved improvements you have made, and the annual increase (if any) spelled out in the cooperative bylaws. This last amount varies from $90 to $200.

A member collects this equity when he leaves the cooperative. The co-op has the first option to buy the apartment. A member can sell his apartment to anyone approved by the cooperative. There are no race, creed, or color restrictions.

The only major problem with cooperative housing is that there are not enough apartments available.

Condominium housing

The condominium is a newer type of unit ownership in a multifamily structure. Under this arrangement the apartment dweller holds direct legal title to the apartment in which he lives and a proportionate interest in the common areas and the underlying ground. Ownership rights in an individual unit are the same as if it were a single-family dwelling. Rules and regulations for managing the property are set forth in the deed and are binding upon the owner. In most states, when a unit is sold, ownership is conveyed by a transfer of title.

With land becoming scarcer and the desire to own real property continuing, interest in condominiums is increasing. This new kind of homeownership will be a factor in maintaining a high rate of owner occupancy in the years to come.

Cooperative and condominium tax benefits

Cooperatives and condominiums offer the prospect of combining the economic and tax benefits of homeownership with the convenience of apartment living. Yet, there are important differences between the various forms of real estate investment, particularly in their tax treatment. One should get professional advice before making a purchase.

Generally, both cooperatives and condominiums offer considerable tax advantage because local taxes and interest on the mortgage can be deducted from income taxes. Also, capital gains taxes can be deferred if a home is sold and the money is reinvested in a cooperative or condominium. And there is the big nontax benefit of building up an equity.

If one buys a cooperative apartment he, in effect, buys stock in a corporation. He does not own his apartment outright. This arrangement complicates tax deductions. For example, a husband who puts up *all* the money to buy a cooperative apartment but enters into a joint ownership situation with his wife may wind up owing gift taxes. The gift-tax law says the creation of a husband-wife joint tenancy in real estate is *not* a gift—which includes a house as well as a condominium. But a cooperative apartment is considered personal property, not real property, and the exemption does not apply. There are ways to overcome this tax responsibility.

Advantages of condominiums over co-ops

Condominiums appear, to some housing experts, to have certain advantages over cooperative housing:

1. Owners are under less restrictions when selling their apartments. A cooperative owner must get approval from the board of directors.

2. In a condominium, a default in payments affects only the mortgage of the owner's own apartment. In the case of default in a cooperative unit, all apartment owners may be forced to make up the shortage, if any.

3. Each condominium apartment owner is taxed separately and owns title to his unit.

4. He can rent or lease to anyone.

5. He can also own up to three units, but he must live in one of them.

The earliest condominiums in California were in the $19,000 to $25,000 price bracket. The biggest market currently seems to be in town houses and four-unit buildings with fourteen to sixteen buildings per acre and each unit selling for about $15,000. In the Fairfax Plaza Terrace Townhouses in a Virginia suburb of Washington, D.C., there are three-bedroom units selling for about $28,000. A monthly fee of about $30 entitles the resident to swimming-pool privileges, a group homeowner's insurance policy, all maintenance and yard work, water and sewer service, and trash and garbage collection.

Land costs, high taxes, and rising construction expenses are making it harder and harder for families to buy the typical single-family home. Condominiums offer the perplexed house-hunter one more way to achieve this goal. It's a way of owning a home without suffering all the headaches.

The mobile home: a housing alternative

In 1969, mobile homes were officially recognized as housing by the U.S. Department of Housing and Urban Development. Today, new styles and easier loans are helping to attract buyers in record numbers to mobile homes. In 1972 more than one out of every five new homes built in this country were mobile homes. Young couples in suburban areas and small- and medium-sized towns are taking to mobile homes. So are many older people who cannot or do not wish to pay fancy prices for condominiums and town houses.

Growing popularity of mobile homes

The mobile home is financed as a consumer product. One of the important advantages of the mobile home has been that money for consumer finance was available when money for conventional housing was not. Today, financing is available through commercial banks, savings and loan associations, and dealers. The repayment record has been excellent.

Typical present terms for new mobile-home loans are seven years to repay, a down payment of about one-fifth of the purchase price, and a finance charge of between 11 and 12 percent. Federal Housing Administration insurance is available to most consumer finance lenders for loans to purchase new mobile homes and is handled in the same way as loans to finance repairs and rehabilitation of conventional houses. FHA-insured loans, which insure lenders for up to 90 percent of any loss, provide liberal terms: up to twelve years to repay, a down payment of 5 percent of the first $6,000 and 10 percent of the price above $6,000, and a finance charge of from 7.97 to 19.57 percent. Used mobile homes usually entail higher down payments, higher finance charges, and shorter repayment periods.

A typical two-bedroom mobile home of reasonable quality can be purchased for about $7,000 to $9,000. These homes are completely furnished. There is about 720 square feet of space in a typical mobile home, and there is at least one complete bathroom and standard wiring and heating systems. Most manufacturers abide by the American Standards Association Code to provide better protection against fire, windstorms, and corrosion. Not all manufacturers subscribe to this code, unfortunately.

A mobile home depreciates in value faster than conventional single homes. After about six years, a mobile home has a market value of only about half its original price. After fifteen years it may be sold for 20 to 35 percent of its original price. The average mobile-home cost is about $6,500. "Doublewides" range from about $8,000 up to over $25,000 for deluxe units. The average unit costs about $8.50 to $10 per square foot, complete with furniture, carpeting, drapes, and major appliances. Conventional houses average about $16 a square foot without furnishings and appliances.

On the average, it costs from $35 to $60 per month to keep a unit in a modern mobile-home park. The best parks are like small subdivisions with landscaping and all modern facilities.

The owner of a mobile home—and there are over 6 million of them in America—buys a way of life as well as physical housing he can afford. Payments are manageable. And some families, especially young families, do not expect to live in a mobile home for the rest of their lives. Meanwhile, where else can you get a modern, furnished, two-bedroom home for about $161 a month (this includes monthly mortgage payments on a new $6,000 unit of $104 for five years; park-site rental, taxes, and utilities, $45; maintenance, $5; and insurance, $7)?

In contrast, here is a report on housing costs from the U.S. Department of Housing and Urban Development (HUD). The average new single home cost $24,500 in 1970, and monthly payments on taxes, mortgage, insurance, utilities, maintenance, and repair came to about $265 a month. No doubt, a cost of around $161 a month, compared with approximately $265 per month for an average new single home, is responsible for the great demand for mobile homes in this country.

If you decide to rent

There are many claimed advantages of renting, such as: (1) A renter is free to move; (2) he is not directly concerned with taxes; (3) he is not faced with the risk of shrinkage in capital value; (4) he doesn't have to sign up for a thirty-year debt; (5) in the case of apartments, one check is signed each month for everything—heat, light, water, shelter, and so on; and (6) even if renting is more expensive than owning (which is questionable), the greater peace of mind may be worth the extra cost.

It is very difficult to compare the cost of renting with the cost of owning a home. There are so many variables. For example, when taxes and insurance on the property are increased, the time will come when the owner has to increase rents, and in the long run the tenant pays for the increased costs.

A standard lease is a sort of overkill

One of the facts of life a renter has to face is a little-read document called a *lease.* Too many landlords indulge in a sort of overkill. In other words, leases protect the landlord more than the renter. A typical apartment lease, for example, is likely to incorporate clauses like these:

1.   Tenant agrees to pay all expenses resulting from repairs to plumbing during term of lease.
2.   Owner may terminate this lease at any time.
3.   Owner may enter dwelling at any time.

Landlords have for many years abused so many renters—even the middle- and upper-income apartment residents and the financially secure and politically astute—that renters have organized and are speaking up against poor treatment and unfair leases. *Changing Times* magazine (May, 1972) says that there are 300 affiliates in 90 cities belonging to a national organization born to do battle with landlords who abuse renters' rights. The American Bar Foundation and the National Conference of Commissioners on Uniform State Laws are presently active in getting a "fair shake for both sides." In time, these thorny issues may be ironed out. Meanwhile, renters should read the lease carefully and know their rights and the landlord's rights before the document is signed. Sidney Margolius[3] has spelled out twelve facts you should know before signing an apartment lease. (See Taylor-Troelstrup Reading 61 for details.)

HOW TO INSURE YOUR HOME

At one time you had to buy home insurance in pieces—a fire policy, "extended coverage," a theft policy, a liability policy, and so on. Now you can buy all your home protection needs in one package and save premium costs.

The homeowner's policy A homeowner's policy is a complicated contract. It also comes in several types of protection. Since it is a fairly recent kind of protection, today's policy may differ a little from the policy of a year or so ago.

There are two major parts to a homeowner's policy. The first part consists of four types of property coverage:

1. The "dwelling" includes the structure and extras such as patio, air conditioner, lawnmower, furniture, and outdoor equipment.

2. "Appurtenant private structures" includes other buildings on the lot, like a detached garage and tool shed.

3. "Unscheduled personal property." This refers to household contents, such as chairs, tables, dishes, clothing, carpets, and a boat if stored at home, which are not scheduled by name.

4. "Additional living expense," in case you have to live off the premises while your house is being repaired.

The second part of the homeowner's policy covers three other areas:

1. "Personal liability." This section protects you in the event you are sued by a visitor or neighbor who was injured on your property, or off your property in certain cases.

2. "Personal medical payments" will pay expenses of people injured by you, your family, or your pets, at or away from home.

3. "Physical damage to property" covers damage to the property of others, even though you may not be at fault.

Homeowner's policy: protection varies

In most states five kinds of protection are sold:

1. MIC 1, a "standard form"
2. MIC 2, the "broad form"
3. MIC ¾, a combination of the "dwelling special form" (MIC 3) and the "residence contents broad form" (MIC 4)
4. MIC 4, the "tenants form," used for people who rent a home or apartment
5. MIC 5, the "comprehensive form"

[3] *The New Adult Guide to Independent Living,* 1968, pp. 21–22.

All of these policies provide the same liability protection: up to $25,000 for personal liability; $500 for medical payments to one person; and up to $250 for damage to someone else's property. Once you go beyond the liability protection, the policies begin to differ, primarily in the amount of insurance on the house. The protection varies with the type of property and the policy, as shown in Table 9-6.

If you insured your house for $20,000 with MIC 2 (broad form), the insurance company will pay up to $2,000 for buildings other than your house; $8,000 for personal property at home; $4,000 for living expenses; and $1,000 for trees, shrubs, and plants. There is also $1,000 minimum for property away from home.

The above allowances are ample for most situations. You can reduce the limit on personal property in all policies except MIC 5. Other allowances can usually be cut only by reducing the coverage on the house.

Some guidelines

The homeowner's policy is probably the best one for homeowners. But the policy needs revision from time to time. The desire for protection should be balanced against cost. The premium as well as the coverage goes up from the MIC 1 to MIC 5. For example, in one community it costs $263 to insure a $25,000 home for 3 years without deductible under MIC 1, $338 under MIC 2, and $365 under MIC ¾. The MIC 5 costs $495 even with a $50 deductible. Which one do you really need? MIC 1 offers a lot of protection against basic risks.

The second suggestion is to use the current market value of the house. On big losses, you are entitled to full replacement cost if the insurance is kept up to 80 percent of the cost of replacing the house. If you insure for less than 80 percent of the replacement value of the house, the company will pay only a part of the cost figured on the basis of the ratio of the insurance to the amount of insurance you should have had under the 80 percent rule. If you do not have coverage that automatically increases a homeowner's insurance as property values rise through inflation (using U.S. Department of Labor cost-of-living indices), you are probably underinsured. If you are underinsured, see your in-

TABLE 9-6 Homeowner's Protection According to Policy Type

	POLICY TYPE				
	1	2	¾	4	5
Appurtenant structures	10%	10%	10%	. . . .	10%
Personal property at home	50	50	50	$4,000	50
Personal property away from home (percentage of personal property at home)	10	10	10	10	100
Additional living expenses	10	20	20	20	20
Damage to trees, shrubs, plants (limit, $250 per item).	5	5	5	—	5

surance agent and get coverage up to the 80 percent rule of current value of the house. The replacement cost feature applies only to buildings.

The third reminder is that payment for property other than buildings is reduced by an allowance for depreciation, regardless of how much insurance you have.

Fourth, as a rule one company's homeowner's policy is identical to that of another company. Premium rates vary on the type of house (frame construction costs more than brick or masonry). The kind of fire protection in the community makes a difference in premium rates, too. Some companies offer discount rates. But equally as important as the premium rate is the reputation of the company for paying claims. In the final analysis, your policy is only as good as the company.

Personal property "floater"

An ordinary homeowner's policy may not adequately cover your personal property. It usually limits coverage on the valuables. Most property insurance policies are written on a "named peril" basis. It covers only losses caused by something specifically listed in the policy, such as fire, or theft, or windstorm. Floaters are issued on an "all risk" basis. They cover all losses except those specifically excluded. For example, a camera would be protected by a floater policy if the camera were lost, stolen, run over by a car, dropped in a lake, damaged by wind, hail, or storm, or shattered by a fall. In other words, you would be unprotected only if the damage came from a cause specifically ruled out.

Exclusions

There are some excluded areas of protection. A standard floater does not insure against wear and tear, inherent defects, vermin damage, or losses from military actions and a few other risks. Accidental breakage of a fine arts object is excluded if you, the owner rather than a thief, dislodged the object from a table or shelf.

There are several ways of using a floater. A single object such as a piece of art may be insured. It can be added to another floater. For example, a homeowner's policy can cover ordinary personal belongings, and highly valuable articles can be protected on the floater. This "scheduling" of special articles can be attached to the basic policy.

You can also protect your wedding presents by a floater for a given number of days while you are on your honeymoon.

Cost of a floater

The premium depends upon where you live, the value of the article insured, and the kind of object insured. Usually, there is a minimum charge. As a rule the more goods you insure, the less the cost per $100 of face value of the articles. Some standard rates for a pay-in-advance three-year floater are shown in Table 9-7.

SELLING YOUR HOUSE

If you own your own house, you should keep records against the day it is sold. If you keep the right kind of records, you could end up several hundred dollars or possibly thousands of dollars ahead. This is true even if you sell and then buy

TABLE 9-7 Standard Rates for a Pay-in-Advance Three-Year Floater

ARTICLES	ANNUAL RATE PER $100	MINIMUM PREMIUM
Jewelry	$1 to $2.40, depending on location	$10
Silverware	$0.25	5
Stamps, coin collections	1.00	10
Musical instruments	0.75	10
Wedding presents	0.75	10
Furs	$0.30 to $1.80, depending on location	5

a more expensive place. The deferment rule allows you to buy a more expensive residence within twelve months or build a more expensive one within eighteen months, without paying tax on the profit you made from your previous home at that time. However, this tax is only deferred, not wiped out. If the day comes when you purchase a residence for less money, or if you do not buy one, you must at that time pay the tax on all the untaxed profits that have accumulated over the years—except for certain tax considerations for the seller who is over 65.

How to profit when selling your house

The records and proof should cover purchase cost, certain improvements, and selling costs of the home you have owned over a lifetime. Here is what qualifies for these three categories:

1. Purchase cost and settlement costs. The Internal Revenue Service says that these include attorney fees, abstract fees, utility connection charges, transfer taxes, cost of surveys, payments for title insurance, and any sum that may be owed by the seller, such as back taxes.
2. Sales expense may include repairs done within ninety days before the sale and paid for within thirty days after the sale. (This includes repair work and painting.) Broker and attorney fees are also an expense.
3. Improvement costs may be added to the base price; maintenance costs may not. For example, blacktopping a gravel driveway is an improvement, while resurfacing an old blacktop drive is maintenance; cutting a new door where there was none is an improvement, but replacing a worn door is maintenance.

Let's illustrate how this works for a family. The Johnsons paid $25,000 for a house in 1965 and sold it for $30,000 in 1972. If there had been no expenses eligible to reduce the tax, they would have had to pay a tax on the $5,000 capital gain. Since the Johnsons were in the 22 percent tax bracket, 11 percent of the $5,000, or $550, could have been claimed for taxes.

But the Johnsons kept itemized records and proof of purchase, improvement, and selling costs. These totaled:

Purchase cost	$25,520
Improvements	1,000
Sales expense	1,600
	$28,120

The Johnsons' base price was then $28,120, and so their profit was only $1,880 instead of $5,000. However, they were still responsible for a tax on this profit, but 11 percent of $1,880 is only $206.80. Quite a saving for the Johnsons.

DO NOT PLUNGE INTO DEBT FOR A DREAM HOUSE

Next to food, housing is the greatest need of every family. Today, families spend from 25 to 35 percent of their total income on shelter. With such a large percentage of income involved, it is wise to give close attention to the problems of securing satisfactory shelter at an economical cost. Every family must decide whether to rent, buy, or build a home.

Since a home is the base of family operations, it deserves high priority in the family spending plan. It is wise to investigate whether renting a house or apartment, buying or building a house, or renting or buying a mobile home is the intelligent choice for your family. You must figure the maximum amount that you can expend for shelter and still leave adequate income for other aspects of family living before you allow your dreams to plunge you into debt.

QUESTIONS FOR DISCUSSION

1.   Would you select a variable home mortgage if it were available to you? Give reasons for your answer.

2.   The average *conventionally* financed built single house sells for around $36,000, and buying it takes a $10,000 or so down payment plus at least $200 per month to carry the loan, not to mention the outlays for insurance, taxes, furnishings, and upkeep. All in all, the deal calls for an income of about $16,000 annually. Assuming the above situation (a fair assumption), how many families in this country can afford this expenditure for a house?

3.   Is it cheaper to rent than to own a house for your family to occupy?

4.   What are the factors influencing the cost of housing a family?

5.   What are the factors which affect housing choices?

6.   A standard renters' lease is a kind of overkill. Explain, giving specific information to support your discussion of this statement.

PROJECTS

1.   Interview a homeowner you know. Ask such questions as, "What were your biggest problems in acquiring a home to fit your family needs?" "How did you solve these problems?" "What advice would you give to others who are contemplating owning a home?" Evaluate the answers to these questions. Ask yourself, for example, "Could these problems have been solved better?" "How?"

2.   Compare commercial versus government-insured home financing as to availability, interest rates, building requirements, and advantages and disadvantages.

3.   Arrange a panel discussion of two young couples who have recently moved into the community, asking them to relate their experiences with (a) moving household goods and (b) finding housing they could afford.

4.   If there is communal housing in the community, invite a couple of the officers to class to discuss the advantages and disadvantages of this kind of housing. Perhaps it will be possible for two members of the class to visit with the people in their housing unit.

5.   Investigate the cost of closing the deal when buying a house. Invite a local real estate dealer, a home mortgage banker, and a lawyer experienced in handling housing deals to class to discuss this problem. What can be done to reduce closing-the-deal costs?

6.   Study an amortized mortgage loan on a house. Find out how much equity the buyer possesses after the fifth year and after the tenth year of a $20,000 thirty-year mortgage loan.

7.   What you don't know *can* hurt you. Study a house mortgage contract and pick out parts that could hurt the mortgagor. Give supporting evidence.

8.   Visit with families living in mobile homes. What experiences have they had as owners or renters? What do they say are the advantages and disadvantages of mobile-home living? If they had to do it over again, would they still choose to own or rent a mobile home?

9.   In June, 1972, the Federal Home Loan Bank Board, in response to pressures from young couples, authorized savings and loan associations to grant mortgages on $45,000 homes with only $4,500 down (the previous high was $36,000). What was the reasoning behind this authorization? Do you agree with it?

SUGGESTED READINGS

"Can We Ever Build Cheaper Houses?" *Changing Times,* October, 1970, pp. 15–19.

Chirman, David, and Edna L. Hebard: *Condominiums and Cooperatives,* John Wiley & Sons, Inc., New York, 1970.

Hall, Florence T., and Evelyn Freeman: "Survey of Home Buyers' and Sellers' Closing Costs in Seattle, Washington Area," *Journal of Home Economics,* January, 1972, p. 20.

"Home-Loan Escrow Accounts: Service or Swindle," *Changing Times,* July, 1972, pp. 6–9.

Mobile Homes, Council of Better Business Bureaus, Washington, 1971. (Free, 16 pp.)

"The Moving Man Cometh (Maybe): A Report on Proposed ICC Rules," *Consumer Reports,* April, 1970.

Nader, Ralph: "Falling-Apart Houses," *The New Republic,* May 27, 1972, p. 11.

"New Way to Buy a Home-Flexible Interest Rate," *U.S. News and World Report,* Apr. 27, 1970, pp. 90–92.

Shelton, John P.: "The Cost of Renting versus Owning a Home," *Land Economics,* February, 1968.

Your Rights and Responsibilities as a Tenant, Community Legal Assistance Office, Cambridge, Mass., 1968. (Free, 18 pp.)

CHAPTER 10

CHAPTER 10
FAMILY TRANSPORTATION

The automobile has broadened our horizons. No longer are we satisfied with public transportation. More and more of us own one or more cars. Over 100 million Americans are licensed car drivers. Our social patterns have been influenced by mass ownership of automobiles. Car ownership has changed our pattern of recreation, increased our standard of living, and brought us many conveniences and new services. Drive-in restaurants and theaters, multi-million-dollar shopping plazas, country inns, and suburban bowling alleys are dependent upon people with cars. Many public and private beaches and parks have come into existence because their patrons have cars.

Owning a car has become a necessity for many, a convenience for some, and a pleasure for most of us. Why do over 80 percent of American families own cars? More families can afford a car today because their real incomes have increased and their work hours have decreased. By use of a car more people can live farther from their place of work. Furthermore, installment financing of cars, with payments stretched from twelve to thirty-six months, brought automobiles within reach of middle-income and even below-middle-income people. And for some, a car took them away from the miserable surroundings of their homes. Then there are those who want tomorrow today.

But since the mid-1960s, ominous signs have been appearing: Auto volume no longer surges, profit margins have contracted, and prices—stable in the early 1960s—now go up annually like clockwork. More car buyers have stopped trading up, and the small-car trend has started to grow. Industry analysts now engage in probing studies and wonder about the industry's future.

AUTOMOBILE OWNERSHIP: A SYMBOL OF STATUS OR MATURITY?

In 1950, about 60 percent of all families owned cars. In 1971, about 80 percent did—a porportion that had held steady since 1965. Four out of every five families own at least one car, and about 30 percent have two or more. In 1950, only 8 percent did. In 1960, about 16 percent owned two or more cars.

Many Americans are totally dependent upon cars for transportation because mass urban public transportation has made practically no headway up to now. People are using their cars more and spending more hours of their lives inside the mobile machines.

"A crack in the car's image"

This increasing familiarity is breeding a certain kind of contempt for cars among many owners. "Increased exposure to invitations of traffic congestion decreases the uniqueness and novelty of driving an automobile," concedes an official at one auto company. Says one marketing official in Detroit: "It is quite clear that for a very large proportion of the automobile-owning public, the attitude toward the car has changed rather significantly." The chairman of General Motors put it this way: "America's love affair with the automobile isn't over. Instead it has matured into a marriage."[1]

Status versus maturity

For many decades we were told that the automobile was an indicator of the owner's social status, his position, his place in the scheme of things. The car was thought of as a "portable" status symbol. Only a few people can be aware

[1]"End of the Affair," *The Wall Street Journal*, Mar. 30, 1971.

of one's bank balance. investments, and country-club membership, but a car is proof of one's position and accomplishments that is there for all to see. In a way, a car seemed to tell us what we were or wanted to be as a person—or what we thought we were.

Dr. George Katona, a consumer psychologist who directs the University of Michigan's survey research center, says the growing headaches of automobile ownership are creating a "grudge" among drivers against dependence on cars. Dr. Katona says his surveys show that drivers believe that auto insurance costs are "exorbitant," that repairs are "far too difficult and expensive," that gasoline and depreciation are too costly, and that parking is a worsening chore.

Dr. Ernest Dichter, president of the Institute of Motivational Research, says "people feel that Detroit doesn't give a damn" and there's "an incestuous breeding among designers and . . . the industry has lost interest in the needs of the consumer." Research by one automobile company reveals that the new utilitarian attitude toward cars is especially strong among people in their early twenties. If this is true, it is viewed as highly significant because young buyers are becoming a bigger factor in the market for cars.

Buyers want smaller, more practical cars and less styling emphasis. This attitude is most threatening to Detroit, implying a reversal of the cycle toward bigger, more complex, and more profitable cars. Robert McCurry, sales vice president of Chrysler, said, "Now many people buy the smallest car that will do their specific transportation job." Adds Lee Iacocca, president of Ford, "Nobody has to draw us any pictures to show that the tide has turned. More and more customers are putting the emphasis on utility and functionalism."

The above statements appear to be based on facts. Because of the demand for efficient small cars, imports make up 14 percent of the American market. Small cars, including imports, accounted for only 16 percent of the new-car sales in 1966. In 1971 the figure was 33 percent and is expected to rise to 50 percent before 1980. There is also a trend in deemphasizing annual design changes, according to *Automotive News,* a trade publication. Dr. Dichter summed it up more bluntly: "The image of the American car has a big crack in it."

SHOULD A TEEN-AGER HAVE HIS OWN CAR?

The teen-ager: wheels of his own

There is little doubt but that teen-agers evaluate the status of boys and girls partly by whether they have a car. Boys feel it is difficult to date without wheels of their own.

For most youth it is much more important to arrive at driver's-license age than at voting age. The car is technology in their hands, a machine to command, power at the touch of a toe, danger, skill, privacy from family, privacy with his date, courtship. They are probably the true pleasure drivers. They can drive around for hours, never bored or tired. When they return home and parents ask what they did, their answer is like a child's. Instead of "Nothing," they reply, "Oh, just drove around with the boys."

Teen-agers and cars

Most girls can get along without a car of their own. But to most boys a car of their own can be almost a necessity. Without a car, a boy feels handicapped socially. His need is not merely transportation, because way down deep he wants the status, independence, and manhood that go along with wheels of his own.

A teen-ager with his own car can be dangerous because his exposure to traffic would be increased. The nation's 21 million under-24 drivers, about 20.6 percent of our driving population, were involved in 33.4 percent of the accidents and suffered 33.1 percent of the fatalities.[2] That makes the car the number one killer of teen-agers, deadlier than all diseases combined.

Why a teen-ager should not have a car of his own [3]

After completing a driver-training course and satisfying a state driver examiner, your teen-ager may know a lot about driving, except how. He will learn more about how to drive by being given errands to run. Until he convinces you that he is a responsible fairly skilled driver, he has not earned the privilege of having his own car. There are other reasons why he may not earn the right to own a car. There is evidence that his schoolwork may suffer. There is evidence, as noted at the University of South Carolina, that after freshmen were forbidden to have cars, their grades went up, but older students who had cars continued to have academic problems.

Another consideration is this—a youth who owns his own car usually will not account for his whereabouts while he is gone. You will end up knowing less about his companions than ever before.

His expenses increase rapidly. Insurance alone can cost up to several hundred dollars annually. It is a good idea to check on insurance costs, since they vary greatly from state to state. In some states a youngster can secure only limited insurance, particularly in liability coverage. Girls have better accident records, and most companies have lower rates for them than for boys. Too, teen-agers log more in-town driving than most parents, and the cost of operating the car will be higher per mile. For these and other reasons, should you flatly deny him a car of his own?

An alternative choice

Let him have his car, but try to reason with him along these lines. Try to steer him away from a "bargain" car with souped-up engine, drag-racing shift, and wildly changed suspension. These can be and often are roaring beasts on wheels or a lethal weapon in the hands of youth. Why not discuss a standard car with a stick shift and clutch (boys prefer this)? The youth might be less tempted to reach cruising speed by spinning the rear wheels even on dry pavement if he had a column-mounted shift lever, which costs less and is cheaper to repair. He should have a mechanically safe car, whether new or used. So, go along with him on his search for that "dream" car. Parents are likely to have to be in on the deal anyway if he is under legal age in the state. It might be well to hire a reliable car mechanic to take the car on a test drive and to examine the vital parts carefully before buying the car. After purchase and use, it might be a good idea to give the car an occasional check and inspection yourself.

FAMILY SPENDING FOR TRANSPORTATION

With higher incomes and increased leisure, individuals and families have chosen to spend more and more dollars for transportation—largely, auto-

[2]*Changing Times,* October, 1968.

[3]House of Representatives, Committee on the Judiciary, *Auto Insurance Study,* Oct. 24, 1967, Government Printing Office, Washington, 1967, pp. 4–5.

mobiles. In 1971, about 9 to 10 percent of family take-home pay was used for transportation.[4] Only food, housing, and clothing costs exceed the cost of transporting family members today.

The average cost of transporting family members can be misleading because of variable factors such as income, cost and age of car, number of cars, annual mileage, number and age of drivers, urban or country driving, and kind of driving. A family of two nearing retirement age is apt to use fewer dollars in transportation, whereas a young family is likely to spend above the national average of 13 percent of take-home pay. Families with net income of over $5,000 spend, on the average 14 to 17 percent of their income on transportation, and most of it is for the family car.

The cost of operating a car

Americans spent more than $20 billion in 1972 for new cars, but most of them do not know how much it costs to own and operate a car. Many of these new-car owners may be aware that, except for a home, they will never purchase anything nearly as expensive as their automobiles. However, the purchase price is only the first in a long line of costs. In a 1972 study of the cost of operating an automobile, the Federal Highway Administration said the typical owner of a standard-size 1972 automobile would spend $13,553 to buy and operate the car for 10 years—an average of 13.5 cents a mile (Figure 10-1). This average cost of 13.5 cents a mile for 10 years for a new standard car in 1972 compares with 13.6 cents a mile in 1968.

The owner of a 1972 compact car will pay $10,808, or 10.81 cents a mile, over the 10-year 100,000-mile period. The owner of a 1972 subcompact will pay $9,444, or 9.4 cents a mile, over the decade from assembly line to junkyard.

According to the Federal Highway Administration, "During this period, the standard size car owner will pay $2,787 for 7,350 gallons of gasoline.

"He will pay $2,147 to keep the vehicle maintained and in repair, $1,350 to insure it, and over $1,800 for garaging, parking and tolls.

"His state and federal automotive-tax bill, most of which goes to support the roads he drives on, will amount to $1,319—about 9.7 percent of total costs."

[4] *Autumn 1971 Urban Family Budgets,* U.S. Department of Labor, Bureau of Labor Statistics, April, 1972, pp. 1–3.

FIGURE 10-1   Cost of operating an automobile. Figures based on new 1972 cars driven over a ten-year 100,000-mile period.

Suburban-based Operation
Cents per Mile

	Original vehicle cost depreciated	Maintenance, accessories, parts, & tires	Gas & oil (excluding taxes)	Garage, parking, and tolls	Insurance	State & federal taxes	Total cost
Standard size	4.4¢	2.6¢	2.1¢	1.8¢	1.4¢	1.3¢	13.6¢
Compact size	2.7¢	2.2¢	1.8¢	1.8¢	1.3¢	1.0¢	10.8¢
Subcompact size	2.1¢	2.1¢	1.4¢	1.8¢	1.2¢	0.8¢	9.4¢

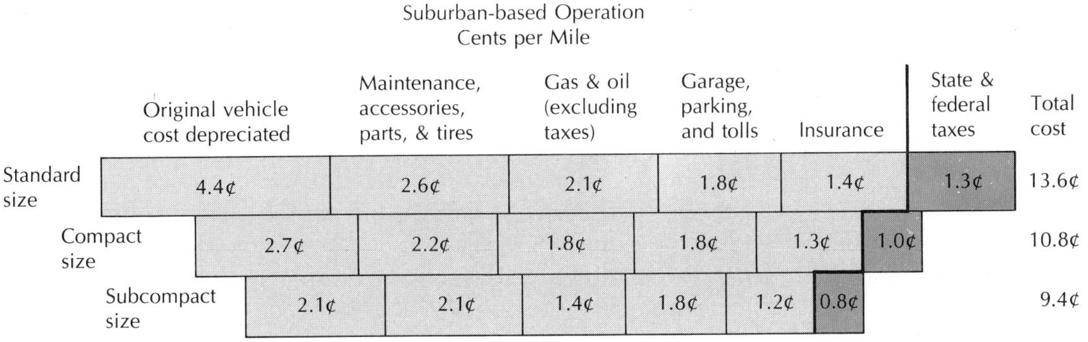

SOURCE: U.S. Department of Transportation, Federal Highway Administration, Office of Highway Planning, Highway Statistics Division, April, 1972.

The study also reported that nationwide sales records of 1972 standard-size cars and compacts showed that 70 percent or more had power steering, more than 90 percent had automatic transmissions, and 90 percent had radios.

More than 80 percent of the standard-size cars had air conditioning. For the subcompacts, power steering was virtually nonexistent, but 45 to 50 percent had automatic transmissions, and more than 80 percent had radios.

The study revealed depreciation to be by far the greatest single cost of owning and operating an automobile. First-year depreciation is relatively high—16 cents a mile for the standard-size car in suburban use, 11.2 cents for the compact, and 7.8 cents for the subcompact.

Automobile factors and assumptions

A description of the vehicles chosen for study and the costs of major repairs, repetitive maintenance operations, replacements, insurance, and other items are given in Table 10-1. In this estimate of the costs of owning and operating a new car for the life of the vehicle—ten years and 100,000 miles—it was assumed that each car was bought new, without a trade-in. There was no change in ownership of the cars. As the cars became older, they were driven at a reduced mileage rate per year. Automobile finance charges were not included in the costs. A conservative interest rate of 6 percent could have been used, about $260, or nearly 2 cents per mile during the first year of the life of a standard-size car. The compact car would cost about 1 cent per mile, and the subcompact would cost about 9/10 of 1 cent per mile.

Depreciation is by far the greatest single cost of owning and operating a car. Year by year, as the car gets older, depreciation decreases, but the outlay for maintenance and repairs rises. Referring to Table 10-1, daily owning and operating costs during the first year of operation are as follows: standard-size car, $6.37; compact car, $4.49; subcompact car, $3.09.

Depreciation—the greatest cost of owning a car

Since depreciation is the greatest cost of operating a car, some experts argue that a family car, averaging 10,000 miles annually, should be kept three or four years before it is traded or sold. The "annual trader" always has a new car, but depreciation for a standard-size automobile over a ten-year period costs him about $12,260 (ten times the first-year depreciation). The two-year trader pays $10,630 in depreciation (five times the depreciation for the first two years). This is a savings of $1,630 over the annual trader's costs, and it appears that the two-year trader can save even more by becoming a three-year trader. However, after the first year he faces a series of outlays for tire replacement, repairs, and incidentals that begin to offset his savings in depreciation. A careful study of the dollar costs will be very rewarding to the average driver, particularly the young driver, who can easily overestimate his financial ability to own a car.

Car repair and maintenance costs

The older the car, the greater the increase in repair and maintenance costs. The estimated costs of repairs and maintenance for three kinds of new 1972 cars are as shown in the accompanying table.[5]

It is obvious from the table that repair and maintenance costs for a new standard-size car are modest the first year (14,500 miles), increase moderately the second year (13,000 miles), increase twice as much the third year (11,500 miles), and substantially increase the fourth year (10,000 miles).

[5] U.S. Department of Transportation, Federal Highway Administration, April, 1972.

TABLE 10-1 Automobile Operating Costs: Bases for Estimates

ITEM	STANDARD-SIZE AUTOMOBILE	COMPACT-SIZE AUTOMOBILE	SUBCOMPACT-SIZE AUTOMOBILE
Automobile description	1972 model 4-door sedan equipped with V-8 engine, automatic transmission, power steering and brakes, air conditioning, tinted glass, radio, clock, whitewall tires, and body protective molding.	1972 model 2-door sedan equipped with 6 cylinder engine, automatic transmission, power steering, radio, and body protective molding.	1972 model 2-door sedan equipped with: standard equipment plus radio and body protective molding.
Repairs and maintenance	Includes routine maintenance such as lubrications, repacking wheel bearings, flushing cooling system, and aiming headlamps; replacement of minor parts such as spark plugs, fan belts, radiator hoses, distributor cap, fuel filter, and pollution control filters; minor repairs such as brake jobs, water pump, carburetor overhaul and universal joints; and major repairs such as a complete "valve job."		
Replacement tires	Purchase of seven new regular tires and four new snow tires during the lives of the cars was assumed		
Accessories	Purchase of floor mats the first year, seat covers the sixth year, and miscellaneous items totaling $2 per year was assumed		
Gasoline	Consumption rate of 13.60 miles per gallon was used	Consumption rate of 15.97 miles per gallon was used	Consumption rate of 21.43 miles per gallon was used
Oil	Consumption was associated with gasoline consumption at a rate of 1 gallon of oil for every 186 gallons of gasoline	Consumption was associated with gasoline consumption at a rate of 1 gallon of oil for every 166 gallons of gasoline	Consumption was associated with gasoline consumption at a rate of 1 gallon of oil for every 135 gallons of gasoline
Insurance	Coverage includes $50,000 combined public liability ($15,000 to $30,000 for bodily injury and $5,000 for property damage), $1,000 for medical payments, uninsured motorist coverage, and full comprehensive coverage for the ten-year period. Deductible collision insurance was assumed for the first five years ($100 deductible)		
Garaging, parking, and tolls	Includes monthly charges of $10 for garage rental or indirect cost of the owner's garaging facility plus parking-fee average of $54 per year and toll average of $6.94 per year, both of which were assigned in proportion to annual travel		
Taxes	Includes federal excise taxes on tires (10 cents per pound), lubricating oil (6 cents per gallon), and gasoline (4 cents per gallon) plus the Maryland tax on gasoline (7 cents per gallon), titling tax (4 percent of retail price), and registration fee ($20 for 3,700 pounds or less shipping weight, or $30 for vehicles over 3,700 pounds)		

KIND OF CAR	REPAIR AND MAINTENANCE COSTS			
	First year	*Second year*	*Third year*	*Fourth year*
Standard	$81.84 (0.56 per mile)	$115.37 (0.89 per mile)	$242.65 (2.11 per mile)	$296.00 (2.96 per mile)
Compact	$79.41 (0.55 per mile)	$107.14 (0.83 per mile)	$170.61 (1.48 per mile)	$218.93 (2.19 per mile)
Subcompact	$76.15 (0.53 per mile)	$114.59 (0.88 per mile)		

The repair and maintenance costs for a new compact and a new subcompact car over a four-year period follow similar patterns. (See Taylor-Troelstrup Reading 62 for records of all costs of owning three new 1972 cars.)

The great automobile repair fraud

According to Donald A. Randall and Arthur P. Glickman, authors of *The Great American Auto Repair Robbery*, $33 billion is spent annually on repairs and maintenance of automobiles in America. Of this $33 billion, about $10 billion is wasted on improperly done repairs, incompetent service, and unnecessary repairs.

A study by the American Automobile Association in St. Louis, Missouri, pointed out that rechecks of 2,000 cars recently repaired showed that only 35 percent of the work was done properly.[6]

The White House Office of Consumer Affairs has stated that the automobile has become the number one cause for complaints by the American consumer, supplanting home appliances.

There is no doubt about the alarming number of dishonest, incompetent, and fraudulent car repairmen. Honest repairmen do exist, however, but how do you find one? You may pull into a garage or gas station and not be overcharged at all, but how can you tell whether the repairman is competent? What is the solution?

Preventive efforts

Several kinds of preventive measures and actions have been taken or suggested that may reduce dishonesty and incompetence in the car repair business. We should bear in mind, however, that individual mechanics involved in fraudulent acts should not receive all the blame. Some of it must be placed upon companies whose policies directly and indirectly encourage these abuses.

Who is the devil?

For instance, many service station mechanics receive a commission for the parts they sell on repair jobs and for the hours they have worked. This encourages fraud. The Auto Club of Missouri said that many companies set a quota on the parts a mechanic must sell each day. Tire companies tell their mechanics that each one must sell $150 worth of parts each day.

Here is what is being done to encourage honest, competent car repair work:

1. Ford began a program in September, 1972, for dealer warranty of car

[6] *Everybody's Money*, Winter, 1971, p. 10.

Warranty wars?

repair work among its 6,700 dealerships. Under the plan, heavily advertised, Ford will warrant repair work on Ford products of any age for 90 days or 4,000 miles. If the car fails, the job will be repeated, with the dealer paying for the labor and Ford paying for faulty parts.

As another part of the plan, Ford is offering $2 million in annual prizes to mechanics receiving the highest ratings on customer "report cards," mailed to Ford for computer processing. Prizes range from $25 to trips to Hawaii.

Ford has also instituted a new training program for mechanics. Trouble-shooters now visit dealers, and special plastic bags are provided in which old parts removed from cars are returned to customers.[7]

2. California has enacted an Automotive Repair Act which creates a Bureau of Automotive Repair within the state's Department of Consumer Affairs. This law requires all car dealers and service stations that solicit major repairs to register their facilities with, and be licensed by, the state agency. The law contains provisions for suspension and revocation of licenses and for criminal penalties of fines or imprisonment.

Several other states have enacted auto repair laws, but none are as stringent as the California law.

At the federal level, Senator Vance Hartke of Indiana has introduced a bill for motor vehicle repair industry licensing.

Two prison sentences

The *Washington Post,* on June 26, 1970, released news that a former owner of three Washington-area car repair shops was sentenced to ten years in prison for defrauding customers by charging them for work not actually performed or parts not replaced. At the same time, Montgomery County Circuit Judge John P. Moore sentenced the former service manager at the firm's Bethesda location to six years in prison for the same offenses.

How do you measure a mechanic's wanting to "do good?"

3. A certification program to certify competent car repair people was initiated by the National Institute of Automotive Service Excellence in June, 1972, by the National Automobile Dealers Association and the Motor Vehicle Manufacturers Association. The Educational Testing Service of Princeton, New Jersey, was contracted to create four tests. The first successful mechanics were certified in January, 1973.

Will this program work? One weakness is that it is voluntary. The testing institute will not guarantee the mechanic's honesty. It will certify the mechanic, but not his work. Nevertheless, the effort is worth watching. This program is industry's answer to complaints from consumers and legislators regarding the quality of auto repair work. (Read the *Time* magazine article "Highway Robbery" Taylor-Troelstrup Reading 70.)

REPAIRABILITY OF CARS

Could repair costs be reduced if the auto industry designed "repairability" into its products? In August, 1972, a study conducted by the Insurance Services Office, a statistical research firm, compared the costs of repairing thirteen major

[7] *The Wall Street Journal,* Sept. 12, 1972.

types of collision repair parts for six two-door models and for low- and high-priced General Motors, Chrysler, and Ford cars.[8] It also calculated price increases for new parts from 1970 to mid-1972. The thirteen repair groups were front bumper, frame, grille, cooling system, air conditioning, hood, front fender, wheel and front suspension, steering, rear quarter, rocker panel, door, and rear body. The results were as follows:

1.   Parts for the 1972 Impala cost 30 percent more than parts for the Ford Galaxie and 38.7 percent more than parts for the Plymouth Fury III. The total cost of all Chevy parts was higher than the total cost of all Lincoln Continental parts.

2.   GM also led the other major manufacturers in the percentage of cost increases for 1970 parts between 1970 and 1972.

Similar results had been obtained in a study conducted by the Liberty Mutual Insurance Company. This study placed 46 percent of GM cars in the high-cost-to-repair category, compared with 10 percent of Chrysler cars and only 2 percent of Ford cars. It also placed only 17 percent of GM cars in the low-cost-to-repair class, compared with 62 and 61 percent of Ford and Chrysler cars, respectively.[9]

All cars of any manufacturer meeting the 1973 federal bumper standards will qualify for car insurance discounts—some as high as 20 percent.

Leasing a car   To decide whether leasing a car for family use is advantageous, you will have to do a little pencil work. Assume, for example, that you are interested in a medium-priced four-door sedan, eight cylinders, air-conditioned, power brakes, automatic transmission, power steering, and radio. The car dealer assumes all the risks, depreciation, repairs, sales tax, license costs, personal property tax, insurance premiums, and all maintenance costs for two years and a maximum of 30,000 miles during the two-year period. You pay for the gasoline and oil changes.

The first problem is to get some facts on the total costs for operating a medium-priced car as described above. The U.S. Department of Transportation prepared an estimate of operating a new 1972 medium-priced car for the first two years (Table 10-2).

These costs of operating a new, medium-priced 1972 automobile are estimates considered to be in the middle range by the Transportation Department. You may have to change some costs, depending on local and state taxes, insurance rates, and other variable factors. Even so, the total costs of $2,325 the first year and $1,795 the second year are probably fairly accurate figures to use. Changes in cost after 1972 will, of course, have to be made.

Now look at a two-year lease contract. In 1972 you could probably have leased a similar model for about $165 to $175 per month for a maximum of 30,000 miles of driving. Assuming a leasing cost of $170 per month, the total cost for two years would be $4,080. Using the U.S. Transportation Department study of the costs of operating a new 1972 medium-priced car as described above, the

8 *Consumer Newsweek,* Aug. 21, 1972.
9 Ibid.

TABLE 10-2 Estimated Cost of Operating a Standard Four-Door Sedan (Two Years)

ITEM	FIRST YEAR (14,500 MILES) Total Cost	SECOND YEAR (13,000 MILES) Total Cost
Costs excluding taxes:		
Depreciation	$1,226.00	$ 900.00
Repair and maintenance	81.84	115.37
Replacement—tires and tubes	17.90	16.05
Accessories	3.21	3.08
Gasoline	286.75	257.16
Oil	11.25	11.25
Insurance	164.00	156.00
Garage, parking, tools, etc.	208.36	199.22
Total	$1,999.31	$1,658.13
Taxes and fees, state:		
Gasoline	$ 74.62	$ 66.92
Registration	30.00	30.00
Titling	177.15	—
Subtotal	$ 281.77	$ 96.92
Taxes and fees, federal:		
Gasoline	$ 42.64	$ 38.24
Oil	0.22	0.22
Auto, tires, tubes, etc.	1.38	1.24
Subtotal	$ 44.24	$ 39.70
Total taxes	$ 326.01	$ 136.62
Total all costs	$2,325.32	$1,794.75

SOURCE: *Cost of Operating an Automobile,* U.S. Department of Transportation, 1972.

total costs for two years will add up to $4,120. Other things being equal, it appears that you will save a small sum by arranging for a two-year lease rather than to buy and trade in. But this is not the whole story. There are several less obvious points to consider when you lease.

You might buy a "lemon" and have expensive repair bills not included in the warranty. Warranties for 1972 were for only one year, in contrast to two-year guarantees in previous years. You also take a chance on the trade-in allowance. At the time you are ready for a trade-in, the market may be soft; or extra heavy driving may cut down your trade-in.

In leasing you may avoid a lump-sum outlay and thus keep your money free for investment. If this is true, and say you can earn $250 in investing over two years, the overall purchase price goes up accordingly.

In leasing, as in buying, it pays to look around. You can do better in leasing a smaller car provided it suits your needs. A Volkswagen can be leased for two years for about $75 a month. You may also prefer to lease a car by the month or by the day.

A final word—if you lease, be sure to read the contract carefully. Contracts are not standard. Automobile manufacturers are presently encouraging dealers to push leasing of cars. Leasing may be to your advantage. You better know exactly what you are getting in return for the monthly payments. If you lease a car, be sure to check the odometer even though the car is new. Odometers are usually inaccurate on the short-of-a-mile side. And since a leasing deal is based ultimately on mileage (usually 15,000 miles a year), it is to your advantage to check the odometer.

SHOPPING FOR A CAR

How to buy a new car

The January through April issues of *Consumer Reports* will contain the ratings of new models. But before you shop around for a new car, sit down with your family and decide what sort of car will fit your needs and budget.

But no matter how hard you bargain, you will probably pay more for next year's model than you would have paid for last year's equivalent.

In contrast to the way the big three auto manufacturers administer prices, the automobile salesroom operates much like a Levantine bazaar. You must go prepared to bargain or risk being fleeced. With few exceptions, new cars carry no set selling price.

No set selling price on new cars

Dealer strategy in many a sales booth is to play down the price of the car and play up the trade-in deal and the financing terms. Don't play that game. Insist on negotiating one deal at a time. First, isolate the price of the car together with the optional accessories you want. It is wise to decide in advance on the make, model, and equipment you want. Essentially, the same automobile, sold with variations in trim and nameplate, may be delivered with a range of sticker prices as wide as $560.

Remember that the sticker price is not the selling price on most cars. Cars customarily sell for less than the total on the sticker. The federal law requires every seller to attach to the left rear window of each car a list price and prices for all extras, such as freight charges and cost of accessories.

If you are negotiating for a car already in the dealer's possession, read the sticker, deduct the freight charge, and then apply a discount of 22 percent for a full-sized car or 18 percent for a compact or intermediate. The result should be quite close to the dealer's cost. [10] If the car must be ordered, have the salesman itemize the sticker price anyway, including the accessories you want.

Here's the way the figures would work out. Say the sticker price for a full-sized V8 was $3,270 with automatic transmission and power steering. Deducting 22 percent, you arrive at a wholesale price of $2,551. Figure $150 to $200 for the dealer, and set your bargaining sights on a final price in the $2,700-to-$2,750 range. If you are dickering for a car that wholesales for $3,500 or more, figure on $300 to $400 over wholesale. You will also, of course, have to add shipping charges and local sales taxes to the final agreed-on price.

Whether or not you can bring yourself to bargain, you make the salesman put his price in writing. The time to do so is before you put down a cash deposit or give him the keys to your old car. Get from him on his company's standard order form an itemized statement of the model you are buying, number

[10] *Car Tax 1972: The New Car Price Authority,* Tax Publications, Inc., New York, 1972. This annual publication gives dealers' costs and manufacturers' suggested retail prices for each model and optional equipment.

of cylinders, engine size, accessories, transportation and makeready charges, sales tax, registration fees, and any special features (such as color) the salesman has promised. Then request that the statement be signed by an official of the firm. That way, a salesman will not be able to "low-ball" you—quote a lower price than he will demand when you come for the new car, on the excuse that the official would not approve his price quotation. And he probably will not try to "pack" the final price with phony or unordered extras.

Ad claims leave readers in the dark

Unfortunately, reading, hearing, or seeing automobile ads will leave readers in the dark about the merits of the car being advertised. When the Federal Trade Commission demanded, in midsummer, 1971, that seven major auto makers document four dozen of their advertising claims so that the public could for the first time see the facts behind the claims, the public showed little interest because the FTC made no effort to translate the technical language into language that would be meaningful to the average citizen. After much pressure from consumer groups, the FTC hired an independent engineering firm (Bolt, Beranek, and Newman) to evaluate the auto firms' documentation of car advertising claims for 1972 cars. The engineering firm found the advertising claims to be "irrelevant, grossly inadequate or contradictory in 20 out of 54 cases." The report which was issued in July, 1972 was so uncomplimentary to the car firms that the FTC declined to release it. A copy of the report was brought to Bess Meyerson's attention, and the New York City Consumer Affairs Commissioner made a public statement on October 6, 1972, forcing the FTC to admit that it had been "sitting on it" since July, 1972.

The important point is that consumers who are in the market to purchase a new car are still not apt to be enlightened by automobile advertising.

Shopping for a used car

Most used cars are on the market because the owners were dissatisfied with them. Nevertheless, a carefully chosen used car can provide relatively low-cost transportation because its high early depreciation has already taken place. Most repairs are likely to cost less than the yearly depreciation on a new or nearly new car. But the older the car, the more likely it is to be in need of repairs.

For average family use, choose from recent models of the compact, intermediate, or lower-priced standard-size cars. Such cars are likely to provide a maximum of trouble-free service per dollar spent; they should burn less fuel than larger cars; and when repairs are needed, the cost is less. Stick to the simple cars—without power-operated options, extra carburetors, boosted compression ratios, and other features.

Do not be fooled by odometer readings or by shiny appearances. Used-car dealers are more likely to spend money on paint, polish, and new floor mats than on mechanical repairs.

Used-car guarantees take various forms. The dealer may guarantee the cost of repairs, including or not including replacement parts, for a specified period, usually 30 days. Or seller and buyer may agree to share repair costs. Whatever the form of guarantee, it should be signed by an officer of the firm. If you are financing your purchase, here are some points to remember.

Carrying charges on used cars nearly always are higher than for new cars.

Shop around for your financing loan. Usually the best source is a commercial bank or credit union.

Buy your insurance separately, not as a part of the time-payment sales contract.

Read the whole contract carefully. Do not sign until all details are written in and you understand them all. Never, of course, sign a blank contract.

Get a signed copy of the contract and file it. If, later, you feel the dealer did not act in good faith, get in touch with your local Better Business Bureau, the frauds division of the attorney general's office, or a lawyer.

If you are not acquainted with average prices on used cars, see the most recent *Annual Guide* of *Consumer Reports.* Dollar figures are usually given for used cars for the last five or six years. The *Annual Guide* will also advise you on on-the-lot tests, driving tests, and a list of used desirable models and undesirable models. For the person not mechanically minded, it may be worthwhile to invest in a final examination by a reliable garage, auto diagnostic center, or independent mechanic. The charge is usually modest, $5 to $25. If there are defects, the mechanic can offer suggestions and give you reliable repair estimates and help you decide whether the car is a good buy. Whether you buy or reject the car, consider his fee as good insurance and continue your search.

Some states require annual and semiannual inspection of all cars using public roads. If your state has inspection requirements, ask the used-car dealer to present evidence for the last inspection. It may be that the previous owner decided to sell the car rather than make all the repairs needed to continue driving the car.

It may be that your state requires used cars to be inspected within seven days or so of registration, but that they do not legally have to be inspected *before* they are sold and registered. If the latter is true, a buyer of a used car may be faced with spending more money to put it into safe operating condition. A car that has been inspected usually carries an inspection sticker. Look for this sticker before buying.

FINANCING A CAR

The most economical way to finance a car is to pay cash. The next best way is to pay as much down as possible in addition to your trade-in allowance. Then arrange to pay the balance in as short a time as possible. The shorter the interest period, the less you pay.

What price credit?

The price you must pay for money to buy a car will vary with the age of the car, where you live, the lender you deal with, and the going rate at the time. The cost of a car loan is generally quoted either as a percentage discount rate or as a finance charge of so many dollars.

Take a little trouble and save a lot

After July 1, 1969, however, the Consumer Credit Protection Act of 1967 required the lender to disclose the cash price of the car, the down payment or trade-in allowance, an itemization of all other charges, the total money actually borrowed, the total finance charge, the number of payments and their amounts and due dates, any extra charges for late payments, and a description of any lien or other security interest kept by the lender on your property. The yardstick for comparing prices will be a figure labeled "annual percentage rate."

The new Consumer Credit Protection Act requires the lender to give you the dollar amount of the finance charge and the annual percentage rate. These facts enable you to shop separately for the lowest-price credit. As a general rule, banks and credit unions are likely to charge lower interest rates than dealers. Pick the deal most advantageous to you (Table 10-3).

When checking the lenders, you are likely to discover these financial facts of life relative to car loans:

1. Auto dealer loans are apt to be pretty expensive.
2. Banks and credit unions are apt to offer the best deals.
3. Consumer finance company loans are likely to be more expensive.

Read the contract Be sure the dealer's contract shows these things:

1. An item-by-item listing of the cost of the car and the accessories
2. Charges for such things as taxes, freight, and dealer preparation
3. The down payment separated into trade-in allowance and cash
4. The unpaid balance

Be sure the addition and subtraction are correct. Check the credit contract to be sure it is filled in and that it shows the following:

1. The total amount to be financed.
2. The annual percentage rate.

TABLE 10-3   What Your Car Loan Will Cost

NUMBER OF MONTHS:		TWELVE		TWENTY-FOUR		THIRTY-SIX	
ANNUAL RATE, PERCENT	LOAN AMOUNT	LOAN COST	MONTHLY PAYMENT	LOAN COST	MONTHLY PAYMENT	LOAN COST	MONTHLY PAYMENT
8	$1,000	$ 43.86	$ 86.99	$ 85.46	$ 45.23	$128.11	$31.34
	2,000	87.72	173.98	170.91	90.46	256.22	62.68
	3,000	131.58	260.97	256.37	135.69	384.33	94.02
9	1,000	49.42	87.46	96.43	45.69	144.79	31.80
	2,000	98.84	174.92	192.87	91.38	289.58	63.60
	3,000	148.25	262.38	289.30	137.07	434.37	95.40
10	1,000	54.99	87.92	107.48	46.15	161.62	32.27
	2,000	109.98	175.84	214.96	92.30	323.24	64.54
	3,000	164.97	263.76	322.43	138.45	484.86	96.81
11	1,000	60.58	88.39	118.59	46.61	178.59	32.74
	2,000	121.16	176.78	237.18	93.22	357.19	65.48
	3,000	181.74	265.17	355.76	139.83	535.78	98.22
12	1,000	66.19	88.85	129.76	47.08	195.72	33.22
	2,000	132.37	177.70	259.53	94.16	391.43	66.44
	3,000	198.56	266.55	389.29	141.24	587.15	99.66

NOTE: This chart will help you decide how much you can afford to spend on a car. It shows what you can save by shopping for the lowest interest rate, by shortening the loan period, or by increasing the down payment. Insurance and other extras aren't included.

SOURCE: *Changing Times*, April, 1972, p. 9.

3.   Any other fees or charges.

4.   The total finance charge—the sum of interest in dollars plus other charges.

5.   The number of monthly payments and the exact amount of each. (Some lenders may have low regular monthly payments, but sock you with a big "balloon" payment that can be twice as much, or more, as the other payments.)

You should also know whether the contract has an acceleration clause that makes all payments due at once, should you fail to make any payments on time. See whether there are penalty charges for late payment and what is considered late payment. Find out what happens if you don't pay promptly. Will you receive fair notice of the lender's intent to repossess the car? And if the car is repossessed and then sold for less than you still owe, will you have to repay interest as well as the balance due?

Owning a car is like having a taxi in which the meter never stops ticking. Even when the car is parked, it costs you something in depreciation, insurance, and financing. Make the meter run a little slower; shop for financing carefully.

The Car-Puter system In case you are too busy to take the time, as suggested earlier, to figure the wholesale cost of the car and model you prefer, thus putting you in an informed position to bargain effectively with the dealer, you may be interested in the Car-Puter system, which makes new cars available to consumers for $125

$125 over factory costs above factory costs.

Arnold Wonsever, president of United Auto Brokers, created this international computerized system, which gives the consumer, for a $7.50 fee, a complete breakdown on the factory price of the car model he wants, including all options desired, along with bargaining power. The prospective purchaser can take his computer print-out to the dealer of his choice, asking that the car be provided at $125 over factory cost. If the dealer refuses, the consumer can buy that car through a Car-Puter affiliated dealer at that price.

So far, neither Consumers Union nor Ralph Nader has found flaws in the Car-Puter system or in Mr. Wonsever's honesty. They prefer to take a "watch and see" attitude toward the system.

Any consumer can get the same information by using the detailed system suggested in Chapter 2 or the shortcut percentage system suggested in this chapter. However, there is no guarantee that the dealer will be willing to sell the car model you want at about $125 over factory cost.

Car warranties More than 9.4 million new vehicles were recalled by automobile manufacturers in 1971 for safety defects—an increase of 8 million over 1970, when 1.2 million cars were recalled, according to the National Highway Traffic Safety Administration. In the first five months of 1972, Ford recalled 436,000 Mercury Montegos and Ford Torinos to install new rear axles and bearings, while General

"They can't make one that works" Motors recalled 350,000 Vegas to prevent a part from falling into the engine linkage and jamming it open.[11] The point of sifting through this wreckage of inefficiency is not to harp on the "bad news" about automobiles, but to point up the need for better warranties for vehicles. To reassure customers that they

[11] *The New York Times,* Apr. 26, 1972, p. 1; May 9, 1972, p. 16.

stand behind their products, many producers offer explicit written warranties on workmanship, materials, and performance.

The warranty concept includes the seller's promise to the buyer, explicit or implied, that the car is for use and salable for the offer. Sellers create an express warranty by describing goods or by displaying a sample exhibit which serves as the basis for exchange. Even if not expressly stated as a warranty, advertising claims and sales claims are evidence of merchantability under the Uniform Commercial Code. Merchantability means that goods are reasonably fit for their intended use and that the buyer relies on the skill and judgment of the seller in selecting and furnishing suitable goods.

Sellers have attempted to limit their legal responsibility by expressly warranting only certain parts and excluding all parts not expressly warranted. Many explicit warranties are efforts to camouflage disclaimers and limitations of the seller's responsibilities which the law would otherwise require. Most express warranties promise to repair or replace defective items, but labor costs for repair may be borne by the retailer rather than by the manufacturer. Damage which might result from the use of a defective product or even destruction of the product itself may be specifically excluded from warranty on the grounds that only certain parts were warranted. In the event of a fire or the destruction of the appliance, this would provide little relief to the injured consumer. Similarly, the exclusion of transportation charges for repairs, the limitation of the warranty period, or the limitation of costs to parts only may substantially injure consumers (rather than competition). Consequently, courts have found for consumers in a number of cases in which the manufacturer has expressly disclaimed responsibility for these losses.

Manufacturers use warranties primarily as a sales tool or as a liability-limitation device. Retailers have also used warranties to generate revenues, reduce sales resistance, and limit their liability.

In 1972 all domestic car manufacturers offered guarantees of 12,000 miles or twelve months, whichever comes first. Tires were excluded from auto warranties because they are covered by tire companies.

The American Motors buyer protection plan promised to repair or replace anything that goes wrong with a 1972 car. Other domestic companies provided free service for only ninety days, but excluded ordinary "wear-and-tear" items like brake linings, clutch plates, windshield wipers, and light bulbs from the guarantees.

The American Motors plan apparently reduced complaints from AMC owners by a substantial amount. Officials of the Department of Transportation and the Center for Auto Safety report significant drop-offs in complaints since the plan started.

AMC scored another first with its offer to reimburse its car buyers up to $15 for food and lodging expenses if a 1973 car is kept overnight for warranty repairs more than 100 miles from the owner's home. If repairs take more than twenty-four hours, the use of a free loan car would be provided. The company has also offered to sell a "double" guarantee for 24,000 miles or twenty-four months, whichever comes first, for $149. All maintenance items like tune-ups and oil changes will also be free.

So far, the big three auto makers haven't tried to compete directly with AMC's unusual warranty. If the other three domestic car manufacturers improve their warranties, Congress is likely to postpone action on the proposed quality-control act suggested by the FTC.

The major purposes of a good warranty are to reduce complaints, and improve the "image" of the company to the end that more cars will be sold. It appears likely that car manufacturers are trying to progress beyond the "snake-oil huckster" morality that condoned the use of warranty language that released companies from responsibility for their deeds. As new vision is granted to consumerists, we can hope that they will hold producers and distributors, as well as courts and regulatory agencies, to standards of social accountability consistent with the responsible use of the scarce and dwindling resources of this good earth.

"Implied warranty" Consumers have a right to collect damages for personal injuries resulting from defects in cars regardless of any time or parts limitation imposed by the warranty, according to the Federal Trade Commission and recent court decisions. Philip Elman, of the FTC, said:

> Section 5 of the FTC Act, prohibiting unfair practices in interstate commerce, precludes automobile manufacturers from using time and mileage limitations, exclusion of successive purchasers and other restrictions and conditions in new car warranties, to limit their liability to remedy any defect in manufacture, whenever and wherever they appear. [12]

Court decisions are supporting Mr. Elman's interpretation in personal injury cases and in the right to obtain satisfaction for repairs authorized by the warranty. In 1967, the owner of a $6,700 Lincoln Continental sued Ford and its dealer in Miami, Florida, for recovery of the price of the car because, he claimed, it was a "lemon." Ford defended itself by quoting the limitations of liability in its warranty. But the Florida Supreme Court ruled that, despite the expressed warranty, the customer may recover damages "on the basis of implied warranty of a product due to its defects and lack of fitness and suitability." [13] The owner of a Chrysler Imperial who took the car back to the dealer thirty-eight times over a sixty-day period to fix a rain leak collected $2,800 from Chrysler Corporation. [14]

It seems that consumers have more legal rights than they think they have. Of course, the consumer is not likely to get the protection he needs unless he sues until Congress enacts some legal remedies, such as some sort of inexpensive compulsory arbitration procedures for settling warranty disputes.

AUTOMOBILE INSURANCE

One of the most controversial consumer battles going on today, at both the state and the federal level, concerns a concept in automobile insurance known as "no-fault." For many years we have accepted the "liability-tort" system, under

[12] *U.S. Consumer,* Nov. 27, 1968.
[13] *Consumer Reports,* April, 1968.
[14] *U.S. Consumer,* Nov. 27, 1968.

which a driver buys insurance to protect himself against possible claims of accident victims. But too much is wrong with this system. In essence it has broken down, and yet for most motorists, unfortunately, "fault" insurance is the only kind available. Thus it is necessary to know how to get the best deal from present expensive, inefficient liability-tort automobile insurance.

No-fault—a controversial idea

As of 1972, only seven states had enacted some form of no-fault auto insurance—Massachusetts, Illinois, Delaware, Florida, New Jersey, Connecticut, and Michigan. In one state, Illinois, the state Supreme Court declared it unconstitutional. None of these states has genuine no-fault insurance. Congress, too, is involved—the Magnuson-Hart bill (S945) seeks to develop a computer model to motivate states to pass their own bills on the basis of generating pressure sufficient for the legislatures to meet the federal bill standard or be forced to accept the federal law. Meanwhile, most owners of automobiles will have to protect themselves via the expensive and inefficient liability-tort insurance plans.

Consumer discontent with increasing costs, long settlement periods, and policy cancellations has led to discussions and investigations of the present system of automobile insurance. Government inquiries, at both the federal and local levels, have been initiated. More will be said about auto insurance reform proposals following a review of how to shop for car insurance policies which are presently available in most states.

Kinds of insurance coverage

There are five kinds of insurance coverage that a prudent person should weigh carefully: liability, medical payments, uninsured motorist, collision, and comprehensive. Liability and collision insurance are the most expensive.

Liability insurance

Liability insurance covers bodily injury liability and property-damage liability. Bodily injury liability coverage pays the sum for which the car owner becomes legally liable if his car injures someone. Property-damage liability pays the amount for which the car owner becomes legally liable for damage to property —another car, a telephone pole, a building. Liability insurance is the heart of an automobile insurance policy. No prudent person would drive even temporarily without liability insurance, and in some states it is compulsory. Liability insurance also pays the cost of legal defense. The practical question is what liability limits to carry.

The insurance company pays no more than the amounts specified in a policy. Liability limits are usually described by a series of three numbers separated by diagonal lines—for example, 10/20/5. This set of numbers describes a policy that pays a maximum of $10,000 for bodily injury to one person, a maximum of $20,000 for bodily injury to more than one person, and a maximum of $5,000 for property damage in one occurrence.

Insurance companies offer liability up to 300/500/100 and even higher. The difference in the cost of liability of 10/20/5 (around $100) and liability of 50/100/5 coverage is usually small. No matter where you live, be sure to meet the requirements of the financial-responsibility laws of the states in which you drive.

The relative costs of various liability coverages are:

If 10/20/5 liability coverage costs $100, then—
20/40/5 coverage will usually cost about $109
25/50/5 coverage will usually cost about $112
50/100/10 coverage will usually cost about $119

Medical payments insurance

This insurance ($2,000 coverage may cost around $10) pays medical and hospital bills, and funeral expenses if there is a death in an automobile accident, regardless of fault. This is good insurance since it protects all passengers in the car. It is not a duplication of your medical and hospital insurance.

Comprehensive physical damage insurance

This insurance pays for loss if your car is stolen, damaged, or destroyed by fire, hail, hurricane, and most other causes, and also pays for losses due to vandalism. This policy does not pay for collisions, mechanical breakdown, wear and tear, or freezing.

Driving without comprehensive insurance is a gamble, but full comprehensive coverage is quite expensive. A $50 deductible provision (the car owner pays the first $50 loss) may be available at about 55 percent of the full-coverage rate. The cost of such a policy depends on where the car owner lives and on the age of the car.

Collision insurance

This insurance covers damages to a car if it is upset or hit by another car or fixed object. Collision coverage is valuable primarily for losses due to an upset that is not the fault of someone else or where the question of fault is debatable.

Full coverage on collision is expensive. Collision rates vary with the age of the car. The rate for new models is based on the original factory price of the car. Last year's models may pay off at only 87.5 percent of the original factory price. The premium remains the same. A point is eventually reached where the premium is out of all proportion to the coverage. Consequently, a car more than four years old may have too little coverage compared to the premium paid.

Full collision coverage is rarely offered and is very expensive. Coverage with the first $50 or $100 of the damage deductible is generally purchased—in which event you pay the first $50 or $100 of the repair costs and the company pays any balance.

If full-coverage collision insurance is priced at $300, then—
$50 deductible coverage will cost about $75
$100 deductible coverage will cost about $45 to $60
If $100 deductible collision insurance is priced at $50, then—
$250 deductible coverage will cost about $30
$500 deductible coverage will cost about $30

Uninsured motorist insurance

This more recent form of coverage insures the driver and passengers against injury by a driver who carries no insurance or by a hit-and-run driver. It is automatically included in some policies. The premium is small because the risk is small.

Premiums based on classes of drivers

Insurance companies set up classes of drivers and assign each class a rate based on its own accident and claims record. The class depends on the use made of the car and on the age of the male driver. Premiums vary also according to the place of residence, and for comprehensive and collision coverage they vary with the value of the car.

Premiums are generally lowest if the car is driven only tor pleasure, with no male driver under 25 years of age. A single male driver under the age of 25 will pay about two or three times as much as a single male driver over 25.

Preferred risks

For years many insurance companies have cut rates for drivers who passed stiff eligibility tests. The criteria among companies vary, but these are the most common: (1) driving record, (2) occupation, (3) driver under 25 years or over 65, (4) alcoholism or physical handicap, (5) condition of car, and (6) merit rating if the insured has avoided traffic trouble. Discounts in premium, if a driver qualifies, generally range from 10 to 25 percent below the company standard rates.

Special or package policies

Some insurance companies offer a package of various kinds of insurance, which usually costs less than if selected separately. Strictly speaking, however, the differences in premiums on standard policies and on the special or package deals are not comparable because of the differences in coverage. Then, too, maybe a car owner wants only liability coverage. The premium for a standard liability policy would be less than the package would cost. On the other hand, if a car owner wants to combine comprehensive and collision insurance, the package savings may run to around 15 percent.

Some companies combine the special or package deal and the merit-rating plan. In 1962, one large automobile insurance company announced that good school grades would get California students and their parents a 20 percent discount in auto insurance. California was selected as the first state for the program because state laws there permitted immediate introduction of the new plan.

What insurance coverage do you need?

If insurance is purchased through the dealer who sells the car, you will usually get only collision and comprehensive coverage. If the car is a late model, buy liability insurance before driving it off the lot. Here is the order in which some automobile experts rate the need for various kinds of coverage.

1. *Liability.* A must for all drivers. Awards of $50,000 are common, and verdicts run much higher at times. Buy 50/100/5 if you can afford it.

2. *Comprehensive physical damage.* A must on a new car. You might omit comprehensive on an old car if you can absorb the loss. Repair costs are usually higher than the value of an old car.

3. *Collision.* A good idea for a late-model car that you own outright. Repair costs run high. If you need to economize, you might omit it for an older car. If you need this insurance, buy a $50 or $100 deductible policy.

4. *Medical payments.* Some motorists can do without this protection. It may be worth the premium if the family is large or in case of carpool driving.

5. *Uninsured motorists.* Inexpensive but the risk is very small.

Shopping for insurance rates

To aid you in comparing automobile insurance rates, make out a chart (similar to Table 10-4, Policy Specifications Chart) for each company you select for bids. Then select the coverages you want. When asking for and comparing rates, be sure that they are for the same coverage.

After receiving the bids, record them on a blank similar to Table 10-5, Rate Comparison Blank. The lowest rate quoted is not necessarily the best buy. Give some consideration to membership fees, service, discount for two or more cars, premium rates, cancellation and renewal record. Also check on the financial stability record of each company in *Best's Insurance Guide*. The Consumers Union recommended list of automobile insurance companies will still be useful.[15]

Safe-driver policies

Other things being equal, including comparative costs, give some preference to a policy *without* a safe-driver or merit rating plan, says *Consumer Reports*. The magazine points out that you could easily lose the advantage of a lower rate. These plans charge lower rates to drivers with good records and raise the rates of others. Many of these plans base your rate on the driving records of members of your family over a period of two or more years. Some plans raise the rate on the basis of accidents or claims. Some exclude certain types of accidents which are not your fault. Your driving record may thus earn you the minimum rate under one plan and subject you to large surcharges under another.

Many companies use a point rating system for each chargeable accident,

[15] *Consumer Reports,* June, 1962.

TABLE 10-4   Policy Specifications Chart

TYPE OF COVERAGE	FAMILY OR INDEPENDENT POLICIES	SPECIAL OR PACKAGE POLICIES
Liability	Limits: ____ / ____ / ____	$____,000
Medical	$500	$____,000
Uninsured motorist	Yes	Yes
Collision	$____ deductible	$____ deductible
Comprehensive	Full coverage	Full coverage
Towing	Yes	Included with collision or comprehensive
Other	None	None

SOURCE: *Consumer Reports,* June, 1962.

TABLE 10-5   Rate Comparison Blank

Name of company					
Safe-driver or merit rating (yes or no)					
Liability	$	$	$	$	$
Medical	$	$	$	$	$
Uninsured motorist	$	$	$	$	$
Collision	$	$	$	$	$
Comprehensive	$	$	$	$	$
Towing	$	$	$	$	$
Total	$	$	$	$	$
Membership fees	$	$	$	$	$

SOURCE: *Consumer Reports*, June, 1962.

and one, two, or three points for serious traffic-law violations. Under this system, your rate might be set as follows:

POINTS	EFFECTIVE RATE
0	None
1	30% surcharge over base rate
2	70% surcharge over base rate
3	120% surcharge over base rate
4 or more	180% surcharge over base rate

Auto insurance reform needed

Clearly, reform is needed. The current system of tort liability is "an absolute scandal," said Virginia Knauer, Special Assistant to the President for Consumer Affairs, on June 16, 1972, when talking to the National Association of Insurance Commissioners. Under our present system, she said:

"Outrageously expensive"

One out of four accident victims never gets a dime. The accident victim who does get paid has to wait an average of 15 months for his money. Out of every dollar spent for liability insurance premiums, accident victims get back only 44 cents. Lawyers and claims adjusters get about 25 cents out of every premium dollar. The system is appallingly inefficient and . . . it is outrageously expensive.

Since 1960, the cost of insuring a car in this country has risen an average of 83 percent, according to the Consumer Price Index. If your family includes a teen-age driver, premiums of $1,000 a year are not unheard of, as shown by Table 10-6.

No-fault car insurance

Of all the proposed reforms to reduce the cost of delivering benefits, the

TABLE 10-6   How Annual Premiums Escalate*

	INCREASE	TOTAL
Married couple (45 years old with a good driving record, living in a Chicago suburb, and driving a 1972 Ford Galaxie for pleasure only).		$237
Family moves to the city of Chicago.	+$217	$454
Husband now drives more than 10 miles to work.	+$182	$636
Husband has one accident involving more than $100 damage.	+$181	$817
Their son (18 years old) completes driver training and is permitted to drive the family car.	+$409	$1,226
Son is involved in an accident, involving more than $100 damage.	+$227	$1,453

* Insurance includes $10,000 per person or $20,000 per accident bodily injury liability, $5,000 property damage liability, $500 medical payments, $100 deductible collision, and comprehensive. (From rates published by Insurance Services Office of New York.)

no-fault concept for personal injury compensation has received the most discussion.

Some states, as we said, have already adopted it as law; others are currently examining it in various forms.

"An idea whose time has come"

In short, with no fault insurance the element of "blame" is minimized. In the event of an accident, you deal directly with your own insurance company. The need for costly, time-consuming litigation to determine who's at fault is substantially reduced. That, of course, releases the courts and judges for more important legal matters—such as those involving schools, enforcement provisions, taxes, felonies involving drugs, and homicide and crime in the streets, to name only a few.

A case in point: the Massachusetts story

Massachusetts adopted a no-fault plan in January, 1971. How is it working after a year's experience? Here's what a national weekly news magazine reported in its January 3, 1972, issue:

> After one year, this State's No-Fault auto-insurance plan seems to be working better than many expected. Though some experts say it's too soon to make a final judgment, this much appears certain:
> • Premiums are coming down dramatically for insurance against bodily injuries.
> • Settlements to injured motorists are being made faster than under the old system.
> • Inflated claims and bitter lawsuits are fewer and far between.

Specifically, the article said, "Bodily-injury premiums were cut 15 percent when the plan started. A further 27.6 percent reduction in these premiums has been decreed for 1972."

The article also quoted Massachusetts State Insurance Commissioner John G. Ryan: "Now we are taking the profit out of auto accidents. And the claims that are being made aren't inflated. Most people only want to get what everybody else is getting." Mr. Ryan said that during the first nine months the no-fault plan was in effect, the number of bodily-injury claims paid was down 50 percent from the year before and that the average cost per claim dipped from $419 in 1970 to $165 in 1971.

Phony no-fault laws

In most of the states presently having no-fault insurance, the laws are labeled "no-fault," but in fact invite just as many lawsuits as before. These phony no-fault laws, supported largely by the trial lawyers' lobbying, will undoubtedly be recognized for what they are worth in due time. Meanwhile, the federal Magnuson-Hart bill and other federal bills are likely to receive more attention from the public.

No-fault insurance — what the experts say

Consumers Union, the nonprofit publisher of *Consumer Reports,* has recommended fourteen objectives which should be met by any reform plan.[16] The article also tells which of the major reform plans incorporate these principles and which do not. (See the full text in *Auto Insurance: The Road to Reform,* Taylor-Troelstrup Reading 69.)

As the experts see it, there are advantages and disadvantages to no-fault insurance.

[16] *Consumer Reports,* April, 1971, pp. 225–226.

Major advantages

1. It speeds up compensation for losses. You deal directly with your own insurance company, and in most cases there is no need to determine fault.

2. It reduces congestion in the courts. The need for court decisions in most accident situations is substantially reduced.

3. It provides for more proportionate compensation. Payments are directly related to losses; i.e., medical expenses, lost wages, etc., are not dependent on the question of fault or the willingness and ability of the injured party to pursue legal action.

4. It results in lower insurance premiums because of reduced administrative and legal costs.

Major disadvantages

1. Most no-fault systems restrict in some manner an injured party's right to sue. Any restriction will cause some injured parties to be denied adequate compensation in situations where it can be argued that the injured party should not be further compensated.

2. There are wide variations in proposed no-fault systems. The proposals differ greatly in features and potential benefits.

3. There is no consensus on the question of what the ideal no-fault package of benefits should be.

4. The relationship between fault and liability is reduced. Critics of no-fault assert that this is morally undesirable and would encourage some persons to drive recklessly.

Nevertheless, no-fault's strengths far outweigh its weaknesses. The least that should be done is to encourage legislatures to investigate no-fault, adopt genuine no-fault principles in law, and put no-fault on a trial basis for two or three years. With experience, one hopes the optimum plan will emerge. If the legislatures buckle under pressures from the Trial Lawyers' Association and other pressure groups who stand to gain by the present tort-liability system, the only alternative is a uniform federal no-fault plan for all states.

Motor Vehicle Safety Act of 1966 In carrying out the safer-car idea, the federal law requires the National Highway Safety Bureau to write standards of safety in vehicles that are "reasonable and practical." The first safety standards for cars were supposed to be issued on or before January 31, 1967, covering 1968 cars, and before January 31, 1968, to cover 1969 and 1970 cars. No more such restrictive deadlines exist for new-car standards. Henceforth the bureau can initiate new standards at its leisure. The bureau policy is to seek out standards in areas where something can be accomplished quickly. Tamperproof odometers and radiator caps were not very important requirements in improving the safety of the car. The bureau works now on basic needs, such as requirements for bumper effectiveness, for auto-body energy-absorption and crush characteristics, and for limiting intrusion of the car structure into the interior. Engineers also say that there is need for new standards for steering performance, for greater protection to occupants in rollovers, against penetration of carbon monoxide into the passenger compartment, and for tire standards, to suggest a few. Ralph Nader, crusader for safer cars, wrote a letter to the bureau in September, 1968, in which he accused the bureau of laxness in determining compliance with its tire standards, seat belts, outside rear-view mirrors, and brakes. This delay in carrying out needed changes to make cars safer may be due to lack of funds for research and enforcement as much as to inertia and pressure from the automobile industry.

Auto recalls: caveat vendor

For all its vaunted management talent and technological capability, the auto industry is having increasing trouble building cars that hold together. Since the federal government went into the car safety business in 1966, more than 26 million cars and trucks have been recalled for safety defects, about 10 percent of them foreign imports (end of 1971).[17]

In 1971 alone, American manufacturers recalled 8,790,286 cars. The largest single safety defect campaign was General Motor's recall of 6.7 million Chevrolet cars and trucks because of potentially dangerous engine-mount failure. And GM doesn't seem to be faring too well with its Vega, which was recalled for the third time in July, 1971.

Ford owners have had their troubles too. Owners of 1972 Ford Torinos, Mercury Montegos, and Ford Rancheros received two recall notices relating to failure of rear-axle bearings. And on June 20, 1972, Ford announced its largest recall—4,370,000 1970 and 1971 passenger cars and Ranchero car-style pickup trucks—to correct a safety defect in the shoulder harness.

"A stitch in time saves nine"

Under present law, the manufacturer does not have to pay for necessary repairs. The car owner must pay for the manufacturer's error unless the company offers to pick up the tab. (It is estimated that GM will spend between $25 million and $30 million on the engine-mount recall.) A bill to make the auto industry pay for all recall repairs was introduced by Senators Walter Mondale (Democrat from Minnesota) and Gaylord Nelson (Democrat from Wisconsin) in 1971, but it met Commerce Department opposition and was given no immediate chance of passage.

Under present law, defect notification letters are sent out by registered mail when a car or tire manufacturer determines that its equipment is defective. Letters are also sent when the National Highway Traffic Safety Administration finds a defect that could be a safety hazard. Letters must describe the defect and explain what safety risks are involved and the measures that must be taken to repair the defect. Transportation officials report that many notification letters have fallen short of the requirements, and they have thus offered regulations establishing guidelines for these letters.

U.S. 1973 safety standards for cars

The 1973 federal safety standards include four items. One is that front bumpers must be able to withstand up to a 5-mile-per-hour frontal impact, and the rear bumpers up to a 2.5-mile-per-hour rear impact, into a flat, vertical, fixed barrier without impairment of the normal operation of the car's latching, fuel, cooling, lighting, and exhaust systems. Oldsmobiles have a hydraulic front-bumper system which retracts on minor impact, with the grille moving out of the way, while most other automobiles have some type of impact-absorbing bumper.

---

[17] *The New York Times,* June 25, 1972, sec. 3, p. 1. Data from the National Highway Traffic Safety Administration (NHTSA).

The second requirement is that "automobile interiors must have a burn rate limit of not more than four inches per minute under special specific laboratory criteria."

Another standard says that "all cars must meet a side door minimum strength requirement." This allows for a "peak crush resistance of not less than twice the vehicle's curb weight or 7,000 lbs., whichever is less. Ford Motor Company has equipped its cars with a steel "Guard Rail." This rail has energy-absorbing qualities which in an accident can cause vehicles to be deflected away from each other.

The fourth requirement provides for "illumination of all controls for heating, air conditioning, windshield wiper speed control and hazard warning control (if not located on the steering column)."

These small but important safety features will have at least two good effects for consumers. First, many lives will be saved, and injuries will be less serious. Second, it is estimated that "at least half the motorists buying 1973 cars can expect to pay 10 percent less for collision insurance than those driving comparable 1972 models," according to the Insurance Services Office, which sets or advises on insurance rates for some 40 percent of the nation's cars.[18]

Social responsibility
All adults have social responsibilities in the American system. During the past decade, however, exposure to unsafe new automobiles by the millions; fraudulent car repairs by a countless number of mechanics; selfish trial lawyers thinking only of their shrinking incomes, should true no-fault car insurance replace the inefficient, costly liability-tort system; the improper use of flat-rate manuals that tell the time it takes to make every conceivable repair job; the failure of auto designers to protect cars against damage resulting from low-speed collisions, while gearing their efforts toward the consumer in the showroom; the successful attempts of the automobile executives to reduce the pollution-control standards established by the federal government; the brazen effort of a government agency (the FTC) to sit on an engineering report which it had contracted for and which contained evidence of very little substantiation of automobile advertising claims; willful violation of car warranties[19]; Ford's "doctoring" of the 1973 test cars to make sure they would pass the emission standards of the federal government—all such exposures make a mockery of social responsibility.

Consumers, too, have social responsibilities relative to our total automobile transportation system. They are:

1. *Drive safely.* In 1970 there were an estimated 16 million accidents involving 27.7 million vehicles. And in the first eleven months of 1971 there were 50,170 fatalities, as compared with 49,940 for the corresponding period in 1970 (National Safety Council figures).

2. *Use the safety belts that are in your car.* Studies by the Highway Safety Research Center of the University of North Carolina indicate that lap belts reduce serious and fatal injuries by 43 percent.

---

[18] *The Wall Street Journal,* July 7, 1972, p. 19.
[19] The innovative buyer protection plan for 1972 American Motor cars shows promise of eliminating some of the problems which have surfaced most often since 1969.

3. *Don't drink and drive.* According to the National Highway Traffic Safety Administration of the Department of Transportation, 50 percent of the traffic fatalities in 1971 involved alcohol.

4. *Make your views known.* Let your congressmen, elected state and local representatives, and government agencies established to carry out the intent of the laws and regulations know how you feel when the political system breaks down.

Of course, social responsibilities are difficult to define, but industry and business will end up increasing their social responsibility in self-defense, if for no other reason. Senator Warren G. Magnuson recently said this: "Today industry must submit annually to a fiscal audit; tomorrow it will undoubtedly be forced to submit, if not done voluntarily, to a new kind of audit: A social audit."[20]

QUESTIONS FOR DISCUSSION

1. What steps usually take place before a car recall is put into effect? What role is played by the NHTSA? The manufacturer? The dealer? The car owner?

2. What are some of the things that are wrong with the current liability-tort car insurance system?

3. Is proving fraud in car repair a difficult task? Explain.

4. Could repair costs be reduced if the auto industry designed "repair-ability" into its products? Explain.

5. What are the different ways in which one can finance a car? Which method is most advantageous to you?

6. What are the provisions of the Clean Air Act, authored by Senator Edmund Muskie (S.4012), which became Public Law 91-36 on July 10, 1970? What auto pollution standards have been set forth as a result of this act? What has been industry's position regarding these pollution standards?

PROJECTS

1. Draw up some guidelines to follow in buying tires for your car. How would you go about researching this matter? What sources of information would you consult? What is the government doing in the area of the labeling and grading of tires? What standards has the government set forth for tire safety? (See the *Federal Register*, Dec. 23, 1971, p. 24824; "Tires," *Consumer Reports*, August, 1971.)

2. What are the provisions of the National Traffic and Motor Vehicle Safety Act of 1966? What safety standards have been established by the NHTSA

[20] Ralph M. Gaedeke and Warren W. Etcheson, *Consumerism*, Harper & Row, Publishers, Incorporated, New York, 1972, p. 6.

for bumpers (see pp. 206–207)? For crash survivability (see pp. 246–250)? For children's car seats (Standard no. 13)? (See National Highway Traffic Safety Administration, *What to Buy in Child Restraint Systems;* available from the Superintendent of Documents, Government Printing Office, Washington, D.C. 20402, 20 cents.) What changes have been made in the original safety regulations? Why have they been made?

3.   Using the model outline in Taylor-Troelstrup Reading 17, dealing with how to purchase a new car, find out how much the car dealer paid for the model and accessories desired, shipping charges, etc. Add all these costs, and you know how much the dealer paid for that particular car. Allow the dealer a profit of from $125 to $200. How much do you think you saved by taking the time necessary to "bargain" informatively?

4.   What suggestions can you make for improving the auto insurance industry? If you were asked to propose a plan for reforming the industry, what features would you include?

5.   Virginia Knauer, advisor to the President on consumer affairs, wrote: "Too many consumers have paid for unnecessary repairs made with unsatisfactory results. I am sure you will agree with me that these experiences on the part of many Americans are intolerable. We must remove this burden and one way we can do it is by stimulating service competition through independent, objective evaluations." She asked consumers to draw up a list of recommendations for a public rating system for garages to use in future discussions with dealers and auto manufacturers. In another letter, dated October 1, 1971, and sent out to auto manufacturers and the NADA, she urged manufacturers to "provide additional incentives for better dealer service above and beyond fair compensation for in-warranty repairs."

If these letters were addressed to you, what recommendations would you suggest? Be as specific as possible.

6.   More than 9.4 million vehicles were recalled by manufacturers in 1971 for safety defects, an increase of 8 million over 1970, according to NHTSA figures. How is the car owner notified of his car's defect? Who pays for the repair? What steps usually take place before a recall is put into effect? (See "Chevrolet's Failing Engine Mounts," *Consumer Reports,* February, 1972, pp. 118–121.)

SUGGESTED READINGS

Automobile Insurance . . . for Whose Benefit? State of New York Insurance Department, New York, 1970.

How to Buy a Used Car, Consumers Union, Inc., Mount Vernon, N.Y., 1972.

"How to Find an Honest Repairman," *Family Circle,* March, 1972, pp. 99, 132, 134, 136.

Maynes, E. Scott, and C. Arthur Williams, Jr. (eds.): "Fault or No Fault?" *Proceedings of a National Conference on Automobile Insurance Reform, 1970,* University of Minnesota, Department of Conferences and Institutes, Minneapolis, 1971.

Nader, Ralph, Lowell Dodge, and Ralph Hotchkiss: *What to Do with Your Bad Car,* Grossman Publishers, New York, 1971.

O'Connell, Jeffrey: *The Injury Industry and the Remedy of No-Fault Auto Insurance,* Consumers Union, Inc., Mount Vernon, N.Y., 1972.

Randall, Donald A., and Arthur P. Glickman: *The Great American Auto Repair Robbery,* Charterhouse Books, Inc., New York, 1972.

Report of the Federal Trade Commission on Automobile Warranties, February, 1970.

CHAPTER 11
BUYING GOOD HEALTH CARE AND SERVICES

*A*merica's health care system is seriously ill, a victim of long neglect and in desperate need of an adequate cure. Saving it will not be easy, but its rescue is essential.

The present health care crisis results from an accumulation of closely related and complex problems that center around a severe shortage of medical manpower, a frightening increase in medical care costs, and the resultant lack of effective services.

Putting this clinical assessment in human terms means that thousands of Americans are dying who could be saved, hundreds of thousands are going without proper medical care, and millions are burdened with bills they just cannot afford to pay.

America can be proud of its world leadership in health technology, but when it comes to delivering health care, we rank behind many less affluent nations of the world. Some of our rankings are shameful: tenth in female life expectancy, thirteenth in infant mortality, and seventeenth in life expectance for males. In delivery of health care to our people, America is an "also-ran."

The reasons for these figures can be found in other, more telling statistics:

1. The United States is short an estimated 50,000 doctors and has a total medical manpower deficit of 512,000 physicians, nurses, technicians, and other health professionals. There is also great disparity in the distribution of the available doctor supply.

2. Nationwide, there are 141 doctors for every 100,000 people, but the availability varies greatly from state to state. New York has 219 physicians for every 100,000 people; Minnesota, 143; and Mississippi, 73. More than 130 counties in this country have no doctors at all.

3. Ten years ago the average American spent $145 a year for medical care. In 1971 he spent $345—an increase of more than 150 percent, compared with a Consumer Price Index increase of less than 33 percent over the same period of time.

4. In 1964 the average daily cost per hospital patient was $38. In 1971 it reached $92 ($100 in Minneapolis), and not all these costs were covered by insurance. About one out of every five Americans under 65 has neither hospital nor surgical insurance. More than half of all Americans in the same group have no coverage for medical bills incurred outside a hospital.

All these facts make it painfully clear that we must restore health to our health care system. But how should we do it? How can an individual or family cope with these high costs?

Budgeting for health care: families live in fear

The need for better health care is felt by nearly every individual and family in this country. It cuts across all political, social, economic, and geographic lines—it affects rich and poor, black and white, old and young, urban and rural dwellers.

Almost every family knows the cruel burden of worry, frustration, and disappointment that marks our search for better health care at a price we can afford. The average American lives in dread of illness and disability. He lives with the uncertainty of not knowing whether to seek medical care, when to seek it, or how to obtain it. He lives with postponements and delays. Above all, he lives in fear of the cost of health care.

Private health insurance —more loophole than protection

Despite massive sales of private health insurance, most of the expenditures for personal health services must still be borne out-of-pocket by the patient at the time of illness or as a debt. Nearly all private health insurance is limited. Despite the fact that health insurance is a more than $15-billion industry, benefit payments meet only about one-third of the private costs of health care, leaving about two-thirds to be paid outside the framework of health insurance.

Families cannot obtain adequate health security from private health insurance. Why? It provides sickness insurance, not health insurance; acute care, not preventive care. It gives partial benefits, not comprehensive benefits. It fails to control costs and quality of care. It ignores the poor and the medically indigent.

Far too often, the catastrophe of serious illness is accompanied by the fear of financial ruin. Private health insurance today is more loophole than protection.

These are not the problems of some small sector of our society. These are not the problems of only the poor, the handicapped, or the chronically ill or of those in the inner city, small towns, or rural areas. These are the problems of people throughout our country.

Can a family budget for health care today?

There is unpredictability of risk for the individual and some predictability of risk for a group; the larger the group, the more accurate the prediction can be. Therefore, under our present systems or ways of securing health care, perhaps most persons and families can budget for only a small part of their health care expenditures. How much? Some experts say a family should set aside from 8 to 12 percent of its take-home pay (including personal deduction for a group health care plan by the employer). But it takes more than building up a reserve fund in a 5 percent savings account. For many families there are multiple decisions that need to be made:

1. What is the best kind of health care protection available to me in the community or area?
2. How much does it cost? Can I afford it?
3. What are the limitations or loopholes?
4. Is the available health care plan for profit? Nonprofit? Prepaid? Is it cooperative? Blue Cross–Blue Shield? Preventive medicine?
5. How inclusive is the health care protection?

Many other questions are likely to come to mind when you are deciding how much to set aside each month for health care. For example, family members who use alcohol, drugs, and cigarettes; who do not practice good, nutritional eating habits; who neglect regular health examinations and dental care; who use over-the-counter drugs and high-cost prescription drugs without some investigation; who habitually drive dangerously—all are, without much doubt, good candidates for above-average medical care and costs. For these persons, especially, budgeting for health care is a gamble because there are too many unknown cost factors.

Good health practices are a basic responsibility of the individual. This means a proper diet and adequate exercise and rest for each family member. It means regular physical checkups, as well as consulting a physician or dentist promptly when the need arises. You may be so lucky as to live in a community or area that has a group health cooperative (GHC)—a consumer-owned nonprofit health maintenance medical care system that offers prepaid comprehensive medical care for a family of four for about $44 per month plus membership. Or you may be near a Kaiser-Permanente, the largest noncooperative group health plan in the country, which may cost a little less than the GHC but which does not offer quite as much coverage for drugs, X rays, lab fees, house calls, and psychiatric care. You may also be fortunate enough to live in the New York City area, where the well-known Health Insurance Plan of Greater New York (HIP) provides prepaid, comprehensive health care for subscribers. HIP, too, practices preventive medicine. The most recent health care service available in communities in increasing numbers is the health maintenance organization (HMO). These are health maintenance centers that provide comprehensive health services to an enrolled group of individuals or families for a prepaid annual fee. The HMO, too, emphasizes preventive care, outpatient service, continuity of care, and cost effectiveness.

These examples of health care and health maintenance systems will be examined in detail later. Unfortunately, only a small percentage of people live close enough to them to be able to utilize their facilities. The rest of us have to consult solo practitioners, who operate under the very expensive fee-for-service system, or group-practice organizations, which emphasize efforts to *cure* present ills, rather than practice *preventive* health care service.

The medical maze

Thus we have mostly fragmentation of services among specialists, physicians, hospitals, nursing homes, clinics, solo practitioners, health insurance, laboratories, pharmacies, public and private institutions, for-profit and nonprofit services, and free care for members of the armed services and others. Such disorganized service is very costly and, on the whole, not conducive to good medical care and service. Each of these parts acts as an independent business. This system does not organize itself around a "patient" to offer preventive care, nor does it adequately organize itself around him to meet his health needs if he becomes ill.

Most physicians are in solo practice in this country. If you need a specialist, one physician refers you to another. You probably have to review your health history for the specialist. Sometimes the same X rays and other tests are repeated by the second physician. Neither physician sees it as his business to keep track of the entire course of your care or the total cost to you. There are exceptions, of course.

Solo practice—expensive and inefficient

Similarly, hospitals, nursing homes, laboratories, and other health organizations frequently act as independent businesses. Financing arrangements are no less difficult. The health insurance agent is not obligated to tell you accurately how his policy fits into Blue Cross–Blue Shield, Medicare, or any other policies. So, in fact, a patient has no way of figuring his benefits from various kinds of health protection until he sees his bills. And then he must assume all responsibilities for evaluating the contracts and must do what he has to do pretty much on his own. For the elderly, the disabled, and those with limited income and education, this is almost an impossible job.

This lack of coordination reveals the inefficiencies and higher costs of our fragmented system. The combination of solo practice and specialization contributes heavily to the fragmentation. We had more "one-man businesses" in health care in 1970 than we did in 1963—in fact, about fifteen thousand more.

One of the tragic results of this fragmentation is the fact that such a health care system operates in ways which keep us from getting information that might enable us to choose the best care. There is no *Consumer Reports* in health care as generally practiced here at this time. Health care institutions do not advertise to inform us of their advantages, and insurance companies, even Blue Cross and Blue Shield, do not make public their criteria for reviewing bills for reasonableness of the care offered, nor do they reveal those who offer questionable services. The attitude is "don't rock the boat." Computer screening of insurance claims by Blue Cross–Blue Shield, for example, could detect fraud, excessive services, and unreasonable charges. But this information is not given to the insured person. Finally, fragmentation does not lend itself to review of medical practice by capable health professionals—a neglect that does not assure quality care.

HOW CONSUMERS GET CLOBBERED

Senator Hart's antitrust subcommittee in 1971 and 1972 zeroed in on Medicare frauds and health costs and other medical abuses involving the aged. This subcommittee found (1) hospital officials who load their hospitals with costly, often unnecessary medical equipment bought from firms that pay them "consultant fees"; (2) doctors who charge unknowing patients for fake services and who otherwise run up bills beyond what the insurance will allow; and (3) blood banks which receive free blood from volunteers and then, for a big fee, allow hospitals to sell the extra blood.

Compelled to buy prescriptions blindfolded

No competition permitted

Many prescription-drug price surveys have been taken by federal, state, and private organizations in the last twenty-five years. In all these surveys, the evidence was clear—price gouging. Surveying prices in Chicago in 1967, the American Medical Association discovered differentials as high as 1,200 percent. Later studies, including one by Consumers Union[1] and others by newspapers, a congressional subcommittee, and a drug chain, turned up spreads for one or more drugs as much as 840 percent. In other words, you might pay $1 to have a prescription filled in one drugstore and $12 to have the same prescription filled in another drugstore in the same city. How could this be? The answer is that there is no price competition because drug prices cannot be advertised in thirty-four states; some states even forbid drugstores to advertise the fact that they give discounts. The cost to the public of the lack of price competition is enormous—in a single recent year, over $4 billion was spent for prescription drugs.[2] In its

[1] *Consumer Reports,* May, 1970; March, 1972, pp. 136–140.
[2] *Consumer Reports,* March, 1972, pp. 136–140.

March, 1972, issue, *Consumer Reports* describes the ordeal of Osco Drug, Inc., a retail chain with 178 pharmacies in seventeen states. About a year ago, the city of Boston adopted a law requiring drugstores to post prices of a list of about one hundred prescription drugs. Osco, which had been considering posting drug prices in all its stores, put up price lists in its new Boston stores. Public response was so favorable that last fall, Osco began posting price lists in all 178 of its stores.

All hell broke loose. In half a dozen states, the boards of pharmacy (which are official state regulatory bodies traditionally dominated by proprietors of independent pharmacies) began proceedings to suspend Osco licenses. In other states, the pharmaceutical associations threatened legal action. Osco found itself blacklisted in pharmacy schools when it went recruiting. Its pharmacists were threatened with loss of their individual licenses. Other drugstores began refusing to give Osco the prescriptions of customers who wanted to transfer their business to Osco.

"Here were vigilante tactics with a vengeance," comments *Consumer Reports,* which went on to report similar experiences endured by smaller cut-rate prescription drugstore chains.

Most of the thirty-four state laws are on the books because the pharmaceutical organizations lobbied them into the statutes. The pharmacists take a pretty moralistic tone about them. A recent policy statement by the American Pharmaceutical Association says:

> By definition, prescription medication is available only upon the prescription of a lawful prescriber Increasing the demand for such drugs by promotional activities aimed at the public serves no useful purpose. Rather, evidence indicates that such promotion tends to subject prescribers to pressures which stimulate the sale of the drugs and focus the attention of patients on matters other than what is best for their health.

This is nonsense. Nobody takes antibiotics for the fun of it, and there is plenty of evidence that people who take tranquilizers or amphetamines for kicks can get all they want either legally or illegally. Advertising drug prices won't increase demand, but it *will* increase consumer awareness and give consumers the information they need to spend their health dollars wisely. What the pharmacists' organizations really fear is price competition.

The U.S. Justice Department, taking note of these price differentials, recently stated: "Differentials such as these can only exist when they are unknown to potential consumers, for given a choice, most consumers would refuse to pay 10 or 12 times the going price for a drug available elsewhere."

Uninformed buying

It is intolerable that people should be blindfolded when they go to buy medicine. If supermarkets suddenly stopped putting prices on food, there would be riots in the parking lots. People don't buy food entirely blindfolded; why should they be compelled by law to buy medicine blindfolded?

The March, 1972, issue of *Consumer Reports* lifted a corner of the blindfold by reporting the prices of ninety-eight common prescriptions sold at Osco's Chicago drugstores. (See Taylor-Troelstrup Reading 76 for this list.) It makes a handy yardstick for judging whether you are being grossly overcharged.

Consumer Reports gives this advice to drug shoppers: "Ask your physician to write on a piece of paper separate from the prescription itself the name of the drug, the strength . . . and the quantity. Given that information, pharmacies should be willing to quote a price over the telephone. Those that refuse may not be worth patronizing."

Battle against fixing drug prices gaining ground

Since state legislatures have, to date, been reluctant to lock horns with the powerful American Pharmaceutical Association and the state boards of pharmacy on the issue of fixing high drug prices, it remains for the Department of Justice to initiate price conspiracy suits against pharmaceutical companies. This was done in 1969 when Justice sued five major pharmaceutical firms—American Cyanamid, Bristol Myers, Pfizer, Squibb, and Upjohn—and won the case. On December 19, 1969, these five firms presented a check for $2,966,063 to New York City as the first installment of a $93-million settlement for "overcharges" on city hospital and welfare department purchases of drugs. Twelve other cities and two counties received $3 million in refunds.

In addition to governmental actions, more than five thousand claims by individuals have been verified, ranging from $1.19 to $9,000.

On June 24, 1970, a federal judge approved an $82.5-million offer by the same five major drug companies to settle damage suits brought against them by sixteen states, cities, counties, druggists, and thousands of individual consumers who charged these firms with "fixing high prices on tetracycline and other wonder drugs."[3]

Since 1970, 40,000 claimants in 43 states have been receiving notices from the federal court handling the mammoth drug-price refund case and will eventually get about half of what they paid for certain "wonder drugs" purchased between 1954 and 1966. These original civil suits, based on conviction of the five firms for price-fixing, were settled by the drug firms before the conviction was overturned by the U.S. Supreme Court. Claimants in the other seven states (California, Hawaii, Idaho, North Carolina, Oregon, Washington, and Kansas) may never collect anything because they failed to file claims in time.[4]

Perhaps the solution to future excessive high prices of drugs may be found in a bill introduced in the Senate by Senator Nelson (Amendment 1659) on September 29, 1972, which is designed to force holders of exclusive patents on patent medical drugs to license them if the markup is more than 500 percent of the cost of manufacturing them and if the drug is important to the public. Many widely used medicines have markups in the thousands of percent. One example cited by Nelson was Smith, Kline and French's Thorazine (generally known as chlorpromazine). SKF has an exclusive license for United States sales and charged the Defense Department $32.62 for 1,000 25-milligram tablets. The same drug is sold in Canada, said Nelson, for $2.60.[5]

Meantime, what can you do?

Physicians could be of some help if they took the time and had the will to advise their patients on drug prices. This would be easy for them to do because a reference book, *Physicians' Guide to Prescription Prices*, intended for compari-

---

[3] *The New York Times*, June 25, 1970, p. 1.

[4] *Consumer Newsweek*, Oct. 9, 1972.

[5] See ibid. for a long list of comparative drug prices in the United States and eight other nations.

Price competition is too important to be left to professionals

son of prices only, has been available to them since 1971.[6] Do not hesitate to discuss prices with your physician before he writes a prescription. A query to your doctor may also save you some money if it results in his recommending a generic product instead of a higher-priced prescription drug.

It pays to shop around, but this takes time and energy that people should not have to expend. In larger communities, shopping around pays considerable dividends. Revco Discount Drug Centers, a fast-growing chain based in Cleveland, offers senior citizens a 10 percent discount. Skaggs also gives a 15 percent discount to senior citizens, and there are other chains that offer a 10 to 15 percent reduction on prescriptions. In a statewide plan, Colorado Prescription Service members pay a small fee in return for reduced prescription rates. Consumer groups, cooperatives, and labor unions have reduced drug prices for their members. And, as mentioned earlier, the 178 or more pharmacies in the Osco Drug chain, covering seventeen states, post reduced prices of some one hundred of the most common prescriptions. Dart Drug, a chain in the Washington, D.C., area, is also posting drug prices despite local laws prohibiting such advertising. Such laws exist in thirty-seven states. Pathmark, a division of Supermarkets General and one of the largest food and drug retailers in the country, is posting prescrpition drug prices despite the laws. A survey by Douglas Bloomfield, an aide of Representative Benjamin Rosenthal (New York), showed that retail prices in cities where such advertising is banned are as much as 400 percent higher than in cities where advertising is allowed.

Drug prices at mail-order houses are also lower than those at independent corner drugstores. A few such mail-order houses are Getz Prescription Company, 916 Walnut Street, Kansas City, Missouri 64199; Rugby Laboratories, 420 Doughty Boulevard, Elmwood, New Jersey 11696; and NRTA-AARP Pharmacy, 1224 Twenty-fourth Street, Washington, D.C., 29037 (for retired persons).

The fastest solution to this anticompetitive disease is clear: repeal of state restrictions against honest price advertising, congressional action if need be, and appointment of consumer majorities to state pharmacy boards. Drug-price competition, like war, is too important to be left to the professionals.

Few nonprescription drugs called effective

Out of 125 over-the-counter drugs reviewed by the National Academy of Sciences-National Research Council, only 25 were "considered effective without qualification for their intended purposes," according to notices published on May 23 and 24, 1972, in the *Federal Register* by the FDA, for which the reviews were made.[7]

The notices listed products in nine categories: antihistamines, menstrual products, vitamin and mineral preparations, laxatives, antidandruff and ophthalmic preparations, sunscreens, vaginal contraceptives, topical antibiotics, and other items.

A $3-billion business—mostly ineffective

The items were all introduced to public sale between 1938 and 1962. Many well-known products not on this list were introduced prior to 1938 when proof of effectiveness was not required. Products marketed after the 1962 Kefauver drug amendments must be proved effective prior to sale. (For more details about many of these nonprescription drugs, see Taylor-Troelstrup Reading 77.)

---

[6] Published by the Wilcom Educational Company, Medical Press Division.

[7] Drug Efficacy Study Information Control (BD-67), FDA, Bureau of Drugs, Rockville, Md.

Early in 1973, the FDA called for:

1. Sharp limitations on claims for these products
2. Formula changes to prevent hazards
3. More testing to prove the effectiveness of ingredients and eliminate unnecessary ones

There is likely to be a very bitter battle over the proposed changes. The market for antacids alone was $109 million in 1971 out of a total $2.9-billion over-the-counter drug market, according to *Drug Topics,* a pharmaceutical trade publication.

The antacids requirements are being developed by an advisory committee outside the FDA headed by Dr. Franz Inglefinger, editor of the prestigious *New England Journal of Medicine.* This is the first of twenty-five panels that will provide standards for the effectiveness of an estimated 100,000 to 500,000 over-the-counter drug products. Thus its deliberations will provide a precedent for FDA action embracing the entire nonprescription field.

It is still easy to buy a supplemental hospital insurance policy by mail. But you don't have much after you buy it, say most state insurance commissioners. The vast bulk of mail-order hospital insurance is sold by National Liberty Corporation through its subsidiaries, the National Home Life Assurance Company and the National Home Assurance Company of New York, and by Union Fidelity Life Insurance Company, based in Pennsylvania.

These health and accident companies use Madison Avenue hocus-pocus ads which mislead people into buying near-worthless coverage. For example, an ad for the National Home Assurance Company of New York features the TV personality Art Linkletter and begins: "Dear friend: You know me. I wouldn't recommend anything I didn't believe in. And I think National Home's $600-a-month plan is just about the best protection you can give your family."[8] Pennsylvania Insurance Commissioner Herbert Denenberg wonders whether Art Linkletter's "dear friends" know him very well. Denenberg thinks they should be told that this folksy endorser is paid $50,000 a year for his image—and is both a stockholder and director of National Home. What is wrong, of course, is that promises to pay large sums—$600 a month up to a maximum of $50,000—without giving *specific* explanations of what must happen for the jackpot to disgorge are dangerously noninformative.

At the Pennsylvania hearings, Denenberg pointed to an ad for Union Fidelity Life Insurance (a firm that pays only $175 on an average claim) and asked an officer of the company whether it had ever paid out the full $50,000 it regularly advertises. The officer replied that the largest payment he knew of was $10,000.[9] Actually, you would have to be in the hospital more than seven years to collect $50,000.[10]

Three things seem to worry the state regulators of mail-order health insurance:

Mail-order hospital insurance

Be suspicious of all mail-order hospital insurance

"That's why I'm rich"—Linkletter

[8] *The Nation,* Apr. 17, 1972, p. 488.
[9] Ibid.
[10] *The Wall Street Journal,* June 22, 1972, p. 30.

1. Advertising claims.
2. The policies don't cover preexisting physical conditions for the first two years, and this clause is invoked to reject many policyholders' claims.
3. The insurers' profit margin is a disproportionate ratio between what is paid by the firms and what these companies are promising.

Newspapers, TV, and direct-mail ads make such claims as "$1,000 a month tax-free cash when you go to the hospital" or "protect your family with this $600-a-month extra cash plan." The companies "should relate them to daily payments," says Washington's commissioner, "nor do they say that, often, benefits don't start until the sixth day, which is beyond the five-day average for hospital stays."[11]

Some ads hammer hard on the point that hospital benefits are tax-free. All insurance payments are tax-free. What the ads don't say is that hospital indemnity policies have *less* tax advantage than some other health policies. But premiums for policies that provide a fixed sum for a specified period, as the hospital indemnity policies do, are not deductible.

Changing Times (April, 1972) says, "Selling has gotten so bad that a few states have taken action against certain companies for misleading advertising." The FTC has also been looking into possible deceptive practices.

Getting the facts: a puzzle
"Inherently complex"

Denenberg, with a Ph.D. in insurance, says that health insurance is "not merely a matter of sorting apples from oranges: it is more like separating out a whole basket of fruit, much of it rotten." Despite the complexity of health insurance contracts, there are some basic questions that should be asked about any policy you may be considering. *Changing Times* (April, 1972) believes the following questions will cut through the essentials and help you avoid the most common pitfalls:

1. What does the policy *specifically* cover?
2. Does it apply to both accident and sickness?
3. How much will the policy really pay?
4. How much of actual costs (hospital, etc.) will be covered?
5. When do the benefits begin?
6. On what basis can you renew the policy?
7. How does it supplement Medicare?
8. Is the company licensed in your state?
9. What percentage of the premium is returned to the policyholder in benefits? (Blue Cross returns 97.9 percent; some mail-order policies return 20 to 30 percent.)
10. Does the policy reduce benefits when you qualify for Medicare without reducing premiums?

What to do?

Perhaps the best advice is to be suspicious of mail-order policies that promise much and cost very little. Better yet, why settle for present mail-order policies before first investigating other medical care and health services?

Medical-hospital services: laboratories and other costs

It's never been much of a secret that hospital patients experience some of their worst suffering at the pay window on the way out—where they are hit by staggering bills. It's the rise in hospital costs that has been the biggest single

[11] Ibid.

factor in the tremendous increase in health care costs. Hospital charges rose 170 percent between 1960 and 1970. Doctors' fees in the same period rose about 60 percent, and health insurance kept pace with these increases. The average hospital charge for a room is about $84 per day in this country.

Hospital costs

All hospitals, public or private, share similar problems. They have difficulty balancing their budgets. Many private hospitals are forced to pass to public hospitals the burden of treating the poor or those patients whose insurance benefits have run out. These extra burdens on public hospitals are so serious as to threaten the hospitals' very existence.

This situation has led to two systems of hospital care. We have well-equipped private hospitals, fully staffed with few patients waiting in line, but just blocks away there are public hospitals that are crumbling and understaffed. Two systems of care will, in time, turn into two levels of care—a two-class system.

Within these two systems of health care, there is no serious pressure toward efficiency or toward economizing on special-equipment costs by forming sharing agreements with other hospitals for open-heart surgical units and other expensive equipment.

Other situations in hospitals add needlessly to higher costs, such as certain monopolistic practices. For example, there are pathologists, who run the hospital laboratories; radiologists, who interpret X-ray photographs; and anesthesiologists, who administer anesthesia during surgery. These specialists usually are not salaried employees of the hospital. Rather, they are given a percentage of

"Strictly a monopolistic money-making proposition"

the profits of their department. In a nonprofit prepaid group practice hospital like the Group Health Cooperative of Puget Sound, such specialists receive salaries of around $40,000 to $60,000, but in most of our hospitals such specialists *insist* on a percentage of the department income because each can net from $100,000 to as high as $500,000 annually.[12] Dr. Kenneth J. Williams, medical director of the Catholic Hospital Association, says the lack of any ceiling or control on pathologists' compensation "borders on the scandalous."[13]

A comparison of the prices charged by the Washington Hospital Center (where Dr. Vernon E. Martens runs the laboratories on a percentage basis) and two local, independent labs, also in the Washington, D.C. area, is as shown in the accompanying table.

[12] Congressional testimony and interviews with hospital administrators quoted by Ronald Hessler in six articles in *The Washington Post*. See *The Washington Post*, Nov. 1, 1972, article no. 4.
[13] Ibid.

TEST	HOSPITAL CENTER	LAB A	LAB B	AVERAGE: DIFFERENCE (PERCENTAGE)
Routine urinalysis	$5	$2.50	$1.00	186
Complete blood count	7	3.75	2.00	143
Pregnancy test	11	3.75	3.50	204
Mono test	6	3.50	5.50	33
Routine tissue	18	10.00	15.00	44
Twelve channel (SMA12)	25	5.00	5.00	400

The average difference shows the additional price charged at the hospital center over the average price charged by the two independent labs for the same test. [14]

Some hospital practices are "scandalous"

Why don't hospitals use independent lab tests to cut charges to patients? Dr. Jacques M. Kelly, head of the National Health Laboratories, Inc., says that despite the 1969 Justice Department decree, pathologists continue to have a "lock" on hospital labs and an "ex officio" agreement that they won't do business with an independent lab unless they own it. [15] Incidentally, Consumers Union, nonprofit publisher of *Consumer Reports,* believes that arrangements under which a hospital agrees to franchise its laboratory services to a pathologist, giving him a share of its profits, is a violation of Section 2 of the Sherman Antitrust Act, which prohibits a contract or conspiracy in restraint of trade. This could be a class action suit. At this writing no legal court action had been taken by Consumers Union.

We have summarized some of the major areas in which consumers of health care can be and are being clobbered to the tune of hundreds of millions of dollars each year. Some of these practices border on the outrageous; in other instances misleading ads appear in the press and on radio and TV; and in a few situations there is outright fraud. The reader should remember to be suspicious of mail-order health insurance, to shop around for prescriptions, to forget most of the nonprescription drugs, and to be aware of the inefficient way in which many of our hospitals are administered. Outside these abuses, which are costly to health care patients, what can the individual consumer do?

BUYING INSURANCE FOR ILLNESS AND ACCIDENTS

The cost of health care

Health care in this country is very, very expensive. Not only do we discover that health care cost is exorbitant, but most of us also find out too late how inadequate health insurance policies are. Many of us cannot buy insurance because of health problems. Some of us live in parts of the country that doctors have abandoned to set up more profitable practices elsewhere. Many of us are exposed to poor health care facilities. Four out of five Americans have some kind of health insurance. On the other hand, one out of seven Americans has no health insurance at all because he can't afford it or because he has an uninsurable health problem. As a matter of fact, comparatively few Americans can buy adequate health care protection at a price they can afford. And many people do not live close to one of the better prepaid, group health care organizations and therefore cannot have the advantage of better health care at lower cost. Far too many people have to depend on the fragmented solo medical practice, which is very expensive and inadequate at best.

Paying for health care

We have allowed hundreds of life insurance companies to create thousands of complicated policies that trap Americans in gaps, limitations, and exclusions on coverage, and that offer disastrously low benefits which spell financial disaster

[14] Ibid.
[15] Ibid.

for a family when serious illness or injury strikes. We have allowed doctor and hospital charges to skyrocket out of control through wasteful and inefficient practices to the point where more and more Americans are finding it difficult to pay for health care and health insurance.

The average American lives in fear of health care costs

This was the conclusion of the Chairman of the Senate Health Subcommittee, Edward M. Kennedy, after hearings held in Washington and in nine cities across the nation and several European countries in 1971–1972.[16] Faced with such a serious condition, what can a family or individual do? We have to use the health care systems that are available to us. First we shall examine the five basic types of coverage available from insurance companies: disability income insurance, hospital expense insurance, surgical expense insurance, regular medical expense insurance, and major medical expense insurance.

1.   Disability income insurance

This is the oldest kind of health insurance. It provides regular weekly or monthly cash payments to insured persons whose wages or income is interrupted by total or (in some policies) partial disability due to illness or accident. The basic features in these contracts are the specified amount, a waiting period, and the length of time the benefits will continue. Normally, the income allowed is limited to about one-half to two-thirds of the individual's normal earned income.

The longer the waiting period, the less the premium cost. Waiting periods vary from eight days to a year. Sometimes disability due to accidents is payable on the first day. Long-term disability provides benefits for periods ranging from two years to age 65. Benefits are usually based on 50 to 60 percent of earned income. Usually the benefit is reduced by the amount received from workmen's compensation, Social Security, and the Veterans Administration. Some contracts have death and dismemberment benefits.

2.   Hospital expense insurance

This covers (1) daily room and board up to a daily limit stated in the policy and also routine nursing care and minor medical supplies and (2) additional charges such as those for lab tests and X rays, anesthesia, drugs and medicines, and use of the operating room. This does *not* necessarily mean that full-expense benefits are paid. Maternity benefits are available in the form of a lump sum. Some contracts have a deductible clause stating that the insured person pays the first $50 or $100 of hospital bills.

3.   Surgical expense insurance

This helps to pay the surgeon's fee.

---

[16] Edward M. Kennedy, *In Critical Condition: The Crisis in America's Health Care,* Simon and Schuster, New York, 1972, p. 16.

4. Regular medical expense insurance

This covers the cost of physicians' services not related to surgery. These are basic costs and could involve X-ray and lab tests performed in a physician's office. To cover the expense of serious illness, families have to turn to major medical expense insurance.

5. Major medical expense insurance

First written in 1949, this insurance is in the experimental stage. The contract covers catastrophic illness or accidents involving amounts ranging from $5,000 to $25,000 or more per illness. The company pays for the hospital-medical-surgical costs up to the maximum stated in the contract. It may limit benefits such as the cost of the hospital room, the surgeon's fee, and possibly a few other costs.

This maximum benefit is subject to two cost-sharing features—the deductible and coinsurance. The deductible is the amount which the insured pays *before* benefits commence. It may range from $250, or less, up to $1,000. The purpose of the deductible is to eliminate the small claims which add to the premium cost of insurance and which the family usually can budget in its savings program.

After the deductible, the company will pay 75 or 80 percent of the remaining costs up to the maximum benefit. Under the coinsurance system, the insured pays 20 or 25 percent of the amount in excess of the deductible. In this way the insured has a stake in the amount and some control of medical expenses incurred—and the cost of the policy is also lower than it otherwise would be.

To get more complete coverage than under major medical expense insurance, the comprehensive major medical expense contract combines basic hospital-surgical expense and major medical expense benefits. It may be combined into a single overall plan with a low deductible of $100 or less.

The coverages and premium cost are affected by sex, age, physical condition, occupation, personal habits, and place of residence. Administrative costs are about 13 percent for group policies, in contrast to usually over 50 percent on individual contracts. Some 75 million insured are in the lower-cost group plans, in which employers pay part or all of the premium. Group plans do not require physical examinations, and usually the contracts are noncancelable.

The best-known group plans are Blue Cross (BC) and Blue Shield (BS). They, too, have comprehensive major medical insurance plans. We shall have more to say about these nonprofit plans after evaluating the for-profit plans sold by life insurance companies.

Health insurance companies: investigate contracts

1. Hospitalization

How many days in the hospital does your policy cover?

How much does the policy pay per day for room and board?

How do these daily benefits compare with hospital room and board charges in your community?

How much does the policy pay for related expenses in the hospital—X rays, anesthesia and its administration, and the like?

Are there waiting periods before certain conditions are covered?

Is there a deductible which you must pay toward hospital expenses before benefits start?

Is the policy renewable?

What are the limitations or exclusions in the policy?

2. Doctor bills

Are the benefits in line with physicians' and surgeons' fees in your community?

What types of surgical and physicians' services does the policy help pay for?

What are the limitations or exclusions in the policy?

How much does the policy pay for each doctor visit in the office or in the hospital?

How many such visits are allowed per confinement?

Are you covered for house calls?

Is there a deductible before benefits start?

3. Major medical insurance

What is the maximum amount your policy will pay?

Will the maximum benefit be in effect again for you upon recovery?

How large a deductible must you pay?

Is there a deductible for each claim for a different illness or injury? Or is it on a calendar-year basis, with one deductible in a given year charged against the total bills?

What percentage of the total cost above the deductible does the policy pay—75 percent? 80 percent? What percentage do you pay?

What provisions exist for renewing your policy?

What top benefit limits, if any, exist for such expenses as hospital room and board, surgery, or other specialists' consultation and treatment?

4. Disability income insurance

Is there a waiting period before benefits begin?

Does the waiting period vary depending on whether sickness or an accident is involved?

How does the policy define total disability?

Will it pay benefits for partial disability?

Is it a requirement of the policy that you be confined to bed at home, or confined to your home, for benefits?

What is the amount of weekly or monthly benefits?

How long do the regular payments continue for accident? For illness?

What provisions exist for renewing the policy?

What exclusions or limitations exist in your policy?

How will workmen's compensation, or Social Security, or disability income from your employer affect income from your insurance policy?

Private, for-profit health insurance failing to do the job

It is comparatively easy to document the evidence that the private health insurance industry has failed to adequately protect Americans from disastrous health care costs by spreading the risk among all the 175 million Americans who pay billions of dollars in health insurance premiums. The files of the Senate Antitrust Subcommittee hearings in the 1971–1972 sessions and the testimony gathered by the Senate Health Subcommittee 1972 hearings in Washington and in nine American cities are quite clear about the failure of private health insurance to contribute effectively toward adequate health care for all Americans at an affordable cost. Edwin P. Hoyt saw the health crisis coming in the 1960s

Health insurance—a story of failure

and wrote a book in 1970 called *Your Health Insurance: A Story of Failure.* Dr. Herbert Denenberg, Insurance Commissioner of Pennsylvania, and one of the nation's experts in insurance, said recently that the "country would be better off without any supplemental health insurance because of the misleading claims and high costs associated with it." He went on to say that "as bad as the Blues [Blue Cross and Blue Shield] are, compared with commercial insurance companies, they look like angels."[17] Leonard Woodcock, president of United Auto Workers, in expressing his dissatisfaction with health benefits for his union members, said that "private health insurance covers only a fourth of personal health care expenditures." Then he added that in the past, these companies had rendered "important and needed services" but that "they have outlived their usefulness."[18]

Of course the private health insurance companies are not alone in being ineffective in encouraging greater efficiency in managing health agencies. Hospitals, doctors, and other providers have also been guilty of inefficient management of health care facilities.[19]

When private, for-profit insurance companies are presently doing a poor job in providing adequate health care at an affordable price, what can a consumer do?

Prepaid, nonprofit Blue Cross–Blue Shield protection

Blue Cross (BC) and Blue Shield (BS) are doctor- and hospital-administered prepaid, nonprofit health care and service plans. Their activities are coordinated at the national level, but their insurance (individual or group) plans are slightly different in each geographic area. Blue Cross covers largely hospital bills; Blue Shield covers most surgeons' and physicians' bills. BC and BS are managed separately, but they do work together to provide package policies for both hospital and most doctor bills. There are likely to be some costs not covered by either plan. On the whole, BC and BS nonprofit groups pay more benefits per premium dollar than for-profit, private insurance policies. According to Dr. Milton I. Roemer, a witness at the Senate Antitrust and Monopoly Subcommittee hearings on health care delivery systems, the cost-benefit ratio was more

---

[17] *Consumer Newsweek,* May 15, 1972, pp. 1–4.

[18] Ibid.

[19] See Kennedy, op. cit., for recent evidence of negligence and inefficiency in our health delivery system.

Subscribers to group practice plans get more for their money

unfavorable for commercial insurance plans than for "provider" systems such as Blue Cross or group practice plans such as health maintenance organizations. The same study showed also that subscribers to group practice plans get more for their money and are more satisfied than even subscribers to BC or health insurance policies.[20] We will shortly take a look at a couple of the group practice plans which seem to offer more health care coverage at lower cost to subscribers.

Even though BC and BS pay about the highest percentage of premium income paid out in claims (about 95.9 percent, in contrast to 83.3 percent paid by insurance companies) from both individual and group plans, there are some limitations to BC and BS. Separately, BC pays out about 97.9 percent of premiums in claims, in contrast to about 91.1 percent paid out under the BS plan.[21]

Blue Cross subscribers are well served, especially those having group contracts. Blue Shield, although it pays less in claims of subscribers than BC, has also served subscribers well on the whole. Both BC and BS, however, could offer even more and better service to subscribers at lower premium rates if certain weaknesses were corrected.

Doctors and hospitals in control of BC and BS

Originally, both BC and BS were established to keep hospital beds filled and to assure that all hospital and doctor bills would be paid. Both groups have tried to put pressure on physicians and hospitals to hold down costs. They have failed. The reason is that BC and BS are controlled by doctors and the American Hospital Association. Consumers are kept off the boards or have been selected by them because they are nonactive in the sense of representing the interest of consumers of health care. Thus hospital administrators, trustees, and others find themselves establishing policies governing their own or sister institutions.

Policed by state medical societies and the American Hospital Association

Indeed, the fee schedules and administration for BS plans are proposed by either the medical society or a committee in which physicians constitute a majority. The fee schedules are then approved by the physician-nominated boards. Thus both organizations are set up to protect the interests of the provider of health care rather than the interests of the patient, the final user of health care.

"Income-conscious healers"

Blue Cross has done little to press a hospital or physician to greater efficiency. Many plans pay the hospitals their costs plus a percentage. There is no incentive to try to be efficient under such plans since the higher the costs, the greater that percentage is, and thus it is to the benefit of the hospital to be inefficient.

Some BS plans request physicians and surgeons to accept the fees listed in the subscribers' contract. Many, if not most, physicians charge more than the fee figures considered reasonable by the local doctors. However, most doctors bill patients directly, and the patient pays the difference, if any. This is not the way BS was originally planned, but it is the way it has worked out. And, as Barry P. Wilson, a Washington, D.C., BC-BS spokesman, said in a recent report: "Some of these prices are almost as ridiculous as some of the drug prices."[22]

Finally, BC traditionally has offered coverage only for inpatient hospital

[20] *Consumer Newsweek,* June 12, 1972.
[21] Social Security Administration figures quoted in *Changing Times,* April, 1972, p. 16.
[22] *The Washington Post,* Nov. 1, 1972.

care, even in cases where a procedure might be done equally well on an out-patient basis (in clinics or a doctor's office). Under such a plan, subscribers are forced to use more expensive inpatient hospital care. The result is unnecessary overutilization of hospitals (which charge the highest costs) and higher BC premiums. Similarly, BC plans have failed to insist that hospitals prescribe generic drugs—whose use would cut drug costs by an estimated 65 to 95 percent. [23]

Thus we see that BC and BS, which write almost as many health care contracts as all 1,800 commercial companies combined, are stymied in their efforts to improve efficiency in hospitals, to force doctors not to charge more than the reasonable fees suggested in the contracts, and to exercise effective control over unneeded surgery and hospitalization, inferior care, and prolonged hospital stays. Put all these inefficiencies together, and you arrive at one conclusion: There must be a better health care system. There is. But first, let's take a look at new ways to pay dental costs and to secure preventive dental care.

DENTAL INSURANCE AND PREVENTIVE DENTAL CARE

Now it's dental insurance that is headed for explosive growth, with the emergence of nonprofit groups, private insurance plans, dental societies, group health dental cooperatives, and the federal government's "Denticare" prepaid system for older people.

Costs are up and up   The major reason behind new developments in dental insurance is an effort to reduce rapidly increasing dental costs and to encourage more people to get adequate dental care at an affordable cost.

What has happened to dental care costs? They have climbed much more rapidly than the overall cost of living, according to the U.S. Bureau of Labor Statistics (see Figure 11-1 for details). Many Americans have neglected dental care because of the high costs. The average cost of having a tooth filled increased from $5.75 in 1960 to about $8.40 in 1970, and the cost of having a tooth pulled went from $6.50 to about $10 during the same period. Some dentists charge $25 today to pull one tooth.

Various kinds of dental   There are signs of explosive growth in dental insurance. Here is the latest on
insurance plans   the dental care front:

.1   In 1970, a Blue Cross–Blue Shield prototype plan was started in the New York area which now covers over 150,000 people served by some 6,000 dentists. Since then, forty-nine other BC-BS plans have been set up providing dental care to about 300,000 subscribers.

2.   The Delta Dental Plans Association sponsors insurance through the state dental associations. Delta contracts cover about 2.5 million persons in twenty-nine states today.

3.   Unions are negotiating for dental plans with their companies.

4.   Pressure is growing to have the federal government provide for "Denti-

---

[23] Herbert Denenberg, *Guidelines for Inclusion in Blue Cross Contract with Delaware Valley Hospital Asso.,* 1971.

FIGURE 11-1 Dental costs climbing rapidly

U.S. average, 1960=100—

Dentist's Fees

145.9

131.6

100   100

1960   1961   1962   1963   1964   1965   1966   1967   1968   1969   latest
(July, 1970)

SOURCE: U.S. Bureau of Labor Statistics.

care"—free dental services for the elderly. Care of teeth is not included in the federal Medicare program, and only a few states include such care in their Medicaid plans.

5.   More than fifty commercial insurance companies are writing dental care policies which offer benefits to over five million people. Most of these are group policies.

6.   An additional one-half million persons receive prepaid dental care through private plans arranged by dentists in group practice.

Four common arrangements   Four common arrangements for payment show up in dental insurance plans now on the market:

1.   *Full coverage.* The dentist is paid his "usual, customary, and reasonable" fee in full, possibly after a "deductible" charge paid by the policy holder.

2.   *Fixed coinsurance.*   A specified percentage of the dentist's bill is paid. The patient pays the rest.

3.   *Sliding-scale coinsurance.*   The percentage paid by the subscriber declines as the policy remains in force over a period of years. Since most Americans have neglected their teeth, they usually need a great deal of work at the start of treatment and less work as time goes on.

4.   *Indemnity.*   A fixed amount is paid for each service the dentist renders: so much for cleaning, so much for a filling, etc.

Insurance men say it is difficult to set average costs for a dental care policy because dentists' fees vary according to locality. Premiums differ by type and length of coverage.

One expert notes that the monthly premium for a married man with a family might range from $5.50 to $33, depending on breadth of coverage.

Dental cooperative provides preventive control

The Group Health Cooperative of Puget Sound, Washington, has established a Group Health Dental Cooperative and recently instituted a Dental Preventive Control Program. These are prepaid, nonprofit, comprehensive plans based on the assumption that in dental care, it is better and cheaper to prevent than to repair. Unfortunately, most dental schools train dentists to repair rather than stop damage to teeth.

It is better to prevent than repair—and it costs less

This fine program is so new that no valid evaluation data are available. No doubt, it will prove difficult to change people's habits for the better—seeing the dentist at least twice a year, for example. The dental cooperative, however, has a dental control program in the hands of specialists consisting of a dental director, another dentist who specializes in pyorrhea treatments, a dental hygienist who specializes in preventive controls, and dental assistants trained in teaching subscribers how to prevent damage to teeth and surrounding areas.

COMPREHENSIVE NONPROFIT PREPAID GROUP HEALTH PLANS

In 1967, John Gardner, Secretary of Health, Education, and Welfare, prepared a *Report to the President on Medical Care Prices,* in which he concluded:

> Group practice, especially prepaid group practice, should be encouraged. . . . Groups of doctors practicing together can make more efficient use of equipment, auxiliary personnel, and consultation than doctors practicing alone. Where the patient has paid in advance for comprehensive medical care under a group practice plan, less incentive exists to use high-cost hospital services where lower cost alternatives would meet the patient's needs just as well.

Dr. William H. Stewart, Surgeon General of the U.S. Public Health Service, said: "The American people . . . want to know when and how they shall receive better health care at prices they can afford to pay. We who believe in group practice have an answer. It is not the whole answer, nor the only answer, but it represents a valid and important approach."[24]

In the April, 1968, issue of *Group Health and Welfare News,* Dr. W. Palmer Dearing, executive director of the Group Health Association of America, said: "Group practice prepayment plans provide a rational organization of medical services with good quality and cost control."

The question is: Is this a promising route?

Comprehensive prepaid group health care

Group Health Association estimates that there are about 10 million Americans presently receiving this kind of health care in some 220 group plans that have some of the following characteristics:

[24]"Who Can Afford to Be Sick?" *Look,* Oct. 15, 1968.

1. *Group practice.* This means simply doctors practicing as a team, general practitioners and specialists together.

2. *Prepayment.* You pay for health care (generally monthly) on a "level-premium" basis just as you pay for insurance.

3. *Comprehensive care.* You go to the medical center on some regular basis and the doctors' job is to take care of your health *before* you get sick. This is called "preventive medicine." If medical attention—treatments, surgery, etc.—is needed, all of the costs are paid for by your monthly premiums.

4. *Consumer control.* Generally, a group health association or foundation is formed and a board of directors is selected which hires an administrator who hires the staff. The doctors have full charge of the *practice* of medicine.

Comprehensive prepaid group health plans have proved that their "cost of medical care is less and can be more effectively contained than the cost of individual fee-for-service medical services," according to a study by the General Accounting Office (GAO), Congress's investigatory arm. The 1972 study goes on to report that comprehensive group health organizations emphasize preventive medicine and better use of hospitals and clinics.[25] The Group Health Cooperative of Puget Sound is one of the best health care group plans in the United States. There are over 220 other prepaid group health care plans in all parts of the country.

The Group Health Cooperative of Puget Sound

The Group Health Cooperative of Puget Sound, after twenty-five years of steady growth, has over 148,000 enrolled persons, 145 full-time physicians on salary representing all specializations, 301-bed hospitals, several neighborhood outpatient clinics (completely staffed), home health service and equipment second to none; it provides for hospital coverage every day of the year and for continuous hospital coverage regardless of length of stay.[26]

One of the best preventive practice group health care plans in the country

Compared with noncooperative health plans, and by almost any measure of comparison, it comes off well. Under many prepaid insurance schemes, benefits are obtainable only when the patient is hospitalized (most expensive) and is kept much longer than necessary. GHC's reliance on outpatient care and on salaried doctors rather than fee-for-service arrangements accounts for startling differences in costs. In 1970 the national per capita cost of health care was $226, while for GHC members it was only $143. The biggest savings were in hospital expenses, which averaged $37 per GHC member, compared with $112 nationally.[27]

Doctors are well paid by GHC. They must serve a probationary period prior to taking on regular assignments. The salary schedule is confidential, but informed estimates place the range from about $22,000 to over $40,000, not including bonuses, fringe benefits, and other supplemental income. The staff also receives half the amount of carefully controlled fees charged private patients, fees for completing insurance forms, and legal fees for court testimony. They also receive life insurance, full medical coverage, malpractice insurance, ninety

[25] *The Wall Street Journal,* Nov. 24, 1972.
[26] See *View,* Twenty-fifth Anniversary Issue, Spring, 1972; also *View,* Mid-Winter, 1972.
[27] *View,* Mid-Winter, 1972.

days' sick-leave pay, and disability income insurance. In addition, they are entitled to a month's vacation and a five-day postgraduate leave each year, and there is a good retirement plan that goes into effect at age 65. The elected board of directors has overall supervision, but a contract forbids lay interference in medical decisions.

Doctors' salaries are high

This plan provides complete prepaid preventive medical care–dental care; mental health care; blood transfusions; renal analysis (artificial kidney machine); family planning services; ambulance services; services at home, clinics, and hospitals; and X-ray, laboratory, and pharmacy services—and the best equipment money can buy. Dr. Arthur Shultz, chief of staff, says, "If we were to charge standard fees for the services we perform, the cost would be astronomical."

Costs to patients (GHC)

A family of four could have complete coverage for about $44.15 per month in 1971: $15.65 for each adult under 65, $7.15 for the first child, and $5.70 for the second child. An additional *initial* capital dues membership of $175 is charged solely to cover construction, equipping, or acquisition of a hospital and other capital facilities. This can be paid monthly if desired. There are no further dues. There is a special maternity fee of $200, which covers all hospital care and physicians' services. This fee is applicable if full adult dues have been paid for thirty days or more prior to conception.

Quality service at a lower price

As Figure 11-2 shows, the gap between what the average person in this country paid in 1971 and what the average GHC member paid for services continued to widen. That is, those outside GHC paid $91 more in 1971 for the same type of health care services. In 1970, the difference was $84.

The solution to ever-increasing costs of medical care has not been found in this country. GHC, however, shows that it can deliver quality services at a lower price. The question is: Will there be more health care co-ops like GHC if middle- and upper-middle-class groups don't become a lot more effective locally and nationally than they now are? After all, there are still twenty-two states that do not permit health care centers like GHC!

HMO: HEALTH MAINTENANCE ORGANIZATION

What is an HMO, and why are so many health centers so concerned about this concept? The concern is due partly to the fact that an HMO appears to be a good way to deliver health care at low cost and partly to the fact that neighborhood health centers are interested in innovation and new approaches. However, health centers are concerned primarily because the federal government (from which most HMO funds flow) is advocating the HMO concept so strongly. The Nixon administration has sponsored legislation and HEW has been awarding grants for planning, research, and demonstration projects throughout the country. After awarding several million dollars in grants, HEW suddenly made no new grants in midsummer, 1972.

HMO: A system of health care delivery

A good idea, but . . .

HEW describes an HMO as an organized system that provides comprehensive health services to an enrolled group of individuals and families for a prepaid annual fee. It emphasizes preventive care, outpatient services, continuity of care, and cost effectiveness (which GHC is offering to Puget Sound members).

FIGURE 11-2   **Annual per capita costs of selected health services**

Group Health Cooperative compared to United States average, 1969-1971(*)

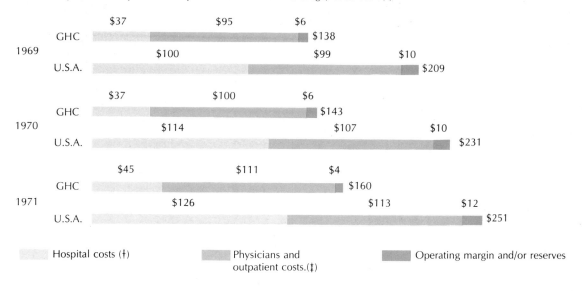

| | Hospital costs (†) | Physicians and outpatient costs.(‡) | Operating margin and/or reserves |

(*) Excludes dental, nursing home, eyeglasses, construction, research, and public health costs.
(*) Includes visiting nurses, physicians office expenses and outpatient lab x-ray and drug costs.
(‡) U.S. data exclude operational costs of psychiatric, tuberculosis, and other long-term hospitals.

Annual per capita costs of GHC Health care delivery are significantly lower than United States average.

SOURCE: *View,* 25th Anniversary Issue, Spring, 1972, p. 14

An HMO can be regarded as a health insurance company which pays out services instead of money when a subscriber makes a claim and which provides coverage of all the health services that one is likely to need, but which stipulates that members must obtain these services from only one provider.

The idea is not new. The Kaiser plan has been operating in this fashion for years in California and other states, as have the Group Health Association of America and the Group Health Cooperative of Puget Sound, discussed above. What is new is the federal pressure to get the medical providers interested in the HMO idea. The providers have become interested, at least in the planning grants, but most of them have gone to the traditional elements in the health "establishment." And the establishment isn't too interested in innovation!

Advantages of HMO   One of the principles of prepaid service is the elimination of nonessential services. If the medical provider is paid a fixed amount per patient in advance, regardless of the amount of health care he gives, there is no incentive to give unneeded care, to perform unnecessary operations, or to require too many return visits because he would receive no more money. The theory is that the doctor would give enough care to make the patient well, and no more. Furthermore, the doctor would have an interest in keeping the subscriber to the prepaid plan healthy by practicing preventive medicine and providing regular checkups in order to avoid the more expensive treatment of the subscriber's illness. The Kaiser plan, group health plans, and group health cooperatives, to mention just a few, provide ample evidence to support this theory. The federal government would doubtless realize considerable dollar savings if the millions of Medicaid and Medicare members now receiving health care under the expensive fee-for-service method were to switch to prepaid care and dramatically decrease their hospital use.

Drawbacks of HMO

The chief criticism of the HMO concept concerns insufficient assurance of quality controls. The system builds in a disincentive to deliver enough care. It is true that the general level of health of prepaid subscribers is higher than that of people who do not prepay. However, most of the prepayment experience has been with middle-income persons, who have fewer health problems than those whom OEO and HEW have been providing health care through the neighborhood health centers or through Medicaid and Medicare and whose illnesses are often of a different nature.

There is also a deficit in HMO budgets because patient income comes mainly from Medicaid and Medicare, and this sum does not nearly cover the cost of operations. Prepaid members having incomes above the OEO poverty levels must pay a fee based on a sliding scale according to income and family size. In practice, the health centers turn no one away who cannot pay. Therefore, it seems as if the federal grants must be continued.

Absence of consumer participation a serious defect

Another weakness is the absence of consumer participation in HMO policy-making decisions. The recent Nixon administration bill makes no mention of consumer participation in HMO, but the Roy bill and the Kennedy bill provide for consumer participation in policy making.[28]

According to several experts in the field of prepaid comprehensive group health care organizations, HMO must demonstrate that it will be capable of providing comprehensive health services "efficiently, effectively, and economically." These recommendations were made to HEW and Congress in 1972.[29]

Apparently, HMO is still in an experimental, developmental stage. It appears doubtful, at this time, that Congress can agree on the changes needed for HMO to function efficiently, effectively, and economically.

National health insurance: the next step

It is no secret that Americans now favor some kind of a national health plan. What lies behind this shift in national attitudes is widespread frustration—especially among the middle class—over high taxes for ever more costly and fragmented health care programs; the inadequacy of the most costly private insurance plans; the inability of Blue Cross–Blue Shield, HMO, and other forms of private health insurance to control soaring medical costs; and the ability of millions to get good health services when and where they want them. Some exceptions to the above can be found in a few nonprofit prepaid preventive medical group health care plans led by group health cooperative plans such as the Group Health Cooperative of Puget Sound.

Inadequate health care under present systems

[28] Roy bill, HR 11728, 92d Cong., 1st sess.; Kennedy bill, S.3327, 92d Cong., 2d sess.

[29] Reported in *National Clearinghouse for Legal Services,* Northwestern University School of Law, Chicago, May 15, 1972, pp. 18–21.

High costs under the present system

Few people realize that the United States government is already spending more on health care than any other country—some $70 billion annually. It is expected to increase this amount to a total of $95 billion by 1975.

The United States government pays more for health care than Great Britain under its national health system

Between private and tax sources, the average American is paying about $345 per year for medical care, compared with $100 per person in Great Britain. In the United States some 70 million persons have all or part of their medical care paid for by the government—veterans, Medicare and Medicaid recipients, members of the armed forces, and others. Thus we are already providing limited socialized medicine to vast numbers of people, but in expensive and fragmented ways.

Most European countries have had national health insurance for many years, whereas Great Britain has a "national health system." According to Dr. David S. Murray, one of the architects of the British health system, the health system in his country is based on the "right of every citizen and every visitor" to have universal health care coverage. There are no special categories, he says. [30]

The national health system in Great Britain

Residents of Great Britain are free to pick their own family doctor. The physician is compensated by the government on the basis of a fixed payment per individual per year whether the person receives medical care or not. A commission adjusts the "capitation" payment from time to time to ensure that physicians generally receive an income equivalent to that of other professionals such as engineers and lawyers.

Dr. Murray gave this example of a health care system's operation: "If a patient needs an operation and the hospital in his locality is filled we will provide transportation to another area where his or her condition can be treated. Emergencies are treated at the nearest facility."

The Kennedy-Griffiths "Health Security Act"

While there are five health bills before Congress, the principal one is the Kennedy-Griffiths bill. (For a summary of these bills, see Taylor-Troelstrup Reading 74.)

Leaving aside the point that health care, like education, ought to be available to all as a matter of right, it is plain that the practical and equitable solution to the cost crisis is national insurance, a fact that most other industrialized democracies recognized years ago. Under the Kennedy-Griffiths bill, which is modeled on a plan advanced by the Committee for National Health Insurance, physicians' services and hospital services would be paid for in full; exceptions would be some nursing-home care, treatment of mental illness, some dental care, and some drugs and medical appliances. Half of the money would be paid through a tax on employers and employees; the other half would come from general taxes. Some tax experts say that it might be cheaper to pay the entire amount by means of simple taxation.

An important feature of the bill is the provision for funds ($800 million in the first year) to improve the health care system by training more health care personnel and providing various incentives to establish more efficient methods of providing health care. This program would become operative before the insurance went into effect, for it is evident that until the health care system

[30] Lecture reported in *View,* Winter, 1971, p. 12.

became greatly enlarged and modernized, it could not meet the increased demand the insurance would generate.

The Kennedy-Griffiths bill may not be the one that is finally enacted, but the day when national health insurance proposals can be easily turned aside by special-interest lobbyists has gone forever. (See Taylor-Troelstrup Reading 74 for a comparison of six national health proposals.)

THE MEDICARE PROGRAM

Medicare is a Social Security health insurance program set up to help millions of Americans 65 and older, and many severely disabled people under 65, pay the high cost of health care. It is in two parts—hospital insurance and medical insurance.

The hospital insurance helps pay for hospitalization costs and for certain types of follow-up care *after* discharge. The medical insurance helps pay for doctors' services, outpatient hospital services, and many other medical items not covered by hospital insurance.

Financing Medicare   Medicare hospital insurance is financed by special contributions from employees, their employers, and self-employed people. Each group pays the same rate—1 percent of the first $12,000 of annual earnings (1974 rates). The medical insurance is voluntary and is financed by monthly premiums and by the federal government, which by law must pay at least one-half of the total program costs. The basic premium is $6.30 per month for the twelve-month period which begins in July of each year.

Hospital insurance   Hospital insurance helps pay for the cost of certain medical services such
benefits   as:

1.   Up to 90 days of inpatient care in any participating hospital in each benefit period. For the first 60 days, it pays for all covered services after the $72 deductible. For the sixty-first through the ninetieth day, it pays for all covered services after an $18 daily deductible. Care in a psychiatric hospital has a lifetime benefit of 190 days. There is also a "lifetime reserve" of 60 additional days if more than 90 days of hospital care is needed in any benefit period.

2.   Up to 100 days of care in each benefit period in a skilled nursing facility. Hospital insurance pays for all covered services for the first 20 days and all but $9 a day for up to 80 more days.

3.   Up to 100 home health "visits" from a participating home health agency for each benefit period.

4.   Covered costs in a hospital or nursing home, including a semiprivate room, nursing services, drugs, supplies, appliances, and other services.

Medical insurance   Medical insurance benefits help pay for the following services
benefits   1.   Physicians' services no matter where you receive them—in the doctor's office, the hospital, at home—including the medical supplies usually furnished by a doctor in his office, the services of his office nurse, and the drugs he administers as part of his treatment.

2.   Outpatient hospital services in an emergency room or an outpatient clinic.

3. Up to 100 home health visits each calendar year.

4. Outpatient physical therapy and speech pathology services under periodical review by a doctor.

5. A number of other services prescribed by your doctor such as diagnostic services, X-ray treatment, surgical dressings, artificial limbs, and oxygen.

6. Certain ambulance services.

7. Certain services by chiropractors.

8. Home and office services by independent physical therapists, with certain payment limitations.

Medical insurance pays for these services

Each year, as soon as covered medical expenses go over $60 (the annual deductible), medical insurance will pay 80 percent of the *reasonable charges* for all covered services for the remainder of the benefit period. The insurance, however, does not cover routine physical checkups, prescription drugs, eye examinations and glasses, hearing aids, immunizations, dentures and routine dental care, orthopedic shoes, and the first three pints of blood received in each calendar year.

At the present time, Medicare will cover about half of the medical and hospital services incurred in a benefit period. Sometimes a patient who is hospitalized for a short period may pay as little as 10 percent of the bills.

Supplementary insurance is needed

It is usually beneficial to have "Medicare-Extended" coverage from a Blue Cross–Blue Shield organization or from a reliable private health insurance company. It is good policy to avoid purchasing supplementary health protection from most mail-order insurance companies.

WHAT ABOUT FUNERAL COSTS?

Regardless of our skill in giving our loved ones the best health care possible, death is an inevitability. Consequently, a family should be knowledgeable about the cost of services and merchandise provided by the funeral director, burial receptacles, interment or cremation, monument or marker, and miscellaneous expenses for flowers, burial clothing, transportation of the body, and so on.

Cost of services and merchandise

The National Funeral Directors Association, representing some 14,000 of the 25,000 funeral directors in the nation, said that the average adult funeral in 1966 cost about $820. About 26 percent of the funerals cost over $1,000.[31] These figures do not include vault, cemetery or crematorium expenses; monument or marker; or miscellaneous expenses.

You save only if you get less

The U.S. Department of Commerce figures for the cost of a "regular adult funeral" would average out at $1,160.[32] Regardless of the difference in the price of funerals, the fact remains that "one funeral director has the same things to sell that another one has." So said Charles L. Arnold, vice president of the Missouri Funeral Directors and Embalmers Association, when testifying before the Senate Subcommittee on Antitrust and Monopoly. He said: "The difference in price is in overhead. The funeral director determines his overhead costs by

[31] Sidney Margolius, *Funeral Costs and Death Benefits,* Public Affairs pamp. no. 409, 1967.

[32] U.S. Senate Hearings, Subcommittee on Antitrust and Monopoly, part 1, *Antitrust Aspects of the Funeral Industry,* Government Printing Office, Washington, 1967, p. 1.

dividing annual operating costs by the number of adult funerals he performed in a year."

The Senate subcommittee got information for comparative figures from one funeral home in Missouri that performed between 100 and 200 funerals annually. This home had twelve types of caskets, ranging from a low-priced wooden casket to caskets made of mahogany and fiber glass. The price of the cheapest casket was $50 and the price of the basic service with that casket was $150. Progressing upward in cost, he reported these figures, giving the wholesale cost first and the basic funeral price second: $54 and $150, $72 and $397, $120 and $863, $167.50 and $939, $175 and $997, $246 and $1,237, and finally, $439.15 and $1,989. So the "operating spread," between casket cost and funeral price, reported by this funeral firm ranged from $96 to $1,549.85.

Interment or cremation

Interment or cremation charges are in addition to the basic costs paid to the funeral director for goods and services he provides. In most cemeteries, the cost of an individual grave space, says the National Funeral Directors Association leaflet, ranges from $75 to $350. Costs of opening and closing the grave run from $45 to $150, and the price of individual crypts in indoor mausolea start at about $600. Outside garden crypts begin at about $350. Vaults of metal or concrete cost from $100 upward.

The cost of cremation is around $100. Urns to hold the ashes or remains cost from $50 to $250. Columbaria niches to hold such urns range from $35 to $750. Cremation is the cheapest and quickest way to reduce the body to the elements from which it came. There need be no ashes unless a relative requests them, and hence no need for urns.

Monument or marker

Bronze markers vary in price from $75 to $300, and stone monuments begin at $60. The cost can run very high, depending on material, design, and craftsmanship. This industry, however, is facing a future that is "grave" because more and more people prefer either cremation or burial in memorial parks that restrict or forbid tombstones.

Miscellaneous expenses

The cost of flowers, burial clothing, transportation of the body, additional limousines or flower cars, honorarium for the clergyman, and newspaper death notices make up some of the miscellaneous items paid through the funeral director or directly by the family.

The funeral industry and its problems

The National Funeral Service Journal, a trade journal, stated that a funeral director "must condition the public mind to associate established funeral customs with all that is desirable in the American way of life." The basis for doing this, the writer said, lies in "cultivating certain subconscious opinions regarding the funeral service." And he added that "chief of these is the acceptance of the funeral as a valid status symbol—which in fact it is." In short, it is argued, with some justification, give the public what it wants.

There seems to be little doubt that the funeral industry as a whole has some special difficulties. The death rate, for example, is going down, and the funeral market is limited by the death rate. Meanwhile the number of funeral homes grows. Some 25,000 funeral homes share 1,750,000 deaths annually, for an average of seventy funerals each. In fact, 60 percent of the funeral homes average one funeral a week, while the famous Forest Lawn Memorial Park in Los Angeles has about 6,000 funerals a year.

There is no doubt, too, that the funeral industry faces increasing costs. Chapels are luxuries with wall-to-wall carpeting, expensive organs, "slumber rooms," and the "selection room" where coffins and burial garments are displayed. A hearse costs about $15,000 to $20,000. Labor costs have increased. Furthermore, calls have to be answered around the clock. According to NFDA (the National Funeral Directors Association), the average funeral home represents an investment of $116,459 for land, buildings, equipment, cars, inventory, and service charges outstanding. The total annual pretax income for the owner of an average funeral home comes to $20,671, says the NFDA.

Prefinanced burial plans

Funeral directors have other problems that need attention. Many of them have been accused by the Federal Trade Commission of using high-pressure promotion in getting people to sign up for prefinanced funeral plans and burial plans. The abuse, said the FTC, was that the first 20 percent went to the sales firm; 80 percent went into a trust fund. Income from the trust also went to the sales firm, and the sales firm in due time split some of the income with the funeral home named in the burial agreement. Some firms, say the FTC, pay half of the first 20 percent to the salesmen. The NFDA and the Better Business Bureaus have opposed this kind of preneed plans.

There is nothing wrong with preplanning a funeral and burial. Consumers have been well-advised to engage in careful preplanning. Clearly, the consumer should be aware of, and perhaps should be protected by, state laws against being high-pressured by promoters into making hasty decisions to buy prefinanced plans. Certainly, a salesman deserves some commission for services rendered. But the interest on the payments in the trust fund should go back to the trust fund, just as in mutual fund investment. Furthermore, for the protection of the people involved, trust funds should be carefully regulated and supervised by the state.

Advertising

It doesn't pay to advertise?

Another problem concerns the right of a funeral director to advertise truthful pricing information.[33] A case in point receiving national attention occurred in Wisconsin. A Wisconsin funeral home prepared a simple 3- by 5-inch printed card showing the range of prices it had charged for 1,036 adult funerals con-

[33] Ibid., pp. 12, 43.

ducted over a period of time. The funeral home director said he wanted to inform the public about funeral prices. The printed card was available to visitors at the funeral home. The cards were also available at civic and community meetings.

After prolonged discussion, the Wisconsin Funeral Directors Association (membership in the National Funeral Directors Association) finally suspended the funeral home from membership in WFDA. Later, the NFDA took similar action by reaffirming the price advertising prohibition contained in their code of ethics.

In 1964, the U.S. Justice Department announced a proposed consent judgment intended to encourage price competition among funeral directors in advertising their services. The judgment prohibiting the National Funeral Directors Association from engaging in any activity to limit advertising of prices for funeral services was accepted by the association. The judgment also provided for local and state groups to offer readmission to any funeral director who had been expelled or suspended or who had withdrawn because of restrictions on price advertising.[34]

Public protests against high costs

With all the built-in extravagance attached to the rites of death, is it possible for a prudent person to have a dignified and inexpensive funeral? Many people think it is possible. Doctors, lawyers, clergymen of all faiths, union officials, cooperative organizations, and consumer groups are protesting against funeral practices that are needlessly costly and often relegate spiritual values to a place of minor importance.

Reducing funeral costs

Here are suggestions for the average consumer confronted with arranging for a funeral:

1. Discuss the funeral arrangements with your minister, rabbi, or priest. It is generally wise for the clergyman to accompany a member of the family to the funeral parlor to help resist any pressure toward overspending.

2. Arrange for the service to be held at your church.

3. Select an inexpensive casket and consider limiting or omitting flower displays.

4. Omit embalming and hold the service as soon as possible.

5. Arrange for cremation or for delivery of the body if it has been willed to a medical or scientific society. These methods of disposition appeal to many public-minded and sophisticated persons today.

6. Permit the funeral to center around the spirit rather than the body by having the casket closed during the service. Many families prefer to have the casket removed from the actual service.

7. Keep the graveside service, if any, private—only for the family and close friends.

8. Request the funeral director, in advance, to provide a detailed, itemized estimate of the funeral costs.

9. Join a memorial association if possible.

[34] *The Wall Street Journal,* July 18, 1968.

Memorial associations

Membership in a memorial or funeral society can be a solution if there is such a society in your community. In 1950 there were about eight memorial associations in the United States and Canada, and in 1964 there were about 115 in these two countries, with a membership of some 200,000 persons.

Memorial societies a better choice

Memorial societies [35] are nonprofit, and life membership fees·average $5 for an individual and $15 for a family. A few societies are merely educational, acting as sources for information; others contract with funeral homes to provide a dignified, simple, and modest burial. The cost of embalming and cremation, without a formal ceremony, may average $250. For a modest coffin and private burial before a memorial service, the charge is usually around $350, not including a cemetery lot. More elaborate ceremonial arrangements are negotiated with the funeral home.

The society assists members in advance planning, helps with subsequent memorial services, and may be of aid in case of contractual misunderstandings.

A twenty-story mausoleum

The newest thing in funerals is the crypt above ground—high above ground. Some funeral directors think it may provide the answer to the high cost of dying. The idea is to combine mortuary, funeral (minus casket), and entombment facilities under one roof.

Instead of a casket, the corpse would be placed for viewing on a mattress-like base resting on a bier resembling a bed; this would be available in a variety of furniture styles—Early American, French Provincial, and so on.

High-rise—the newest fashion in burial plans

Before entombment, the body would be placed in standardized fiber-glass encasement. All biers would cost the same and would be included in a standard package price—ranging from $1,100 to $1,200, as against a so-called typical, complete funeral cost of about $1,200. Of course, a complete funeral for some folks would far exceed $1,200. The innovators claim that maintenance costs would be lower and that there would be no need for caskets or for digging and covering graves. Funerals could also take place around the clock and in any kind of weather. The idea is an interesting one and may result in lower-cost funerals, providing real competition is permitted. The next step could be the sale of franchises to enterprising businessmen.

QUESTIONS FOR DISCUSSION

1. Families cannot obtain adequate health security at a moderate price from private health insurance companies because the contracts provide sickness insurance, not health benefits. Explain what this statement means.

2. Health care systems in this country are largely a commercial enterprise. Explain.

3. How do you feel about laws that will not allow prescription drugs to be advertised? (Thirty-four states still have such laws.)

---

[35] Information on memorial associations may be obtained from the Continental Association of Funeral and Memorial Societies, 59 East Van Buren Street, Chicago, Ill. 60605.

4.   What is your reaction, in the light of ever-increasing hospital costs (an average per-day room charge of about $84, up to about $125), when some specialists such as pathologists insist on getting a certain percentage of the income from all lab fees? Under such arrangements, incomes for laboratory heads run from $200,000 to $500,000 a year. What can be done about such arrangements?

5.   It would seem that Blue Cross, which pays back in health care costs about 97.9 percent of premium costs, and Blue Shield, which returns about 91.1 percent of premium charges, are about the best prepaid nonprofit private plans we can hope for. Is this a fact? Why haven't BC and BS been able to hold down hospital and medical service costs?

6.   Can you find out why most of the health care plans (even BC and BS) do not permit layman control of the overall policies of the organization?

7.   What are the prospects that federally aided HMOs will deliver quality health care to subscribers at a cost that all can afford?

8.   Our health system should be based on the principle that every citizen has a right to universal health care coverage. Do you agree? Explain your position.

PROJECTS

1.   Prepare a report on the Group Health Cooperative of Puget Sound. This comprehensive prepaid nonprofit health care plan is considered one of the best in this country. What accounts for its success? Send for some of the literature explaining the plan in detail, including subscriber fees, salary arrangements with doctors, the nature and quality of the services, and so on. Write to the Group Health Cooperative of Puget Sound, 200 Fifteenth Avenue, East, Seattle, Washington 98102.

2.   Read *The Death of a President,* by William Manchester, which gives an almost unbelievable account of how two funeral directors (one in Dallas and one in Washington, D.C.) literally took over the burial arrangements of President John F. Kennedy. Here you will see funeral directors at about their worst.

3.   Make a list of six or more common prescription drugs. Go to as many pharmacies as possible and ask the pharmacist the cost of each drug. Some pharmacists may not give you all the prices. (This resistance to giving price information is in direct conflict with our free enterprise system.) Compare prices for the same prescription drugs.

Read the article entitled "Drug Pricing and the Rx Police State" in *Consumer Reports,* March, 1972. Select prescriptions from the list of some 94 prescription drugs given in this article. Then ask a physician to write down the name of each drug, the strength (50 mg, for example), and the quantity. Given that information, pharmacies may be willing to quote the price over the telephone.

4.   Visit a funeral home and ask the director or assistant to assume that you are making arrangements, for the first time, to bury a member of your

family. Take notes as you discuss each kind of service and the costs. Then assume that you have a limited budget—say $1,000. What kind of a burial could you arrange for $1,000?

5. The soaring cost of health care has reached the crisis stage. We now have several proposals for congressional action—the Kennedy-Griffiths bill (the social insurance approach), the Javits bill (a combination approach), and the Fulton-Broyhill bill (backed by the American Medical Association), and the Pettengill-Aetna bill (both the private insurance approach). Compare these three different approaches and decide which one will best meet our health care crisis.

SUGGESTED READINGS

Borsody, Robert P.: "Health Maintenance Organizations and the Neighborhood Health Centers," *Clearing House Review,* July, 1972, pp. 120–129.

Denenberg, Herbert: "Insurance in the Age of the Consumer," *Best's Review,* April, 1970, p. 38.

Ferguson, Allen, Jr.: *National Health Proposals,* University Extension, Berkeley, Calif., 1971.

Foran, Eugene: *Funeral Facts and Figures,* National Funeral Directors Association, 1970. (38 pp.)

Georgopoulos, Basil: *Organization Research on Health Institutions,* Institute for Social Research, Ann Arbor, Mich. Summer, 1972.

Goodwin, David: *Stop Wasting Your Insurance Dollars,* Simon and Schuster, New York, 1969.

"HMO Projects," *Medical Economics,* Mar. 16, 1971.

Hoyt, Edwin P.: *Your Health Insurance: A Story of Failure,* The John Day Company, Inc., New York, 1970.

Kennedy, Edward: *In Critical Condition: The Crisis in America's Health Care,* Simon and Schuster, New York, 1972.

Landphair, Theodore: "The Key is Managed Grief: How Funeral Directors—and Students—View Their Careers," *The National Observer,* June 8, 1970, p. 22.

"National Health Insurance and Health Security," *Congressional Record,* proceedings and debates of 91st Cong., 2d Sess., pp. 1–25.

Prescription Drug Pricing, Consumer Federation of America, New York, September, 1972.

CHAPTER 12
BUYING PROTECTION: SOCIAL SECURITY, LIFE INSURANCE, AND ANNUITIES

Every year in the United States, 200,000 more men die than women, and the ratio is increasing. In every adult age group, women already outnumber men. One reason is that medical science seems to have benefited women more than men. Deaths connected with childbearing, which used to help balance the hazards of being a man, have been reduced to near zero. More women are staying alive.

What about the men? Twenty percent more men than women die of cancer. While this disease kills more women in their middle years, it strikes the men when they are under 30 and over 55. Still more important is heart disease, which is responsible for 40 percent of all deaths. Between ages 40 and 75, nearly twice as many men as women die of heart disease.

Accidents account for more than three-fourths of the extra male deaths between ages 10 and 35. Between ages 20 and 24, more than six times as many men as women die in accidents—largely automobile accidents.

By 1975, at the present death rate, women will outnumber men in the United States by 3,600,000. Life insurance agents say that wives, generally, object to the purchase of life insurance because they do not want to think about the possible death of their husbands. But no widow objects to the life insurance payment when such death occurs. In a way, it is not life insurance that costs money; it is the things that the widow and children will need, and life insurance can provide that cost money.

THE CONSUMER'S INTEREST IN BUYING PROTECTION

But, some say, there is little or no need for personal life insurance because of pension plans, employee group life insurance, and Social Security. It is true that most families have one or more of these protections in the event of premature death of the major breadwinner. But the fact remains that these protections are only minimal.

Social Security—no cure-all
Employee group insurance seldom reaches $5,000 in protection, and then only while the breadwinner is employed by the company. Retirement or a change in employment usually ends employee group insurance protection.

Present Social Security benefits do not meet the minimum needs of the average retired couple, and the cash grant of $255 for burial is hardly enough for this purpose. Social Security is not enough insurance against death unless the covered breadwinner dies before the children are 18 years of age. The widow under 65 could then in 1973 receive a maximum of $531.18 a month for herself and one child, and a maximum of $620.40 a month for herself and two or more children under 18 years of age. When the children reach their eighteenth birthday, all payments in their behalf cease.

Social Security will not pay off all a man's illness and burial expenses, and it will not pay off his mortgage or other debts; it will, however, pay income to a widow under 65. It will provide educational funds for children who stay in school or college until age 22. Social Security will not supply money for emergencies or opportunities; it will not pay a retirement income to a man who wants to retire before 62 or to a wife before age 62; it will not allow income benefits to be taken in a lump sum; and it will not allow invasion of principal in case of emergency.

Social Security, however, can do a great deal. Social Security, as presently constituted, is not intended to be a complete financial protection program. Social Security does provide for "basic" protection for a modest retirement income (really insurance), disability income insurance, and Medicare. So Social Security occupies a vital part in family financial planning. No family can plan its life insurance program intelligently without figuring out the size and duration of the Social Security benefits. But overestimating Social Security benefits is more dangerous than underestimating them.

Defense against the threat of insecurity

Elmo Roper, a leading authority in measuring public opinion, concluded on the basis of twelve years of opinion polling that what the average American wants most in life is a sense of security.

A sense of security is important

No two families can successfully work out the same security program. But they can begin by noting the major hazards to security and then find the best means for protection against them. The major hazards to financial security and the most common defenses employed are these:

Unemployment.   Unemployment compensation; a savings fund for contingencies

Illness.   Medicare; health and medical insurance; a savings fund for emergencies.

Accident.   Social Security; accident insurance; in special cases, state workmen's compensation; a savings fund

Old age.   Social Security old-age insurance; retirement pensions; a savings fund; annuities

Premature death.   Life insurance; survivors' insurance under the Social Security Act

The particular needs of each family will be apparent to its members. For example, a government employee protected by civil service may not need unemployment insurance. A carpenter, on the other hand, is constantly faced with seasonal unemployment. Most professional people, such as teachers and doctors, usually have continuous work and should build their financial defenses around other insecurities than unemployment.

The needs of a family with several children are large compared with the needs of a childless couple. The latter could minimize its life insurance expenditures and build up larger emergency and retirement income funds.

The first important step, then, in planning a security program is to evaluate each hazard in terms of a family's particular needs. Then select the defenses that will best protect against the insecurities. This is, of course, easier said than done. But few informed persons would disagree with the following statements:

1.   Protection of family dependents through insurance should be the first consideration. In purchasing insurance, the primary objective should be to get the most protection for the lowest cost that safety permits.

2.   Investment for the education of children and for retirement should be a second but important consideration.

3.   The financing to meet the minimum needs of a family should be the safest and best that is available—namely Social Security, United States savings bonds, and insurance.

Financial security goals   Every family has a level of basic living costs. How much it can save is determined by the difference that exists between this level and its income. The closer
these two come together, the more difficult it is to save.

How much you can save is primarily controlled by how determined you are
to save for future use. One thing is certain: unless you plan to save early and
methodically, you are not likely to achieve your goals. There can be no evasion
in setting aside the sum agreed on for savings.

No one is likely to argue that the savings pattern should be the same for all
families having similar net incomes and spending units. For some families, it
is important to concentrate on certain kinds of savings because they will sacrifice many things before touching these savings. Some families are unable to
save at all, while some go to the other extreme and deny themselves daily
"good living." It goes without saying that a happy medium between reckless
extravagance and niggardliness makes for greater satisfaction and happiness.

1. Insurance

There should be life insurance and disability insurance on the breadwinner
to protect the family from loss of income in case of death or of partial or permanent disability. Health and medical insurance is necessary to protect the
family group against hospital and surgical-medical bills.

2. Emergency fund

A cash reserve fund should be built up to a minimum sum equal to two months'
income.

3. Educational fund

Since most families hope to give their children a college education, the way to
build such a fund is to begin as early as possible, but after goals 1 and 2 have
been achieved.

4. Retirement

Old-age benefits under Social Security are a base for retirement, but not sufficient to maintain the standard of living to which most families are accustomed.
Therefore, Social Security should be supplemented by investments and perhaps
an annuity purchased just prior to retirement.

5. A mortgage-free home

Some families may aim to achieve this before adding to a retirement fund.

The United States, in its early history, was a developing country with a vast
frontier and a predominantly agricultural economy. One of the early forms of
"social security" was the availability of up to 160 acres of free land, given by

the government to any person who wished to be a farmer. American citizens have always been encouraged to provide their own security, to take advantage of the opportunities in a young nation rich in natural resources and with a rapidly growing population.

That everyone should plan for his own security remains a cherished heritage of the American people. Essential to the purpose is an economy that provides full employment at a high wage level. Today the great majority of Americans have savings, life insurance, a home, and other forms of personal property that contribute to security as well as to a high standard of living.

Individual effort by itself, however, is not sufficient protection against the insecurities of a society now highly industrialized and urbanized. Such a society, while increasing the productive capacity of the nation manyfold and providing the basis for an ever-increasing standard of living, has created a dependence on cash income that was unknown in the earlier history of the United States. Also, the small, mobile family of today, while well suited to an urban-industrial economy, is less able than the three- or four-generation family of the past to provide mutual care and support.

Therefore, the American people acted through their government to establish a Social Security system that protects against the risks common to all and against which citizens as individuals are unable to provide adequate safeguards. The system serves as a foundation on which individuals may build additional protection through their own efforts and with the help of their employers.

How Social Security works

The basic idea of Social Security is a simple one: During working years employees, their employers, and self-employed people pay Social Security contributions, which are pooled in three special funds. When earnings stop or are reduced because the worker retires, dies, or becomes disabled, monthly cash benefits are paid from these funds to replace part of the earnings the family has lost.

Part of the contributions go into a hospital insurance fund; and when workers and their dependents reach 65, money from this fund helps pay their hospital bills.

Voluntary medical insurance, also available to people 65 or over, helps pay doctor bills and other medical expenses. Money to pay medical insurance benefits comes from a fourth special fund. Half of the money in this fund comes from the premiums paid by people who have signed up for medical insurance, and the other half is paid by the federal government.

About 28 million men, women, and children were receiving monthly cash Social Security benefits in early 1973. Their total included about 1.2 million disabled workers and nearly 1 million of their dependents. Nearly 2.4 million children of deceased workers were receiving benefits at that time, and about half a million widowed mothers were receiving benefits because they were caring for their children entitled to benefits. About 2.8 million older widows and dependent widowers were also receiving benefits.

Protection stays with you

The Social Security protection you earn stays with you when you change jobs, when you move from city to city, when you move to another state.

More than nine of every ten working people in the United States are building protection for themselves and their families under the Social Security system. Almost all other people are either covered by another federal, state, or

FIGURE 12-1 **How Social Security works**

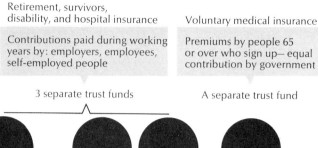

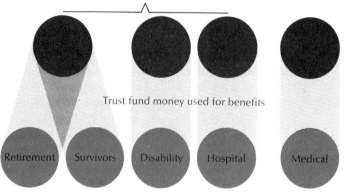

local government retirement system or are protected under Social Security as dependents of other workers.

Nearly any job you take is covered by Social Security; your earnings from any business you go into are covered, too; and you earn protection under Social Security while you serve in the armed forces. Through 1967, only your military basic pay counted toward Social Security benefits. Beginning with January, 1968, additional earnings credits, generally amounting to $100, were counted for each month of active duty. No additional deductions are made from your pay for these additional credits.

Financing Social Security
Your wages and self-employment income are entered on your individual record by the Social Security Administration. This record of your earnings will be used to determine your eligibility for benefits and the amount of cash benefits you will receive.

The maximum earnings that can count for Social Security and on which you pay Social Security contributions are shown in the accompanying table. Earn-

YEAR	AMOUNT
1937–1950	$3,000
1951–1954	3,600
1955–1958	4,200
1959–1965	4,800
1966–1967	6,600
1968–1971	7,800
1972	9,000
1973	10,800
1974	12,000

ings over the maximums may have been reported to your Social Security record and may appear on your earnings statement, but cannot be used to figure your benefit rate.

When you work for more than one employer in a year and pay Social Security contributions on wages over the maximum amount that can count for Social Security, you may claim a refund of the excess contributions on your income tax return for that year. If you work for only one employer and he deducts too much in contributions, you should apply to the employer for a refund.

A refund is made only when more than the required amount of contributions has been paid.

Table 12-1 shows the schedule of contribution rates now in the law. Table 12-2 shows the contribution rate schedule for self-employed people.

Working wives add to Social Security benefits

When a wife works, there's more than the total family income to be considered. Her potential Social Security benefits could be substantial. While it is fairly well known that a wife's retirement benefits would equal her husband's, assuming she earns over $12,000 in 1974, she's entitled to other benefits that might be even more important.

For example, a wife who has enough coverage under Social Security can start drawing retirement benefits at age 62, even if her husband is still employed. A wife who has not worked gets nothing until her husband retires. In addition, should a working wife become disabled, she receives benefits for her-

TABLE 12-1 Contribution Rate Schedule for Employees and Employers (Each)

	PERCENTAGE OF COVERED EARNINGS		
YEARS	For Retirement, Survivors, and Disability Insurance	For Hospital Insurance	Total
1971–72	4.6	.6	5.2
1973–77	4.6	.9	5.5
1978–85	4.5	1.0	5.5
1986–92	4.5	1.1	5.6
1993–97	4.5	1.2	5.7

TABLE 12-2 Contribution Rate Schedule for Self-employed People

	PERCENTAGE OF COVERED EARNINGS		
YEARS	For Retirement, Survivors, and Disability Insurance	For Hospital Insurance	Total
1971–72	6.9	.6	7.5
1973–77	6.9	.9	7.8
1978–85	6.7	1.0	7.7
1986–92	6.7	1.1	7.8
1993–97	6.7	1.2	7.9

A working wife earns more than just income

self and her children, regardless of her husband's earnings. A nonworking wife receives nothing for herself or her children. Of course, a widow who has not worked under Social Security can get disability benefits starting at age 50 based on her husband's coverage.

If a working wife dies, her children receive benefits to age 18—or age 22 if they are full-time students—no matter how much the father earns. Children of a nonworking wife, however, receive nothing.

Changes in your Social Security

There have been and will continue to be big changes in Social Security and Medicare as a result of amendments to the Social Security law in July, 1972, and in October, 1972. Most of these provisions were written to take effect shortly after passage of the amendments, and other changes will go into effect after 1973.

The 20 percent across-the-board increase in monthly benefits showed up in the October, 1972, checks. In January, 1973, pensioners got a second hike in their checks as a result of further changes voted in mid-October, 1972.

On January 1, 1973, employers and employees both began paying a tax of 5.85 percent on as much as $10,800 of earnings, a maximum of $631.80 each and an increase of $163.80 (or a 35 percent increase over the amount paid in 1972). Self-employed persons pay 8 percent on the same base, or as much as $864.

The rate is scheduled to rise only a few tenths of 1 percent over the next few decades, but the base will soar to $12,000 in 1974 and, beginning in 1975, by whatever amount is necessary to keep pace with increases in the average covered earnings of workers. Current and future benefits will rise according to changes in the Consumer Price Index.

Other Social Security changes

A few of the more important changes Congress made in Social Security and Medicare are these:

1. The no-loss ceiling was raised from $1,680 to $2,100, reducing the benefits for working after retirement $1 for each $2 earned over that amount and removing the $1-for-$1 trade-off entirely. Future adjustments will be made as average earnings rise.

2. Future retirees will obtain a 1 percent increase for each year their retirement is delayed between the ages of 65 and 72.

3. Up to 1972, men and women were permitted to draw benefits at age 62 on their own wage credits, but men received smaller amounts, despite the fact they have a shorter life expectancy. This was due to the fact that in determining the average monthly wage on which benefits were based, females needed to include earnings only to age 62, while males had to include income to age 65. Congress extended to men the same rules that apply to women—inclusion of earnings only to age 62.

4. Conversely, although it costs as much for a widow to live as it did for her late husband, widows claiming benefits at age 62 or later received only 82½ percent of their spouses' primary benefit. Now widows may claim the full 100 percent at age 65.

5. Medicare benefits were extended after July 1, 1973, to persons of any age on the Social Security *disability* rolls after two years of entitlement.

6. As of January 1, 1973, the annual deductible for the medical insurance

part of Medicare is $60 instead of $50. This means that after you have $60 in doctor bills or other covered expenses in 1973, medical insurance will pay 80 percent of the reasonable charges for the rest of the year. The same change was made for home health care.

7.   As of July 1, 1973, medical insurance covers certain colostomy care supplies and some services by independent physical therapists and chiropractic services.

8.   There are now additional Social Security credits of $100 for each month of active military service from 1957 through 1967.

There will no doubt be other changes in the near future. The biggest change may come in the form of a national health insurance proposal such as that put forth in the Kennedy-Griffiths bill or a combination of other proposals mentioned in Chapter 11.

Social Security cash payments

Because of the thousands of possible combinations, no simple table can show what each person or couple will receive in Social Security. Table 12-3, however, gives approximate monthly cash benefits or payments. There are three main times for action: (1) when you reach age 65, whether you intend to retire or not; (2) when a working member of your family dies or becomes disabled; and (3) when you reach age 72, when benefits cease being affected by income. Check with one of the Social Security offices nearest you.

So, until we get a complete, comprehensive social insurance system for all our people, the present Social Security protection, as amended from time to time, is the best, per dollar of premium, available in our country.

TABLE 12-3   Social Security Benefits

AVERAGE YEARLY EARNINGS AFTER 1950*	$923 OR LESS	$1,800	$3,000	$4,200	$5,400	$6,600	$7,800	$9,000
Retired worker 65 or older; disabled worker under 65	$ 84.50	$134.30	$174.80	$213.30	$250.60	$288.40	$331.00	$354.50
Wife 65 or older	42.30	67.20	87.40	106.70	125.30	144.20	165.50	177.30
Retired worker at 62	67.60	107.50	139.90	170.70	200.50	230.80	264.80	283.60
Wife at 62, no child	31.80	50.40	65.60	80.10	94.00	108.20	124.20	133.00
Widow at 60	73.30	96.10	125.10	152.60	179.30	206.30	236.70	253.50
Widow or widower at 62	84.50	110.80	144.30	176.00	206.80	238.00	273.10	292.50
Disabled widow at 50	51.30	67.30	87.50	106.80	125.50	144.30	165.60	177.30
Wife under 65 and one child	42.30	67.20	92.50	157.40	217.30	233.90	248.30	265.90
Widowed mother and one child	126.80	201.50	262.20	320.00	376.60	432.60	496.60	531.80
Widowed mother and two children	126.80	201.50	267.30	370.70	467.90	522.30	579.30	620.40
One child of retired or disabled worker	42.30	67.20	87.40	106.70	125.30	144.20	165.50	177.30
One surviving child	84.50	100.80	131.10	160.00	188.00	216.30	248.30	265.90
Maximum family payment	126.80	201.50	267.30	370.70	467.90	522.30	579.30	620.40

* Generally, average earnings are figured over the period from 1951 until the worker reaches retirement age, becomes disabled, or dies. Up to five years of low earnings or no earnings can be excluded. The maximum earnings creditable for Social Security are $3,600 for 1951–1954; $4,200 for 1955–1958; $4,800 for 1959–1965; $6,600 for 1966–1967; and $7,800 for 1968–1971. The maximum creditable for 1972 was $9,000. The maximum creditable for 1973 is $10,800, and beginning in 1974, it will be $12,000. However, average earnings cannot reach these amounts until later. Because of this, the benefits shown in the last column on the right generally will not be payable until later. When a person is entitled to more than one benefit, the amount actually payable is limited to the larger of the benefits.

We said earlier that Social Security is not intended to protect people from the cradle to the grave. It does, however, provide a good base for planning further protection against the economic hazards common to all of us. One of these economic hazards is the possibility of the premature death of the major breadwinner or breadwinners.

LIFE INSURANCE

Social Security provides a minimum subsistence for survivors. It is intended to keep them from actual minimal need, not to give them all the basic comforts of life. Life insurance will help complete a protection program. In evaluating family needs, these questions are pertinent:

1. Which family members should be insured?
2. How much insurance should be carried?
3. What kind of insurance is best?
4. Which insurance companies should be selected?

But first, something about the nature of life insurance and the money value of the major breadwinner.

The lengthening life-span

Longevity in the United States has changed but little in recent years. The average length of life in 1965 was 70.2 years, the same as in 1964. It had previously reached that figure in 1961, after which an unusually high prevalence of acute respiratory disease resulted in slight setbacks for two years.

The improvement since the turn of the century has been great. On the basis of today's mortality conditions, three-fourths of the newborn may be expected to reach their sixty-third birthday and half may attain 75 years of age. Around 1900, according to mortality conditions prevailing at that time, less than half the newborn were expected to reach age 63 and only a fourth had prospects of living to 75. However, the bulk of this progress was achieved in the earlier part of the century, in sharp contrast to the relatively stationary situation in the past decade. Between 1900 and 1956, expectation of life at birth, for all persons, increased by over twenty years, but since then it has improved by less than a year.

Life insurance—a supplement to Social Security

In 1965 the expectation of life at birth for white females was 74.7 years, an increase of only a year since 1956. Among white males the corresponding figures were 67.3 years in 1956 and 67.6 in 1965, a gain of just three-tenths of a year. White men 20 years old in 1965 had, on the average, 50.2 years of life ahead of them.

The longevity of nonwhite persons is considerably less than that of whites. Among nonwhites the expectation of life at birth in 1965 was 61.1 years for males, the same as in 1956. Among nonwhite females the figure rose from 65.9 years in 1956 to 67.4 years in 1965, increasing 1½ years.

Sharing risks

Insurance is a plan by which large numbers of people, each in some danger of unforeseen loss, are brought together for mutual protection so that when one person suffers a loss, it can be made good by the premiums of all the others in the group. For example, term insurance is a year-to-year wager on survival. The insurance company statisticians, from a study of life expectancy tables and interest rates over the years, have figured out a system that works like this:

Of 1,000 men, age 30 and apparently healthy, two will die within the next year. If each of these men buys a $10,000 policy good for five years, insurance companies can sell it to each of them for about $55 a year. This will put enough money in the "kitty" to pay the salesmen's commissions, the insurance companies' overhead, and $10,000 to each of the ten men who will die within the five years. The total five-year premiums of around $275 each, for those men who continue to live, remain in the "kitty."

The odds on the term insurance bet change each year as a man gets older, and the premiums have to go up at five-year intervals for a five-year term contract. At the age of 40, a $10,000 term contract costs about $85 a year; at age 50, about $160. Other kinds of life insurance, like ordinary life, have built-in savings in the policy, so the statisticians have to include interest in the cost calculations.

The principle of the law of probability, or the law of averages, is basic in figuring premium rates. Insurance companies have actuaries—skilled mathematicians—who study the proportion of people who die at certain ages. They figure rates of mortality based on hundreds of thousands of cases and the results are compiled in mortality tables, which insurance companies use as the basis for figuring the rate to charge for a particular kind of insurance policy.

When to buy life insurance

If a man is single and has no dependents, the only life insurance needed is enough to cover debts and final expenses. It is true that the younger a man is when buying life insurance, the lower the annual premium for any policy. This argument has several weaknesses. In the first place, the final cost remains about the same because the younger a man is when buying insurance, the longer he pays. Buying early may mean several years of needless expense if there is no need for protection. The odds are almost 65 to 1 that a healthy man of 20 or 25 will live at least five years.

On the other hand, delay in buying life insurance risks the development of some health condition that may make it impossible to get insurance other than group insurance, or makes it necessary to pay a higher premium as a poor medical risk. From the standpoint of insurability, then, the sooner you buy, the better.

It might be better for a single person, in reasonably good health and with no dependents, to delay purchasing life insurance (except enough to cover debts and final expenses) unless he is eligible for one of the United States government life insurance programs for veterans.

For a newly married couple, with the wife working, about the same protection is needed as when single. If the wife is not working but could, some income should be provided for the readjustment period. In case there are sizable debts, it would be wise to cover them with reducing term insurance.

Here is one case. A young couple has been married a year or so. The wife is a college graduate but has never worked. They have purchased a home with a small down payment and a large, economy-size mortgage. A baby is on the way. Do they need life insurance? The question appears silly. A better question would be "How much life insurance?" Failure to insure the husband's life to a reasonable amount would be an unpardonable irresponsibility in this case, because there are dependents who need financial protection.

Consider another case. This young couple has been married a year. The wife taught high school before marriage. Her folks are moderately wealthy. They expect no child as yet; they rent an apartment and have no big obligations. Do they need life insurance? There is probably no immediate need for life insurance unless each of them thinks it advisable to have a $2,000 ordinary life policy for funeral purposes. Conditions can change, of course. In the second example, if their present situation continued for many years, they might be considered irresponsible if they did not methodically and prudently invest each year to supplement their Social Security retirement or disability income.

Who needs life insurance?
There are many uses for life insurance, but its primary purpose is to *protect* dependents financially against the untimely death of the major breadwinner or breadwinners. It is well to remember that economic dependency in marriage has been decreasing. Most wives today can probably support themselves before they have children and, to a greater extent, after the children have grown up. Thus, life insurance must produce the income, together with Social Security and any other private resources, that will meet the financial responsibilities of the husband's dependents after his death. And what are those responsibilities?

1. Children come first

In most families children are dependent on their father's income for shelter, food, clothing, and other common needs. In this country a college education or a good vocational education usually extends a child's dependency to his twenty-second year or beyond. A part of this protection includes the mother, unless she has a career-type job that pays a decent salary. Most widows will probably need some outside support for their families, especially at the beginning. Therefore, a husband may justifiably feel that his insurance program should provide for some of his wife's upkeep at this stage of family life. A small income for the years between child rearing and retirement may be desirable. Ideally, when retirement is just around the corner for both parents or for only one, good planning will see to it that all the assets—Social Security, pensions, savings, investments, annuities and so on—will provide for the rest of their lives without the need for life insurance to protect against loss of income.

Unfortunately, the insurance industry seems to ignore the logic of insuring primarily the chief wage earner or earners. Almost 20 percent of all individual coverage sold is family-plan coverage, which spreads thin the coverage of the chief provider (inadequately covered) and covers the wife and child or children. *Consumers Union* shopping survey of life insurance and sellers gives a good illustration of the wrong kind of recommendations. Only one of the fifteen agents recommended pure term insurance, though this kind of insurance provides the maximum amount of life insurance protection for the premium dollar.[1]

[1] See what agents from five of the largest companies recommended in the case of a 38-year-old father, with a $10,000 income, some savings, $5,000 equity in his house, and a wife and two children in *Report on Life Insurance,* rev. ed., Consumers Union of U.S., Inc., Mount Vernon, N.Y., 1972, p. 16.

The father was underinsured at $24,145 coverage at annual premiums from $210 to $1,144. The hitch, of course, is obvious. Insurance companies pay low commissions on sales of pure term insurance, and so the desire for higher commissions was greater than the desire to plan a good program at a cost the father could afford. The best advice when planning a life insurance program is to start out with well-drawn-up specifications of your own. This is what this chapter is all about.

Be prepared to have an agent tell you that your child's future insurance costs will be reduced if you buy when he is quite young. The insurance cost may be lower than it would be later, but the payments include money wasted during the years when no insurance is needed. Did the child have economic dependents? If not, the largest amount of insurance necessary might be a $2,000 term policy for burial costs in case of premature death. Put the insurance on the major breadwinner. Most major providers are woefully underinsured today (the average life insurance on a breadwinner is only about $24,000).

Caveat emptor on campus

Students have become favorite prospects for insurance agents. Most college students are contacted several times, especially during their senior year. Much pressure is put on college students, despite the fact that those without dependents don't need life insurance. As a rule, he does not need life insurance unless a college student has children.

Consumers Union investigated the very successful effort to sell college students life insurance on a "buy now, pay later" arrangement, which goes something like this:[2] the company pays the first annual premium, and sometimes the second, with a loan to be paid off five or so years later. (The commission for such a policy is a generous 50 to 75 percent of the first annual premium.) The student signs a promissory note and a policy-assignment form, so that if he dies, the insurance company is the first beneficiary. Built into the policy is a separate savings account into which deposits are paid. After five years, the balance in this account will equal the sum owed. At this point, the insurer takes possession of the savings account—something like an installment loan. Since repayment of the loan depends on the student's paying future premiums, the company takes another precaution—an acceleration clause. If the student fails to pay any premium on time, the lender can demand payment for the *entire* loan—perfectly legal.

The best advice is: "Don't buy", says Consumers Union.

2. Should a wife be insured?

A regular working wife and mother whose earnings contribute regularly to the family income should be insured, but not a full-time mother at home. It is true that a wife makes a valuable economic contribution at home, but compared with the lifelong cost of feeding, clothing, transporting, doctoring, and entertaining a wife, the wages of a housekeeper may not even approach the cost-of-living items. Some "wife insurance," perhaps a decreasing term policy, would help tide a family over the transition period.

[2] *Consumer Reports,* January, 1972, pp. 50–51.

3. When is a husband adequately covered?

The amount of coverage is different for every family. Well-trained insurance agents today know how to find an answer by using the company computer. The arithmetic is elementary, and anyone can make the calculations at home *before* selecting the insurance company and policies. But first let's take a look at the four basic types of life insurance.

Four basic types of life insurance policies

Despite the many differing policies offered by life insurance companies, there are only four types of life insurance policies: (1) term, (2) straight life or ordinary life insurance, (3) limited payment life insurance, and (4) endowment insurance. All these types have in their contracts one or two elements. Term insurance is pure protection in the event of death. The other three types have one additional feature—savings. It is the savings feature, primarily, that makes these other types more expensive. So forget about the advertising or selling gimmicks like "modified life," "whole life special," "special protection policy," "pure endowment," "joint life," "last survivor life," "family protector," "contingency life," "retirement income," "family income," "preferred risk," and many other catchy but confusing terms.

Remember the basic principle when planning a life insurance program for your family—to gain the most protection at the lowest cost. Table 12-4, What Various Policies Cost, shows that term insurance gives much more short-term protection per premium dollar.

Term insurance—maximum protection at low cost

Term insurance is so named because it is sold for a term—usually for a period of one, five, ten, or twenty years, often with option to renew without another physical examination. Such policies are called *renewable term*. The rate is increased at the beginning of each new term because the rates are based on the age of the insured, and because there are no extra premium charges for savings, as there are in all other contracts.

In term insurance, there are no savings or investment features. It cannot be used as loan collateral or be surrendered for cash. You pay premiums only as long as you keep the protection. But this kind of insurance gives the family the highest protection for a limited period for the least cost, and it can be made the backbone of protection for dependents in event of premature death of the breadwinner. It provides almost twice as much protection per dollar cost as ordinary life—the next cheapest policy—during the early years of family life.

TABLE 12-4   What Various Policies Cost ($1,000 Policy), a Mutual Company

TYPE OF POLICY	AGE AT ISSUE		
	25	35	45
10-year renewable term	$ 4.93	$ 6.84	$12.89
Straight life (ordinary)	12.71	17.07	25.18
Payment to 65	14.37	20.79	35.30
20-payment life	23.33	27.97	35.30
Endowment at age 65	16.94	24.97	42.64
20-year endowment	39.35	39.73	42.64

It is generally wise to purchase renewable term insurance rather than nonrenewable insurance because it is adaptable to situations where temporary or decreasing protection is needed. Term insurance is best planned on a reducing basis so that it may be reduced or terminated as dependents no longer require a large amount of protection. It should be increased to maximum protection as each child is born and decreased to the point of no insurance on the father for the children after they are economically independent, perhaps around the age of 22.

Term insurance is best for young families

The maximum protection of the wife in the early years of marriage may be reduced gradually to zero when the husband reaches his retirement age at 65 or earlier. Then he could give up all life insurance with the possible exception of a $2,000 ordinary life policy (for last illness and burial) acquired shortly after marriage.

Figure 12-2, Life Insurance Program Using Reducing Renewable Term Insurance, shows how the purchase of renewable term insurance works out.

Before buying term insurance. The breadwinner should fully understand a reducing term insurance program before embarking on it. It does not build up an educational fund for the children in the event that the insured person lives. Nor does it necessarily provide a retirement fund or funds for other purposes. Additional savings must be used to plug these gaps in family financial planning. But the savings in excess premiums that would otherwise go into more expensive life insurance can be placed in more productive kinds of investment.

The theory of term insurance is that the family would have insurance for less money plus a larger cash fund if needed. But there are these questions to consider: Will the family save and invest the difference between level premium insurance, such as ordinary life, and reducing term insurance premiums? Will they be able to save beyond Social Security benefits, which are inadequate for comfortable living during retirement years?

If the breadwinner is uncertain about carrying out the use of reducing

FIGURE 12-2 Life insurance program using reducing renewable term insurance

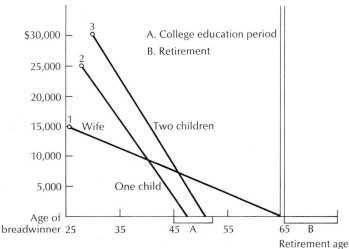

renewable term insurance, it is better to pay a little more for combined term insurance and ordinary life and a savings plan, described later. However, the family would get about the same benefits by the purchase of renewable term insurance and separate ordinary life policies, or by purchasing all renewable term insurance with the privilege of converting to ordinary life insurance without a physical examination after the children are financially independent.

Buying term insurance. After considering the problems involved in a term insurance program, keep the following main points in mind when buying term insurance:

1. Purchase only renewable and convertible term insurance.
2. Buy several term policies rather than one or two large ones. This gives greater freedom in dropping policies that are no longer needed and allows more convenient distribution of premium due dates.
3. Be examined by your own doctor before applying for term insurance. The physical examinations are usually more severe than for other contracts. If possible, you want to avoid rejections by the company doctor. A good agent can be helpful in this matter. If you have once been rejected, other companies will know it because your record will be on file at the Medical Information Bureau, created by the insurance companies.
4. Since there are no loan values on term insurance, maintain an emergency fund to pay the premium in case you fall ill or lose your job.
5. Compare the net cost of policies sold by several companies, because the final cost varies considerably among a few companies.
6. Select agents who are trained to give honest, intelligent technical help in servicing your general plan.
7. Select insurance companies that are sound financially and have a record of efficiency in selling the kind of insurance contract you want. Some companies are very efficient in selling one kind of contract and less efficient in selling other kinds of insurance policies. Never accept the trite statement that all the good companies charge about the same premium rate.
8. Compare premium costs between stock and mutual companies. Do not assume that a mutual company has lower-cost insurance because it has regularly returned a good dividend. Likewise, do not assume that a stock company policy is cheaper because the premium is lower. A stock company's premium is net and final—no dividends.

Buy term, invest the difference. Is the family better off in protection of dependents and with more cash-in value at age 65 of the breadwinner? Yes, if the difference in the cost of straight life and a decreasing term policy is invested. Interesting details discovered by *Changing Times* magazine (October, 1962) are shown in Table 12-5, which compares "straight life" with "thirty-year decreasing term" and "term-to-65 plus mutual fund investment."

The buyer is age 35. In case A, he buys a $10,000 straight life policy for $237 a year and leaves the dividends to gather interest. In case B, he buys a $10,000, thirty-year decreasing term, for $76 a year. In case C, he buys a term-to-65 policy for $120 a year. In both B and C, he invests the difference between the cost of the straight life policy and the two kinds of term insurance in a

TABLE 12-5   Invest the Difference

A. STRAIGHT LIFE—IF BUYER DROPS POLICY AT END OF YEAR

Age at Start of Year	Premiums Paid to Date	This Cash Value	Plus These Dividends
35	$ 237	0	0
50	3,792	$2,940	$ 923
64	7,110	5,600	3,253

Results at 65:

Total outlay	$ 7,110
Insurance in force if premiums continued*	$10,000
Insurance in force if premiums stopped	$10,000 for 15 years, or $ 7,330 for life
Cash if insurance surrendered	$ 8,853

B. 30-YEAR DECREASING TERM PLUS MUTUAL FUND INVESTMENT

Age at Start	Premiums Paid to Date	Amount Invested to Date	Insurance in Force	Savings at 10 Percent
35	$ 76	$ 161	$10,000	$ 163
50	1,216	2,576	5,000	5,853
64	1,824	5,286	383	27,374

Results at 65:

Total outlay	$ 7,110
Insurance in force if premiums continued	———
Insurance in force if premiums stopped	———
Cash value of mutual fund	$ 27,374

C. TERM-TO-65 PLUS MUTUAL FUND INVESTMENT

Age at Start of Year	Premiums Paid to Date	Amount Invested to Date	Cash Value of Policy	Savings at 10 Percent
35	$ 120	$ 117	0	$ 119
50	1,920	1,872	$740	4,271
64	3,600	3,510	0	19,542

Results at 65:

Total outlay	$ 7,110
Insurance in force if premiums continued	———
Insurance in force if premiums stopped	———
Cash value of mutual fund	$19,542

*Plus $3,253 in dividends.

mutual investment fund that charges an 8 percent sales commission. Dividends and capital gains are reinvested in the fund.

In case of death, the conclusions are: (1) death proceeds would be greater by a wide margin under the term-to-65 policy than under straight life; (2) straight life would yield a little higher death proceeds than decreasing term in the early years unless the mutual fund investment yielded more than 10 percent interest compounded annually; (3) the term-to-65 is likely to produce more death benefits than the decreasing term.

If the breadwinner lives, the conclusions are: (1) both term programs will amass a nest egg much larger than the total value of the straight life (thirty-year term, $27,374; term-to-65, $19,542; straight life, $8,853). *Warning:* The difference in premiums must be invested each year without fail, and earnings and dividends must be plowed back.

Ordinary life or straight life insurance

Ordinary life or straight life insurance is payable at death of the insured, but one need not die to win on this contract. The same premium is paid as long as the insured lives.

Since ordinary life is a combination of term plus savings, a reserve is accumulated, and in a few years the policy has cash-surrender, loan, and other values. Consequently, the premium is about twice as expensive per $1,000 as term insurance, when first taken out.

Generally, the cash value at age 65 is ample to provide a paid-up policy equal to all the paid premiums. Many companies permit the cash value to be used to provide a guaranteed annuity, if by the age of, say, 70 to 75 there is no longer the need for protecting a dependent in event of the death of the insured.

A *family income policy* combines decreasing term with ordinary life insurance. It provides, in addition to the regular life insurance payment, income payment to the beneficiary if the insured dies within the stated period. The payments begin at death of the insured and extend to the end of the period. If the insured is living at the end of the period, the premiums usually decrease.

The advantage in this policy is that while the children are young there is greater protection than the family usually can afford on a permanent basis. The highest income is provided for the dependents during the first twenty years, when the need is greatest in case of premature death of the breadwinner. If the policyholder lives, the term insurance ends twenty years after purchase of the policy, and the premium is reduced accordingly. Only the ordinary life insurance remains permanently in this contract.

Limited payment life insurance

Limited payment life insurance is payable only at death of the insured. The premiums are payable only for a stated number of years or until the insured reaches a certain age, such as 60 or 65. Payments are usually limited, however, to ten, twenty, or thirty years. Thirty-payment life, for example, provides for premiums to be paid for thirty years, after which the policy is paid up. The face value, however, is not paid until the insured dies. The premium rate must be considerably higher on this kind of policy than on ordinary life because it is fully paid up in a stated number of years.

Policies of this type are considered to be more appropriate for persons whose incomes may be expected to decrease appreciably in later life. It is not suitable for most young married couples, because the premium is so costly that they cannot afford to buy enough for adequate protection for dependents. Term insurance, in particular, and ordinary insurance will give a young family much more protection at lower cost at a time when the highest protection is most needed—the first twenty years of married life.

Endowment insurance

Endowment insurance is a combination of temporary life insurance and periodic savings. If the insured dies, the beneficiary receives the face value of the policy. If the insured lives, however, the face value or amount is paid to him, or to some designated person, either in a lump sum or in the form of income. The protection offered not only is small compared to the cost but ceases when the policy matures.

This kind of policy should not be considered as permanent protection for dependents. It provides the least protection for a given premium, but includes the highest investment element of the above general types of policies.

Endowment policies can be purchased on a basis of ten, fifteen, twenty, twenty-five, or thirty years, or to mature in cash at specified ages. Since the company must have the stated amount (say $2,000, in a twenty-year $2,000 endowment) available for payment at the end of twenty years, the premium rate must be higher than on a twenty-year family income policy.

In the latter case, the company might not have to pay the beneficiary for several years after the insured had stopped making premium payments, provided the insured continued to live. The company could use these funds to earn additional interest. The endowment policy, on the other hand, calls for payment at the expiration of a certain number of years. Consequently, higher premiums are necessary for endowment policies.

Settlement terms of life insurance policies

The method of payment of life insurance policies is important. There are several options, and choosing the right settlement option helps to accomplish the purpose of the insurance. Before purchasing an insurance policy, the settlement terms that are available should be discussed with a competent life insurance underwriter. Most policies have the following four optional settlement plans, which may be decided by the insured or by the beneficiary.

Option 1

The beneficiary may receive a lump sum. This may be a good option if the money must be used to pay expenses for sickness, taxes, and burial. On the other hand, a lump sum coming into the hands of a beneficiary who cannot manage it carefully may prove to be an unsatisfactory option. It is easy for the beneficiary to become a victim of poor investments suggested by well-meaning but uninformed friends or even by an investment counselor.

Option 2

Choose the right settlement option

The principal sum is retained by the company, and interest (about 2½ percent) is paid to the beneficiary for a certain number of years or for life. At the end of the period, the principal is paid to the children, or according to the terms of the contract—a good option, as it is not final, and allows time to consider.

Option 3

A third option provides for the payment of insurance in installments—annual, semiannual, quarterly, or monthly. Usually, the company will specify the minimum installment or the minimum number of payments it guarantees. It might be, for example, a guarantee of $100 a month for thirty years, or that principal and interest will be paid until exhausted. This option may fit nicely for the protection of children.

Option 4

The annuity or life-income settlement provides regular life income to the beneficiary. The company may guarantee either a specified number of payments or payments that will equal the principal. If the beneficiary dies before the guaranteed payments have been made, the remainder goes to the estate, or as directed. Guaranteed payments cost more, however, because the risk is greater to the company.

Table 12-6, Monthly Installment Payments for Each $1,000 of Insurance, shows the amount due under options 3 and 4, as reported by an American life insurance company.

If option 3 is selected, the guaranteed income to a beneficiary will be $6.53 a month for fifteen years for each $1,000 policy. A $15,000 policy would provide an income of $78.36 a month for fifteen years.

If the widow is age 65 and is eligible for full Social Security coverage, she may wisely elect a monthly life annuity of $4.67 per $1,000 of insurance. A $15,000 policy would provide $70.05 a month for life, which would be in addition to her monthly Social Security benefit. The monthly life annuity would cease on her death.

There is no single option, of course, that will fit all needs. These four options, however, are planned to meet all possible choices.

TABLE 12-6 Monthly Installment Payments for Each $1,000 of Insurance

OPTION 3		OPTION 4		
Number of Annual Payments	Amount of Payments	Attained Age of Payee		Monthly Life Annuity
		Male	Female	
1	$84.19	20	25	$2.69
3	28.69	25	30	2.89
5	17.59	30	35	2.96
7	12.84	35	40	3.13
9	10.21	40	45	3.34
11	8.53	45	50	3.59
13	7.38	50	55	3.88
15	6.53	55	60	4.24
17	5.88	60	65	4.67
20	5.16	65	70	5.20
25	4.34			
30	3.80			

Restrictions and double-indemnity clause

Before buying a particular policy, compare the contract with policies of other companies. Policies vary with regard to restrictions and advantages. Some companies, for example, will not accept the risk of death in air travel. Others will accept financial responsibility for travel on regularly scheduled commercial planes.

Some companies, for an extra premium, will include a double-indemnity clause that will pay double the face value of the contract in case of accidental death.

In case of total or permanent disability before age 60, some contracts provide for waiver of future premiums.

The disability income payment, not common any more, pays a stated income in case of total or permanent disability. This kind of contract is far more expensive.

Loan value and dividends

Most level premium policies have a loan value after the second year or so. The loan value and the rate of interest charged are stated in the policy. Sometimes a loan may be obtained from a commercial bank at a lower rate of interest than most insurance companies charge. Consequently, it is a good idea to compare the total interest charges of a bank and of the insurance company before a decision is made for a loan on a life insurance policy.

If it is difficult to pay the premium, some policies contain an automatic premium-loan provision. If the policyholder takes advantage of this provision, the loan should be repaid as soon as possible; if long continued, the interest can destroy to a considerable extent the protection value of the policy.

Dividends may be paid by mutual or participating companies. The policy holder may use them in any of four ways: (1) accept them in the form of cash, (2) allow the company to retain them at interest, (3) apply them to future premiums, or (4) use them to purchase more life insurance.

How much life insurance should you buy?

Independent insurance advisors say that Americans lose millions of dollars annually because they do not know how to plan a protection program to fit their needs and pocketbook. Many families get a poor insurance deal because they (1) carry more insurance than they need, (2) carry insurance that is too expensive, (3) carry too little insurance, (4) purchase insurance that is too cheap, (5) insure the wrong members of the family, (6) borrow on their insurance from the insurance company, (7) select poor companies and agents, (8) fail to relate life insurance to total family savings and protection needs, or (9) cannot determine the costs of cash-value life insurance.

How much life insurance do you need?

Consumers Union, publishers of *Consumer Reports,* hired insurance experts to study this complex problem and reported the findings in *Report on Life Insurance.* [3]

Step 1

Take inventory of your assets:

Life insurance. Include amounts payable at death of all policies of the major wage earner. Deduct from face value any loans against the policies.

[3] Consumers Union, Mount Vernon, N.Y., rev. ed., 1972. The author wishes to give credit to Consumers Union for the excellent material used in this section.

Widow's pension benefits. If there is a death benefit for an employee's beneficiary, enter that lump sum below.

Cash on hand. Enter total deposits in savings and checking accounts and present value of U.S. savings bonds.

Equity in real estate. Enter the present value of all real estate after subtracting the amount due on mortgages.

Securities. Enter present market value of stocks, mutual shares, debentures, and other commercial bonds.

Other. If there is a ready market for antiques, jewels, and art work, enter present sale value. Money in trust funds should be counted, but omit a possible future asset like a possible inheritance from someone now living.

Step 2

Now take inventory of your liabilities. But first you have to figure out the monthly income your life insurance funds would have to contribute at future periods to meet your family income goals. You will also have Social Security income before age 62 if you are a widow with children under 18 or 22 or if children are in college. After one child graduates from college, Social Security income decreases. Therefore, insurance income must be planned to fill in the gaps. Information on Social Security benefits can be secured from your local Social Security office. The worksheets prepared by Consumers Union in their 1972 *Report on Life Insurance* will be especially useful at this stage of planning.

Step 3

The next step is to convert long-term income and education funds into present values. You may wish to provide $100 a month for 120 months. This does not mean that you need $12,000 worth of insurance, because the insurance is likely to be paid in a lump sum and the diminishing principal can earn interest. Therefore, the insurance sum need not be $12,000. The present value—the face value of the life insurance necessary to produce it ($100 per month for 120 months) is a discounted amount. Thus to provide $100 a month for ten years starting now, you will need $100 × 99, or about $10,000. Table 12-8 will be useful in helping you to find out your survivor's income need.

TABLE 12-7 Inventory

FAMILY ASSETS	FAMILY LIABILITIES
Life insurance _____	Family income fund _____
Widow's pension benefit (omit Social Security) _____	Education fund _____
	Widow's retirement fund _____
Cash on hand _____	Widow's income fund _____
Equity in real estate _____	Uninsured debts (omit home mortgage) _____
Securities _____	
Other _____	
Total _____	Total _____

TABLE 12-8 Survivor's Income*

YEARS OF INCOME NEEDED	MULTIPLIER	YEARS OF INCOME NEEDED	MULTIPLIER	YEARS OF INCOME NEEDED	MULTIPLIER
1	12	11	107	21	170
2	23	12	114	22	175
3	34	13	121	23	180
4	44	14	128	24	185
5	54	15	135	25	189
6	64	16	142	26	194
7	73	17	148	27	198
8	82	18	154	28	202
9	91	19	160	29	206
10	99	20	165	30	209

*Table 12-8 was prepared by Consumers Union insurance experts and can be found in their *Report on Life Insurance,* rev. ed., 1972.

Step 4

After you have decided how much monthly income you will need in addition to Social Security, and for how long, find the desirable number of years in Table 12-8. Then apply the multiplier to the monthly income figure. The resulting sum is what you need to provide that monthly income. Table 12-8 is constructed on the assumption that the lump sum will be invested at a modest 3½ percent net annual interest after income taxes. Thus, to provide $100 a month for ten years starting now, you would need $100 × 102, or $10,200.

Table 12-8 shows the proper multipliers for determining how much money at 3½ percent interest will be needed to create a fixed monthly income for any number of years up to 45. Simply apply the appropriate multiplier to your monthly income goal. For example, to figure out the lump sum needed to provide $100 a month for twenty years, look up the twenty-year multiplier in Table 12-8. It is 174. The lump sum needed is $17,400 ($l00 × 174).

Table 12-9 shows the interest discount factors to which an entire fund may be reduced if it will not have to be touched for some years. For example, if the $17,400 income fund would not be needed until five years from now, look up the five-year factor in Table 12-9. It is 0.84. The lump sum needed now is $14,616 ($17,400 × 0.84).

If your heirs are not to start spending certain insurance funds for a number of years, these funds should be discounted for the interest they can earn in the interim. In Table 12-9, find the number of years before the income will be needed. Then multiply the adjacent discount factor by the lump sum needed. The result is the amount that, when invested at 4 percent net, will grow to the lump sum needed in the appropriate number of years. Thus, to provide $12,000 for college—but starting sixteen years from now—your insurance policy should supply only 0.53 × $12,000, or $6,360 to $6,400.

TABLE 12-9   Discount Factors for Money Needed Later*

YEARS BEFORE INCOME IS NEEDED	DISCOUNT FACTOR	YEARS BEFORE INCOME IS NEEDED	DISCOUNT FACTOR	YEARS BEFORE INCOME IS NEEDED	DISCOUNT FACTOR
0	1.00				
1	0.96	16	0.53	31	0.30
2	0.92	17	0.51	32	0.29
3	0.89	18	0.49	33	0.27
4	0.85	19	0.47	34	0.26
5	0.82	20	0.46	35	0.25
6	0.79	21	0.44	36	0.24
7	0.76	22	0.42	37	0.23
8	0.73	23	0.41	38	0.23
9	0.70	24	0.39	39	0.22
10	0.68	25	0.38	40	0.21
11	0.65	26	0.36	41	0.20
12	0.62	27	0.35	42	0.19
13	0.60	28	0.33	43	0.19
14	0.58	29	0.32	44	0.18
15	0.56	30	0.31	45	0.17

*Table 12-9 was prepared by Consumers Union insurance experts and can be found in their *Report on Life Insurance,* rev. ed., 1972.

How to use the four-step sheet

An illustration for planning your own insurance needs

We shall follow the methods used in the Consumers Union study. The Smith family is made up of Tom, age 25; his wife Mary, 23; and two children, Johnny, age 2, and Amy, age 2 months. Tom earns $10,000 annually and nets $700 a month after deductions.

This family plans that, in the event of the father's death, the mother would stay at home until Amy, her 2-month-old, is 18 years old; that's when the mother's own Social Security income would stop unless Amy goes to college. The mother would support herself after that until she retired at age 62.

The insurance objectives of the Smith family: $525-a-month family income for eighteen years; a $12,000 college fund for each of the two children; and a $400-a-month retirement fund for the mother.

The father's Social Security survivors' benefits were $482 a month (1972) for his widow and two children under 18; up to $413 a month for his widow and one child under 18; $206 a month for a child age 18 to 22 in college (using the conservative figure of forty benefit months, or about $8,000 for each of the two children); and $227-a-month lifetime income for the mother beginning at age 62.

Figure 12-3 projects the Smiths' Social Security benefits. Note that if John goes to college, his mother and Amy will not receive the full $413 a month for widow and one child. This is because their maximum monthly income was $482; with John receiving $206, $276 is left for his mother and sister.

The Smiths figured their family income, education, and widow's retirement fund as follows:

FIGURE 12-3   The Smith's projected Social Security benefits

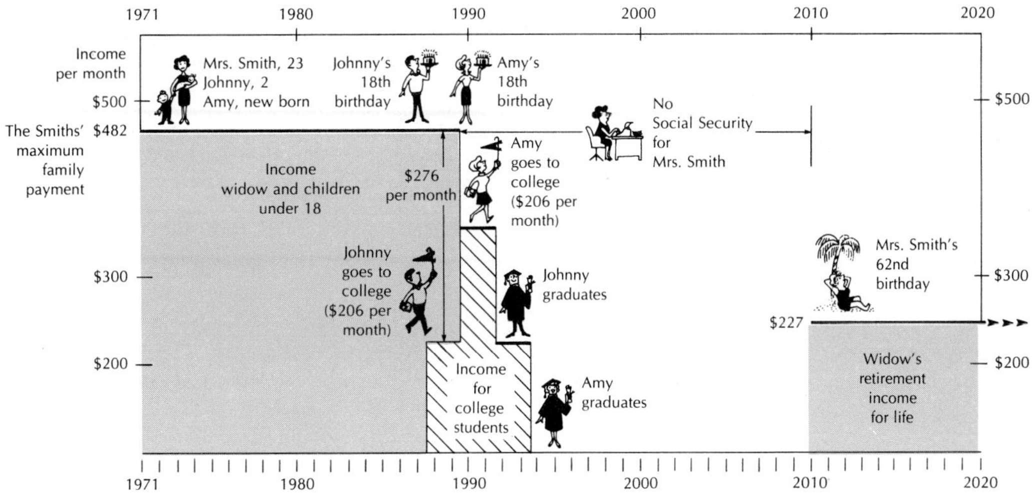

Courtesy of Consumers Union.

FAMILY INCOME FUND

Monthly income needed: $525

Number of years: eighteen

Social Security monthly income for first sixteen years: $482

Monthly balance needed, ($525 minus $482): $43

Sixteen-year multiplier (from Table 12-8): 142

Lump sum needed now ($43 × 142): $6,106 (round off at $7,000)

(Note: No interest discount factor from Table 12-9 is used because income drawn from this fund would be needed as soon as Tom Smith died.)

Social Security monthly income starting sixteen years from now and continuing for about two years: $276

Monthly balanced needed ($525—$276): $249

Two-year multiplier (from Table 12-8): 23

Lump sum needed sixteen years hence ($249 × 23): $5,727 or $6,000

Sixteen-year discount factor (from Table 12-9): 0.53

Lump sum needed now ($6,000 × 0.53): $3,180 or $3,200

Total lump sum needed now ($7,000 + $3,200): $10,200

EDUCATION FUND

For son Johnny (now age 2 years): $12,000

Social Security's contribution: about $8,000

Balance needed: $4,000

Number of years before it will be needed: sixteen

Sixteen-year discount factor (from Table 12-9): 0.53
Lump sum needed now ($4,000 × 0.53): $2,120
For daughter Amy (now 2 months): $12,000
Social Security's contribution: about $8,000
Balance needed: $4,000
Number of years before it will be needed: eighteen
Eighteen-year discount factor (from Table 12-9): 0.49
Lump sum needed now ($4,000 × 0.49): $1,960
Total lump sum needed now ($2,120 + $1,960): $4,080 or $4,000

WIDOW'S RETIREMENT FUND
Monthly income needed: $400
Age when it would begin: 62
Number of years: rest of life
Social Security monthly income: $227
Monthly balance needed ($250—$138.60): $111.40 ($400—$277): $173
Twenty-year multiplier (from Table 12-8; using this multiplier gives roughly the price, at age 62, of a life annuity): 165
Total lump sum needed now ($173 × 165): $28,545
(Note: Although this income will not be needed for thirty-nine years, the fund should not be reduced by the interest discount factor in Table 12-9. Its interest should be dedicated to coping with inflation, and some of its principal could be spared for emergency use.)

The Smiths' balance sheet

If we assume that the Smiths' present assets consist of $10,000 in group life insurance and $3,000 in checking and savings accounts and they have no sizable debts, their balance sheet looks like the accompanying table.

FAMILY ASSETS		FAMILY LIABILITIES	
Life insurance	$10,000	Family income fund	$10,200
Cash on hand	3,000	Education fund	4,000
		Widow's retirement fund	29,000
Total	$13,000	Total	$43,200

Deficit to be made up with new life insurance ($43,000 minus $13,000: about $30,000)

Although Social Security survivors' benefits will provide much of the Smiths' income needs, a part of the new life insurance could be used for the father's funeral expense. As future life unfolds, there is great flexibility in how the balance might be used during Mrs. Smith's middle years (Mrs. Smith would be 41 when Amy is 18) until she retired at age 62, a twenty-one-year period without Social Security income. And at age 65 she will be eligible for Medicare (hospital and medical insurance).

Can the Smiths afford $30,000 of new life insurance?

It seems a lot for a young father making $10,000 a year. According to insurance industry data, the average insurance coverage for insured heads of families with an income like the Smith family was less than $23,000.

What could $30,000 of life insurance cost each year?

KIND	ANNUAL COST
Ordinary or straight (nonparticipating)*	$365.00
"Modified ten" (ordinary life):	
Low premium the first ten years	245.00
Higher premium the rest of the years	480.00
Twenty-five-year decreasing term insurance	100.00

*Lower premiums than participating policies; however, they may cost more in the long run.

Although Mr. Smith can buy $30,000 of the twenty-five-year decreasing term life insurance, the death benefit goes down to zero in twenty-five annual steps. The family goal, however, was to obtain adequate coverage for the present when the family needs the most protection, and this policy provides it.

In the event Mr. Smith remains healthy for ten to fifteen years longer, his insurance needs may increase if there is another child—or substantial increases in his salary and, with it, an increase in his standard of living, such as purchasing a house. As long as Mr. Smith remains insurable or his firm provides group life insurance for employees, he can cope with new insurance needs as they arise. He can buy more decreasing term insurance. A more flexible way, as we learned earlier, would be for Mr. Smith to start out insuring himself with $30,000 of five-year *renewable* term insurance for about $125 annually, and the death benefit will not decrease unless he wants it to decrease. Every five years the policy can be renewed at its full amount or at any smaller amount selected by the policyholder down to a minimum of $5,000. Generally, however, the price of the policy goes up at the end of every five years.

An important feature of this kind of insurance is that it is guaranteed renewable until age 65. The company must renew this policy without requiring another medical examination.

The Smiths' selection

This type of policy may be the best kind for the Smiths. This type of policy (five-year renewable term) goes up in price very slowly at first (in fact, the premium goes down the second five-year period at Mr. Smith's age). In later years, the premium goes up steeply, but by then Mr. Smith has possibly passed the peak of his financial responsibilities. The chances are that increases in income have enabled him to pay for most or all of his home, or to have invested some savings in stocks or bonds. At this stage of his life he actually needs less life insurance because the children are on their own economic power, and the parents will soon be eligible for modest Social Security income and very likely a company pension. The sensible policy would be for the Smiths to reduce their insurance coverage as each child leaves home, and to carry only a modest amount of insurance when both children are on their own. After the father reaches his early fifties, very little insurance is needed because there are only a few years left before they reach age 62 or 65 for Social Security and age 65 for a company pension and Medicare.

It's hard to tell the best buy in life insurance

Life insurance companies have been reluctant to provide consumers with a sound method or standard for judging relative costs of life policies. Agents still try to make you believe that all companies charge about the same rates. This is not true, even though the premiums are about the same.

Three major associations of life companies appointed a committee to look into the problem. The experts investigated twelve methods of figuring insurance costs and chose the "interest-adjusted" formula as the "most suitable."[4]

Experts disagree with the interest-adjusted method, although the formula is an improvement in comparing premium cost per $1,000 of coverage. Dr. Joseph E. Belth, professor of insurance at Indiana University, figured a method of determining comparative costs that takes into account premiums, dividends, cash values, interest rates, mortality tables, and lapse rates. The idea is to add up all costs and benefits over, say, a twenty-year period and then state the excess costs for each company's policy. Dr. Belth took a straight life policy for a 35-year-old man *over a twenty-year period*. He figured the costs versus the benefits for such a 1968 policy with fifteen of the largest companies that pay dividends (participating) to policy holders. The February 4, 1970, issue of *The U.S. Consumer* (now called *Consumer Newsweek*) published the net cost over a twenty-year period to a policyholder, using Dr. Belth's data: Northwestern Mutual, $276.64; Connecticut Mutual, $326.68; Massachusetts Mutual, $390.33; New England Mutual, $422.38; New York Life, $428.51; Mutual Benefit, $430.85; Equitable of New York, $463.48; Penn Mutual, $465.86; John Hancock, $491.57; Mutual of New York, $505.97; Lincoln National, $516.67; Connecticut General, $517.33; Aetna Life, $588.89; Prudential, $611.65; and Metropolitan Life, $617.98.

The Belth studies

Thus a policyholder with Northwestern Mutual would pay less than half what policyholders with Metropolitan would pay for the same insurance over the 20-year period. Dr. Belth has published a report on his research entitled *Life Insurance Price Measurement*.[5] What makes the Belth studies important is that the leading insurance associations have now accepted almost all his points. What we need now is wide publicity for this report and a go-ahead sign by insurance management to insurance agents at the local level. So far, companies have been reluctant to permit local insurance agents to use even the "interest-adjusted cost" information, which recognizes only one of the hidden cost variables. (See Taylor-Troelstrup Reading 81 for level prices for $10,000 participating straight life policies issued by fifteen major companies to standard males aged 35 in 1968.)

It pays to shop around

You will note that the twenty-year level prices per $1,000 of protection in 1968 for a male aged 35 ranged from a low of $6.41 (Northwestern Mutual) to a high of $10.06 (Metropolitan). The important conclusion is that a comparison of only premium costs is meaningless and deceptive. Price competition in cash-value life insurance was and is a fiction as far as the consumer is concerned.

The Denenberg report:
Shopper's Guide to Life
Insurance

Another study and report on the search for the best buy on straight life insurance was prepared by Dr. Herbert S. Denenberg, Insurance Commissioner of Pennsylvania. The study covers 166 of the largest insurance companies doing business in Pennsylvania. Which of these companies have the lowest-cost insurance policies over a period of twenty years (see Table 12-10).[6]

[4] See *Changing Times*, March, 1971, pp. 6–11 for details.
[5] For a detailed report, see Joseph M. Belth, *Life Insurance Price Measurement*, Indiana University, Graduate School of Business, Bureau of Business Research, 1969.
[6] Herbert S. Denenberg, *A Shopper's Guide to Life Insurance*, Pennsylvania Insurance Department, Harrisburg, Pa., April, 1972.

TABLE 12-10 Premiums and Insurance Cost for the Ten Lowest-Cost $10,000 Straight Life Cash-Value Insurance Policies

COMPANY[b]	MALE AGE 20 OR FEMALE AGE 23 [a]			MALE AGE 35 OR FEMALE AGE 38 [a]			MALE AGE 50 OR FEMALE AGE 53 [a]		
	Annual Premium	Average Yearly Cost of Insurance	Ranking[c] At Age 20–23	Annual Premium	Average Yearly Cost of Insurance	Ranking[c] At Age 35–38	Annual Premium	Average Yearly Cost of Insurance	Ranking[c] At Age 50–53
1. Bankers Life Company (Iowa)	$149.70	$24.70	4	$229.10	$42.00	1	$400.30	$119.20	2
2. Home Life Insurance Company (New York)	150.70	23.10	3	228.40	43.10	2	405.10	125.90	5
3. National Life Insurance Company (Vermont)	152.70	28.30	10	230.30	46.30	5	389.80	125.80	4
4. Connecticut Mutual Life Insurance Company	135.00	22.40	1	218.50	46.70	6	397.70	132.70	11
5. Phoenix Mutual Life Insurance Company	157.00	26.60	7	233.60	48.60	7	392.50	127.70	6
6. Northwestern Mutual Life Insurance Company	157.40	28.70	11	234.80	45.50	3	405.40	129.40	8
7. Central Life Assurance Company (Iowa)	155.10	22.90	2	235.70	46.10	4	404.00	136.30	15
8. State Mutual Life Assurance Company of America (Mass.)	149.50	28.80	12	231.60	49.00	9	408.30	132.70	11
9. Modern Woodmen of America[d]	138.80	27.50	9	214.10	48.90	8	377.80	134.80	13
10. Lutheran Mutual Life Insurance Company	144.80	27.30	8	226.10	49.50	10	394.90	135.00	14

NOTE: All are participating policies.
[a] Usual premiums for a female are the same as those for a male three years younger.
[b] Listed according to the average of the interest-adjusted costs at three ages.
[c] Ranked at each age according to the average yearly costs of insurance over a twenty-year period.
[d] Fraternal organization; policy available only to members.

The lowest premium cost may be the highest real cost!

Considering cost only, Table 12-10 shows the ten best buys in straight life insurance policies sold by the 166 largest companies doing business in Pennsylvania. As shown, a comparison of only premiums can be misleading, as it doesn't take into consideration cash values and dividends. Incidentally, the study also shows that participating policies are better buys than nonparticipating policies. You may save 170 percent or more by shopping for your insurance, says Denenberg. Once again, it pays to shop around for life insurance.

How about renewable term insurance?

We have learned that the best kind of cash-value insurance (combines protection and savings) is straight life insurance. Insurance authorities also believe that the most protection for the lowest cost is obtainable through renewable term insurance. This is pure protection—no savings—and is much less costly. When used properly, as in the case of the Smith family, term insurance is the only way most American families can adequately protect their dependents.

Consumers Union recommends the use of five-year renewable term policies for the major protection of dependents. In the case of the Smith family, for example, decreasing five-year term insurance at a rate of $100 a year was the only source available that they could afford to cover an insurance need of $30,000. The lowest-cost straight life insurance for $30,000 would have cost the Smiths about $365 annually or more, which would have been too heavy a burden.

Table 12-11 shows the lowest cost of five-year renewable term policies based on standard 1972 rates for a man aged 35 whose policy size was $50,000 or the most protection available from the various sources.

Handsome rewards for the careful shopper

The five-year renewable term insurance of the National Life Insurance Company of Montpelier, Vermont, priced at $6.87 per $1,000, was the lowest among the commercial insurance companies and is sold in all fifty states; it may be the lowest-cost policy available to many people. The other four sources are open only to certain people. The National Life Insurance Company may be used as a bench mark when looking around for a twenty-year price illustration of their five-year renewable term policies. If other insurance companies cannot give you this kind of information, strike them off your buying list.

Veterans' insurance

Until recent years, any discussion of low-priced life insurance began with this advice to veterans: "Don't drop your GI life insurance." Veterans of World Wars I and II and the Korean war could keep their $10,000 military policies as cash-value or term policies at very low rates plus dividends, excepting the latter for veterans of Korea.

Sad to report

Veterans of the Indochina conflict, however, cannot convert their $15,000 coverage, for only $3 a month, to term insurance, but only to straight life or some other expensive cash-value policy issued by a private life insurance company at regular commercial premium rates at the time of conversion. To deny servicemen the same conversion rights that veterans of World Wars I and II and the Korean war had is to deny them the option to purchase the best kind of insurance to adequately protect their dependents—renewable term insurance.

Variable life insurance: a new idea

Payoff tied to stocks

Life insurance executives are acutely aware that in the past, the erosion of values through inflation has been the main factor behind the sagging interest in straight life policies. The purchasing power of a $10,000 ordinary life policy, for example, dwindles to $4,120 over a thirty-year period of inflation at 3 percent annually.

TABLE 12-11 Participating Five-Year Renewable Term Policies

	POLICY SIZE	TWENTY-YEAR GROSS PREMIUM	TWENTY-YEAR DIVIDENDS*	TWENTY-YEAR NET PAYMENT	AVERAGE ANNUAL NET PAYMENT	AVERAGE ANNUAL COST PER $1,000
Institute of Electrical and Electronics Engineers, group plan	$50,000	$7,572.00	$3,180.24	$4,391.76	$219.59	$4.39
Massachusetts Mutual Savings Banks	41,000	6,498.50	2,575.21	3,923.29	196.17	4.78
New York State Mutual Savings Banks	30,000	4,138.50	1,263.00	2,875.00	143.78	4.79
Teachers Insurance and Annuity Association of America Individual Policy	50,000	9,497.50	4,313.00	5,184.50	259.23	5.18
National Life Insurance Co. (Montpelier, Vt.)	50,000	9,750.00	2,882.50	6,876.50	343.38	6.87
Berkshire Life Insurance Co. (Pittsfield, Mass.)	50,000	9,280.00	1,973.00	7,307.00	365.35	7.31
Prudential Insurance Co. of America (Newark, N.J.)	50,000	10,050.00	2,627.50	7,422.50	371.13	7.42†
Metropolitan Life Insurance Co. (New York City)	50,000	10,450.00	2,766.50	7,683.50	384.18	7.68†
Nationwide Life Insurance Co. (Columbus, Ohio)	50,000	10,222.50	2,034.00	8,188.50	409.43	8.19

NOTE: This table compares twenty-year premium costs of policies from six conventional insurance companies and four other sources open only to certain people (see accompanying discussion). The prices shown are based on standard rates in 1972 for a man who bought the insurance at age 35 and whose policy size was $50,000 or the maximum coverage available when the maximum was under $50,000. Companies were selected to illustrate a wide price range against which to compare the price of any five-year renewable term policy you may want to consider.

*Based on 1971 dividend scales and IEEE's average dividend credit for the years 1966 to 1970.

†Includes waiver of premium for total disability.

If, on the other hand, the investment pool backing up a variable life policy rose in value by more than 3 percent, the policy would maintain its full purchasing power. The $10,000 variable policy would pay out about $24,000 after thirty years, and that would buy about what $10,000 would have bought at the start. In other words, if the stocks go up in value, so do the prospective death benefits. If the stocks go down, so do the benefits—but not below some fixed guarantee.

So, this is an inflation hedge. It's hoped to be a big selling point for insurance companies. Of course, the consumer will pay an extra price for his variable life insurance policy.

Whatever the pros and cons in regard to variable insurance policies, the Securities and Exchange Commission and other segments of the investment industry have raised some unanswered questions that cloud the future of variable insurance. The mutual fund industry, for one, opposes it vigorously. The tax status of the variable insurance policy is unsettled at this writing. It is still an interesting idea in life insurance.

Finally   After working out your insurance protection plan as suggested by Consumers Union on the basis of years of study by independent life insurance experts, look the plan over regularly and see whether your family's needs have changed. Look ahead and try to see where your financial pathway will lead. Keep track of changes in Social Security, price changes indicated in the Consumer Price Index, increases in your standard of living, and changes in your net worth.

Don't be "life insurance poor"—pouring a disproportionate percentage of your income into expensive life insurance (ordinary life policies and even more expensive policies) and thus forcing your family to a lower standard of living now so that you can leave a wealthy widow later on. You *can* "have your cake and eat it," to a considerable extent, because the burden of life insurance need be no greater than absolutely necessary for *protection* of dependents.

ANNUITIES: SHOULD YOU BUY THEM?

Life insurance and annuities are exact opposites. Life insurance pays the beneficiary on the death of the policyholder. An annuity pays the policyholder for life. In life insurance, the company is betting that the policyholder will live. In an annuity, the company is betting that the annuitant will not live. This means that if a family is young and growing up, life insurance protection for the family comes first.

The word *annuity* implies an annual payment. Today, however, any fixed periodic payment—yearly, monthly, or weekly—for a given period of time or for life is an annuity. The essential feature of annuity payments is their payment as long as the annuitant lives. The annuitant pays a certain amount per month for a given number of years, or pays a lump sum just prior to retirement, and in return receives an income for life, or variations of a deferred annuity.

No medical examination is required because the insurance company counts on the annuitant's death earlier than statistics indicate. The purchase price for women is higher than for men, because women usually live about five or six years longer than men.

The more frequent the payments to the annuitant (monthly, quarterly, or yearly), the higher the purchase price. The annuity policy is primarily for the benefit of the annuitant and only secondarily of benefit to others. One can, however, select a "joint and survivorship" form that pays an income for life to two or more persons.

Kinds of annuities   All annuities have three variables: how you pay for them, when you collect, and how you collect. Similarly, every annuity has a three-part name. A glance at Figure 12-4, What Kind of Annuity? shows these three classifications and the various types of annuities available.

An *immediate annuity* is paid for in one lump sum, and annuity payments begin without delay. For example, to buy such an annuity for $100 a month at age 65, a male annuitant would have to spend approximately $13,750. Generally, people buy an immediate annuity just prior to retirement, to continue as long as they live.

A *deferred life annuity* is one that begins to pay the annuitant at a later specified date, say at age 65. As in the immediate life annuity, it can be pur-

FIGURE 12-4 What kind of annuity? Check one label in each column, string together three you have checked, and you will have a description of the type of annuity that suits your plans. (Annuity experts might use shortcut descriptions or rearrange the three elements, but these will do.)

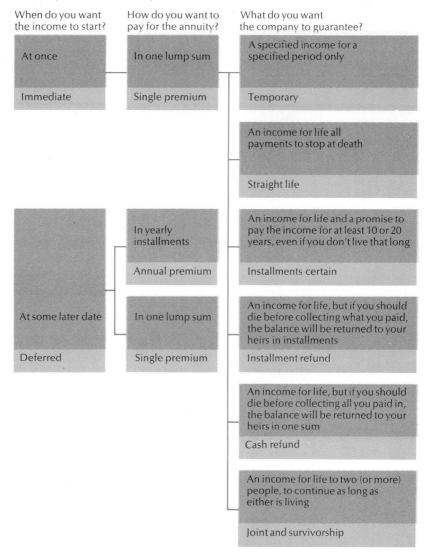

When do you want the income to start?	How do you want to pay for the annuity?	What do you want the company to guarantee?
At once	In one lump sum	A specified income for a specified period only
Immediate	Single premium	Temporary
		An income for life all payments to stop at death
		Straight life
	In yearly installments	An income for life and a promise to pay the income for at least 10 or 20 years, even if you don't live that long
	Annual premium	Installments certain
At some later date	In one lump sum	An income for life, but if you should die before collecting what you paid, the balance will be returned to your heirs in installments
Deferred	Single premium	Installment refund
		An income for life, but if you should die before collecting all you paid in, the balance will be returned to your heirs in one sum
		Cash refund
		An income for life to two (or more) people, to continue as long as either is living
		Joint and survivorship

chased in one lump sum years before benefits begin, or by installments covering perhaps many years.

Sometimes a deferred life annuity is paid to the annuitant until he dies, and then the remainder is paid to a named beneficiary until the entire cost of the annuity has been recovered. In other instances, if the annuitant dies, a lump sum is paid to a named beneficiary. The lump sum paid is the difference between the income payments received and the total premiums paid by the annuitant.

Both immediate life and deferred life annuities may be *joint and survivor-*

ship annuities. Under this annuity policy, an income is guaranteed during the joint lifetime and is continued until the death of the survivor. This plan may fit a man and wife who have no other dependents but may not be a good one for a husband with an invalid wife. It may not be a good policy if the annuitant had been rejected for life insurance, which might indicate that he may not need financial assistance after age 65 or so.

In any event, it is wise to have a thorough physical examination before taking out an annuity, especially if the annuity is to be taken out shortly before retirement or before the beginning of payments to the annuitant. For healthy persons reaching age 65 or older, it may be advisable to purchase an annuity just prior to retirement, because the older the annuitant, the higher the return.

One of the principal advantages of joint life-and-survivorship annuity is that most of the need for life insurance (beyond the great need when children are still on the family payroll) is eliminated. For example, if husband and wife have an annuity or a combination of annuity, Social Security, and some income from stocks, bonds, or real estate, which provide sufficient income, they need carry only permanent insurance (straight life) to cover funeral expenses, because the wife will be supported by the annuity income even after the husband's death. This arrangement eliminates paying heavy life insurance premiums during the retirement period when income is usually less than in the earnings years.

Cost of annuities

The cost of an annuity is based largely on the amount of income it will pay. Annuity rates are usually quoted in either of two ways: the amount of income the annuitant receives per unit of premium, or the amount the annuitant receives per unit. Table 12-12, The Cost of Annuities, gives some averages of costs from both points of view. The amount the annuitant pays for a given income depends on the income plan selected, on the age when payments begin, and on the sex of the annuitant.

It is well to remember these facts about costs: (1) A woman pays more than a man because she lives longer; (2) for each dollar of income, a cash-refund joint life-and-survivorship plan costs most, and a straight life plan costs least; (3) the older the annuitant when the income begins, the less he will pay, as in the case of an immediate annuity; (4) with a deferred annuity, the younger the annuitant when he buys, the smaller the annual premiums will be; (5) a straight annuity is the cheapest. The more generous the guarantee, the greater the cost.

Why buy an annuity?

An annuity is really an investment. You have to compare annuities with stocks and bonds, savings accounts, and other kinds of investment in order to pick out the advantages and disadvantages. The chief advantages are these:

1. Annuities are the safest way to obtain a retirement income. You get guaranteed payments that cannot be reduced.

2. You are freed of the job of managing your investments.

Think of annuities as an investment

3. You can never outlive your capital.

4. A deferred annuity makes it easier to save for old age, and more difficult to use your savings.

5. There can be tax advantages, because your annuity premiums draw interest during your working years, but you delay paying an income tax until you collect it. By then your tax bracket is apt to be lower.

TABLE 12-12 The Cost of Annuities

IMMEDIATE SINGLE PREMIUM ANNUITY (Income to Begin at Once)

Age		Each $1,000 Buys This Monthly Income			Each $10 of Monthly Income Costs		
Male	Female	Straight Life	10 Years Certain	Installment Refund	Straight Life	10 Years Certain	Installment Refund
50	55	$4.93	$4.88	$4.73	$2,030	$2,050	$2,110
55	60	5.51	5.41	5.20	1,838	1,847	1,920
60	65	6.30	6.08	5.81	1,605	1,644	1,721
65	70	7.36	6.87	6.56	1,375	1,455	1,524
70	75	8.80	7.73	7.50	1,145	1,293	1,331

DEFERRED ANNUAL PREMIUM ANNUITY (For Men Age 65 When It Starts*)

Age at Issue	Each $100 a Year Buys This Monthly Income			Each $10 of Monthly Income Costs This Much a Year		
	Straight Life	10 Years Certain	Installment Refund	Straight Life	10 Years Certain	Installment Refund
30	$33.17	$31.33	$30.38	$ 30.15	$ 31.92	$ 32.92
35	26.49	25.01	24.50	37.75	39.98	40.82
40	20.57	19.42	19.03	48.61	51.49	52.55
45	15.34	14.49	14.20	65.19	69.01	70.42
50	10.71	10.12	9.92	93.37	98.81	100.81
55	6.62	6.26	6.13	151.06	159.74	163.13

* A woman would receive 15 to 20 percent less in annuity income per $100 of annual premium than a man of comparable age at issue.

SOURCE: *Changing Times.*

The chief disadvantages are these:

1. Your income will not increase if inflation erodes the dollar's value, unless you select a "variable" annuity described later in the chapter.

2. You will leave less to your heirs because you use up your capital.

3. You earn a comparatively low rate of interest on your investment.

4. You cannot get at your capital in an emergency once annuity payments begin.

Annuities versus investments

If you are about to retire and need an income of $100 a month in addition to Social Security and other investment income, you will be interested in putting a large part of your capital into either an annuity or investments. Table 12-13 will be useful when making this decision.

Should you buy an annuity?

The answer depends on your investment skills and temperament and your financial circumstances. Keep these points in mind:

1. Have enough life insurance before you invest in annuities—first things first.

2. You may consider buying an annuity just prior to retirement rather than paying monthly premiums during your working years because the interest from annuities is comparatively low.

3. Figure your retirement income before buying annuities—how much you may need and where it will come from.

4. You can make more money through the regular investments during your working years.

5. Consider variable annuities, because with these most of your premium money is invested in common stocks. Common stocks keep up with inflation or go even higher, and you get a larger monthly annuity as the earned income increases.

6. If you have enough money, diversify. Put some of your savings into other investments and some into annuities just prior to retirement.

Combination of annuities and investments

Should you put most or all of family savings into annuities? There are limitations to the judicial use of annuities. The major limitation is that they provide for a *fixed income* unprotected from inflation. For the same reason, placing all savings in investments might be too risky.

By judicious combination of annuities and investments, a greater fixed income could be obtained as well as a hedge against inflation. For example, if an elderly couple had $40,000 available at a retirement age of 65 (for the husband) and 62 for the wife, they might invest all the money at 5 percent, which would net an annual income of $2,000, hardly sufficient to live on. Their income could be divided as follows:

	ANNUAL YIELD
$17,300 for straight life annuity for wife (at age 62)	$1,000
$13,750 for straight life annuity for husband (at age 65)	1,000
$9,250 in good preferred stock yielding 6 percent	550
Total	$2,550

TABLE 12-13 Annuities versus Investment

START WITH YOU		SUPPOSE YOU BUY AN ANNUITY	SUPPOSE YOU INVEST OR BANK THE SAME AMOUNT AND TAKE $100 A MONTH TO LIVE ON		
If you are:	Your life expectancy is:	$100 a month guaranteed for life costs:	You can live on dividends or interest only if your money earns:	With lower earnings, you can tap both interest and principal and your money will last:	And if still living, your life expectancy will then be:
A woman age 62	19½ years (49% live at least 20 years)	$17,300	7%	At 3%, 19 years At 4%, 22 years	At 81, 9 years At 84, 7½ years
A man age 65	14½ years (27% live at least 20 years)	$13,750	8¾%	At 3%, 14 years At 4%, 16 years	At 79, 7½ years At 81, 7 years

SOURCE: *Changing Times.*

Thus a greater income can be obtained by a combination of annuities and other investments.

Another way to achieve the same objective has been in operation since 1952. In that year, the Teachers Insurance and Annuity Association offered college teachers the opportunity to place three-fourths of their pension contributions into selected common stocks through the College Retirement Equities Fund (CREF) and the remainder in regular annuities (TIAA).

This way to finance retirement has been called "inflation-proof annuities." The combined annuity (*fixed* dollar annuity plus the *variable* annuity based on the purchase of common stocks) has produced more income since its inception than the fixed income annuity. This was to be expected because stocks went up between 1952 and 1969.

Variable annuities—pro and con

Despite the arguments, pro and con, over the variable annuity, offered by security dealers, investment bankers, mutual funds, and insurance companies, the two most important considerations from the buyer's point of view concern the tax angle and the final cost in making the investment.

When you buy a variable annuity, the dividends and capital gains are reinvested nearly tax-free by the insurance company. That makes the capital grow faster than is possible when you buy stocks or invest in mutual funds, because in these instances you pay taxes on capital gains and dividends in the year of purchase.

As for cost, variable annuities will probably carry a commission charge, or load, of around 12 percent over a long period of time. This means that about 12 percent of the premiums would go into commissions and expenses. For ordinary life insurance the figure is over 15 percent. On most mutual funds, the load ranges between 4 and 9 percent. On common stock purchased on a major stock exchange, the commission is lower.

By 1969 over 212,000 persons were contributing to the College Retirement Equities Fund. An ever-increasing number of large corporations are also providing variable pensions for their employees, including Warner-Lambert, Boeing Airplane, Pan American Airways, and New Jersey Power and Light, to mention a few. Among the major life insurance companies, Prudential is offering variable annuities on an individual or a group basis.

How the variable annuity works

If a buyer decides to set aside, say, $25 each month over a number of years for a variable annuity, the funds would be invested in common stocks. Each payment, after deduction of expenses, would be credited to the buyer's account units, determined by the current dollar value of a unit. The dollar value would go up or down depending on the market value of the stocks; the company makes no guarantees. When the buyer retires, all his variable contract account units would be converted into a fixed number of units. But instead of paying him each month in a *fixed* number of dollars, the variable contract provides for the *current* value of the units credited to him. Thus the dollar value of an annuity unit would change each month according to the investment results on the account.

The potential hazard of the variable annuity, then, is that stock prices may decline and the investor may get back less than he put in. But in testimony before the Securities and Exchange Commission in 1962, the Prudential Insurance Company argued that the danger is minimal; that the payments into a variable annuity over any modern fifteen-year period would have provided a greater return than fixed annuities. One reason for the delay in launching the variable annuity programs is that they have been ruled by the courts to be subject, not only to state insurance regulations, but to SEC regulations also.

The chief advantage of the variable annuity is that it serves as a hedge against diminished purchasing power due to inflation. The chief disadvantage is that income may be reduced during a period of stock market decline.

QUESTIONS FOR DISCUSSION

1. Who needs life insurance? Why?

2. Assuming you are old enough to buy life insurance (the legal age is 18 in most states) and an unmarried college student, would you be wise to purchase a policy prior to graduation?

3. Like so many major buying decisions, decisions concerning the purchase of life insurance are much more difficult than they ought to be. Why is this true?

4. Are the death benefits in a cash-value policy (such as straight life) different from the death benefits in a term policy?

5. Should you buy term insurance (as suggested by many *independent* life insurance advisors) and invest the difference? (If only the consumer could find out which companies' prices are lowest, he could maximize his return from cash-value policies, or he could minimize his outlay for term insurance and thus put more of his budget into savings or investments—the percentage return on outside investment that would have to be earned, after taxes, to surpass the guaranteed, rigid, tax-sheltered cash value of the more expensive straight [ordinary] life insurance.) Before you tackle this question, read the revised edition (1972) of Consumers Union *Report on Life Insurance,* pp. 113–116.

6. Under what set of circumstances might you be interested in buying a variable annuity just prior to retirement?

PROJECTS

1. If you are a college student with no dependents and find yourself swamped with life insurance salesmen on campus, urging you to sign up for a "buy now, pay later" life insurance program, keep a record of the sales pitch. Then read the informational article entitled *Insurance for the College Man* in *Consumer Reports,* January, 1972. This article and the information provided in Chapter 12 should give you a good background as to the wisdom of buying life insurance while you are still in college and have no dependents. Report your findings to the class. The life insurance agent has become a familiar figure on many campuses.

2.   Paul Harvey claims on TV and radio that his Chicago-based life insurance sponsor can sell you a policy that will give you "all your premium back," if you live long enough, and meantime offer you protection, Is this promise possible? Assuming it is possible, can you conclude that this policy (a cash-value policy) is the best one to use for protection of dependents? Support your answer with facts and logic.

3.   In this chapter the statement was made that where benefits are concerned in our Social Security system, there are three main times for action: (1) when you reach age 65, whether you intend to retire or not; (2) when a working member of your family dies or becomes disabled, and (3) when you reach age 72. What are the specific situations as you come to these stages?

4.   *A Shopper's Guide to Life Insurance,* recently issued by the Pennsylvania Insurance Department, shows large differences in costs among straight life (cash-value) policies of the same type. For example, the cost of $10,000 worth of straight life insurance for a 20-year-old man or a 23-year-old woman varies from $22.40 to $53.10 per year, depending on which company sells the policy. These are *not* premium costs. Using the *Shopper's Guide,* find the names of these two companies. Then find out the premium rates for each of these policies. What have you learned about the truth of identical life insurance policy (cash-value) costs? Are consumers entitled to have important information about a product before they buy it?

SUGGESTED READINGS

Belth, Joseph M.: *Life Insurance Price Measurement,* Indiana University, Graduate School of Business, Bureau of Business Research, Bloomington, 1969.

Denenberg, Herbert S.: *A Shopper's Guide to Life Insurance,* Pennsylvania Insurance Department, Harrisburg, Pa., April, 1972.

Fogiel, Max: *How to Pay Lots Less for Life Insurance,* Research and Education Association, New York, 1971.

"How Much Life Insurance Do You Need?" *Changing Times,* January, 1972, pp. 37–40.

Report on Life Insurance, rev. ed., Consumers Union, Inc., Mt. Vernon, N.Y., 1972.

Department of Health, Education, and Welfare, Social Security Administration. See the most recent leaflets on Social Security benefits for students, for young families, and for disability and also those on Medicare and medical aid to retired persons.

CHAPTER 13

CHAPTER 13
SAVINGS AND INVESTMENTS: ESTATE PLANNING, WILLS, AND TRUSTS

W

e might as well admit, at the start, that saving money is not easy. So many people feel like the wife who said: "But why should we save for the future, Roscoe? If there is anything we want in the future, it'll be available on the credit plan."

Saving money takes discipline, planning, cooperation, and plain hard work. But it is so important to family security and happiness that it is worth this effort. Savings based on a well-planned and purposeful program, balanced with present needs, can be an exciting experience when a family has agreed on its financial security goals.

THE IMPORTANCE OF SAVINGS TO THE CONSUMER

Every family needs to accumulate funds for use during the more expensive stages of the family life cycle—especially the high school and college period—and for recreation, pleasure, rewards, vacation, household furnishings and equipment, or new furniture. In addition, every family needs to build a reserve fund for the expenses of illness, death, loss of income, and other unforeseen emergencies. It needs savings to ensure financial security in old age or for protection should the breadwinner become incapable of further earning. The payment of life insurance and disability insurance premiums and payments toward the purchase of a home are usually classified as protection for the family.

Putting the American way of life into action

The major goal of family savings is to achieve family happiness through protection. There is, however, another desirable reason why a family should plan its own financial security above the minimum Social Security benefits. A family that plans its own financial security program—insurance, emergency fund, educational fund, retirement, and possibly its own home—and begins to accumulate its own wealth is not likely to fall for the philosophy, "Let the government take care of us."

A family that has planned and saved, sometimes even at the expense of better current living, has too much at stake to support legislation that may substitute government funds for family funds In other words, family-planned and -earned financial security is one of the concrete ways by which we can put into action our belief in the American way of life.

What are savings?

An economist might describe savings as "accumulating wealth through the postponement of consumption." He looks at savings as the first step in creating wealth—that is, the first step in increasing the economy's ability to produce more and better things.

If you decide to bank some of your money for later spending, the bank will lend a part of it to a manufacturer who needs more capital to install new machinery. This is a form of savings that diverts your present spending to new machinery to produce more goods for everyone. This is one function of savings.

What if you, and most Americans, decide to spend all your income in buying things? This would result in less money for producers who want money to expand, and the demand for savings would exceed the supply. This, in combination with other factors, can produce inflationary pressure.

What if you, and most other Americans, decide to double your savings at a time when business does not want to expand? The supply of savings exceeds demand. This, in combination with other factors, can produce a recession.

This is an oversimplified description of the role you play when you drop coins in a piggy bank or put dollars in your bank account. We can draw several useful conclusions from all this:

1. Saving as an operation has an overriding public significance as well as a personal and private one.
2. Savings are not "money not spent." They are money spent at one time instead of another time.
3. The important idea is that savings consist of money that is not spent for "current consumption."

What has this to do with you and your spending patterns? For one thing, it leads to the idea of what savings are: the difference between your current consumption expenses and your current income. Thus, money you spend for food, clothes, and taxes is not savings. Another lesson to learn from the economist's approach is that of choosing how to spend. When most people choose to save, it actually means choosing to spend more on capital goods, as when you buy a house or stocks, or on future enjoyments, such as college education for your children, retirement, or a trip around the world later on. When you save, you deny yourself something you could have now in order to have something later.

Why families save   The greatest incentive to save is provided when savings have a purpose, such as for an emergency fund, an education, homeownership, or a new car—those objectives in life for which money is necessary. Families with the foresight to establish both short-range and long-range goals for the use of money are the ones who seem to get ahead most rapidly. They find that planning helps them place the proper emphasis on the desired goals.

According to researchers, there are three basic purposes for which families save:

1. Short-term spending plans—saving for something wanted badly in the near future, a car, a home, a vacation.

Saving is not obsolete   2. Long-term spending plans—college education for children, retirement, buying into a business.
3. Financial security—a rainy-day fund, investments, an estate for children or grandchildren, retirement.

According to research in the behavioral sciences, a family's major future obligations for retirement and for the education of children may lead to concern but not always to saving.[1] Families may have some long-range concerns, but except for the major contractual commitments in insurance, mortgage,

---

[1] James N. Morgan, "Planning for the Future and Living with Risk," *The American Behavioral Scientist,* May, 1963, p. 40. See also "Is Saving Obsolete?" *Changing Times,* October, 1972, pp. 7–11.

and retirement programs, may appear to be operating on a relatively short-run strategy. According to the researchers, a substantial number of persons are unable to plan. Those who say they are unable to plan are less likely to have hospitalization insurance or liquid assets. They also have less education.

Families with higher incomes do most of the saving and hold most of the assets. Families in the middle range of incomes, $7,000 to $10,500, do less saving, apparently because they prefer to have a higher standard of living immediately—a new car every other year, shrubbery for the yard, a bedroom for the new baby, a long vacation trip, and so on. Often, however, the choices are not this clear-cut.

Who are the savers? Families that have received a substantial increase in income are likely to be savers. Their living has been adjusted to a certain standard, and it takes time before they move up to a higher standard of living.

Other factors influence a family's ability or desire to save:

1. Occupation. More lower-income wage earners and clerical workers on steady jobs eke out savings than professional and salaried people—perhaps because of the fear of losing their jobs. High-income salaried people often save quite a bit.

2. Medical expense. Families having constant large medical bills are not savers. The fewer the medical bills, the higher the savings.

3. Age and family cycle. Generally, young single persons and people past 65 produce relatively few savers. The heaviest proportion of families with savings comes from the 35-64 age bracket. Couples under 45 with young children and persons over 45, with or without children, are those who seem best able to save.

4. Once a person gets into the habit of saving money, he tends to retain the habit. Conversely, a person who is used to satisfying impulses of the moment and to avoiding choices and decisions finds it hard to save.

5. Contractual savings is the easiest way to save for many people. Commitments to mortgage payments, insurance premiums, pension contributions, and regular monthly investment plans almost always produce continued savings.

6. The big influence on the nature of savings is the great change in the financial tools that families have to work with. Two or three decades ago, the family that did not save might find itself on charity and in the county poorhouse. But private pension plans, Social Security, and other government financial aid programs have reduced the need for saving to prevent poverty. Families now plan protection largely by investing in life insurance, disability income insurance, and medical aid insurance. In a strict sense, Social Security taxes and health insurance premiums are not savings. but the benefits from these affect retirement and emergency fund requirements and savings.

Where to put your savings How comforting it would be to invest in something that never loses value, grows steadily year by year, pays a high tax-exempt return guaranteed to rise with the cost of living, and can be bought and sold any time at no cost.

Unfortunately, no such ideal investment exists. In real life we have to compromise and spread our money around. And it's at that point we often run into trouble.

Some people gamble when they should be conserving capital. Some who are capable of accepting a certain amount of risk play it too safe and immobilize all their excess cash in savings accounts.

To be most effective, savings should be allocated to meet specific objectives. For example, a fund for family emergencies or home repairs should be accumulated where it will be safe and immediately available. If you're building a retirement fund, you may want to broaden out to securities with growth potential. But when you retire and need supplementary income, your best bet may be bonds and other high-yield securities.

You can choose the investment that suits your needs by focusing on six crucial factors:

1. *Safety of principal.* This is the degree to which you are assured of getting back the same number of dollars you originally invested.

2. *Liquidity.* The liquidity of an investment is measured by the speed and ease with which you can cash it in. Real estate may take a long time to sell, and so it rates low on liquidity. A savings account rates high because generally it can be drawn on as soon as you can get to the bank. Stocks can be sold in a matter of minutes, though it usually takes a few days for payment to come through.

3. *Yield.* Interest and cash dividends represent the two most common forms of yield, and both are customarily calculated as a percentage of the amount invested. A $100 stock or bank account that pays $5 a year has a yield of 4 percent ($5 divided by $100).

4. *Capital gain potential.* A bank account doesn't fluctuate in price from day to day; securities do, and their potential for gain or loss extends far beyond their yield.

5. *Extra payments.* You pay nothing extra to open a bank account. You will pay commissions, though, to buy securities, and the purchase of real estate could involve several hundred dollars.

6. *Convenience.* It takes little time and only a check to invest in some fields. Some investments, however, take considerable investigation and supervision. You don't risk much in choosing a federally insured savings institution, as you would in buying a common stock. Each investment medium—common stock, preferred stock, corporate bond, and so on—presents a combination of these six factors. For a quick view of how the major types of investments compare, each group is rated in Table 13-1 according to the six characteristics.

Differences are ranked on a 1, 2, 3, 4 scale, with 1 denoting the highest degree of the characteristic. For example, in the cost column a 4 indicates the most expensive and a 1 the least expensive type of investment in terms of commissions and fees. Bond ratings refer to top-quality obligations.

Savings accounts   Selecting a good place to save isn't as simple as it may seem. The American Bankers Association estimates that there are at least fifty-four widely used ways of computing interest. Recently, a research thesis prepared for Kansas State University demonstrated that a high-paying system can produce 171 percent more interest in dollars and cents than a low-paying one with the same percentage rate.[2]

---

[2] Reprinted in *Changing Times*, February, 1971.

TABLE 13-1 A Savings Rating System

| | SAFETY OF PRINCIPAL | LIQUIDITY | CAPITAL GAIN | | | |
			Yield	Potential	Cost	Convenience
Savings accounts	1	1	3	4	1	1
Certificates of deposit	1	1	3	4	1	1
U.S. savings bonds	1	2	3	4	1	1
Corporate bonds	2	2	1	3	4	3
U.S. government bonds	1	2	2	3	4	2
Municipal bonds	1	2	2	3	4	3
Common stock	4	2	4	1	4	3
Preferred stock	3	2	2	3	4	2
Convertible stocks and bonds	3	2	2	1	4	4

SOURCE: *Changing Times,* February, 1972.

Truth-in-savings law needed

Obviously, we need a full-disclosure law for savings rates that would do for savers what the truth-in-lending law of 1968 did for borrowers. Before the lending law, borrowers faced the same problem confronting savers—the percentage rate on the loan did not necessarily indicate how much the loan really cost. The 6 percent personal loan usually worked out to about 12 percent simple interest.

Most of us are savers as well as borrowers. And it's clear that you can lose as much by choosing the wrong savings account as you can by choosing the wrong loan. Meanwhile, take the precaution of checking which system your savings institution is using. But how in the world can an ordinary person spot the highest-paying deal? Generally, you can obtain a good yield—although not necessarily the best—by selecting an account where (1) the interest rate is calculated from the day of deposit to the day of withdrawal and (2) there are no penalties for withdrawals. If it's one of the lower-paying varieties, shop around for a better deal.

Certificates of deposit

Certificates of deposit are comparable to savings accounts but usually pay a higher rate, providing the money is kept in the institution for the prescribed period—six months, a year, two years, and so on. Presently, you can earn 5.75 percent to 6 percent on savings on higher-interest certificates.

U.S. savings bonds

E bonds can be redeemed any time after two months from their issue date; with H bonds, you wait six months. In both cases, early redemption reduces the rate from 5 ½ percent guaranteed for bonds held to maturity.

E bonds can be purchased for as little as $18.75. H bonds start at $500 and are subject to federal income taxes but not to state and local taxes. E bonds have the same exemption, but the interest that accumulates each year need not be declared on your federal income tax until the bonds are redeemed. Moreover, you can postpone paying taxes on all or most E-bond interest by using the bonds to purchase H bonds. In that case, the accumulated E-bond interest need not be reported for taxes until the H bonds are cashed or have matured.

The government has extended maturities of E and H bonds and of the notes known as *Freedom Shares,* and so all three types are continuing to earn interest.

How much do you want to save?

Why not try this idea: Save now, pay later. Decide how much you need for specific objectives—a trip to Europe, a college fund—you name it. Then find in Table 13-2 the amount of money you must set aside monthly, at various rates

TABLE 13-2   How Much Do You Want to Save?

FIND YOUR SAVINGS GOAL IN THIS COLUMN	HERE IS THE REGULAR MONTHLY SAVING NEEDED TO REACH THAT GOAL IF YOUR MONEY IS INVESTED AT							
	3%	3½%	4%	4½%	5%	6%	7%	8%
$ 500 in 5 years	$ 7.80	$ 7.70	$ 7.60	$ 7.50	$ 7.45	$ 7.25	$ 7.10	$ 6.95
10 years	3.60	3.50	3.40	3.35	3.25	3.10	2.95	2.80
15 years	2.20	2.15	2.05	1.95	1.90	1.75	1.60	1.50
20 years	1.55	1.45	1.40	1.30	1.25	1.10	1.00	0.90
30 years	0.85	0.80	0.75	0.65	0.60	0.50	0.40	0.35
$1,000 in 5 years	$15.55	$15.40	$15.25	$15.05	$14.85	$14.55	$14.20	$13.90
10 years	7.25	7.05	6.90	6.70	6.50	6.20	5.90	5.60
15 years	4.45	4.25	4.10	3.95	3.80	3.50	3.25	2.95
20 years	3.10	2.90	2.75	2.60	2.45	2.20	1.95	1.75
30 years	1.75	1.60	1.45	1.35	1.25	1.00	0.85	0.70
$2,000 in 5 years	$31.15	$30.80	$30.45	$30.10	$29.75	$29.05	$28.40	$27.75
10 years	14.40	14.05	13.70	13.40	13.05	12.40	11.80	11.20
15 years	8.85	8.55	8.20	7.90	7.60	7.00	6.45	5.95
20 years	6.15	5.80	5.50	5.25	4.95	4.40	3.95	3.50
30 years	3.45	3.20	2.90	2.70	2.45	2.05	1.70	1.40
$3,000 in 5 years	$46.70	$46.15	$45.65	$45.15	$44.60	$43.60	$42.60	$41.65
10 years	21.60	21.10	20.55	20.10	19.55	18.60	17.65	16.80
15 years	13.30	12.80	12.30	11.85	11.40	10.50	9.70	8.90
20 years	9.20	8.75	8.30	7.85	7.40	6.65	5.90	5.25
30 years	5.20	4.80	4.40	4.00	3.70	3.05	2.55	2.10
$4,000 in 5 years	$62.30	$61.55	$60.90	$60.20	$59.50	$58.10	$56.80	$55.50
10 years	28.80	28.10	27.40	26.75	26.10	24.80	23.55	22.35
15 years	17.75	17.10	16.40	15.80	15.20	14.00	12.90	11.90
20 years	12.30	11.65	11.05	10.45	9.90	8.85	7.90	7.00
30 years	6.95	6.35	5.85	5.35	4.90	4.10	3.40	2.80
$5,000 in 5 years	$77.85	$76.95	$76.10	$75.25	$74.35	$72.65	$71.00	$69.40
10 years	36.00	35.25	34.25	33.45	32.60	31.00	29.45	27.95
15 years	22.20	21.35	20.55	19.75	19.00	17.50	16.15	14.85
20 years	15.35	14.55	13.80	13.05	12.35	11.05	9.85	8.75
30 years	8.65	7.95	7.30	6.70	6.15	5.10	4.25	3.50
$6,000 in 5 years	$93.40	$92.35	$91.30	$90.30	$89.20	$87.20	$85.20	$83.30
10 years	43.20	42.20	41.10	40.15	38.10	37.20	35.35	33.55
15 years	26.60	25.60	24.65	23.70	22.75	21.00	19.35	17.85
20 years	18.40	17.45	16.55	15.70	14.85	13.25	11.85	10.50
30 years	10.40	9.55	8.75	8.05	7.35	6.15	5.10	4.20

of interest, to reach your goal. To accumulate $2,000 in five years at 5 percent interest, for example, you need to invest $29.75 a month for five years.

The two assumptions built into this table are these: interest is compounded semiannually and the money does not earn interest until six deposits have been made. Quarterly deposits will put your goal ahead of schedule.

How long will your savings last?

Solving problems like these is complicated for most people. You can get a quick answer from Figure 13-1. It is based on a $10,000 fund, but you can adapt it to other amounts. How long will $10,000 earning 5 percent a year last if you withdraw $150 each month? Find $150 on the left-hand margin, then draw a horizontal line over to the curve representing the 5 percent growth rate. From this point drop a vertical line to the bottom scale, and find the answer, 6½ years.

You can handle other amounts with the aid of a ratio. If, for example, you want to find out how long a $25,000 sum will last if you want to withdraw $150 a month. Set up a ratio: $25,000 is to $10,000 as $150 per month is to $X per month. You will discover that X works out to $60. So your answer will be the

FIGURE 13-1   How long will your savings last?

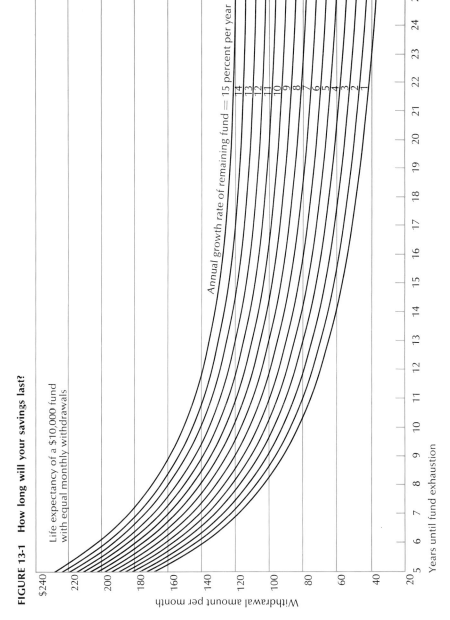

Life expectancy of a $10,000 fund with equal monthly withdrawals

Annual growth rate of remaining fund = 15 percent per year

same as for $60-a-month withdrawals from a $10,000 fund—about twenty-three years.

If you want to use a $10,000 sum for a fixed monthly amount for twenty years, assuming the fund grows 10 percent a year, locate twenty years on the bottom scale and then draw a vertical line up to the 10 percent curve. From there draw a horizontal line over to the left margin. You will find it hits $94 per month. This is what you can withdraw.

If the sum were $25,000 instead of $10,000, you would multiply $94 by 2½ times, since $25,000 is 2½ times $10,000. The answer— $235 a month.

The fund will remain the same if your withdrawals equal the monthly earnings. The data below show the maximums that you can withdraw each month from a $10,000 sum without running out of money. By using ratios again, you can figure the monthly amounts for sums larger or smaller than $10,000.

PERCENT GROWTH PER YEAR	MAXIMUM MONTHLY WITHDRAWAL THAT WILL MAINTAIN CAPITAL
1%	$ 8.30
2	16.52
3	24.66
4	32.74
5	40.74
6	48.68
7	56.54
8	64.34
9	72.07
10	79.74
11	87.34
12	94.89

Savings and inflation

Not only must consumers be concerned with the need for full disclosure of interest received on savings, but they should also be aware of savings and investments that lie dormant at a fixed rate of interest. Savings and investments are safe only in the sense that if you deposit or invest $1,000, for example, you will be able to withdraw $1,000. But if you had deposited $1,000 thirty years ago and withdrew it today, the present value of that $1,000 would be less than $350 in terms of its original purchasing power.

Savings are affected by inflation

Not only capital has been affected. The value of the interest earned on savings accounts and by bonds must also be adjusted downward as inflation continues to take its toll.

Will prices again double or triple? The prestigious Conference Board, in its economic model for 1990 prepared for the White House Conference on the Industrial World Ahead, assumed a "moderate" rate of inflation of 3 percent. It also projected a high rate of 4.5 percent and a medium rate of 3.75 percent. This projection is in contrast to a 5.9 percent inflation in 1969–1970, a 4.2 percent inflation in 1970–1971, and a 3.5 percent inflation in 1971–1972.[3] Given

[3] U.S. Department of Labor, The Conference Board, 1972.

3 percent as a minimum rate, the purchasing power of the dollar would be cut in half before the end of this century. Consumers would be paying double or triple today's prices. The point to be observed is that you should be aware of the dangers of the erosion of interest and capital when making savings and investment decisions. For example, common stocks and convertible stocks and bonds, and real estate in general, tend to increase in value for a period of years and serve as a hedge against inflation. On the other hand, savings accounts, United States savings bonds, corporate bonds, and municipal bonds do not increase in value because they pay a *fixed* rate of interest regardless of inflation.

THE SMALL INVESTOR

Before considering the pros and cons of specific kinds of investments and savings accounts for the ordinary, small investor, who generally seeks advice from so-called experts, it may be a healthy thing to comment generally on how to get advice on the stock market.

Once a would-be composer went to Mozart for help with a sonata. "You're only 21," Mozart told him, "why not start with something simple?"

Miffed, the young man retorted, "But you were only 7 when you wrote your first sonata."

"Yes," Mozart said, "but I didn't have to ask anyone how."

I think of this anecdote whenever a reader asks "how" to invest in the stock market. Anyone who must pose such a question has no business in the market in the first place. But even those who don't need to ask how certainly should seek advice.

An honest and competent advisor, by soundly guiding you about what to do and when to do it, can help you achieve financial security over the years. Then there are the dishonest or incompetent advisors, who can cause the quick loss of your life's savings.

"Most investors lack the time, interest or talent to take the full responsibility for their own investment decisions," says John Springer in his book "If They're So Smart, How Come You're Not Rich?" As a result, many seek the advice of "investment experts"—advisors who can literally make or break you.

Springer, a former Associated Press writer and a successful investor, has written a hard-hitting, well-researched book that might just spare you the latter experience.

"Much trouble with the advice-giving mechanism," he says, "stems from the absurd situation that allows virtually anyone to set himself up as an adviser."

In his book, Springer gives the following eight suggestions to help the reader make a wise choice of an investment advisor or, equally important, avoid an unwise choice:

The road to wise investing

(1) Reject the idea that "professional advice" is automatically superior.
(2) Recognize that only a small percentage of specific investment advice is truly objective.
(3) Remember also that it is difficult to get disinterested advice about mutual funds from a broker or fund salesman.

(4)   Maintain your options. Think twice before entering a binding, long-term commitment.

(5)   Learn the reasoning behind an advisor's recommendation and double-check wherever possible.

(6)   Beware the advisor who plugs one stock exclusively.

(7)   Know your legal rights.

(8)   Above all, don't expect miracles.

If you're already investing, you can check the record your advisor has made over a three- or four-year period against the Dow Jones stock averages for the same time. (These may be found in the back of the annual *Wall Street Journal Index* in most good-sized libraries.)

Some 31 million Americans are now investing in stocks and bonds directly, and there are 6,500,000 shareholders in mutual funds. Most of the individual and all the fund investors are counting on the experts for help.

If this is what you're planning to do—or are already doing—you should, at the very least, know your expert. Among other things, you might paraphrase John Springer's title and ask, "If that advisor's so smart, how come he's not rich?"

Corporate and government bonds Bonds have always been something of a mystery to many people. It wasn't until a few years ago, when bond yields rose far above savings account rates, that smaller investors began buying bonds in significant amounts.

Bonds are generally issued in face amounts of $1,000 or more. They are traded much like stock on the New York Stock Exchange and over the counter through dealers.

Each bond pays a fixed rate of interest, expressed as a percentage of the face value. For example, a 5 percent $1,000 bond pays $50 a year, usually in semiannual installments of $25. That 5 percent "coupon rate," as it's known, is only one of the facts needed to evaluate the yield.

Bond prices fluctuate in line with interest rates. If you buy that $1,000 bond when it drops to $950, your "current yield" will be not 5 percent but about 5.3 percent (the $50 annual interest payment divided by $950). Also, the institution that issued the bond has pledged to repay the entire $1,000 when the bond is redeemed at the end of its stated lifetime. By holding it until then, you can earn the extra $50, and your "yield to maturity" will exceed the 5.3 percent current yield.

Once you have bought a bond, your return is fixed, but don't ignore the possibility of gain or loss should you decide to sell before maturity. If interest rates fall, you can sell the bond at a higher price. If rates rise, you will have to accept a lower price. And the price can drop like a rock if you've blundered into buying a bond issued by an institution that fails to earn enough to keep up interest payments or assure redemption.

Those risks can be moderated by selecting high-quality bonds that mature in a relatively short time. Bonds are rated by two major financial reporting services, Standard & Poor's and Moody's. The Standard & Poor's ratings run from a top of AAA to a bottom of D (for bonds in default). High-quality bonds normally pay lower interest rates than lower-quality bonds of the same variety.

A wide array of short-term (maturing in up to five years) and long-term (over five years) bonds are issued by companies, the United States Treasury and federal agencies, and state and local authorities. The federal bonds rank highest in safety of principal.

Municipals, known as *local* and *state issues,* offer a special advantage— interest payments that are exempt from federal income taxes. Their real yield, therefore, depends on your particular income tax bracket. To a person in the 32 percent tax bracket, a 5 percent municipal bond rate is equivalent to a taxable interest of 7.35 percent.

Bonds can be purchased and sold through brokerage firms. Banks, for a service fee, will usually purchase certain government securities for their clients. The usual charge for $1,000 bonds is $5 for the first forty-nine bonds and $2.50 thereafter. Some banks and brokers will not take orders for less than five bonds ($5,000).

Common and preferred stock

As a bondholder, you're a creditor of the institution that issued the bond. As a stockholder, you're a part owner of the company, with all the potential risks and rewards that such a position entails.

The value of your shares will rise or fall almost every day. You hope, of course, that yours will rise more than they fall, and often it works out that way. Stocks listed on the New York Stock Exchange increased by an average of 5 percent a year between 1960 and 1970. On the other hand, if you had bought any one of the 254 listed issues at the beginning of 1970, you would have lost 30 percent or more by the end of the year.

Preferred stock carries a fixed dividend rate, and for that reason preferred stock prices move with interest-rate trends. Common stock dividends range from nothing to a yield of 6 percent or more, and they can change from quarter to quarter, year to year. Technically, companies may pay as much as they like to common stock owners. In practice, dividends are restricted by two consider- ations: Bondholders and preferred stock owners must be paid their interest and dividends before any income is distributed to common stock holders. Many companies, especially growth companies, retain a substantial amount of earn- ings to finance expansion.

Financial analysts separate common stock into cyclical and growth cate- gories. The earnings of cyclical companies are determined largely by the overall savings in the economy. Growth companies are those which produce special products or services that usually maintain earnings in poor periods and increase revenues faster than most others in good times. The public utilities and rail- roads, for example, are cyclical types of companies that usually pay higher yields than growth stocks.

Brokers' commissions depend upon several factors such as the number of shares bought or sold and the dollar amount of the transaction. On orders for round lots (orders of 100 shares), minimum commissions as of March, 1972, are as specified in the accompanying table.

AMOUNT OF MONEY	MINIMUM COMMISSION
$100–$800	20% plus $6.40
800–2,500	1.3% plus $12.00

The minimum commission on an order of 100 shares is $65. This is also true for an odd-lot order (less than 100 shares). The commission on odd-lot orders involving $100 to $800 usually is 2.0 percent plus $4.40 at this writing. It is possible to buy stocks without commissions. You purchase them from brokerage firms engaged in underwriting, trading large blocks of stocks for sellers, and so on. Such firms get commissions from the companies, and if the stock is one you want, there is no commission to buyers.

Convertible bonds and stocks

Companies sometimes sweeten an offering of bonds or preferred stock by making the securities convertible into common stock (of the same company) at a designated price or ratio for a certain period. At first sight, convertibles appear to provide all the advantages of a fixed-income security plus the capital gain potential of common stock. Analyzing convertibles, however, requires more than average investment skill because of the complex price and yield relationships between the different types of securities—common stock and bonds or preferred stock. And once bought, convertibles have to be watched carefully.

Investment companies

From go-go to so-so

Shares in an investment company give you part ownership of a broad portfolio of securities that are selected and managed by experts. The diversification and professional direction are designed to better your chances of succeeding, at less risk and with less trouble.

Many investment companies do, in fact, beat the stock market averages. But not all do, and even the winners suffer occasional losses; thus investment company shares must be chosen with the same caution as the stock of individual companies.

By far the most popular investment companies are mutual funds, which continuously sell shares to the public and stand ready to redeem them at their going value. Another type of investment company, the closed-end fund, issues new shares only when it needs more capital. Its shares are traded like regular stock.

Mutual funds try to manage their portfolios to meet specific investment goals. Many concentrate on growth stocks or growth and income stocks. Balanced funds invest in a mixture of securities designed to minimize risks. Income funds are based largely on bonds and other fixed-income securities.

"Load" funds charge sales commissions, ranging up to about 8.5 percent, and market their shares through agents and brokerage houses. "No-load" funds have no entrance fees and don't use sales agents. To buy no-load shares, you generally have to mail an order directly to the company.

The companies that manage funds charge the fund an annual fee, typically ½ of 1 percent of the fund's average assets, which covers most costs except brokerage commissions and some administrative costs. All those expenses reduce the income available to pass on to shareholders in the fund.

Municipal bond funds are a close cousin to investment companies. They start with a fixed portfolio of municipal bonds against which they sell "units," usually in $1,000 denominations. The tax-exempt interest received by the fund is passed on to the unit holders. They also are entitled to a pro rata share of the principal realized by the fund as bonds in the portfolio are redeemed. The fund is ultimately dissolved when all the bonds are redeemed or sold.

Investment companies may spread risks, but they don't alter the essential

Average annual dividend
and interest yield

nature of your investment. If you buy shares in a common stock fund, you are still investing in common stock, at one stage removed.

Now that we have briefly reviewed the nature of savings accounts, United States government bonds, state and municipal bonds, corporate bonds and industrial stocks, public utility and railroad stocks, and mutual funds, consult Table 13-3 for the average annual dividend and interest yield for the above types of savings and investments for small investors. Notice that each category of investment tends to maintain a special relationship to the others. Corporate bonds, for example, tend to give higher yields than other investments, and growth funds tend to give lower yields.

The small investor: how
about securities?

Investment = risk

Just about everyone who has bought securities learns sooner or later that investing is a high-risk affair, even when the stock market has been rising for a number of years. Sometimes the best thing that could happen to a new investor is to make a mistake quite early in the game; this may show him the odds. The difference, you know, between a small child and a small (new) investor is that once burned, the former seldom returns to the source of his discomfort, while the latter shows a puzzling proclivity to do so.

At any rate, over the years, a family should not venture into securities investing until it has built up a comfortable emergency savings account and has adequately insured the life of the major breadwinner. The next thing to do is to determine your investment objectives: What are you investing for? How much risk are you prepared to take? A bachelor can afford risks, if he likes. A man with a wife and children and a modest sum for investment should try to get into nonspeculative, growth-oriented kinds of investment. Don't shoot for the moon.

**TABLE 13-3 Types of Investments—Average Annual Dividend
and Interest Yield**

	1960	1965	1970
Savings accounts:			
Commercial banks	2.56%	3.69%	4.92%
Credit unions	4.66	4.81	5.50
Mutual savings banks	3.47	4.11	5.03
Savings and loan associations	3.86	4.23	5.09
U.S. government bonds	4.01	4.21	6.59
State and local bonds	3.69	3.34	6.12
Top-rated corporate bonds	4.41	4.49	8.04
Industrial stocks	3.26	3.06	3.67
Public utility stocks	3.59	3.30	5.88
Railroad stocks	5.75	4.26	6.68
Mutual funds growth	1.5	1.2	2.1
Growth and income	2.9	2.4	3.3
Balanced	3.0	2.9	3.8
Income	4.8	3.7	5.2

SOURCES: National Credit Union Administration; Standard & Poor's;
U.S. Savings and Loan League; Wiesenberger *Financial Services.*

Somewhere early in his investing career, he should consult a bank trust officer about his estate plan—such things as a will and executors—because investing should be a part of the overall program.

Suggestion 1. Diversify according to plan. Historically, stocks have grown at a compound rate of about 9 percent annually, including capital gains and dividends. Perhaps a stock may not reach that high for some time. At any rate, a small investor may wind up with an insignificant amount of stock in any one company following diversification unless he sticks to a general plan over a number of years. To start with, some independent investment counselors recommend 50 percent of the money in a no-load mutual fund (stocks) with no sales commission, 10 percent in a growth utility company, 15 percent in consumer-oriented firms (retailing, etc.), and 25 percent in advanced technology companies (computers, electronics, etc.). If you do diversify this way, you had better be willing to spend some time keeping up with the market and with the economy.

Suggestion 2. One of the advantages of a monthly investment plan is that it offers the opportunity of *dollar averaging,* as illustrated below. In dollar averaging, you invest the same fixed sum regularly into the same stock or stocks regardless of current price. Your fixed amount of money buys more shares when the stock is low, fewer shares when the stock is high. Dollar averaging over several years results in the average cost of all shares purchased being lower than the average price at which shares were bought. In other words, your cost per share will be below the average of the prices at the separate times you made your purchases.

According to the National Association of Investment Companies, over 15 million common stocks have been purchased through over 200,000 accounts since monthly investment plans were introduced in 1954. Over 55 percent of the plans in force are quarterly, and most individuals automatically reinvest dividends. The most popular issues subscribed to under these plans are "blue chips" (good-quality common stocks) like General Motors, American Telephone and Telegraph, Phillips Petroleum, and others. This is a plan for steady investors, not for those interested primarily in day-to-day fluctuations of the market.

Figuring profits

Investing small sums regularly in good-quality common stocks has great advantages, but there is one hitch. You should know the true annual growth rate,

TABLE 13-4   How Dollar Averaging Works

	FIRST QUARTER	SECOND QUARTER	THIRD QUARTER	FOURTH QUARTER
Amount invested	$100.00	$100.00	$100.00	$100.00
Price per share	$ 20.00	$ 25.00	$ 12.50	$ 20.00
Number of shares purchased	5	4	8	5
Total number of shares owned	5	9	17	22
Total invested	$100.00	$200.00	$300.00	$400.00
Average cost per share	$ 20.00	$ 22.22	$ 17.65	$ 18.18

and this is not too easy to measure. As an example, suppose you had invested $10 a month for fifty-two months and your holdings are worth $650. Are you better off than if you had put $10 per month for fifty-two months in a savings and loan association paying 4½ percent? Figure 13-2, Progress Chart for Monthly Investment Programs, will give you the answer.

You will need to know your gross profit and the number of months you have been investing. In this example, you invested $520 for fifty-two months, and your stocks are presently worth $650; thus the gross profit is

$$\frac{\$650 - \$520}{\$520} \text{ or } 25\%$$

FIGURE 13-2   **Progress chart for monthly investment programs**

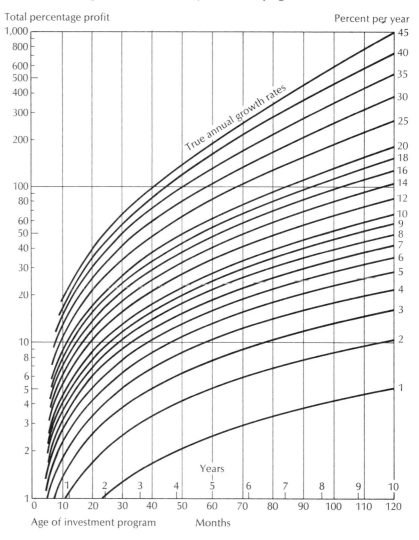

SOURCE: Prepared by Carleton Financial Computation, South Bend, Ind.

Now find this figure on the left side of the chart, and pencil a horizontal line through it. Then, on the bottom line of the chart locate fifty-two months. Draw a vertical line through this figure. These two lines will cross on, or close to, one of the curves labeled "True annual growth rates." In this case, the lines cross above the 10 percent curve. So the true annual rate of growth is slightly over 10 percent, more than double the 4½ to 5 percent you may receive from a savings and loan association.

How do you size up a stock?

How does a small investor size up a stock? When institutional investors like pension plans and mutual funds, with batteries of experts and computers, search for the best stocks from the thousands and thousands available in the markets, what chance does an individual have to select one or two stocks that will do a good job? You don't have their resources, but you still may be able to select good candidates for growth, providing you follow a few basic guidelines:

Separating the sheep from the goats

1. Select a stock that fits your objective (for income, for growth). A good broker can show you a list of stocks that will fit your objective.

2. The company should be well established. Small, new companies are risky. "New" issues, however, are not always from new companies.

3. The firm should have a good mix of products or services. Find out how much each product contributes to sales and profits.

4. The company should have a secure position in its industry. If it is at the edge of the market, it may be vulnerable to pressures from the major suppliers in the field.

5. Find out whether the company invests in research. Success often depends on developing new products and processes, not only on marketing skills.

6. Sales and real earnings should be rising. The trend should be upward.

7. The firm's financial reports should be satisfactory. A real analysis of a company's financial report requires accounting skills that most of us do not possess. Standard and Poor's manuals are apt to show serious deterioration in a company. *Forbes* magazine and *Fortune* make financial analyses of some corporations.

8. The company should have stable management. Sometimes a floundering company is taken over by good, new management.

9. Find out whether the firm is involved in a special situation. The *Wall Street Journal* frequently brings out this kind of news.

10. The stock should be selling at a reasonable P/E. The P/E, or multiple, is the ratio of the current price to the annual net-per-share earnings. A $12 stock with $1 earnings would have a multiple of 12. P/E relates the price to the key factor determining price. Growth stocks usually command the highest multiples. Ideally, you buy a stock when its P/E is at its low point of the year.[4]

11. The stock should not be overly volatile. The more volatile it is, the more you have to watch it.

"Wall Street: security risk"

Many small investors seem to believe that they are well-protected against any loss when dealing with a brokerage firm. Not quite. In 1972 a young lawyer, Hurd Baruch, working for the Securities and Exchange Commission (SEC), pub-

[4] See *Changing Times,* March, 1972, pp. 21–22.

The SIPC

lished a book entitled *Wall Street: Security Risk*. The target—the inability of the SEC to regulate the securities industry effectively. In the late 1960s and early 1970, operational and financial crises shook the foundation of Wall Street. This book tells how badly the securities business policed itself. Among the questionable aspects were its freedom to finance day-to-day operations with billions of dollars customers leave deposited with their brokers, the paper-work jam, and a condition that allowed brokerage house partners to pick up their marbles and go home at the first sign of trouble. Many brokerage houses closed their doors or were forced to merge with a stronger brokerage house because they could not meet the demands of clients for their securities left with their brokers. Millions of securities just disappeared.

Congress is concerned about this mess. The SEC has been investigated, and reforms may be on the way. Congress created the Securities Investor Protection Corporation (SIPC) to insure investors up to $50,000 per account against brokerage house failures. The SEC first opposed the plan and then modified its total opposition, but it fought hard against fundamental industry reforms to the insurance package.

Mr. Baruch recommended that the SEC should become the primary regulator of the securities industry, with all the exchanges relegated to a lesser role; he also felt that the industry should move to a competitive rate structure from the present system of mostly fixed commissions. How do you regulate the self-regulators—the New York and American Stock Exchanges, as well as the regional exchanges?

The important questions now are: Will the SEC chairman fight hard for enactment of the SEC recommendations? What pressures, one way or another, will President Nixon and Congress use? If Congress grants the SEC more power, will it also give the commission the personnel and money it would need to handle new authority properly?

At this writing the only positive action—an important one for small investors —has been the creation of the SIPC, which Congress set up in 1969 to ensure investors up to $50,000 per account against brokerage house failures. The Baruch study claims the same conditions which caused the crisis of 1967–1970 still exist and that the crisis could reoccur at any time.

Alternative forms of investment

In the early 1970s, when stocks apparently were not in a "forever upward" trend and when many small securities investors had left the market, many small investors turned more to other kinds of investments—notably, high-yielding bonds and savings accounts and other alternative forms.

Actually, it isn't true that there are fewer individual traders in the market today. What has been happening is that the institutional volume grew so rapidly between 1965 and 1971, according to William Fruend, New York Stock Exchange chief economist, that it now accounts for 68 percent of all trading in dollars. The individual investor accounts for only 32 percent of trading, says Fruend.

There were about 32,500,000 individual investors trading in 1971. The biggest traders are private pension funds, which now have over $125 billion in assets, with $85 billion in common stocks. Next are the mutual funds, with total assets of $51 billion, all but $3 billion of it in common stocks.

Thus, it is these two institutional trading categories that have caused the individual investor to become less and less powerful in the market. Each year these two fund categories are more influential in setting prices. Some mutual funds now turn over their portfolios 100 percent within one year.

The small investor is "getting out"

Small investors also have been withdrawing gradually from direct stock investments, as reflected in the steady excess of small-lot selling in relation to buying. Many observers feel that this behavior represents more than just caution; instead, they feel, it signifies disillusionment.

"There are all sorts of people that I run into that don't want to buy any stock at all," William McChesney Martin, former chairman of the Federal Reserve Board System, told a meeting of the New York Financial Writers.

Martin, author of a recent report that recommended reforms in the market, added that the integrity of the investment industry must be restored following disclosures of excesses and abuses and sins of omission.

For one thing, the investment community is becoming more sharply aware of the need for the small fellow's orders if liquidity is to be maintained. Without those small orders, prices have a tendency to lurch instead of flow; instead of changing by 25 cents on a trade, some shares change by $1.25.

No longer is there any mystery about what the small investor is doing; he's getting out.

The mystery that remains is this: Why should professional investors—individuals and institutions that have the background, the experience, and adequate resources—want to have someone else making the decisions for them?

The small investor is trying to find other kinds of investing opportunities. Historically, stocks have grown at a compound rate of about 9 percent a year, including capital gains and dividends. The stock market, as a whole, cannot match that average now. This is why so many small investors are still disillusioned about the securities market.

The small investor: should he buy corporate bonds?

We learned earlier, but it bears repeating, that bonds (usually in $1,000 units) are debts of the corporation, in contrast to common stocks; that income from a bond is fixed and the interest is payable usually twice a year; that there are long-term and short-term bonds; that the owner of bonds cannot share in the prosperity of the company; that long-term bonds are not good buys during inflation; and that certain short-term, high grade bonds for income should be considered by the small investor.

The following is a sampling of high-grade, high-income utility bonds today: American Tel & Tel, 8.7s; Columbia Gas, 8 3/8s; Florida Power, 9s; IT & T, 8.9s; Michigan Bell, 8 5/8s; N.Y. Telephone, 7 3/4s; Northwestern Bell Tel, 7 7/8s; Virginia Electric & Power, 8 7/8s; and many others. See the *Wall Street Journal* or a metropolitan newspaper for further listings of good utility bonds.

Many of these high-coupon issues are selling at premiums (above $1,000), and so the actual return from a 9 percent or 8 1/2 percent coupon will be reduced by the fact that you pay more than $1,000 for the bond. The yields, however, are still excellent, as are the quality ratings. The trust department in your local bank is a good local source for advice, as are good brokerage firms, Moody's Investment Service, Inc., and Standard & Poor's Corporation.

The small investor: should he buy in Ginnie Mae?

Later on in life when you have $25,000 available (the smallest amount at this writing—the minimum until recently was $100,000), you may want to free yourself from the necessity of making individual decisions by investing in securities backed by the Government National Mortgage Association, called "Ginnie

Mae" in the marketplace. The federal government is in back of this investment and each month pays you interest on their investment and a small return of principal. Their money is yielding about 7.16 percent at this writing. The securities are actually backed by the Federal Housing Administration and the Veterans Administration. Owning these Ginnie Mae securities is like owning a mortgage on real estate and receiving the house payments each month, but without the worry about whether the occupants will make their payments.

Low risk, high yield

Since these attractive guarantees were first offered in 1970, many banks, savings and loan associations, and pension funds have flocked to the Ginnie Mae securities. The interest, however, is taxable; on the other hand, the risk is almost nil. Furthermore, such an investment is easier to bail out of than a conventional real estate investment. Most of these thirty-year mortgages have an actual life of only twelve years because there is such a vigorous demand or secondary market for these securities. Ginnie Mae securities are especially useful to ordinary investors when regular monthly income is needed—usually after retirement.

The small investor: should he buy load or no-load funds?

There are two kinds of investment companies—open-end and closed-end. *Open-end trusts* (called "mutual funds") are those whose shares are redeemable at any time at approximate asset value. These trusts will also sell new shares at any time. Thus, the number of outstanding shares is always changing. There is generally a loading charge of about 8.5 percent when you buy this type of share; when you sell, you usually receive the net asset value of the shares without deduction or charge. In purchasing mutual shares, the loading charge of 6 to 9 percent can wipe out earnings of 3 to 4½ percent a year for a couple of years. Therefore, never buy mutual shares unless you can afford to keep them for several years. There are a few funds, such as Scudder, Stevens and Clark and Loomis Sayles, both of Boston, the De Vegh Fund of New York, and the Haydock Fund of Cincinnati, that do not have a loading charge at all. As a result, these funds are not popular with brokerage houses.

Closed-end trusts, on the other hand, have a fixed number of shares outstanding. Since these trusts do not issue new shares or redeem old ones, you acquire shares by buying from someone who wants to sell. This is why closed-end shares are sold on stock exchanges or over the counter just as industrial stocks are traded. You pay a regular broker's commission when you buy or sell these shares.

Closed-end shares are affected by the law of supply and demand. They may sell for more than net asset value or for less, depending on demand or popularity. At times, closed-end trusts invest heavily in one company and get involved in its management. So if you want diversification, investigate before you invest.

Both kinds of investment trusts are in the business of investing money entrusted to them by their shareholders. It is difficult to say that one type is better for all investors than the other. There are differences, however, that are worth investigating.

Major objectives of investment trusts

The major objectives of investment trusts are given in the latest edition of Arthur Wiesenberger's book *Investment Companies*. This comprehensive volume covers both open-end and closed-end trusts. Here are some of the major objectives of investment trusts:

1. Long-term growth of capital and income.
2. Long-term growth of capital only.
3. High current income.
4. Stability and dependable income.
5. Concentration on a particular industry, such as Chemical Fund, Inc., Atomic Development Mutual Fund, and the Axe Science and Electronics Corporation.
6. Concentration on a particular type of security, such as bonds or preferred stocks. There are very few such funds. Examples are the Bond Fund of Boston and the Franklin Custodian Funds—Preferred Stock Services.
7. Heavy investment in special situations thought to be undervalued.

No-load funds do better

Some fund managers earn their keep; some don't

Do investors get more for their money with no-load mutual funds? That question has been debated for years, if "debate" is the word for the name-calling and backbiting that's gone on. It looks, finally, as if we may have an authoritative answer.

No-load funds don't charge the buyer a sales commission or load because they don't reward salesmen or brokers with a cut of the customer's money for selling their shares. Load funds, which do, typically take 8 1/2 percent off the top to cover their sales expenses. Thus $1,000 handed over to a no-load fund buys $1,000 worth of shares; in a load fund, only $915 is left to be invested in shares.

Champions of the load funds have insisted, however, that it doesn't make any difference how much you start out with—it's how much you've got at the end of the road that counts. Take a look, they insist, at "performance." That's generally illustrated by showing how much an investment ($10,000 for easy arithmetic) has appreciated over a ten-year period.

Load-fund supporters appeared to get at least a draw when the Securities and Exchange Commission released in 1971 its massive study of institutional investing. The SEC said it "concluded that there is no appreciable difference between the 'performance' of load funds and no-load funds."

To Yale Hirsch, who publishes the yearly *Mutual Funds Almanac* and a quarterly *Scoreboard* giving performance data for some 530 funds, that didn't sound right, and in September, 1972, he started running a massive study of his own. When his figures showed a substantial tilt in favor of the no-loads, he took them to the SEC and asked, "How come?"

Alan Rosenblat, chief counsel of the SEC division involved, now admits that the SEC study hadn't taken sales charges into account, and that "investors in no-load funds actually had better investment returns than investors in load funds."

How much better is shown in a special report published by the Hirsch Organization in Old Tappan, New Jersey, covering thirty-four periods of five to twenty years.

In all time periods, the average no-load fund outperformed the average load fund on the basis of "net appreciation." Overall, there was a difference of 30.7 percent in favor of the no-loads.

It's the sales charge, or the absence of it, that makes the difference, Hirsch concludes. Obviously, the investor with $1,000 pumping away for him is going to stay ahead of one with $915 invested, unless the latter's load fund is running quite a bit faster.

A lot faster, in fact, because as Hirsch sums up the results of his study, "the no-loads have a helluva head start"—certainly in some degree accounting for the fact that after twenty years, the average no-load fund was 28.2 percent ahead.

Large investors buy mutual funds

It is widely believed that mutual funds are made up primarily of the pooled assets of millions of small investors with a desire for professional portfolio management and diversification.

Even the Investment Company Institute, trade association of the funds, seems to accept the notion. This is how it describes the role of its members: "Management investment companies seek to do for the individual what he might do for himself if he had the time, the inclination, the background, the experience and sufficient resources. . . ."

Not made up of small investors

But who are those investors who increasingly have been buying fund shares in lots of $100,000 or more? Small investors? People of insufficient experience and resources?

Third-quarter figures in 1971 showed that more than one-third of the industry's sales were made up of single investments of $100,000 or more, compared with 21 percent a year earlier.

Small investors who earlier found themselves pummeled by volatile price changes resulting from the infighting of big institutions in the stock market will be watching for the same thing in mutual funds now.

But clearly they are doing more than just watching. In several recent months, for example, despite purchases by big investors, the industry has suffered an excess of redemptions over sales. This was also true in 1972.

After viewing the figures, Standard & Poor's Corporation made this observation: "This means two things: One, $100,000-and-over buyers almost doubled their purchases of funds, to $370 million in the 1971 period from $205 million in the third quarter last year; and, two, small investors at the same time actually cut back on their fund-buying, to $730 million in the latest quarter from $770 million."

To summarize:

1. You get convenience, diversification, and—you hope—efficient management.

2. It is difficult to select a fund with a good performance record--but no-load funds have proved to be the best in performance over a ten- to twenty-year period.

3. Never select a fund that performs irregularly—for example, one that has a good three-year period and then rather suddenly goes down and down.

4. Investigate carefully, and you may find a winner.

5. Small investors should remember that large investors (in lots of $100,000 or more) are buying over one-third of the fund shares. Small investors actually cut back on purchasing of fund shares in 1971 and 1972.

6. Past performance is no sure guide to future performance.

The small investor: should he buy real estate?

"They are making more people, but they are not making any more land." This remark may explain why more and more people are investing in land and buildings. To house our growing population, we have been building houses and apartments at a rapid rate. On top of housing demand, we are consuming more recreation areas, and industrial and government uses of land are increasing—including acre-devouring highways and airstrips. The result? An ever-continuing land boom. Why, then, is real estate not a sure-fire investment? Real estate "as a whole" will rise in value over the years. As a practical matter, you do not invest in real estate "as a whole." You have to make a selection of a particular piece of real estate, which involves location, price, terms, taxes, mortgage, seller, lender, agent, and so on. If you have the patience to learn, to secure facts, and to seek professional advice, you are likely to have success. But you should know that real estate investing is usually more difficult than investing in stocks. Within a short time you can get most of the information you need about a stock. To get a comparable perspective on a piece of land or a building, you may have to spend many days digging out all the facts. Real estate, as a rule, cannot be sold readily in case one needs cash. Also, a building is tied to one location. A change in the area, such as relocating of a road or highway, can result in depreciation of the value of the investment. Finally, real estate usually consumes a large amount of cash—$5,000 to $10,000 or so—and this makes it hard, for small investors in particular, to spread the risk over several situations.

Offsetting disadvantages is the fact that many real estate investments make a good profit, some of which may be tax-free. (See Taylor-Troelstrup Reading 89 for the stories of amateurs who do make money.)

Where to begin

Most people start with the purchase of a home for their family. Most homes purchased for family use are not likely to produce a net gain as an investment. However, if you are fortunate enough to buy for your family a home that will sell fast, if you make a small down payment, if you obtain a no-penalty mortgage in case you pay off in advance, if the house does not need much fixing-up, and if there is considerable inflation in real estate, you *might* make some profit. There are, however, many ways to make a good profit in real estate.

Real estate opportunities

Here are a few opportunities for alert investors in real estate:

1. *Leverage.* Raw land is jumping in price on the edges of many cities, small and large. Raw land in the path of development can be purchased by the acre. With a relatively small amount of cash you can control a much larger investment by using leverage. You can usually buy raw land with about 20 to 25 percent down. That gives you "leverage," and this is what it means: Say you buy a lot for $1,000 cash and sell it a year later for $2,000. There is not much profit in that deal. On the other hand, if you arranged a 20 percent down payment—$200 —and paid $25 a month toward the purchase, at the end of the year the amount you put down ($200) plus twelve months of $25 payments ($300) adds up to a $500 total investment, plus interest cost, instead of $1000. If you sold the lot for $2000, you could pay off the balance owed on the land and still have a profit with only about half the investment. By using "leverage," your percentage of profit would have roughly doubled.

2. *Taxes.* When raw land is sold, if it has been held over six months, the profit is generally subject only to the capital gains tax—about one-half of the ordinary rate, with a maximum tax of 25 percent, not counting the surtax. It is also possible to further reduce the immediate tax on the sale of the land if the owner

receives less than 30 percent down payment on the sales price in the year of the sale. Then he can spread his capital gain over the life of the installments and pay his tax in smaller amounts over the years.

3. *Prepaid interest.* If the seller will accept prepaid interest, there will be good tax benefits. The initial down payment, consisting of prepaid interest, is deductible in the year paid, even if it is paid several years in advance. Thus, land can be purchased with money that would otherwise go for income taxes. And the higher your tax bracket, the more you benefit. There is danger, however, in case the land does not appreciate fast enough to cover the annual interest cost, property taxes, and other expenses.

4. *Inflation hedge.* Undeveloped land offers a growth potential that can outstrip losses in the dollar's purchasing power. Well-selected land will keep your investment well ahead of inflation.

Investors of modest means can share in the ownership of real estate through a real estate investment trust. A REIT is similar to a mutual fund, except that the holdings consist of real estate rather than stocks and bonds.

The first REITs were organized in the middle 1880s in Massachusetts. With the large increase in corporate profits in the 1930s, REITs (which were taxed as corporations) waned as an investment. In 1960, however, Congress passed a law which provided that justified REITs will be exempt from federal taxes on that portion of the income distributed to their shareholders if 90 percent or more of the ordinary income is so distributed. The second important requirement is that the trust must derive 75 percent of its income from real estate assets, such as apartments, shopping centers, office buildings, and nationally based business sites. Usually the annual operating costs, including trustee compensations, are limited to $1\frac{1}{2}$ percent of the net assets. Another rule is that they cannot invest more than 5 percent of the assets in undeveloped land. And no one person can own more than 10 percent of the shares.

Since the passage of the federal law in 1960, some sixty new REITs have sprung up in the country. Most of the shares were originally offered at from $5 to $10 each. In due time, the shares may be active enough to be sold over the counter and on the regular stock exchanges.

What's the attraction?

If successful, REIT investments pay out a higher and more stable income (5 to 9 percent) than is offered by common stocks (averaging about $3\frac{1}{2}$ percent). There is a good possibility that some income may be tax-free. The attractive tax-free possibility centers on the "depreciation reserve." The Internal Revenue Service allows money to be put into a "depreciation reserve" tax-free. This reserve, theoretically, is built up so that eventually money will be available to replace the building.

Assume the land and building were purchased for $1 million, with cash payments of $400,000, a 6 percent mortgage on the $600,000 balance, annual payments of $45,000 on mortgage, rent income of $100,000 a year, and a total operating cost of $19,000 as shown in the table on page 477.

You can see from this example that a property that made no profit, paid no income tax, but was able to return to its owners a 9 percent return on a cash investment of $400,000. If a tax loss could be established, the gain would be greater.

PROFIT AND LOSS FOR INCOME TAX PURPOSES

Rent income		$100,000
Expenses	$36,000	
Depreciation, 5%	45,000	
Operating expenses	19,000	
Total expenses		$100,000
Net profit or loss		0
Cash flow		
Rent		$100,000
Cash disbursements:		
Mortgage	$45,000	
Operating expenses	19,000	
Total expenses		$ 64,000
Balance for distribution		$ 36,000

Appraisal of REITs

In appraising these trusts it is well to keep in mind that real estate is a business built on borrowed money and wise use of depreciation and amortization, and that properly located land and buildings become more valuable as the country grows. REITs are more closely controlled by federal and state laws than ordinary real estate stocks. The true value of REITs is yet to be tested, but they have survived since the 1961 federal act mentioned earlier and are already rewarding many people who desire higher income. It is well to remember that the quality of a REIT is no better than its management.

ESTATE PLANNING: WILLS, TRUSTS, AND TAXES

To many, "estate planning" is exclusively a rich man's problem. Actually, however, anyone who owns a home, a normal amount of life insurance, and a few shares of stock can probably benefit his family by seeking professional advice. In the case of a father of minor children, an integrated financial plan, including a properly drafted will, is almost essential to prevent the hardship of unnecessary administrative expenses, forced sale of assets, and inflexible use of resources.

Since legal advice and drafting of legal documents such as wills and trusts are usually necessary to fulfill any estate plan, most of such planning is done by lawyers, although trust officers of banks, accountants, and life insurance agents are often helpful in working out solutions. And recently there have grown up firms, operating on a fee basis, devoted entirely to estate planning for those with sizable estates.

Regardless of which of these professionals is consulted first, the process of analysis is basically the same. The planner must analyze his client's existing assets and sources of income, together with his family responsibilities and goals. Then he examines the probable results if his client should suddenly die. If the results would fall short of the client's expectations, the planner will suggest one or more methods whereby estate shrinkages or other problems can be avoided.

Disposing of your estate

There are seven methods by which you may dispose of your estate. The first four are ways of disposing of your estate upon your death. The other three are ways of disposing of it during your life.

1. Disposing of your estate at death:
   a. You may neglect to make a will or otherwise dispose of your estate, in which case the law will dispose of your estate.
   b. You may put your property in the joint names of yourself and some other individual (your wife, husband, sister, son, etc.).
   c. You may make a will which provides for outright distribution of your estate to your beneficiaries.
   d. You may make a will which leaves all or a part of your estate in trust.
2. Disposing of your estate during your life:
   a. You may dispose of all or part of your estate *now* by placing it in a *revocable* living trust.
   b. You may dispose of all or part of your estate *now* by placing it in an *irrevocable* living trust.
   c. You may dispose of all or a part of your estate *now* by making an outright gift.

The necessity for making a will

A will is the means by which you can definitely and positively direct the economical and orderly disposal of your estate to persons of your own selection. You should make a will as soon as you are married or whenever you have dependents. Furthermore, your will should be kept up to date.

Do not be among the 70 percent of those who die in this country without a will. Modern young people should face the necessity of making a will as part of their family objectives and financial security goals. Replace any unpleasant thought of death of the testator by the happier thought of providing for those you love who will go on living.

When a person fails to make a will—that is, dies *intestate*—an administrator is appointed by the probate court to distribute the estate to the heirs of the *decedent*—the person who has died. Usually, problems of heirship arise to plague everyone. Jerome K. Jerome has said that if a person dies leaving a will, then all his property goes to whoever can get possession of the will; but if a man dies without a will, then all his property goes to the nearest villain. Jerome was exaggerating somewhat. Each state, however, has a different law of descent. If a person dies without a will, his real estate in one state will go to one set of heirs, and to another set in another state.

If a man in Illinois fails to leave a will, for instance, the law will divide his estate. If he leaves a wife and children, the wife will get only one-third of the estate; the other two-thirds will go to the children. If the children are minors, their inheritance becomes involved in guardianship proceedings. If he leaves a wife and no children, the wife gets all the personal estate, but only half of the real estate. The balance of the real estate will be divided among the parents, brothers, and sisters. If he leaves no wife or children, the entire estate goes to the parents, brothers, and sisters. If no survivors exist, the estate will go to the county, nothing to charities.

Legality of wills

Most states will give some protection to a man's wife against his creditors and the handing over of certain properties to other people. Certain kinds of property, usually the home, are exempt from creditors forever or for several years, depending on the state law.

Each state determines the qualifications of a person eligible to make a will. In the first place, each state requires that the person reach a minimum legal age —18 in many states now. In addition, some states prescribe a lower legal age for personal property and a higher age for real property.

Another requirement provided for in the laws of the various states pertains to having a sound mind and to acting on one's own volition, free from undue influence. The question is a technical one. Wills have been contested successfully and unsuccessfully on the basis of competence to make a will. The courts have usually held that a testator is of sound mind if he is capable of understanding what he has written into the will. If he fails to provide for near relatives without any rational explanation, the will may be inoperative. In cases of disinheritance, it is therefore important to name names and give reasons.

Wills made on deathbeds or when the testator is very ill are vulnerable to attack. No one should take this chance. Make a will when you are in good health.

Writing your own will. The greatest creator of litigation is the man who believes he has sufficiently mastered the technicalities of drafting a will and writes his own will. It is said that St. Ives, the patron saint of lawyers, extends to none a heartier welcome in the life beyond than to the so-called "lawyer's best friend," the Jolly Testator Who Makes His Own Will!

Contests over wills may go on for years. You remember the famous will contest of *Jarndyce v. Jarndyce,* recounted by Charles Dickens in *Bleak House.* It will bear rereading. We are told, incidentally, that Dickens himself was a little bitter over the time consumed by some necessary litigation in his own life.

Essentially, a will is a legal document. It is advisable, therefore, that a good attorney be hired to draw it. A will need not be long. Lawyers have sample forms available. Many good wills do not use the standard forms provided for such purposes. Well-known Americans have drawn wills in only one or two sentences.

Formalities of making a valid will

Certain formalities are to be observed in making a valid will. In the first place, hire a good lawyer who is capable of advising you properly. He will draw up a will that will do exactly what you—the testator—intend. In most states, the following factors are necessary in making a valid will:

Signature. The will must be signed by the maker or testator. If the will covers more than one page, the testator usually signs each of the pages. It must be signed in the presence of the witnesses. The signature should be exactly as written in the body of the will. Wills have been thrown out of probate courts because the name was incorrectly spelled in the signature of the maker of the will.

Witnesses. Most states require two or three witnesses. It is wise to have younger persons, but of legal age, act as witnesses. If the wife or the beneficiary of the will or the spouse of a beneficiary acts as a witness, such persons may be disinherited. The will should state that all witnesses signed in the presence of each other. The addresses of all witnesses should be included in the document. Even if the state requires only two witnesses, it is generally wise to have three witnesses in the event that one dies before the will is probated.

Alterations. Do not take a chance on a will being voided because of alterations or erasures. It pays to have the entire will redrafted. As a rule, witnesses do not read the will. They usually are present only at the signing of the document. If called to testify later on with regard to alterations or erasures in the will, most witnesses would be unable to state whether the erasures existed at the time of the signing.

Terms. In addition to making the will legal, care should be taken so that the will distributes the properties in the way desired by the testator. This is not difficult in a simple case but becomes technical in the event of an involved will. The first step in making a will is an appraisal of the properties or the entire estate. Careful estimates of estate shrinkage from taxes, administrative costs, and immediate expenses should be made. Provision for meeting such expenses by the use of life insurance is an excellent idea. After expenses have been cared for, the disposal of the estate is next on the agenda.

Disposal of an estate

If a will is to do exactly what the maker wants it to do, expert advice is necessary. For example, if the testator has contacts in two states, perhaps an apartment in New York, though his principal business is in another state, it is possible that both states will want inheritance taxes after his death. Such double taxation has been upheld. The heirs to the Campbell Soup fortune could tell you that Pennsylvania and New Jersey each took $15 million—just out of one little can of soup!

Make sure your will does what you want it to

Also, out-of-state real property needs to be handled carefully. Usually, it is wise to get rid of such real property or place it in a revocable trust. In this way, the property will be taxable to the estate but will not be a part of it, thereby eliminating a substantial estate expense.

Some lawyers include in wills a direction to pay debts. This has little meaning, since all debts must be paid anyhow. And it may be harmful because the direction to "pay all my just debts" means all debts, moral and legal. There is no point in inviting a lawsuit.

In making gifts, use fractional parts of the estate rather then fixed amounts or particular items. If a son is willed $25,000 and the rest (say $100,000) is willed to the wife at the time an estate is worth $200,000, and death occurs without the will being changed, the estate may have shrunk to $35,000. The son, in most states, will still get $25,000 and the wife the remainder—$10,000. Worse yet, the tax comes out of the residue.

Joint wills between spouses, as a rule, are undesirable, because they have the effect of preventing revocation without notice during the life of both parties and any revocation of the survivor.

Another important factor in drawing up the terms of a will is the determination of the portion of the estate that will bear the taxes. In some states, the taxes are paid out of the residue of the estate, which is the portion remaining after special gifts. Gifts in contemplation of death are taxable but are never a part of the estate itself. The point is to be careful so that the residue, which is so often left to the wife, is adequate. One method of accomplishing this purpose is to require the insurance beneficiaries to pay their share of the taxes and that each devisee or legatee bear his pro rata part. Exactly what should be done depends on the particular estate and the law pertaining to these matters.

If the testator, for instance, has provided $500 a month for his wife by certain insurance options, federal laws require such insurance to pay its pro rata share of the estate tax unless the will provides otherwise. The effect of this may be to reduce the widow's income to $375 a month, which is less than the husband considered adequate. Consequently, the tax apportionment clause should be drafted as a part of the estate plan so that the benefits of the legacies will be carried out as intended.

Duties of the executor. An independent executor should be designated and given as broad powers as the trustee. If the testator, for example, got a loan commitment from the bank so that ready money would be available for taxes, which must be paid in cash, then the executor should be given the power to draw on this money. It may be wise to require the beneficiaries to join in the execution of the notes, at least to the extent of the properties they will receive from the estate. This power makes borrowing much simpler.

Another requirement is early distribution of the estate. Income taxes can be saved in this way. The executor should also be under no duty to post bond—it saves expense. He should be given discretion about whether or not the estate income should be paid during the executorship. This power will mean substantial income tax savings for the family.

Whether the executor is a person or a corporation, the major qualifications are (1) ability and experience in business; (2) financial responsibility; (3) some knowledge of accounting; (4) experience in administering estates; (5) adequate facilities for safekeeping of securities, correspondence, and the like; and (6) time to do a good job.

It is customary to name a member of the family or a close friend of the family as the executor. Under certain conditions, such persons may be satisfactory. The fee of an executor or trustee is fixed by law or by court and is the same for individuals as for corporations, though the individual may waive the fee. Therefore, it is generally wise to select the best person or corporation.

The administration of an estate is a highly specialized business. An inexperienced person must hire a lawyer to do the work for him. These are some of the things that an executor must do:

1. File the will in the probate court.

2. Select and retain legal counsel. It is usually customary to name as counsel for an estate the lawyer who drew the will.

3. Aid the attorney in presenting to the court an application for letters testamentary, the oath of the executor, and proof of the legal heirs.

4. Assemble, take possession of, and safely hold all personal assets.

5. Withdraw bank deposits; locate and assemble securities; arrange for collection of interest and dividends.

6. Collect all debts due to the estate—through litigation, if necessary.

7. Take charge of real estate, if the will so provides; ascertain status of taxes and mortgages against the property; inspect the condition of the property; provide for management and collection of rents.

8. If life insurance is payable to the estate, file the necessary papers, collect on all policies, and determine what to do with the proceeds.

A common disaster clause

Simultaneous deaths (such as the death of a husband and wife in one accident) are not uncommon. In the event there is no will, all the property would pass to the children, if any. If there were no children, there may be a legal battle over which person died first. If the court had evidence that the husband died first, and if the wife had a will, this property would be disposed of according to her will. In the absence of a will, any property she left would go to *her* relatives.

Many inequities result from simultaneous deaths. Therefore, a will should provide for the disposal of the property if both husband and wife die in the same accident. A common disaster clause may read: "Any person who shall have died at the same time as I, or in a common disaster with me, or under such circumstances that it is difficult to determine which died first, shall be deemed to have predeceased me." In case there is only one bequest, to the wife perhaps, and in case she does not survive the testator, the property may be left in the will to a daughter or son, or to both of them. This is a useful clause in cases of common disaster.

Letter of last instruction

Your executor or lawyer should have a letter of last instruction that is not a part of your will. This letter is usually opened at death and contains the following information:

1. Exact location of will.

2. Instructions about funeral and burial. Veterans should remember that they may request burial in a national cemetery and save their estate some expense.

3. Location of all documents, such as birth certificate, Social Security card, marriage certificate, discharge papers, and the like.

4. Lodge or fraternal membership certificates.

5. Location of all safe-deposit boxes.

6. List of insurance policies and where deposited.

7. Pension statements and records.

8. List of all bank accounts, stocks and bonds, real and other property, and their locations.

9. Instructions concerning a business, if any.

10. Statement of reasons for disinheritances, if any.

Wills should be reviewed

Many persons hesitate to draw a will, feeling that such a document, once executed, exists for all time. Nothing is further from the truth. A will is operative and binding only at the date of the maker's death. Before death, you can make any number of wills, each of which in succession should include terms that revoke and cancel all prior wills. Or you may supplement or modify an existing will by the addition of a *codicil,* which is an amendment to a will. Whenever your family or financial conditions change, a new will should be made to meet the new conditions.

You should reread and reconsider your will each year, or oftener if necessary. A will that may be just at the time of its making may be very unjust a few years later. Take the case of a single man, the sole support of an aged and widowed mother. He marries, dies by an accident, and his wife survives. His estate consists solely of personal property of a substantial sum. When he executed his will, he was engaged to marry the woman he later did marry, but no mention was made of her in his will.

Unfortunately for the mother in such a case, the law in Illinois provides that a will executed prior to the testator's marriage is revoked by the marriage. The decedent's mother would not receive any of the estate, since it consists solely of personal property and belongs to the widow in its entirety under the law.

The moral is obvious. Review your will at least once a year in the presence of your attorney. If you are married, both husband and wife should review their wills together. There may have been changes since a year ago in the size of the family, in residence, or in tax laws. The kindest thing to do for dependents and loved ones is to be sure that your will follows your intentions.

Where to deposit a will

After you have executed a will, the safest place for deposit is with the trust company you may have named as executor or in a safe-deposit box. As a safe-deposit box may be sealed for a while after death, it is preferable to place the original will with the trust company and to place the receipt for the original will and a copy of the will in the safe-deposit box. Most banks make no charge for the safekeeping of wills in which they are named as executor or trustee.

Taxation of estates   Since the tax burden is a factor of great importance in planning the disposition of an estate, consideration of estate taxation is a desirable preliminary to estate planning. The tax burden upon an estate depends upon the value of the assets that are included in the estate for tax purposes and upon the rates of taxation. The property includable in an estate for tax purposes is the following:

1. All property in the name of the deceased.
2. Property in joint names, except to the extent that the surviving owner can show that his or her funds purchased the joint property.
3. Insurance on the decedent's life which he owns.
4. Gifts (either outright or in trust) made by the decedent during his lifetime, if such gifts were made within three years of death and in contemplation of death or if the decedent retained any interest in or control of the gift.
5. Property in respect to which the decedent had a taxable power of appointment (the right to dispose of the property by his will or by deed).

From this total may be deducted the decedent's debts, executor's fees, other costs of administering his estate, the "marital deduction" (50 percent of the net estate), and the $60,000 estate tax exemption.

Trusts   With your objectives clearly in mind, analyze your current and expected future assets, then consider how to best conserve those assets and pass them on to your family with the least amount of shrinkage. Many people rely solely on life insurance for an "instant estate," but in many cases other solutions may be available to the prudent family.

Today more families are turning to trusts, in one form or another. Even if you bequeath no more than $25,000, a trust can provide many benefits. In fact, a trust is the most flexible instrument in estate planning. Essentially, it is an arrangement whereby property is legally transferred to another person, bank, or trust company (the trustee) who handles it for you or your beneficiaries.

Life insurance trust

A young couple in their 30s, for instance, can start an estate easily with a "life insurance trust." This is administered by your bank or other trustee, not an insurance company. In this elastic program, a trustee is named to manage the insurance proceeds after death for heirs inexperienced in handling large sums. They then will receive both income and principal as needed.

Funded trust

If the estate is set up as a "funded trust," other assets (such as securities) can be coordinated with the insurance to receive the same expert management. Such a trust does not have to be mentioned in a will or go through probate. Estate administration expenses can be reduced considerably and taxation can be averted; that is, taxes need not be paid first by the wife and then again by the children who inherit the same funds from her.

Testamentary trust

You can have a trust tailor-made for you. Under a will, for example, you can create a "testamentary trust" to make certain your property is managed expertly and used as you desire. The trustee—usually a bank—is given broad investment powers, with directions for paying income and principal to your heirs.

Living trust

If you want to control your assets during your lifetime, consider the increasingly popular "living trust." With this legal instrument, you can make the income payable to yourself while you are alive or have it reinvested for your future benefit. This type of trust will not be subject to probate.

In an emergency, you can withdraw part or all of the money from the "living trust." At your demise, the trust can be continued for other members of your family. It has all the advantages of a will with none of the shortcomings (disappointed relatives rarely will challenge it). Nevertheless, you should have a will, too.

A "living trust" can be revocable—can be altered or canceled at any time—but this type is subject to estate taxes. You can, however, make the trust irrevocable, unchangeable for a specified term. Here, taxes on income are at the lowest rates. Often, the federal estate tax can be bypassed or substantial savings made by removing assets from the estate.

When a "living trust" is handled by a bank as trustee, you also have experienced investment management at a modest cost. If you become seriously ill, the trustees can pay the bills for you. Settlement of the estate is simplified and no delays are incurred. For minor children in a family, the "living trust" can provide guardianship protection.

Budget trusts

Lately, a number of banks have introduced what may be called "budget trusts," which permit people of modest means to build year by year for their family's future. Under one such plan, you begin with an investment of $100, then follow with monthly installments as low as $25.

Some drawbacks. Sure, trusts have some drawbacks. An irrevocable trust ties up property you may need later. Amending a revocable trust yourself, without the guidance of professionals, can foul up the arrangement. Attorneys and bank trust officials usually recommend extreme flexibility, so that you do not run into complications.

Some advantages. Is estate planning worth all the thought and trouble? Just look at the federal taxes. If you have a total estate, including life insurance, of $150,000 or more, $16,000 can be saved in federal estate taxes alone for the ultimate benefit of your children after the death of your surviving spouse. To do this, consult your attorney and develop an estate plan that will take full advantage of the so-called marital deduction.

Most states also have inheritance taxes. Here, again, proper planning can result in important savings. In some states, for example, life insurance payable to your spouse or any specific beneficiary (other than your estate) is exempt from state inheritance taxes.

Using gifts to save estate taxes

Let us consider a widow with one son. The mother intends to leave all of her assets to her son. Her taxable estate is $300,000. Her estate tax on $300,000 will be $62,700. Let us assume she makes a gift of one-third of the assets. Here is how the gift tax would be calculated:

Gift	$100,000
Less annual exclusive	3,000
	$ 97,000
Less lifetime exemption	30,000
Subject to tax	$ 67,000
Tax	$ 8,595

This gift has diminished her estate by $108,595 ($100,000 gift, plus $8,595 tax). The taxable estate is now $191,405. Her estate tax on $191,405 will be $30,121 (before state inheritance tax credit). Using the accompanying table, compare the tax effect on the gift.

Estate tax—no gift	$62,700
Estate tax on	
$191,405	$30,121
To which add gift	
taxes paid	8,595
Total taxes	38,716
Saved her son	$23,984

Cost of settling an estate

The exact sum that will be spent to settle your estate depends upon whether all or part goes to a wife or husband, whether property passes by will, trust, or joint ownership, the kind of property, and other factors. Table 13-5 gives a rough guide showing average payments for estate taxes and expenses. The estate-size figure represents the value of the property left, minus debts and the $60,000 tax-free exemption. "Other expenses" include court costs, fees to accountants, and other costs.

The total cost of settling an estate is more than many people realize. This is why estate experts strongly recommend capable legal advice when making a will. It may be that trust funds will be recommended. As we have pointed out earlier, there are important tax gains and other advantages of trusts. The fees for trustees in carrying out the instructions of the trust or trusts are not as large as some people imagine.

Fees for trustees

There are no standard fees for trustees. The amount depends on state law. Generally, fees are a percentage of the trust's income or capital, or both. In New York State, for example, the trustees' annual fee is limited by law to $\frac{1}{2}$ of 1 percent on the first $50,000 of capital, $\frac{1}{4}$ of 1 percent on the next $450,000, and $\frac{1}{5}$ of 1 percent on anything over $500,000. Also there is a charge of 1 percent on any principal paid out of the trust fund. There may be other expenses incurred by the trustee that would be charged to the trust fund.

TABLE 13-5   The Cost of Settling an Estate

SIZE OF ESTATE	EXECUTOR'S FEES	ATTORNEYS' FEES	OTHER EXPENSES	ESTATE TAX
Up to $20,000	$1,755	$1,824	$ 446	$ 181
$20,000 to $40,000	2,227	2,244	566	1,174
$40,000 to $90,000	3,017	2,961	715	3,971
$90,000 to $140,000	4,413	4,213	1,014	11,206
$140,000 to $240,000	6,049	5,785	1,401	23,421
$240,000 to $340,000	8,732	8,175	2,106	43,036

SOURCE: *Changing Times,* January, 1968.

SUMMARY

In choosing an executor and trustee for your estate, consider the many legal, investment, and tax questions your spouse will be facing for the first time. Many widows find it difficult to take care of even simple financial duties, such as keeping records for tax purposes. A bank with a well-staffed trust department is uniquely equipped to assist beneficiaries facing such problems, in cooperation with your lawyer, accountant, or insurance man.

In planning your estate, here are some cardinal points to keep in mind:

1.   Make sure your program is flexible—able to meet whatever contingencies may arise.

2.   Do not choose a plan solely to reduce taxes, though you should take advantage of all savings. The primary purpose is to fulfill your family's needs and objectives.

3.   This is not a do-it-yourself project. Consult a competent lawyer and choose a bank with a well-equipped trust department.

4.   Review your estate plan and your will at least once every three years.

Remember, without a well-conceived estate program, the more you are worth, the more your dependents may lose; the less you are worth, the less they can afford to lose.

QUESTIONS FOR DISCUSSION

1.   Tax avoidance will be a major estate-planning goal only if the estate is a big one. Explain. Be as specific as you can.

2.   Mutual funds were very popular among ordinary investors until about 1969 to 1973. What happened to discourage small investors in mutual funds?

3.   It goes without saying that nearly all experts agree that we can expect some inflation—not over 3 percent annually, one hopes—in the foreseeable future. Assuming this is true, how can a small or ordinary investor best protect the purchasing power of his investments?

4. Would you recommend real estate investment trusts (REITS) for a small investor? Support your answer.

5. There are at least three basic purposes for which families save money. Can you think of other important reasons for family savings?

6. We need a full-disclosure law for savings rates that would do for savers what the truth-in-lending law of 1968 did for borrowers. What evidence is there to support this statement?

7. Why are reforms needed in the Securities and Exchange Commission? In light of what happened in the securities industry during the crisis of 1967–1970, why is there so much opposition to basic reforms on the part of the SEC and brokerage houses?

8. What is the major purpose of estate planning? Is it necessary for everyone to do this kind of planning?

PROJECTS

1. In the dollar-averaging formula for buying securities we learned that when the market is high, the investor gets fewer shares, and when the market is low, he acquires more shares for the same amount of money. The net result over the long term of a fluctuating market price is that the final average cost per share will be less than the mathematical average of all the prices in effect on the various purchase dates. Conversely, when a mutual fund investor, for example, asks a fund to mail him $100 a month, every month, from his mutual fund, he must be prepared to see more shares liquidated (in order to raise that $100 each month) when share prices are low than when they are high. So, in the long run he will sell more shares when prices are low, and fewer shares when prices are high—the reverse of the system which proved so advantageous when he was buying the shares. This is a serious drawback. How could such an investor in mutual funds do much better for himself?

2. Write to a broker and request information on the monthly investment plan; then give a report to your class.

3. The estate or inheritance taxes at the state level frequently lay heavy burdens on those with little ability to pay. In New York State, for example, a resident is taxed on all estates valued at $20,000 or more. A wife and husband, for example, held title to their modest residence "in joint tenancy," and the court held that half the value of the home was an asset of the wife's estate and hence was taxable. The husband was also taxed on his half, even though the home had been purchased wholly out of his earnings. Since they are living on Social Security income largely, the tax weighs heavily indeed. Should the state exempt the value of a homestead held "in joint tenancy"? Present your findings to the class.

4. During the retirement period, a husband died, leaving a good will. It provided for an "irrevocable" trust of $60,000 to his wife, with their local bank as trustee. The widow receives a monthly check of between $235 to $250, which is about a 5 percent return on $60,000. The bank charges 1 percent, or

$600 annually for handling the trust. If her husband had left the $60,000 free, she could have invested that sum in bank certificates yielding 6 percent. Wouldn't it have been wiser for him to have left the $60,000 directly to her? Investigate this situation as if it had happened in your own state. What recommendation do you come up with? Present this recommendation to the class.

5. Some people assume that a way to avoid probate is for a husband and wife to own property jointly (the right of survivorship). Is that always a safe assumption?

SUGGESTED READINGS

American Research Council, Inc.: *Your Investments,* 18th ed., McGraw-Hill Book Company, New York, 1970.

Baruch, Hurd: *Wall Street: Security Risk,* Arcropolis Books, Ltd., London, 1972.

Friend, Irwin, Marshall Blume, and Jean Crockett: *Mutual Funds and Other Institutional Investors: A New Perspective,* McGraw-Hill Book Company, New York, 1970.

"Let's Rewrite the Probate Laws," *Changing Times,* January, 1969.

"The Need for Truth-in-Savings," *Everybody's Money,* Summer, 1972, pp. 24–25.

"Pitfalls to Watch for in Planning Your Estate," *U.S. News & World Report,* Dec. 18, 1972, pp. 48–50, 55–57.

Report on Life Insurance, rev. ed., Consumers Union of U.S., Inc., Mount Vernon, N.Y., 1972, pp. 108–112.

"Settling an Estate Could Be Faster and Cheaper," *Changing Times,* November, 1972, pp. 6–9.

"Why So Many Lawsuits against Mutual Funds?" *Changing Times,* November, 1972, pp. 27–31.

Wiesenberger, Arthur: *Investment Companies,* Arthur Wiesenberger & Company, New York. (Published annually.)

CHAPTER 14
EXPENDITURES AND TAXES FOR GOVERNMENT SERVICES

Nothing is certain but . . . and taxes.

We are all familiar with Benjamin Franklin's remark: "In this world nothing is certain but death and taxes." And the older one grows, the more certain he feels that Old Ben was so right. The tax burden on the family increases yearly despite efforts on the part of the taxpayer to take advantage of every legal deduction. It is said that one newlywed, filling out his income tax return, listed a deduction for his wife and in the section "Exemptions for children" penciled the notation, "Watch this space." He should meet the man with six "little deductions" who said, "It's got to be sort of a game with us. Every time the government raises taxes, we counter with another exemption."

Taxes in the United States are levied by three forms of government—the federal government, the states, and local governments. All three governments have been collecting more and more taxes as the years have passed.

We have proved ingenious in devising ways to tax ourselves. We levy taxes on what we earn, spend, and own. We even tax ourselves on some of the things we use, and occasionally we have taxed ourselves on the right to vote. Every American baby enters life unencumbered, but almost immediately he is tied into the tax system, if only as an exemption.

In this chapter, we choose not to teach you how to fill in a federal income tax return. The federal Internal Revenue Service furnishes various tax forms, distributes free material on how to fill in the tax forms, and even prepares an excellent teaching kit for instructors and students. With all of this information available free for the public, our emphasis will be on criteria for good taxes, federal tax reforms, local and state tax problems, and the need for revenue sharing.

TAXES AND YOU

Justice Oliver Wendell Holmes, Jr., said, "Taxes are what we pay for civilized society." As citizens, each of us has certain obligations to our society. One of these is to support the government (our society) through the payment of taxes. But more than that, as informed citizens we should know why we pay taxes, what the tax money is being spent for, and whether we can improve our tax system.

Many of us think of taxes in terms of their being too high. In reality taxes are probably higher than most college students imagine, because in addition to the federal income tax there are many other federal, state, and local taxes. Some of these are sales taxes, inheritance taxes, state and sometimes local income taxes, personal property taxes, and real estate taxes—just to mention a few.

There are other taxes that are not so obvious. The state license plate on your car, the local license permit, and your driver's permit are forms of tax. And for every cent you pay to run your car, you give a certain amount in gas tax to your federal, state, and maybe local government. But we know we receive something, too.

What do you get for your money?

Right around home you can easily see what services you get from your state and local taxes. In most places these taxes pay for streets, police and fire protection, water, sewers, parks and recreation facilities, help for the needy, public schools, and teachers' salaries.

The federal services are a little harder to see but nonetheless important. They also provide protection, but usually on a national basis. We are all familiar with the support taxes provide for our national defense. Taxes also help ensure that our foods and drugs meet safety and effectiveness standards. Taxes finance research projects that find the causes of man's diseases and continue to improve our agricultural products. They finance our relations with other nations. Through the Peace Corps and the Agency for International Development we are able to help many people to help themselves in many parts of the world. In addition, taxes help provide for most of our interstate highways, national parks, wildlife refuges, and conservation areas. Also, federal taxes provide assistance for older people, people out of work, and those who cannot afford medical care. The list is much longer, but these examples will remind you of what we get for our tax money.

Complexity of the tax structure

Our tax structure has grown increasingly complex, partly because the federal, state, and local governments compete for sources of tax funds. In raising revenue, certain understandings have been worked out: the federal government depends largely on the income tax, the states on the sales tax, and local units on the property tax. There are, however, enough exceptions to these guidelines to create serious problems of competition for revenue sources and problems of cooperation when functions and jurisdictions overlap. This problem is so serious that Congress set up the Advisory Commission on Intergovernmental Relations in 1959. This commission published two large volumes of recommendations in the hope of bringing together representatives of the federal, state, and local governments for the consideration of these intergovernmental tax problems. In December, 1972, the ACIR rejected the states' request for relief for property-tax help. This commission affirmed that school financing is a matter for the states and localities to worry about.

Citizens expect more services

The complexity of the tax structure, and of tax policies, is also attributable to the great growth of goods and services the present-day governments are expected to supply. Financing the tremendous demands for education, highways, welfare services, and old-age and unemployment insurance and the increasing costs of defense and foreign aid have put new pressures on our capacity to generate the necessary revenue in a fair and equitable manner.

Another factor, besides overlapping tax jurisdictions and growing demands, that has contributed to the complexity of tax policy has been the recognition that the ways in which government collects money and the timing of its tax decisions have an important impact on our economy—on the stability of its performance.

FEDERAL, STATE, AND LOCAL GOVERNMENTS FACE FISCAL CRISIS

No matter where you live, you are aware that local and state taxes are headed in one direction—up. Hard-pressed for revenue to meet the growing demands for services, most states and localities face a fiscal crisis.

Resistance to rising state and local taxes has been partially blunted by reductions in federal income taxes, although the latter were largely offset for many taxpayers by sharply increased Social Security payroll taxes. This suggests

Tax pains are growing

that federal taxes cannot be further reduced and that higher taxes may in fact be necessary. If prudent expenditure policies at all levels of government are not pursued, "tax revolt" may increasingly become an unpleasant fact rather than an overused catch phrase. This is why many thoughful citizens are beginning to insist on getting some realistic answers to the question: Whose tax burden is heaviest?

Whose tax burden is heaviest?

Unfair taxes

Tax Freedom Day fell on April 27, the 118th day of 1972. The Tax Foundation, a private research foundation, figures that it took all the income of the average taxpayer during the first 117 days of 1972 to pay all his taxes for the year, direct and indirect—federal, state, and local. And overall, that's just about the proportion of our total income—one-third—we pay in taxes.

But who cares about "overall"? You're not the average taxpayer. Each of us is sure that he is saddled with more than his share of the tax burden.

Lower-income groups, for example, feel ground down by regressive taxes that take a larger proportion of their income than they do of their more affluent neighbors' income. People with yearly incomes of $6,000 receive 12 percent of all income in the United States but pay 16 percent of the sales taxes and 17 percent of the property taxes.

The $9,000-a-year man finds the 5.2 percent Social Security levy biting into every paycheck, while his $18,000-a-year boss enjoys an end to Social Security withholding at midyear.

The rich man reminds everyone that the federal income tax is progressive, with rates rising from 14 to 70 percent, taking a larger share of his income than of a poorer man's. Also, a major reform of the 1969 Tax Reform Act cost 18,000 wealthy individuals $117 million in additional taxes in 1971. And, furthermore, what benefits do the rich get from all the schemes that shift their income to the poor?

The middle-income man complains that he's squeezed by both regressive and progressive taxes. He feels he subsidizes the poor while he's denied tax shelters enjoyed by the more affluent. And when he hears talk of taxpayers' revolt, he's convinced it's talk about redressing his inequities.

Fairness in taxes has always been debated. "To tax and to please, no more than to love and to be wise, is not given to man." So said Edmund Burke, speaking on American taxation in 1774. But now, with rising cries of tax reform and with arguments over the merits and demerits of the value-added tax (VAT), a kind of national sales tax, interest increases in the tax burdens we bear.

Fairness in taxation

Talk about redistributing income and wealth among citizens, talk about cutting up the pie differently, can really stir all of us. Carl Sandburg pointed this up in "The People, Yes":

"So, you want to divide all the money there is and give every man his share?"

"That's it. Put it all in one big pile and split it even for everybody."

"And the land, the gold, silver, oil, copper, you want that divided up?"

"Sure—an even whack for all of us."

"Do you mean that to go for horses and cows?"

"Sure—why not?"

"And how about pigs?"

"Oh to hell with you—you know I got a couple of pigs."

In tackling fairness in taxation, one must cover some slippery statistical ground. Calculations must be made about taxes we pay but are unaware of—for example, parts of the corporate income tax and the business property tax that are passed on to consumers in the form of higher prices.

Income concepts also need adjusting to fairly ascertain tax burdens. For example, readily available Census Bureau data on money income exclude realized capital gains. For this reason primarily, original census data on 1968 incomes, for example, showed only 200,000 families and individuals with incomes of $50,000 or more. They accounted for only 2 percent of money income reported in the census survey. But Roger A. Herriot and Herman P. Miller of the Census Bureau—in their landmark studies of tax distribution—report that after making appropriate income adjustments, they found that there were 900,000 families and individuals with total incomes in excess of $50,000 and that they accounted for 11 percent of total income in 1968.

The net tax burdens still elude researchers until they consider who receives and who pays for various benefits made via government transfer payments such as Social Security, veterans' benefits, unemployment compensation, welfare, Medicare and Medicaid benefits, and public employee retirement and disability payments.

The accompanying table from the Herriot-Miller studies shows, for 1968, relative net tax burdens after making all these adjustments. Taxes paid are expressed as a percent of total income.

INCOME GROUPS	TAXES PAID
Under $2,000	25.6%
$2,000–4,000	24.7
$4,000–6,000	27.9
$6,000–8,000	30.1
$8,000–10,000	29.9
$10,000–15,000	30.9
$15,000–25,000	31.1
$25,000–50,000	33.6
$50,000 Up	46.6
Total	31.6

Tax structures not progressive

For the bulk of American taxpayers, the tax structure clearly is not very progressive. The narrow tax-rate range of 25 percent to 31 percent for incomes of less than $2,000 to as high as $25,000 "can hardly be viewed as the basis for a substantially progressive tax structure," says J. Fred Bateman, of the School of Business at Indiana University. Within those groups are 96 percent of all families and unrelated individuals, and their total income before taxes and transfer payments accounts for more than 80 percent of all income.

For most Americans, taxation is proportional; that is, taxes take equal proportions through a wide range of incomes. Note that tax rates through the $6,000 to $25,000 levels show a spread of only 1.2 percentage points. For over 60 percent of us—a group that in 1968 accounted for 72 percent of all income—it seems that progressive taxes, like the income tax, are counterbalanced by regressive taxes like those on property, leaving us, like it or not, with proportional taxation.

The Herriot-Miller studies offer some evidence to support the suspicions of middle-income families that their share of the tax burden grew during the 1960s. The evidence can be seen in the accompanying table, which shows the share of total taxes paid by various income groups (families and unrelated individuals) in 1962 and 1968.

INCOME GROUP	1962	1968
Lowest fifth	3.7%	3.7%
Second fifth	8.9	9.4
Middle fifth	14.4	15.2
Fourth fifth	21.3	22.1
Highest fifth	51.7	49.6
Top 5%	28.1	24.8

This table indicates that during the prosperous mid-1960s, the situation of the middle 60 percent of income recipients was worsening. Their burden was growing, not because the poorer paid a smaller share of the taxes, but because the top 20 percent paid proportionately less. The Tax Reform Act of 1969 may be changing relative positions again, but as of now we can't accurately measure its impact.

Writing in *Business Horizons*, Professor Bateman says:

Middle-income groups would appear to be in a difficult situation. Many of their spokesmen would probably support higher sales taxes, arguing that such levies force the lower-income recipients, whom they feel gain most from government spending, to pay a reasonable share of the cost of government. Yet persons earning moderate incomes also fear greater progressivity in the tax structure because they realize that this conflicts with their goal of upward income mobility.

Paradoxically, middle-income groups appear to have not only felt the effect of the progressive income tax as their incomes grew, but also have found their tax burdens increasing as a result of regressive taxes as well.

Middle-income tax burdens grew in the 1960s

At this point, some people may wonder into which of the above income groups they fit. The next table from the Herriot-Miller study may be helpful. Income is for 1968, before taxes and transfer payments but including realized capital gains and adjusted for various forms of "nonmoney" income.

INCOME GROUP	INCOME RANGE
Lowest fifth	Under $3,800
Second fifth	$3,800–$8,200
Middle fifth	$8,200–$12,100
Fourth fifth	$12,100–$17,500
Highest fifth	Over $17,500
Top 5%	Over $29,700
Top 1%	Over $60,000

"People with money always feel poorer than they are," says Joseph A. Pechman, director of economic studies at The Brookings Institution and a taxation expert.

Who reaps benefits from government spending?

Attempts to distribute the tax burden fairly must, of course, consider who reaps what benefits from all government spending. The difficulties in measuring the "utility" or "satisfaction" of such spending are insurmountable. And there can be disagreement about how to allocate the benefits from something like national defense. Since each of us has but one life, do we have an equal stake in the defense of the country? Or, since the rich man has more material things to lose, does he enjoy a greater benefit from protection by the armed forces?

Middle- and lower-income persons benefit because national defense spending exceeded their total taxes

It's obvious that the general pattern of distribution of spending benefits is highly regressive—or pro poor. But it is somewhat surprising to find that, under most reasonable assumptions about how to distribute such unallocable expenditures as national defense, people with annual incomes up to $10,000 in 1968 generally realized benefits from government spending that exceeded their total tax outlays.

Formal economics can be helpful—but only up to a point—in any true overhaul of the tax system on equity grounds. In essence, the arguments over progressive versus regressive tax structures, the level of welfare, and Social Security benefits are all disputes over the optimum distribution of money incomes, as was recently noted by Professors Lester Thurow and Robert Lucas in a study for the Congressional Joint Economic Committee.[1]

The fundamental problem is one of making a social value judgment about the degree of equality or inequality that is morally desirable in the American economy, the study stressed.

To Colbert, the chief minister of Louis XIV, taxation was "the art of plucking the goose in such a way as to produce the largest amount of feathers with the least possible squawking." In the election year 1972 the squawking was near deafening. But no one knows how far voters may want to go in reforms that would bring a sizable redistribution of income.

The fundamental tax problem is a social value judgment

What is the right or desired distribution of income? Fundamentally, say Lucas and Thurow, the answer cannot be found in economic analyses. It is, they say, a moral problem that "revolves around our collective judgments as to the proper degree of equality or inequality. . . . In essence the fights over progressive versus regressive tax structures, level of welfare, and social security benefits are all disputes over the optimum distribution of money incomes."[2]

Those in the richest quintile have eight times as much income as those in the lowest quintile

Lester C. Thurow, in his study of American taxation, says that substantial equalization may come about "in the process of taxation or in the process of distributing public goods and services." He found that in the United States, the "pre- and post-tax distributions of income are not noticeably different." When all our taxes (local, state, and federal) are added together, "progressive taxes seem to be cancelled by regressive taxes leaving a proportional tax system," adds Thurow. As a result, taxes reduce everyone's income by the same percentage and

[1] Lester C. Thurow and Robert E. B. Lucas, *The American Distribution of Income: A Structural Problem,* Congress of the United States, Joint Economic Committee. Superintendent of Public Documents, Washington, Mar. 17, 1972.
[2] Ibid., p. 3.

leave relative incomes unchanged. Thurow concludes that "either pre- or post-tax, the richest quintile has approximately eight times as much income as the poorest quintile."[3] Again, the fundamental problem is one of making a social value judgment about the degree of equality or inequality that is desirable in the American economy. In our political system such social value judgments must be made by the President and Congress.

Income redistribution goals not set yet

We could have three income redistribution goals. First, we could alter the distribution of income—make it more equal or unequal. Second, we could alter the distributions of minority or majority incomes so that they would be about the same—make black income distribution identical with white income distribution and so on. Third, we could increase economic mobility--to ensure that a son's income will not be determined by his father's income or to ensure that the poorest man this year will not be the poorest man next year.

The present poverty program, for example, is trying to alter the distribution of income. If it succeeds, the percentage of total income to those now in poverty should rise from about 2.8 to 4.6 percent in a two-year period.[4] Equal opportunity programs are designed to bring minority and majority income distributions into conformity. If they were to succeed, a white man's family's probability of having an income over $25,000 annually would be about equal to that of a black man's family, rather than five times as high. Public education is to some extent designed to improve economic mobility. Children of poor families, for example, are to be educated to prevent them from also being poor.

Until each of these three possible income redistribution goals has been set, it is unlikely that we can design actual plans and policies for altering the distribution of income.

Solutions

The tax team of Thurow and Lucas concludes that there are no easy solutions. Any set of programs that actually altered the structure of incomes (this can be done) would require enormous political pressure on its behalf. From the point of view of economics, tax-transfer policies are by far the easiest to implement, and yet these are probably the most difficult to implement politically. Unfortunately, there simply are no governmental policies that will just slightly affect the economy and yet cause large changes in the market distribution of earnings.[5]

TAX REFORM IS IN THE AIR

Just about everyone agrees that the tax system needs to be revised. In what ways? The answers are starting to appear from the welter of conflicting plans.

In the 1972 presidential election, President Nixon promised a plan to give homeowners some relief from the already high and still rising state and local property taxes. George McGovern proposed a wholesale redistribution of income in this country.

---

[3] Lester C. Thurow, *The Impact of Taxes on the American Economy*, Frederick A. Praeger, Inc., New York, 1971, chap. 4.

[4] Thurow and Lucas, op cit., p. 5.

[5] Ibid., p. 46.

The impact on the business scene—on investment and the stockmarket—would vary widely. Mr. Nixon would place emphasis on these goals:

1.   Keep the overall tax load about where it was in 1972.
2.   Simplify the law without a big switch of tax burdens from one group of people to another.
3.   Shift more of the load for schools from the localities, with their heavy dependence on the property tax, to the federal government.

Mr. McGovern stressed other ideas that would have quite different results:

1.   Put a bigger share of the federal tax burden on wealthy individuals and corporations.
2.   Use the money raised from these sources to pay for the expanded federal spending—to augment support for schools, as one example—and steer clear of any national sales tax (value-added-tax, or VAT). President Nixon advocated such a tax at one time, but later withdrew his support.

Edwin S. Cohen, Undersecretary of the Treasury during Nixon's first term would simplify the individual income tax by:

A painful operation for middle-income people

1.   Ending special treatment given to long-term capital gains—profits on sales of stocks and other property held more than six months—and, in the future, treating such income the same as wages and salary.
2.   Abolishing all the deductions that people are presently entitled to take that have nothing to do with the way they earn their income—for example, deductions for contributions to churches, charities, medical expenses, for state and local taxes, for interest paid on home mortgages, and so on.
3.   Increasing personal exemptions and reducing tax rates to partially offset losses from abolishing present deductions. Net effect: a cut of $1.3 billion in the total take from the individual income tax. The Cohen plan would reduce taxes for lower-income people, raise them for people making $10,000 to $50,000 a year, and reduce them about 9 percent for those making incomes from $50,000 to $100,000.

Plugging the loopholes

Wilbur D. Mills, chairman of the tax-writing House Ways and Means Committee, and Senator Mike Mansfield introduced bills in both houses of Congress which would pass a "death sentence" on fifty-four provisions of the present tax law and, in one way or another, enable individuals and corporations to save on taxes. Eighteen of these fifty-four provisions would expire on January 1, 1974; eighteen would expire on January 1, 1975; and the rest would expire on January 1,1976. (See Taylor-Troelstrup Reading 91 for a partial list of these provisions and the annual taxes involved.)

The objective of the Mills proposal is to close the "loopholes" in the present federal tax law such as percentage depletion for oil, gas, and other minerals; the present deduction for research and development; the present deduction for municipal bonds; and so on. It is estimated that tax loopholes shield about $166 billion today.[6]

[6] Testimony of Joseph A. Pechman and Benjamin A. Olsner of The Brookings Institution before the congressional committee on Jan. 15, 1972.

Finally, the U.S. Treasury Study[7] reports that personal income in this country totals about $860 billion annually but that only about $405 billion is reached by the federal income tax. The reasons for this, says the U.S. Treasury, are the following:

The political war over taxes is spreading

1.   Personal exemptions, deductions, and exclusions now result in the writing off of about 53 cents of every dollar of personal income.
2.   The tax rates on this limited base, ranging from 14 to 70 percent, must bring in $85 billion of the revenue.

The tax base needs to be broadened and simplified so that deductions and exclusions would be wiped out (close to the Mills-Mansfield plan), but personal exemptions should be retained and increased. The tax base would be increased from $405 billion to $600 billion. Then, tax rates could be cut to a range of 12 to 35 percent and still produce nearly as much revenue as under the present law.

Getting back to income distribution goals

We need to keep our eye on the ball

The several major proposals for tax reform have been presented primarily so that you can square these specific ideas for tax change with basic concepts and facts presented earlier by outstanding tax experts like Herriot, Miller, Thurow, Lucas, and others. We need to ask ourselves questions like this: Should we try to reform taxes, piece by piece, *before* determining the basic goals for income redistribution and distribution of public goods and services?

Criteria for a good tax

When exploring the impact of particular taxes, economists generally focus attention on productivity, equity, administrative efficiency, and economic effects:

1.   *Productivity:* How much income does the tax generate? As the economy grows, does the tax yield increase?
2.   *Equity:*   Is the tax fair? Do people feel that it treats equals equally?
3.   *Administrative efficiency:*   Is it easy to collect, difficult to evade, and not too expensive to collect?
4.   *Economic effects:*   How does it affect a person's incentive to work or to invest? How does it affect the total performance of the economy?

Evaluation of the federal income tax

Congress viewed the income tax law it passed in 1913 as a constructive response to the demand for a realistic and productive system of revenue which all good citizens "will willingly and cheerfully support . . . the fairest and cheapest of taxes." Has the optimism expressed in this statement by the House Ways and Means Committee been borne out by experience? How does the tax measure up to the criteria, mentioned earlier, of productivity, equity, simplicity, and economic usefulness?

Productivity

Certainly its productivity cannot be criticized. It has been an especially suitable tax in a growing economy because its yield has risen with the increase in gross material product.

[7] *U.S. News & World Report,* June 19, 1972, pp. 25–27.

Equity

Equity is more difficult to assess. Even if one concedes that in principle it is as fair as any other tax, or perhaps fairer, in practice many of its features are questionable on grounds of fairness. The major questions are:

Does the income-splitting provision unduly discriminate against single persons?

Does the capital gains provision encourage dubious schemes for converting income into capital gains?

Should the income from state and local securities continue to be excluded from taxable income?

Should deductions be permitted students for costs of college education?

Should tighter curbs be placed on deductions for entertainment and travel?

It has been suggested that in principle, since the tax is a tax on income, deductions for interest paid, casualty losses, and so on, should be permitted only for items related to the production of income.

Despite these criticisms, the tax scores high for its fairness, since it reflects the widespread agreement that ability to pay is a reasonably fair criterion. Those in the lowest income brackets pay a smaller fraction of their income in taxes than do those in higher brackets, the rate being 14 percent on the first $1,000 of taxable income, 15 percent on the next $1,000, 16 percent on the third $1,000, and so on up the ladder. Moreover, the special features introduced to take into account the additional expenses, such as those incurred in raising a family or in meeting heavy medical expenses, are in accord with public attitudes about fairness in tax treatment.

Administration

The income tax has been reasonably easy to administer because it is largely self-reporting. Taxpayers have filed their returns and made their payments with a minimum of surveillance. Compliance has been voluntary and virtually complete. Two innovations of the past twenty-five years have improved the system still further. One was the introduction in 1943 of withholding—the principle that income is taxable when earned and should be deducted from the employee's pay. The tax withheld is turned over to the federal government at intervals ranging from fifteen days to three months, depending on the amount. As a result, the government gets its revenue regularly and promptly, and taxpayers are prevented from building up large tax liabilities, formerly burdensome to meet each year. Taxes on dividends and interest are not withheld, but statements are made to the Internal Revenue Service listing payments to individuals and organizations, as a reference in auditing individual returns. The other major change contributing to administrative efficiency has been the development of computer technology. Modern data-processing techniques have made it possible to check cheaply and efficiently on the accuracy of returns filed.

Economic impact

What about the economic impact of the individual income tax? First, recent studies have shown that this tax has served as a kind of automatic stabilizer, helping to smooth out fluctuations in the level of economic activity. It does so because its yield varies with income. In slack times, when their incomes are lower, taxpayers retain proportionately more out of their income, and in good times, when their incomes are greater, they retain proportionately less. Because changes in after-tax income were relatively smaller than changes in gross national product, owing in large part to the effects of the income tax, the duration and severity of the postwar recessions of 1948, 1953–1954, 1957, and 1960 were checked.

The evidence about the effect of progressive rates on individual incentives to work, and to invest, suggests that there is little discouragement to wage earners in the lower and middle income brackets. At higher income brackets, incentives other than income have strong effects, and the effect of tax loopholes has greatly offset the nominal progressivity of the tax schedule. A frequently quoted study by the Harvard Business School[8] substantiates the view that taxes are not a significant discouragement to investors and top executives, and a more recent study[9] of the economic behavior of the affluent also bears out this belief.

A good deal of criticism of the individual income tax persists, both by those who consider it the fairest and best of our taxes, and by those who would prefer to place greater reliance on other forms of taxation, such as the value-added tax, which is widely used in Europe. But the place of the individual income tax in the federal revenue system seems reasonably secure. Overall, it gets good marks when tested for its consistency with the nation's total economic policy.

Similarly, the overall federal tax system has its defenders and detractors. In many areas, tax reform is overdue, and there is a continuing need to reexamine particular taxes for their productivity, their fairness, their administrative simplicity, and their economic impact. To say that the American tax system is the best in the world—as some experts do—is not to say that it cannot be improved.

PROPOSED TAX REFORMS

Congress has been studying many kinds of improvement in federal taxes. According to U.S. Treasury Department studies, the following tax reforms are high on the agenda of Congress for the years 1973 to 1975:

1.　An increase in the standard deduction. The 1972, 15 percent deduction, up to a maximum of $2,000, would be raised to eighteen percent with a maximum of a possible $2,500.

[8] Lynn L. Bollinger, *Effects of Taxation: Investments by Individuals,* Harvard Graduate School of Business, Cambridge, Mass., 1953.
[9] Robin Barlow et al., *Economic Behavior of the Affluent,* The Brookings Institution, Washington, 1966.

2.   Tax abuses of some private tax-exempt foundations would be curbed, including the small foundations used frequently to operate family businesses at lower tax cost.

3.   A major tax-avoidance gimmick is the deduction of farm losses from business income. This is how it works with "city cowboys": a high-income taxpayer buys cattle. He then takes generous deductions permitted full-time farmers, writing them off against nonfarm income that otherwise would be taxed at rates up to 70 percent. Ronald A. Buel, a *Wall Street Journal* reporter, mixed a little humor in his article on March 19, 1969, when he wrote:

> I'm a rich cowhand, of the Wall Street brand
> And I save on tax, to beat the band
> Oh I take big deductions the law allows
> And I never even have to see my cows
> Yippie-i-o-ki-ay!

Well, maybe not for long.

4.   Tax-exempt bonds, the basic borrowing instrument of cities, school districts, and states to finance public projects, would be discouraged. One plan provides for the U.S. Treasury to provide an "interest subsidy" to help municipalities to meet interest costs.

5.   Wealthy individuals (many escape all of the federal income tax) would be required to pay a minimum tax (see Table 14-1).

6.   Unlimited charitable deductions by some taxpayers—one of the techniques by which some millionaires avoid all taxes—would be discontinued over a period of years.

7.   Capital gains tax rules would be tightened.

8.   Depletion allowances in excess of cost of drilling for oil would be minimized or eliminated.

These are among many of the proposals for an overhaul of the federal tax system.

Middle-income class hurt

Table 14-1 shows clearly why the middle-income classes are likely to revolt against income taxes because certain provisions of the tax laws unfairly lighten the burden of those who can afford to pay. In other words, the federal income tax is unfair to this income group. According to the U.S. Treasury study (Table 14-1 reveals this clearly), the "effective" rates are the basic measure of tax bite— the tax actually paid as a percent of income. If you look at the left-hand vertical column of Table 14-1, you will see it broken into income classes—0 to $3,000, etc., up to incomes of over $1 million per year.

Most of us (68 percent), as the table shows, in the lowest income levels pay from 0 to 5 percent of our income in taxes. From a level of $3,000 to $20,000, most Americans pay from 15 to 20 percent of their incomes in taxes.

The rich escape

Now look at the remaining levels up to $1 million and more. From $20,000 to $50,000, the tendency to cluster around a rate drops sharply. Then, from $100,000 to $500,000, there is almost no cluster point. These wealthy taxpayers are ranged widely—with 2 percent paying rates from only 0 to 5 percent. And a

TABLE 14-1 Percentage Distribution of Returns by Effective Tax Rate Classes (by amended gross income classes, 1969, levels)

Amended Gross Income ($000)	EFFECTIVE TAX RATE CLASSES													
	0-5	5-10	10-15	15-20	20-25	25-30	30-35	35-40	40-45	45-50	50-55	55-60	60-65	65-70
0- 3	68.0	0.3	1.4	6.0										
3- 5	14.5	2.3	10.9	63.0	5.6									
5- 7	3.9	2.0	22.2	71.6	0.1									
7- 10	0.9	1.0	22.2	70.5	5.3									
10- 15	0.7	0.8	6.3	85.2	6.6	0.4								
15- 20	0.6	1.5	4.8	71.2	19.8	2.2								
20- 50	0.9	1.6	7.0	27.9	45.2	13.5	3.0	0.6	0.2					
50- 100	1.2	0.8	3.3	7.5	12.7	21.6	31.2	16.4	3.9	1.2	0.2			
100- 500	1.9	1.3	1.9	6.1	17.9	15.9	11.5	14.1	14.4	8.7	4.1	1.9	0.3	
500-1,000	2.1	0.7	0.8	0.7	31.9	32.8	6.3	4.3	3.0	2.4	3.1	4.6	6.7	0.4
1,000 & over	2.5	0.4	0.3	0.4	36.6	37.8	4.3	1.7	1.8	2.1	1.2	1.3	6.1	3.4

SOURCE: Office of the Secretary of the Treasury, Office of Tax Analysis.

similar unfair tax situation prevails with only 2.5 percent of the $1 million-and-more class paying taxes at the 0 to 5 percent rate and only 9.5 percent of the group paying 60 to 70 percent rates.

What has happened? The answer lies in the way income is treated for tax purposes. It is up to Congress to deal with these unfair tax situations.

A most regressive tax: Social Security

Social Security taxes were raised ten times between 1960 and 1972. As recently as 1950, they accounted for only one-twentieth of federal revenues; today they account for almost one-fourth and are the second largest source of government funds. Throughout these increases the regressive pattern of Social Security taxation established in the 1930s has been preserved as if set in concrete.

Social Security tax not related to ability to pay

By 1974, employers and employees will both be paying Social Security taxes at a rate of 5.85 percent on the first $12,000 of earnings—a total of $702 each. In fact if not in appearance, workers will bear the full burden of $1,404 a year, since economists agree that the employer's share would otherwise be apportioned to wages. The 5.85 percent rate applies equally to the worker earning $4,000 a year and to the one earning $12,000. However, the executive who earns $50,000 will also pay the maximum of $702; his tax rate, therefore, is not 5.85 per cent but 1.4.

"The wage ceiling and the flat percentage rate is what makes the Social Security tax such a regressive tax in that it falls heavier on those with lower incomes than those in the high income bracket," Senator Gaylord Nelson, Wisconsin Democrat, has pointed out. "The Social Security taxes violate the first principle of sound taxation in that they are not related to ability to pay."

This is not to say that benefits have risen too rapidly; on the contrary, they are still inadequate for the millions who depend on them for their entire livelihood. It isn't necessary, as Senator Nelson observed, "to levy an unjust tax on the American worker to provide a just retirement for the elderly American."[10]

The growing role of government

Considerable attention in recent years has centered upon the ability of state and local governments to support the growing demands upon them. Re-

[10] *The Progressive*, December, 1972, p. 9.

ceipts from their principal revenue sources, property and sales taxes, do not grow as rapidly as the total economy, especially in periods of inflation. Efforts to meet inflation—swollen costs and demands for new and improved services— have therefore led to serious inequities both between regions and between individual groups in the population. In recognition of this problem, federal aid to state and local governments grew by more than 200 percent between 1965 and 1973, from $11 billion to $36 billion, and more is in the works (Table 14-2).

The federal government deficit in 1972 may be closer to $35 billion than the $39 billion originally projected in the budget document. Whatever the final deficit figures may be, it is estimated that total receipts in 1973 may increase some $25 billion as a result of higher Social Security taxes and growth in personal income and corporate profits. In spite of this increase in income, expenditures are estimated to grow by nearly as much, resulting in another large deficit for 1973. The prospect for 1974 and subsequent years is not much better. On balance, it would appear that a deficit averaging between $20 billion and $30 billion is the prospect for the next few years.

A new revenue source: VAT

VAT aims at an old target—the consumer

In order to cope with these large deficits, the Nixon administration has turned its attention to new revenue sources such as a value-added tax (VAT). This is no more than a national sales tax. VAT is a tax assessed at each stage of the fabrication of products, from raw materials to finished goods, as a percentage of the value added to the product at each stage. In the end, the consumer picks up the total of the added taxes when he buys the products in the stores.

TABLE 14-2 Federal Receipts and Expenditures, Fiscal Years 1965–1973 (billions of dollars)

	1965	1966	1967	1968	1969	1970	1971	1972*	1973*	PERCENT CHANGE 1965–73
Receipts:										
Personal taxes	$51	$58	$64	$71	$90	$94	$88	$91	$98	92
Corporate profits	28	31	31	34	37	33	33	33	41	46
Indirect business tax	17	16	16	17	19	19	20	20	21	24
Payroll taxes	25	28	36	38	44	49	53	59	68	172
Total receipts	120	133	147	161	190	195	194	203	228	90
Expenditures:										
Purchase of goods and services	64	72	85	95	99	99	95	103	107	67
Defense	49	54	68	76	78	78	73	73	77	57
Nondefense	15	17	18	19	21	21	22	30	30	100
Transfer payments	30	34	39	45	51	57	70	80	87	190
Aid to states and cities	11	13	15	18	19	23	27	36	41	273
Interest	8	9	10	11	12	14	14	13	15	87
Subsidies	4	4	5	4	4	5	6	5	6	50
Total expenditures	118	132	154	172	186	197	212	238	256	117
Surplus or deficit (—)	2	1	—7	—12	4	—3	—18	—35	—28	

*Estimated.
NOTE: N.I.A. basis.
SOURCE: U.S. Treasury.

Assuming a VAT of 3 percent, which is the figure being discussed in Washington, revenues generated could be as much as $18 billion.

Any sales tax, including VAT, tends to bear most heavily upon low- and middle-income families, who spend a larger proportion of their incomes upon goods that would be subject to the tax. To partially guard against this obvious inequity, various ideas are under consideration to provide a tax rebate to consumers that would be relatively largest at the lower-income end of the scale and smallest at the upper-income end.

But why the VAT? It is a cumbersome tax to levy and to collect. One obvious consequence will be a sharp jump in the Consumer Price Index. It also goes against most good tax principles. It would seem far more sensible to raise personal income taxes, say many economists. If the planned reduction in local property taxes to be financed through the VAT does not have enough public support, and if an increase in income taxes does not get public approval, then perhaps the need for the revenue transfer taxes could be reexamined. There must be some suspicion that the real reason attention has focused upon a VAT is because its impact upon those paying the tax is not clearly visible or understood.

Patterns of taxes and expenditures

A close study of Tables 14-2 and 14-3 will reveal two outstanding features. One is the extent to which the growth in total spending at all levels of government has been financed through taxes upon individuals. The second is the extent to which the growth in expenditures has been concentrated in income transfers. What is involved here in these two patterns is a remarkably large amount of income redistribution among segments of the population over the past several years.

Higher taxes concentrated on middle-income taxpayers at the state level

Recognizing some limitations such as business passing taxes on to the con-

TABLE 14-3 Receipts and Expenditures, State and Local Government, 1965–1971 (billions of dollars)

	1965	1966	1967	1968	1969	1970	1971*	PERCENT CHANGE 1965–71
Total receipts	$75	$85	$94	$107	$120	$133	$152	103
Social insurance	4	5	6	6	7	8	9	125
Property, sales, and business taxes	48	52	57	64	70	77	86	79
Personal taxes	12	14	15	18	21	24	27	125
Federal aid, etc.	11	14	16	19	22	24	30	173
Total expenditures	74	84	95	107	119	133	149	101
Transportation and housing	16	18	19	21	21	23	26	63
Education	30	35	39	43	48	53	59	97
Health, labor and welfare	16	17	20	24	27	30	34	113
Policy, fire, etc.	8	9	11	13	15	16	17	113
Other	4	5	6	6	8	11	14	250
Surplus or deficit (—)	1	1	—1	0	—1	0	3	

*Preliminary.

SOURCE: U.S. Department of Commerce.

sumer in the form of higher prices, a reasonable estimate is that of the $124 billion total increase in taxes levied by all levels of government between 1965 and 1971, approximately $105 billion, or 85 percent of the total, was paid more or less directly by individual households. As a consequence, the percentage of total personal income going to pay taxes increased from 20.7 percent in 1965 to 25.1 percent in 1971.

The pressing need at state and local government levels for higher taxes has been met largely by imposing or increasing income taxes or by raising real estate and sales taxes. The resulting growth in tax revenues has tended to bear proportionately more heavily on the middle-income taxpayer, who earns enough money to pay income taxes, who in most cases owns his own home, and who still spends much the largest part of his income on products subject to sales taxes.

And, of course, federal outlays in the form of transfer payments, as we pointed out earlier, have skyrocketed—increased aid to states and cities, Social Security and medical benefits for the elderly and the indigent, and direct income support in the form of unemployment benefits, welfare systems, and so on.

PROPERTY TAX RELIEF: A HOT ISSUE

A drive to ease property tax burdens on homeowners, small farmers, and businessmen is sweeping the state capitals, city halls, and county courthouses. In some states and localities, moves have been made to reduce real estate taxes by shifting some of the load to income and sales taxes or other sources of income. In others, the push is for reforms designed to spread the property tax burden more equitably by equalizing assessments, curbing exemptions, and eliminating corruption. In Missouri, for example, voters gave the Legislature power to lighten the real estate tax which elderly people pay directly on their homes or indirectly through rent. Oregon's new "circuit-breaker" law gives property tax relief to low-income people of all ages. In Louisiana, the statewide property tax has been replaced by a tax on natural gas production. Texas exempts $3,000 of the assessed valuation of owner-occupied homes. In short, the real action appears to be in the state capitals.

New ways to pay for schools

The need for change to equalize support for schools, as well as other local services like police protection, can be seen in this illustration. In one community, tax support for schools came to $577 per pupil, counting some money from the state. A few miles away, another town was spending $1,232 per pupil. The assessed value of the average home in the former community was a high 5½ percent. In the latter community, the assessed value of the average home was only 2½ percent. In other words, by making less than half the effort to support local schools, residents spent more than twice as much money per pupil.[11]

Obviously, something is wrong. In fact, the California Supreme Court said so. This court said that paying for schools with money raised mostly by local property taxes meant that districts with high-priced property could afford ex-

[11] *Changing Times,* April, 1972, p. 25.

cellent schools, while poorer districts had to tax themselves at high rates just to manage mediocre levels of support. This is discrimination against children in poorer districts, said the California Supreme Court, and is therefore unconstitutional. The shock waves from that decision have been felt in every state capital ever since. A federal court in Minnesota and another federal court in Texas have found methods of financing schools unconstitutional for much the same reasons. In New Jersey, a superior court judge outlawed that state's school-support system via local property taxes. Suits asking similar rulings have been filed in many other states.

State governments know that local districts need help, and some of them have worked out "equalization" plans to try to close the gap between rich and poor communities by simply funneling money to the poor ones. But the problem remains unsolved. The best guess is that (1) local property taxes will diminish; (2) state support will increase; and (3) increased federal aid will be a part of the solution.

Federal revenue sharing   In December, 1972, the first federal revenue-sharing checks were mailed to state and local governments. The wide variations in per capita allotments startled many mayors and governors. Why, they ask, do some states and cities get much more than others in relation to their populations? For example, some big cities got $24 per resident, while others got only about $10 per resident.

The official reason for the variations was twofold: (1) States and communities that had low incomes were regarded as neediest and got more dollars, and (2) places that made the most vigorous efforts to help themselves by means of a heavy tax load also got a special bonus.

Following the distribution of the early December, 1972, checks, the proposals for large-scale property tax relief across the country—financed from Washington—suffered a setback. The Advisory Commission on Intergovernmental Relations, which includes some mayors, governors, county officials, and members of Congress, rejected a moderate set of suggestions drafted by the staff of the commission. The commission staff proposed "circuit-breaker" laws

Who will have decision-making power?   that would rebate property taxes to low-income homeowners and renters, especially the elderly; grant $1 billion or $2 billion annually to help the states equalize the funds available for education from one school district to another; and grant $10 million to $15 million a year to encourage the states to improve the administration of property taxes. This rejection was a harsh setback for property tax help. In fact the commission affirmed that (1) property taxes and school problems are matters for the states and localities to worry about, rather than the federal government; (2) homeowners generally are not overburdened by the residential property tax; and (3) there would be no assurance that the federal grants would actually lead to a lowering of property taxes unless stern rules were issued from Washington. That, of course, could put the federal government deep in the business of telling the states and localities how to finance their operations.

The issue of local control will be a hot one. Will more federal aid mean that local and state boards will have to surrender much of their decision-making power to Washington? Does a switch to greater state support necessarily mean more state control over local schools? These are the questions that state and local politicians and officials will be trying to answer in the years ahead.

What's going to happen?

Despite these hot issues of controls and decision-making power, the tax structures at all governmental levels will ultimately be modified.

No one knows what the final solutions will be relative to tax reforms at the federal, state, and local levels. Independent tax experts are sure that there can be many improvements in terms of equity, efficiency, fairness, cooperativeness, administration, simplicity, productivity, and economic usefulness. There will be differences of opinion over some of the means to the end. There are fewer differences, at least among tax experts, concerning the importance of getting reasonable agreement on basic income redistribution goals. These goals must be set up first. Until the goals have been set up, it is unlikely that we can design actual plans and policies for altering the distribution of income at the federal, state, or local levels that are based on the principles of equity, efficiency, and fairness.

QUESTIONS FOR DISCUSSION

1.   What are progressive tax principles? Regressive tax principles?

2.   The Herriot-Miller tax studies showed the narrow tax rate range of 25 to 31 percent for incomes less than $2,000 to as high as $25,000. Do these data prove that we have a progressive tax structure in this country? Explain your answer.

3.   A good tax is one that will "produce the largest income with the least amount of squawking." Do you agree? Defend your point of view.

4.   Tax experts say that our fundamental tax problem is a social value judgment. What does this mean?

5.   Why should we set our income redistribution goals *before* we pass tax reform legislation?

6.   Is our Social Security tax progressive or regressive? Explain your answer.

7.   If Congress or a state passed a value-added tax (VAT), would this tax qualify as a good tax?

8.   Property tax relief is a hot issue today. Why?

PROJECTS

1.   The Internal Revenue Service prepares, each year, an excellent teaching kit on filing in Forms 1040A and 1040. All the forms and instructions are supplied by the Internal Revenue Service. These provide a very practical exercise in learning how to prepare your own tax return.

After filling in the forms, you may be in the mood to discuss more realistically the criteria for good taxes and needed tax reforms.

2.   Almost every year Congress amends the income tax law. Research this problem. What are the important changes made in the federal income tax rules covering this year's income tax reports? (Read *Your Federal Income Tax* and *Your Income Tax.*)

SUGGESTED READINGS

Economic Report of the President, Government Printing Office, Washington. (Published annually.)

Lasser, J. K.: *Your Income Tax,* Simon and Schuster, New York. (Published annually.)

"Many Companies Work to Avoid Local Taxes," *The Wall Street Journal,* July 17, 1972.

People and Taxes. (Monthly newsletter published by Ralph Nader's Tax Reform Research Group, Washington.)

Thurow, Lester C.: *The Impact of Taxes on the American Economy,* Frederick A. Praeger, Inc., New York, 1971.

———— : *Poverty and Discrimination,* The Brookings Institution, Washington, 1969.

———— and Lucas, Robert E. B.: *The American Distribution of Income: A Structural Problem,* Congress of the United States, Joint Economic Committee, Superintendent of Public Documents, Washington, Mar. 17, 1972.

Your Federal Income Tax, Superintendent of Public Documents, Washington. (Published annually.)

CHAPTER 15

CHAPTER 15
SELLER-BUYER COMMUNICATION: PRIVATE AIDS

Any marketing practice that renders rational choice more difficult is a subversion of the American economy.

Mildred E. Brady

C ommunication, or lack thereof in the market, is really what present-day consumer controversies are all about." So said Professor Gwen Bymers at the American Home Economics Association's 1971 annual meeting.[1]

THE COMMUNICATION GAP: CONSUMER DISSATISFACTION

Consumer dissatisfaction with business has become widespread because consumers are ill served by our present production and marketing systems. A recent national poll by Opinion Research Corporation shows that 68 percent of Americans feel more consumer protection laws are needed, and a recent Harris poll reveals that 53 percent believe Ralph Nader is doing more good than harm. A recent national survey shows that 95 percent of students and 92 percent of nonstudents are convinced that business is too profit-minded and should concentrate on social needs.

One way consumers voice their complaints is by writing letters. The federal Office of Consumer Affairs in Washington, D.C., receives more than seven thousand letters of complaint a month. The Better Business Bureaus are receiving more and more communication critical of products and services—especially automobiles and appliances. Consumers Union, publisher of *Consumer Reports,* also receives thousands of consumer complaints each month concerning: poor quality, poor service, dishonored promises, unsafe products, polluting products, deceptive advertising, and fraud.

An examination of the complaints reveals a common thread—the buyer's right to know and the peripheral issue of the use the consumer makes of the information. The real communication gap is implicit in the question: What is it the consumer has a right to know, and who has the right to decide this? The dimensions of the gap can be seen in the rising level of distrust in the market mechanism that is a growing force, as we pointed out earlier, not only among the youth but also throughout society. We apply the label *consumerism* to the effort to secure corrective measures.

The rise of consumerism

Traditional economic theory suggests that our economy should market the best-quality products at their single, lowest prices. Our consumer markets are, however, characterized by the coexistence of high and low prices, high and low quality, and high and low price per unit of quality, as well as by unkept advertising promises. The price-per-unit-of-quality differences do not compensate for differences in money prices. Perhaps the important reason for this failure of markets is the inability, and to a lesser degree the unwillingness, of consumers to obtain and to act on genuine price-quality information.

Why is the consumer so ill served? The villain is the information gap between seller and buyer. At times, this gap is due to inability to obtain accurate information regarding quality and prices. At other times, consumers fail to act on accurate information. When the information is poor or is lacking entirely, the reward-punishment mechanism at the heart of market economy does not work well.

Consumerism, then, is the by-product of the delivery of poor-quality, high-

[1] *Journal of Home Economics,* February, 1972, p. 59.

priced goods. Consumerism is also grounded in another marketing failure—the increasing volume and unsatisfactory resolution of consumer complaints and grievances such as those concerning performance failures, misrepresentations and deceptions, frauds, misunderstandings, and failure to be sensitive to the environmental effects of products and services. In some instances the technical complexity of some products, the difficulty of placing responsibility for consumer complaints, the impersonality of present-day buyer-seller relations, and the power and dominance of sellers in disputes with buyers account for unsatisfactory resolution of consumer complaints.

Conditions for an effective, free competitive market

The minimum conditions for a free, effective competitive market are many buyers, many sellers, knowledge, and mobility. These conditions make a competitive market possible—they do not guarantee it.

The consumer's role in a well-functioning market is to identify and reward good performance by sellers. To perform his role, the consumer must know:

1. What products, brands, and sellers exist and where they may be found
2. What characteristics of a product are desirable
3. The extent to which particular product-brand-seller combinations possess the desired characteristics
4. The prices of the product-brand-seller combinations

Consumers must not only possess accurate information but also be able to act on it, at low cost.

Communication in the market—advertising and labeling—produces a double-edged sword. Accurately informed consumers are the key element in the existence of workable competition, but control over information and its dissemination can also be an effective instrument for control over a market and may lead to monopoly. We have already learned in Chapter 1 that access to mass media with more advertising dollars than other competitors can deter the entrance of competing products. When this happens, consumers need to be concerned with this communication gap because it may be a gap about "who is to decide what it is the consumer has a right to know." Perhaps Professor Tibor Scitovsky, in his book *Welfare and Competition,* is right when he says that the "scope of advertising depends on the ignorance of the people to whom it is addressed." In other words, the less informed the buyer is, the more he tends to rely on advertising, informative or noninformative. Advertising, unfortunately, seldom helps the poorly informed buyer because it is too general, irrational, repetitive, and suggestive and because it contains so little relevant information.

Consumers require more relevant information today

Today, consumers require much more relevant information than they did fifty or so years ago. Why? First, there are more products, more brands, and usually more sellers. Second, we have more money to spend. Third, variants of brands have proliferated, as every car and appliance buyer knows. Fourth, model changes have become more frequent. Finally, the car has given most consumers access to more product-brand-seller combinations.

Affluence and cars have given consumers access to more goods, but we still have the same number of hours in a week. In other words, time is worth more now; hence the cost of shopping has increased greatly, and the task of securing price-quality information has become more difficult. The culprits are the technical complexity of modern products and services, the lack of relevant information, and the personal research time necessary to obtain accurate product and service information—in short, a serious breakdown in seller-buyer communication in the market. This is what consumerism is all about.

Virginia Knauer, President Nixon's Special Adviser for Consumer Affairs, offers a good definition of consumerism as

> . . . nothing more and nothing less than a challenge to business to live up to its full potential . . . to give consumers what is promised, to be honest, to give people a product that will work, and that is reasonably safe, to respond effectively to legitimate complaints, to provide information concerning the relevant quality characteristics of a product, to take into consideration the ecological and environmental ramifications of a company decision, and to return to the basic principle upon which so much of our nation's business was structured—"satisfaction guaranteed, or your money back."[2]

THE NEED FOR MORE RESPONSIBLE CORPORATE LEADERSHIP

Communication between business and consumers is essential. Business often says that consumers don't understand its problems, but what about feedback in the other direction? Communication is a two-way street. What about business asking the consumer what is bothering him? Or listening to him when he has a problem? What about doing something about legitimate grievances immediately? Something is being done by a few corporations—a direct telephone line to the president's office. Appointment of a director of consumer affairs, training hard-core unemployables, new plants in the ghettos—all are good social projects. Is this social grandstanding or the beginnings of social accountability?

The shadow of the top man

Virginia Knauer said, "The responsiveness of a firm to the consumer is directly proportionate to the distance on the organizational chart from the consumer to the chairman of the board." The pragmatic truth is that the chief executive makes or breaks a company's corporate responsibility. Unfortunately, most top corporate heads are only "occasionally in touch" with the real world of the company they're supposed to direct. Ralph Cordiner, a member of top management of General Electric, "didn't know his people were conspiring to fix prices." For anyone interested in an encyclopedia of corporate irresponsibility, which should be required reading for those who would understand the antics of ITT, the Justice Department, and the White House, *America, Inc.,* by Morton Mintz and Jerry S. Cohen, would be enlightening.

Social responsibilities of business corporations

Enlightened self-interest

For many corporations "social responsibility" is now a major concern. It is, however, far from a reality. Top corporate executives are still likely to agree with economist Milton Friedman, who argues that the "corporation's responsibility is to produce profits."[3] Others profess a social conscience, but don't really mean it—they just recognize a public relations fad when they see it. But a few major corporations are taking a few steps forward, which they contend

[2] Speech given in Indianapolis, Jan. 14, 1972.
[3] *The Wall Street Journal*, Oct. 26, 1971, p. 1.

represent sincere efforts to gear social dimensions into their daily operations. So far, the vast majority of these actions are in the realm of dealing with minorities. Most executives acknowledge that they are acting from "enlightened self-interest."[4]

In 1971 the Research and Policy Committee of the Committee for Economic Development (CED), a business-sponsored group, in a statement on social responsibilities of business, said: "Inasmuch as business exists to serve society, its future will depend on the quality of management's response to the changing expectations of the public." The statement goes on to say that business can and should do many things to improve society in such areas as education, the environment, civil rights, and culture and the arts.

As that lists suggests, a number of the major responsibilities of business are deemed to be much more than purely social. In a vigorous dissent to the document, Philip Sporn, a member of the research and policy group, argued that if business were doing its primary job better, it would be drawing less flak for shirking its "new" social responsibilities.

> In the case of the railroad industry, what society wants and has not received is an imaginative modern system of transportation. . . . If many of the electric utilities in the country are in trouble [Mr. Sporn formerly headed American Electric Power] it is not because of new requirements but because they have not taken care of their basic responsibility to give an adequate power supply. . . . That they have also been careless of their obligations to do so with minimal adverse effect on the environment has not helped them to get public absolution of their failure to discharge their primary responsibility.

> And if our automobile manufacturing industry is in difficulty, it is due to the fact that for too many years the manufacturers and purveyors of automobiles have, for competitive reasons, failed to realize that they could not continue to build the same automobiles, making them larger and more expensive . . . while at the same time neglecting safety and the Frankenstein of environmental pollution they were raising.

The CED statement expresses strong confidence in modern corporations and modern managements, a confidence that Mr. Sporn does not entirely share. The statement, for instance, comments that "the great growth of corporations in size, market power and impact on society has naturally brought with it a commensurate growth in responsibilities; in a democratic society, power sooner or later begets equivalent accountability."

As Mr. Sporn acidly replies, growth in size can also bring with it "elephantiasis, arrogance, contempt for law." What happens depends a great deal on the caliber—and character—of managements, and he feels that this sometimes leaves more than a little to be desired.[5]

For corporate accountability

"The entire press of business in the '50s was to produce, produce, produce. The '60s was a decade of 'don't give a damn' attitude on the part of producers. The '70s will be a decade in which the producers will pay attention to the consumer." So said Margot Sherman, senior vice president and consumer affairs

[4] Ibid.

[5] *The Wall Street Journal,* July 15, 1971, p. 6.

coordinator of McCann-Erickson, Inc., of New York, a large advertising agency. She concluded her remarks by saying "people are people, not markets."[6]

Rockefeller predicts a "social audit"

It is no secret that "business is plainly in trouble." Today's criticism "focuses not so much on size as on performance—they are making communities dirtier, more polluted, and less congenial." So said David Rockefeller, chairman of Chase Manhattan Bank, in a speech at an Advertising Council dinner in New York.[7] He went on to say that "corporations are too heavily oriented toward profits at the expense of service," that "waste goes unchecked," and that "output is sometimes unfit for human use." The question, he thinks, comes down to this: "Will business leaders seize the initiative to make necessary changes and to take on new responsibilities voluntarily, or will they wait until these are thrust upon them by law?" Finally, Rockefeller foresees the day when corporations will be required to publish a "social audit" certified by independent accountants.

Ralph Nader, a constructive critic of business, is probably one of the best friends the private market has in this country because he is teaching the American public what it should expect in the way of responsible action from the business community.

Ralph Nader suggests

In an interview with Ralph Nader, the *New York Times* (Feb. 1, 1971) reported the following changes that are needed for "corporate accountability":

1. Rewrite the rules governing the chartering of corporations so that one state (Delaware) cannot mess up forty-nine states. He supports the late Senator Joseph C. Mahoney's proposal for federal chartering of corporations. The federal charters would (a) require "social cost accounting" such as disclosure of dumping waste into water or air or on land; (b) require a "complaint procedure" that works; (c) require disclosure of how much research a company does to improve the safety of its products; (d) reform the whole area of "trade secrets," which today amount to trade secrets *against* consumers; (e) provide for the suspension of violators—for example, the suspension, without pay, of the president of General Motors for six months when he is found guilty of selling unsafe cars (this would be a tremendous built-in deterrent); and (f) require that firms whose advertising is found to be fraudulent be forced to suspend advertising for six months or so.

2. Have a concept of "social bankruptcy" under which a company would be thrown into receivership after it was proved that its unsafe drugs and products had caused illness or death.

Enlightened profit maximization

These suggestions may appear "far out" to some people. Business, however, has been going in the direction of more and more corporate responsibility. In 1970, General Motors, for example, announced a proposal to "publish facts and figures revealing its progress in auto-pollution control, auto-safety and minority hiring."[8] General Foods President Herbert Cleaves promised efforts by his company to "improve human nutrition and combat hunger," combat

---

[6] *Columbia Missourian,* May 9, 1970, p. 15.

[7] *The Wall Street Journal,* Dec. 21, 1971.

[8] *Of Consuming Interest,* Nov. 25, 1970, p. 3.

pollution, improve the quality of goods, and provide more useful information on products at the point of sale.[9] Several large food chains have appointed directors of consumer affairs and have initiated unit pricing, product information, and nutrient labeling. Such innovations have been partially accomplished at Giant Food, Inc., Grand Union Company, Jewel Stores, Kroger, and the Berkeley, California, Food Cooperative, to mention a few.[10]

It would seem, then, that there *can* be such a thing as "enlightened profit maximization," wherein recognition is given to some socially determined good. It is possible that profits may become necessary but not sufficient condition for the survival of a firm. This human concept could be one of history's momentous turning points.

REDRESSING THE BALANCE BETWEEN BUYER AND SELLER

Thanks to the technical advances spawned by World War II, the marketplace grew steadily more complex. Our new expression of the electronic age, the TV set, gave industry a powerful tool for reaching the market with advertising. The marketplace became more concentrated, with the explosive growth of the supermarket and the discount store and the disappearance of the last personal link between the manufacturer and the consumer—the neighborhood store. Mass production joined mass consumption, which meant that the consumer bought more and more goods and services which he understood less and less. Soap became detergent, rubber became polyethylene, and cars became sex symbols. The quality of life slowly deteriorated as countrysides were taken over by housing developments and ribbons of paved highways, worms in apples gave way to pesticides, and air and water pollution spread. Twenty-two billion dollars of advertising simply added to the complexity of the marketplace. Federal agencies which were established partially to protect the consumer interest in such a complex marketplace barely creaked along. Antitrust legislation was never able to come to grips with the problem of concentration. Without consistent effective support from Congress, and without effective leadership of his own, the consumer had little hope of exerting influence to redress the balance between buyer and seller. He lacked the ability to find out exactly what he was buying.

Consumers' rights and responsibilities

President Nixon, in his Consumer Message to Congress on October 30, 1969, outlined basic consumers' rights:

Consumer rights—Nixon

> I believe that the buyer in America today has the right to make an intelligent choice among products and services. . . . The buyer has the right to accurate information on which to make his free choice. The buyer has the right to expect that his health and safety are taken into account by those who seek his patronage. . . . The buyer has the right to register his dissatisfaction, and have his complaint heard and weighed when his interests are badly served.

[9] Ibid.

[10] *Of Consuming Interest,* May 10, 1972, p. 3.

What the consumer seeks as his rights in the marketplace actually serve to strengthen the free enterprise system. He seeks competition among producers because it assures him competitive prices and a wider choice of kind and quality of merchandise. He seeks to abolish practices that work to his disadvantage as a consumer and weaken and destroy a free enterprise system—practices such as monopoly, fixed prices, unfair competition, and unjust and deceptive practices.

The consumer should understand his role in the economy and exercise his right to dissent when the marketplace serves him badly. The aim is to create a marketplace which is fair to both the buyer and the seller. It is manifest that unfair, deceptive, shoddy business practices; fraud; and a lack of reasonable standards for, and information about, products and services are the worst enemies of the honest businessman and the free enterprise system. In short, the consumer is asking to be given all the important information about a product or service so that he can decide whether he wants it.

These are reasonable requests on the part of consumers. The basic question confronting industry and business, as well as government, is this: Will business redress the balance between buyers and sellers, or does it need government regulation?

REGULATION AND RESPONSIBILITY: THE PRICE OF FREEDOM

There is no doubt that most industry leaders and businessmen prefer self-regulation to legislation by lawmakers. The practical question still remains: Do they prefer self-regulation enough to change "let the buyer beware" to "let the seller beware"?

Let the seller beware: equal bargaining power in the marketplace

Self-regulation

Betty Furness, former Special Assistant to the President for Consumer Affairs, put it this way to the American Bar Association: "I hope the past has taught us much and that a new era of consumer relations will be achieved without hammering out such a code over the piled up bodies of the defenders of the status quo." She was, of course, referring to the reluctance of industry and business, by and large, to give consumers equal bargaining power in the marketplace. President Kennedy said it this way in 1962: "If consumers are offered inferior products, if prices are exorbitant, if drugs are unsafe or worthless, then his [the consumer's] dollar is wasted, his health and safety may be threatened and the national interest suffers."[11] The report to the White House by the Consumer Advisory Council in 1966 clarified these consumer handicaps in the marketplace by reminding industry and business that the "consumer today must be a chemist, electrician and nutritionist to fathom what he is buying, what it will do, how well it will perform and endure and how to take care of it." What consumers are demanding, in short, is either that a determined effort be made to aid the consumer in his agony of wonder and complexity or that new laws which nobody wants be enforced.

[11]Quoted in James Bishop, Jr., and Henry W. Hubbard, *Let the Seller Beware*, The National Press, Inc., Washington, 1969, p. 108.

Well, the day of *caveat venditor* is here. The question is whether the present mix of government regulation and industry self-regulation and consumer pressures is adequate.

THE NEED: A MORE EFFICIENT PRODUCT PERFORMANCE INFORMATION SYSTEM

The concern here is with the economic interests of the consumer. The question is whether the right to information goes beyond the right not to be deceived, to include the provision of performance information that will ensure a wise purchase. Much of the business view is that the buyer should be guided by his judgment of the reputation of the manufacturer and the quality of the brand, as opposed to the view of consumer spokesmen that information should be provided by impartial sources and should reveal performance characteristics.

Brands and trademarks

Brands on trial

The legitimacy of brands and trademarks has been under attack for many years. A brand or trademark identifies a product and its source, and at times it says something about its worth. If a retailer mishandles both product and the trademark, the value of the product may diminish in the consumer's eyes, and sometimes the manufacturer may seek to punish such a retailer by refusing to sell the product to him. This maintains the good reputation of the branded merchandise and perhaps even enhances it. As the reputation of the branded product is promoted via heavy advertising, the price of the product, at times, can be increased without any reduction in net profits. In short, the brand has then gained consumer acceptance by way of a particular impression about it. This may actually be a lower-quality, higher-priced product than one of a small competitor with a low advertising budget. Nevertheless, brands and trademarks are valuable aids to manufacturers because they assure a steady market at prices set by the manufacturer—usually higher prices.

Are brands and trademarks useful to consumers? Brands can prevent confusion regarding the origins of goods of competing firms. A brand owner can refuse to sell his product to a retailer who he believes (rightly or wrongly) would tend to adulterate the reputation of his brand. On the other hand, branded goods tend to have higher price tags and, at times, to be of lower quality according to independent testing standards than nonbranded and store-branded competing goods. But who really knows the quality of branded goods except the manufacturer? And he won't tell! For this reason, more and more educated consumers feel the need to consult *Consumer Reports* and *Consumers' Research Magazine* to obtain reliable information as to quality and other comparable characteristics based on standards.

Guarantees, warranties, and services

One helpful step has been taken by those industries which are willing to underwrite the reliability of their products. This is the warranty. A warranty does not guarantee that the product will operate or perform as advertised, but it promises that the machine, appliance, or product will be repaired at little or no charge if it fails to operate.

A warranty is usually a written guarantee to repair or replace defective parts. In practice, the terms "warranty" and "guarantee" are used interchangeably. An implied warranty law was expressed in a landmark case by a New Jersey state court. The court wrote that it did not see a rational difference "between a fly in a bottle of beverage and a defective automobile." Accordingly, the court held that when a "manufacturer puts a new automobile into a stream of trade and promotes its purchase by the public, an implied warranty that it is reasonably suitable for use as such accompanies it into the hands of the ultimate consumer."

But warranties are not always what they appear to be. The problem has many faces. Some warranties are intended to leave the consumer guessing. One type of warranty is filled with indigestible technical words that only an engineer can comprehend. Another device is the partial warranty. For example, such a warranty may list many parts or show them on a diagram. The list and the diagram seem complete to the layman, but when an important part, such as the transmission in a washing machine, dies, the company may charge for repairs. If asked whether the warranty covers the repair cost, the company will answer "no." The diagrammed parts listed in the warranty are "the parts that don't break down."

Some rob you with a fountain pen

Another kind of warranty may state that "no other warranty, either express or implied, can be construed to apply to the machine." This very common wordage is an attempt to free the manufacturer from the responsibility of living up to other claims made in advertisements. The knowledgeable consumer knows that the implied warranty still makes the company liable because courts have upheld the original case cited earlier. Furthermore, the manufacturer, not the repairman or middleman, is liable. Unfortunately, many consumers are unaware of the role of the implied warranty and simply chalk up a bad guarantee to "experience." Thus the warranty provides a handy means of bypassing the courts, and it gives extra advantage to the seller.

Some warranties cover everything; some exclude labor costs and certain parts. Many assume no responsibility for normal wear and tear. Some prorate the cost of replacement of parts which wear out before their time, such as car batteries. Some, notably car warranties, require specific action on the part of the purchaser to keep the warranty in force.

In recent years there has been an effort to write guarantees and warranties in nontechnical language and to state clearly the nature of the warranty. American Motors, for example, was one of the first firms to clarify the guarantee in simple language. Recently, too, some firms that have had difficulty repairing products satisfactorily and within a short time have introduced training schools for repairmen. Other companies try to correct mistakes at the factory. Since engineering and quality control have at present little to do with the salability of a product as opposed to its performance, the compulsion to take this step is not very strong. The very large number of cars recalled from the marketplace is a good illustration of lack of corporate responsibility. On the other hand, a few corporations advertise a direct, free "hot line" to the president's office for dissatisfied complainants.

One industry has proved its willingness to respond constructively following very many complaints. Early in 1970, representatives of the major appliance industry appointed a Major Appliance Consumer Action Panel (MACAP). The

It is cheaper to win a war than to lose it

sponsors are the Association of Home Appliance Manufacturers, the Gas Appliance Manufacturers Association, and the American Retail Federation. The eight panel members (all fairly good consumer representatives) are charged with reviewing complaints that have not been solved at the local level and where the parties are deadlocked in their attempts to reach a satisfactory solution.

The panel meets monthly; members receive expense money only. The panel handled over four thousand cases between 1970 and 1972. During that period there were only a handful of instances in which the manufacturer involved did not follow the panel decision. In only fifty-two instances did the panel rule the complaint to be unjustified, according to the chairman of the panel, Dr. Virginia F. Cutler, of Brigham Young University.

This attempt to aid the consumer is hopeful. Much depends on the attitude and integrity of business, the kind of consumers selected to serve on the panel, and the machinery for enforcement of panel decisions.

CONSUMER PROTECTION BY PRIVATE JOINT ACTION

The basic role of standards

There is a naive and erroneous concept of a standard as a step toward regimentation, as a limitation on variety, as an inhibition to creativity. That standards have such effects simply is not true. Quality standards and dead sameness of end product are not synonymous. On the contrary, *meaningful* variety, as opposed to *meaningless* product differentiation, is directly dependent on the development and effective use of standards. In fact, only through the use of standards can we, as consumers, fully realize the fantastically fruitful, productive potential of modern industrial techniques. Why? Because the basic role of standards and specifications is simply to supply a common language understood and respected by producer, distributor, seller, and buyer, a language by means of which open and fair bargaining can take place and the necessary exchange of goods be facilitated. In other words, standards and specifications function as the language of careful description in the production and exchange of goods in somewhat the same way that mathematics is the language of the sciences from which our productive techniques have taken on their particular mid-twentieth-century character.

The development of a common language between buyer and seller of goods for the ultimate consumer is long overdue. To date, however, industry in general has given nothing but a negative response to effective standards and specifications. This negative attitude was pointed up by Tom M. Hopkinson, a member of a public relations firm, when he reported on his independent poll of New York marketing, advertising, publicity, and product promotion executives representing twenty-six organizations in seventeen different industries. In his personal interview, time after time, these executives told him, "It's for legal to decide," when they were asked whether there were any special ethical, moral, or public relations considerations in marketing areas heavily concerned with the "consumer interest." Only three out of thirty-one executives could see any such relationship.

Thus, he concludes, the philosophy of the day, in considering borderline cases involving public taste, fair dealing, and full and accurate consumer information, too often seems to be: "This is the deal—can we get away with it?"

So business managers apparently have conflict-of-interest problems and are primarily concerned with getting people to buy, not with keeping them properly informed. This is not to say that there have not been efforts on the part of business to establish standards for some consumer products, and, in a few instances, efforts made to enforce voluntary standards. But these efforts are minimal.

Certifications and seals
of approval

The major forms of industrial joint self-regulation are product standards and certification programs including seals of approval. In substance these programs are communication tools, i.e., devices for reducing the cost of transmitting information from sellers to buyers. An estimated twenty thousand sets of industrial standards are currently in effect in the United States, and there are some thirty-six thousand federal government standards. Over four hundred organizations are involved in writing these standards (for example the Carpet and Rug Institute, which is a producer group, and the American Society of Mechanical Engineers, a professional society). Products that conform to the standards are usually certified by means of being awarded seal, grade stamp, or endorsement or by being enrolled on an approved list.

The cost-saving and safety features of these programs can be beneficial to consumers. There can be, however, less desirable aspects such as restraint in trade through such practices as price-fixing, controlling supply, excluding competitors, and preventing the introduction of new, lower-cost technological processes or improved, lower-priced carpeting products. In addition, these programs can promote widespread consumer deception by inducing reliance on certification marks as evidence of quality without disclosing the basis of the standards used, the competence and impartiality of the certifying body, or the grade performance rating of the product certified in comparison with that of other products of the same general class.

Private certification not
the answer

Activities of this kind have increased in recent years. Consumer groups, government leaders, and others like Ralph Nader have been expressing concern over product safety, for example, and over what many believe is the deteriorating quality of many consumer goods. The consumer's principal source of product information, advertising, has focused less on products' objective performance than on their psychological associations.

Certification based on
unstated standards

The current trend, unfortunately, is not a reassuring one. In response to increasing demands of consumers in such areas as product safety, product performance, and the like, industries are turning to certification programs rather than supplying solid information that would minimize consumer deception and focus competition on price and quality. The only information consumers will get is a certification via a private certifying body's "seal" of approval based on unstated standards.

After extensive hearings both the National Commission on Product Safety and a subcommittee of the House Select Committee on Small Business were sharply critical of the performance of private standards organizations, the former with respect to lack of consumer protection, and the latter with respect to both lack of consumer protection and anticompetitive results. Criticism was not limited to a few organizations. Rather serious deficiencies were found in the performance of every standards and certification organization studied.[12]

National private professional standards associations, however, have maintained more respect from independent testers. The American National Standards Institute, Inc. (formerly the American Standards Association), and the American Society for Testing Materials are examples of private professional associations that are performing, on the whole, valuable services in establishing reasonably good standards for products used by industry, consumers, and governmental agencies.

Major shortcomings of certifications and seals of approval

1. The American Gas Association

This association is financed by gas companies and businesses engaged in the manufacture of gas appliances. The AGA Laboratory Seal of Approval is available to members of the AGA who have met certain minimum standards of utility, durability, and safety of gas burners and other gas-using equipment. A member may also qualify for a Certified Performance marker if his gas appliance meets additional specifications for performance, convenience, and efficiency.

Do the AGA standards adequately protect consumers? A court case in point, involving Radiant Burners, throws some light on this question.[13] The plaintiff charged an unlawful combination to exclude from the market gas appliances not receiving a seal of approval from AGA's testing laboratories. It asserted that AGA's approval was not based on "valid, unvarying, objective standards." The plaintiff alleged that its own gas burners, denied the seal of approval, were "more safe and more efficient, and at least as durable, as burners which AGA had approved." The United States Supreme Court agreed with the plaintiff. In essence, it established the principle that decisions by a group to grant or withhold the seal must be fairly made—that tests must be available to all manufacturers of gas appliances. There is also the serious question of whether bases for exclusion are appropriate for private group action at all as well as the question of whether consumers' interests can be protected without proper representation in AGA's decisions. There remains also the question of whether the safety standards are adequate or are based on minimum requirements in order to reduce costs to meet competition in the marketplace. Perhaps it would have been better if the AGA had confined itself to the publication of testing reports which would have forced local governments or the federal government to determine the standards. The main conclusion is that the prospect for satisfactory private solution of the problems of protecting consumers is directly dependent upon the extent of conflicts of interest among the members of the AGA group. The greater the conflicts of interest among the manufacturers, the greater the

---

[12] *Final Report of the National Commission on Product Safety,* Government Printing Office, Washington, June, 1970, pp. 47–66; Subcommittee No. 5 of the Select Committee on Small Business, House of Representatives, no. 1981, 90th Cong., 2d Sess., 1968.

[13] *New York Bar Association Antitrust Law Symposium,* Commerce Clearing House, Inc., New York, 1967, pp. 36–46.

chance that the standards established will prove unsuitable as a device for protecting consumers. It is doubtful whether private agreement among competing manufacturers is the *best* way to decide standards for consumer goods and services.

2. *Good Housekeeping* and *Parents' Magazine* Seals

No quality guarantee

These are regarded by many people, especially women, as reliable guides in purchasing consumer products.[14] Originally, *Good Housekeeping* told readers that the products advertised in the magazine had been tested and approved without charge to the manufacturer. It was claimed that a large percentage of goods tested were rejected. And the manufacturer whose product was accepted was permitted to use the *Good Housekeeping* Seal of Approval in his advertising and as a label on the product tested. Consumers were guaranteed that the seal on a product was as represented in the advertising. If the product was not satisfactory, it would be investigated and, if defective, would be replaced or the money refunded.

The FTC in 1939 charged Hearst Magazines, *Good Housekeeping's* publisher, with using unfair methods of competition and with engaging in deceptive acts and practices. The details in the FTC charge were these: (1) *Good Housekeeping* represented its shopping service as free, when the facts showed that respondents received a kickback of from 3 to 7 percent from the sellers of merchandise purchased through such service; (2) whoever used the seals had to purchase them, plus all plates from the magazine; (3) the tests were usually not adequate to ensure the claims made for the products; (4) in some cases, the products weren't even investigated; and (5) many of the ads contained false, deceptive, and misleading statements. The FTC therefore issued an order in 1941 requiring Hearst to cease and desist from representing in its advertising that the statements were true and permitting the use of the seals only if adequate tests had been made.[15]

And still no quality guarantee

Good Housekeeping then conveniently adopted a guarantee seal in 1941 which said merely that it would replace the product or refund the purchase price if the product was defective or not as advertised. Five years later the magazine discontinued its seals of approval. And in 1962 the phrase "as advertised therein" in the guaranty seal was deleted. The reworded seal, which the FTC promptly approved, now states, "If product or performance defective *Good Housekeeping* guarantees replacement or refund to consumer."

Misleads the buyer

In 1969, a San Diego woman alleged that a pair of shoes advertised in *Good Housekeeping* and bearing the Seal of Approval were constructed in a faulty manner that resulted in severe injuries when she tripped and fell. The Orange County Superior Court held that the seal is an inducement to buy and made Hearst a party to the lawsuit. The court, separating fact from opinion, rejected Hearst's contention that the granting of the seal is an expression of opinion rather than a statement of fact.[16]

[14] *National Commission on Product Safety—Hearings,* vol. 7, September–October, 1969, pp. 33–34.

[15] Federal Trade Commission, *Decisions,* vol. 32, Docket 38–72, pp. 1440–1463.

[16] *Magazine Industry Newsletter* Oct. 29, 1969. p. 2.

It is strange indeed that on the one hand, *Good Housekeeping* says its seal is a guarantee of safety, while on the other hand Mr. Peterson, of *Good House-keeping,* when testifying before the National Commission on Product Safety, said his magazine "does not guarantee the safety or wholesomeness of any product."[17] It would seem that this magazine's seal misleads the public. *Good House-keeping* should resolve to make the seal mean what the public *thinks* it means, or it should not be used.

To increase sales

The *Parents' Magazine* Guarantee Seal is granted only to products which are advertised in the magazine and which "Parents' Magazine believes are suitable for families with children."[18] There is nothing in the magazine's long statement about how good the product is and nothing about the standards or the rating system used. Certainly the magazine wouldn't use high standards and thus discourage potential advertisers. A seller cannot advertise in the magazine using the Guarantee Seal unless he buys a minimum of 286 lines, or the equivalent in dollars, of advertising in twelve consecutive issues. This amounts to an aggressive advertising policy. It is also a form of exploitation of a good rating because the magazine's promotional leaflet tells prospective advertisers that the use of their seal increases sales.

If complaints are received, *Parents' Magazine* notifies the manufacturer, and if the latter fails to settle the case, the magazine settles with the consumer and presumably collects from the manufacturer.

As in the case of *Good Housekeeping*, the FTC in 1966 ordered *Parents' Magazine* to stop misrepresenting the basis on which its seal is granted. The FTC discovered that some manufacturers were given a Guarantee Seal solely on the basis of a recommendation of magazine staff members without testing their products.

In the light of the evidence available it is difficult to understand why many people still believe that *Parents' Magazine* and *Good Housekeeping* seals are endorsements of the general quality and safety of a product when, in truth, both magazines have denied this when confronted at federal hearings.

TRADE ASSOCIATION STANDARDS AND SEALS OF APPROVAL

Underwriters' Laboratories is a nonprofit testing organization sponsored by insurance companies. UL tests products submitted by manufacturers for safety. Its staff periodically inspects production at the factories and spot-checks items such as electric cords bought on the open market.

Valuable as the UL service is, it has serious limitations. Products are evaluated for safety rather than for the quality of the product itself. Furthermore, UL approval on a cord does not extend safety approval to the appliance. Finally, its standard for the amount of current leakage considered permissible to come into contact with the user of the product is less stringent than those of other testing organizations. Consumers Union testing, for example, often disagrees with UL standards and passes critical judgment on items bearing the UL seal.

In mid-1968, UL announced plans for reorganization that would broaden

[17] *National Commission on Product Safety—Hearings,* pp. 61, 66.
[18] See the long statement in *Parents' Magazine* concerning the seal.

its membership base to include consumer and government groups. One year later, UL had only two "consumer" representatives (a magazine writer and a banker) out of a total of 113 members.

The National Electrical Manufacturers Association has written a number of standards for consumer items as well as for industrial equipment. NEMA is best known for finally clearing up the bad situation in room air conditioners. Units used to be sold on the basis of "tons." But one 1-ton unit may have 65 percent more cooling power than another 1-ton unit. Under pressure, especially from Consumers Union, NEMA finally adopted the recommended BTUs (British Thermal Units), which measure cooling output more accurately. Manufacturers willing to follow NEMA standards could apply the Certified Seal on their product.

Electrical Testing Laboratories, with the aid of the Illuminating Engineering Society, worked out standards for an IES seal on the ETL Certificate of Compliance shield. This certificate can be placed on any lamp that has met the required standards. Perhaps as many as fifty different lamp manufacturers use this certificate. ETL maintains a continuous checking service in the factories. The manufacturer pays about 3 cents a lamp for the testing service and around 10 cents a lamp to an advertising agency hired to promote the use of IES lamps.

ETL will test any product in its line for a manufacturer for a fee, but permits use of its seal only on products whose standards are printed on the label where the consumer can read them. These standards are based on performance requirements, not on construction specifications. ETL has the final word when granting its seal of approval.

LIBERALIZING STANDARDS AND INFORMATION

A few large retailers have developed rather extensive programs of merchandise testing and of informative labeling. Among them are Macy's of New York, Gimbel's of Philadelphia, Marshall Field of Chicago, Lit Brothers of Philadelphia, Kaufmann's of Pittsburgh, and various mail-order houses, such as Sears, Roebuck and Company and Montgomery Ward. Moreover, certain large chain stores—notably A & P, Safeway, and J. C. Penney—test, grade, and label some of their store-brand products.

Sears, Roebuck and Company has maintained its own laboratories and staff of technicians since 1911. This is reportedly the largest privately owned merchandise testing laboratory in the world. The company sets up minimum standards arrived at through agreement among the general merchandise office, the buyers, the merchandise comparison office, and the technical laboratories.

The primary function of the testing is to aid buyers in the selection of merchandise. The company gives special attention to its own trademarked goods. A close analysis of the descriptions in its catalogs reveals the influence of the laboratory technicians upon the advertising department.

J. C. Penney Research and Testing Laboratory in New York City was established in 1930. Most of the merchandise handled by the J. C. Penney stores is tested. The laboratory is equipped to do physical, chemical, and some types of biological testing. Besides setting up standards and testing the products, the laboratory also checks all returned goods to discover whether the article had some inherent fault that did not show up in previous tests. Staff members also spend time in the various mills and factories that produce merchandise for the J. C. Penney stores.

Macy's Bureau of Standards, established in 1927, is primarily interested in the adaptability, performance, durability, and care of merchandise sold by Macy stores. It is concerned largely with these factors from the consumer's point of view. The bureau has also established many standards for goods sold under Macy's brand names. It studies and recommends more effective garment, rug, and fur cleaning, waterproofing, mothproofing, and so on; prepares informative labels for the merchandise; assists in the training of buying and selling management personnel; and is continually working on adequate but easy-to-understand terminology for informing the buying public.

Macy's service supplements the store's guarantee policy, making it more reliable and less costly to both consumer and owner, and more enforceable than most so-called product guarantees.

In other consumer-related moves, some companies are liberalizing their warranties and guarantees and are providing more information. Some makers of color television sets, for example, have extended their warranties on solid-state models from ninety days to a year and at least one manufacturer, RCA, is experimenting with two-year free-labor warranties. Ford and General Motors have added special ninety-day warranty coverage of some expensive services such as wheel alignment and balancing and brake adjustments.

Maytag Company now places information tags on all its products. The tags are quite informative, telling where the specific model fits into Maytag's line, what features it has, and how much electricity it uses; the tag also provides installation instructions and information on special safety precautions and warranty coverage.

Even some food chains are responding to consumer demand for more informative labels, as we learned in Chapter 7. Giant Food, Kroger, Jewel Stores, and the Cooperative Food Stores in Berkeley, California, were among the first food stores to use open dating, unit pricing, nutrient labeling, and ingredient labeling.

Consumer protection via self-regulation—an evaluation

It is generally agreed that consumerism is here to stay.[19] Therefore, attention is now centered on various forms of response to the consumer movement. Indicative of this direction is the creation, by business, of the Consumer Research Institute to "objectively" study consumer problems and evaluate alternative responses. Questions like these are being asked:

Consumer Research Institute

1. Is it socially wiser to accept the present state of consumer dissatisfaction than to pay the cost of reducing this dissatisfaction?
2. Can industry reform itself without government pressure?
3. Which is likely to be more effective and economical—Better Business Bureaus, trade association complaint bureaus, or corporate divisions of consumer affairs?

[19] Chamber of Commerce of the United States, *Business and the Consumer: A Program for the Seventies,* Washington, 1970, p. 10.

4.   Should consumers be encouraged to obtain self-protection by means of class-action suits?

5.   Should private business associations involved in setting product standards and granting seals and certificates of approval provide for consumer voting power to allow consumers to block unsatisfactory standards?

6.   Can consumer education suffice to eliminate market abuse?

7.   Should consumer participation at the basic level of standards writing, where most decisions are made, be permitted?

Underlying these questions are certain basic issues: What should be the role of private versus government efforts to protect consumers? What should be the role of consumer-goods testing organizations and professional consumer organizations?

Voluntary action seldom adequate protection for consumer

Voluntary action is seldom adequate. Even though some companies observe voluntary guidelines, others must be coerced to observe them. And it isn't just the fringe firms who are guilty of questionable ethics and who will not follow guidelines. Too often the nation's most reputable companies are guilty.[20]

To be meaningful, self-regulation must be enforceable industry-wide. To do so requires collective action—possibly a form of boycott against the offender if he refuses to reform. But boycotts in restraint of trade are illegal under the Sherman Act. Should the Sherman Act be amended if restraints are meritorious? Is that the way to free private enterprise on behalf of the consumer interest?

Is there a way out of this dilemma of trying to protect consumers in the short run while preserving the long-run benefits of freedom? Lewis L. Stern says the answer is to (1) provide for maximum consumer involvement in the writing of product standards; (2) provide for automatic review of standards at frequent intervals; (3) permit the sale of products not conforming to the relevant standards, provided that the nonconforming products are labeled with the relevant standards and the manner and extent to which they do not conform to these standards; and (4) permit collective action among firms to boycott any firm whose products conform to neither the industry nor the labeling requirement.[21]

Consumer protection a threefold responsibility

It may be that to make self-regulation work, Congress, the FTC, and the Department of Justice will have to play a role to make enforcement possible when it is clearly in the consumer interest. A continuing threat of government regulation will always be necessary to make self-regulation work. Government regulation, in turn, needs consumer advocates to make it function effectively. Hence consumer protection is a threefold responsibility, involving self-regulation, government pressure, and consumer-advocate pressure.

PROFESSIONAL ASSOCIATIONS AIDING CONSUMERS

Professional associations and organizations are another source of consumer protection, and they have done outstanding work in promoting consumer education. The effective programs of some of these associations will give an idea of what they are accomplishing.

[20]"The Editorial Viewpoint," *Advertising Age,* Mar. 30, 1970, p. 14.
[21]*Journal of Marketing,* July, 1971, pp. 47–53.

The American Council
on Consumer Interests
(ACCI)

The American Council on Consumer Interests was born at a conference of twenty-one educators in the consumer field on the University of Minnesota campus in April, 1953. The Preamble of the Constitution of the ACCI reads: "This organization is concerned with problems of our economy considered from the point of view of the ultimate consumer of goods and services . . . People, as consumers, need information to use the economic resources available to them in a way to secure maximum satisfaction."

The need for the council grew out of the fact that teachers and research workers interested in consumption specialize in many fields, including economics, sociology, psychology, education, natural sciences, home economics, business administration, business education, and public welfare. Publications on consumer problems come not only from educational institutions but also from business, consumer, labor, farm, and government groups. It is difficult to keep abreast of the contributions from all these sources.

Activities

The American Council on Consumer Interests is the only national, independent, professional consumer organization in the United States. Through its quarterly *Newsletter,* its annual conference, and its official *Journal of Consumer Affairs,* the ACCI keeps its hundreds of members informed on the latest developments in the consumer field.

From 1954 to 1967, the ACCI published seventeen pamphlets on current, critical consumer issues. Since 1966, the organization's research and publication efforts have been centered on its professional *Journal of Consumer Affairs.*

American Home
Economics Association

The AHEA is primarily an educational organization with over thirty-five thousand members engaged in the fields of family economics, home management, family relations and child development, foods and nutrition, textiles and clothing, housing and household equipment, and art. The organization is active in extension service and in college clubs, with over twenty thousand students majoring in home economics. Through its publication, the *Journal of Home Economics,* and joint projects with trade associations, the American National Standards Institute, and legislative activities, the AHEA has been an important information center.

The Consumer Interests Committee promotes important consumer programs and serves as a clearinghouse for all consumer activities. The textile section was a prime mover in seeking a way to set standards for consumer goods. Today, the efforts of the AHEA revolve around consumer legislation, consumer education, and promotion of standards of quality for consumer goods.

Some of the most outstanding work of the AHEA has been in the field of food facts and fallacies. This is in keeping with one of its major contributions — giving information to consumers. The AHEA has supported programs for consumer protection against misrepresentation and misleading advertising. Work in the areas of trading stamps, credit charges, fictitious pricing, good labeling, and bait advertising has received a large share of attention.

The AHEA is preparing to take even greater interest in improving the position of the consumer. To commemorate its golden anniversary (in 1959), the committee on philosophy and objectives set forth the new direction for home economics. Among the twelve objectives, three were specifically related to the consumer. This organization of over thirty-five thousand, with members in al-most every county or small political unit in fifty states, could become the most effective consumer educational force in the United States.

There are several medical, surgical, and dental associations that have estab-lished standards of materials and practices. These standards are of direct value to consumers.

The American Medical Association, an organization of physicians, is active in the improvement of quality and standardization of medical products. Most of the testing and education is done by five committees. Some of the findings are reported in its publication, *Journal of the American Medical Association.*

The Council on Pharmacy and Chemistry, one of the five AMA committees, judges products claimed to have therapeutic values. The accepted and unac-cepted products are described in the *Journal* and published annually in a sepa-rate brochure.

The Council on Physical Therapy investigates and reports on the merits of nonmedical apparatus and devices offered for sale to consumers as well as to physicians and hospitals.

The Council on Foods and Nutrition checks the health claims made by pro-ducers for their manufactured foods. It concerns itself only with foods sold for dietary purposes. It merely "accepts" foods that offer truthful advertising and labels. The use of the seal is granted to products that are accepted. It defi-nitely does not "approve," "recommend," or "grade" food products. Foods sub-mitted for analysis are accepted or rejected, and the facts are so published in the *Journal.* No attempt is made to equate quality and price relationships.

The Committee on Advertising of Cosmetics and Soaps was formed to ad-vise the manager of the *Journal* on advertisements of cosmetics and soaps that are submitted to him.

The Bureau of Investigation has for its primary purpose the investigation and dissemination of information on "patent medicines," quacks, medical fads, and other aspects of pseudo medicine.

The American College of Surgeons is actively engaged in standardization of surgical dressings on the basis of use and characteristics. The college also develops standards for hospitals with respect to services, treatments, and rec-ords.

The American Institute of Homeopathy published the first *Homeopathic Pharmacopeia* in 1897. The standards set up by this organization are for the use of the pharmacist as well as the physician. The Federal Food, Drug, and Cos-metic Act recognized these standards as well as those found in the *United States Pharmacopeia* and in the *National Formulary.* These are not government publi-cations. They are published by scientists, doctors, and pharmaceutical manu-facturers.

These standards are reviewed periodically to incorporate the latest scien-tific information. When new drugs are discovered, the experts study the evi-dence of their effectiveness, the right dosages, and the best processes for their manufacture, packaging, and labeling. This information is made available to doctors and pharmacists.

In general, a drug or standard preparation with the letters U.S.P., H.P., or N.F. on its label has been processed, packed, and labeled according to stand-ard specifications.

American Dental
Association

The American Dental Association is a professional association with a membership of a high percentage of the more than 100,000 dentists in the United States. Its Council on Dental Therapeutics evaluates dental therapeutic agents and dental cosmetic agents sold by companies directly to the public or to the profession. In the council's *Accepted Dental Remedies* are up-to-date descriptions of basic drugs used in dentistry. The council does not evaluate medicated mouthwashes sold to the public, because it feels that they are useless when used without professional supervision. Toothbrushes and cleansers for dentures are also not considered for acceptance. The council, however, continues to give consideration to dentifrices that claim to have evidence against tooth decay or any other mouth disorder.

Until 1960, the best the council had to say about dentifrices was summed up in the terse statement: "The function of a dentifrice . . . is to aid the brush in cleaning the teeth."

In 1960, there was one exception, when the official *Journal of the American Dental Association* published a report that began, "After careful consideration of the results of clinical studies conducted on Crest toothpaste, manufactured by the Procter & Gamble Company, the Council on Dental Therapeutics has recognized the usefulness of the dentifrice as a caries (decay) preventive agent . . ."

There were resentful reactions on the part of toothpaste manufacturers because the ADA allowed its name to be used. Many dentists also resented such commercialization of their professional organization.

Actually, the ADA recognition of Crest, according to a report in 1961, *The Medicine Show,* by Consumers Union, was "hedged and tentative." In view of the ADA's long-standing invitation to dentifrice manufacturers to seek the kind of recognition given to Crest, it would seem to be a fair conclusion that no such evidence exists up to now. The patent on Crest formulation is held by the Indiana University Foundation, where the experiments were conducted at a cost of over $3 million financed by Procter & Gamble, who have an exclusive license to produce and market the toothpaste.

The Procter & Gamble promotion and advertising of Crest were objected to by the ADA as "gross exaggeration and a misleading distortion." Then why was nothing done about these claims? The two federal agencies that have some control over dentifrices, the Food and Drug Administration and the Federal Trade Commission, did not have enough power. Until Congress changed the law, in 1962, the FDA could only review the "safety" of the product, not its efficacy. Now that the FDA has the efficacy power, it can seize a product if its label is false or misleading. And the burden of proof is the company's headache.

The curbing of misleading advertising is the responsibility of the FTC. To prove the claims as false in regard to Crest is almost an impossibility because hearing examiners and judges (not ordinarily trained in scientific disciplines) have usually considered laboratory evidence, even if inadequate, more convincing than testimony by experts. The American Dental Association has complained about the ineffectiveness of the FTC under present rules. The remedy, said the ADA, is an amendment that would shift the burden of proof to the advertiser, and until this happens, consumers must be wary of claims for dentifrices. Incidentally, the ADA does recognize the suitability of baking soda mixed with powdered salt as a cleansing agent.

The contributions of AMA and the ADA could be much greater. At the present time, the chief weakness is their inability to reach the consumer. Modern advertising reaches millions, whereas statements by medical associations may reach only a few thousand. Perhaps the greatest benefit is in the professional use of the standards set up, rather than in giving direct information to the consumer. A good consumer-education program in the schools could inform families of the importance of this kind of information and on how to get up-to-date consumer information.

The danger of professional occupational monopolies

A recent Nader report concluded that doctors, lawyers, pharmacists, and similar professionals systematically fix prices, limit the number in their ranks, and otherwise engage in practices that limit competition.[22] Such monopolies result in excessive fees and prices and gross inefficiencies. More specifically, the questionable practices are these:

1. Price-fixing can and does exist when the state legislature is persuaded by a profession to license its practitioners to work in the state. Under the guise of protecting the public from quacks, some professional organizations raise prices via suggested fees for specific services.

The good qualifications to practice are offset by limiting competition— result: price-fixing

2. The American Medical Association has opposed almost every effort to get more and better medical services at lower cost to consumers.

3. Both doctors and lawyers abstain from informational advertising that would permit rational choices among those professional services. The professionals could at least identify their area of specialization without subjecting the profession to commercialism.

The Nader study says that to allow a licensed profession the unilateral power to define, control, and implement its own prerogatives in the marketplace is little different from granting monopoly power to an industrial corporation. We have already learned that not all doctors and lawyers approve of the closed-shop techniques mentioned in the Nader study.

Better Business Bureaus (BBBs)

The BBB movement started in 1912 when "vigilance committees for truth-in-advertising" were set up in local advertising clubs. These committees became bureaus and expanded the scope of their activities to include misleading and deceptive business practices as well as advertising. The name Better Business Bureau was adopted in 1915. At the present time, there are over 144 BBBs in the United States and eleven in Canada. They are nonprofit, private organizations supported by business contributions and designed to "promote public confidence in responsible business."

What the BBBs actually do varies from bureau to bureau. In general, however, they can perform the following services: (1) receive consumer complaints; (2) furnish factual information about the reliability of concerns and offerings, including the number and type of complaints against certain companies or merchants; (3) act as a mediator between consumer and business, informing business of wrongdoing, deception, and fraud; (4) expel the businesses which fail to stop abuses; (5) alert news media and law-enforcement agencies such as the FTC of unfair trade practices; and (6) monitor local advertising.

---

[22] Mark J. Green, Beverly C. Moore, and Bruce Wasserstein: *Ralph Nader's Study Group Report on Antitrust Enforcement.* Grossman Pub., Inc., N.Y., 1972.

Although many consumers still think highly of the BBBs, they have in recent years slipped in public esteem and have been severely attacked by critics from within and without the organizational structure. Radio station WMCA features a program entitled "Call for Action" which serves as an information clearing-house for New Yorkers who don't know where to find help in solving their problems. In early 1971, reporters conducted a three-month survey. They followed through on 200 consumer complaints called in to the station. Of the four New York agencies surveyed, the BBB was the only one to receive failing grades in both aspects of handling consumer complaints—success and effort. Of those who took their complaints to the BBB, 65 percent had received no help at all within three months, 19 percent were referred to other agencies or received other helpful advice, and 16 percent had their cases solved to their satisfaction.

A more detailed study was conducted in the summer of 1971 by a senior law student at New York University in conjuction with interns from Congressman Rosenthal's office. The findings were basically the same: "BBB services are of little value to the buying public. In some instances, their efforts actually have a counter-productive impact on consumers."

Just how valid are these criticisms? What exactly are the functions of the BBBs? How can they help the consumer? What are they not permitted to do? What problems do they have? What are they doing to improve and revitalize their services to the business community? To consumers? Let's take one question at a time.

They cannot (1) give legal advice or intervene in a case under litigation, (2) endorse products and brands, (3) recommend one company over another, or (4) judge the fairness of prices.

Problems and criticisms

The BBBs are suffering from their own popularity. Many of the bureaus are understaffed and just can't handle the volume of calls that come in each day. The Chicago bureau, for example, has twenty-three full-time employees who field up to 800 requests for information and 200 complaints a day. "We estimate that at least 40 percent of the people calling us can't get through because the lines are busy," observes the bureau's president.

The Rosenthal study Even when a caller does make contact, however, the result is often disappointing. According to Rosenthal's study, there are some basic reasons for this: (1) BBB telephone reports "almost never" give information on actions taken by federal, state, and local law-enforcement agencies against businesses for consumer abuses; (2) many bureaus place the stress on whether or not a business cooperates with the bureau rather than on the nature of the complaint or whether it was resolved to the satisfaction of the consumer; (3) members and nonmembers of the bureau often call anonymously requesting reputation reports on their firms; and (4) the bureaus fear libel and slander actions. The report goes on to point out that although the overall quality of BBB telephone services is poor, this does vary from bureau to bureau. Commercial activities which may be acceptable to one bureau may cause another to report adversely on a firm. Written BBB reports, however, "frequently contain accurate and useful information."

Trying to serve two masters

According to William D. Lee, Deputy Assistant Secretary of Commerce, 80 percent of the millions of calls received by Better Business Bureaus are made for the purpose of asking for information, not to register complaints. And just how are these complaints being handled? The Rosenthal study found that "BBB claims for an extremely high rate of success on handling complaints are completely unsupported and highly exaggerated." They are successful "only in those few instances when the dispute is free of controversy." His study disclosed no instances in which a bureau aggressively prodded a firm to adjust a consumer complaint after it had refused to do so. In many instances, the bureau would accept the word of the firm complained against that the complaint had been satisfactorily resolved.

An integral part of the problem seems to be the fact that BBBs are trying to serve two masters. Loyalty is divided between business and the consumer. "BBBs serve as the agents of the business community and reflect all the biases of that community against the consumer movement and government regulations of anti-consumer practices in the marketplace," concluded Rosenthal.

Improving the BBBs

To restore respect for the BBBs

Faced with a continuing barrage of complaints against business in general, a burgeoning consumer movement, and government attempts to regulate the marketplace, the Better Business Bureaus began their own investigation. Each of the bureaus was assessed, and a study of the strengths and weaknesses of the BBBs was conducted by a management consulting firm. As a result, a new national organization was formed in August, 1970, the Council of Better Business Bureaus. "Its dual mission is to become an effective national self-regulatory force for private enterprise and to demonstrate a sincere and visible concern for consumers." Elisha Gray II, chairman of the finance committee, Whirlpool Corporation, is chairman; H. Bruce Palmer, past president of the National Industrial Conference Board, is president. A board of directors was recruited, a drive for money was started, and major goals were established.

"The council offers no magic formula for solving consumerism problems," commented Palmer. "Our first objective is to restore the Better Business Bureaus to full effectiveness and to the full measure of respect." In order to meet this objective, the council is implementing five major projects:

1. Improving and expanding local services by increasing staff, adding telephones, and introducing new techniques such as mobile units and foreign-language materials to bring the services of the bureau to consumers in disadvantaged communities. The CBBB has already allotted $2.5 million toward the improvement of phone service.

2. Establishing consumer arbitration panels to resolve voluntarily disputes between consumers and business.

3. Establishing a national consumer information data bank, eventually linked to every local bureau. Information stored there would be available to manufacturers, consumers, regulatory agencies, and others.

4. Expanding consumer education efforts.

5. Monitoring and reviewing national advertising in all media.

The big question is: Can the BBBs overcome divided loyalty?

CONSUMER-FINANCED NONPROFIT TESTING AND RATING AGENCIES

For any desired product, the consumer encounters a multiplicity of brands and models. Is there some rational basis for choosing one over the other? Not the wild, unsupported (and often unsupportable) advertising claims, hundreds of which impinge on the consumer's senses every day. Not the kind of judgment a consumer can make from even a careful examination at the point of sale. Not the sweet purrings of an attractive salesperson, often less informed about product differences than the customer and possibly biased by "push money" (money paid for urging a certain brand on customers). Not even your own experience, or your neighbor's, can be a rational basis for selecting many products that are bought infrequently, such as refrigerators and automobiles, which are changed radically from year to year.

How useful is comparative testing and rating to the customer?

The best all-round answer was given by Dr. Arthur Kallet, when he was director of Consumers Union:

> Suppose a buyer were in the market for an automatic washing machine and suppose that the buyer knew an intelligent housewife who had actually used in her own kitchen, each with several loads of clothes, the twelve leading washing machines on the market. Which would the buyer find more useful, the hyperbole of the advertisement and sales claims for the different washers? Or the housewife's off-the-cuff reaction as to ease of loading and unloading, ease of setting controls, ease of adding detergent, cleanness of the clothes, effectiveness of dryer, noisiness, etc.? Substitute for the housewife engineers able to examine and test all of the machines side by side under simulated home-use conditions, keeping accurate records of the behavior and operation of each machine, scoring each factor studied in terms of its effect on the utility and desirability of each machine. There is, of course, room for error, but even in the absence of standards and of a multiplicity of test samples of each model, there are enough differences in design and construction affecting performance and convenience to make purchase decisions based on such tests far more reliable than decisions based on brand names, price, advertising, or the chance recommendation of a neighbor or a salesman. [23]

Consumers' Research, Inc. (CR)

In the early 1920s there was an outburst of inaccurate and misleading advertising. The prosperity following World War I brought forth a tremendous flow of consumer goods on the market, aided by mass production techniques worked out by Henry Ford and others after him. This flow of products was pushed by new methods of advertising and by what Thorstein Veblen called the "higher salesmanship." Many of the new products were shoddy and poorly designed, calling for critical examination. In a way, the testing of consumer goods at this time was an inevitable response to confused disappointment in the mass-produced outflow of products. Consumers began to ask: Is there "soapier soap," "coffee-er coffee"?

This confusion set the scene for what became a best-seller—*Your Money's Worth*, by Stuart Chase and F. J. Schlink—in 1927. The book revealed the multiple methods used by business to deceive consumers, and shortly after it ap-

[23] Dickson Reck (ed.), *National Standards in a Modern Economy*, Harper & Row, Publishers, Incorporated, New York, 1956, p. 279.

peared thousands of letters flooded the offices of the publishing company. People were concerned. Primarily, they wanted to know, "How can I select the best product?" To the authors and a small group of their friends, these letters expressed the development of a new attitude—a consumer-minded attitude—on the part of the American people. Out of Mr. Schlink's attempt to answer the queries, the Consumers' Club was organized in White Plains, New York. In 1929, the club became Consumers' Research, Inc., and in 1933 it moved to Washington, New Jersey, its present home.

This testing agency publishes twelve monthly issues of *Consumers' Research Magazine* and its *Annual Bulletin.* The subscription cost of the former is $8 and of the latter, $2.95. Consumers' Research claims around 100,000 mail subscribers and is bought on newsstands by an additional 10,000 readers. Its financial resources are about $750,000 annually. Besides product ratings, the *Magazine* carries ratings of motion pictures and phonograph records, short editorials, and the Consumers Observation Post. CR does not have an aggressive sales promotion department. Sales are largely dependent on recommendations by subscribers.

Most of the testing is hired out to well-known testing laboratories and to specialized consultants. Listings in the *Magazine* are usually arranged in alphabetical order: A, recommended on the basis of quality; A-A, highest recommendation; B, intermediate with respect to quality; and C, not recommended. Price ratings, 1,2, and 3, are given in some ratings, 1 being low and 3 high price. Quality judgments are wholly independent of price with one exception—automobiles.

Evaluation of Consumers' Research Magazine

1. The control of CR limits its potential effectiveness. Although nonprofit, the board of trustees is limited to five persons, including the president and his wife. It is a self-perpetuating organization, which excludes fresh ideas that might come from a board elected from among its subscribers. CRs full-time staff comprises approximately eighty persons, including about fifteen technical experts. The board does not permit the employees to belong to any other organization without written permission. Consequently, there is no labor union in the plant.

2. Some people question the reliability of the test reports in the *Magazine* by arguing that large corporations pay fees to secure the highest ratings. There has never been proof of these accusations, and their reliability can be questioned for at least two reasons. First, a successful court suit on this count would be the easiest method to destroy the testing organization, and there are plenty of businessmen who would jump at this opportunity. Second, over a period of years, the products of large corporations receive about the same percentage of "not recommended" and "recommended" ratings as other producers.

3. The financial resources of CR are limited to the sales of its publication (no advertising income is permitted). Testing of consumer products is expensive, and consequently CR is not able to test as many products as the subscribers might like. To rate more consumer goods, CR frequently borrows test samples of large, expensive items from manufacturers who sign affidavits that the goods

were typical and selected at random. Typewriters, for example, were rented.[24] Consumers would feel more assured if all the products tested had been purchased in retail stores by persons unknown to the stores, rather than samples that may not have been selected at random. As a matter of policy, consumer products to be tested should be purchased in different sections of the country, to protect against the possibility of a better- or poorer-quality shipment to other sections.

4. Branded products available in one section of the United States are not available in other sections. California and the West Coast in general have many branded products not available elsewhere. Subscribers in some sections are unhappy because their needs are not served.

5. Consumer testing agencies restrict most of their tests to branded goods nationally distributed. This policy, a practical one to testers, excludes the testing of local unbranded products.

6. Some subscribers would prefer to have CR test most of the products by its own staff in its own laboratories. When representatives from industry want to discuss and examine the data on the testing of their products, it is more satisfactory to talk with the scientists and experts who did the testing. When tests are farmed out to many different laboratories, adequate discussion by fellow testers and experts is usually impossible.

7. A certain number of social-minded subscribers do not want to purchase products from businesses that have poor working conditions and low wages for their employees. CR insists that this social concern should have no place in reporting the results of testing. This decision is more reasonable today than it was when CR was established in 1929, because the federal government has set up minimum wage standards for goods sold interstate. Furthermore, unionization of plants and the nature of competition make this limitation appear less important even to social-minded people.

When the Technical, Editorial, and Office Assistants Union attempted to unionize the CR plant, and agreement seemed unlikely, a strike was called in September, 1935, which lasted four months. The National Labor Relations Board ordered CR to bargain with the employees and to reinstate three discharged employees. CR refused to comply with the order. A group of CR's subscribers, organized to aid in settling the strike, decided to set up a new consumer testing agency appropriately named Consumers Union.[25]

Consumers Union of U.S., Inc. (CU) Arthur Kallet, former secretary of Consumers' Research, and ten former CR staff workers set up the new testing agency, Consumers Union, in two small rooms in a dingy corner of Manhattan. Mr. Kallet was director of CU until his retirement in 1957. He remained on the board of directors for a few years following retirement. In 1955, CU moved to spacious new quarters in Mount Vernon, New York.

Consumers Union, a nonprofit organization, was established in 1936. It is

[24] Sylvia Lane, "A Study of Selected Agencies That Evaluate Consumer Goods Qualitatively in the United States," unpublished doctoral dissertation, University of Southern California, Los Angeles, 1957, p. 106.

[25] Helen Sorenson, *The Consumer Movement*, Harper & Row, Publishers, Incorporated, New York, 1941, p. 47.

chartered under the Membership Corporations Law of the State of New York and derives its income solely from the sale of its publications (over two million subscribers and 150,000 newsstand buyers in 1973). In addition, the expenses of occasional research projects of a public service nature may be met in part by nonrestrictive, noncommercial grants.

Consumers Union has no connection with any commercial interest and accepts no advertising. Its ratings and reports on products are solely for the information and use of the readers of *Consumer Reports* and may not be used in advertising or for any commercial purpose. The pocket-size, 400-page *Buying Guide* is issued in December. It condenses articles in previous issues of *Consumer Reports* and includes some new material and buying advice.

The purposes of Consumers Union, as stated in its charter, are "to provide for consumer information and counsel on consumer goods and services . . . to give information and assistance on all matters relating to expenditure of family income—to initiate and cooperate with individual and group efforts seeking to create and maintain decent living standards.

Any subscriber may become a member of Consumers Union by so requesting at the time he subscribes to *Consumer Reports* or by written application at any time. Any subscriber becomes a member also by voting in the annual election of directors; ballots are mailed to all subscribers. Membership entails no financial or other obligation, except that members are expected to exercise their right to vote in the annual election of the board of directors.

CU is served by its board of directors, numbering twenty-one in 1973, which functions through committees. The board deals with broad policy considerations. The operation of CU, which includes testing, publishing, and servicing of the readership, is supervised by the director and a management staff of twenty-three, including the heads of thirteen departments. The total staff numbers more than three hundred persons. All except the management staff work under a contract between CU and the American Newspaper Guild, AFL-CIO (American Federation of Labor and Congress of Industrial Organizations).

CU publishes information on more than 200 different consumer products each year. In deciding what products to test, CU polls its readers with questionnaires. If sizable numbers reply that they want reports on hi-fi equipment or clothes dryers, the staff gives full consideration to these products in preparing a list of upcoming test projects. After the staff has approved a project, a market survey is made to find out trends and pricing practices in the industry involved and to determine which brands and models—in terms of availability and consumer interest—are to be tested.

To obtain samples of products for testing, CU has a "ready reserve" of some eighty-five shoppers located in some sixty cities scattered throughout the United States. On orders from CU, these typical buyers go to the regular retail stores, and without revealing CU connection to the seller, buy the specified brands at the merchant's regular price. The products are immediately shipped to CU.

CU tests over 90 percent of all the products in its own laboratories. To conduct its complex testing and rating work, CU now has seven technical divisions—appliance, audio, automotive, chemistry, electronics, textiles, and special projects. In tests of boys' clothing—polo shirts, blue jeans, and shoes—CU's engineers used ninety-six boys, aged 6 to 12. As many as seven hundred women volunteers participated in comparison tests of forty-four brands of nylon hosiery. A panel of fifty-six men use-tested eight widely sold brands of electric shavers.

Consumer Reports

Consumer Reports has a reputation among publishers for being the most carefully prepared and edited magazine in the United States. Only the best professional writers are employed. Not only must the articles be interesting, readable, and not too long, but they must also be accurate in reporting the data derived from scientific testing. The testers have the final word on the technical accuracy of the articles. The introductory paragraphs in each article tell what was tested and why, pointing out the limitations of the test, if any, and giving advice on how to use the test results for maximum satisfaction.

The reports present ratings of the brands in the order of their estimated overall quality and performance. In the range of ratings, the highest is rated by a check mark for an "Acceptable" brand that is also outstanding in quality and performance. The lowest rating, "Not Acceptable," is for a brand that was particularly poor in performance or displayed a safety hazard during the testing of the sample. If an Acceptable brand is sufficiently low in price to represent an outstanding value, it may be designated as a "Best Buy." Thus, the consumer gets comparative information that cannot be obtained from the advertising or labeling of products, no matter how truthful, or from over-the-counter inspection, no matter how careful.

A public service department investigates broad areas of public concern, among them radiation hazards, air and water pollution, and car accidents. The staff gathers information, working with scientific and technical consultants and with government agencies. Its recommendations and findings are presented for remedial action by consumers and by appropriate departments or agencies of government. By initiating investigations early—before public agencies begin investigation—the public is made aware of the dangers. Usually, the public agencies take over from that point and carry on the needed investigations.

The monthly publication also carries regular reports on health and on economics. The health reports cover such vital subjects as cancer research, new drugs, food fads, and alleged weight reducers. They also point out the real or potential dangers of certain chemical additives and pesticide residues in foods, and are widely recognized and commended by many authorities.

Regular articles on economics relate the product on the market to the broad marketing realities that consumers face. Typical subjects include the consumer's need for standard grades and labels in meats and other foods; packaging practices that mislead shoppers; pros and cons on installment buying and credit cards; the costs of price-fixing laws to consumers; and government actions affecting customer welfare.

In addition to these services, CU rates movies, represents consumer interest in hearing of congressional committees (usually invited), and often confers with federal agencies (the FDA, the FTC, and the National Bureau of Standards) on problems of common concern.

In another service, CU sponsors conferences at universities and colleges on conducting workshops on consumer welfare problems. CU has also made modest grants to universities for special research on consumer matters.

Influence of CU ratings

Consumers Union does over 90 percent of testing in its own laboratories. This has an advantage for manufacturers who care to send their own testing experts to Consumers Union headquarters to review test methods and results. Many manufacturers have improved their products because of the Consumers Union rating.

While there are criticisms directed at test methods and evaluation of test results, Consumers Union has had a definite impact on sales and product quality. Westinghouse, for example, credits a favorable rating for a 20 percent jump in washing machine sales in 1966. A Norge executive said, "Consumers Union put us in the washing machine business." A West Coast hi-fi dealer said 5 to 10 percent of his customers arrive with an opinion influenced by *Consumer Reports*. [26]

The studies cited in the accompanying table are evidence of how useful Consumers Union's comparative testing and rating were in earlier years (1957 to 1963).

[26] *Business Week,* Dec. 23, 1967.

How Useful Is Comparative Testing and Rating?

QUESTION	ANSWER
Do brand ratings influence buying patterns of households that refer to them?	Yes. (Sargent study,[a] Lane study,[b] Dear CU letters[c])
Do households that consult consumer publications do more shopping around than nonconsulting households?	Yes. (Sargent study[a])
Do people who consult consumer publications have higher formal education than nonconsulting persons?	Yes. (Sargent study[a])
Is CU rendering a valuable social service in helping some 4 million readers to stimulate quality improvement?	Yes. (Sargent,[a] Lane,[b] Beem[c])
Do CU ratings encourage product improvement?	Yes. (Werner,[d] Dear CU letters[e])
Do CU ratings influence consumer purchases? (Asked of retailers.)	Yes. (*Home Furnishings Daily,* Oct. 7, 1959, p. 30; Dear CU letters;[e] Nelson Foote[f])
Do CU ratings save readers money?	Yes. (CU returns of 40,000 readers:[g] 32.6 per cent saved $50 to $100 a year; 37.7 per cent saved $10 to $50 a year; 29.7 per cent saved less than $10 a year.)

[a]Hugh W. Sargent, "Consumer Product Rating Publications and Buying Patterns," *University of Illinois Bulletin,* Urbana, Ill., December, 1959.

[b]Sylvia Lane, "A Study of Selected Agencies That Evaluate Consumer Goods Qualitatively in the United States," unpublished doctoral dissertation, University of Southern California, Los Angeles, 1957, pp. 491, 535.

[c]Eugene R. Beem and John S. Ewing, "Business Appraises Consumer Testing Agencies," *Harvard Business Review,* vol. 32, no. 2, pp. 113–126.

[d]M. R. Werner, "A Detective Agency for Wary Buyers," *The Reporter,* reprint, 1958.

[e]Consumers Union, Mount Vernon, N.Y., 1961.

[f]Lincoln Clark (ed.), *Consumer Behavior.*

[g]*The Wall Street Journal,* Mar. 15, 1962, p. 1.

CU's own effectiveness has been enhanced by the spread of the consumer movement that it has helped promote. "What we say now will be echoed by other groups or by sympathetic politicians," said Morris Kaplan, late technical director, "and that means that industry worries more about what we say. They are afraid it will get picked up and spread around, so they are more likely to follow our recommendations."

Almost no businessman will openly criticize CU's techniques. Even if they grumble, manufacturers rush to correct defects pointed out in *Consumer Reports*. After publication of a critical article in the January, 1971, issue, the owners of 180,000 General Motors cars received letters advising them of a faulty gas-tank cap. The letters also contained a certificate for a replacement cap.

CU has big impact

A good rating by CU can be as important to a product as a favorable review is to a new Broadway play—and manufacturers have had the lesson driven home. Not long ago, when *Consumer Reports* recommended a $4 pair of electric scissors that turned out to be unavailable in most stores, some twenty-five thousand readers wrote the maker to complain.

CU has also gained influence in Washington, particularly in the area of product safety. As a result of a CU suit, the Food and Drug Administration ordered some thirty-nine dangerous toys off the market or required warning labels on them, and a number of carpets and rugs were banned because of tighter new federal standards concerning flammability based largely on CU testing. And if the federal government decides to set safety standards for all consumer products, as President Nixon has proposed, it will undoubtedly have to rely heavily on CU's methods and experience.

Most of the studies thus far undertaken allude to the great surprise of retailers when they first note the marked effects of favorable ratings. Thus a store's inventory of a top-rated brand of air conditioner, television set, or high-fidelity speaker may be completely wiped out within several days after the test results are published in *Consumer Reports*. An automobile salesman accustomed to having customers ask many questions about his product may be surprised to find that prospective buyers, checkbook in hand, are interested in a particular model with particular options and are concerned solely with one question—the price.

From its experience since 1936, CU has learned much concerning the areas in which consumers wish product information. Cars, of course, are at the top of the list, followed by major appliances and small appliances. The field of medicine and health is also high on the list.

Consumers Union more than Consumer Reports

Perhaps most people think of CU only as a private, nonprofit consumer product testing and reporting organization. This function still is the primary reason for CU's existence. Over the years, however, it became clear that government and business were more interested in serving business than in handling consumer complaints. If a legislator introduced a bill that would, for example, require more truth in the marketplace or the reduction of hidden product hazards, industry lobbyists would work to pigeonhole the bill in committee—or, failing that, to riddle it with holes, strip it of penalties, or withhold funding to enforce it. As a result of political power plays, legal challenges, or threats, regulatory agencies might be persuaded not to act. Consequently, a whole new ball game was evolving which needed attention and some kind of effective challenge.

The emergence of Ralph Nader in 1967 as a catalyst of the new consumer consciousness stimulated Consumers Union to investigate approaches for protecting the consumer interest and establishing a more competitive marketplace other than those undertaken through *Consumer Reports*. Out of this investigation came the Consumer Federation of America (CFA); Consumer Interests Foundation, Inc. (CIF); a Washington, D.C., legal office; and a special publications program.

Developing "consumer consciousness"

1. The Consumer Federation of America (CFA)

CU played an important role in organizing the CFA in 1967 for the purpose of unifying community, state, regional, and national consumer organizations. The CFA has 196 member organizations, representing such diverse constituencies as local, state, and national consumer groups; women's clubs; unions; farm groups; cooperatives; and affiliations of senior citizens. It is dedicated to promoting the rights of consumers and, among other activities, has waged active campaigns for securing decent warranties, reforming the FTC, revising unfair credit codes, and creating an independent consumer agency at the federal level. Recently, it played an important role in getting all manufacturers of baby foods to use open dating on their products. Through its Washington office and its periodic bulletin, *News from CFA*, the federation serves as a clearinghouse for information on issues, activities, and programs affecting the consumer interest. CU is a charter member of the CFA.

Effective lobbying

Other activities of the CFA include monitoring proposed bills in Congress; lobbying for good consumer legislation; providing spokesmen for some 35 million members of 200 local, state, and national organizations; supporting consumer-oriented government policies; publishing a monthly digest of government actions and activities in the consumer interest; representing consumers before congressional hearings; and sponsoring an annual consumer assembly, a national forum focusing on consumer issues, concerns, and problem solving.

The CFA has announced the chartering of a new tax-exempt research arm— the Paul H. Douglas Consumer Research Center. Efforts are now under way to build the center's funds so that it can provide information to the public on consumer laws, decisions, and administrative enforcement; provide technical assistance to local and state consumer organizations; publish a newsletter; conduct seminars to provide leaders of diverse citizens' and professional organizations opportunities to secure authoritative information and alternative solutions to consumer problems; and assert the rights of consumers before federal administrative and regulatory agencies and the courts.

2. Consumer Interests Foundation, Inc.

Established in 1972, this organization concentrates on the problem of finding money for research on such major concerns as the environment and carrying out a systematic identification of major researchable problems affecting the consumer interest. For example, very little research has been done on social effects of advertising, energy utilization, product safety, consumer complaints, and many other consumer-related problems. After important, researchable topics are selected, specialists will be consulted, and eventually a final report will be prepared. This will identify the problem and the additional research needed, and organizations and/or individuals to conduct the research will be recommended. The CIF is located in Washington, D.C., and has a board of trustees; David Swankin was the first director. At the present time, the CIF is concentrating on identifying consumer-related issues that need research, on raising funds, and on establishing a priority list of consumer issues focusing on the present needs of the consumer movement as well as on projected major developments over the next ten years. The CIF hopes to become a completely independent consumer research center.

3. CU's Washington office

Established in 1972, the Washington office, presently manned by three lawyers, will focus mainly on efforts to enforce present laws and federal agency decisions which are concerned with the consumer interest. This office has already instituted a few lawsuits. For example, a suit has been filed to force the government to halt sales of Serc, a prescription drug it has ruled ineffective. This suit is a challenge to the broad assertion of administrative discretion in handling all inefficacious drugs by the FDA. The office may also consider taking action on enforcing product safety standards, unit pricing, and drained-weight disclosures on cans and frozen food packages.

4. CU's special publications program

There are two basic criteria for publication: (1) The book should fill a significant gap in consumer information and (2) it should meet certain standards of research, accuracy, lucidity, and lack of gross bias. CU relies heavily on recognized authorities, consultants, and nationally known writers. The writer of one of the recent books, *Licit and Illicit Drugs,* for example, worked with forty consultants in various disciplines. *Overweight,* another recent book, was not published—even though it was written by a recognized nutritional authority, Jean Mayer, of Harvard—until it was reviewed by other well-known nutritional authorities and medical consultants. The reviews usually result in important corrections.

Most of the books have been an appendage to *Consumer Reports* and have been produced usually as a result of an article appearing in that publication (for example, on life insurance, wines and spirits, and family planning). A few of the books have come from other publishers who permitted CU paperback editions (*Silent Spring* and *The Real Voice,* for example). The large, 400-plus-page *Buying Guide* is an annual paperback summarizing material covered in the past year's *Consumer Reports.* A few other consumer articles also appear in the annual *Buying Guide.* A total of eighteen books appeared prior to May 31, 1972.

RALPH NADER AND COMPANY: CONSUMER-ADVOCATE CATALYST

Ralph Nader is sometimes called a "consumer crusader." Actually, he is the consumer-advocate catalyst who recently sparked the renewed interest in consumer-industry-government affairs and the revitalized concern about the impact

of America's products, technology, and institutions upon the health, safety, and economic status of her citizens.

He is a blend of talents and abilities—attorney and lawyer for everybody, prolific writer and lecturer, challenger of misused corporate and lobbyist power, prodder of government agencies, organizer of bright college students into investigative teams, and founder of the Center for Auto Safety and more recently at least eight other organizations (see Figure 15-1).

What was originally a one-man show in Washington, D.C., now has a cast of hundreds. Beginning with a single issue—auto safety—Nader has come to focus on a broad range of consumer and environmental issues.

Nader came to Washington with little more than a highly developed desire to do what he could as a consumer advocate. This tireless and selfless young lawyer, highly motivated because he truly cares about the tragically

FIGURE 15-1   This list of Nader research and project groups was up to date as of September 14, 1972.

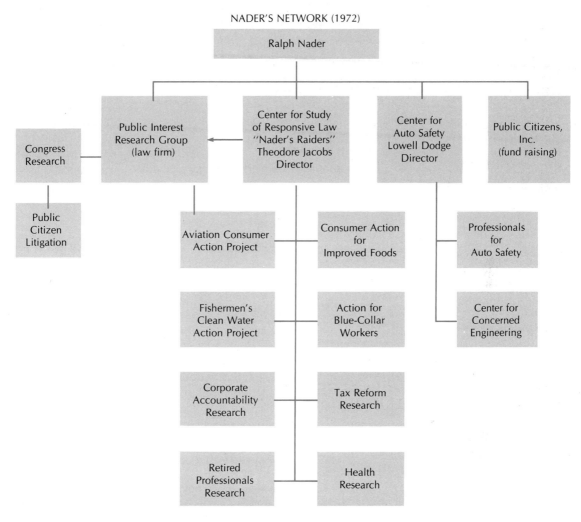

NADER'S NETWORK (1972)

SOURCE: Educational Division of Consumers Union.

dwindling health and safety of mankind and about the state of the total ecology, is dedicated to helping reform our socioeconomic institutions so that they will serve more humane purposes. He moved toward national prominence in early 1966 as a result of reforms suggested in his book *Unsafe at Any Speed.*

Soon thereafter, in the spring of 1966, congressional hearings were held to probe the auto safety issue. Much of the thrust at the hearings came from Nader himself, who was a key witness and sharply articulated the factual and philosophical basis for emphasis on safety in car design, reform of the auto industry, and the establishment of a strong representative federal agency and motor vehicle safety standards.

During the hearings a startling set of events developed. Ralph Nader was in the process of being investigated by representatives of General Motors.

General Motors' costly mistake

On March 9, 1966, GM admitted that it had hired detectives to follow him night and day, claiming that this action was prompted by Nader's criticisms of Corvair automobiles in his speeches. Two weeks later at the hearings, James M. Roche, then president of GM, apologized both to the committee and to Mr. Nader. These acts of harassment were settled "out of court" for $425,000.

Nader a household word

Before GM's mistake, Nader was a single crusader and *not* a well-funded, well-staffed, and well-advertised person. But GM's harassment made Nader a household word. Several small foundations, some businessmen, and Consumers Union provided him with an improved financial base from which to expand his activities. All his personal earnings from lectures, magazine articles, and the General Motors settlement went into building an organization to carry out more fact-finding investigations, followed up by public reports of his findings. As a result of these early investigations, he asked some very basic, logical questions:

1. Does this affect the health, safety, or economic position of the consumer?
2. Is the responsible industry aware of its misdeeds?
3. Is it diligently working to correct the problem?
4. Is there a responsible agency of government chartered to represent the consumer interest, and is it being responsible in resolving the problem?
5. Are the facts being adequately and accurately conveyed to the public?
6. Does the public have the right to seek redress for any grievances and preventive correction of the basic problem itself?
7. How can I best serve as an advocate for the consumers' interest?

One man can make a difference

Thus the logic of a few basic questions can usually point out the basic deficiencies in a particular consumer-interest area. Often it has been desirable to seek a broader hearing on a subject, especially where important national dilemmas of health, safety, and economics are concerned. Our democratic system provides for congressional hearings held by committees and subcommittees, and Nader made liberal use of these to air matters of public concern and to help encourage corrective legislative action. On many occasions he was a key witness, submitting verbal testimony in addition to meticulous formal written statements. At such hearings Nader has testified on automobile safety, the auto industry, wholesale meat quality, natural gas pipeline safety, radiation control, wholesale poultry quality, coal miners' working conditions, misuse of chemical additives in food, excess fat in hot dogs, unclean and polluted fish, deadly overuse of X-ray equipment in medical and dental work, the abusive influence of powerful lobbyist groups, suppression of information by governmental agencies, and so on.

Nader believes in working through established channels of communication. He believes in our competitive system and strives to suggest changes that will make it work as it was intended to.

Public Citizen, Inc.

Nader's newest idea is Public Citizen, Inc. It calls on individuals to make small contributions—$10 per person to support public-interest work. Nader sends out form letters to those on a limited mailing list, asking the recipients

The public has faith in his integrity and credibility

to become Public Citizens. In the letter he tells about the thousands of young lawyers, engineers, medical personnel, and others who are willing to work for a modest income. He says "If these young people are willing to sacrifice their material rewards to pioneer the future, other public-spirited citizens should do their share." The preliminary mailing in 1971 to some 180,000 persons brought in over $100,000. The first Public Citizen ad in the *New York Times* brought in about $50,000. This was proof that the public really cares about Nader's efforts to make our competitive marketing system work as intended.

Bess Myerson, Commissioner of the Department of Consumer Affairs for New York City, referred to Nader as "a remarkable man who in the last six years has done more as a private citizen for our country and its people than most public officials do in a lifetime." This man has shown that change can be brought about with weapons available to any citizen—the law, congressional hearings, federal agency records and reports, and the force of public opinion. His job has been to bring issues out in the open, where they cannot be ignored. Most important, he thinks, is the "generational thing." A whole new generation is growing up under the influence of this consumer advocate for real competition in the marketplace.

A whistle-blower, a public citizen—it's all the same. This is an old idea being pushed with a new urgency. And the fact that it's being pushed by Ralph Nader might make the difference. After all, anyone who can fight General Motors and win. . . . (See Taylor-Troelstrup Reading 95, "Washington Pressure/Nader Network Switches Focus to Legal Action, Congressional Lobbying.")

SOME PRIVATE NEWS PUBLICATIONS IN THE CONSUMER INTEREST

Consumer Newsweek, formerly *U.S. Consumer,* is published by Consumer News, 813 National Press Building, Washington, D.C., 10004. This four-page newsweekly features news you can use from the nation's capital. A recent copy, for example, printed a report of the National Business Council for Consumer Affairs (a business advisory group in the Department of Commerce) giving background information on current consumer credit bills including the Credit Billing Act. Usually each issue includes two or three of the most important consumer news items to come out of Washington during the week.

Of Consuming Interest is a four-page, twice-monthly leaflet published by Federal-State Reports, Inc., P.O. Box 986, Court House Station, Arlington, Virginia 22216. A typical issue might contain news on a no-fault insurance bill, the banning of nitrate-nitrite color additives, industry self-regulation, product safety agency, business' need for a director of consumer affairs, and prepaid legal services.

Media & Consumer, first issued in December, 1972, reprints interesting consumer news stories from many other sources. Although this fine twenty-page publication was originally intended to provide fellow journalists with a place to print controversial news stories, teachers, writers, and publishers who are concerned with current consumer news and the disclosure of consumer abuses will find *Media & Consumer* a storehouse of information.

Changing Times was first issued in January, 1947. During the first 1½ years of publication this monthly magazine seemed to be designed primarily for businessmen, but gradually it broadened its content, until today it can be described as a magazine for consumers. Most of the articles are on such subjects as budgeting, investing savings, buying insurance, borrowing money, buying or building a home, running a car, and protecting health. Often, excellent charts and tables are included. On the whole, the articles are objective, readable, and to the point.

Occasionally an article appears that omits information that would be important to the consumer, tempting one to say that the magazine has forsaken the consumer interest; but perhaps it would be more accurate to say that the magazine was not designed to be a 100 percent consumer magazine. Consumer-minded citizens can get their money's worth from this modestly priced publication—at least its subscribers, mostly nonbusiness people, think so. Like *Consumer Reports* and *Consumers' Research Magazine*, *Changing Times* accepts no advertising.

New subscribers receive an up-to-date ninety-six-page book, *99 New Ideas on Your Money, Job and Living,* which is a collection of consumer articles and ideas taken from recent issues of the magazine. The address is *Changing Times,* Editors Park, Maryland 20582.

The National Consumers League (NCL), with headquarters in Washington, D.C., depends on dues and contributions from its members. It is frankly committed to legislative action in the interest of consumers. The NCL has never been a mass movement, and yet it has been in the thick of successful battles to protect and promote the welfare of all consumers. The NCL, for example, led the fight for the original Pure Food and Drug Act. Later it fought for drug safety and efficacy, truth-in-lending, truth-in-packaging, and better health insurance. An important function of the league is the publication of *Fact Sheets,* legislative alerts, and other information regarding consumer protection needs. Finally, the NCL has been active in presenting the consumer point of view at hearings before congressional committees and federal agencies.

CONSUMER RESEARCH ORGANIZATIONS

We have selected three consumer research organizations—the Weights and Measures Research Center, the Center for Consumer Affairs, and a recent organization called the Consumer Research Foundation—to examine because these are voluntary, nonprofit organizations run by enlightened, professional, consumer-oriented personnel.

The Weights and Measures Research Center

Dr. Leland J. Gordon has been director of the Weights and Measures Research Center at Denison University (Granville, Ohio) since 1955. As an economist, he had become aware of the importance of adequate and well-enforced standards of weights and measures. As early as 1959, Gordon recommended changes in weights and measures legislation and in enforcement at the state and local levels. Since then he has made two national surveys of state weights and measures legislation, administration, and enforcement—in 1963 and in 1966. In 1968 Dr. Gordon made a study of the implementation of the Fair Packaging and Labeling Act and tells the story as it was in July, 1968. All of these studies were distributed by Consumers Union, Mount Vernon, New York 10550.

Consumers Union has made modest grants for the operation of the center. In June 1974, the Weights and Measures Research Center was transferred to the Center for Consumer Affairs, University of Wisconsin Extension Division in Milwaukee.

The Center for Consumer Affairs

The Center for Consumer Affairs was established in March, 1963, by the University of Wisconsin Extension Division. Mrs. Helen Nelson, an economist, is director of the center. Its objectives are:

1. To identify and analyze problems of concern to consumers
2. To develop among consumers an understanding of the economic system of the United States
3. To foster appreciation of the consumer's responsibilities and opportunities in the economy.

The Center for Consumer Affairs plans the following activities:

1. Sponsoring workshops, clinics, and institutes on consumer affairs
2. Offering credit and noncredit courses on consumer financing, consumer marketing, and family finance
3. Sponsoring action-oriented research on topics like consumer credit, burial costs, trading stamps, family financial counseling, and legal protection for consumers
4. Developing the usual aids for use in consumer education
5. Conducting experimental work in family financial counseling and training of counselors

Since consumer affairs have many dimensions, the center plans to use people trained in economics, law, social work, psychology, home economics, communications, sociology, political science, and possibly others.

The Consumer Research Foundation

CRF was established in Berkeley, California, on February 6, 1967, as a nonprofit organization dedicated "to research and education for the benefit of consumers." The foundation is organized, for example, to conduct research in:

1. Consumer problems affecting low-income families, senior citizens, and young families.
2. Consumer needs involving credit, food buying, housing, medical care, transportation, money management, etc.
3. Developing consumer education and teaching materials for the schools.
4. Preparing programs tailored to individual family needs for budgeting and money management.
5. Professional presentation of technical information concerning consumer interests before public and private forums.

One of the first research jobs completed by CRF was a *Critique of the Uniform Consumer Credit Code.* This information analysis of the proposed 127-page uniform code for consumer credit law being submitted to most of the state legislatures in 1968 and 1969 will be useful to anyone interested in understanding how the code, if passed by a state legislature, may eliminate some of the protection the consumers had in the recently enacted Federal Consumer Credit Protection Act (better known as the Truth-in-Lending Bill). This research also points out how the proposed code will improve protection of the users of consumer credit in states with poor consumer credit protection.

As is the case with most nonprofit organizations, Consumer Research Foundation depends on memberships, donations, grants, and research contracts to carry on its programs.

Three new consumer research centers were opened in 1972/73. The Consumer Interests Foundation, Inc., initially financed by Consumers Union, will eventually be an independent consumer research organization, as described earlier on page 544.

The Paul H. Douglas Consumer Research Center, chartered under the aupices of the Consumer Federation of America in 1972, is presently raising funds for research and service to and for other consumer organizations in this country. A brief description of this organization can be found on page 544.

The National Consumer Congress (NCC), a neophyte organization that grew out of the nationwide meat boycott in 1973, is moving rapidly to build upon a strong grassroots support. Under the direction of Ellen Zawel, with temporary headquarters in Washington, D.C., six regional boards were set up together with six national sets of officers which comprise the national executive board.

The first two months of the NCC was spent in developing a viable mass membership consumer organization. The national office will coordinate regional efforts, provide technical aid, assist with consumer education and leadership training programs, and sponsor a Consumer Resource Center which will function as a clearinghouse on consumer issues and prepare a monthly newsletter *(Common Sense)*. The key emphasis of NCC seems to be "mass mobilization."

QUESTIONS FOR DISCUSSION

1. What is it that the consumer has a right to know, and who has the right to decide this?

2. Consumerism is grounded in marketing failures. Explain.

3. What is the consumer's role in a well-functioning market?

4. Why do consumers today require much more relevant information on goods and services than consumers fifty years ago?

5. Why has top business leadership neglected social responsibilities?

6. What is your reaction to David Rockefeller's statement that the day will come when corporations will be required to publish a "social audit" certified by independent accountants?

7. When General Motors is found guilty of selling unsafe cars, why not suspend the President of GM for six months or so without pay?

8.   How would consumer rights as outlined by President Nixon in 1969 actually serve to strengthen our free enterprise system?

9.   Warranties are not always what they appear to be. Explain.

10.   Why do we need standards for consumer goods? When there are good standards for consumer products, is it important for the consumer to know what the standards mean?

11.   Why are the *Good Housekeeping* and the *Parents' Magazine* seals unreliable?

12.   Is it important for real consumers to participate in standards-writing decisions?

13.   After reading why the Council of Better Business Bureaus is attempting to restore the local BBBs to full effectiveness, explain how the local BBBs can overcome the problem of divided loyalty, stemming from the fact that public and business interests support them financially.

14.   What are the contributions of Consumers Union to consumers and to our free competitive system?

15.   "Ralph Nader—one man can make a difference." Explain.

PROJECTS

1.   Make a study of Ralph Nader. What has he accomplished so far? How would you characterize his role in the consumer movement? What are his strengths? His weaknesses? Can one man make a difference? Report your findings to the class.

2.   What is it that the consumer has a right to know, and who has the right to decide this? This is a tough question that needs to be discussed when considering seller-buyer communication. This chapter addresses itself to this question. Try to write an editorial using the question as a basis for whatever point of view you believe is best.

3.   Professor Tibor Scitovsky, in his book *Welfare and Competition,* wrote: The "scope of advertising depends on the ignorance of the people to whom it is addressed." You may be interested in finding out what he meant by this statement.

4.   Select several business leaders concerned with manufacturing consumer products in your area. Ask them about their responsibility in handling consumer grievances and complaints. What has the corporation done in recent years to improve its communication with consumers? If the corporation claims it is doing a good job in handling buyer complaints and grievances (which actually may or may not be true), what are the motivations behind its present policies? (Enlightened self-interest? A public relations fad? Social grandstanding? Or a sincere effort to gear social dimensions into its daily operations?)

5.   When David Rockefeller, a wealthy businessman, predicts that corporations will someday be required to publish a "social audit" certified by indepen-

dent accountants, just what does he mean? You might like to read more about his reasoning in *The Wall Street Journal,* Dec. 21, 1971.

6. The Brand Names Foundation, financed by manufacturers of brand-name products, spends hundreds of thousands of dollars to educate the public to purchase brand-name products. Why? Are brands helpful to consumers? Do labels on brand-name products indicate their quality? Can you be sure of the quality? How is one to know which of the 100 or so brands of cold breakfast food is best for his purpose? What are the advantages to a manufacturer of brand-named products? What are your conclusions?

7. After studying the *Good Housekeeping* and *Parents' Magazine* Seals of Approval, how do you account for the fact there are well-educated people who still believe these seals are a guarantee of quality? Ask twenty-five of your friends what these seals of approval mean to them. Square the answers with what you learned in this chapter.

SUGGESTED READINGS

Aaker, David H., and George S. Day: *Consumerism: Search for the Consumer Interest,* The Free Press, New York, 1971.

Gaedeke, Ralph M., and Warren W. Etchesen: *Consumerism: Viewpoints from Business, Government, and the Public Interest,* Canfield Press, San Francisco, 1972.

Herrmann, Robert O.: "Consumerism: Its Goals, Organizations and Future," *Journal of Marketing,* October, 1970.

McCarry, Charles: *Citizen Nader,* Saturday Review Press, New York, 1972.

Mintz, Morton, and Jerry S. Cohen: *America, Inc.,* The Dial Press, Inc., New York, 1972.

Morris, Ruby Turner: *Consumers Union,* Litfield Publications, New London, Conn., 1971.

——— and C. S. Bronson: "The Chaos of Competition Indicated by Consumer Reports," *Journal of Marketing,* July, 1969, pp. 26–34.

"The Passion That Rules Ralph Nader," *Fortune,* May, 1971, pp. 144–147, 219-220, 224, 226, 228.

Schrag, Philip E.: "Consumer Rights," *Columbia Forum,* Summer, 1970.

Scitovsky, Tibor: *Welfare and Competition,* rev. ed., Richard D. Irwin, Inc., Homewood, Ill., 1971.

Warne, Colston: "The Impact of Consumerism on the Market," *The San Diego Law Review,* February, 1971.

CHAPTER 16

CHAPTER 16
CONSUMER PROTECTION: THE FEDERAL GOVERNMENT AND THE CONSUMER

Government agencies seldom create anything that may rock the boat.

A deputy commissioner of the Food and Drug Administration, John L. Harvey, said in 1955: "It is abundantly evident that the complexities of modern civilization require a greater degree of protection to the consumer than is now available. Obviously, he is largely beyond self-protection."[1] Seven years later, in 1962, the late Senator Estes Kefauver told a group of consumer leaders in Washington, D.C., that "the consumer is the forgotten man in our governmental structure." In 1969, Representative Benjamin S. Rosenthal said: "Until the consumer interest is the primary motivation of a statutory agency of government . . . , the consumer will remain a second class citizen in the marketplace."

Protection of the consumer interest, in an era of technological revolution, cold war, strontium 90, subsidies, and recessions, continues to languish as a do-it-yourself program in many respects. In our democratic society, government at all levels inevitably succumbs to powerful lobbies seeking special privileges. Consequently, if consumers are to receive any protection, they must organize and become articulate in making their demands known. Unity of consumers, however, seems unlikely in the foreseeable future.

The main reason for this lack of unity is that consumption is a function common to all and peculiar to none. We are all consumers, but we think of ourselves first as workers, teachers, retailers, farmers, manufacturers, doctors, lawyers, and so on, and only secondarily and incidentally as consumers. Psychologically, community of interest with these primary income groups far overshadows the broader interests of being consumers. The primary-group interest comprises a vertical division of our economy. All members can unite to promote the interests of the group. On the other hand, since consumption is a function rather than a group, and comprises a horizontal division across an entire population, there are no group members to promote the interests of all concerned. It becomes apparent, then, that in our democratic society, where government responds to pressure groups, inarticulate consumers are at a distinct disadvantage. And lacking organization, consumers are largely at the mercy of effectively organized groups. On the other hand, consumers may have been losing battles, but they have not lost the war. Victor Hugo said: "There is one thing stronger than all the armies in the world and that is an idea whose time has come." Such an idea is consumerism.

REDRESSING THE BALANCE BETWEEN SELLER AND BUYER

Democratic government is powerless to act, for the most part, in the absence of expressed need. The consequence for consumers is that government action is inevitably tardy, sporadic, and ineffective.

Interest groups are organized primarily to improve the relative position of their members; they are not organized to improve the position of all members of society. The interest groups attempt to present their own special intents as being identical with the interests of the general public, but their behavior frequently indicates a pathetic ignorance of consumer welfare.

This is not entirely a criticism; freedom to organize and speak are guaran-

[1] *Food-Drug Consumption*, March, 1955.

teed by the United States Constitution. Prevalence of active groups is a barometer of social action. Recognition of antisocial behavior, however, is important to an understanding of consumer problems. It is also important to recognize this aspect of the problem if the unrepresented consumer is to survive the fierce conflict of interests.

Marketplace as regulator

As long as the marketplace was an adequate regulator and coordinator of economic activity, admittedly in the distant past, less need existed for government to act as protector of consumer interests against exploitation by producer interests. But as industrialization developed with its urbanization, consumer dependence on source of supply beyond their own control continued to increase rapidly. This increasing consumer dependence, in turn, has been responsible for partial public realization that the health of each individual is becoming inseparably bound up with the health of the entire community.

Today's market leaves consumers more defenseless

As merchandising and marketing practices grow progressively more complex, the unassisted consumer becomes progressively more defenseless. Consumer education is not even in the race with technological and marketing advancement. In fact, it appears that the consumer is becoming more confused and illiterate as a buyer in an increased ratio with modern business and marketing advancement.

What concerns the public

In 1968, the ORC Public Opinion Index report of the Opinion Research Corporation released a study that found seven Americans in 10 thought that present federal legislation was inadequate "to protect their health and safety." The majority also believed that "more federal laws are needed to give shoppers full value for their money."

Careful reading of current literature on major problems facing consumers indicates that drug safety, drug prices, and auto insurance rates are areas that need congressional investigation. There is also public support for more government investigation of packaging and labeling, auto safety, and car service and repair. There is strong support for federal action toward generic versus brand-name drugs. Other consumer areas that the public thinks need federal attention are these: manufacturers' warranties and guarantees, cigarette advertising, consumer credit, and tire safety, to mention a few.

Will consumerism go away?

E. B. Weiss, director of special merchandising service for Doyle Dane Bernbach, said in 1967: "Consumerism will not go away. To the contrary, it will gain momentum . . . either marketing will cooperate in providing the new standards . . . or politicians will go it alone."[2]

Henry Ford II put it this way in January, 1967: "The real question for businessmen is not how to stop the growth of government. To meet our nation's growing problems and aspirations, both government and business must expand their responsibilities and activities."[3] Elisha Gray II, chairman of the Council of Better Business Bureaus, said in 1972: "The blunt truth is that to a large degree government has been pushed into consumerism . . . by default . . . the default of business."

It would appear, then, that business may have to accept some new respon-

[2] E. B. Weiss, *A Critique of Consumerism,* Doyle Dane Bernback, Inc., New York, 1967, p. 8.
[3] Ibid., p. 9.

sibilities—and may have to formulate a new and more socially responsible and sophisticated philosophy of marketing.

Failure of education to help consumers

A traditional national respect for the "acquisitive spirit" has relegated intelligent consumption to a position of relative unimportance. In fact, there is much evidence to support the contention that extravagant spending is a badge of honor; conspicuous consumption—emulation of people of great wealth—is an indication of financial power and success. As a result, certain types of wastefulness have received social approval.

The attitude of consumers regarding intelligent consumption is, to a large extent, the product of our educational system, which, in turn, is largely a product of the traditional American pursuit for the highest material standard of living. Much of the responsibility for the retarded development of intelligent consumption must rest on our educational system, which is weighted in favor of the producer interest as against the consumer interest. In short, our system does a good job of teaching how to make money, not how to spend it intelligently.

The solutions to improving the consumption habits of people are not simple at all. The late President John F. Kennedy emphasized this in his special "consumer message" to Congress in 1962:

> The march of technology has increased the difficulties of the consumer along with his opportunities. . . . Rational choice between and among [products] would require the skills of the amateur electrician, mechanic, chemist, toxicologist, dietician, and mathematician. . . . Marketing is increasingly impersonal. Consumer choice is influenced by mass advertising utilizing highly developed arts of persuasion. The consumer typically cannot know whether drug preparations meet minimum standards of safety, quality, and efficacy. He usually does not know how much he pays for credit; whether one prepared food has more nutritional value than another; whether the performance of a product will in fact meet his needs; or whether the "large economy size" is really a bargain. Additional legislative and administrative action is required, however, if the Federal government is to meet its responsibility to consumers in the exercise of their rights. These rights include—

> 1. The right to safety. . . .
> 2. The right to be informed. . . .
> 3. The right to choose. . . .
> 4. The right to be heard—to be assured that consumer interests will receive full and sympathetic consideration in the formulation of Government policy, and fair and expeditious treatment in administrative tribunals.[4]

Failure of federal regulatory agencies to regulate

Back in 1872, Congress evidenced its first interest in consumer problems when it enacted a law to protect consumers from frauds involving the use of the United States mails. Since then, legislation and executive action in the name of consumer protection has produced a sprawling, uncoordinated maze of laws and agencies, frequently working at cross purposes and usually cursed by a too-little-too-late timidity. Thus, consumer interests have not been served.

[4] Message from the President of the United States Relative to Consumers' Protection and Interest Program, 87th Cong., 2d Sess., House of Representatives, Doc. no. 364, Washington, D.C., Mar. 15, 1962.

Tug-of-war between private interests and consumer interests

The regulatory agencies were set up by Congress under its power to regulate commerce in the public interest. But though many of their decisions (as, for instance, those of the Interstate Commerce Commission affecting railroad rates, the Federal Power Commission in setting gas rates, and the Federal Trade Commission in its decisions with respect to unfair business practices) are of direct concern to consumers, consumers are not regarded as an interested party. Even if consumers were allowed to appear in these cases, under existing circumstances they would not be in a position, generally speaking, to prepare and present significant data.

In actual practice, the regulatory agencies are preoccupied with settling conflicting claims among rival groups of producers. Thus, the Interstate Commerce Commission is caught in disputes between railroads and trucks, the Civil Aeronautics Board between large certificated carriers and the smaller airlines, the Federal Communications Commission between rival applicants for television and radio licenses, the Federal Power Commission between gas producers and public utility companies, and the Tariff Commission between companies that want tariff protection and those that do not.

One can go on almost indefinitely with such a roster of conflicting producer groups that are fighting to make their views prevail with the agencies of regulation. Is it surprising then that, amid this constant tug of war between contesting private interests, there is little room for the consumer to be heard? And, unlike these private pressure groups, which are well organized, highly disciplined in the art of exerting influence, and omnipresent when decisions are to be made, consumers are scattered, unorganized, and often unaware that decisions of vital import to their standard of life are being made. The initiative for action has been left increasingly to the companies that are being regulated. As the late Dr. Walton Hamilton, after a lifetime of study of these agencies, said in his last book:

> The result is that the commission on all its levels becomes busy, in fact over-busy, but largely with detailed problems of the moment, problems which have been raised by complaining parties. It has adequate legal authority to raise questions on its own motion, but amid all the bustle of everyday activity there is very little leisure in which to do it. The larger questions of holding the regulated industry to its function, of improving its capacity to serve the public, of looking to the hazards ahead and guarding against them, and of making of it a more effective instrument of the general welfare are neglected. Matters of policy get immersed in the quagmire of detail. The agency fails to direct the activities of the industry to public objectives, and the industry is left to effect for itself such structure and practices as serve its purpose.[5]

Private interests "close and cozy"

There have been some changes in a couple of the federal agencies since Hamilton wrote the above criticism in 1957. A few now have a consumer representative. In 1970 the Federal Trade Commission created a new Bureau of Competition (in charge of antitrust law enforcement) and a Bureau of Consumer Protection (in charge of enforcement of consumer-type statutes assigned to the FTC). However, it is very hard to change or overhaul a federal agency. In 1971,

[5] Walton Hamilton, *The Politics of Industry*, Alfred A. Knopf, Inc., New York, 1957, p. 155.

John Gardner, then Secretary of the U.S. Department of Health, Education, and Welfare (HEW), warned of how hard it would be to overhaul the federal bureaucracy. He said that "special interests" would try to block changes in the departments and told a congressional committee: "It took them [special interests] years to dig their particular tunnel into the public vault, and they don't want the vault moved."[6] Republican Senator Charles Percy, in 1972, put it this way: "Too often in the past agencies established as watchdogs for the public interest have become lapdogs for private interests."

A good illustration of the close and cozy relationships between business and federal agencies was brought to public attention by Ralph Nader's Health Research Group in 1972. In an eighteen-page report, the group accused the FDA of kicking around two medical officers who had offended the pharmaceutical industry by building "unassailable records of protecting the public from harmful drugs." The FDA was also charged with using the guise of a "reorganization" in the Bureau of Drugs to assign growing responsibilities to "outside consultants who are actively involved in research supported by the drug industry." The report also said the actions raise the "unresolved question" of whether the FDA protects "the public or the industries it regulates."[7]

One of the most interesting features of the Nader study of the FDA is the number of alleged incidents in which FDA officials, through a variety of strategems, lies, and pressures, have tried to quash scientific evidence that called their actions into question. If the incidents occurred as described—and some of them seem to be well documented—this report may well contain the most titillating material yet published on the hazards of being a scientist under the thumb of a public relations-conscious government agency.[8]

Public interest versus ultimate consumer interest

Although charged to act in the public interest, regulatory commissions can fulfill that obligation only if the public interest is defined with respect to each issue. But there are few opportunities and few effective spokesmen to define the public interest, and in the heat of controversy the general welfare is all too often overlooked. The major issue, then, is how to place the public welfare in the forefront of governmental regulatory activities. Without the balance wheel of concern for the general welfare, government by regulatory agencies tends to solve only short-term, shortsighted private struggles for privilege.

In most of the issues raised before government regulatory agencies, the interests of the ultimate consumer have been those most consistent with the general welfare. In many countries, notably Great Britain and Sweden, where governmental regulatory agencies have been subject to detailed investigations (the Final Report of the Committee on Consumer Protection, 1962, and Sweden's Cartel law), the public interest is specifically defined as the interest of the ultimate consumer.

As government by regulatory agencies has expanded, the necessity for an

[6] *The Wall Street Journal,* June 19, 1972. Special editorial prepared by Arlen J. Large.
[7] *The Washington Post,* Apr. 3, 1972, PA5 (CF).
[8] *Nader's Raiders on the FDA: Science and Scientists "Misused."*

increasing emphasis, within government, on the interests of the ultimate consumer has become urgent. The effective expression of the ultimate consumer's interest is now essential to the very functioning of government and to the economy.

Lee Loevinger, recently of the Federal Communications Commission, said it best:

> Unfortunately, the history of every regulatory agency in government is that it comes to represent industry or groups it's supposed to control. All of these agencies were fine when they were first set up, but before long, they became infiltrated by the regulatees and are now more or less run by and for them.

REPRESENTING THE CONSUMER INTEREST IN GOVERNMENT

A new approach to regulation: an affirmative declaration

Can the FTC play a dual role?

Federal agencies need more consumer input

To appreciate the inadequate and haphazard character of current consumer protection activities calls for (1) a brief review of existing programs at the federal level and (2) a look at new approaches to regulation.

The federal agencies having regulatory responsibilities in the consumer interest have a most difficult role—a dual role really. How can these agencies effectively keep consumers from making unwise purchasing decisions or from being misled, misinformed, or noninformed via information and protection and yet ensure that they will continue to obtain the benefits of the producing power of our abundant economy? The FTC, for example, is bound by law and custom to adhere to the philosophy of industrial freedom and the promotion of competition. In more recent years the FTC has, by law, been given certain responsibilities to protect the consumer interest. Can it successfully play such a dual role? This difficult dual role also applies to most of our regulatory agencies.

In some of our federal agencies, notably the FTC and the FDA, efforts are being made to obtain more responsible consumer input to assist the agencies in their efforts to improve consumer protection. There is a great desire for response from consumers. The agencies want to know what we think about, say, nutrient labeling. They are aware, as we are aware, of the cost of implementing the growing number of consumer protection programs, and so they are groping for new solutions, as Helen Nelson, director of the Center for Consumer Affairs, University of Wisconsin Extension, pointed out in 1972.[9]

Some of the federal agencies, especially the FTC and the FDA, appear to be moving toward requiring an affirmative declaration. We are accustomed to saying that "anything goes" as long as the seller doesn't do this or that. There is some thinking in Washington now about turning this around and telling the seller that he *must* do this and this—that he must, for example, give the consumer certain information to enable him to make a *value* judgment. A good illustration is the nutrient labeling program proposed by the FDA in 1973. The agency is hopeful of being able to tell food manufacturers that the labeling on a box of frozen spinach soufflé, for example, must indicate the protein content, the number of calories per serving, and the amounts of Vitamin A, Vitamin

---

[9]"Consumer Education and Political Action: Allies or Opponents?" annual meeting of the American Council on Consumer Interests, Dallas, Apr. 14, 1972.

C, iron, calcium, and so forth, that the product contains. In other words, the manufacturer must make an affirmative declaration of the nutrients that the product provides.

This is a new approach. We have affirmative declaration in the case of light bulbs, which was the FTC's first move in this direction. Then the FTC said, "All right, now let's try it for gasoline. We'll require that the octane rating be posted on the service station pump." And they issued a regulation to that effect. The oil companies apparently felt that this would give consumers an edge in that they could buy gasoline in a more informed manner, so they went to court to prevent us from making these better purchasing decisions. A lower court supported the oil companies. The case may go all the way to the U.S. Supreme Court, where the issue will be whether the FTC in its role as arbiter of competition in the marketplace has the authority to require oil companies to give consumers information about the octane ratings of gasoline.

Now the FTC is anxious to see whether consumers will support more affirmative declarations and on which products. We should be ready to advise the FTC on what sort of information will be of the greatest value to us as consumers.

Consumers are beginning, slowly, to say: "Give me the information and let me decide for myself. Enough of 'protecting' me and not telling me anything about the product or the service." And from the regulatory agency's point of view, the beautiful advantage of this approach is that the consumer can help enforce it.

It is possible that the final order for nutrient labeling of foods may be watered down by pressures from lobbyists for the canning industry to secure lengthy delays in its implementation. In any case, consumers should continue to support the new affirmative-declaration approach by federal agencies as an alternative to the slow, cumbersome process of amending the powers of a federal agency through legislation.

A new approach to regulation: publicity—tell it like it is

There is no substitute for facts

Dr. Herbert S. Denenberg, Insurance Commissioner of Pennsylvania and formerly professor of insurance at the University of Pennsylvania's Wharton School of Finance and Commerce, has again proved that it is possible for a government agency to regulate—in this case, the life insurance industry—by publishing facts and figures in addition to holding administrative hearings. He was unable to obtain legislative reform from the state legislature, and so he had the courage to take consumer protection out of the hands of government alone and restore it to its logical repository—the consumer and his marketplace. The result was that the Pennsylvania Insurance Department, operating on a shoestring, has been transformed into one of the biggest bargains in the consumer's budget.

Bargains are not easy to find in government agencies. In fact, Denenberg says, "Government might be called the 'number one consumer fraud' in terms of its failure to deliver."[10] He characterizes the relationship between the regulators and those they regulate as "close and cozy." Their personnel are "interchangeable." A young lawyer looks on a brief stint in government regulations as an internship for a lucrative career in industry. Denenberg says that "about twenty insurance commissioners now in office have previous employment rec-

[10]"A New Approach to Regulation," *The Progressive*, December, 1972, pp. 17–19.

ords with the insurance industry, and former commissioners line the executive suites of insurance companies. All too often the public's concerns go unrepresented."

It is a well-known fact that there are many obstacles to obtaining new legislation from Congress, and often such an undertaking is hopeless. A case in point right now is the Hart-Magnuson no-fault auto insurance bill, which was sent back to the Senate Judiciary Committee to lie quietly dormant for the time being. A well-organized lobby can kill a bill even though the vast majority of consumer groups support it. A few thousand trial lawyers who thrive on auto accident cases have more influence than millions of people.

Denenberg has proved by his own success that the most effective way to overcome the veto power of special-interest groups is through intense citizen pressure developed by campaigns that educate the public and mobilize public opinion. For example, in the case of the no-fault bill in Pennsylvania, Denenberg's Insurance Department overcame the powerful trial lawyer's power by a *That is what democratic* hard-hitting public education campaign. Reams of material flooded to the mass *government is all about* media with facts in the form of shoppers' guides to no-fault. Their question-and-answer pamphlets were widely circulated by the 1½-million-member Pennsylvania AFL-CIO.

Pennsylvania's *Shopper's Guide to Life Insurance* generated enough pressure for billion-dollar premium reductions. The high-cost insurance companies listed by name in the *Guide* were under "unbelievable pressure" from the public, their agents and brokers, security analysts, and others. Almost immediately after the release of the *Guide* list, the lowest-cost companies, most of them smaller companies, began to publicize the results and gained an advantage in sales. Within four months, the *Guide* had had a remarkable policing effect. Nine of the ten gimmick life insurance policies which were confusing to consumers and difficult to compare with standard policies in measuring premium costs were withdrawn from the market.

Denenberg said, "If we had to get special legislation to eliminate gimmick *All this for one thin dime* policies, it would take years. If we tried to attack these policies in the courts, it would take a platoon of lawyers and years of litigation." He said, "We did it all with a little booklet that costs about ten cents apiece to print."[11]

One man can make a As with Ralph Nader, one man *can* make a difference when he is armed with *difference* the facts and is able to get these facts distributed in the mass media and by other organizations that care enough. That is what democratic government is all about.

A new approach to The consumer's plight is not the result of a lack of federal agencies. Con-
regulation: appropriate gressman Benjamin Rosenthal has pointed out that "there are approximately
actions and more 50 federal agencies and bureaus performing some 200 or 300 functions affecting
efficiency the consumer."[12] Thus it cannot be said that the consumer has been left at the mercy of malevolent producers.

Among the federal agencies directly concerned with consumer affairs, for example, are the following: the Federal Trade Commission, the Consumer and Marketing Service (Department of Agriculture), the Federal Communications

[11] Ibid., p. 19.
[12] *Hearings on S. 1177 and H.R. 10835*, p. 19.

Commission, the Federal Housing Administration, the Federal Power Commission, the Food and Drug Administration, the Interstate Commerce Commission, the National Bureau of Standards, the National Commission on Consumer Finance, the National Highway Safety Bureau, the National Transportation and Safety Board, the Office of Consumer Services, the President's Committee on Consumer Interests, and the Securities and Exchange Commission. Indeed, the history of consumerism—consumerism has, after all, been a recurrent theme in American politics for years—is a history of the growth of a large state and a federal bureaucracy.

Recent studies of federal regulatory agencies indicate that there are about three recurring ingredients on the failure side of the performance of agencies:

1. Too many bureaucrats tend not to work a full day or to be as productive as they might be. [13]

2. Appointments to high positions and subsequent policy decisions are all too often based on partisan political considerations rather than the public interest. One of the Nader reports indicates that appointments to the Interstate Commerce Commission (ICC) are generally political plums. [14] It was also charged that the location of an FTC office—in Oak Ridge, Tennessee—was chosen solely for political reasons. [15]

3. Over a given time an agency tends to respond most favorably to the organized interests which put the most resources into influencing it. The interest of a single consumer or a few consumer organizations is small as a rule. Producers are better organized and in a position to put effective pressure on the agency. Agencies are all too often "captured" by the very interests they are supposed to regulate. [16] In 1972, for example, a court ruling supported a charge long made by critics of the FDA—that it "has been more protective of the drug industry than of the public." [17]

The usual suggested cures offered by consumer advocates are these:

1. Better people must be appointed to responsible positions in federal agencies.

2. An unsafe product should be taken off the market without regard to its potential benefit.

3. The marketing of products which fail to meet particular quality standards should be outlawed.

4. Advertising which would cause the amount of advertising to decline sharply should be restricted.

5. The force of government should be put behind an independent agency, empowering it to intervene in the proceedings of most of the other agencies.

[13] Edward F. Cox, Robert C. Fellmeth, and John E. Schulz, *The Nader Report on the Federal Trade Commission,* Richard W. Baron, New York, 1969, p. 148.

[14] Robert C. Fellmeth, *The Interstate Commerce Commission,* Grossman Publishers, Inc., New York, 1970, pp. 1–4.

[15] Cox et al., op. cit., pp. 137–139.

[16] Fellmeth, op. cit., pp. 15–22.

[17] *The Washington Post,* Aug. 26, 1972, p. A15.

There are, no doubt, merits in the above suggestions. E. Scott Maynes, of the Center for Economic Research, Department of Economics, University of Minnesota, suggests another approach in a discussion paper.[18] Maynes says that at least two steps are involved in using government regulation effectively: (1) using appropriate rules or corrective actions and (2) allocating enough resources (money, able people, etc.) to assure that the rules are enforced and the corrective actions carried out.

The key question in the "appropriateness problem," Maynes says, is whether the proposed actions will achieve the desired end. The obvious corrective measure may *not* yield the desired end. Maybe there are alternative means.

If the appropriateness question is solved for a particular policy, the second step, the efficiency problem, must be faced by the agency: What amount of resources is required to see that the corrective actions are carried out with some acceptable level of success?

In general, Maynes feels that federal regulation will be more efficient when:

1. The number of units to be regulated is smaller.
2. The number of actions to be monitored is smaller. It is easier for the Price Board and the Wage Board to check prices and wages of a small number of important firms than to check those of all producers.
3. The action being regulated is fairly simple. It will be easier, and hence more efficient, for an agency to check a given set of safety features in new cars than to check on the accuracy of public utility rates which yield a "reasonable rate of return" on investment.
4. The agency is smaller. The larger the government agency, the more it will suffer from all the classical defects of bureaucracies.
5. The agency is younger. The older the government agency, the more set in its administration it becomes.
6. The agency is independently and adequately financed. Agencies depending only on legislative appropriations are commonly vulnerable to "starvation," preventing them from functioning effectively and efficiently.
7. The agency is armed with meaningful enforcement powers. A $5,000 fine to a giant corporation found guilty of monopoly is only a tap on the wrist. A fine plus two or three years in prison for top officers is something else.

While this list may be incomplete, it does help citizens, legislators, and congressmen to form better judgments regarding the best form of government regulation for particular purposes.

In the light of these seven proposals for improving the effectiveness of federal agencies in carrying out their regulatory responsibilities in the consumer interest, let's examine three agencies that assume large responsibilities in the consumer interest—the Federal Communications Commission (FCC), the Food and Drug Administration (FDA), and the Federal Trade Commission (FTC).

---

[18] This paper may appear in Eleanor B. Sheldon (ed.), *Understanding Family Consumption*, J. B. Lippincott Company, Philadelphia, 1973. Parts are reproduced with the permission of the author.

A look at three federal
agencies

Although there are about thirty-nine federal agencies and departments having some responsibility in protecting the consumer interest, we shall center our attention on three federal agencies—the Federal Communications Commission, the Federal Trade Commission, and the Food and Drug Administration. The FDA is probably the most consumer-oriented agency in the federal government today and as such deserves more of our attention.

The Federal Communications Commission (FCC)

During the last half century, producer groups have captured American radio and television. Modern communication is harnessed to sales objectives primarily. From the look of TV schedules, one would hardly guess that the broadcasting industry and its regulator, the FCC, are undergoing as far-reaching a public reexamination as any since the revelations a decade ago of rigged quiz shows, payola, and faked commercials.

Congress passed the Communications Act of 1934 establishing the Federal Communications Commission. The concept called for a nationwide system of locally based stations to ensure that broadcasting would be attentive to the specific needs and interests of each community and that local groups and leaders would be guaranteed an adequate opportunity for expression of diverse and even antagonistic viewpoints. FCC was given the sole power to issue broadcasting licenses, but Congress decreed that each license should automatically expire after three years. It also instructed the FCC to "prescribe the nature of the service to be rendered" by each station "as public convenience, interest or necessity requires."

In 1965, not one of the forty very-high-frequency television stations (channels 2 through 13) licensed in the nation's ten largest metropolitan areas was independently owned: thirty-seven belonged to firms with other TV-station holdings, and the other three belonged to newspapers. This situation was unchanged in 1973.

FCC in trouble

The FCC is in trouble today because of its long and implacable neglect of duty. The Senate has held hearings. A House group is proposing to legislate better programming. A blistering attack on the FCC majority has come from two of its commissioners, Cox and Johnson, while a third commissioner, Bartley, would split the FCC into three agencies. The Antitrust Division of the Justice Department is proposing that the FCC deny license renewals to any station owner who owns another station or a daily newspaper.

The view of the present majority of the FCC is expressed by a former commissioner, who said when the American people do not like what they see or hear, "they can and they do turn it off." Too often, however, it is not a choice between one program and another but a choice among a number of poor programs and none at all.

The consumer stake

Consumers have a far larger financial stake in broadcasting than does any private segment of the industry. They have spent an aggregate of more than $20 billion for their radio and TV sets, plus about $3 billion for antennas. They spend more than $1.25 billion a year for maintenance and repairs. Consumers also pay for advertising that in turn pays all broadcasting costs. In 1972 close to $6 billion in radio and TV advertising revenues was built into the price of sponsors' goods and services.

The FCC's mail had grown from 8,000 expressions of public opinion in 1961 to 67,700 in 1967. It appears that half of these letters were complaints about program content or advertising.

TV and the radio code: Matters of "leadership and conscience" on the publicly owned but privately occupied commercial airwaves fall under the purview of the Television and Radio Code Boards of the National Association of Broadcasters. The code loftily says, "Material which is excessively violent or would create morbid suspense, or other undesirable reactions in children, should be avoided." But *Consumer Reports* for October, 1968, quotes a report which appeared in *The Christian Science Monitor* six weeks after the murder of Senator Robert F. Kennedy which counted 372 acts of violence or threats of violence portrayed on the three television networks during a week of prime-time evening and Saturday morning shows. Some stations subscribe to the code without living by it, and others—37 percent of all television stations—find it so restrictive that they do not even subscribe to it.

A public opinion survey done for the National Association of Broadcasters reveals the stunning fact that more people find commercials annoying than amusing. Many people polled also believe the government sets rules for sex and violence and for the number of commercials permitted. The government does not, though it could. (Starting September 15, 1968, the television industry's code had authorized four commercials in a row instead of three during programs, and three instead of two during station breaks.)

License review: The entire ritual of license review is a sham, according to FCC Commissioners Cox and Johnson. Programming deficiencies—even the most flagrant indifference to the local-service obligations imposed by the Communications Act—raise no eyebrows. In 1966 a United States Court of Appeals decision stated that: "After nearly five decades of operation the broadcast industry does not seem to have grasped the simple fact that a broadcast license is a public trust subject to termination for breach of duty."

In dissenting from FCC approval of a new FM station in 1967, FCC Commissioners Cox and Johnson pointed out that the station owner frankly proposed to devote up to thirty-three minutes per hour to commercials. They sent questionnaires to fifty-one stations applying for license renewals and found that only 10 percent of the commercial TV stations devoted as much as two hours a week to local affairs. Ten percent carried between one and two hours, 60 percent devoted less than one hour, and 20 percent carried no local public affairs at all.

Intervention by other means: Intervention by other agencies of government or by private citizens has accomplished what the FCC should be doing on its own. The Justice Department intervened to challenge the merger, under the antitrust laws, of the American Broadcasting Company and the International Telephone and Telegraph Company. Private citizens in Chicago stopped, temporarily at least, the FCC-approved sale of WFMT-FM Chicago to a subsidiary of the *Chicago Tribune,* which already owns other Chicago TV and radio outlets.

In 1959 Consumers Union submitted a thirteen-point proposal to the FCC designed to make it more responsive to the public interest. At the head of the list was the establishment of a Television and Radio Consumers Council with full power (1) to review all commission licensing decisions; (2) to request, if necessary, additional data on a licensee's performance; and (3) to publicize its findings. Consumers Union's proposals, if accepted, would go far in making television and radio more responsive to the public interest.

Cigarette advertising: On February 5, 1969, the FCC said that the evidence of a link between cigarette smoking and lung cancer, as well as other diseases, was so overwhelming that it had no choice but to rule cigarette advertising off the airwaves, under its legal responsibility to regulate broadcasting "in the public interest, convenience and necessity." This was probably the most courageous act in the history of the FCC.

The FCC doesn't plan to force radio or TV to carry counteradvertising, but it may add a proviso involving the finding that broadcasters have an affirmative responsibility to carry at least some consumer education programming. This anticonsumer attitude, announced on December 12, 1972, will no doubt be challenged. Counteradvertising simply is a public way of expressing the firm's regret for running an ad that the FTC charged was misleading.

Federal Trade Commission (FTC)

At the very top of the FTC pyramid, the commission is composed of five members, appointed by the President and confirmed by the Senate for terms of seven years. The President also appoints the chairman.

The official manual of the FTC assigns the responsibility for controls over false and misleading advertising to the Bureau of Deceptive Practices. The FTC's well-publicized activities in the control of false and misleading advertising have led many elements of the general public to overlook the fact that the commission was originally created to combat concentrations of excessive economic power accumulated by trusts and monopolies before and around the turn of the twentieth century. The FTC received wide authority to investigate "unfair methods of competition in commerce."

Dual responsibilities: Over the years the FTC has had to work out overlapping and duplication of its activities with those of other federal agencies such as the Food and Drug Administration with respect to misleading advertising of foods or proprietary drugs, the Post Office Department in the matter of lotteries and frauds via the mail, and the Federal Communications Commission in regard to obscene, profane, and fraudulent or deceptive advertising.

New consumer powers: New and potent powers were given the FTC. The commission can now center its attention on the direct protection of the consumer, whereas formerly it could protect him only indirectly through the protection of the competitor. The Wheeler-Lee amendment also gave the FTC authority to proceed against false advertising of "foods, drugs, cosmetics and devices by United States mails, or in interstate commerce by any means." Also, "criminal proceedings" may be instituted when intentional efforts to defraud or mislead are made in connection with a product which is injurious to health. Finally, in *all* cases of alleged deception or misleading advertising, an FTC order to "cease and desist" becomes final if no judicial appeal is made within sixty days.

The FTC tries to educate business with sets of "basic ground rules" aimed at seeking voluntary compliance. The FTC effort at voluntary compliance centers around its *Trade Practice Conference Industry Guides, Advisory Opinions,* and *Trade Regulation Conference Rules* for more than 160 industries, and it has published eleven sets of *Advertising Guides.*

Ralph Nader recommends: Early in 1969, a 185-page report by Ralph Nader and investigators recommended a thorough overhaul of the agency's policies, practices, and staff. Among the findings and recommendations are these:

1. The Commission "fails woefully to enforce its laws properly. It relies too heavily, nearly exclusively, on voluntary non-binding enforcement tools. These cannot be expected to work at all unless backed up by stricter coercive measures, which are almost completely lacking now."

2. The "methods of becoming aware of consumer problems are woefully inadequate. It relies almost exclusively on letters of complaint from the public to detect possible violations of its laws, yet cannot obtain monetary satisfaction for injured individuals." This causes it to "proceed in purely random fashion."

3. There is a preoccupation with the trivial while ignoring large-scale deception by big firms, particularly the ones that advertise heavily on television.

4. There is too much secrecy about what it is doing.

5. The Chairman (Paul Rand Dixon) ought to resign because he allegedly has "institutionalized mediocrity, rationalized a theory of . . . inaction, delay and secrecy, and transformed the agency into the Government's Better Business Bureau." (Dixon did resign shortly after Mr. Nixon became President.)

6. A "limited number of engineers, doctors and product experts" should be employed, and office procedures should be modernized.

7. Congressional committees "should undertake a full-scale study" of the FTC.

Coincidentally, the FTC issued a report that illustrated some of the points brought out in the Nader report. The FTC report on supermarket games of chance, for example, has been in the works for more than two years. Despite ample evidence for prosecution, the FTC decided to lick the problem by only issuing trade regulation rules. One rule proposed by the FTC to clean up the practices would be to prohibit rigging of games and misrepresenting the chances of winning. Another rule was aimed at gasoline games. This rule would prohibit oil companies from pressuring retailers to participate in the games.

In short, the Nader report says that the FTC, with the most responsibility to protect consumers from unfair and deceptive selling practices, is wasting much effort on trivial matters, giving the impression that it is vigorously policing the marketplace while actually letting the biggest culprits get away with unfair and illegal activities. The American consumer, continues the Nader report, is not getting the protection he needs or thinks he is getting.

Changes in the FTC since 1969

Changes began to appear in 1969 after an American Bar Association panel studied the comatose agency at the request of President Nixon. The group confirmed reports by critics of the FTC (notably Ralph Nader's "raiders") and recommended some strong medicine for revitalizing it. The agency perked up under Caspar Weinberger, who was named chairman in 1970, and the work he started has been continued by the present chairman, Miles Kirkpatrick, who headed the ABA study group.

The ABA study

Operating bureaus were cut from four to two—the Bureau of Competition, which handles antitrust cases, and the Bureau of Consumer Protection, headed by Robert Pitofsky, who was counsel for the ABA panel. He is only one of many zealous staff people brought in to help revitalize the agency. Others work under him as heads of divisions involved with consumer credit, national advertising, and industry rules and guides.

The commission also created a new type of staff position, the consumer protection specialist, and sent over one hundred of these "paralegal" specialists to work in teams with attorneys in the FTC's eleven regional offices. They do investigative work previously handled by attorneys, check business practices, and maintain contact with other consumer enforcement agencies and consumer groups.

Stronger regional offices

The revamping extends to the regional offices, which were given new authority to investigate problems in their areas, hold public hearings, and argue their own cases before FTC hearing examiners.

In the past year or so, for example, the Cleveland and New York regional offices have held hearings on consumer problems of poor people, deceptive practices by auto dealers, and unfair credit collection practices.

But roadblocks remain. The FTC faces rough going with one rule, and, depending on the final outcome of a court case, the commission could be seriously hampered in the future. The case, mentioned earlier, began in 1971 after the agency announced a rule that would have forced oil companies to post octane ratings on gas pumps. The FTC estimates that the average motorist spends from $50 to $75 extra a year on high-octane gas that he doesn't need.

The suit brought by thirty-four oil companies and two trade associations blocked enforcement of the rule and challenged the right of the FTC to issue trade rules at all. The U.S. District Court in Washington, D.C., recently ruled that the FTC cannot force the companies to post octane ratings because it doesn't have statutory authority to issue trade regulation rules. The commission is appealing the decision.

The FTC needs more authority

In an earlier case, however, the U.S. Supreme Court held that the FTC has broad powers to stop unfair practices. It's not clear whether this would apply to its rule-making authority. In any event, the oil companies' action shows how the FTC can be stalled.

Also highly troublesome are the procedures the FTC has to operate under.

If a company has a proposed complaint announced against it, time is on its side because in most instances the FTC doesn't have authority to seek temporary injunctions to stop misleading practices.

A company accused of deception can try to work out a settlement with the FTC staff, but if it doesn't like a proposed settlement, it can take the case to an FTC hearing examiner; if it doesn't like the examiner's decision, it can ask the five FTC commissioners to review the case. Finally, if the commissioners stand by the decision, the company can take the case to court, where it might drag on for years.

FTC staff people argue that if the commission had greater power to seek temporary injunctions, companies would settle cases more swiftly. In 1971 the Senate passed a bill, which the House is now considering, that would give the commission such power and also give it the right to initiate court suits that could result in various penalties for unfair or deceptive practices. The legislation would also clarify the FTC's rule-making authority.

Despite its "new look," the FTC still doesn't move very fast. Many of the trade regulations now awaiting final action by the commission were proposed a year or more ago. The rule on cooling-off periods, for example, was first proposed in September, 1970. FTC lawyers say it may be five years before all the "experimental" approaches now being taken are tested all the way through the commission and the courts.

Moreover, the agency is small when viewed against the huge industries it's supposed to regulate. The consumer protection bureau has a staff of about three hundred attorneys, scientists, and consumer protection specialists. The budget for the whole agency is $25 million. This budget covers many duties, and policing advertising is only one of them. In a recent year, 100 companies alone spent close to $3½ billion for advertising in major media. The single largest national advertiser, Procter & Gamble, spent almost $190 million that year on major media ads—nearly eight times the FTC's total budget for fiscal 1972—plus some $75 million on all other advertising and sales promotion.

And there's always the possibility that more conservative commissioners could be named to the FTC. If that happened, it could mean the end of the FTC's "new look." In early 1973, President Nixon did show his hand. He wants a conservative FTC. This means that small business and consumers will be sacrificed, and big private interests will be favored.

The Food and Drug Administration

The protection of the ultimate consumer from the questionable and rapacious practices of producers is not a modern invention. In the precapitalistic feudal economy, the consumer was protected by guild regulations covering the size, weight, and quality of products.

During the era when the United States economy was largely agricultural, most consumers were fairly well protected by common law—recourse to the courts. But in the last quarter century or more, the legal protection provided by common law has been entirely inadequate. To try to meet these new conditions, due to the mass production and mass distribution revolution, a few states in the latter part of the nineteenth century attempted to protect consumers against abuses in the sale of food and drugs. In 1848, the first federal inspection action was taken on imported drugs, medicines, and related products. Later, importation of impure tea and adulterated food was stopped.

In the 1890s, attempts were made to authorize limited supervision by federal regulation of interstate sales of foods and drugs. This campaign was led by Dr. Harvey W. Wiley, of the Bureau of Chemistry in the Department of Agriculture, in 1890.

Pure Food and Drug Act of 1906: In 1906, the Pure Food and Drug Act was passed by Congress. It took Upton Sinclair's *The Jungle* (a novel about the unsanitary conditions in the Chicago meat-packing plants) and the exposé of political and economic corruption by the muckrakers in the family magazines, notably *McClure's,* to get the average citizen stirred up sufficiently to overcome the influence of business in Congress against food and drug regulations.

The Pure Food and Drug Act of 1906 had several weaknesses that began to appear as time went on. For one thing, women began to use cosmetics in the "roaring twenties." The cosmetic trade, quite untouched by moral and safety principles, had scores of cases of poisoning in the 1920s, caused by hair dyes, face bleaches, face creams, rouges, powder, and hair tonics.[19] In 1937, in *The American Chamber of Horrors,* Ruth de Forest Lamb described the cosmetic industry in detail. Thus the public was made aware of the need to have federal regulation of the cosmetic industry.

Another weakness in the original act was its failure to regulate advertising as well as labeling. The truth, even if presented on labels, could be and was misrepresented in false and misleading advertising. With the advent of radio and television, this problem became acute.

Federal Food, Drug, and Cosmetic Act: A third weakness in the 1906 act was the failure to provide for the safety of drugs and medical preparations for human use before making them available to the public. In 1936, the public became aware of this weakness when seventy-three persons died from the use of a patent medicine, Elixir Sulfanilamide. So in 1938, the 1906 act was amended to include the federal regulation of cosmetics and to prohibit the sale of drugs and medicines until they had been proved safe for human consumption. The effort to include the regulation of false and misleading advertising under the Food and Drug Administration was defeated, but the Wheeler-Lea Act provided for regulation of untruthful advertising in another federal regulatory agency, the Federal Trade Commission.

By the early 1940s, the great increase in the use of chemical food additives led to the demand for protection from dangerous chemicals in food. The FDA did not have authority to prevent their use unless it was first demonstrated beyond a reasonable doubt that the chemical additives were dangerous to human beings. Finally, in 1958, this was corrected. Chemicals in the form of food additives must now be proved harmless to human beings before they can be used in food as preservatives or emulsifiers.

Drug Amendments of 1962: On October 10, 1962, the Drug Amendments of 1962, overhauling and strengthening the drug provisions of the Federal Food,

[19] Stuart Chase and F. J. Schlink, *Your Money's Worth,* The Macmillan Company, New York, 1927, p. 22.

Drug, and Cosmetic Act, became law. The amendments deal mainly with drugs sold only on prescription and with "new drugs." A new drug is one that is not generally recognized by qualified experts as safe and effective for the uses recommended in its labeling.

Here are some of the major changes in the law:

1.   Before the new amendments, only safety clearance of new drugs was required. Now there must be substantial evidence that any new drug is effective as well as safe before it can be approved for marketing.

2.   All manufacturers must now have adequate controls—test procedures and checks—with trained personnel and proper facilities, to assure the reliability of drugs. Absence of such controls will of itself violate the law, without the necessity for proving that a particular shipment of the drug was defective.

3.   Previously cleared drugs may be ordered off the market immediately if new information indicates an imminent hazard to health. And any prior approval may be withdrawn, after a hearing accorded to the manufacturer, in any case where tests or experience show that the drug is not safe or will not be effective for its intended uses.

4.   The FDA is given 180 days instead of 60 days to consider a request for safety clearance of a new drug, and the new drug cannot be marketed without FDA approval.

5.   Manufacturers are required to report promptly to the FDA on experience with new drugs, including any adverse effects they learn about after the new drug goes on the market. This also applies to previously cleared new drugs and antibiotics.

6.   A firm legal basis is provided for regulations to prevent testing of drugs on humans unless and until specified safety conditions, including thorough animal testing, are met.

7.   Manufacturers are required to get assurance that the patient's consent will be obtained if experimental drugs are to be used, unless this is not feasible or unless the investigator believes that obtaining such consent would be contrary to the patient's best interest.

8.   All drug producers must register annually with the FDA, even if their output does not actually move in interstate commerce.

9.   The FDA is directed to inspect each registered establishment at least once every 2 years.

10.   The scope of authority for inspection of manufacturers of prescription drugs is broadened to include legal access to pertinent records, files, papers, processes, controls, and facilities.

11.   Authority is provided for the federal government to establish an official name for a drug when this is desirable in the interest of usefulness and simplicity. Drug labels must bear the established name of the drug and, for prescription drugs, the quantity of each active ingredient.

12.   Prescription drug advertisements must include a brief summary of side effects, contraindications, and effectiveness, as well as the established name for the drug and the quantitative formula.

13.   The FDA batch testing and certification of safety and effectiveness is extended to all antibiotic drugs for humans. This adds some thirty groups

of antibiotic drugs and their derivatives to the five previously subject to this requirement. Manufacturers pay fees to cover the costs of the FDA tests.

Consumers have every reason to hail the Drug Amendments of 1962 as a major advance in the cause of safe, effective, and honestly promoted drugs.

A final set of drug control rules by the FDA included these requirements for drug manufacturers:

1. Prove to the satisfaction of the FDA that new drug products are effective as well as safe.

2. Adopt the "good manufacturing practice" guidelines of the FDA at all drug-production and drug-testing facilities.

3. Include in all advertising of branded drug products the drug's technical, or generic, name as well as brand name, and list any side effects it may have had on previous users.

The last requirement was hotly opposed by many drug firms. The FDA's purpose is to acquaint consumers with the generic term so that they can shop for drugs and get the lowest price possible.

In recognition of the protests of drug companies, the final set of rules omits an earlier proposal that would have permitted the FDA to pass on certain advertising before it is used. Another change gives drug producers the right to demand a prompt ruling on the safety and effectiveness of a new drug if the FDA fails to clear it for use within the specified 180 days.

The Drug Abuse Control Amendment of 1965: There is widespread abuse and illegal traffic in depressant, stimulant, and hallucinogenic drugs. Lives are being shackled in chemical chains because the users do not recognize the potential dangers of these drugs. The users can become physically and emotionally dependent on these drugs, but the drugs do not yet have the social stigma that is usually associated with the use of narcotic drugs. The use of LSD has been openly and irresponsibly promoted for alleged mind-expanding effect. Experience has shown, however, that users of LSD may lose their capability to think clearly, to reason, and to create or otherwise use their minds productively. There may be other effects not known at this time.

These are some of the reasons why a federal amendment to the Food, Drug, and Cosmetic Act was passed in 1965. The amendment prohibits (1) the sale or disposition not covered by legal prescriptions; and (2) illegal possession for resale. The penalties are quite severe. The FDA has some two hundred specially trained investigators to carry out enforcement provisions of the law. [20]

Some current problems: The FDA faces a critical challenge in its effort to revamp federal drug marketing requirements to more fully assure that all versions of the same drug, regardless of trade name, are equally effective. The FDA also faces problems of high cost of drugs and stricter testing of antibiotic drugs:

1. *Efficacy of drugs.* In the 1962 amendments to the 1938 Food and Drug

[20] See *Fact Sheets*, 1 through 10, from the FDA Bureau of Drug Abuse Control.

Act, the FDA was instructed to ensure that all drugs sold to the public were effective as well as safe. But there are legal and scientific difficulties posed by the large number of drugs on the market. In the past the FDA relied largely on the evidence presented by the manufacturer. Furthermore, the FDA must end the sale or curtail claims for ineffective drugs originally marketed between 1938 and 1962. The removal of hundreds of drugs from the market is based on an exhaustive scientific review by nongovernment experts at the National Academy of Sciences of the usefulness of 2,900 drugs sold in as many as 17,400 different formulations. Some FDA officials estimate that about 290 drugs, sold in 1,740 different formulations, will be kept off the market. It will be up to the drug manufacturers, however, to prove that these drugs are effective and safe. An overly permissive approach by the FDA could allow ineffective products to remain on the market. In 1968, for example, the FDA conceded significant shortcomings in its certification procedures for antibiotic drugs which must be tested by the government before release to the market. The agency said it had received manufacturers' samples that were not adequately labeled or that reflected careless handling by the companies. Evidence of the shortcomings led to reassignment of three ranking members of FDA's division of antibiotics and insulin certification, which handles this activity, according to a *Wall Street Journal* story. The FDA also issued a letter to 250 makers prescribing stricter standards which must be followed in submitting antibiotic samples to FDA for testing.

2. *Drug prices.* In Chapter 11 we presented some of the evidence of excessive prices for some drugs on the market today. According to a special HEW "task force" study of the cost of drugs, which was presented to Secretary Cohen of the Health, Education, and Welfare Department in 1968, much of the blame for high cost of drugs was due to the lack of price competition. Our patent system gives patent owners exclusive rights for 17 years to manufacture or sell licenses for the patented product. In addition, the report says that profit margins are exceptionally high. The special "task force" thinks drug prices can be substantially reduced by shortening the legal life of a patent and by compulsory licensing of other manufacturers in exchange for royalties after a specified number of years. The United States and Belgium are alone, among industrial nations, in not specifying some forms of compulsory licensing of drug patents. [21]

Strengthening the FDA: Consumer leaders generally agree that the FDA, over the years, has been the most consumer-minded agency or commission in the federal government. Consequently, the report on the Food and Drug Administration by the Citizens Advisory Committee, October, 1962, under the chairmanship of Dr. George Y. Harvey of the University of Missouri, should be studied carefully. This hard-hitting and industry-oriented committee report evoked reaction among agency officials ranging from a "wait and see" attitude to frank statements that the report was "naive and unrealistic." [22] The committee, however, believes that the FDA will be strengthened by carrying out the following recommendations:

[21] *Report of the Task Force on Prescription Drugs,* U.S. Department of Health, Education, and Welfare, 1968.

[22] According to *Drug Trade News,* Nov. 12, 1962.

1.   Substitute "preventive policy" in place of "after-the-fact" enforcement.
2.   A change in the role of the commissioner of the FDA, with a major change toward decentralization of decision making.
3.   Upgrading of the scientific program by setting up a Food and Drug Institute headed by a scientific director to attract better scientists and to result in improvement of analytical methods.
4.   Improve FDA-industry relationships.
5.   Establish a National Advisory Council to the commissioner, appointed by the Secretary of Health, Education, and Welfare, authorized to make annual reports to the Secretary.
6.   Upgrade personnel and provide better training opportunities for the staff.
7.   Provide more effective program planning.
8.   Educational program should emphasize education of the consumer, of industry, and of the state food and drug agencies rather than publicize the FDA.
9.   Secure closer cooperation between the FDA and the Public Health Service and other governmental agencies.
10.   Develop FDA programs to strengthen the state laws and administrative agencies and to maximize consumer protection by coordinated harnessing of federal, state, and local regulatory programs.

More suggestions: Other suggestions to improve the FDA have been made recently. Dr. George Nichols, Jr., a Harvard University medical professor, proposed that a central agency, jointly financed by the federal government and the pharmaceutical industry, should take over the testing of new drugs.[23] George S. Squibb, former vice president of E. R. Squibb & Sons, a drug manufacturer, claims that drug research by drug companies is often "poor, wasteful, extravagant, unproductive, unimaginative and pointless." Furthermore, he thinks that pharmacists should be permitted to substitute lower-price drugs of identical formula when a doctor prescribes a higher-price drug.[24] An intensified inspection of drug plants has been in the plans of the FDA, but funds have limited this important activity. Vincent A. Kleinfeld told the food, drug, and cosmetic division of the American Bar Association in 1967 that drug manufacturers should appoint a top lawyer as an Ombudsman to police drug firm ads. This watchdog could prevent drug firms from making false claims or breaking the law in their advertising and promotion activities.

Keep the FDA independent: Implementation of these recommendations could lead to improvement in the effectiveness of the FDA. It is possible, however, that the drug industry, with profit motives in mind, might acquire too much influence over FDA policies. Politicians, too, might acquire unhealthy influence over the organization. Many consumer leaders are much concerned about producer-oriented and politically administered federal agencies that have been organized, theoretically, to protect the public.

There are two basic reasons for keeping the FDA independent of political

[23] *The Washington Post,* Jan. 18, 1968, p. A26.
[24] *U.S. Consumer,* Dec. 17, 1967.

and industrial pressures. (1) The FDA is basically concerned with protecting consumer health and safety. (2) To the extent that the FDA—through its declarations of standards of quality and standards for fill of containers and its prohibition of mislabeling and misrepresentation—enables the consumer to become a better-informed buyer in the market, it meets one of the basic prerequisites of a free enterprise competitive economy and thus is of basic significance to all consumer citizens.

The Bureau of Product Safety

The Bureau of Product Safety (FDA) was established in 1970 for the purpose of effecting a reduction in the frequency and severity of injuries involving consumer products used in and around the home, and in recreational and institutional environments—more specifically, to administer the Federal Hazardous Substances Act, the Child Protection and Toy Safety Act, and portions of the Public Health Acts. Later, the Poison Prevention Packaging Act was also assigned to the bureau. Each year, in this country alone, an estimated thirty thousand people die as a result of 20 million accidents associated with the mechanical, electrical, and thermal properties of consumer products. However, until now, no country in the world has been able to describe the circumstances surrounding product-related injuries or to determine the frequency and severity of such injuries. The bureau's National Electronic Injury Surveillance System (NEISS) represents a key step in understanding product-related injuries.

Reducing product hazards

The importance of having accurate product injury information cannot be overemphasized. We must know and understand the problems before we can move toward intelligent solutions. As NEISS identifies the problems, the other units of the bureau swing into action. The three technical divisions—the Chemical Hazards Division, the Children's Hazards Division, and the Mechanical, Electrical, and Thermal Hazards Division—conduct technical analyses to identify and evaluate various ways of reducing product-related injuries. Laboratory tests are conducted, contracts for outside technical services are negotiated, and expertise in other government agencies is called upon. The end results are the establishment of test methods and standards designed to protect the consumer. Informational–educational programs are also developed, in conjunction with standard-setting programs, where these may contribute to consumer safety. The legal arm of the bureau, the Compliance Division, considers what enforcement action is necessary once standards have been established.

With the on-line, day-to-day operation of the innovative NEISS system an accomplished fact, the Bureau of Product Safety can move toward the reduction of consumer product injuries—using timely information to help solve and effectively prevent complex injury problems.

The FDA accommodates industry

In 1972, efforts were made to create an independent consumer product safety agency divorced from the interests of industry and having only the public as its constituency. The problem with the current FDA regulatory system is that it was established to accommodate the needs or wishes of industry and not those of the average citizen. As a case in point, the FDA has no authority to force food processors to report quality-control information, data which could alert authorities to the presence of unsafe food on the market. As yet, the FDA does not have the power to seek injunctions against the sale of items which violate standards. Injunction power is very important because it permits dangerous products to be taken off the market immediately; the courts can then settle the issue later.

The FTC, under this law, will ultimately remove flammable fabrics, garments, and carpets from its authority. The responsibility for fair practices in the labeling of wool, fur, and textiles will remain with the FTC.

Can the Bureau of Product Safety be independent within the FDA, a regulatory agency in the Department of Health, Education, and Welfare? The willingness of HEW Secretary Richardson to give regulatory authority to the administrator of a proposed new safety agency in all matters except those with "broader policy implications" opened the door for two Senate committees to recommend amendments to legislation to create an independent consumer product safety agency which would be incorporated into the HEW structure.

Time will tell whether HEW will:

Protecting people's "body rights"

1. Assure "virtual regulatory independence" by having the "administrator report directly to the HEW secretary" (Senator Charles Percy of Illinois).

2. Permit "independence of politically dictated timidity"; "openness" or an end to "secrecy" within the agency; an "end to White House dictated clearance of regulatory decisions"; or "end to political clearance for a safety regulatory job"; and the "right of citizens to have access to agency records and proceedings and through citizen suits" (Senator Magnuson of Washington).

3. Include a "fixed term of office for the agency head; his removal only for cause; permitting him to appoint those who will serve under him; flexibility of an absence of interference in his budget and legislative recommendations" (Senator Percy). [25]

A new approach—will it work?

Several other restrictions are written into the law, signed by President Nixon on October 28, 1972, that, it is hoped, will make the agency independent of political and industry pressures. [26]

OVERHAULING GOVERNMENT ISN'T EASY

In 1971 former HEW Secretary John Gardner warned how hard it would be to overhaul the federal bureaucracy. Special interests, he said, would block changes in departments. He told a congressional committee: "It took years to dig their particular tunnel into the public vault, and they don't want the vault moved."

Don't move the public vault!

It's all too true. Of President Nixon's plan to amalgamate seven old agencies into four new ones, only one section has made some headway. The new Department of Community Development should have been the easiest of the four to create, requiring only a new sign on the door of the Department of Housing and Urban Development. But the farther this bill progressed, the more it was beset by special-interest groups trying to preserve their pipelines—home builders, farmers, highway contractors, veterans, and so on.

Efforts are being made to take the FDA out of the Department of Health,

[25] *Of Consuming Interest,* May 10, 1972, pp. 2–3.

[26] *Consumer Newsweek,* Nov. 6, 1972 (whole four-page issue).

Education, and Welfare. One bill in Congress proposes that it be turned into an independent consumer agency. Many industry spokesmen take the position that the FDA is overcontrolling drugs and new foods. On the other side, consumer advocates are unhappy with filth tolerances in food factories and many other abuses. Reorganization supporters tend to identify with the thinking of government officials who distribute the cash and worry whether it's doing any good. Reorganization foes tend to sympathize with recipients of the government help.

While proposing to make the Federal Housing Administration (FHA) a part of a new department, the administration didn't dare touch the companion mortgage-guarantee program run by the Veterans Administration. The American Legion complained.

Moving the Department of Transportation to a new agency affects mass transit and highway construction. This thought set alarm bells clanging among many highway-related groups.

But the biggest ruckus came from the farmers. The administration proposed a "rip-off" of two Agriculture Administration subagencies, the Farm Home Administration and the Rural Electrification Administration. The complaints were thunderous in 1971 when Mr. Nixon suggested this as part of a bigger plan for abolishing the Agriculture Department entirely, a breathtaking idea that was soon dropped. Many consumer advocates would like to see the Meat and Poultry Inspection Service out of the USDA (which is generally more concerned with producers than with consumers). Many consumers say it should be placed within the FDA, which is already concerned with inspection of food plants and food products. In fact, many citizens think it would make more sense to take all the health-related activities of government and place them in a separate Department of Health. There will be, of course, opposition to that change, too.

Goals versus function

The federal government historically has been organized along functional lines according to which bureaucrats have assignments to do something: to test new drugs for safety and efficacy, for example.

Structuring bureaucracy toward goals may create superdepartments, but the hope is that more conflicts can be settled at lower planning levels by officials who care little about special constituencies.

Whatever the outcome in reorganizing federal agencies, the fact is that there will be changes in the federal bureaucracy. A case in point is the effort to place most of the consumer protection departments in one large agency—the functional approach.

CREATION OF A CONSUMER PROTECTION AGENCY

In late 1970, the Senate voted overwhelmingly in favor of a new consumer protection agency operating independently of other federal departments. The President would appoint the agency's director, but couldn't fire him because of a disagreement over policy or politics. The director would have to be confirmed by the Senate.

The Senate bill 1177 is much like the House bill 10835 with several exceptions: The administrator has the right to participate in informal, as well as formal, hearings in federal departments and agencies, and all federal agencies must give advance notice to the administrator of informal hearings. In addition, the administrator has the right to go to court to enforce his authority to intervene in informal proceedings. He also has independent discovery powers and may conduct his own investigations.

The issue of participation in informal hearings is one on which opinion is sharply divided. Consumer advocates argue that this right is a necessity for adequate consumer representation. The White House says that the requirement is "superfluous" and an "unmanageable burden." Consumer advocates and the White House also differ on the issues of enforcement powers and discovery powers. The former say that the administrator must have the right to go to court to enforce his authority to intervene in informal hearings and that independent discovery power is necessary. The latter would withhold the power to enforce and to make independent discovery investigations, adding that such discovery power would encourage "freewheeling investigations."

On November 14, 1971, the House passed bill 10835, which establishes a Consumer Protection Agency with an administrator and deputy administrator appointed by the President and confirmed by the Senate. It authorizes the agency to represent consumers in formal proceedings conducted in other federal agencies and provides for intervention as a part in any nonpunitive adjudicative proceeding. In punitive proceedings, it may participate as amicus curiae. The agency may also intervene in or institute a court review of a proceeding by another federal agency in which it has participated and, in certain instances, intervene in a situation in which it did not participate.

Agency's job   The agency's job will be to represent consumer interests in regulatory proceedings before other government agencies. If the Agriculture Department were reconsidering its rule on the fat content of hot dogs, for example, the Consumer Protection Agency presumably would argue officially for a low-fat product.

The administration also has proposed a consumer protection unit, but wants it lodged within the Justice Department. Consumer groups contend that this would make the unit vulnerable to political pressure from the White House.

Despite the Senate's decision to give the new agency independent status, the bill as passed was denounced as "unacceptable" by consumer advocate Ralph Nader, who watched most of the debate from the Senate gallery.

Nader's objections   Mr. Nader lamented the failure of a floor effort by Senator Hart (Democrat of Michigan) to take the new agency entirely out of the executive branch and give Congress a bigger say over its operating policies. Mr. Nader also complained that the bill "hamstrings" the new agency's ability to receive consumer complaints and release information about faulty products.

But if Senator Hart failed to liberalize the bill, even the most loyal administration backers made no serious effort to put the new consumer unit in the Justice Department, where President Nixon wants it. The legislation was a compromise product of two separate Senate committees, whose members vowed to resist any floor changes from either left or right. Arguing against any major amendments, Senator Cotton of New Hampshire, ranking Republican on the Senate Commerce Committee, said the bill as written is "reasonable, safe, and effective."

The Senate bill also upgrades the job presently held by Virginia Knauer, the

*Pressure groups killed
the bill with words
—filibuster*

President's Special Assistant for Consumer Affairs. Her office would be replaced by a statutory three-member council of consumer advisors, which would attempt to coordinate federal programs benefiting consumers.

The House Rules Committee, shortly before adjourning in December, 1972, submitted its bill for a vote on the floor, where it would have broad bipartisan support. The lengths to which special business interests went to block passage of the proposed consumer agency offered another example of the low position on the totem pole that is the lot of the consumer. Senator Charles Percy, Republican, a sponsor of the bill but certainly no foe of business, said he never had seen such intensive lobbying in Congress as was mounted by corporate forces opposed to giving the consumer a voice in the federal bureaucracy.[27]

In 1973, the consumer protection agency bill will come up in both the House and the Senate. A good consumer bill will give the agency full authority to intervene in all federal agency proceedings and activities that may affect consumers and in any court proceeding arising out of such agency action.

In looking for solutions to consumer problems, the individual must not be left out. Perhaps research could be turned toward new means for assuring a grievance channel between buyer and seller, between investigator and investigated, between serviceman and customer. Perhaps a mechanism could be developed that could assure a day in court—albeit a new and different kind of court—for the average customer who does not get his money's worth.

"There has been an empty chair for the consumer everywhere," Representative Benjamin Rosenthal of New York testified before a congressional committee last year. The time has come to fill that chair.

CIVIL JUSTICE FOR CONSUMERS: CLASS-ACTION SUITS

For a number of years, Congress has been conducting hearings and studies which document an immense amount of fraud, deception, and hazard arising out of market exchanges between manufacturers, retailers, and consumers. One can use the word "immense" even without accepting Senator Philip Hart's estimate that consumers spend approximately $200 billion in one year (out of about $750 billion) for which they receive no value. The annual cost of product-related injuries may exceed $5.5 billion.[28] This immense sum excludes about 59,000 deaths and 4½ million injuries resulting from motor vehicle accidents annually. At the time he signed the Product Safety Commission bill, President Nixon pointed out that 125,000 citizens are injured each year by faulty heating devices, 100,000 are hurt and maimed by faulty power mowers and faulty washing machines, 40,000 are gashed when they fall through glass doors, and 30,000 are shocked and burned by defective wall sockets and extension cords.[29] The issue here is that in most instances where industry is guilty of fraud and negli-

[27] Paper written by James C. Millstone for the Commission on a National Institute of Justice, which was established by the American Bar Association. *St. Louis Post-Dispatch,* Dec. 12, 1972.

[28] *Final Report of the National Commission on Product Safety,* Government Printing Office, Washington, June, 1970, p. 1.

[29] News release, Office of the White House Press Secretary, Nov. 20, 1967.

gence in that it markets faulty and dangerous consumer products, most consumers cannot afford to take the corporation into court, and justice is therefore denied. Our complex court system offers advantages to those commercial professionals who use it regularly and can achieve economies of scale, but it presents a forbidding front to *individual* consumers who have a grievance against a retailer or a corporation. Two proposals gaining increased attention could remedy this imbalance: consumer class actions and the creation of neighborhood arbitration tribunals.

Our courts: shocking imbalance

Vast portions of consumer fraud and hazard problems involve thousands of little claims in the $10 to $500 categories, and some up to $3,000. The reality of our court system is that it is structured by formidable price and time mechanisms that effectively shut out the large majority of consumer grievances from any prospect of consideration. The process is too expensive, too time-consuming, and too esoteric for self-help without a lawyer. Shocking imbalance, therefore, has been the shameful mark of injustice. The most significant development in the area of seeking justice for consumers with legitimate complaints is the rise of the class-action suit.

Class-action suits

In a class action, one consumer sues a retailer or a corporation to get a refund or a debt cancellation not only for himself but also for all other victims, who need not be identified until an advanced stage of the case, when they can be located through a search. Because only one case per fraud or injury involving use of a dangerous consumer product need be brought, rather than one case per victim, consumers achieve the economies of scale which the court system usually reserves for the commercial professionals; the legal and investigative fees and expenses are spread among all the beneficiaries of the case, if they win, rather than being imposed repetitiously on each of them. Since a single lawyer or group of lawyers handles the case, the investigative work and legal research need be done only once for all the represented consumers.

Advantages

Class actions have the great advantage of mobilizing thousands of lawyers as "private attorneys general" to enforce the consumer protection laws. Lawyers are well compensated for instituting class-action suits. If they win, the courts award them counsel fees amounting to between 10 and 30 percent of recoveries, sometimes amounting to tens of thousands of dollars or more.

Opposition is intense and immense

At present only a few states permit class actions on behalf of consumers. In most of the other states, legislation appears to permit such cases, but the courts have protected business by giving the statutes tortured meanings, practically prohibiting the suits. In Congress, Robert C. Eckhart of Texas has conducted a crusade for several years for a federal bill to permit consumer class actions, but has been blocked by intensive lobbying by the National Association of Department Stores, car dealers, food manufacturers, canners, and the American Bar Association, as well as meeting with opposition from President Nixon, Chief Justice Warren Burger, and others. Burger said the courts had enough to do without having to decide consumer cases.

Despite this opposition, class actions are making progress. In the few states which permit these suits, they have produced significant gains for consumer justice. An Illinois consumer class action forced one of the largest mail-order houses to credit the accounts of thousands of its credit customers, to which it had unlawfully added certain insurance charges. In California, an action is pending to force one of our automobile companies to pay for replacement of defective wheels on 200,000 trucks; shortly after it was filed, the company offered to pay for new wheels for 40,000 of the trucks for which the defective wheels were most likely to cause accidents. And consumers; local, state, and federally run hospitals; and health-care units all over this country have benefited from the settlement of a treble-damages class action against drug companies that for a period of years unlawfully fixed the prices of antibiotics.

While these cases illustrate the potential use of the class-action device, class actions are in their infancy, and the time for further development is at hand. Congress and the President may yet agree on a reasonably good class-action law that would *not* require successful federal legal action *before* a group of citizens could take a business to a federal court on behalf of other citizens.

National Legal Services Corporation

The Legal Services Program of the Office of Economic Opportunity (OEO) has represented the nation's poorest consumers in our large cities since 1966 effectively enough to have gained the enmity of political figures the country over. Largely because of its desire to reform laws and regulations that discriminate against poor people as a class—for example, by stalling highway construction projects undertaken before the displaced poor are given help in relocation—the program has been fighting for its life almost since its inception. The prospect of justice for the consumer is not enhanced by what has happened to the effort to insulate the program from political retaliation.

White House opposition

It is notable that the report of the Task Force on a National Institute of Justice mentioned that the proposal to create a nonprofit, federally chartered National Legal Services Corporation that would be independent of political control had "already received congressional approval." This task force spoke prematurely, perhaps failing to gauge the strength of opposition to an independent entity that might imaginatively and creatively represent the poor without interference. What actually happened, after the task force report was published, was that Congress withdrew the corporation plan rather than compromise its independence, as demanded by the White House.

Thus the idea of a National Legal Services Corporation to replace the OEO Legal Services Program appears defeated for the time being. This is sad because the Neighborhood Legal Services, a nationwide network of offices which is funded by the OEO through the use of federal aid and which handles cases for the indigent, is likely to expire.

The poor need free legal consumer service

In an eloquent statement made in June, 1965, Nicholas Katzenbach, then Attorney General of the United States, said: "Seldom in his struggles with a finance company, a merchant, a landlord, or a rigid official, is the poor man even aware that he has rights which perhaps are being violated. If he knows, he may have no way to protect them. And finally, even if he is aware of legal services, he might well be deterred by irrational fear of cost, shame or further exploitation."[30]

What will replace these legal services if the OEO receives a knockout blow?

[30] Warren G. Magnuson and Jean Carper, *The Dark Side of the Marketplace*, Prentice-Hall, Inc., Englewood Cliffs, N.J., 1968, p. 55.

Will the National Legal Services Corporation bill be revived? Nobody at this time (1973) knows. What we do know, however, is that several million poor people will suffer. The adversary system on which our courts are based fails whenever one side goes unrepresented and judgment is entered by default.

CONSUMER REPRESENTATION AT THE WHITE HOUSE LEVEL

Since 1962, however, there has been renewed federal interest in the consumer's plight. Steps were taken by both President Kennedy and President Johnson to give the consumer a spokesman. In 1962 President Kennedy, declaring that consumers have a "right to be heard" and to have their interests given "full and sympathetic consideration in the formulation of Government policy," cre-

The Consumer Advisory Council

ated a Consumer Advisory Council as an adjunct to the Council of Economic Advisers "to examine and provide advice to the Government on issues of broad economic policy, on government programs protecting consumer needs, and on needed improvements in the flow of consumer research material to the public." The council was given more formal status by an Executive order issued by President Johnson on January 3, 1964. In addition to the council, which was composed of twelve private citizens, President Johnson established a Committee on Consumer Interests. This committee was composed of private citizens who served on the Advisory Council and representatives of ten federal agencies.

A Special Assistant for Consumer Affairs

A Special Assistant for Consumer Affairs was appointed by the President early in 1964. The holder of this White House position (Mrs. Esther Peterson, succeeded by Betty Furness and Virginia Knauer) was the principal spokesman for the consumer in the federal government and also served as chairman of the President's Committee on Consumer Interests.

Kennedy and Johnson institutionalized the consumer

These organizations—CAC, PCCI, and SACA—were supposed to represent consumers at the federal government's highest policy-making levels. But there was no clear sense of purpose. The President's Committee on Consumer Interests was to consider federal policies and programs of primary importance to consumers, while the Consumer Advisory Council was directed to "advise the Government on issues of broad economic policy of immediate concern to consumers." Both groups were served by the same staff, which in turn reported to the Special Assistant, and the holder of that office was chairman of the President's Committee on Consumer Interests and an ex officio member of the Advisory Council. If this committee implemented programs developed by the council and approved by the President, its function would be understandable. The committee's job, however, was not to implement, but rather to advise, and that was also the responsibility of the Advisory Council.

The Nixon administration and the Office of Consumer Affairs

In December, 1968, Father Robert McEwen, president of the Consumer Federation of America, asked Mr. Nixon to "appoint somebody for the consumers." Mrs. Patricia Hitt, President Nixon's top woman in government in early 1969, assured 500 conferees at the third annual Consumer Assembly (organized by the Consumer Federation of America) on January 31, 1969, that the new administration "will develop programs . . . designed, not to weaken, but to strengthen the response to consumer needs."[31] On April 9, 1969, President Nixon

---

[31] *The Washington Post*, Jan. 31, 1969.

appointed Mrs. Virginia Knauer, director of the Pennsylvania Consumer Bureau, to succeed Betty Furness as Special Assistant for Consumer Affairs.

The Office of Consumer Affairs

In 1971 the Office of Consumer Affairs in the Executive Office replaced PCCI. Under the Nixon reorganization, CAC was continued and given advisory responsibilities to the director with respect to (1) policy matters relating to consumers, (2) the effectiveness of federal consumer programs, and (3) ways in which unmet consumer needs can best be met through federal action.[32]

Problem number one: organizational structure

Consumer representation must be permanent

At present, the Office of the Special Assistant for Consumer Affairs exists by virtue of an Executive order which directs the office to study consumer interests and problems and to make recommendations to the President. In addition, it has been charged to work with federal agencies in coordinating plans and programs affecting consumers and to work with the federal government, state and local governments, private organizations, and individuals in areas of consumer interests. However, the President's message recognized and touched candidly on the weaknesses of the offspring of this Executive order; he stated, "This position has been created by Presidential order rather than by statute, however, and it is neither as visible nor as effective as it should be."[33]

The President was referring, among other things, to the fact that the Office of the Special Assistant for Consumer Affairs simply has not had the staff or the technical resources to deal with the hundreds of issues affecting consumer interests. These issues need investigation, thoughtful consideration, proposed solutions (voluntary or legislative), and vigorous advocacy before industry groups, administrative agencies of government, and Congress. The Office of the Special Assistant for Consumer Affairs has been hampered, over its life, in responding to the needs for consumer protection by virtue of the fact that there have been too many issues and too few people to deal with them. Critical issues brought to the Special Assistant for Consumer Affairs by individual consumers, consumer groups, Congress, the press, industry, and others have been so numerous that the limited time available to deal with each individual issue inevitably produces a sense of frustration and a feeling that justice has not been done to the importance of the issue. The establishment of a statutory office with an expanded budget would go a long way toward curing this lack of "horsepower."

Lacks horsepower

Problem number two: industry response to a consumer issue

Another problem we have encountered in responding to the needs of consumers is attributable to the traditional reaction of many industry representatives toward discussion of the very existence of a consumer issue or irritation. An article in *Business Week* traced seven specific stages of industry response to a consumer problem.[34] The traditional phases of reaction include denying the existence of the problem, blaming the problem on marginal companies cutting corners to survive, criticizing those who proclaim the existence of the problem, hiring a public relations firm to launch a campaign, working to blunt proposed legislation, launching a fact-finding committee to see whether a problem really exists, and, finally, deciding actually to do something about the problem.

Industry denies existence of consumer complaints

We can verify the existence of these reactions concerning many consumer

[32] News release, Office of the White House Press Secretary, Feb. 24, 1971, p. 4.

[33] Message from the President of the United States, *Congressional Record,* 91st Cong., 1st Sess., House of Representatives, Oct. 30, 1969.

[34] "How Business Responds to Consumerism," *Business Week,* Sept. 6, 1969, pp. 94–108.

Well, there may be consumer issues

issues even if they do not, in fact, crop up in relation to every consumer issue. This reflex series of reactions, however, is tending to become more of a historical curiosity. More and more associations, individual companies, and company spokesmen are speaking out candidly and strongly on the need for the corporation to base more of its decision making on the promotion and protection of the public interest. This emerging attitude is, in large part, attributable to the recognition that traditional reactions to consumer issues may not work anymore—if they ever worked at all.

One lesson needs to be emphasized

Consumer representation at White House level must be strengthened

One lesson that should be learned from experience in consumer representation at the White House level is that such representation, to be effective, must be permanent, well staffed, continuous, and at a high level. The director of the Office of Consumer Affairs should have a direct line to the Executive Office of the President. Virginia Knauer, Special Assistant to the President for Consumer Affairs, in 1970 said, "We need an office that can *effectively* advise the President on consumer matters."[35] The President's aid, therefore, in charge of domestic issues should permit the director reasonable access to the President. The director and Consumer Advisory Council members themselves should maintain high-level liaison with all departments and agencies responsible for consumer protection and service programs.

OTHER GOVERNMENT ACTIONS IN THE CONSUMER INTEREST

Consumer education gets a boost

One important piece of consumer legislation went largely unreported while legislators and the administration argued about busing.

The higher education law which the President reluctantly signed in late June, 1972, includes a section on consumer education. Major provisions include:

1. Setting up a director of consumer education
2. Giving the director authority over a grant program to improve consumer education not only in the schools but also in communities
3. Funding the office in fiscal 1973 with $20 million, in 1974 with $25 million, and in 1975 with $35 million.

Recognizing that there are neither sufficient funds nor trained personnel to teach consumers, Congress concentrated its assistance on developing curricula and training teachers. The purpose of the law, Congress said, is:

- To encourage and support the development of new, improved curricula
- To demonstrate the use of such curricula in model educational programs
- To evaluate the effectiveness of these model programs
- To provide support for initiating and maintaining consumer education programs at all educational levels
- To disseminate educational materials and other information for use by citizens throughout the nation

[35]"Federal Role in Consumer Affairs," *Hearings before the Subcommittee on Executive Reorganization and Government Research of the Committee on Government Operations,* U.S. Senate, 2d Sess., Jan. 20, 1970, pp. 245–251.

- To provide training programs for teachers and other education personnel, public service personnel, community and labor leaders and employees, and government employees
- To provide for community consumer education programs
- To provide for preparation and distribution of consumer materials by the mass media

Consumer product information coordination center

Consumers Union, a private, nonprofit, consumer products testing organization and publisher of *Consumer Reports,* began a campaign in 1965 to persuade the federal government to release information concerning its tests of products likely to have significance for consumers. CU, with a small budget of $13 million, is able to test only some two hundred products annually. The federal government makes many, many more such tests, the results of which would be of value to most consumers. This was a citizens' struggle for access to information possessed by the government.

A partial consumer victory

In the case of *Consumers Union v. the Veterans Administration,* conducted in early 1971, CU won a partial victory when the court accepted its legal obligation to release all data on its tests of hearing aids. It was only a partial victory because the court refused to rule that not only the VA but also all other federal agencies must release almost all other information of possible value to consumers. The only exceptions, CU argued, are *genuine* trade secrets, which are specifically protected by an exemption under the Freedom of Information Act. The court also left standing a ruling that the court, in its wisdom, could decide whether or not the release of information would be good for consumers.

The U.S. Court of Appeals, on August 31, 1971, struck down the lower court's notion about freedom of information and made the victory complete. Actually, the case, *Julius G. Getman v. the National Labor Relations Board,* was not interested in consumer information. But CU's attorneys, upon learning that the NLRB was raising the same unresolved argument used against CU by the VA, submitted a brief in CU's behalf as a friend of the court and participated in the oral argument.

Higher court supported CU's contention

The appeals court opinion held that a court "has no equitable jurisdiction to deny disclosure on grounds other than those laid out under one of the Freedom of Information Act's enumerated exemptions."[36]

Despite this victory, the federal government has continued torturing the law in search of new grounds for secrecy and probably won't relent until the Supreme Court settles the matter.

The Product Information Coordinating Center

The handwriting on the wall is there for all to see. It will be only a matter of time, for when tax moneys are used to test products of interest to the federal government and consumers, all citizens obviously have a right to this information. Probably with this in mind, President Nixon issued an Executive order on October 26, 1970, establishing the Product Information Coordinating Center (PICC). The center is charged with the responsibility of "disseminating general product information that the Federal Government acquires in buying consumer

[36] *Consumer Reports,* June, 1972, p. 339.

products." The hitch is, however, that test data, quality features, and comparative testing information are *not* made available to the public. This takes us back to CU's original position—release of "all data" on government testing of products of interest to consumers. [37]

THE CHANGING CONSUMER ROLE OF THE FEDERAL GOVERNMENT

It is generally agreed that consumerism is here to stay. This is the implicit assumption or explicit conclusion of the business community. [38] Thus the basic issue is: What should be the role of government and private effort to protect consumers? This question is a critical aspect in the resolution of the consumerism question.

Federal regulation is a mixed blessing. It should, but often does not, serve the public interest. It serves to define, clarify, and make acceptable or unacceptable norms of conduct. But it is at times insensitive, inept, and burdensome. Usually it is fashioned by compromise and twisted by interpretation. By the same token, self-regulation by business is seldom adequate. Sellers, for example, recognize the wrong but accept no responsibility for it. Some businessmen who reject the concept of responsibility may do so to maximize profit.

The need for action stems from the imbalance of power in favor of business and industry. Furthermore, urbanization, the increasing size of corporations, and the complexity of the consumer-goods market have contributed to the relative decline of the consumer. The present void of avenues for redress through the market system means that government is brought into the picture to effect a balance between consumer and producer. And, too often, federal efforts are likened to a shotgun approach. [39] It cannot be assumed that legislators have the appropriate answer at hand to make the best decisions.

Market regulations derived from laws or Executive order receive power from government—the power to coerce. At times laws are inadequate, born of compromise usually, and too often federal agencies are budget-starved into non-enforcement positions. Before successful changes can be effected, more facts are needed to assure that the power is used with fairness and effectiveness.

A good consumer wants all important information about a product or a service

And "let me decide"

There is no doubt about the need for important information to aid in establishing effective recourse for the consumer in the marketplace. As long as this void remains a marketing fact, government will be asked to redress the balance. An informed consumer is an asset in the marketplace from the point of view of both consumer welfare and the promotion of effective competition. It is up to all citizens to see that federal regulation is based on meaningful research.

[37] For what it may be worth, copies of all released publications are available from Consumer Product Information, Washington, D.C. 20407.

[38] *Business and the Consumer,* Chamber of Commerce of the United States, Washington, 1970, p. 6.

[39] J. N. Uhl, "Consumer Education and Protection: A Synergistic Relationship," in L. L. Mather (ed.), *Economics of Consumer Protection,* The Interstate Printers & Publishers, Inc., Danville, Ill., 1971, p. 103.

QUESTIONS FOR DISCUSSION

1. Business and industry generally prefer self-regulation to government regulation. What is the rationale for this preference?

2. What is the role of the federal government in protecting the rights of consumers?

3. Do you favor an independent consumer agency at the White House level? What powers and responsibilities would you give to this agency?

4. In recent years the Federal Trade Commission has been more responsive to consumer needs, in contrast to protecting private business and industry. Can you document this statement with facts? (You might begin by researching "counter advertising.")

5. Hans Thorelli, professor of business at Indiana University, predicts that public policy in the next ten years will take a more relaxed stand in regulating business activities. Do you agree?

6. What is the meaning of regulation via an affirmative declaration?

7. What is your reaction to Professor E. Scott Maynes's suggestions for improving government regulatory agencies?

8. Why is the "injunction" power a very important weapon in the hands of the FDA? Why doesn't Congress give the FDA the right to use injunctions?

9. What are the reasons for instituting class-action suits? Why has Congress been reluctant, up to now, to pass legislation supporting class-action suits?

10. A federal judge's ruling said that the FTC does not have the authority to issue trade regulations. Thus the ruling at this time casts a shadow of uncertainty over other FTC trade regulations. What are the implications of this ruling in terms of the FTC's handling of unfair trade practices?

PROJECTS

1. Research the kinds of consumer legislation being considered by Congress today.

2. Read about a recent class-action case and report to the class. Suggested topics are illegal prices for antibiotics, the illegal manner in which Sears, Roebuck includes an insurance charge when extending credit, and injuries caused by defective parts in new cars.

3. Mrs. Virginia Knauer, in her job as the President's Special Assistant for Consumer Affairs, is "heiress to a dilemma." Her position is that of the American consumer's spokesman to the President and the President's spokesman to over 200 million consumers in our country. The two tasks are not always compatible. Dig into this problem and show specific instances where she appeared to have difficulty in playing the two roles.

4. Make a study of President Nixon's accomplishments in favor of the consumer interest and against the consumer interest. What general conclusions do you come up with?

5. Read Mary Bennett Peterson's book, *The Regulated Consumer*. Your class may be interested in her views on how seven of the federal regulatory agencies overlook consumer interest.

SUGGESTED READINGS

Consumer Product Information, Consumer Product Information Coordinating Center, Washington.

"Consumer Protection against What?" *The Journal of Home Economics,* May, 1972, pp. 14–17.

Final Report of the National Commission on Product Safety, Government Printing Office, Washington, June, 1970.

Gaedeke, Ralph: "What Business, Government, and Consumer Spokesmen Think about Consumerism," *Journal of Consumer Affairs,* Summer, 1970, pp. 7–18.

"How Airlines Overcharge on Connecting Flights," *Consumer Reports,* May, 1972, pp. 321–324.

Knauer, Virginia: "The Role of the Office of Consumer Affairs," *International Consumer,* Winter, 1971–1972, pp. 7–8.

McLaughlin, Frank E.: "Problems Encountered by the President's Committee on Consumer Interests," in L. L. Mather (ed.), *Economics of Consumer Protection,* The Interstate Printers & Publishers, Inc., Danville, Ill., 1971, pp. 53–59.

A New Regulatory Framework: Report on Selected Independent Regulatory Agencies, Government Printing Office, Washington, 1971.

Peterson, Mary Bennett: *The Regulated Consumer,* Nash Publishing Company, Los Angeles, 1971.

"The Regulators Can't Go On This Way," *Business Week,* Feb. 28, 1970.

Rivlin, Alice M.: *Systematic Thinking for Social Action,* The Brookings Institution, Washington, 1971.

Troelstrup, Arch W.: "The Consumer Interest and Our Competitive System," in *Freedom of Information in the Market Place,* University of Missouri, School of Journalism, Columbia, 1967.

U.S. Government Organization Manual 1972–1973, Government Printing Office.

CHAPTER 17

CHAPTER 17
CONSUMER PROTECTION ON THE STATE AND LOCAL LEVELS; CONSUMER JUSTICE—CONCLUSIONS

The individual consumer voice in the community "should not be only loud and authoritative, but reasonable and responsible."

British Molony Report

*A*fter seventeen months as the President's Special Assistant for Consumer Affairs, Mrs. Esther Peterson was convinced: "The letters that pour in to us, the requests from agencies, indicate that the place where the real consumer protection is needed, and where the action is needed, is at the state level where the people are. One thing has become very clear—consumer representation at the federal level is not enough. The consumer must also receive representation at the state level and also at the local level."[1]

Paul Rand Dixon, former chairman of the FTC, said: "The more effective the states can be in nipping illegal schemes in the bud, the more energy the FTC can devote to dealing quickly and effectively with problems of regional and national significance."[2]

CONSUMER PROTECTION AT STATE AND LOCAL LEVELS

Nationwide review of state and local governmental action in behalf of the consumer, except in rare instances, is not equaled by enthusiasm, money, or needed legislation. The laws in some states are so inadequate that their citizens have virtually no protection at all except that offered by the FTC. Many state officials, particularly attorneys general who are handcuffed for lack of laws while the "gyps" run wild, are painfully aware of legislative deficiencies—on both the state level and the federal level—and soundly support the passage of effective laws and adequate appropriation to do the job.

In the last few years, however, the fact that the groundwork has been laid for state and local action in behalf of the consumer has become evident from new laws, regulations, and court decisions; from the significant increase in the number of consumer offices created and programs developed; from the growing number of consumer legislative committees established; from the strengthening of interstate and state-federal cooperation; and from the volume of consumer bills introduced.

Among the consumer interests usually handled on the city and county levels are weights-and-measures inspection, sanitation and health inspection of public eating places and food stores, and building and construction standards. State agencies regulate such things as consumer credit controls, utility rates, local hauling rates, banking and insurance, safety, milk prices (sometimes), the selling of real estate, the price and distribution of alcoholic beverages, TV and radio repairs, dry-cleaning establishments, dance studios, and burial services.

By April, 1972, forty-six states, the Virgin Islands, and the Commonwealth of Puerto Rico, had consumer offices. The responsibilities and powers of each of these state offices vary from advisory only to actual enforcement of consumer protection laws. Within each state, the responsibility for the consumer office may be in one to three branches of the state government.[3]

[1] Warren G. Magnuson, and Jean Carper, *The Dark Side of the Marketplace,* Prentice-Hall, Inc., Englewood Cliffs, N. J., 1968, p. 3.

[2] Ibid., p. 63.

[3] *Consumer Alert,* Federal Trade Commission, vol. 11, no. 4, April, 1972.

Highly significant is the growing number of consumer offices, not only at the state level, but increasingly at the city and county levels. Some were created by statute or ordinance, and others by executive direction. In April, 1972, at least fifty-three cities and eighteen counties had consumer offices with varying responsibilities and powers.[4]

CONSUMER PROTECTION IN THE STATES

The protection of the consumer is much less satisfactory at the state level than at the federal level. Colston Warne, president of Consumers Union, thinks the main reason for this situation is the "lack of consumer awareness" by citizens in the state.[5] Much of the authority to inspect and regulate is vested in ill-paid and, at times, inadequately trained civil servants.

With the appearance of state consumer counsels, the increased attention to consumer affairs by the attorneys general, and the emergence of new state consumer federations, the consumer viewpoint is no longer entirely absent from legislative deliberations or from legislative committee hearings. Not too long ago, business lobbies were able to blanket the state with laws providing resale price maintenance, to establish industry-dominated boards to limit competition by licensing procedures, and to protect banking, insurance, and utilities from effective public appraisal.

Today, however, the voice of the consumer is more than a whisper in most states. It has become politically popular to champion bills which will make *caveat emptor* almost obsolete. Today offices of consumer protection have emerged in a few states to coordinate existing agencies and to act on consumer complaints. As further evidence of the new trend, inventories have been made of the functions which are performed by state agencies—functions which have traditionally been buried in the bureaucratic maze of state departments. Meanwhile, state consumer groups have succeeded in reinforcing existing consumer laws in the fields of health and safety. Increasingly, state consumer groups, aided in some instances by city consumer organizations, have also pressured for the realignment and the invigoration of existing state agencies. They have also pressured for protection against the hazards which have resulted from new technology—for safeguards against dangerous chemical additives and preservatives as well as for environmental safeguards.

State consumer protection offices[6]

Following is a list of state consumer protection offices. The code, in parentheses, indicates where the responsibility lies.[7]

[4] Ibid.

[5] *Consumers Union Report on New City and County Consumer Protection Agencies,* Consumers Union of U.S., Inc., Mt. Vernon, N.Y., p. 2, 1972.

[6] *Consumer Alert,* Federal Trade Commission, vol. 11, no. 4, April, 1972.

[7] AG—Office of the Attorney General; AGR—Department of Agriculture; AGRCO—Department of Agriculture and Commerce (one department); GOV—Office of the Governor; CO—Department of Commerce; L—Department of Labor; IND—independent office.

Alaska (AG)	Nebraska (AGR)
Arizona (AG)	Nevada (CO)
Arkansas (AG)	New Hampshire (AG)
California (AG-IND)	New Jersey (AG)
Colorado (AG)	New Mexico (AG)
Connecticut (AG-IND)	New York (AG-GOV)
Delaware (AG-IND)	North Carolina (AG)
Florida (AG-AGR)	North Dakota (AG)
Georgia (IND)	Ohio (AG)
Hawaii (GOV)	Oklahoma (IND)
Idaho (AG)	Oregon (AG-CO)
Illinois (AG)	Pennsylvania (AG-AGR)
Indiana (AG-CO)	Rhode Island (AG-IND)
Iowa (AG)	South Dakota (AG)
Kansas (AG)	Texas (AG-IND)
Kentucky (AG-IND)	Utah (AG-IND)
Louisiana (AGR)	Vermont (AG)
Maine (AG)	Virginia (AG-GOV-AGRCO)
Maryland (AG)	Washington (AG)
Massachusetts (AG-GOV-IND)	West Virginia (AG-L)
Michigan (AG-GOV-IND)	Wisconsin (AG-AGR)
Minnesota (AG-CO)	Wyoming (IND)
Mississippi (AG-AGRCO)	Puerto Rico (AG)
Missouri (AG)	Virgin Islands (IND)

Trends in state legislation in the consumer interest

The growing number of states enacting or strengthening unfair and deceptive practices acts—one of the basic bulwarks of consumer protection—is highly significant. The trend is to pattern these laws after the Federal Trade Commission Act. At least thirty-six states have laws very similar to this act.

Other trends are discernible: (1) to provide means not only for stopping an unfair and deceptive practice but also for securing restitution for those who have been victimized; (2) to empower a state official to serve as a consumer advocate, especially in rate hearings; (3) to require that the consumer be provided with additional presale disclosure of information and, in the case of door-to-door sales, a cancellation privilege; (4) to eliminate or to limit the holder-in-due course doctrine in consumer sales; (5) to prohibit multilevel and pyramid sales schemes and to regulate franchise operations; (6) to study and enact automobile no-fault insurance; (7) to license auto and TV repair establishments with the licensing bureau given jurisdiction over relationship with customers, deceptive practices, and fraud; (8) to license other consumer service firms not previously licensed and to add consumers to the licensing boards; (9) to provide the consumer with increased warranty and guarantee protection; and (10) to increase intrastate, interstate, and state-federal cooperation in the consumer's behalf.

Little state FTCs

The Federal Trade Commission, which is capable of stopping nearly every type of scheme imaginable, operates under a statute singular in its simplicity. The heart of the statute (Section 45, Title 15, of the U.S. Code) consists of

"Little FTC" laws

only nineteen words: "Unfair methods of competition in commerce, and unfair or deceptive acts or practices in commerce are hereby declared unlawful."

Stopping deceptive practices

The mark of effectiveness that distinguishes this law from many of the state criminal statutes is that it is a civil statute aimed solely at *stopping* deceptive activities without providing that a wrongdoer must be proved guilty of a crime. Under the FTC law, a man cannot be sent to prison; the FTC can simply order him to "cease and desist" from "unfair, false, or misleading business practices." If he doesn't do so, he is subject to civil penalties of up to $5,000 per day for each violation. Proof of intent to deceive is not necessary, and this is the law's strength. And rather than enumerate the schemes to be outlawed, Congress wisely made the FTC law flexible enough to cover any deceptive practice. Unfortunately, only a few states (Washington, Hawaii, and Vermont) have enacted "little FTC" laws. Several states, however, have passed general deceptive practices statutes which are similar to the FTC law.

Many states continue to pass consumer protection laws on a piecemeal "emergency" basis, thus leaving out many actions related to shady selling practices.

Consumer protection bureaus

The most significant achievement of the states is the establishment of consumer protection bureaus, usually under the attorney general. The pioneering was done in New York under Attorney General Louis J. Lefkowitz, who set up a consumer fraud and protection bureau in 1957. Since then most of the states have established consumer protection units of varying effectiveness and power. The bureaus provide a centralized agency through which consumer complaints can be funneled. In states like California, Illinois, New York, and Washington—long experienced in this work—the staff follows up nearly every complaint (over ten thousand annually) and even takes full-scale court action against gypsters if necessary. Prior to 1961, in the state of Washington the apprehension of swindlers was the responsibility of thirty-nine prosecuting attorneys statewide. Similar situations still exist in some states. A culprit chased out of one county could set up business in another. Under the present system, the state mobilizes against the gyps and the action is swift and complete.

Coup de grâce

Several states can impose fines (in legal terms, "civil penalties") for misdeeds prior to the time the injunction is final. New Jersey can levy a fine of $100 for the first violation and $250 for subsequent violations. California can fine $2,500 for each violation. This deterrent is formidable, if strongly used. New York has the power to dissolve a corporation, and in one case the victims shared $100,000 of the company's assets.

The "Robin Hood" method

Several states make great efforts to see that the cheated victims are compensated. The Illinois bureau, for example, between 1962 and 1967 succeeded through the cancellation of debts and the return of money in saving $1,158,089 for consumers in Cook County (Chicago). New York's bureau returns more than this amount every year.

Some legislatures take no action in setting up fraud bureaus because of the unrealistic fear that business will object. Experience shows that only shady business objects.

Complaints

Usually a state consumer protection agency will not spend too much time on one consumer complaint. After all, many state agencies receive several thousand complaints each year. Action is likely to come after many people make the same complaint, especially in cases where it is necessary to gather sufficient proof to initiate a suit. Individual complaints are usually studied in order to review new legislation and to assist local enforcement agencies.

Are most complainants satisfied with the settlement? It appears that most are reasonably satisfied—possibly 60 to 75 percent of the complaints are resolved to the complainants' satisfaction. This rather high batting average encourages consumers to voice their complaints to attorneys general.

There is no charge for filing a complaint with your state justice department. As attorney general William Scott of Illinois told the residents of his state, "Any citizen can now obtain free legal assistance in correcting wrongs in consumer transactions." Several populous states have branch offices to handle consumer complaints. Usually complaints can be made by telephone, by letter, or in person. A few states have "hot lines" or toll-free telephone lines. You will probably be asked to document your complaint with such items as bill of sale, receipt, and warranty. In most states the complaint file is assigned to an investigator or attorney. He decides on the validity. If it is valid and within the office's jurisdiction, he contacts the party complained against.

Mediation between complainant and the respondent often solves the complaint. Law students or attorneys act as mediators. We are told that as many as sixty hearings a week are held in the downtown Chicago office alone. Occasionally a complaint will end up in court—some in the small claims court.

There seems to be a growing use and an increasing number of court tests of the doctrine of *parens patriae* invoked in the consumer's behalf. This doctrine has been applied to that function of sovereignty in which a state sues on behalf of its citizens generally who are not individual parties to the lawsuit. California, Florida, Iowa, Kentucky, and possibly other states permit the attorneys general to sue on behalf of the citizens. Ombudsmen spur aid to consumers in five states—currently in Hawaii, Iowa, Nebraska, Oregon, and South Carolina. The activities of the ombudsmen vary somewhat in each state. The most common service rendered by these people is to expedite consumer complaints. A *New York Times* story on the activities of these ombudsmen concluded that about one-third of the consumer complaints resulted in action on behalf of the citizens, and in several cases state regulations have been changed after investigation of a complaint.[8]

The vast majority of consumer fraud and hazard problems involve thousands of little claims in the $10 to $500 category. These grievances are conflicts which can be resolved in a variety of ways within and without the legal system, or else they are not resolved at all. The reality of our court system is that it is structured for formidable price and time mechanisms that effectively shut out the large majority of consumer grievances from any prospect of consideration. Cases involving large amounts of money are what receive legal representation, and such cases are needed to weather the attrition of judicial expense and delays. Most states do not permit people to join together in order to leap over the hurdle of expense and inadequate or nonexistent counsel. Therefore, a shocking imbalance has been the shameful mark of injustice. Thousands of letters flow into the federal agencies to note a very common absence of any feeling by the

[8] *The New York Times,* May 10, 1972, p. 10.

complainants that the law or the courts can help them. The door of the courtroom says to them, "No Admittance."

Class action useful

Class action would open the doors of the courtroom to bring high-volume, small-dollar abuses to justice. This is a way to protect the consumer without adding more regulation and more budgets.

Class-action suits, then, would be useful in cases in which a merchant is engaged in a scheme to defraud several thousand consumers, but government is unable to react because of limited resources, inadequate legislation, uninterested personnel, or political influence. In a class action, one consumer sues a merchant to get a refund or a debt cancellation not only for himself but also for all the other victims, who need not be identified until an advanced stage of the case, when they can be located through a search of the merchant's sales and credit records. Because only one case per fraud need be brought, rather than one case per victim, the consumers achieve the economies of scale which the court system usually reserves for the professional creditor; the legal and investigative fees and expenses are spread among all the beneficiaries of the case.

At present, only a small number of states have adopted laws permitting consumer class actions. As yet, after several years of effort, Congress has not passed legislation permitting citizens the right to sue in a class-action suit.

The expansion of consumer class actions—the biggest type of consumer case—must be accompanied by the creation of new institutions to handle the many grievances not susceptible to class-action treatment.

If we seriously propose to give the defrauded consumer his day in court, we must remove consumer cases from the low-level civil courts that serve more as collection agencies in most urban areas and create entirely new forums for the smallest type of individual consumer case. Let's call them "consumer courts."

Consumer courts proposed

The basic marketplace experience of today's consumers is too often one of frustration, powerlessness, and, in some cases, outright injustice. Consumers feel basically helpless to influence the actions of the marketplace power structure—the manufacturers, sellers, and advertisers.

FTC Commissioner Mary Gardiner Jones says that the existing court system —especially because of the high cost of litigation—is "no longer an effective or even feasible mechanism for serving the great bulk of needs of our citizens."

Weakness of existing court system

She said, "Our courts are for all practical purposes foreclosed to the individual citizen with a typical grievance involving non-delivery or unsatisfactory servicing of goods, landlord defaults or indifferent performance under a lease, or even personal injury or property damage claims which involve relatively minor amounts." She also said that the "National Committee on Product Safety estimated that court costs are so high it is impractical for a citizen to press a claim over a defective product unless the claim is in the $5,000 to $10,000 range."[9]

Commissioner Jones said that consumer courts—created either as a brand-new legal system or through revitalization of small-claims courts—could serve as a "third-party grievance mechanism" through which consumers could press claims against merchants in cases of fraud or unfair business practices.

Lawyers, usually young lawyers, who have served as defenders of consumer

[9] Speech quoted in *St. Louis Globe Democrat,* Sept. 7, 1970, p. 8E.

rights in the ghettos of urban centers are aware of the institutional paralysis that permits both petty criminals and big corporations to use the law, the courts, and the general feeling favoring the status quo to delay and blunt any attacks made upon them. Philip G. Schrag, a young lawyer, was appointed by Bess Myerson to be New York's "first defender of consumer rights" in that city. His unique experiences ended in disillusionment and frustration when he came to recognize the gap between the promise of the legal system and its actual performance.

"Consumer courts"   In Schrag's opinion, we must create entirely new forums. These forums or tribunals must be "convenient and informal for consumers to participate in their proceedings. They should hear consumer cases involving claims under $3,000. . . . Each should serve an area no larger than a school district . . . so that access is not a problem; they should convene in each district only often enough to keep them busy. At least half the time, they should be open during the evening, or on week-ends, so that people who work need not have to choose between justice and their jobs."[10]

Schrag goes on to say that these tribunals should hear evidence in an orderly but informal manner and should dispense with those rules of procedure which "befuddle ordinary citizens." Participants may have counsel, but assistance of paraprofessional advocates on the tribunal's staff should enable citizens to appear alone without disadvantage. The "judges" need not be judges at all; they could be lawyers or law students acceptable to both parties. The proceedings, then, would be more akin to neighborhood arbitration than to current court practice.

The innovative procedure noted by FTC Commissioner Mary Gardner Jones could take this form as an experiment. Certainly our regular courts have had an opportunity to do the job and apparently have failed. The promotion of consumer courts will require the establishment of new types of courts, the use of new procedures, and the emergence of lawyers and judges who see litigation *not* as an intricate system of postponing decisions but as a way of achieving justice.

Holder-in-due-course doctrine   The holder-in-due-course doctrine in consumer transactions came under heavy attack in the early 1970s. Under this doctrine a merchant who sells goods or services on an installment payment plan may get his money immediately by selling the contract to a bank or a finance company. The new holder of the credit contract has no legal responsibility for the product that has been sold. He is interested only in receiving payments as per the contract. In the event of a defect in the product, the buyer has little recourse. He must continue to make payments until the debt is paid in full. If he defaults in his payments, the product may be repossessed by the purchaser of the contract.

"The mask behind which fraud rests"

The number of states which now restrict the application of the holder-in-due-course doctrine or which outlaw it has grown significantly since 1970. This old doctrine is the basis for most of the consumer grievances in our country today.

[10] *Counsel for the Deceived,* Pantheon Books, a division of Random House, Inc., New York, 1972, p. 199.

REGULATORY AGENCIES IN THE STATES

Inadequacy of state regulation

The regulatory agencies at the state level—those concerned with insurance, banks, utilities, and weights and measures, to mention a few areas of consumer interest—are much less satisfactory in protecting consumers than those at the federal level. There are several reasons for the inadequacy of state regulation: (1) There are few strong and active state consumer organizations able to function as a catalyst in securing the attention of the mass media and in demanding public hearings of legislative committees; (2) those making political appointments of persons to head state regulatory agencies tend to favor business interests via nonregulation as much as, or more than, via regulation according to the regulatory law; (3) enforcement of the laws is carried out by a group of ill-paid civil servants and, in some instances, by political appointees; (4) the focus is almost entirely on the suppression of fraud and the inspection of food; (5) even in these respects, the state's programs are considerably less effective than the corresponding activities of the federal government (recent examples are the poor inspection of meat); (6) drugs are subjected to some sort of inspection and control in most states, but the level of effort is inadequate; and (7) while various industry practices specifically aimed at consumers are recognized as a serious problem, only a few states have established a special enforcement unit to deal with the diverse problems of consumer protection.

Consumer voice stronger

Today, the consumer's voice is more than a whisper at the state level. An effort is being made to support bills which will weaken the rule of *caveat emptor*. Offices of consumer protection have emerged in several states to coordinate existing agencies—some forty-six consumer offices of various kinds by April, 1972. Today, as further evidence of this trend, the federal Office of Consumer Affairs has recently made an inventory of actual functions which are performed by state agencies—functions which have traditionally been buried in a bureaucratic maze of state departments.[11] Some state consumer groups have pressured for more effective existing state agencies, as well as for providing protection from hazards which have resulted from new technology—safeguards against chemical additives and preservatives as well as environmental safeguards for air, water, and soil.

In one year, 1971, twelve state consumer offices were reported established, and some existing offices were made statutory or restructured. A number of other states indicated they were studying the creation of consumer offices in the near future.[12]

There was no clear-cut pattern as to office administration, location, powers and functions, but offices with enforcement responsibility over deceptive practices acts generally were established in the Office of the Attorney General.

Models for state consumer offices

There are likely to be other kinds of organizational models for consumer representation in state governments besides those reviewed here. There might be, for example, an interdepartmental consumer-interest committee chaired by

[11] Office of Consumer Affairs, Executive Office of the President, *State Consumer Action: Summary 71,* Government Printing Office, Washington, 1971.
[12] Ibid., p. 20.

a consumer-advocate counsel. There could be a joint select consumer-interest committee made up of the chairmen of similarly named committees of the state legislature chaired by a permanent consumer-advocate counsel with staff and funds to function effectively.

Among the first consumer offices of various kinds to be established in this country were those in New York, Connecticut, California, and Massachusetts. Although there have been drastic changes in duties in at least two states, the original organization and functions seem to have been far superior to the present models.

1. Pioneer effort in New York State

One of the most significant achievements of the states is the statutory establishment of consumer representation at the executive level. The pioneer effort in this field was the 1955 action of Governor W. Averell Harriman of New York State in establishing a Consumer Counsel to the Governor. In the latter office, Dr. Persia Campbell showed the immense potentiality of according consumer recognition in state administration. Her work included participation in hearings with reference to basic consumer issues, such as resale price maintenance and installment credit legislation, and the issuance of publications regarding the responsibilities and actions of scattered bureaus for consumer protection.

Early in 1959, Governor Rockefeller failed to continue the Office of Consumer Counsel in his executive department. Consumer-interest organizations in New York have been working, without success, for its reestablishment, this time by legislative action.

Finally, Governor Rockefeller established the Consumer Protection Board and appointed Betty Furness as executive director. She resigned in July, 1971, charging that the Legislature had blocked her attempts to get meaningful legislation passed. As of early 1973, there has been no effective replacement, despite heavy consumer group pressure on the Governor to appoint a new Consumer Protection Board chief.

2. The California Office of Consumer Counsel

California had an Office of Consumer Counsel, established in 1959, located in the Governor's Office. Prior to Governor Reagan's administration, the consumer counsel, Mrs. Helen Nelson, carried on a wide range of vigorous and effective programs of consumer representation, information, and education. The consumer counsel worked closely with the Governor and with his executive departments, most notably with the state attorney general's office in the fields of consumer frauds and consumer legislation. In addition, the consumer counsel presented the consumer point of view at hearings held by legislative committees and by state regulatory commissions. The consumer counsel also provided channels for the two-way flow of information and suggestions between the state government and the people of the state with reference to consumer-interest matters.

When Ronald Reagan became Governor of California, the budget as well as the activities of the consumer counsel were curtailed considerably. The hesitancy about continuing this office could also be seen when the Governor appointed an acting consumer counsel. In 1970, the active and effective Office of Consumer Counsel was replaced by a Department of Consumer Affairs with reduced functions and effectiveness.

California, with the support of the Department of Consumer Affairs, did enact important consumer bills such as those concerning (1) the Bureau of Repair Services, (2) warranties, (3) mail-order sales, (4) funeral services, (5) small-claims courts, (6) mobile home warranties, and (7) a three-day cooling-off period.

3. Connecticut consumer representation in the executive branch

At the present time only one state, Connecticut, has a consumer department in the executive branch of government. There the Department of Consumer Protection, established in 1959, and headed by the commissioner, contains units that are responsible for the administration of laws and regulations pertaining, for example, to foods and drugs and to weights and measures. The Connecticut setup has the great advantage of concentrating several consumer protective responsibilities and services within one department of state government. In 1971 real estate transactions were placed under the jurisdiction of the Department of Consumer Protection.

4. The Consumer's Council of Massachusetts: the consumers' advocate

The consumers' advocate

The Consumers' Council was established by the General Court as a statutory body in the executive department of the Commonwealth of Massachusetts in 1963. It is the first statutory body of its type in the United States. Its function is as follows:

- To represent the consumers' interest as the people's advocate in the governmental structure as well as the marketplace
- To coordinate consumer services and to further consumer education
- To keep the public informed on consumer issues
- To conduct studies concerning consumer problems and initiate consumer legislation
- To advise the Governor and the General Court on matters concerning the consumers' interest

The fundamental purpose of the council is to give the people a voice in matters that concern the consumer, whether the marketplace or the government is involved.

The council consists of eight public members appointed by the Governor for the term of his office and five statutory ex officio members. Except for the staff headed by an executive secretary, the council is a nonsalaried body.

The council is given the authority to act "in behalf of the people in any hearing pertaining to increase of rates or cost of services held by an administrative agency of government." It may also appear in behalf of the people before federal and state legislative committees as well as other public hearings. The council also coordinates consumer functions and activities with other state and federal agencies.

Much of the consumer protection action of the Legislature has been the result of constant pressure exerted by the Consumers' Council. In 1970, the Legislature gave the Consumers' Council the authority to establish consumer advisory commissions in the towns and cities in order to coordinate the consumer protection activities of municipal governments with those of the state government.

A new Executive Department of Consumer Affairs was recently established to supervise the State Department of Public Utilities, the Division of Banks and Banking, the Division of Insurance, and the other regulatory agencies.

Consumer protection   At the state level, officials who attempt to protect consumers are incredibly handicapped by inadequate laws. Although some states have recently passed effective laws and set up machinery to enforce them, the picture of state consumer legislation is, on the whole, not good. A survey in 1967, for example, by the FTC showed that only nineteen states could be said to have "good" or "excellent" laws prohibiting deceptive selling practices. In a few states legislation did not exist. Only twenty states outlawed bait advertising.

Absence of laws, however, is not the only problem in the states. For, as the *Columbia Law Review* noted, "The states have adopted a staggering number of statutes noteworthy for their ad hoc and piecemeal approach to the problems of advertising control and for the very slight degree to which they are enforced." Many attorneys general and county prosecutors freely admitted that they had never tried to enforce their *Printer's Ink* mode law (aimed at untrue, deceptive, or misleading advertising). It is not a secret, according to Gale P. Gotschall of the FTC, who confided to the National District Attorneys Association in 1966, that lawyers and judges usually do not feel that a businessman belongs in jail. [13]

One of the major weaknesses in consumer protection at the state and local levels is that state and local legal authorities tend to let the fraud proceed until they have accumulated enough evidence to prosecute. So said Bronson LaFollette, Wisconsin State Attorney General and a leader in fighting consumer frauds. Consumers, however, want frauds stopped *before* they themselves become the victims. [14]

The clearest examples of inadequate consumer protection at the state level are in the areas of weights and measures, in state regulation of public utilities, and in insurance and banking.

1.   The price of pseudo-regulation of public utilities: overcharges

State commissions for the regulation of public utilities have long been characterized by weakness, with rare exceptions. Commissioners without the expertise of or subservient to the utilities, staffs without required skills or manpower or currying favor with the utilities by looking to them for professional advancement, insufficient funds for operation, and inadequate salaries to attract able men have often resulted in failure to protect the consumer from exorbitant rates.

An appalling absence of hard information on these points has hitherto ex-

[13] Reported by Sidney Margolius in *The Innocent Consumer v. the Exploiters,* Trident Press, a division of Simon & Schuster, Inc., New York, 1967, p. 43.
[14] Ibid.

*State regulatory
commissions that do not
regulate*

isted, according to reports of the Consumers Information Committee on Resources and Energy. So in 1968 the Intergovernmental Relations Subcommittee of the Senate Committee on Government Operations set about to get the facts. The state utilities commissions were polled with a questionnaire and all but two responded.

Sixteen commissions had only one rate analyst and six had none. Six had not a single engineer and nine had only one. Twenty-six commissions had no securities analyst. Thirteen had only one accountant and one had none at all. Only three commissions had an economist. Seventeen had a single attorney and four had none.

Thirty-seven state utilities commissions had no permanent research staff, and thirteen reported they did not even have a research library.

Thirty-four said salaries of administrative and professional staff were inadequate to attract and retain competent persons. One hundred and three former staff members of state regulatory commissions are now in the employ of public utility companies.

The net result of these incompetencies is that the regulated electric utilities are overall obtaining profits which the Senate subcommittee reported are substantially higher than the state regulatory commissions set as the maximum.

The extreme example is Montana Power Company, which the state utility commission allows a return of 5.33 percent, the lowest reported in the Senate survey. In 1965 the company's actual return was 11.37 percent, the highest in the nation, and for the previous three years it had been over 10 percent and rising.

These are the prices consumers pay for state regulatory commissions that do not regulate. Most of the people who sit on the state regulating commissions are politicians, bankers, lawyers, and insurance men—the same people whose firms may profit from vast holdings of utility stocks. There are also secret kickbacks to big banks by major utilities known as "compensating balances." (See Taylor-Troelstrup Readings 102 for a case study.) Electric utilities overcharged consumers $1.38 billion in 1970, the latest year for which the Federal Power Commission has comparative figures, according to Arnold H. Hirsch, a Washington, D.C., consultant.[15] Hirsch compiled his figures from *Public Power,* the American Public Power Association magazine.

Hirsch's figures show that the following states allowed the highest rates of return: Montana, Oklahoma, West Virginia, Texas, Kansas, New Mexico, Kentucky, Ohio, Maryland, Arkansas, Idaho, Wyoming, Delaware, Nevada, and Missouri.

States with the best regulation of utilities allowed electric companies an average rate of return of 6.37 percent, Hirsch said. The states were California, Rhode Island, North Carolina, Michigan, and Vermont. Bell system affiliates were allowed 7.12 percent.

Hirsch figured the overcharge as the difference between the actual rate of return for a firm as reported by the FPC and the average rate of return for the five states with the best regulation. Since 1966, Hirsch says, electric utilities have overcharged consumers $5,975,000,000; telephone companies have overcharged them $3,786,000,000. In 1970, the telephone overcharge was $630 million. The figure has declined steadily from a 1966 high of $976 million.

Hidden costs

*Where are the state
regulators?*

[15] *Consumer Newsweek,* May 8, 1972.

2. State insurance departments

It is a well-known fact that state insurance departments, saddled with statutory authority grossly inadequate to implement their consumer-oriented programs and unable to obtain legislative reform, have settled for a safe and comfortable attitude of "don't rock the boat." That was true until Dr. Herbert Denenberg, Insurance Commissioner of Pennsylvania, was appointed by Governor Milton Shapp in 1971 with the directive to "transform the insurance department into a consumer protection agency." The former professor of insurance at the University of Pennsylvania's Wharton School of Finance and Commerce knew what needed to be done—since insurance companies are not telling consumers the truth about insurance costs so that they can select the best product (insurance policy) in the marketplace, and since the legislatures will do nothing, it is the duty of the state insurance commissioner to do what he can and give the cost information necessary so that people can buy insurance intelligently.

A new approach to regulation

This Denenberg did, as we learned in Chapter 16, by disclosing cost facts in *A Shopper's Guide to Life Insurance.* Other guides followed, one on automobile insurance and another on hospital costs, and others will eventually be published, we are told.

What is significant here is that no other state commissioner of insurance had had the courage to expose the *failure* of the life insurance (and other kinds of insurance) industry to give consumers the facts about insurance costs. Other governors must appoint consumer-oriented insurance commissioners to transform the insurance department into a consumer protection agency. Many insurance commissioners have applauded Dr. Denenberg for his successful new approach to regulation when state statute or the Legislature denies the state's Insurance Department regulatory authority over insurance rates.

Walking into the nineteenth century

Bargains are not easy to find in government agencies. Government might well be called the "number one consumer fraud," says Denenberg, in terms of its failure to deliver. That government has strayed from its initial purpose of protecting the public interest to serving special-interest groups is an unfortunate truism. In no other sector of government is this betrayal so prevalent as in the numerous federal and state regulatory agencies. The relationship between the regulators and those they regulate is "close and cozy." But what has been done in Pennsylvania can be done in other states.

3. Weights and measures: weak laws poorly enforced

Some of the inadequacy of weights-and-measures laws and enforcement was pointed up in Chapter 7. In 1966 and 1967, state weights-and-measures personnel found considerable short weights in, and misleading labels on, meat products, packaged foods, gasoline pump meters, petroleum gas meters, and fuel oil in Pennsylvania, California, Virginia, Michigan, Ohio, and New York.[16] Most of the other states no doubt have similar problems with weights-and-measures enforcement. In fact, a study by Leland J. Gordon, director of the Weights and Measures Research Center, found a hodgepodge of weak laws poorly enforced, weak laws strongly enforced, and strong laws feebly enforced. Effective consumer protec-

[16] *Changing Times,* March, 1968.

tion, according to Gordon, might cost $12,500,000 a year, or only about 25 cents a year per family.

A solution to the problem of more effective enforcement of weights-and-measures laws, in addition to improved enforcement at the state and local levels, is to arrange for some kind of effective cooperation of state and federal agencies.

Will federal and state cooperation work?

Unfortunately, there are conflicts, cross-purposes, and some gaps in the protection offered consumers. After Congress passed the important Fair Packaging and Labeling Act (FPLA) in 1966, it was a matter of record that the FDA and the FTC were "looking to the states for the enforcement of FPLA."[17] The question, then, is this: Will federal-state cooperation work in the enforcement of the FPLA? Some state officials are jealous and fearful of the federal agencies such as the FTC and the FDA. As of early 1973, we have to continue to "wait and see" what kind of cooperation there will be between the federal and state agencies in enforcing the FPLA. Meantime, consumers are not receiving the protection the act anticipated.

Meat inspection and standards were poor in the states

Another illustration of the weakness of state agencies established to protect citizens' health and pocketbooks came to public attention shortly after the federal Wholesome Meat Act of 1967 became law. This act was to ensure standard high quality of all meat sold in the country by requiring 15,000 plants which had previously processed meat for sale within state borders and which had weak or sometimes no standards to have inspections that would at least meet federal inspection requirements within two years of that date (1967) or else be taken over by the federal government. On December 15, 1969, the original deadline, only three states met the standards—California, Maryland, and Florida. North Dakota came under federal inspection immediately. Another deadline, to December 15, 1970, was set for states that appeared to be making sufficient progress—forty-six states fell in this category. The final deadline came in January, 1971, with two-thirds of the states still in limbo. Clifford Hardin, Secretary of Agriculture, waited long for the state inspection agencies and was now faced with a clear-cut legal mandate to certify these states or take action. For another four weeks he allowed fifteen states to continue to process meat without federal standards. In February, 1971, fifteen states were taken over by federal meat inspectors.

State meat inspection too often tied to patronage

Why should the states have objected to federal takeover, considering the financial benefits this would bring to them? The federal government would pick up all the costs instead of only 50 percent. Basically, the real objection had to do not with interference in state or local affairs but that state meat inspection is closely tied to the position of the state commissioner of agriculture, which can be a source of extraordinary political power with patronage benefits.

It is also obvious that the cooperation between the states and the federal government in establishing decent standards for fresh meat under state inspection has not been entirely successful, even with the federal government picking up 50 percent of the state's cost for meeting the higher standards. It appears that state-federal cooperation is a difficult concept to understand.

State-federal cooperation in consumer protection has increased since 1971,

[17] Leland J. Gordon, "Fair Packaging and Labeling—When?" July 15, 1968, p. 24.

State-federal cooperation

according to Virginia Knauer, Special Assistant to the President for Consumer Affairs. The National Association of Attorneys General at its Winter, 1971, meeting unanimously adopted a resolution calling for an Interstate Consumer Protection Compact. With its adoption, each attorney general has agreed to file suit on behalf of another attorney general to collect on or enforce a consumer protection order, judgment, or decree. In the past, the inability to enforce orders, judgments, and decrees has often frustrated the complaining consumer and has damaged the respect in consumer litigation by the attorney general.[18]

Another example is the FTC's Office of Federal-State Cooperation, established in 1965. Through this office, the FTC works with state officials, exchanging information on deceptive and fraudulent practices of firms and individuals. This stimulates states to handle their own problems before they grow into national scandals.

VOLUNTARY CONSUMER ORGANIZATIONS AT THE STATE LEVEL[19]

As of November 1, 1968, there were forty-four voluntary consumer organizations existing at the national, state, and local level. Thirty-one of these were in twenty-nine states. These are voluntary groups drawing membership, for the most part, from individuals and group organizations. They seek to promote consumer interests through consumer education and the initiation of needed legislative action.

In two states there are two voluntary consumer organizations. Colorado has Colorado Consumers Association and the Colorado Housewives Encouraging Consumer Knowledge. In Ohio there are the Consumers League of Ohio and the Ohio Consumers Association.

Activities of typical voluntary consumer associations

The purposes of state voluntary consumer associations are to ensure the protection of the consumer in the marketplace through:

1. *Legislation*   To promote sound consumer laws and to provide for their effective enforcement

2. *Education*   To make consumers aware of practices in the marketplace and to provide the knowledge necessary to buy wisely

3. *Representation*   To provide consumers a voice before those agencies of government which regulate or affect consumer goods and services

4. *Coordination*   To work for coordination of other organized groups and individuals interested in consumer protection and education

5. *Information*   To gather, exchange, and disseminate information of value to consumers

---

[18] *State Consumer Action: Summary '71,* p. 74.

[19] For details, see *Consumer Protection,* published by Consumers Union of U.S., Inc., Mount Vernon, N.Y., 1966; see also the President's Committee on Consumer Interest, *Forming Consumer Organizations,* Washington, January, 1969. The latter publication gives the names and addresses of all voluntary consumer associations as of Nov. 1, 1968.

The consumer associations, typically, engage in such activities as giving testimony at hearings, speaking and enlightening members of other community or statewide organizations, preparing position papers or letters for members of the legislature or for legislative committees, pressing for consumer representation in the executive branch of state government, and working for the creation of consumer fraud or protective bureaus in state government. The Virginia Citizens Consumer Council, for example, installed a phone called "Dial-a-consumer" to spread important consumer information. Radio, newspapers, and TV are playing up "Dial-a-consumer." The VCCC has a novel way to make the consumer's voice heard. It sells 1-inch orange and black stamps carrying a slogan, "Consumers Care, Let the Seller Beware." They suggest placing the stamps on envelopes when paying bills, on letters of complaints, on merchandise that is returned, on appliances, under car hoods, and on front doors.

Membership

Membership in most state consumer associations is on an individual or organizational basis. Many of the national organizations, such as the AFL-CIO, American Association of University Women, American Home Economics Association, General Federation of Women's Clubs, League of Women Voters, National Congress of Parents and Teachers, NAACP, CUNA International, and Cooperative League of the U.S.A., have encouraged their state chapters to participate in state and local consumer organizations.

Membership dues in the state consumer associations usually range from $1 to $5 a year for individuals and from $10 to $25 for organizations.

Inadequate financing

The most effective state consumer organizations have a part-time or full-time paid executive secretary. It usually takes several years of successful growth to achieve even a part-time paid executive. The Association of California Consumers, an active association, felt that they "must have a regular lobbyist in Sacramento, for consumers cannot be represented on a hit-and-miss basis." Some of the consumer organizations have reached the stage of growth where they need a full-time executive secretary. It is extremely difficult, however, to secure sufficient income for paying even part-time leadership.

Federal aid?

Because it is extremely difficult to become an effective consumer organization without some outside financial aid, Senator Hart of Michigan has proposed legislation which would establish independent consumer councils with local branches in each state. The consumer councils would be operated by local citizens and financed partly by federal funds; also, they could accept grants from foundations and other private sources. These consumer councils, possibly using the facilities and personnel of the American Arbitration Association, would, among other services, try to settle disputes for consumers that "are too small for legal action and too big to ignore."

Senator Jacob Javits of New York said on January 31, 1969, that he was going to reintroduce a bill called the Consumer Protection Assistance Act to provide effective consumer action at the local level. This act could provide for federal matching grants to assist states in establishing and strengthening their consumer protection programs. The federal grants would cover "up to 50 percent of the cost of the state plan, which would have to be approved by the Secretary of Commerce." The state consumer programs must include a "consumer protection office within the state to deal with dishonest practices." The act would also require states to license or otherwise regulate such businesses as those of appliance repairmen, car repairmen, home movers, and home improvement contractors. There are other requirements, all of which would identify the businesses that practice deception and intimidation.

THE CONSUMERS' VOICE IN CITY AND COUNTY GOVERNMENT[20]

By 1972, at least fourteen cities and eleven counties had established consumer protection agencies by ordinance or proclamation. They are shown in the accompanying table.

CITIES	COUNTIES
Akron, Ohio	Burlington County, N.J.
Belleville, N.J.	Camden County, N.J.
Boston, Mass.	Dade County, Fla.
Columbus, Ohio	Montgomery County, Md.
Elizabeth, N.J.	Nassau County, N.Y.
Jacksonville, Fla.	Orange County, N.Y.
Long Beach, N.Y.	Prince Georges County, Md.
Louisville, Ky.	Rockland County, N.Y.
New York, N.Y.	San Bernardino County, Cal.
Philadelphia, Pa.	Santa Clara County, Cal.
St. Petersburg, Fla.	Ventura County, Cal.
Seattle, Wash.	
Virginia Beach, Va.	
Yonkers, N.Y.	

In addition, at least four other cities and six other counties have taken some action to protect consumer interests, according to the CU report. The cities are Detroit, Michigan; Indianapolis, Indiana; Rochester, New York; and St. Louis, Missouri.

The six counties that have taken some consumer action are: Allegheny

[20] The most recent information on city and county consumer protection agencies is *Consumers Union Report on New City and County Consumer Protection Agencies,* Consumers Union of U.S., Inc., Mount Vernon, N.Y., 1972. Parts excerpted by permission. Copyright Consumers Union of U.S., Inc., publishers of *Consumer Reports.*

County, Pennsylvania; Monroe County, New York; Multnomah County, Oregon; Onondaga County, New York; Sedgewick County, Kansas; and Westchester County, New York.[21]

Highlights

Consumer complaints

Consumer complaint handling is by far the major activity of local-level agencies. The most frequent types of complaints in city consumer offices concerned automobiles, appliances, home improvements, and mail-order selling, in that order.

In counties the most frequent types of complaints concerned automobiles, appliances, home improvements, and mail-order selling.

In both city and county jurisdictions the complaint load was surprisingly low. The reasons for the light loads are these: (1) Many people do not know the office exists; (2) some people hesitate to make complaints; (3) in a few states complaints tend to go to the state consumer agency; (4) in the large cities the Better Business Bureaus pick up many complaints; and (5) most of the city and county consumer offices are of recent origin. One wonders why Chicago received only some 2,000 complaints a year when New York City handled over 170,000 complaints in one year.

Most of the local-county agencies attempt to mediate consumer complaints. Prosecutions are as yet few or are nonexistent in most cities and counties.

Local consumer protection: a recent phenomenon

A total of ten of the twenty-six consumer offices began operations between 1966 and 1970; seven of these were preexisting weights-and-measures departments which expanded into broader consumer programs. Eight offices came into existence in 1970, and seven more in 1971.

Most of these offices, especially those with only one or two full-time staff members, had to set up a priority list in their daily program of activities. Since they were unable to do all the work outlined in the ordinance, the number one priority usually concerned handling complaints and cooperating with schools in their consumer education programs.

Complaint handling: basic procedure[22]

The type of complaint received varies considerably. Most consumer offices require that the transaction occurred within the city or county, is not of a private-dispute nature, falls within the office's general subject matter jurisdiction, and is not specifically within the jurisdiction of another city or county agency. There are also variations upon this general theme: the merchant must live in the city or county, the complaint must not involve landlord disputes, the complaint must not be about business licensed by the state, the complaint must appear likely to constitute an ordinance violation, and so on.

Most of the local consumer offices will accept complaints by telephone, by letter, or in person, requesting a signed statement only when it appears likely that future legal action will be involved.

---

[21] *Consumers Union Report on New City and County Consumer Protection Agencies.* These ten jurisdictions were listed separately for one or more of these reasons: (1) office on paper only, (2) no legal authorization, (3) limited to conducting research, and (4) program not primarily a local government program—rather, an extension of a state program.

[22] *Consumers Union Report on New City and County Consumer Protection Agencies,* pp. 19–22.

Office procedure for complaint disposition varies little. All essential data are obtained and checked using methods ranging from a telephone call to a full-fledged investigation. If the complaint has merit, the businessman is contacted, advised of the complaint, questioned, and perhaps "requested" by the office to cooperate. Most complaints are settled at this stage.

If the businessman is noncooperative or the complainant is dissatisfied with the proposed compromise, the mediation effort stops. The next step varies depending on the powers and priorities of the office. Even if the office has the power to take further action, it may recommend that the complainant take private action. The office may call a conference or a public hearing to impress the businessman with his culpability or to effectuate a compromise.

Subpoena power essential

If the office has subpoena power, it may remind the merchant of that fact to convince him of the willingness of the office to take further action if necessary. According to directors of these offices, subpoena power is essential to office credibility and is one of the most effective devices. The office may issue a warrant for the arrest of the violator or may issue a cease-and-desist order if the severity of the conduct so warrants. The office may also refer the case to a proper agency for prosecution or, if it has the power to do so, begin the action itself by initiating a complaint. So far only eleven offices have been involved in any litigation prosecution activity.

In nineteen of the twenty-six jurisdictions, the consumer office is in some way connected with the local office of weights and measures. This may be good or not so good, depending upon personnel, attitudes, management, and budget. Weights-and-measures personnel have been used to work in the single area of weights and measures. When the whole consumer operation suddenly becomes an integrated whole, a broad administrative agency, it is understandable that some friction and confusion occur.

Understaffed and underfinanced

Local and county consumer protection agencies are understaffed and underfinanced. The budget and staff of county consumer offices range from $376,000 and a staff of forty-nine in Nassau County, New York, to $5,000 and staff of two in Prince George's County, Maryland.

The budget and staff of city consumer offices range from $4,440,000 and staff of 362 in New York City to $25,000 and a small staff in Seattle, Washington. In nine of the cities, the budget was not available, but the staff was listed as consisting of only one in Long Beach, New York; Belleville, New Jersey; and Elizabeth, New Jersey.

With budgets so low, the staff has to be restricted; thus it is no wonder that case loads are so small. The office has to restrict its operation to case-to-case complaint handling even if the city or county ordinance authorizes other duties.

Selected powers of city and county consumer offices

The selected powers of city and county consumer offices generally include investigating consumer complaints, initiating investigations, holding public hearings, issuing subpoenas, promulgating rules and regulations and issuing cease-and-desist orders. In one county consumer office (Prince George's County, Maryland), the power to revoke licenses is in the ordinance. In all but two of the county consumer offices, and in all but three of the city offices, the power to bring prosecutions is granted.

Sanctions [23]

About nine of the local consumer protection laws include penalty provisions which provide for a maximum of a $500 fine per violation; five provide for imprisonment for a maximum of sixty to ninety days; five can seek injunctions or temporary restraining orders in the case of repeated and multiple violations of the laws; and restitution may be required as part of the settlement in three of the offices. The injunction is an important tool not only because of economy of office record, but also because it is an effective deterrent. One other power is the power to recover costs of investigation. Only three offices have this power at present.

County consumer protection offices

Camden County, New Jersey

There are many variable activities among the county consumer offices. The Camden, New Jersey, Department of Consumer Affairs has a small budget—$19,000—and a small staff, although there were over five hundred complaints in less than one full year. The Camden office has an effective volunteer program. As part of this program, five businessmen with accounting, financial, and legal background give talks to local organizations.

Another volunteer group of about seventy-five Camden men and women assist the office in making studies of market price comparisons, warranties, and meat labeling. The results are printed and distributed to civic groups and to the local media.

Dade County, Florida

In Dade County, Florida, the nine staff people are appointed by the county manager. The budget is $109,000. The functions are typical of county offices—handling complaints and initiating investigations of possible violations. The staff can be deputized and vested with police powers and can arrest and impound material evidence. The staff can also enforce the weights-and-measures ordinances and enforce deceptive trade practices laws.

The most frequent complaints concern: retail merchandise (cars, magazines, home furnishings), repairs (cars, home improvement, roofing, television, and air conditioners) and advertised specials (food and general merchandise).

In 1969 and 1970 there were 12,301 telephone complaints and 3,943 mail complaints, 1,736 of which were weights-and-measures complaints. A total of $75,000 in cash and merchandise adjustments was returned in 894 cases. Twenty-eight cases were prosecuted, resulting in $2,765 in assessed fines; 735 cases were referred to other governmental agencies; there were 5,826 office investigations; and 438 deceptive ads were checked. In addition, from January to August, 1971, sixty-six prosecutions were brought under relevant laws. Eight out of ten cases have been won.

City consumer protection offices

Akron, Ohio

A few highlights of activities in several cities will point up the uniqueness of the various programs.

Akron, Ohio, has a Commission on Consumer Protection, established by the City Council in 1971. The commission is composed of the mayor, a housewife, a businessman, a labor union representative, and a representative of the lower-income group.

The commission is an advisory group. It can recommend legislation,

develop educational programs, review activities of the office, and make recommendations.

New York City

New York City established a Department of Consumer Affairs[24] in December, 1969. Barbara Trecker, writing in the *New York Post,* asked Ralph Nader
who he thought was doing a good job in the consumer field. The first name
mentioned was Bess Myerson. Bess Myerson was named commissioner on
March 3, 1969. The department was a new one, the first of its kind ever organized in any municipality. It became the first city agency in this country
to develop a comprehensive program for consumer protection and education.
It had a budget of $4,440,000 and a staff of about 362, plus a well-trained,

Budget and staff

dedicated group of some 300 volunteers. Although it sounds like a large
staff with ample funds, Ralph Nader said that the "tragedy is how much
more she could be doing if she had an adequate staff and budget, because
the problem is so enormous."[25]

The Department of Consumer Affairs is responsible for all laws relating
to the sale and offering for sale of goods and services within New York City.
The office was authorized to conduct investigations, hold public and private
hearings, and issue subpoenas. As its basic administrative apparatus, the
department was given powers and personnel of two preexisting city agencies,
the Department of Markets and the Department of Licenses. Each year the
department collects about $3.5 million in license fees and fines for violations
of its regulations. The act creating the new department authorized it to go
to court seeking remedies for violations, temporary and permanent injunctions, and, finally, mass restitution for all consumers injured by deceptive
schemes. The act is said to "constitute the most effective and comprehensive
set of remedies against abuses in the marketplace available to any jurisdiction
in the country."[26]

The department has also represented consumer interests before administrative and legislative bodies on such issues as regulation of public utilities,
medical insurance rates, class-action legislation, oil import quotas, and other

*Rules and regulations
power*

important issues. Perhaps the most important authority is its power to pro-
mulgate rules and regulations—such as those concerning deceptive collection
practices, reservation of motor vehicles for rental, and disclosures in the
extension of consumer credit, to mention a few.

Since November, 1970, four neighborhood offices have been established.
These are complaint-oriented but also do some spot checking for compliance
with consumer regulations.

*Local and county
consumer protection
offices: forgotten
agencies*

Dr. Colston Warne refers to local and county consumer agencies as the
"most neglected area of consumer concern."[27] While weights-and-measures
control has been embedded in legislative codes since the time of Hammurabi,
scant attention has been paid even to the operation of county and local
inspectors of weights and measures in the United States.

[24] Ibid., pp. 83–91.

[25] John Calascione, "City of New York: Department of Consumer Affairs," *International
Consumer,* Winter, 1971–1972, pp. 11-12, 19.

[26] Ibid., p. 12.

[27] *Consumer Union Report on New City and County Consumer Protection Agencies,* p. 3.

There has nevertheless been a change in the area of consumer protection in cities and counties. There has been increased dissatisfaction with the inadequacy of local complaint handling, the Better Business Bureaus notwithstanding. Our "credit economy" has led to many credit abuses. Inflation has caused many more consumers to react vigorously, especially in major metropolitan areas, where low-income consumers have felt the inflationary pinch. Consequently, consumers have developed enough political muscle to create community consumer protection agencies in Office of Economic Opportunity (OEO) and Model Cities programs. Politicians have reacted to this new consumer awareness, championing reforms demanded by consumer groups.

Low-income consumers and the OEO

So, adding it up, the consumer movement has recently found a new point of focus at the community level. This movement is still in its infancy. The mass media still concentrate on consumer news at the federal and state levels of government except in one or two cities, New York City in particular, where Bess Myerson was a dynamic leader under Mayor Lindsay, and a strong supporter of his Department of Consumer Affairs. Betty Furness succeeded Bess Myerson in 1973.

Finally, with the rapidly accelerating rate of urbanization in American society, there will likely be mounting pressures at the city and county level for establishing more consumer protection agencies, possibly with some state or federal financial aid.

Federal executive boards[28]

Federal Executive Boards, made up of local federal agency heads in twenty-five cities across the country, work together locally to implement presidential policy in their communities. The priority project for fiscal 1971 was consumer protection.

Federal-local cooperation

On February 28, 1971, representatives of each FEB gathered in Washington to discuss with Virginia Knauer and her Office of Consumer Affairs staff and with representatives of the Office of Management and Budget, which through an FEB secretariat serves as liaison to the FEBs, the progress they had made and the problems they had encountered. All groups must, by the end of the fiscal year, provide OMB with a progress report.

Federal local agency heads cooperation

Honolulu, for example, has a weekly radio program; New York has undertaken to interview those citizens against whom default judgments have been brought to delve into the problems that may have led to the judgment; Pittsburgh held a consumer fair in a local department store auditorium; Albuquerque has set up consumer corners in local public libraries where educational material is available; Boston conducted a symposium which brought together attorneys general from six New England states to discuss, with people from the area, including the military, the consumer laws on the books and ways of using them more effectively; Kansas City brought together representatives of all agencies, federal, state, and local, within the jurisdiction of the Eighth Circuit Court to meet with members of the bar, in and out of government, in that area, to discuss ways of rendering consumer protection laws most effective; and a number of FEBs are working with local groups which coordinate consumer-related activities to publish directories which will show the consumer which agency or office to call about a specific problem.

[28] *Of Consumer Interest,* Mar. 10, 1972.

An informal count of those present showed that ten cities are planning such a directory either collated by agency or grouped under "problem" headings—credit, housing, health, and so on.

Low-income consumers

One of these is the Metropolitan Northern New Jersey FEB, which will undertake to publish a directory as part of its involvement with the Paterson Consumer Affairs Committee, a federally funded group within the Paterson, New Jersey, Model Cities area. In this case the emphasis is on low-income consumers, and the FEB intends to participate on demand, rather than to go in with prepared programs. An attempt was made, through the Paterson Outreach Worker's Association, which consists of such people as visiting nurses and other workers who go into the communities, to learn the needs in the communities and then to match up the expertise available in the federal agencies with those needs. Even then, the federal experts will participate only to the extent of training the trainers, who will be drawn from the community itself.

Local voluntary consumer groups

In this country, the consumers' voice in local communities is only a whisper at best and practically nonexistent in most of our communities. Why is this true? No one seems to have an answer. The failure of local consumer group action programs in this country is in contrast to successful local group action in England, where they have been functioning since 1961. Today in England there are some eighty local consumer groups with about eighty thousand members. An examination of how local consumer groups function in England may give us some ideas that will be useful in our own country.

Local consumer groups in England

These groups are independent, nonprofit, nonpolitical party organizations of interested people in a community that aim to raise the standard of consumer goods and services, to give their members facts which will save them money, and to express the consumers' point of view publicly. The groups' local magazines (usually mimeographed) might say which shop in town sells the best at the cheapest, or which local shop is giving the biggest discount on the best washing machines, or which local garage does the best repair work at a fair price. Some groups have managed to get local swimming pools improved, public libraries made more convenient, hospital hours extended, footpaths established, and a host of other services established for their members.

For several years Consumers' Association, publisher of *Which?* (a magazine similar to our *Consumer Reports*), budgeted about $20,000 annually to support the National Federation of Consumer Groups with offices in the CA headquarters. CA, mainly because of lack of funds, has withdrawn its financial aid to help local consumer groups get started.

Consumer Ombudsman in Sweden

The Swedish consumer has known this public figure since 1809. This unique official, who is appointed by the legislature but is completely independent, hears all consumer grievances and acts immediately. If the grievance is real, he takes the issue directly to the proper government agency.

Consumer advocate in government

The Ombudsman makes all valid complaints public—a feature of his office which has a desirable effect upon all public officials and civil servants.

This political concept might provide us with a practical model which we could adapt to help solve our own administrative problems. The presence of an agent for all consumers, inside the bureaucracy itself, would have a salutary effect on all state workers.

On January 1, 1971, a new law, the Marketing Practices Act, came into effect. The Consumer Ombudsman (KO) took office on January 1, 1971. He is appointed by the King in Council, but unlike the parliamentary Ombudsman, he is not answerable to the legislature, being subject to the official responsibility that holds for all civil servants. He now has new responsibilities, but also continues to function as a source for receiving consumer complaints. If complaints have merit, he discusses the problem of the business or person selling the product or service and tries to settle the matter by a voluntary agreement. If this proves to be impossible, he can refer the matter to the Market Court. The decision of this court is final. In minor cases, the KO can issue a cease-and-desist order. If this order is accepted by the entrepreneur, it has the same effect as a prohibition by the Market Court.

The new law does appear to give the Consumer Ombudsman more power and new responsibilities, but at the same time he carries on with his duties of processing complaints from consumers and groups at the local level.

COLLEGE-STUDENT CONSUMER ACTION

Student complaints and grievances

College and university students belong to a local group while attending college. During their years in college, most of their consumer functions and experiences are generally centered in and around the campus and the local community. In this environment, students are exposed to fraud and deception on the part of door-to-door salesmen and auto repairmen, dishonest ads for summer jobs overseas as well as in this country, fraudulent do-it-at-home schemes, "rip-offs" by their landlords, fast-talking life insurance salesmen (pushing them to "buy life insurance now and pay later"), and car and property taxes for out-of-state students. They are also involved in many other consumer issues, such as those concerning local merchants, landlord grievances, complaints against the college or university, subscription sales, renting typewriters, traffic tickets, and dry cleaning and laundry establishments.

Only recently have students begun to realize the need to organize to protect their consumer rights. Since Ralph Nader's exposé of the automobile industry in the sixties, and later his efforts to promote campus organizations for the protection of students' consumer rights, there has been a growing interest in consumer protection on many campuses. Ralph Nader believes there are presently some fifty colleges having student consumer protection organizations.

Kansas State University

At Kansas State University in Manhattan, the Consumer Relations Board of the Student Governing Association handled 380 student complaints in one year. Examples of cases settled or pending involved:

1. An apartment complex—$5,600, case won
2. A discount store—$500, case won
3. Blue Cross–Blue Shield—$30,000, case pending

During one year, 1971, the Consumer Relations Board saved the students over $45,000. The CRB was so pleased with its progress that it published a seventy-two-page booklet, *University Consumer Protection*, which describes the organization and its procedures.[29] The editor of this fine informational booklet, Dr. Richard L. D. Morse, head of the department of family economics, has this to say in the foreword:

> Students are searching for relevance and involvement. As consumers they share many problems experienced by other groups of low income, highly mobile persons, isolated from familiar markets and services. Also most are changing their life pattern and orientation from single to married status and from dependence to independence. Such transition and confusion make them especially vulnerable to consumer problems ranging from simple misunderstandings to outright fraud.

CONSUMER JUSTICE[30]

Today, consumers in the United States are basically concerned with "consumer justice." Ideally, consumer protection in the marketplace is a three-way partnership involving consumer decision making in the marketplace (through consumer education, standards for products and warranties, informative labeling, etc.); efficient production and distribution of consumer products (through effective competition); and effective government laws and enforcement to give consumers and ethical businesses the opportunity to buy and sell informatively (through standards, safety, and fair prices based on competition).

Consumer injustice   We have not been successful in achieving "consumer justice" via a three-way partnership. The consumer movement's relentless documentation (as pointed up in earlier chapters) reveals that consumers are being manipulated, defrauded, and injured, not just by marginal businesses or fly-by-night hucksters, but in many instances by large, blue-chip business firms whose practices are unchecked by laws or by the older regulatory agencies. Because this kind of injustice still prevails in the marketplace, seven out of ten Americans (as pointed out earlier in the January, 1967, confidential nationwide survey by Opinion Research Corporation) think present federal legislation is inadequate to protect their health and safety and that more consumer protection is needed.

What has taken place in the last few years may be seen as an escalating series of disclosures by more and more independent Congressmen, by congressional investigations, and by individuals like Ralph Nader. As these charges get attention, the consumer movement escalates, as noted earlier, and demands increase for new legislative action at the federal, state, and local levels. This, at least, has been the case with exposure of defects of vehicles, air and water pollution, gas pipelines, overpriced or dangerous drugs, unfair credit, harmful pesticides, cigarettes, land frauds, electric power rates and reliability, household improvement rackets, exploitation in slums, auto and durable-product warran-

[29] Available from the Student Governing Association, Kansas State University, Manhattan, Kan. 66502.

[30] Reprinted with permission from *The New York Review of Books*, Copyright, 1969, *The New York Review.*

ties, radiation, high-priced auto insurance, flammable fabrics, and boating hazards.

Consumer justice emerging

A more concrete idea of a just economy is beginning to emerge. Consumers are beginning to have a broader definition of consumer rights and interests. It appears quite clear that consumers must not only be protected in the voluntary use of a product such as a car or a flammable textile product, but also from involuntary consumption of industrial by-products such as air and water pollutant, excessive pesticide and nitrate residues in foods, and antibiotics in meat.

These demands on the part of consumers are ethical rather than ideological. Their principles and proposals for solutions are derived directly from solid documentation of common abuses whose origins are being traced directly to the policies of some of our largest corporations.

It is becoming apparent that the reform of consumer abuses and the reform of corporate power and policies are different sides of the same coin. New approaches to the enforcement of consumer rights are necessary.

New approaches needed

We need to strengthen present consumer protection and to try new approaches to the enforcement of the rights of consumers. The following major forces need our careful attention:

1. Rapid disclosure of the facts relating to the quality, quantity, and safety of a product is essential to a just marketplace. Buyers must be able to compare products via some kind of national standards in order to reward the superior producer. This process is the justification for a free market system.

2. The practices of refunding dollars to consumers who have been bilked and recalling defective products are finally becoming recognized as principles of deterrence and justice. Over 6 million vehicles were recalled between September, 1966 (the date of the auto safety law), and 1969. The FDA now requires drug companies to issue "corrective letters" to all physicians if their original advertisements are found to be misleading. The threat of liability suits is causing companies to recall defective and unsafe products "voluntarily" in some cases even where no law or regulation exists. In 1968, Sears recalled about 6,000 gas heaters after public health officials warned of lethal carbon monoxide leakage. Likewise, General Electric made changes in 150,000 color TV sets which had been found to be emitting excessive radiation by Consumers Union and reported in its *Consumer Reports* magazine. The duty to refund, however, remains less well recognized than the duty to recall defective products. The usual FTC orders to "cease and desist" after it learns about the defects do not require the company to refund to the consumer. Without this sanction, a major deterrent is lost. The mere order to "go and sin no more" is easily evaded. The recent development of filing treble damage suits against violators of antitrust laws has strengthened private actions against malpractices by established corporations. In the early 1960s, for example, customers and governments collected about $550 million in out-of-court settlements after General Electric, Westinghouse, and other large companies were found guilty of carrying on a criminal antitrust price-fixing conspiracy. The second development is in the use of "class actions" in which suits are filed on behalf of large numbers of people who have been mistreated in the same way. Class actions help solve the problem when thousands

of consumers have been cheated in such small amounts that it does not pay to take individual legal action. Presently, some two thousand poverty lawyers, supported by the U.S. Office of Economic Opportunity (OEO), are beginning to use this important technique.

3.   Disputes in courts and other judicial means need to be conducted under fairer ground rules and with adequate representation for consumers. The OEO neighborhood poverty lawyers, representing the poor against landlords, finance companies, car dealers, and other sellers of goods and services, is a hopeful legal sign. For the first time, these lawyers are having success in court in exposing illegal repossession of goods, unreasonable garnishment, undisclosed credit and financing terms, and many other illegal practices. What is important is that these recent cases are documenting a general pattern of abuses and injustices in the legal system itself. This may prod law schools to more relevant teaching, as well as guide legislatures and courts toward reform of laws, court procedures, and remedies. Furthermore, this trend is resolving many consumer conflicts in neighborhood arbitration units which are open in the evenings when dependents need not be absent from their jobs in order to attend.

4.   The practice of setting government safety standards and changing them to reflect new technology and uses is spreading, although much more should be done. Many years after banking and securities markets were brought under regulation, products such as cars (with casualties of 53,000 dead and $4\frac{1}{2}$ million injured annually), washing machines and power lawnmowers (with 200,000 persons injured annually), chemicals, and all pipeline systems did not have to adhere to standards of safety performance other than what companies set up themselves. But with the passage of the auto safety law in 1966, other major consumer products have been brought under federal safety regulation. To avoid more piecemeal safety legislation, Congress in 1967 passed an act establishing the National Commission on Product Safety to investigate many household hazards, from appliances to chemicals. The commission must recommend by 1970 a more detailed federal, state, and local policy toward reducing or preventing deaths and injuries from these products.

5.   To set up effective standards of safety, the government will have to conduct research—or contract for its own research—on safety of products and methods of improving unsafe industrial products. Without this additional power, the government will have to rely on what industry claims is safe, and the government's efforts will be crippled. Also, the existing safety laws do not permit government to find out quickly and accurately whether industry is complying with the law. The National Highway Safety Bureau, for example, has little idea whether or not the 1969 cars meet all the safety standards, since no government testing facilities yet exist.

6.   In theory, business, free competition, and corporate responsibility are supposed to protect the consumer; in practice, all have long ignored him. Price-fixing, for example, is common throughout our economy. The Department of Justice does not have the manpower to cope with this problem. All of us know that price-fixing means higher prices for consumers. An even greater danger exists when the failure of large industry to compete prevents the development of new products that might save lives and the improvement of consumer

products. Ideally, one of the potent forces for consumer justice would be the exercise of corporate "responsibility." The casualty insurance industry, for example, should have a strong interest in safer cars. It chose to raise premiums instead. The insurance industry has not raised its voice to demand legislation to improve the design and inspection of cars; nor has it encouraged the rating of cars according to their safety.

7. Professional and technical societies (American Society of Safety Engineers, etc.) have up to now been little more than trade associations for the industries that employ their members. It is rather shocking, for example, that none of these societies has done much to work out public policies to deal with pollution of air and water. With few exceptions, societies of law and medicine have done little to protect the public from victimization. Engineers and scientists, however, had no procedure for undertaking these new roles. The societies may have to create special independent organizations willing to get facts and take action in the interest of the public. There are the beginnings of such societies. The Committee for Environmental Information in St. Louis and the Physicians for Automotive Safety in New Jersey have shown how people with even small resources can accomplish much in educating the public and in an action program.

8. The courts have been making progress in rulings that give injured persons fairer chances of recovering damages. The expansion of the "implied warranty," mentioned earlier in the book, is one example of the trend toward more justice for the consumer because under this concept the injured need not prove negligence if injured through the use of a defective product. The law of torts (personal injuries) still does not protect the consumer against the pollution of the environment, which indiscriminately injures all the people exposed to it. Pollution in Los Angeles is a serious health hazard, but how many of their people sue? True, some eighty residents in Martinez, California, are suing Shell Oil's petroleum refinery for air pollution. Shell claims, perhaps justly, that it is abiding by the state's mild pollution-control regulation. It may be that justice in the courts must be paralleled by better state laws.

9. The most promising development in recent years is the growing belief that new institutions are needed within the government whose only function is to protect consumer interests. Reference, here, is to the Office of Consumer Counsel in the Justice Department, created by the Johnson administration, and to the creation of other consumer organizations within large government departments. The Office of Consumer Services in the Health, Education, and Welfare Department is one such example. Perhaps some day we may have a Department of Consumer Affairs in the President's Cabinet. Clearly, something needs to be done to expose present regulatory agencies (FTC, ICC, FCC, and others) and challenge them to take more vigorous action. Senator Lee Metcalf introduced legislation to create an independent U.S. Office of Utility Consumer's Counsel to represent consumers before regulatory agencies and courts. Even such an independent office would, in time, have to be encouraged continuously by consumer organizations at the local, state, and national levels to avoid the dangers of bureaucratic attitude and atrophy.

10. Finally, there is urgent need to stimulate professional people, such as lawyers, engineers, doctors, and economists, to develop local consumer

service organizations similar to the OEO neighborhood poverty lawyers, mentioned earlier, that could handle consumer complaints, give information, and work out plans for public action.

Consumer voice still feeble

The voice of the consumer is being heard in the land. Legislators are listening. Alert businessmen are beginning to pay attention. And, as we have noted earlier, the consumer is beginning to organize at the local, state, and national levels.

The current consumer movement dates from a statement on March 15, 1962, by the late President Kennedy when he declared that every consumer has four basic rights—the right to be informed, the right to safety, the right to choose, and the right to be heard. Thus, the President breathed life into the consumer movement, and President Johnson continued to champion the consumer by word and by initiating legislation. Consumers' organizations sprang up, and states, too, got into the act. So did many cities.

The growth of the current consumer movement has not followed traditional patterns. In the past this type of protest originated at the grass-roots level and eventually converged on state capitals and on Washington. The current consumer crusade *started* in the nation's Capital, was fanned impressively by an independent consumer crusader, Ralph Nader (also in Washington), and is currently spreading slowly to the grass roots of America.

Whither the consumer movement?

The progress of the consumer movement since 1962 is impressive when judged by the growing number of laws passed by Congress, by some state legislatures, and by a few local governments. Notwithstanding the progress in consumer legislation since 1962, in particular, the wide publicity the mass media have given to the single consumer crusader, Ralph Nader, and the recent alarm of industry over the publicity about auto safety, drug costs, and other scandals, the consumer movement is still a feeble force in American power politics. Almost any way you look at it, the interests of consumers are low on the list of election issues. Too, the government's expenditures to protect those interests are negligible. Some would argue that this situation will always prevail in view of the tremendous financial and political power in the hands of industry in and out of government. But new approaches to influencing corporate behavior are emerging. It is possible that more people, not merely a few articulate consumer leaders, may begin to react with greater concern to the enormity of their deprivation—the hundreds of ways in which their income is being milked. The current assault on the health and safety of the public from many industrial products, drugs, and foods has resulted in violence that even dwarfs crime in the streets. Since 1965 about 260 people died in riots in American cities; but every two days some 300 persons are killed and 20,000 injured while driving on our highways. Add to these violence records the economic loss each year—$500 million loss in security frauds, another $500 million in home repair frauds, and even more loss in dishonest and fraudulent repair bills, to name only three of hundreds of ways in which our income is unjustly taken from us—and we have an astronomical annual financial loss to Americans.

What the current consumer movement is beginning to say—and must say much more stongly if it is to grow—is that "consumer justice" must prevail. The rule *caveat emptor* (let the buyer beware) should not be relied upon to reward deception and fraud. The modern rule, *caveat venditor* (let the seller beware) and *cognoscat emptor* (let the buyer be informed), should prevail.

QUESTIONS FOR DISCUSSION

1. Why is consumer legislation at the federal level not enough?

2. Can you see any difficulties in dual (federal-state) control in consumer protection laws? (Examine how the federal Fair Packaging and Labeling Act is enforced in your state.)

3. The failure of state laws to protect consumers lies in the slight degree to which they are enforced. How do you account for this tendency? You might investigate how your consumer frauds bureau (if there is one) or your public utilities commission functions in behalf of consumers in your state.

4. The primary weapon against gypsters is the authority to obtain a "court injunction." Does your state give this authority to your attorney general? How do court injunctions work?

5. If your state has a voluntary consumer association, find out as much as you can about its activities, financing, and effectiveness in promoting the consumer interest.

6. There are some people who would destroy the Office of Economic Opportunity. Do you think the OEO Economic Opportunity and Community Action programs, presently in some 150 cities, fill unmet consumer needs in these cities?

7. What is your reaction to FTC Commissioner Mary Gardiner Jones's suggestion that states need "consumer courts" to handle consumer complaints? Why? Would these be better than small-claims courts?

PROJECTS

1. If you have a consumer organization in your community, invite its president and other enthusiastic members to attend a class discussion of its purposes and activities and the results of its combined efforts. Possibly the class might attend one or more of its general and committee meetings. That is where you will see the best in organized consumer education functioning on the local level.

2. Think of all the ways in which people might learn how to develop pride in being intelligent and skilled consumers. Does this pride tend to decrease as the family income increases? If a manufacturer takes pride in his products and an athlete takes pride in excellent performance, why shouldn't an individual take pride in being a good consumer?

3. The statement is made that the foundation of consumer education is to help each of us to (a) develop a sense of values, (b) determine what we most

want out of life, (c) set our goals and see them in proper balance, and then (d) act according to our developed principles. What are your reactions to this? Support your views in an objective manner.

4.   Prepare a paper on consumer protection legislation and enforcement in your state.

5.   Investigate the consumer protection services rendered by your local community. Does the federal government enter into any aspect of these local services?

6.   In 1972 there was an ombudsman in each of these states—Hawaii, Iowa, Nebraska, Oregon, and South Carolina. If you live in one of these states, write this consumer official. Ask him to describe his functions, the nature of the consumer complaints he handles, the results of his efforts to aid citizens, his budget and staff, and his powers.

SUGGESTED READINGS

Barber, Richard J.: "Government and the Consumer," *Michigan Law Review,* May, 1966.

Bishop, James, Jr., and Henry W. Hubbard: *Let the Seller Beware,* The National Press, Inc., Washington, 1969.

Consumer Guardian, Consumer Research Advisory Council, Detroit, Mich.

Consumers Report for 1971–1972 to the People of Pennsylvania, Pennsylvania Insurance Department, Harrisburg.

Consumers' Voice, Consumers Education and Protective Association, Philadelphia.

Digest of Proceedings, Consumer Assembly of Greater New York, New York, Jan. 13, 1968.

"Fixing the Fixers: Curb Repair Frauds," *The Wall Street Journal,* Jan. 11, 1972, p. 1.

Metcalf, Lee, and Vic Reinemer: *Overcharge,* David McKay Company, Inc., New York, 1968.

CHAPTER 18

CHAPTER 18
THE INTERNATIONAL CONSUMER MOVEMENT [1]

[1]The sources of information on the consumer movements in the world are many. The author's visit to countries in Western Europe and to Japan in 1962, 1963, and 1972 gave him valuable information and insight. Much information comes from unpublished sources. Notable among the unpublished sources is the material collected by Dr. Colston E. Warne, of Amherst College and president of Consumers Union of U.S., Inc. Dr. Warne has been most generous in permitting the author to use his excellent material on the consumer movements of the world. The consumer organizations in various countries have also been generous in their efforts to be informative and to discuss common problems. Jan van Veen, executive secretary of the International Organization of Consumers Unions, has given generously of his knowledge about the international consumer movement since 1965.

Intelligent American consumers should be interested in and knowledgeable about the consumer movement in the rest of the world. There is a rapidly developing European consumer movement. An unprecedented number of consumers protection organizations has emerged in Europe, some stimulated by the cooperative movement, some given governmental assistance, and some arising from independent efforts. The same forces that have brought into existence consumer organizations in Europe have spread to Canada, where the Consumers Association of Canada has embarked on a consumer testing movement. The consumer movement has likewise spread to the Near East, Iceland, Australia, New Zealand, and Japan.

Although the structures of the consumer organizations of the world vary, all have one central element in common—the aim to furnish impartial advice and recommendations concerning trademarked consumer goods. Consumers in all countries are increasingly angered at being misled as to product claims and are bewildered by competing advertising slogans. The spectacular advance of new technologies has created a vacuum in product information which has not been filled by producers. The consumer movement forms a practical answer that can improve living standards by directing consumers toward meritorious products and away from those that contain virtues which exist only in the promoter's imagination.

The heart of the modern consumer movement lies in accurate testing and more testing, and in the issuing of reports on testing that will guide consumers to a higher standard of living.

The consumer movement, however, is more than a testing organization. It is also an educational organization—a new and significant phase of adult education. It punctures false claims, it spreads knowledge of new quality products, it harnesses science for the service of the buyer. The consumer movement also helps restore the capacity of the competitive system to reward those companies that are producing better products. The central aim of the consumer movement is to help organize the economy in ways that will best serve the consumer interest.

Another purpose of the consumer movement is that of becoming a countervailing power in legislation that will afford better protection to all consumers against the more common hazards of the marketplace, such as elaborate packaging, extravagantly promoted brand names, deceptive weights, improper measurements, restraints on retail competition, fictitious prices, unknown credit terms, restrictive patenting and licensing arrangements, tariff barriers, and many other impediments to competition.

Just as the International Labor Office for more than fifty years has been championing the development of international labor standards, the international consumer movement has an obligation to insist that a parallel international organization be developed to promote international consumer standards. Just as the earlier legislation insisted that water supplies be sanitary and that food be unadulterated, so in this period of chemical revolution, new social safeguards on the social front must be developed that will take into account that the increases in technological achievements demand increasing consumer protection.

THE PURPOSE OF INTERNATIONAL CONSUMERISM

Aside from providing information necessary to the wise allocation of consumer resources at the spatial level of analysis, international consumerism should tend to lead toward a more efficient allocation of the world's resources through the movement of goods and services across international boundaries. This should result in greater welfare for the world's population.

International trade and the American consumer

International trade has a substantial impact on you, the American consumer, and on your life-style. We need foreign trade—export markets for our agricultural and industrial products and imports to supplement our domestic production and to stimulate competition and productivity.

Every day of our lives each one of us plays a part in the intricate machinery of international trade. We may be awakened in the morning by a Japanese clock-radio; dress in English-tailored clothes or Italian shoes; run our German-made automobiles on Middle Eastern or Venezuelan fuel; sip French wine at dinner, with Central American fruit for dessert; and light our homes by means of wires manufactured from African or Chilean copper. In similar fashion, foreigners consume and use countless American products, including bread from United States grain. They ride in American-made jet aircraft or on roads bulldozed or paved by American earthmoving machinery. They go to discotheques wearing American blue jeans while they dance to American-made records. The list is endless.

As consumers, each time we buy a product made in a foreign country or made from raw materials imported from a foreign country, we participate in the vast and complex interchange of international trade.

No single nation on earth has all the raw materials or productive capacity to supply its citizens with everything they need and want. What a country needs or wants, but does not have or cannot produce at a reasonable price, it buys from other nations. And in order to pay for its imports, it must sell its products on the world market.

A growing dependence on imports

Suppose all trade between nations stopped tomorrow. What would our lives be like? To start with, we'd probably miss our morning coffee—or tea—or even hot chocolate. More than likely there would be enough gasoline to meet our needs for awhile, but soon the use of cars and other vehicles which depend on oil products would have to be limited. Although the United States is one of the world's leading oil-producing nations, the persistent warnings of an energy crisis underline our growing dependence on imports. In 1973, we experienced a shortage of oil and gasoline products and began looking for more oil abroad.

Copper, too, would be scarce, and so installation of new electrical and telephone systems would be restricted. Many of the alloys we depend upon for high-grade specialty steels would be unavailable, as would French wine, Scotch whisky, foreign perfume, Scandinavian crystal, and a host of other items we have come to enjoy. Our choice in thousands of other products, including electrical appliances, flatware, watches, automobiles, and furniture, would be sharply limited.

But more important, the chances are very good that many of us would be out of a job. Millions of Americans owe their jobs to the products we import:

the dock workers who unload these products, the salemen who sell them, the truck drivers and railroad workers who move them, the repairmen who service them, the clerks and bookkeepers and secretaries who work for businesses involved in foreign commerce, and the executives who run these businesses.

Even more people would be affected who are employed in industries which produce products for export to our trading partners around the world. Our computers, aircraft, nuclear power plants, automobiles, plastics, engines and turbines, coal, tobacco, wheat, soybeans, and other farm products which we sell to other countries would have no market outside the United States. Employment in these industries would be cut severely, as would employment in supporting service industries.

There is little doubt that the American economy, as we know it, would grind to a halt without international trade. What's more, our standard of living would be drastically scaled down. A nation must both buy and sell abroad to maintain and enhance the economic well-being of its citizens. And the higher its standard of living, the more dependent it is upon international trade.

Worldwide growth of consumerism

When the world consumer movement was born in 1960, its membership came exclusively from the relatively affluent societies of Europe, North America, and Australia. Today, the sleeping giant of consumerism has awakened in countries in all stages of development and in every continent of the world.

This decade is in all probability the crucial one for two-thirds of the human race. The monster problems of undernourishment, undereducation, underemployment, and mass poverty are now well-enough recognized. What has been less recognized is that a country's progress in solving these problems cannot be measured merely by its rate of growth—merely by the number of percentage points added to its gross national product. Gross national product is no measure of wealth or welfare. One example will suffice. Mass production of substandard merchandise, unwholesome food, and unsafe goods turned out by industries sheltered from competition by a well-intentioned import substitution policy may increase the gross domestic product, but only at the cost of gravely and even dangerously diminishing the net consumer satisfaction. And net consumer satisfaction, as the father of political economy, Adam Smith, taught us, is what really matters—the classic and legitimate goal of economic policy. In short, the ultimate test of socioeconomic planning is not its effect on percentage points; the ultimate test is its effect on human beings, on the standard of living of people. An ever-increasing percentage of families throughout the developing world are dependent for that standard of living on the conditions they find in the market. And what they find in the market is gross adulteration of food products, short weight and measure, absence of price posting, lack of identifying labeling, misleading advertising, fraudulent sales practices, and extortionate credit terms. So, clearly, there is a great need, if standards are to be raised and the quality of life improved, for the planners and policy makers to find means to recruit, train, and finance an effective corps of inspectors for market regulation. But in view of the many priorities jostling for position, it is also clear that the consumer organizations in the developing nations will need to play a greater role, even an innovative role, to achieve market protection through direct participation in the regulatory process—through consumer information, consumer education, and consumer mobilization. And these are the areas where more affluent consumer organizations, through the IOCU, must support and assist consumers in developing countries.

Dr. Gordon Bivens, professor of family economics at the University of Missouri, said, "Our future is more closely connected with and interdependent on the developments in other countries now than it ever was before, and it will continue to become more so."[2] Thus, as consumers we need to be concerned about the effect of tariff arrangements on other countries and their potentials for growth as well as the price that we have to pay for services and goods. Also, we need to be thinking about more international standards for consumer services and goods.

TYPES OF CONSUMER MOVEMENTS

Consumer movements throughout the world are of three different types.

In the United Kingdom, Australia, the Netherlands, Belgium, and Canada, as in the United States, consumer testing is undertaken without government support. The private consumer testing agencies in these countries have been most careful to steer clear of business entanglements. They have recruited technical personnel to give impartial assessments of products bought on the open market. The most rapidly growing testing agency among these newer movements, Consumers' Association, Ltd., in the United Kingdom, had a membership of over 600,000 at the end of its fifteenth year, 1972.

The second type of consumer organization undertakes consumer testing through government subsidy. The two most vigorous examples of this type are Norway and New Zealand. Both of these product-testing groups have been in a position to publish comparative product ratings as well as to handle consumer complaints. In New Zealand, the government linked the testing facilities of its Bureau of Standards and of its universities with the consumer testing movement and has developed a quasi-autonomous consumer testing movement supported by voluntary subscriptions. This effort, like the Norwegian, has as its basic objective the governmental establishment of a nonpartisan consumer movement.

Consumer movements throughout the world making great progress

The third type of consumer agency that has emerged in the international picture is the extension of the work of standards associations into the field of comparative product reporting. Notable examples in this field are in England and in Japan. In Japan, until 1963, the newly formed Japan Consumers' Association used a combination of government subsidy, subscriptions to its magazine, donations by manufacturers of products to be tested, and government testing agencies. In 1963, the JCA made a serious effort to reduce possible outside influences when it decided to purchase in the open market the products to be tested. It remains to be seen whether this association can demonstrate complete independence and objectivity and yet become self-sustaining.

Most of the organizations described in this chapter deserve more attention

---

[2] *Distaff,* Winter, 1972, p. 38.

than space permits, but the brief summaries will give a picture of the great progress made on behalf of consumers in these countries. There is ample reason to believe that other countries, notably many of the newly formed nations in Africa, will also be active in promoting the consumer interest.

INTERNATIONAL ORGANIZATION OF CONSUMERS UNIONS (IOCU)

Dr. Colston E. Warne, president of Consumers Union of U.S., Inc., was largely responsible for promoting the creation of an International Organization of Consumers Unions. After many preliminary discussions with consumer leaders in Europe and elsewhere, the Consumers Union of U.S., Inc., appropriated funds for an organizing meeting of consumer union officials at The Hague, Netherlands. On April 1, 1960, the International Organization of Consumers Unions was made a *stichting* (foundation) under Dutch law, and it functions in accordance with legal regulations. The registered office is at The Hague, Netherlands. The financial resources consist of the *Stichting* Fund, contributions from members, and the sale of its publications.

Consumers' declaration When the delegates to the Brussels Conference of IOCU met in 1964, they decided that the organization should be a voice which has so far been largely silent for the consumer interest. The following declaration was drafted, expressing further the sound reasons for an international organization of consumers:

> The purpose of an economy is to produce, for the maximum satisfaction of consumers, goods and services which are: good in quality; sufficient in quantity; safe; reasonable in price.
>
> In practice, consumers frequently find goods of shoddy quality; insufficient legal control to guarantee safety; gluts or scarcities; prices having no relation to quality; confusing advertising; insufficient information; poor retail service.
>
> Consumers should not acquiesce in this state of affairs, but are urged to act, individually and via their consumers' organizations, to get improvement.
>
> To do so, consumers are urged to organize themselves to: fight ignorance with reports and labels based on comparative tests on consumer goods and services; with accurate, unbiased advice on buying consumer goods and services; with the information necessary to assess the validity of advertising claims and the value of the goods inside the packaging; make themselves heard in every section of the government or economy where the consumers' interest is, or may be, involved. This is particularly important where the quality and price of goods or services are involved and essential where there is any question of safety.
>
> To achieve this, the consumer organizations are urged to enrol, wherever possible, the help of governments, educators, the press, radio and television.
>
> They are urged to work not only for well-educated, conscientious consumers, but for those who are uninterested and hard to reach: not only for the consumers in advance countries, but for those in the underdeveloped areas as well.
>
> Consumers everywhere should be able, if they so choose, to buy goods and obtain services whose essential qualities they can discover without great effort on their part, and which are safe, of good quality and reasonable in price.

Objectives of IOCU

The objectives of IOCU are these:

1. To authenticate, assist, and actively promote genuine efforts throughout the world in consumer self-organization, as well as governmental efforts to further the interests of the consumer;

2. To promote international cooperation in the comparative testing of consumer goods and services, and to facilitate exchange of test methods and plans;

3. To promote international cooperation in all other aspects of consumer information, education, and protection, and to collect and disseminate information relating to consumer laws and practices throughout the world;

4. To provide a forum in which national bodies may work exclusively in the interest of the consumer problems and possible solutions to them;

5. To act as a clearinghouse for the publications of such bodies and to regulate (subject to any regulations promulgated by or applicable to the bodies themselves) the use of such published material;

6. To publish information on subjects connected with the interests of the consumer;

7. To maintain effective links with United Nations agencies and other international bodies, with a view to representing the interests of the consumer on the international level;

8. To give all practical aid and encouragement to the development of consumer educational and protective programs in the developing countries, through the United Nations agencies and in other suitable ways;

9. And in general to take such actions as may further these objects.

Rules, services, and responsibilities

The IOCU is a noncommercial organization. Its members agree to refrain from any use of their membership for advertising purposes, for promoting the sale of any product, or for any commercial purpose whatsoever. The name of IOCU or references to IOCU publications and other materials may not be used for advertising or for any commercial purposes.

The following publications are for the use of members of the IOCU:

1. *International Consumer* (English with summaries in French). Quarterly report with news of consumer organizations, consumer test equipment, operational methods of different consumers' associations, the juridical position of the consumer, and other matters of interest about consumers.

2. *News Letter* (English). A monthly review with news from the headquarters office, financial reports, and other confidential items. The *Circular Letter* is sent to IOCU members only.

3. *Consumers' Directory* (every other year). Information about all IOCU members and other consumers' organizations.

4. *Consumers Review* (English). Bimonthly annotated indexes of consumer magazines, consumer protection laws, and educational material.

Structure

Originally only five consumer nonprofit, independent consumer testing organizations served in the important policy-making IOCU Council (U.S.A., England, Belgium, the Netherlands, and Australia). Later Norway and Denmark were added.

In 1972, the five original consumer testing organizations remained on the council. These were now matched by five consumer groups (Norway, Denmark, France, Germany, and Jamaica).

Five more members were elected from a list of Associate Members of IOCU (Canada, Austria, Israel, Japan, and New Zealand). This brings the council to 15 members. This arrangement allows for a balance between its various kinds of consumer organizations and for an opportunity to give representation to more countries which have hitherto had no part in control of the organization. These fifteen groups elect the executive committee which guides the organization.

Membership qualifications
As of January 1, 1973, there were seventy-three consumer member organizations from thirty-five countries in IOCU. Of these seventy-three consumer organizations thirty-four were eligible for the council. There were also thirty-nine corresponding members. These members do not qualify for associate membership, but are active on behalf of consumer interests in their respective countries.

IOCU is not unlike other international organizations in that the constituent organizations must comply with certain qualifications before being admitted as members. For example, national and regional bodies are eligible to be associates of IOCU if they meet with the following qualifications:

1. They are active exclusively on behalf of the interests of the consumer.
2. They are totally unconcerned with the advancement of commercial or party political causes.
3. They are non-profit-making in character.
4. They do not accept advertisements in their publications.
5. They do not allow selective commercial exploitation of the information and advice they give to consumers.
6. Their independence of action and comment is in no way influenced or qualified by the receipt of subsidies.

The first fourteen organizations listed below are IOCU council members (founder, co-opted, or elected members). The remaining seventeen organizations are listed in order of date of admission to IOCU membership.

Consumers Union of U.S., Inc. (U.S.A.)
Consumers' Association (U.K.)
Australian Consumers' Association (Australia)
Consumentenbond (Netherlands)
Association des Consommateurs (Belgium)
Forbrukerrådet (Norway)
Forbrugerrådet (Denmark)
Statens Konsumentråd (Sweden)
Stiftung Warentest (G.F.R., German Federal Republic)
Verein für Konsumenteninformation (Austria)
Consumers' Institute (New Zealand)
Israel Consumers' Association (Israel)
Consumers' Association of Canada (Canada)
Japan Consumers' Association (Japan)

Arbeitsgemeinschaft der Verbraucher e.V. (G.F.R.)
Union Fédérale de la Consommation (France)
Research Institute for Consumer Affairs (U.K.)
American Council on Consumer Interests (U.S.A.)
National Federation of Consumer Groups (U.K.)
Canberra Consumers, Inc. (Australia)
Selangor Consumers' Association (Malaysia)
Central Consumers' Authority (Israel)
National Consumers' League (Jamaica)
Consumers' Association of Ireland (Ireland)
Consumer Federation of America, Inc. (U.S.A.)
Israel Consumer Council (Israel)
Union Luxembourgeoise des Consommateurs (Luxembourg)
The Consumers' Union of Iceland (Iceland)
Organizacion Consumidores de Puerto Rico (Puerto Rico)
Philippine Consumers Movement, Inc. (Philippines)
Kuluttajaneuvosto Konsumentrådet (Finland)

Major activities of IOCU

1. Representation of national consumer organizations at the international level. In early 1973, IOCU had consultative or liaison status with ECOSOC, UNICEF, UNESCO, FAO (in particular with FAO-WHO Codex Alimentarius Commission), ISO, IEC, CEPT, and the Consumer Protection Committee of the Council of Europe.

2. Study and development of technical aspects of consumer affairs (standardization, test methods, and so forth).

3. Fostering of consumer education.

4. Provision of legal, technical, and educational information and other data.

5. Provision of facilities for discussion of consumer problems and objectives (biennial world conferences: 1960 at The Hague; 1962, Brussels; 1964, Oslo; 1966, Israel; 1968, New York City; 1970, Baden; and 1972, Stockholm. There were, in addition, irregular conferences and seminars.)

HIGHLIGHTS OF THE WORLD CONSUMER MOVEMENT

Since the IOCU headquarters at The Hague publishes, once every two years, a rather complete *Consumers Directory* (the latest is 1971–1972), a summary of the major consumer organizations in each of the countries having membership status with the IOCU will not be given here.[3]

International product testing

The multinational company and the multinational product are realities in our time. Consumers in a number of countries want to buy—and therefore want to test—the same products and services. So, why not get together to test such products jointly?

[3] International Organization of Consumers Unions (IOCU), 9, Emmastract, The Hague, Netherlands. The *Consumer Directory* gives the addresses of the organizations in each country and also their founding dates, objectives, main activities, publications, membership, finances, and principal officers. The price of the 1971–1972 directory is $5 postpaid.

Eurolabo

Joint testing is happening today. A consumer laboratory in Belgium tests recordings for a consortium of Belgian, Dutch, and German consumer organizations. The electroacoustical laboratory known as Eurolabo was set up in 1971. This laboratory has tested stereo amplifiers and tuners, tape recorders, cassette recorders, gramophone records, turntables, pickup cartridges, video tape recorders, and television aerials.

Eurolabo's growth has been very rapid over the past two years. Its testing program increased from four to eight product tests a year to twelve or more annually. Shortly it will move into new buildings in order to accommodate the increased demand for international testing of products sold in other countries.[4]

Joint testing of consumer products a success

In 1968 and 1969, Britain's Consumers' Association (similar to Consumers Union in the United States) and Holland's Consumentenbond (acting for several European product testing organizations) began discussions of experimental automobile testing. Six cars were purchased in Holland, partially road-tested there, and shipped to CA's normal testing facilities in England. Finally, in early 1970, tests were finished and a final report appeared in *Motoring Which?* (CA's consumer magazine) in January, 1971, in *Consumentengids* consumer magazine, *Test Achats,* and in the March issue of *Der Test.* The experimental stage was successful. Since the first cooperative testing, other tests were made following a similar testing procedure.

The big advantage of international cooperative testing is in the economical use of very expensive testing equipment, ground facilities, and testing skills.

A number of other consumer organizations are presently cooperating in testing consumer products. Norway, Sweden, and Denmark jointly test washing machines, refrigerators, freezers, and sewing machines. Sweden and the U.K. have joined forces on vacuum cleaners. The United States (Consumers Union) has tested Canadian products. *Motoring Which?* car tests are reprinted in a dozen countries today. The Scandinavians have recently joined with Western Europeans in cooperative product testing. On the other side of the globe, the Australians and New Zealanders have initiated common testing with Israel, the Philippines, and the Fiji Islands.

Joint testing in Scandinavia

The Interscandinavian Committee on Consumer Matters has a special committee working on consumer product testing services. Such products and services as anticorrosion treatment for cars, TV repairs, airline and postal services, and holiday hotels are common to these countries.

The early experiences of international product testing proved that it would be more efficient to start joint testing between two or more neighboring consumer organizations. The joint tests also must be based on an identity of interests—the collaborators must be after the same thing. This means that the number of consumer organizations engaged in joint testing should be small and that they should be able to cooperate with one another.

The lack of adequate international standards for consumer products and test methods is a frequently mentioned problem in joint testing. The National Swedish Consumer Institute, in fact, regards its contribution to the work of the Electrotechnical Commission and to the Standardization Organization as no less important in the long term than comparative testing itself.

[4] *International Consumer,* Spring, 1971.

Financial savings

The most important advantage in joint testing is economies in serving consumers; members of consumer product testing organizations get that much more for their money. Furthermore, since they use their own testing facilities, there is no need to hire government laboratories. Another possible advantage in joint testing is that the test results may have a greater impact on manufacturers, who are more interested than ever when a project involves a number of markets.

International informative labeling [5]

The concept of informative labeling spread first to other lands in Scandinavia and then farther afield. In 1966 the International Labelling Centre (ILC) was established in The Hague to promote international cooperation in this sphere, primarily by collecting and circulating information about the procedures, activities, and labeling schemes of the member organizations. Today, the ILC has eight members from eight European countries—Association Française pour l'Etiquettage d'Information (France), Dansk Varudeklarations-Naevn (Denmark), Fundacion Espanola Calitax (Spain), Informatieve Etikettering Nederland (Netherlands), Schweizerisches Institut für Hauswirtschaft (Switzerland), Tavaraselosteliitto (Finland), Varefakta-Komiteen (Norway), and the longest-established, Sweden's Varudeklarationsnämnden.

International guidelines

Member organizations are regularly asked to identify the product groups in which they would most like to see labeling schemes introduced, and the international organization then lays down guidelines for these. So far, five international guidelines have been established (for refrigerators, freezers, vacuum cleaners, electric fans, and slide projectors): the aim is to have national labeling schemes based on the guidelines, ensuring that in the future, identical test methods and uniform labeling will be used to the widest possible extent. The first national schemes based on international ILC guidelines have already been introduced in the Netherlands.

In this connection the ILC has established working relations with institutions such as the International Electrotechnical Commission (IEC), the International Organization for Standardization (ISO), and the International Standards Steering Committee for Consumer Affairs (ISCA), as well as with IOCU and with individual consumer organizations.

With the growth of international trade, it is sometimes difficult for manufacturers to know for which market their product may eventually be destined, and one of the objectives of the ILC is to facilitate international trade. A product can be manufactured and tested in one country and then, through the international labeling system, may be sold with an informative label in any or all of the member countries, without need for further testing or measuring. This enables the consumer to make comparisons between foreign and domestic goods much more easily, which is increasingly important as goods cross national frontiers and more and more consumers travel and shop abroad.

A closer look at one of the national labeling institutes will illustrate the processes and work involved in attaching an informative label to a product.

The Stichting Informatieve Etikettering Nederland (IEN) (the Dutch Foundation for Informative Labeling) was established at the end of 1964. Its founda-

---

[5] For more details, see Isolc van den Haven, "The Growth of Informative Labelling," *Consumer International*, Spring, 1972, p. 10.

The IEN

tion and working approach were based largely on the experiences of the Swedish institute. In the early years of its existence the IEN encountered financial difficulties and got off to a rather slow start, but the last two or three years have brought a much wider appreciation of, and interest in, the work of the institution. The thirty-four projects on which labeling work is now being carried out cover four main groups—electrical appliances, home furnishings, household equipment, and sports and camping gear.

A national labeling center

The IEN works in close collaboration with standards organizations, independent research laboratories, and consumer associations, especially the Dutch "Consumentenbond," and has also established important contacts with representatives of trade and industry. Reports from all these groups are requested and studied closely by the IEN to establish priorities for what products are to be labeled and to decide what information the consumer needs and wants on a label. When this has been agreed upon, the institute's technical staff writes labeling specifications, which include information to be given to the consumer (this must be in a readable and understandable form) and the measuring and testing methods used for the product. The tests are carried out at independent laboratories, such as TNO (the Dutch Organization for Applied Scientific Research, which has very extensive laboratories in Delft for carrying out engineering and industrial tests on a wide range of large-scale projects).

The nature of information labels

Interested manufacturers may then apply for an informative label for a particular product. Agreement must be reached with IEN and a contract signed, usually valid for a period of three years. The manufacturer must then have the product tested and measured in accordance with the specifications, at his own expense, at one of the laboratories specified by the IEN. When the product has been subjected to all the necessary testing and measuring, the results are entered on the standard label, and this may then be attached to the goods.

The IEN may make periodic spot checks on label-bearing goods and, if these reveal that the characteristics of a certain product no longer conform to the information supplied, may withdraw the label.

Correcting misleading advertising

Manufacturers are allowed to mention the informative label in their advertising as long as it is in no way misleading. The institute keeps a close watch for misuse of a label in advertising and has two methods for dealing with abuses—it can take legal action or make a public announcement in the press of any such abuse. It is a term of the contract that should IEN have to take such a step, the manufacturer must pay the costs. (This has proved to be a most successful deterrent; it has never been necessary to take such action either in the Netherlands or in Sweden, whose national labeling institute has had the power to do so for some years.)

It is difficult to estimate how far and along what lines informative labeling will spread—it seems to be a phenomenon peculiar to the consumer societies of Western Europe. Britain did have an informative labeling scheme, "Teltag," under which labels were put on electric blankets, electric kettles, electric coffee percolators, curtains, interlined rugs, and tufted carpets, but this was forced to cease operations in March, 1971, as a result of the closing of the Consumer Council.

In those countries where the consumer interest has relatively high priority in government and where consumer protection legislation is well advanced, it is feasible that informative labeling will become compulsory. This is a possibility in Sweden, where a new consumer agency, recommended in 1973, would take over the functions of the existing governmental consumer agencies and the VDN Institute for Informative Labelling, at present a private organization with its statutes approved by the government. Yet informative labeling does work as a voluntary measure. Experience has shown that when one manufacturer starts to label a product, other manufacturers follow suit. (The IEN reports that within two weeks of the introduction of an informative label for life jackets, about 80 percent of the manufacturers of jackets sold on the Dutch market had applied for labels.)

The future looks bright for informative labeling

Consumer advice centers in Austria and England

Austria[6]

The Verein für Konsumenten Information was the first consumer organization in the world that found a fairly successful solution to the problem of where to reach the poor consumer. It established the Consumer Advisory Centre on one of the main streets of Vienna, where anyone can come in and ask for advice on any consumer problem—products, services, legal matters, and so on.

The Consumer Advisory Centre

The Austrian consumer organization, the Association for Information to Consumers, began as an advice center, and later carried out comparative product tests in its own laboratory. It has published a test magazine for over a decade. It also has a labeling program and conducts an effective consumer education program especially for young children.

At first, advice on only a few consumer products and some services was given in a small advisory center. Within a few years, after there was shown to be great interest on the part of the public, individual consultations were held daily, in Vienna and at some of the federal capitals. Usually the advisory service is provided in the evenings, after working hours. Advice is supplied free.

The main features of the advisory service can be summed up as follows:

How the Consumer Advisory Centre works

Consumers are given information orally, by experts, about what is available on the market, about prices, and, if possible, about the quality of products.

The ideas a consumer has about a prospective purchase take a concrete form during the consultation; it is regularly shown that initially, many consumers have only a vague idea of what they really need and what they can afford.

There is direct contact with the consumer, which has sound psychological advantages. Most consumers want to discuss their purchasing problems objectively in the form of an exchange of views. It is regarded as one of the main advantages of the individual oral advisory service that conversations of this kind take place.

From the point of view of the consumer organizations, the advisory service has still other advantages. The advice center is fitted out as a showroom. Discussions are essentially practical, and the goods are shown to the visitor, but he does not feel pressured to purchase, as he would in a shop. Viewing the

[6]"Advice for All," *International Consumer*, Spring, 1972, p. 2.

products in this way also makes a comparison of the various products possible. Such a wide range of products cannot normally be offered in a shop. Other important considerations when making the purchase can be taken into account; for example, information is given during the consultation not only about price and quality but also about the appearance and measurements of the product as well. The consumer with a measuring tape is a frequent visitor to the advisory center.

The goods on display are exhibited for firms free of charge, which means that all firms have an interest in having their products represented in the center. Sample appliances are thus often made available to the center much earlier than they are obtainable in the shops, and the center is thus informed very quickly about changes in the products available on the market.

Problems concerning foods, the safety of household appliances, appropriate treatment for textiles, etc., are less suitable for individual consultation and are therefore dealt with in a more general way in the form of an exhibition.

Individual consultations

During the discussions, visitors provide valuable information about consumer opinions and purchasing wishes and about changes in the consumption structure. This means firsthand information as to which household appliances are in greatest demand, for example, and which are less in demand and about which product tests are in most urgent need of being carried out. The advisory organizations are confronted with purchasers' points of view and can adapt the information they give consumers to these ideas. Direct contact with the purchaser seems to be an important prerequisite for ensuring that consumer policy is kept at a really practical level.

Various problems, especially those of a personal nature, are connected with individual consultation. Not every good consumer expert is suitable for this advisory work, since apart from technical knowledge, the consultant must have the right psychological approach in order to be able to adapt to the individual purchasers. He or she must always be prepared to answer totally unexpected questions. If it is not possible to give a full answer, it is better to tell the consumer this frankly and promise a proper answer later in writing.

Consultation examples

A typical problem encountered at the center might concern the purchase of a heater. The consumer wants to know whether he has chosen a good one. During the consultation the advisor asks how much warmth is needed in the house so that the purchaser will buy one that is the right size, not too large and not too small. He also asks about prices, and a comparison is made of the operating costs of electricity, gas, oil, and solid fuel. In addition, the consumer is advised of the different kinds of warmth provided by the types of heating being considered. Thus the choice is narrowed down to several models. The final decision is then left to the purchaser.

In problems concerning textiles, the purchaser often asks whether a particular piece of material is suitable for a suit, dress, or coat and whether the material is a good value. During the consultation a short examination is made of the material, and the composition is ascertained. Possible uses for it are thus determined, and the textile consultant, on the basis of his marketing know-how, can tell the purchaser whether the actual price of the material is reasonable, low, or too high.

Unfortunately, some consumers do not come for consultation only before they make a purchase. Many come to the Association for Information to Consumers later, when they have a complaint. The legal advice service and complaints bureau work as follows:

Consumer complaints service

The purchaser is acquainted with the legal position. On the basis of the contract of sale, a view is taken as to whether the purchaser has a claim or whether the seller is legally in the right.

The association often takes direct complaints to the supplier, particularly where the purchaser is in an unfavourable position. Experience has shown that intervention by the consumer organization can be productive for the consumer even in legally hopeless cases.

For consumers who are badly off financially, the association in certain circumstances takes over lawyers' and court fees if a settlement of the dispute out of court is not possible. In exceptional cases the association will also undertake an appeal against a court decision, where principles are involved. In these cases the association has to carry the risk connected with the lawsuit.

The consumer advice center in Vienna handles about 50,000 individual inquiries per year, with 180,000 to 300,000 visitors to the center. The operation of the center accounts for about a quarter of the association's total budget, the remainder being taken up with the testing of goods and the supply of information through the medium of publications.

England: Which? Advice Centre[7]

Two-and-a-half years ago Consumers Association set up an experimental Advice Centre in Kentish Town, a largely working-class area about three miles north of Central London. They wanted to find a way of helping the very many people who at present receive no impartial and independent consumer advice, particularly those with lower-than-average incomes. Many shoppers know too little about the goods and services they are buying, too little about their rights in relation to faulty goods, guarantees, credit buying etc. and too little about how to get consumer complaints dealt with. Nor can shoppers expect to get the help and information they need from retail assistants, many of whom have limited product knowledge and are unaware of the full extent of consumers' rights.

In that two-and-a-half years 40,000 people have brought their consumer problems and questions to the "Which? Advice Centre." Some were about products:

Consumer complaints in England

I want to buy a sewing machine to make clothes for my children and the man in the shop says I'll need a machine costing £65. Isn't there anything a little bit more reasonable?

My husband has just died. I'm moving into a small flat and need a new cooker. What can I get that doesn't cost too much and is suitable for someone living on their own?

Some were about services:

Where can I find a reliable electrician?

[7] Robert Simpson, "Consumer Advice Centres in the UK," *International Consumer,* Spring, 1972, pp. 5-6.

Some were about methods of buying:

> A man came to my door yesterday and got me to sign up for a food/freezer plan. My husband says we can't afford it, but I've signed the paper. Can I get out of it?

> I've seen an advertisement for personal loans you can get to pay off your hire-purchase debts. Do you think they're a good idea?

Some were about consumers' rights:

> I bought these boots about five weeks ago and they leak terribly. The shop says it's all the manufacturer's fault and I should get in touch with him. Is that right?

And some were about almost anying:

> Where can I get a new boat-shaped shuttle for my prewar sewing machine?

> How do you get mildew off a nylon shirt?

The basic idea of a consumer advice centre to answer such questions is not a new one. Centres are already well established in Europe and they encouraged CA to open the first Centre in Britain to provide a full-scale consumer service embracing both pre-shopping advice and post-shopping complaints. Five things seem to have contributed particularly to the success of the Centre:

Reasons for success of the advice center

It occupied shop premises—about 1250 sq ft in a main shopping street. Its services were completely free.

It concentrated on pre-shopping advice—making a genuine attempt to answer the questions and worries of the individual enquirer and to tailor its advice to his or her individual needs and circumstances. The main reason for this approach was quite simply that very many enquirers asked for that kind of advice. But we were also aware that the root cause of many consumer complaints was lack of information before purchase. Although we could help people who had already signed for a dubious food/freezer plan or an unnecessarily expensive hire purchase agreement, the best kind of help was to reach them before they made their mistake.

It never turned away an enquirer, whatever his problem. Even if the enquiry was not really a consumer one ("Where can I get poisoned apple analysed?", or "What does an operation for a rupture involve?") the very least that the Centre would do would be to pass on the enquirer to another organisation or person who really could help.

Last, and probably most important of all, the Centre showed the impact that could be achieved when a properly trained staff was backed up by a detailed and extensive information store and a wide range of leaflet material.

The Which? Advice Centre was a demonstration project. It established the need for consumer advice centres to provide help and information to the less-well-off at local level and it showed how such centres should operate. It enabled CA to campaign effectively for the establishment of consumer advice centres financed by local authorities—so effectively in fact that the first five were opened during 1972 in the London Boroughs of Camden, Havering, Greenwich and Lambeth, and in East Kilbride in Scotland. Having served its purpose the Which? Advice Centre was closed early in 1972 to enable its staff to set up an "Advice Centre Servicing Unit." This is now providing the training courses, leaflet materials, information store and general expertise that will enable the local authority centres to operate.

Local authorities establish consumer advice centers

Soundings taken by CA among other local authorities show a general feeling of sympathy towards the idea. This leads CA to feel that developments so far constitute the first firm step towards the creation of a nationwide network of consumer centres— something which CA believes to be necessary and which it believes consumers want. Consumer information, advice and help should be just as much a feature of the neighbourhood shopping centre as the grocer or the furniture store.

IOCU and the developing countries[8]

Within a relatively short time after its formation in March, 1960, IOCU began to turn its attention to the needs of the developing countries. It soon began to be clear that it had an important contribution to make through the assistance and encouragement of consumer self-organization and activities in these regions.

Two-thirds of world population undernourished

Much of this thinking came to a focus for the first time at the Third IOCU World Congress, held in Oslo in 1964, where the problems of developing countries were included on the agenda and attracted the close attention of many delegates. For as one speaker put it in the Closing Session of the Conference: "In the world of today, the proletariat of the West . . . are not in the West but in the underdeveloped countries." And Dr. Michael Young, then Chairman (and now President) of Consumers' Association, UK, continued: "Here are people who know what poverty means— something like two-thirds of the population of the world are in some degree undernourished. They are not concerned with what they are going to have for breakfast at all. These people, the greater part of our fellow human beings, have no choice."

At that 1964 World Congress, the International Organization of Consumers Unions accordingly resolved:

The IOCU resolution to aid people in developing nations

1. To set up a working committee to help promote consumer organization and activity in developing countries, so as to strengthen their consumer position.

2. To reinforce IOCU's contacts with the United Nations and its associated agencies, particularly with a view to promoting consumer education, developing standards for consumer goods and services, and generally supporting the consumer interest in developing countries.

3. To develop plans for a special IOCU fund to help carry out its programme in relation to developing countries.

4. To urge UNESCO and associated agencies and groups to call a special conference on the consumer problems of the developing countries, to be held, preferably, in one of the continents concerned as soon as possible.

Seminar

Meantime, IOCU held a four-day Seminar in Haifa, Israel for delegates from 14 countries in Asia, Africa and Latin America. The Aid-Committee of IOCU in 1969 had its first regional Seminar when Jamaica acted as hosts to consumer leaders from the neighboring Caribbean Islands. Today, there are nine consumer organizations in the Caribbean area. Under the active leadership of two Americans, Dr. Persia Campbell, Chairman of the Aid Committee, and Florence Mason, the IOCU influence has spread to the South-East Asia and the Pacific, where a Seminar was held at Bombay, India for three days in 1971. Some 40 delegates representing consumer organizations, credit unions and family organizations from 12 countries were represented.

The IOCU and consumer organizations were created precisely for the purpose of fighting economic imbalances. And poverty, as IOCU President Peter Goldman has described it, is "the most glaring consumer problem of all."

Consumer problems in different countries grow more and more alike

The social-economic problems which consumer organizations are pitted against in different countries grow steadily more alike, and more global in their implications.

---

[8] An excellent, lengthy article in *International Consumer*, Autumn, 1971, pp. 20–24. The 1961, 1965, 1966, 1968, and 1969 issues of *International Consumer* contain much good material on the efforts of IOCU to help people in the developing countries help themselves.

Industry is increasingly operating on an international scale, so that more and more markets come to share the same products and are subjected to many of the same marketing processes. Technical standards, so often vital to consumer interests, are now very much an international affair. Many problems, such as the environment, air transport, drug misuse, simply cannot be tackled within national boundaries. These are only some of the reasons why consumer organizations attach growing importance to mutual collaboration, and it is out of this joint effort that the international consumer movement has grown.

THE ROLE OF GOVERNMENT IN CONSUMER AFFAIRS

How best to protect the consumer

We said early in this chapter that although the structures of consumer organizations of the world vary considerably, all have one central theme in common—the aim to furnish accurate, impartial advice and recommendations concerning trademarked consumer goods and regular services. Some consumer organizations argue that no government agency can adequately represent the consumer unless it has a high degree of constitutional and political freedom. Some go even further and maintain that since no government body can ever attain this freedom to the full extent, only the independent consumer organization, embodied in an independent consumer movement, can speak for the consumer without fear or favor.

At the other extreme, there is the view that the state alone has the power to stand up to business and industry on the one hand, and its own agencies on the other, to achieve a square deal for the individual citizen as a consumer of goods and services. The recent Swedish reorganization of consumer agencies, with increased powers for a Consumer Ombudsman and the Market Court, represents a sizable step forward in the creation of a consumer "superagency" that intervenes on behalf of the consumer.

The conclusion expressed by the Political Issues Workshop at the sixth IOCU World Congress on this subject was as follows:

Consumers' interest represented at the center of political power

We have considered the ways in which the consumers' interest should be represented at the centre of political power in each country, both in regard to consumer protection and education itself and in the taking part in or initiation of policies which affect the consumer directly or indirectly. Whilst each country has different traditions of government, we do believe that it would be in the general interest of the consumer for consumer affairs to be the specific responsibility of one powerful minister or ministerial body at the very heart of political power, but that the importance and the effectiveness of such a minister must depend on the presence of effective organs of consumer criticism and consumer thought, such as existing or improved consumer councils, agencies and commissions, and in the last resort on the vigour, strength and activity of consumer movements.

In other words, governments help consumers who help themselves.

Influence of IOCU

The influence of IOCU is not extensive yet. This is primarily because the idea of consumers' unions has not caught the imagination of the "man in the street" or the "woman in the supermarket." Its membership is generally confined to upper-middle-class intellectuals. Although many prime movers of the consumer movement are women, the consumer organizations have been singularly unsuccessful in interesting housewives—the major consumers—in their programs.

Nevertheless, the consumer organizations have prevailed upon governments to recognize the interests of consumers. They have done so even without agreement among themselves as to the nature of this interest. Government consumer programs, or government-financed activities, are now in operation in the United States, in most Western European countries, and in some Asian countries. The programs themselves reflect this ideological vacuum.

While the programs may be weak, with a few exceptions the fact remains that the consumer movement is a reality, and it is growing. As of now, it appears that the world consumer movement will not go away, but will slowly gain momentum.

SUGGESTED READINGS

Calascione, John: "Co-operative Testing," *International Consumer,* Spring, 1971, pp. 9–15.

————:"Enter the Ombudsman," *International Consumer,* Winter, 1971–1972, pp. 15–19.

First Annual Report, Canadian Consumer Council, Ottawa, 1969.

International Chamber of Commerce, Commission on Advertising: "Information for the Consumer," *International Consumer,* August, 1970, pp. 9–11.

Kermode, Graham: "Food Standards for the World," *International Consumer,* Winter, 1971–1972, pp. 20–22.

Mishan, E.J.: "The Limits to Consumption," *International Consumer,* Autumn, 1972, pp. 25–32, 35, 58.

Shears, Phillip: "Industrial and Consumer Testing Compared," *International Consumer,* Spring, 1971, pp. 5–8.

"Soviet Is Publishing Its First Consumer Magazine," *The New York Times,* Dec. 25, 1972.

Thiberg, Sven: "The Quality of Life," *International Consumer,* Autumn, 1972, pp. 38–43.

Thorelli, Hans: "Consumer Information Programmers," *International Consumer,* Autumn, 1972, pp. 15–21.

Valle, Mrs. Inger: "The Consumer in Government," *International Consumer,* Autumn, 1972, pp. 7–12.

Wightman, David: "Development versus Environment," *International Consumer,* Autumn, 1972, pp. 48–51.

APPENDIX A:
A SUMMARY OF WAYS TO SAVE MONEY FROM MARRIAGE TO RETIREMENT

The primary purpose of Appendix A is to describe briefly some of the important consumer choices (which you have read about in this textbook) your family can make, or may have to make, if you are living on a lower budget, a moderate budget, or a higher budget.

The use of three different family-income budgets permits a selection of choices to fit various socioeconomic backgrounds. We learned in Chapter 2, for example, that the American consumer fits no single mold. He has no one level of buying competence. But his choices or purchasing habits reflect his income, his position in the life cycle (birth to death), his education, and his occupation, as well as his nationality and cultural background and environment. Yet the fact remains that family resources are an important factor in influencing choices in the marketplace. Furthermore, a considerable amount of data are available to illustrate the relationship between resources of the family and expenditures. One such source is the recent study by the Bureau of Labor Statistics of the U.S. Department of Labor of three standards of living for an urban family of four persons in autumn of 1971. And since most families live in urban centers (small and large), we are using the cost-of-living data from this important study. [1]

AUTUMN, 1971, URBAN FAMILY BUDGETS

The U.S. Department of Labor's Bureau of Labor Statistics has updated to autumn, 1971, its four-person family budgets at three levels and the place-to-place indices based on these budgets. The new budgets are about 3 percent higher than the previous budgets for spring 1970, as income tax reductions offset about half the effect of the rise in consumer prices over the eighteen-month period. The equivalent budget levels varied widely among cities and regions, with the lowest in small cities and in the South, and the highest generally in the largest metropolitan areas.

Average budgets for an urban family of four in the United States were $7,214 a year at a lower level, $10,971 at an intermediate level, and $15,905 at a higher level (see Table A-1). Further details are shown in Tables A-2 to A-4. These budgets are for a precisely defined urban family of four: a 38-year-old husband employed full time, his nonworking wife, a boy of 13, and a girl of 8. After about fifteen years of married life, the family is well established, and the husband is an experienced worker. The budgets are illustrative of three different levels of living and provide for different specified types and amounts of goods and services. The family has, for each budget level, average inventories of clothing, house furnishings, major durables, and other equipment. The budgets pertain only to an urban family with the specified characteristics; no budgets are available for rural families. The budgets are not intended to represent a minimum or subsistence level of living.

---

[1] Write to the Bureau of Labor Statistics, U.S. Department of Labor, Washington, D.C. 20210, for latest revisions.

TABLE A-1 Summary of Annual Budgets for a Four-Person Family at Three Levels of Living, Urban United States, Autumn, 1971

ITEM	LOWER BUDGET	INTERMEDIATE BUDGET	HIGHER BUDGET
Total budget	$7,214	$10,971	$15,905
Total family consumption	5,841	8,626	11,935
Food	1,964	2,532	3,198
Housing	1,516	2,638	3,980
Transportation	536	964	1,250
Clothing and personal care	848	1,196	1,740
Medical care	609	612	638
Other family consumption items	368	684	1,129
Other items	357	560	937
Taxes	1,016	1,785	3,033
Social Security and disability payments	387	419	419
Personal income taxes	629	1,366	2,614

Consumption budgets

Budgets covering consumption items only—food, housing, clothing, transportation, medical care, etc.—were updated to autumn, 1971, by applying changes in the Consumer Price Index to the spring, 1970, budgets for these components. At the lower level, these items came to 81 percent of the total budget. The remaining 19 percent covered gifts and contributions, occupational expenses, life insurance, and Social Security and personal income taxes. In the intermediate budget, consumption items represented 79 percent of the total budget. For the higher budget, these items were 75 percent of the total budget.

The food budget (for food at home and away from home) was 34 percent of the consumption budget at the lower level, 29 percent at the intermediate level, and 27 percent at the higher level.

Medical care constituted 10 percent of the consumption budget at the lower level and 7 and 5 percent at the intermediate and higher levels, respectively. In contrast to food and medical care, total housing (including not only shelter but also house furnishings and household operation) accounted for a rising budget share as the budget level rose. At the lower level, where the shelter component provided for only a rented dwelling unit, 26 percent of all consumption was allocated to housing. It constituted 31 percent of the intermediate budget and 33 percent of the higher budget. Roughly the same proportion (about 15 percent) was allocated to clothing and personal care at all three levels, and for transportation the proportionate differences between the levels were small. These allocations do not represent how families of each budget type actually spend their money. Rather, they reflect the assumptions made about the manner of living at each of the three levels. New information on actual spending patterns will not be available until the 1972–1973 survey of consumer expenditures is completed.

Consumption budgets for different family types

How family consumption budgets that provide an equivalent level of living vary for urban families of different size and composition is shown in Table A-2.

TABLE A-2   Annual "Consumption" Budgets for Selected Family Types, Urban United States, Autumn, 1971

FAMILY SIZE, TYPE, AND AGE	LOWER LEVEL	INTERMEDIATE LEVEL	HIGHER LEVEL
Single person under 35 years	$2,040	$3,020	$4,180
Husband and wife under 35 years:			
No children	2,860	4,230	5,850
One child under 6	3,620	5,350	7,400
Two children, older under 6	4,210	6,210	8,590
Husband and wife, 35–54 years:			
One child, 6–15 years	4,790	7,070	9,790
Two children, older 6–15 years*	5,814	8,626	11,935
Two children, older 6–15 years*	5,841	8,626	11,935
Three children, oldest 6–15 years	6,780	10,010	13,840
Husband and wife, 65 years and over†	3,176	4,484	6,592
Single person, 65 years and over‡	1,747	2,466	3,626

* Estimates for the BLS four-person family budgets.
†Estimates for the BLS retired couple's budgets.
‡Estimated by applying a ratio of 55 percent to the BLS retired couple's budgets.

Differences in budgets between urban areas

Area indices, representing differences in budgets for an equivalent level of living, reflect not only diferences between the areas in price levels but also regional variations in consumption patterns and differences in climate, types of transportation facilities, taxes, etc.

For the lower budget, the consumption component was about 8 percent higher in metropolitan areas than in nonmetropolitan urban areas. The metropolitan-nonmetropolitan difference was 14 percent for the intermediate budget and 18 percent for the higher budget. Total budget levels were lowest in the South and in small cities. Excluding Honolulu and Anchorage, the interarea differences tended to be smallest in the case of the lower budget and to widen as the level rose.

All indices relate to budgets for established families in each area. They do not measure cost differences associated with moving from one area to another or the living costs of newly arrived residents in a given community.

Changes in budgets, 1970 to 1971

Since spring, 1970, when the three family budgets were last published, the consumption budgets at each level have risen 5 percent as a result of the rise in prices.

The Consumer Price Index rose by 6.3 percent over this eighteen-month period. The reduced impact of inflation on the budgets results primarily from two factors. First, in the intermediate and higher budgets, 75 to 85 percent of the families are assumed to be homeowners who purchased their homes six to seven years ago. Hence a substantial portion of their shelter costs (principal and interest payments) are fixed and do not reflect the current increases in home purchase costs reported by the Consumer Price Index. Second, in the intermediate and higher budgets, the relative importance of public transportation was significantly lower than in the Consumer Price Index, where prices for public transportation outpaced those for private transportation. Changes in the various components of the budgets between spring, 1970, and autumn, 1971, were as shown in Table A-3.

The total budget levels—including Social Security payments and federal, state, and local income taxes—rose by approximately 3 percent over the eighteen-month period. The smaller increase in the overall budgets than in consumption was due to a reduction of personal income taxes at all levels of government. Personal taxes decreased 13, 11, and 9 percent, respectively, in the lower, intermediate, and higher budgets. However, the progressive effect of these income tax adjustments was partly offset by an increase in Old Age, Survivors', Disability and Health Insurance (OASDHI) rates in 1971. As a result, for the illustrative four-person family budget the distribution of income between consumption and taxes changed between 1970 and 1971 as shown in Table A-4.

Methods of calculation   The 1971 consumption budgets were derived by applying price changes between spring, 1970, and autumn, 1971, reported in the Consumer Price Index for individual areas, to the appropriate spring, 1970, final budget for each main class of goods and services. This method of updating is approximate because the

TABLE A-3   Percent Changes in Four-Person Family Budgets, Spring 1970, to Autumn, 1971

COMPONENT	BUDGET LEVEL		
	LOWER	INTERMEDIATE	HIGHER
Food	3.1	3.3	3.4
Housing	6.1	5.5	5.5
Transportation	6.1	5.7	5.7
Clothing and personal care	5.1	5.2	5.1
Medical care	8.4	8.5	8.5
Other family consumption	6.7	7.0	6.9
Total consumption	5.2	5.1	5.2
Other items	4.1	3.9	3.8
Social Security	12.2	8.3	8.3
Personal income taxes	—12.5	—10.9	—9.1
Total budget	3.6	2.9	2.5

TABLE A-4   Percentage Composition of Four-Person Family Budgets, Spring, 1970, and Autumn, 1971

	BUDGET LEVEL					
	LOWER		INTERMEDIATE		HIGHER	
	1970	*1971*	*1970*	*1971*	*1970*	*1971*
Total budget	100	100	100	100	100	100
Consumption	80	81	77	79	73	75
Other items*	5	5	5	5	6	6
Taxes†	15	14	18	16	21	19

* Includes gifts and contributions, life insurance, and occupational expenses.

†Social Security and disability payments, plus federal, state, and local personal income taxes. The 1970 taxes were computed at 1969 rates; the 1971 taxes were at 1970 rates.

Consumer Price Index reflects spending patterns and prices paid for commodities and services purchased by wage earners and clerical workers generally without regard to their family type and level of living. Other items were also updated to autumn, 1971. Personal income taxes and OASDHI were computed from tax rates in effect for 1971.

Importance of Table A-1

For our purpose, Table A-1 is useful in that you can recognize the difference in the amount of money generally available for each major expenditure. These differences in costs will help you understand the importance of making more intelligent choices in the marketplace.

CHOICES FOLLOW A PATTERN ASSOCIATED WITH AGE

Many family choices in the marketplace follow a pattern associated with age. The number of children at home, for example, tends to increase, then stabilize, and finally drop off. Food expenditures, also, change as families move from the newly married couple without children to the period when they have children, or until the children are on their own economic power, and finally to the retirement age.

Recognizing these changing purchasing decisions based on age and on income, from marriage to death, we are attempting to summarize how families can improve their purchasing decisions in the marketplace.

There is bound to be overlap from one family cycle to the next, and from a lower but adequate income to a moderate and higher income. We hope that you will be able to identify yourself with one or more of the age and income levels and thereby discover the secret of converting dollars into contentment.

FROM MARRIAGE TO DEATH

You are getting started in marriage. About half of you have children, and your income is apt to be quite modest. For practical purposes, use Table A-1 as a basis for living standards and for allocation of income for food, housing, and other costs. It is wise to keep in mind that as of March, 1972, the median family income of the head of a family below age 25 was only $6,909. [2]

Slice the food bill

1. Stick to your "buying list."

2. Convenience foods are almost always considerably more expensive. Some of the extra costs are made in the name of "built-in maid service." The major objective of the food industry today, however, is to convert inexpensive ingredients into costly processed foods and to provide them in convenience form, which is often a myth. So, if you want to save $400 to $500 a year on your food bill (family of four), look the other way when tempted to purchase prebuttered vegetables, cheese slices, processed cheese, frozen dinners, stuffed baked potatoes, cheese in spray cans, presweetened ready-

[2] U.S. Bureau of the Census, *Current Population Reports: Consumer Income,* p. 60, no. 83, July, 1972.

to-eat breatfast foods and those with fruit in them, diet margarine, meat products with filler or extenders, dehydrated mashed potatoes, frozen meat and chicken pies, frozen chow meins, chopped poultry with broth, frozen deviled crab, snack foods, flavored cottage cheese, stuffed turkey, and frozen beef patties, to mention a few.

    3.   Private store brands are usually considerably cheaper than and equal in quality to manufacturers' advertised brands.

    4.   Vitamin products, special dietary foods, and food supplements are costly and unnecessary. Food is the best source for vitamins.

    5.   "Diet pills do more harm than good."

    6.   Trading stamps and games do not save you money.

    7.   Check weights, expecially of prepackaged meats, vegetables, and fruit. Short-weighting is common.

    8.   Highly advertised products cost more.

    9.   Orange "ades," "punches," and "nectar" are expensive and contain little food value.

    10.   Nonfat dry milk and "imitation" milk are cheaper than fresh milk and have all the nutrients except butterfat.

    11.   Freezer-meat contracts are an expensive convenience.

    12.   Shop for advertised specials—usually on weekends.

    13.   Buy in quantity.

    14.   Buy USDA grades whenever possible.

    15.   Purchase lean meat—by the cut, not by the cost per pound.

    16.   Food away from home (restaurants) is nice but costly.

    17.   Buy good, nutritional foods—read the new nutrient labels.

These suggestions for converting food dollars into contentment and economic security are valid for almost any age bracket or income level. There are, however, a few additional suggestions for parents who are over 45. Their children are in college (food bills at home should go down if the children are away from home). A retired couple is likely to have food restrictions and may be able to eat more often in restaurants if income permits. Incomes of many people in retirement, however, are so low as to create money troubles. The general suggestions above are as important for them as for young marrieds on lower or moderate budgets. For lower-income older couples, the best suggestion is to do more home cooking (with savings up to about 25 percent).

Housing   Average housing costs in urban centers range from $1,560 to $3,980 at autumn, 1971, prices (Table A-1).

    1.   Renting a house is usually less costly than owning.

    2.   Mobile homes have special appeal to young marrieds and are economical.

    3.   The cheapest way to buy a house is to pay cash.

    4.   If you borrow money to buy a house, shop around for the best deal.

    5.   Select a mortgage which permits prepayment without penalty.

    6.   When buying insurance for your home, furnishings, liability, fire, and theft, buy a package deal. If necessary, take a "floater" policy to cover special items such as art objects and valuable jewelry.

7. Renting furnished for newlyweds or young marrieds is usually less costly. The costs of setting up housekeeping in an unfurnished one-bedroom apartment, for example, are apt to be about $1,500—add some extras, and it may jump to $2,000.

8. Retired couples needing less room and possibly all space on one floor may prefer renting an apartment or purchasing a cooperative or condominium apartment. Some prefer a nice mobile home in satisfactory surroundings and climate.

9. Older people need grab bars at several heights in the bathtub; also, they need large refrigerators because they shop less often and buy more each trip.

Transportation

Average transportation costs of three urban living standards in the autumn of 1971 ranged from $536 to $1,250 annually. The cost of operating a new standard four-door sedan is about $2,400 for the first 15,000 miles and about $1,800 for the second 15,000 miles.

1. Car ownership is very expensive—14 to 17 percent of family income.

2. In large cities, it usually pays to use local transportation and rent a car for special trips.

3. If you can afford a family car, keep a new car at least two years; if run only 10,000 miles a year, it is usually economical to keep a new car for four or five years.

4. Look for repairability and safety when buying a new car.

5. The total cost of leasing a medium-priced car for two years (30,000 miles of driving) may be cheaper than ownership of car.

6. If you buy a new, medium-size car, read the list price on the sticker, deduct freight charge, apply 22 percent discount, and you have the dealer's approximate cost.

7. Pay cash for a car. Next best bet is to borrow the money from the cheapest source—usually your bank or credit bureau.

8. A car warranty "giveth and it taketh away"—so read its limitations in particular—the "implied" warranty may help you recover damages due to defective product.

9. Soon, car insurance is apt to be sold at reduced rates and payable "without regard to fault" and at a lower premium.

10. With proper car design, accidents can be safe or safer. Buy safety.

11. After children are of school age, you may need two cars. This is convenient but very expensive. When children are on their own, get rid of the extra car.

Clothing and personal care

The cost of clothing a family of four varied from $848 to $1,740 a year in the autumn of 1971 in lower, moderate, and higher budgets. Personal care costs about $275 per person per year on the average. And the clothing costs for children more than triple between their first and eighteenth birthdays. The point is—if you have to cut clothing costs, consider the following tips.

1. Follow basic wardrobe planning and spending.
2. Avoid credit costs.
3. Look for and understand fabric standards on the labels.
4. Take full advantage of regular and special sales.
5. Consider costs for repair and care of clothing.
6. Do not hesitate to use good discount stores, reliable mail-order companies, and variety stores.
7. Bulk dry cleaning can save many dollars.
8. A clever woman with sewing ability can create most of her own clothes at half the retail cost for comparable quality and style.
9. Make liberal use of wash-and-wear and "permanent press" clothes.
10. Size tags, especially for women's and children's wear, are not reliable—try the garments on.
11. Neither reliable industry nor consumer standards exist for new synthetic-fiber stretch fabrics—watch out!
12. Check recent issues of *Consumer Reports* and *Consumer Research Magazine* for objective evaluation of standard brands of clothing and shoes.
13. Older women can ease the burden of dressing by purchasing dresses with zippers in the front.
14. Look for sewed-on labels giving specific information on care and cleaning (you are not apt to find sewed-on labels with reliable information as of 1973). Most trouble is with bonded fabrics, press-on linings, plastic zippers, color stains, pleats, felt, buttons, foam lining, and lace.
15. Firms are still making and selling flammable fabrics despite federal legislation.
16. Select self-help features which children can handle themselves and easy-care features.
17. Clean, hang, and store clothes properly.

Medical care

Medical care costs are very high. Hospital bills have more than tripled and doctors' fees have increased almost as much in the last twenty years. Drug prices are much too high when compared to costs. Who can afford to be sick unless adequately protected by health insurance and disability income insurance?

1. Evaluate your health care needs and set up a plan for health care and loss-of-income protection. Change protection as children arrive, as they leave the home, and as retirement is near.
2. Probably the best health-medical protection per dollar costs today for pre-age-65 people is nonprofit, prepaid, comprehensive group health plans such as group health cooperatives, Health Insurance Plan of Greater New York, and others.
3. The next best plan in terms of cost and services for pre-age-65 people is likely to be Blue Cross–Blue Shield Group Hospital-Medical plans. Many insurance companies have good plans also, but these are probably more costly.
4. A married couple, with no dependents, can purchase coverage at a lower premium than when children and other dependents are included. After

children are on their own, cut premium costs by returning to husband-wife coverage. A year before retirement, make inquiry about Medicare from the closest Social Security office.

5. Include major medical coverage, because it is designed to handle costs of serious and long-term illness and accident cases. This plan is a supplement to your "basic plan." Some plans combine basic protection and major medical coverage. Group plans cost less.

6. Loss of income is not included in health and medical care insurance. Do not be without it. Costs are comparatively low and oftentimes your employer will pay for it or for part of the coverage.

7. Social Security carries important financial aid if children under 18, or to age 22 if they are in school, are left fatherless.

8. Dental care insurance is now available—an orthodontist for two years may cost from $800 to $2,000! Prepayment group plans cost less than individual family plans.

9. Join Medicare (hospital and medical insurance) early enough to have it go into effect on your sixty-fifth birthday or as soon thereafter as the law permits. This is a voluntary program, so you have to make application through the Social Security office. The coverage is not complete yet, but it is still the best protection per dollar available to most people. It is generally wise to carry a supplementary coverage, such as Blue Cross–Blue Shield, to plug the gaps in Medicare. The supplementary premiums are comparatively low.

10. In the near future we are likely to have a modified form of national health insurance.

CONSUMPTION COSTS

Consumption costs—food, housing, transportation, clothing and personal care, medical care, and other miscellaneous consumption items—for three standards of living of four family persons accounted for 81 percent, 79 percent, and 75 percent of the *total* budgets of lower-level ($7,214), moderate-level ($10,971), and higher-level ($15,905) living standards in the autumn of 1971.

Budgets and rising prices   Most families and many individuals are extremely concerned about the dramatic increase in the cost of living in the United States in recent years. The Consumer Price Index (CPI), which measures changes in prices for goods and services bought by urban wage earners and clerical workers, increased 38 percent between 1962 and 1972.[3] Housing accounted for about 34 percent of the increase in the index, food accounted for 22 percent, and health and recreation accounted for 20 percent. Apparel and personal care accounted for about 14 percent, as did transportation.

The index for services increased faster than that for commodities—53 percent, compared with 30 percent. The largest difference in individual indices was in transportation. The cost of private transportation rose 26 percent, while that of public transportation increased 64 percent.

[3]*Family Economics Review,* December, 1972, pp. 8–9.

It is well to remember that the CPI measures changes in prices; it does not indicate what families actually spend to defray their living expenses. It also measures changes in the purchasing power of the dollar.

Since the end of 1972, however, prices for food have skyrocketed, with no letup in sight at this time. The increase in the wholesale prices of food in February, 1973, was the largest in twenty-two years. Exasperation over inflation hit such a peak that residents in many communities tried to mobilize "meatless weeks." And well they might have, since hamburger increased from 66.1 cents per pound in February, 1971, to 77.8 cents in February, 1973; eggs during the same period increased from 54.9 cents to 73.8 cents per dozen.

Meat is expecially in the spotlight. Fresh meat is leading almost all other items in the parade of rising food prices. In March, 1973, some cuts of beef and pork were selling for 20 to 60 cents more per pound than a year before; porterhouse steak was selling at $1.99 a pound, up 30 percent from a year before, with no quick relief in sight, despite President Nixon's ceiling on the prices of beef, pork, and lamb, imposed on March 30, 1973.

$149 a week needed to make ends meet for family of four

The public's average estimate of what a family of four needs a week to make ends meet has climbed dramatically from $127—recorded in a November, 1971, survey—to a record high of $149 at the end of 1972.

The public's estimate at the end of 1972, as determined by a nationwide Gallup survey, represented nearly a 50 percent increase since 1967, when the estimate was $101.[4]

When this index of living costs was first reported in 1937, the average (median) amount specified nationally was only $30. By 1947, the figure had risen to $43. Near the end of the fifties, the public estimated that a family of four needed $72 a week to make ends meet. The amount climbed to $101 in the 1967 survey and finally to $149 in the 1972 survey.

For nearly four decades the Gallup poll has asked this question of a nationwide sample of the nation's population: What is the smallest amount of money a family of four needs each week to get along in this community?

The highlights of the thirty-five-year trend on this question are presented in the accompanying table.

Minimum Amount Needed by a Nonfarm Family of Four

YEAR	MEDIAN AVERAGES
1937	$ 30
1947	43
1957	72
1967	101
1969	120
1970	126
1971	127
1972	149

[4] Reported in the *St. Louis Post-Dispatch*, Mar. 11, 1973.

An important factor in the public's overall estimate of the cost of living is the cost of food. The latest survey shows that the typical nonfarm family spends a record $37 a week for food, the median average amount given in response to the question: On the average, about how much does your family spend on food, including milk, each week?

The current figure is more than three times the amount specified in the first survey on the subject, taken in 1937, when the median average of responses was $11.

As reported on February 22, 1973, by the Department of Labor, the Consumer Price Index rose sharply in January, spurred (according to the department) by the largest one-month increase in grocery prices on record.

The point in emphasizing the inflationary nature of our economy in the last decade and more is that individuals and families should be continuously aware of the depreciation of the dollar. Such awareness is a motivating factor in developing the skill and art necessary for effective planning and decision making in the marketplace.

APPENDIX B:
FEDERAL AGENCIES SERVING THE CONSUMER

HOUSE COMMITTEES WITH ASSIGNMENTS OF CONSUMER BILLS

Committee on Agriculture
   Subcommittee on Domestic Marketing and Consumer Relations
Committee on Banking and Currency
   Subcommittee on Consumer Affairs
Committee on District of Columbia
Committee on Education and Labor
Committee on Government Operations
Committee on Interstate and Foreign Commerce
   Subcommittee on Commerce and Finance
Committee on Judiciary
Committee on Merchant Marine and Fisheries
Committee on Ways and Means

SENATE COMMITTEES WITH ASSIGNMENTS OF CONSUMER BILLS

Committee on Agriculture and Forestry
   Subcommittee on Agricultural Research and General Legislation
Committee on Banking and Currency
   Subcommittee on Financial Institutions
   Subcommittee on Securities
Committee on Commerce
   Subcommittee on the Consumer
   (has a Consumer Advisory Council)
Committee on District of Columbia
Committee on Finance
Committee on Government Operations
   Subcommittee on Intergovernmental Relations
   Subcommittee on Executive Reorganization
Committee on the Judiciary
   Subcommittee on Antitrust and Monopoly Legislation
Committee on Labor and Public Welfare

FEDERAL AGENCIES SERVING CONSUMERS

Agriculture Department
Agricultural Research Service
Department of Agriculture
Washington, D.C. 20250

Office of Information
Department of Agriculture
Washington, D.C. 20250

Agricultural Marketing Service
Department of Agriculture
Washington, D.C. 20250, or one of its local offices

Food and Nutrition Service
Department of Agriculture
Washington, D.C. 20250

Civil Aeronautics Board Office of Consumer Affairs
Civil Aeronautics Board
Washington, D.C. 20428

Commerce Department National Bureau of Standards
Department of Commerce
Washington, D.C. 20234

National Business Council for Consumer Affairs
Department of Commerce
Washington, D.C. 20220

Consumer Product Safety Office of Information
Commission Consumer Product Safety Commission
Washington, D.C. 20014

Environmental Protection Director of Public Affairs
Agency Environmental Protection Agency
Washington, D.C. 20460

Federal Communications Office of Reports and Information
Commission Federal Communications Commission
Washington, D.C. 20554

Federal Power Office of Public Information
Commission Federal Power Commission
Washington, D.C. 20426

Federal Reserve System Board of Governors
Federal Reserve System
Washington, D.C. 20551, or contact
one of the Federal Reserve banks

Federal Trade Federal Trade Commission
Commission Washington, D.C. 20580, or any
field office listed in local directory

Division of National Advertising
Washington, D.C. 20580

General Services Administration

Consumer Product Information Center
Washington, D.C. 20407, or any federal information center listed in local directory

Consumer Product Information, Pueblo, Colorado 81009

Health, Education, and Welfare Department

Office of Consumer Affairs
Department of Health, Education, and Welfare
Washington, D.C. 20201

Office of Public Affairs
Office of Education
Washington, D.C. 20202

Food and Drug Administration
5600 Fishers Lane
Rockville, Maryland 20852

Office of Information, Health Services and Mental Health Administration
Parklawn Building
Rockville, Maryland 20852

National Advisory Council on Education of Disadvantaged Children
Seventh and D Streets, S.W., Fifth Floor
Washington, D.C. 20202

National Institutes of Health
Information Office
Office of the Director
9000 Rockville Pike
Bethesda, Maryland 20014

Social Security Administration
6401 Social Security Building
Baltimore, Maryland 21235, or the local Social Security office

Housing and Urban Development Department

Department of Housing and Urban Development
Washington, D.C. 20410, or write to any HUD area office of HUD-FHA insuring office

Interior Department

Office of Information
Department of the Interior
Washington, D.C. 20240 (hot-line telephone—202-343-4761)

Justice Department

Antitrust Division
Department of Justice
Washington, D.C. 20530

Bureau of Narcotics and Dangerous Drugs
Department of Justice
Washington, D.C. 20537

Labor Department Bureau of Labor Statistics
Department of Labor
Washington, D.C. 20210

National Credit Union National Credit Union Administration
Administration Washington, D.C. 20456

Postal Service Consumer Advocate
U.S. Postal Service
Washington, D.C. 20260

Securities and Exchange Securities and Exchange Commission
Commission Washington, D.C. 20549

Transportation Office of Consumer Affairs
Department Department of Transportation
400 Seventh Street, S.W.
Washington, D.C. 20590

Distribution Section, HQ-438
Federal Aviation Administration
Washington, D.C. 20590

Federal Highway Administration
Department of Transportation
Washington, D.C. 20590

National Highway Traffic Safety Administration
Washington, D.C. 20591

White House Special Assistant for Consumer Affairs
Executive Office of the President
Washington, D.C. 20506

Address letters to your congressman to House Office Building, Washington, D.C. 20510; or to your senator to Senate Office Building, Washington, D.C. 20515.

APPENDIX C:
THE METRIC SYSTEM: WHAT YOU NEED TO KNOW

The metric system is based on the decimal system. It is quite simple to learn. For use in daily living you will need to know only ten units. You will also need to get acquainted with some new temperatures. There are, of course, other units which most of us will not need to learn. There are even some metric units with which you are already familiar; those for time and electricity, for example, are the same as you use now.

Basic units

> *Meter:* A little longer than a yard
> *Liter:* A little larger than a quart (about 1.06 quarts)
> *Gram:* About the weight of a paper clip

Common prefixes (to be used with basic units)

> *Milli:* One-thousandth (0.001)
> *Centi:* One-hundredth (0.0l)
> *Kilo:* One-thousand times (1,000)

For example:
> 1,000 millimeters = 1 meter
> 100 centimeters = 1 meter
> 1,000 meters = 1 kilometer

Other commonly used units

> *Millimeter:* 0.001 meter—the diameter of a paper-clip wire
> *Centimeter:* 0.01 meter—the width of a paper clip (about 0.4 inch)
> *Kilometer:* 1,000 meters—somewhat longer than ½ mile (about 0.6 mile)
> *Kilogram:* 1,000 grams—a little more than 2 pounds (about 2.2 pounds)
> *Milliliter:* five of them equal a teaspoon

Other useful units

> *Hectare:* about 2½ acres
> *Tonne:* About 1 ton
> *Temperature:* Degrees Celsius are used.

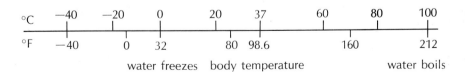

For more information, write to Metric Information Office, National Bureau of Standards, Washington, D.C. 20234.

INDEX